The Evolution of
Christs and Christianities

The Evolution of Christs and Christianities

Jay Raskin

Copyright © 2006 by Jay Raskin.

Library of Congress Number: 2005907733
ISBN: Hardcover 1-4134-9792-6
       Softcover 1-4134-9791-8

All rights reserved. No part of this book may be reproduced or transmitted in any form or by any means, electronic or mechanical, including photocopying, recording, or by any information storage and retrieval system, without permission in writing from the copyright owner.

This book was printed in the United States of America.

To order additional copies of this book, contact:
Xlibris Corporation
1-888-795-4274
www.Xlibris.com
Orders@Xlibris.com
29224

Contents

List of Illustrations 11
Internet Websites for Illustrations 11
Foreword 13
Introduction 17
    A New View 17
    Elaboration of Main Concepts 18
    Narratological Archaeology Applied to Jesus' Mother 23
        Cross Scene Reconstruction 27

Chapter 1: Eusebius the Master Forger 39
    The History that is Not "a Perfect and Complete History" 39
    Eusebius and the Miraculous Founding of Christian Churches ... 46
        1. The Church at Edessa 46
        2. The Church of Jerusalem 49
        3. The Church at Caesarea 61
    The Daughters of Philip and Caesarea and the ERA Hypothesis ... 63
    Saints Who Help Us Understand How Eusebius Worked 70
        1. Gregory and Basil 70
        2. Jerome 73
    Doubts About Eusebius Suppressed 76
    Philosophy and Style 79
    Eusebius' Tell (ET) 80
        Eleven More Cases of Eusebius' Trope
        Three Perhaps Coincidental Uses of Phrases Similar to
            Eusbebius' Trope 92
    In Defense of Eusebius 94
    Checking ET 95
    Did Eusebius Make Interpolations into Other People's Texts? ... 98
        Reconstruction of Tacitus Christian Reference 101
    The Ending of Eusebean History: 103
    The Evolution of Christianity 104

Chapter 2: Non-Eusebean History 109
    Four Broad Stages of Early Christian History 109
    Not Starting with Paul 110
    Tertullian the Master Rhetorician 110

Chapter 3: Mary, the Author of the Word Become Flesh 118
   What are the Gospels? 118
   New Paradigms: Beginning Deconstruction 120
   An Example of the Erasing of Mary from the Narrative 123
   Two Motifs of Mark that May Reflect the Life of Mark 127
     1. The Fear Factor in Mark
     2. Secrecy in Mark: Spread the Word,
        But Don't Tell Anyone About Me!
   Guarding Jesus' Tomb 134
   Differences in the Endings of Mark and Matthew 136
   Time Out of Joint 139
   John Makes Jesus into the Sacrificial Lamb of God 140
   Why did the three Women Come to the Tomb? 143
   A Symbolic Change: Death on the Preparation Day for Passover 146
   The Modus Operandi of Mark and the Earlier Gospel of John 149
   The Number of Women at the Tomb 150
   The Original Ending 151
   Changes in the Preparation Day Gospel of John 152
     First Reconstruction of UrTomb Scene 153
   Why Mark made Jesus Dead for Three Days 157
   The Second Death of Jesus Story: On the Passover Day 158
   The Schizoid Jesus 161
   Crowing Cocks 163
   Why is Mary in the Courtyard of the High Priest? 168
     Reconstruction of Farewell Scene 170
     Reconstruction of Farewell Scene #2 172
   Peter Gets an Earful 172
     Reconstruction of Ear Cutting Scene 174
     Reconstruction of Courtyard Scene 175
     Reconstruction of Jesus's Capture 176
     Reconstruction of Jesus's Capture #2 178
     Reconstruction of Jesus's Capture #3 180
   Mary, Daughter of Annas, Wife of Caiaphas 182
     Reconstruction of Mary's Identity 183
   The Secret Identity of Jesus 183
   Summary of Passover Gospel Reconstruction: Mark is Third Generation 185
   Historical Analysis of Joseph Caiaphas and Mary 186
   Was Mary a Stepmother and Lover of Jesus? 187
   Felix the Egyptian and the Capture on the Mount of Olives ... 189
   Scenario Behind the First Gospel Text: 192

    The Real Name of the Real Man that was Crucified in Mary's tale 193
    The Original Ending of the Gospel of Luke 194
        Reconstruction of the Final Scene in the Gospel of Luke 197

Chapter 4: A New Feminist Paradigm for Understanding the Evolution of the Gospels 201

    Batman Begins as Jesus Begins 205
    He Who Gets Slapped: the Crucifixion as Plot Device 211
    Frankenstein and Jesus 213
    Comparison of Frankenstein to the Passover Gospel
        by Mary Magdalene 214
    Letters of Mary 214
    Jesus and All That Jazz 220
    Chicago as a Paradigm Text for the Gospels 220
    They Both Reached for the Gun 222
    "Never Forget It" 223
    Comparison of the Interview Scenes 225
    A Good Model 230
    And Harry Potter Too! 231
    Jesus the Anti-Christ 232
    Thomas Doubts Mary 234
        Psychoanalytical Reconstruction of Thomas' Doubts 237
    Part II: What is the Gospel? 238
    The Gospels That are Not Gospels 238
    The Memoirs That are Not Memoirs 240
    The Testimony That is a Play 244
    The Mime Play: 247
    Mime Actresses and Mime Plays 249

Chapter 5: Dating the Death of an Unknown Man More Precisely 255

    The Missing Interrogation/Trial scene in John 255
    An Interesting Discovery about Barabas 257
        Pilate and the King of the Jews Reconstruction 259
    History, Josephus and the Death of a Leader of a Samaritan-Jewish
        Revolution 259
    How History was Changed to Get Rid of Pilate a Year Earlier 261
    Passover 36 or 37 or Not Passover at All 263
        Reconstruction of Vestment Passage in Josephus: 266
    Dating Vitellius' Second Visit 267
    Who Died in 36? 268

    The Double Date Switch Hypothesis 269
    The Man Executed by Pilate 272
        Reconstruction of Original Josephus Passage on John 276
    Summary of Years 36-37 Investigation Results 278

Chapter 6: Deconstructing the Gospel of Mark 280
    The Dating Game 280
    Two Problems That are Really One 284
        Reconstruction of Original Tranfiguration Scene 293
    The Apocalyptic Material and Mark's additions 295
        Reconstruction of the Original Coming of Christ Predictions 297
    Does Mark Use the Temple as an Historical Marker? 299
    Six Scenes in the Temple 300
    Two Questions: Which buildings and Which War? 308
    Counter-Evidence: Jesus' Destruction of the Temple 310
    The JDJT Hypothesis 313
    The Logic of First Century Christianity 314
    Did John Baptize with Water or Holy Spirit? 326
    Who is The Son of Man? 331
    An Experiment 340
        Reconstruction of Ur-John Gospel That Mark Worked From 343
    The UrMark Gospel 345
    MQ 355
    Analysis of MQ: The Prophet Versus Christ Hypothesis 358
    Conclusions from MQ 369
    MQQ 369
    Thirty Questions: the John/Jesus FAQ sheet 373

Chapter 7: Deconstructing the Gospel of Matthew 379
    How Matthew Changed a Single Long Speech
        by John the Baptist into Multiple Jesus Speeches 379
        First Evidence of Speeches from a John the Baptist Text 379
        Second Evidence of Jesus' Speeches from a John the Baptist Text 385
        Third Evidence of Jesus Speeches from a John the Baptist Text 389
    An UrMatthew Document: The Teachings of John the Nazarene 390
    Conclusions and New Beginnings: Drawing John the Baptist
        and Jesus Christ from Eleazar and Joshua, Coloring
        from the Book of Malachi 407

Chapter 8: The Birth of John/Jesus 411
    Reconstruction of Birth Narrative 418

Chapter 9: John the Disciple of the Lord, Papias and Eusebius 421
- Papias and John the Disciple of the Lord 426
- Deconstructing Revelation or Revealing the Revealing 432
- Why and Where Patmos? 439
  - Reconstruction of the Opening of Revelation 442
  - Second Reconstruction of the Beginning of Revelation 444
- What Really Happened to John and How He Became John the Christ 447
- The Historical John and the Mythology of John 452

Chapter 10: Paul through a Mirror Darkly 455
- The Seven Inauthentic Authentic Letters of Paul 455
- How Many Trips to Corinth Did Paul Make? 465
- Proof from Acts that Apollos was First to Preach the
  - Gospel to the Gentiles 476
  - Reconstruction of Acts 478
- The Seven Inauthentic Inauthentic Epistles of Paul 485
- How the Seven Epistles of Ignatius Evolved from Seven
  - Asia Minor Epistles of Paul 488
- Timothy, the Useful Real Son of Paul 493
  - Reconstruction of Epistle of Paul to Titus, by Philemon
    - of Laodicea: 496
- Who Was Untimely Born? 501
- The Secret Identity of the Crucified Man 505

Chapter 11: Peter was Simon, But who Was Simon? 511
- Reconstructing Saul's Trip 516
- Hints of Jesus' Simon Identity in the Canonical Gospels 526

Chapter 12: The Shepherd and the Church of God Before Jesus 542
- Tertullian Attacks the Shepherd 544
- The Recycled Proposition Principle 547
- The Smoking Gun Parable 547
- The Shepherd as a Source for the Gospel Writers 551
- The Twelve Commandments of the Angel of Repentence 558
- The Reward of the Flesh: the Founding Myth of All Christianities 562
- Hermas Meets the Shepherd 565
- Summary of What We Learn from this Founding Document 572
- Psychoanalyzing Hermas 573
- Relationship of Paul to Hermas 575
  - Was Paul a Slave? 575
  - Paul and the Obedience School for Slaves 583

Chapter 13: James and the Church of God 587

Chapter 14: Still Jesus after All These Years 595
    Movies, Mickey Mouse and Jesus Christ: The Confusion
        of the Sitz-Im-Leben and the Mise-en-Scene 601

Chapter 15: Bringing It All Back Home 607
    Good News: Jesus did not Die in the Original Story.
        Bad News: He Died in Real Life. 607
    Evolution of the True Gospel 609
    Basis for a New Interpretation of Early Christian Development 611

Endnotes 615
Bibliography 643

LIST OF ILLUSTRATIONS

Map. Times and Relative Locations of Five Different Major Christ Movements in 1st Century Palestine 16
Figure 1. Mosaic. Christ as a Young Beardless Roman Soldier. 37
Figure 2. Sculpture. Jesus as Roman Emperor-God. 108
Figure 3. Fresco. Christ and Woman at Well. 117
Figure 4. Fresco. Christ Healing Woman. 200
Figure 5. Ivory. Jesus Healing Blindman or Is It Mary? 254
Figure 6. Mosaic. Baptism of Young Hermaphrodite Jesus 279
Figure 7. Mosaic. Baptism of Old Jesus. 378
Figure 8. Gravestone. Magician Christ Raises Lazarus with a Wand 410
Figure 9. Fresco. Actor-Magician Christ Raises Lazarus with a Glove. 420
Figure 10. Sculpture. Christ Raises Lazarus, Mary Anoints His Foot. 454
Figure 11. Fresco. Christ as Good Shepherd. 510
Figure 12. Sculpture. Christ as Young Good Shepherd and Lamb of God 541
Figure 13. Fresco. Christ as Lanky Good Shepherd Carrying a Pot. 586
Figure 14. Gravestone. Christ as Husky Good Shepherd Carrying a Pot. 594
Figure 15. Sculpture. Christ with Wand Performing Miracles. 606

INTERNET WEBSITES FOR ILLUSTRATIONS

Websites Retrieved August 25, 2005
Figure 1: *Ravenna Mosaics,*
   http://www.hp.uab.edu/image_archive/ulj/uljc.html
Figure 2: *Late Antique and Early Christian Art,*
   http://employees.oneonta.edu/farberas/arth/arth109/arth109_sl16.html

Figure 3: *Jesus with the Samaritan Woman by the Well*, http://www.aug.edu/augusta/iconography/newStuffForXnCours/catacumbasCristianas/womanWell.html

Figure 4: *Catacomb of Saints Pietro e Marcellino*, http://www.hds.harvard.edu/news/bulletin/articles/branhamfigures.html

Figure 5: *The Murano Diptych*, http://www.aug.edu/augusta/iconography/3001course/muranoDiptychBlind.html>

Figure 6: *The Baptism of Christ*, http://www.ub.uio.no/uhs/ombibl/Sophus/Utstillinger/Mosaikker/Mosaikker.html

Figure 7: R. Ling, *Ancient Mosaics*, Fig. 79, http://shot.holycross.edu/courses/restrictedimg.cgi.en?photoid=2002.03.0371

Figure 8: *Gravestone of Datus*, http://www.christusrex.org/www1/vaticano/PC2-Cristiano.html

Figure 9: *Introduction to Art 1301*, Prestiano, Dr. Robert, http://www.angelo.edu/faculty/rprestia/1301/list_of_illustrations2.htm

Figure 10: *Early Images of Christ:New Clothes for the Emperor or A Battle for the Heavens?*, Cutrone, Emmanuel J., http://ntserver.shc.edu/www/Scholar/cutrone/cutrone.html

Figure 11: *Introduction to Art 1301*, Prestinao, Dr. Robert, http://www.angelo.edu/faculty/rprestia/1301/list_of_illustrations2.htm

Figure 12: Ibid.

Figure 13: *Mosaic, Unit 4: Late Antiquity, Early Christianity*, Octagon Multimedia, http://college.hmco.com/history/west/mosaic/chapter4/image141.html

Figure 14: *Gravestone for Musus and His Wife*, Museo Pio Cristiano—II, http://www.christusrex.org/www1/vaticano/PC1-Cristiano.html

Figure 15: *Christian Iconography*, Stracke, J. Richard, http://www.aug.edu/augusta/iconography/newStuffForXnCours/catacumbasCristianas/sarcophagusChild.html

FOREWORD

My people pray in a foreign language I don't understand.
For all I know they may be asking for the troubles they're always getting.
Woody Allen
Shadows and Fog (1992)

It is fairly easy to see that something has been invented. It is much more difficult to figure out how it was invented. It is easy to know that the magician is really performing a trick. It is much more difficult to figure out how she developed it.

Metaphorically speaking, this book is a kind of intellectual safari into the untamed jungles of early Christian history. Usually on such trips, travelers gratefully accept the assistance of the first Christian historian, Eusebius, the engaging guide who takes us to well-tread, civilized and safe campsites. Like the Gatekeeper of the Law in Kafka's *the Trial*, Eusebius is such an imposing authority that he seems impossible to get around. He is a giant casting a seventeen hundred year old shadow. Still, we will forego his assistance and head into largely unexplored and untraveled territory. Being on our own, we should not be surprised if we occasionally get lost, find ourselves going in circles or reach dead ends. This is a trip for the intellectually adventurous, not the faint of heart.

We will spot and photograph a number of rarely seen species. These include the followers of John the Nazarene, AKA John the Baptist. They worshipped Elijah as the once and coming Christ, before they worshiped John himself. Also we will encounter followers of Simon Magus, AKA Simon bar Caiaphas. They did not believe in the resurrection of the dead or any Christ; although, they came to believe in Simon as the true Word of God. We will also see the powerful, slavish followers of the early Church of God, and their leader, James the Just. They worshipped Joshua of Nun as the once and coming Christ and an alternative to Moses and his confusing outdated laws.

Traveling to the deeper regions, we will even catch glimpses of the mythological griffin named Jesus of Nazareth. In Greek mythology the griffin is part lion, part goat and part serpent. In Christian mythology, Jesus of Nazareth is part Greek philosopher, part Jewish angel, and part Roman God. We will break down the construction to see how each single part most likely grew out of legends associated with perhaps real historical characters. When we get back to civilization we will see the Griffin Jesus in the beautiful Byzantine Mosaics created by Eusebius that the worshiping natives hawk for a hefty price.

The reconstruction of Christian origins in this book is quite different from what one ordinarily encounters. It uses many different approaches and tools to arrive at new solutions to old problems. I believe I have been fortunate enough to make several important and original breakthroughs. I attribute these breakthroughs to the confluence of four unusual elements in my background: my background in philosophy, my background in cinema, my religious and family background, and my use of the new and unique opportunites opened to researchers by the recently developed communications system called *the Internet*.

I received my Ph.D. from the University of South Florida in 1997 after seven years of intensive study. In fact, I had been reading and studying philosophy less intensively since I was 16. So I have really had over 35 years training. Fortunately I read all the ancient philosophers before reading about Christianity. This fortunate accident allowed me to understand the mindset of educated people in the Roman Empire at the time when Christianity began. While this is not a philosophy book *per se*, I do often resort to the tools of philosophy, paying attention to the questions as much as the answers, trying to maintain a state of good cheer and equilibrium, and caring more about self-pleasure and knowledge than public opinion or convincing anyone of propositions.

Why should a philosopher write about Christianity? I categorize Christianity as an ideology and philosophy has always had an interest in ideology. My present definition of ideology is simply this: sets of ideas that are transmitted together over a certain period of time.

My background in film has been surprisingly helpful in this enterprise. I graduated with a BFA in filmmaking in 1976 from the School of Visual Arts and have maintained an interest in cinema and its history ever since. Films are a type of public dreaming. The gospels and most literature of the Bible can also be thought of as public dreams. Understanding the history of cinema has also helped me deconstruct many thorny problems in the New Testament that could hardly have been done without it. For example, scenes are filmed at different times and then intercut to produce certain effects. When one finds the same type of intercutting between scenes in Biblical text, one may often safely conclude that the original scenes were produced at different times and later edited together.

My family situation has also allowed me to see much that others have missed. I was born in a Jewish home in Queens, New York in 1953. I attended a Hebrew School from ages 8 to 13, Hillcrest Jewish Center. While I became an atheist around the age of 15, I still appreciate the opportunity to observe and understand Jewish customs that being born in a Jewish household permits. In 1980, while attending Boston University, I met my current wife Vicky Prodromidou, who is from Salonika, Greece. As a member of her Greek family, I have been able to closely observe Greek customs for over 25 years. This too has also contributed greatly to my understanding. There are only around 15 million Greeks and 15 million Jews in the world. My guess would be that there are only about 10,000 Jewish-Greek intermarriages in the world at the present time. So it is certainly an uncommon opportunity that I have had to observe, examine and weight the similarities and differences in the cultures. Of course one has to factor in the tremendous changes Greeks and Jews have undergone over two millenia. Still, my fortunate marriage and ethnic background has put me in a better position to separate out the Greek and Jewish elements in Christianity than most investigators have had.

Finally, what distinguishes this investigation from other prior investigations is my fortunate timing with the internet. Before the year 2000 there was hardly a good basic library's worth of information on early Christianity on the internet. Since then, a quite fantastic amount of information related to the subject has been put on the net, allowing more information at my fingertips than any researcher could possibly have gathered before now. The associated ability to search any document for any word or phrase instantaneously has also reduced research time by a factor of perhaps a thousand.

I would like to especially thank several people whom I have only met through the internet. Although I have never met them personally, I have spent many thousands of hours on their websites doing research. Peter Kirby has all the important early text for basic research in the field quickly accessible on his website *Early Christian Writings* at *http://www.earlychristianwritings.com/*. Roger Pearse's great website *The Tertullian Project* at *http://www.tertullian.org/* made accessible to me the many works of that greatest of Christian intellects—Q. Septimus Florens Tertullianus. In a way this book ignores Tertullian's tremendous contributions to the consolidation and development of Christianity. I look at the Jewish and Greek forms of Christianity in the first and second centuries and the Roman imperial form of Christianity that came with Eusebius and Constantine in the fourth century, but I leave a blank in the pivotal third century where Tertullian really sets the direction for the movement. I hope to remedy this by devoting a whole book to him in the near future.

A third website that has been indispensable to me has been the Yahoo discussion group JesusMysteries at *http://groups.yahoo.com/group/JesusMysteries/*. Its founder, Clarice O'Callaghan invited me to be a moderator in 2001 and I have spent nearly every day since reading wonderful thoughts and ideas of a multitude of contributors to this discussion group.

I have promised to finish this book so often over the last two years that my wife Vicky and my daughter Aphrodite believe that this book is as much of a myth as Jesus. I dedicate this book to them and their belief in me.

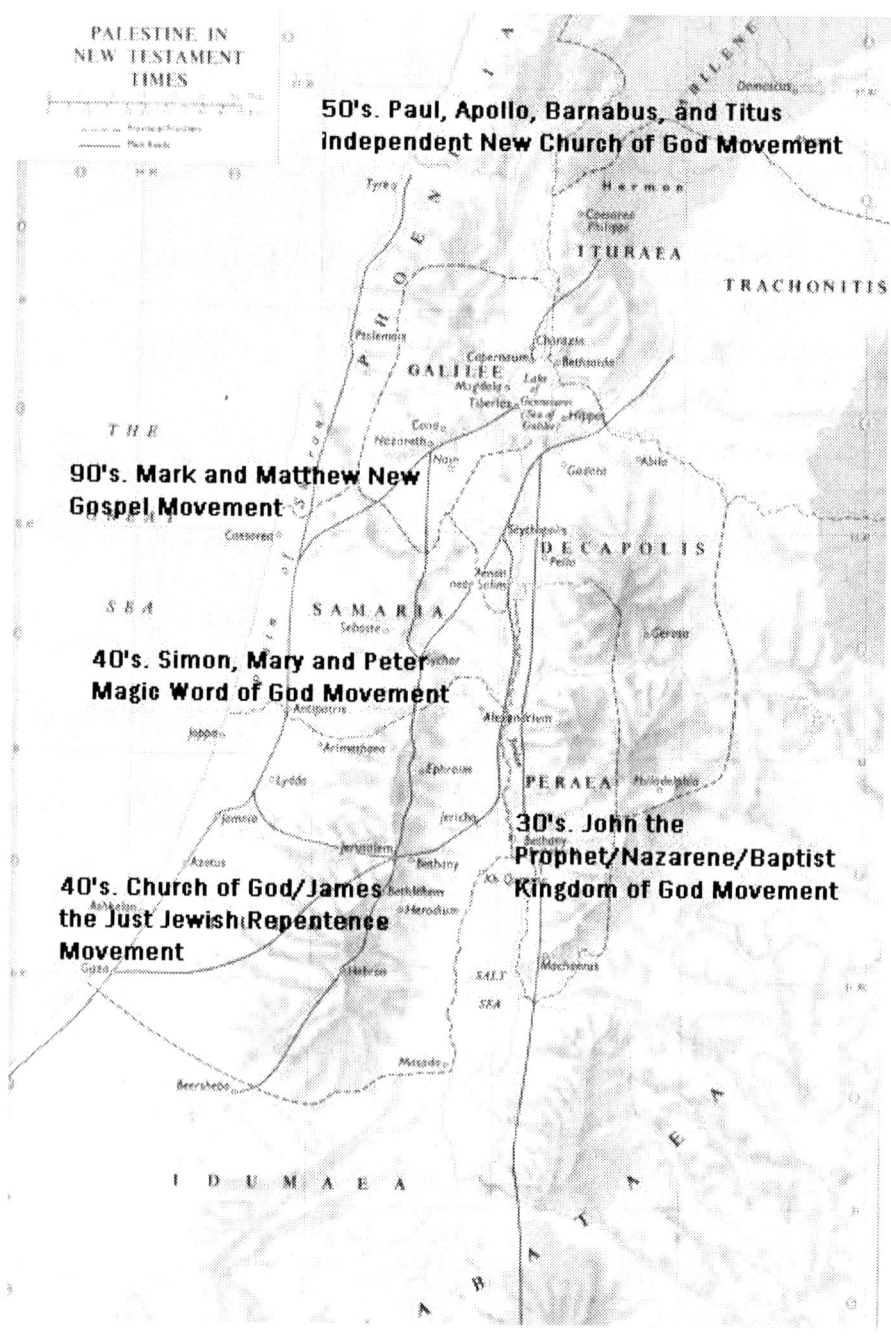

Map. Times and Relative Locations of Five Different Major Christ Movements in 1st Century Palestine

INTRODUCTION

A New View

> A developed mythology shows that man has taken a deep and active interest both in the world and in himself, and has tried to link the two, and interpret the one by the other. Myth is therefore a natural prologue to philosophy, since the love of ideas is the root of both. Both are made up of things admirable to consider[1].
>
> George Santayana

This work offers a new paradigm for Christian history. Although the book has fifteen chapters, in my original plan I divided the work into five sections, with each one demonstrating a major proposition. The five major propositions are: (1) Eusebius was the master constructor of the still dominant paradigm of Christian history, (2) a woman probably named Mary was the original writer of a Christ play, perhaps loosely based on historical incidents, (3) gospel writers changed a great deal of material about John the Baptist into material about Jesus, (4) the model for the crucified man was possibly a Samaritan magician named Simon, (5) an international proto-Christian Church of God existed with James the Just as their dying-founder, Christ figure. In order to demonstrate these things, I had to demonstrate the plausibility of many other interesting propositions. Thus the work has grown wildly into fifteen chapters after this introductory section.

In no case did I start with propositions and seek data to support them. As will be obvious from reading each section, the questions I started with and attempted to answer were quite different. It was only in the course of answering those questions that I was lead to these propositions.

The first section presents what we may call the *Eusebius the Master Forger* hypothesis. We suggest that the entire first half of Bishop Eusebius' *Church History* is made up of quotes from documents he carefully selected and edited to prove that his church was the only legitimate representative of the ideology of Jesus the Christ. This is important because most writers in the field still accept Eusebius as the best primary source for early Christian history. Once we see how Eusebius edited, invented and forged material to fit his ideological schemata about the origins of Christianity, we are forced to reconstruct early Christian history on a basis more consistent with the currently known facts and on a basis less dependent on his ideological prejudices. In the second section, we offer the *Mary, the Writer of Christ* hypothesis. We present evidence that a woman named Mary wrote an important early layer of the gospel material. The later authors of the gospels of *John* and *Mark* worked from this early layer. This evidence is so strong that one feels it is mainly the weight of dogmatic tradition and sexism that has kept more current writers in the field from drawing this obvious conclusion. We propose that she wrote this material as a play and may well have performed it in some of the numerous theaters that the Romans built throughout Judea and their empire. In the third section, we offer the *Rewriting of John the Baptist as Jesus the Christ* hypothesis. We offer evidence that the authors of the gospels of *Mark* and *Matthew* added material originally referring to and quoted by John the Baptist. They transferred many of these references and quotes from John to the Jesus character because they had little actual material with a Jesus character and they wanted to appeal to followers of John. Perhaps the most interesting proposition is the fourth one that the miracles of Jesus were based on tales about and historical incidents involving the Samaritan magician named Simon. The *Jesus Based on the Samaritan Simon* hypothesis is quite exciting especially combined with the third *Jesus-is-John* hypothesis. Nobody as far as I know has understood that the character of Jesus of Nazareth was primarily a late first century hybrid of historical facts and tall tales about the Samaritan magician (Simon) and the Jewish prophet John. In a fifth section, I make the case that an international Judeo-Christian Church of God existed and was a powerful institution before the myth/legend of Jesus of Nazareth existed. This Church seemed particularly interested in slave education and control. The story of the killing of the founder of this Church, James the Just, real or imagined, formed another important source for the killing of Jesus Christ story. Taken together, these hypotheses present a new and different version of early Christian history. They allow us a new and more accurate understanding of the invention and evolution of some of the major texts, practices, and ideologies of early Christianities. They are actually a beginning point for new and hopefully more accurate investigations of the New Testament texts.

Elaboration of Main Concepts

> Verily many things are wondrous, and haply tales decked out with cunning fables beyond the truth make false men's speech concerning them
>
> . Pindar
> *Olympian Odes,*
> "*For Hieron of Syracuse, Winner in the Horse-Race*[2]"

THE EVOLUTION OF CHRISTS AND CHRISTIANIES

The safest thing we can say about early Christian history is that there were many Christs and many Christianities. The New Testament texts tell us this. Josephus, the historian tells us this, and over two hundred Christian and Christian related texts from the first, second, third and fourth centuries tell us this. The multitude of Christs and Christianities is a simple fact. The development and authenticity of them are the points of controversy, both then and now.

The second safest thing that we can say about early Christian history is that forgeries, interpolations and re-editing of documents was the norm. Many texts of the period express doubt about the authenticity of other Christian texts. Many texts contain anachronisms demonstrating that they were produced later than the time of their stated production. There were no consistent or widespread procedures for determining the age or authenticity of documents. Generally, if a document proved a theological point someone wanted to make, it was accepted as genuine. If it opposed it, it was rejected as a forgery or devilish invention. Tertullian, at the beginning of the third century, expresses succinctly the state of the problem:

> For, no doubt, they too are able to retort these things on us. It is indeed a necessary consequence that they should go so far as to say that adulterations of the Scriptures, and false expositions thereof, are rather introduced by ourselves, inasmuch as they, no less than we maintain that truth is on their side[3].

This work presents an alternative history of the development of the ancient cults of Christianity. It is an alternative to the more or less "official" histories that has been developed over the last 1700 years. These histories, more or less, follow the general outline of the early fourth century Bishop of Caesarea, Eusebius Pamphilius. As the Catholic Encyclopedia says in reference to his *Ecclesiastical History*, "It would be difficult to overestimate the obligation which posterity is under to Eusebius for this monumental work[4]."

Eusebius argued that there had been one authentic Christ and one dominant Church or set of apostolic practices and teachings in the first and second centuries. While he may not have been the first to propose it, this line of thought, I dub "Eusebean." Ironically, the need of Eusebius to argue these propositions against a multitude of heretical Christianities allows us to raise the possibility that it is his version of Christian history that is actually a heretical fourth century invention coming from his own Alexandrian-Caesarean school, based primarily on the teachings of Clement and Origen of Alexandria.

We will argue that *Eusebean History* is indeed a fabulous construction of Eusebius. He has not related historical events in his history, but he has created a powerful source for discourse that is Christ-Church centered. Our problem is not just to show that Eusebean history was a fabulous creation of Bishop Eusebius, but to show what most or more probably did happen. Eusebean history will remain a central form of discourse until we provide an alternative source.

Once we see the unreality of Eusebean history, we lose many of our traditional sources for reconstructing Christian histories. A map, even a false one, may give us direction in our travels. Once we perceive the map as false, we may still cling to it and follow it in the hope that at least some of it is true. In this sense, a false map is preferable to no map. Simply pointing out that the old map leads us in circles may be a cynical exercise, if we are unable to provide a better one. The vast majority of this work is concerned with the more difficult task of constructing a more likely version of early Christian history. The important archaeological findings of the Dead Sea Scrolls and different texts at Nag Hammadi in Egypt in the middle of the last century, the development of superior computer and internet tools for manipulating data, plus our more sophisticated understanding of narrative development allows us to do this.

Ironically, once we see that our history is fiction, we must search in fiction for history. In this case we must take apart the gospels to arrive at a true or at least plausible history of the development of Christianity. In using this methodology, we need to be sensitive to what the text tells us and not fall back on interpreting the text in a Eusebean framework. By seeing how the Gospels are put together we may learn about the people who did the work of putting them together. We must understand that this is a two-step process. First we must understand the development of the textual forms of the gospels, especially the earlier source forms. We need to reconstruct them as best we can. Once reconstructed, we can then analyze these new earlier texts and conjecture about the lives and motives of the people who produced the original texts and the people who produced the textual transformations that brought us to the texts we now possess.

Our reliance on a multitude of modern and postmodern literary theories may be obvious to some readers. We think readers may be most surprised by our suggestions for practical paradigms to help reveal the creators behind the creations. For example, various *Nag Hammadi* texts and deconstructions of the canonical texts allow us to suggest a female author for some of the earliest material in the canonical gospels. Thus we need to study feminist literature to help us understand the earliest development of the gospels. In this context, we examine the origins of Baroness Emmuska Orczy's *Scarlet Pimpernel* (1905), Mary Roberts Rinehart's, *The Bat* (1920). Mary Shelley's *Frankenstein; or, The Modern Prometheus* (1819) and Maurine Watkins' play *Chicago* (1927). In each case a woman has made a significant contribution to popular culture, and in each case the significance of that contribution has been degraded[5] or erased by people who later took over the project. We do this primarily to suggest a new way of understanding the origin of the passion of Christ scenes at the end of some of our gospel texts. Before the feminist revolutions of the last half of the last century, such a proposition would have been virtually unthinkable.

Once we have seen past the screen of Eusebean thought and uncovered the important layer produced by Mary, we will still need to understand how the gospel texts took their present form. Just as we find a basic Mary layer at the end of the texts that points to a Mary cult and a more extensive Mary-based version of text, we can uncover a basic John layer in the beginning of the gospel texts. We must suppose that there was a John the Baptist/Christ cult with its own texts. What we will see that may be surprising is how much of their text has actually been transferred to the Jesus character from the John character. In support of the idea that John the Christ transformed into Jesus the Christ, we should take note that thousands of Mandeans (followers of John the Baptist) who believe that John was the Christ still survive amazingly in Iraq today. It seems probable that we should connect this long lasting cult with the original John the Christ cult movement of the first centry, although it is possible their current texts may not date back that far.

If most of Jesus' speeches come from John, Simon, a Samaritan magician, seems to provide us with the miracles and naturalistic philosophy that the later gospel writers worked from. The popularity of Simon the Magician seems to have hardly outlived his own life. If the texts attributed to Mary and Thomas referring to "The Savior" is actually referring to him, then we may assume that he recognized himself as "the Christ" or "the Standing One" in his lifetime. If *Acts, the Clementine Homilies* and *Clementine Recognitions* had not cast him into the role of anti-Christ we should hardly have guessed he played a role at all in the development of Christianity. In an ironic sense the Church Fathers who branded him as the "father of heresies" were quite correct. He was even the father of their own heresies. If there is an historical source to the Jesus literary character, Simon the Samaritan magician seems to be it.

Even if we may suggest the original gospel text was loosely based on some historical character, we should always keep in mind that the gospel authors never present themselves as giving their readers historical information. If they were presenting historical information, we should expect that they would immediately introduce themselves, their relationship to the events, and how they have acquired the information that they are relating. They would start out with something like, "I am Mark, the seventh disciple of Jesus. I first met him while fishing in Capernaum in the fourteenth year of Tiberius' reign. He was a short man with a . . ." We get nothing resembling this. The writers make no attempt to tell us who they are, their relationship to the events, or their sources of information. It is true that the writer of the prologue to the gospel of *Luke* claims a "perfect understanding of all things from the very first," but he never tells us who he is or how he arrived at this "perfect understanding." Therefore this has to be viewed as a rhetorical statement. Rather than reassuring us that the author is in a position to tell us a true story, it seems to suggest quite the opposite. It is a preamble similar in nature to the one we find in Lucian's *True History*:

> Know ye, therefore, that I am going to write about what I never saw myself, nor experienced, nor so much as heard from anybody else, and, what is more, of such things as neither are, nor ever can be. I give my readers warning, therefore, not to believe me.

Likewise, with rhetorical cunning, the writer, or at least the editor of the *Gospel of John* adds in his epilogue the interesting information that the "disciple whom Jesus loved, who had lain close to his breast at the supper" happens to be "the disciple who is bearing witness to these things, and who has written these things." Again, this is not clear precise historical information but a rhetorical game. In order to know who "has written these things," we have to know who the beloved disciple was. Was it John, as this text shyly informs us, or Mary, as story logic and other texts suggest? Again we are encountering literary playfulness here, not historical reporting of facts.

There are some things that we are certain about in this reconstructed alternative *Non-Eusebean* history and some things we are speculating about. In some cases the evidence appears logical and conclusive, while in other cases it merely appears most probable. We are certain Eusebius forged some of the texts now commonly attributed to Hegessipus (unless Hegessipus wrote his memoirs over a eighty year period) and we are certain that Eusebius edited the *Testimonium Flavianum* now found in the text of Josephus (as he himself gives different versions of it in different works). We are less certain that he interpolated material into works by Justin Martyr, Clement and Ignatius, and changed the authorship of Tertullian's *Against Heresies* to Irenaeus. It is possible that the suspicious evidence is wrong in these cases, or that someone chronologically close to Eusebius did these things. We are fairly certain a woman wrote the original passion text describing the coronation of a messianic character that is included in all the canonical gospels. It is too focused on the romance of Jesus and Mary to be by a man. We are less certain her name was Mary. Her name could have been Salome or Selena (the concubine of Simon, known also as Helena) or something else. We are certain that she was the only member of her group to claim to see the executed leader of their group after his death. We are less certain that this Mary was herself a mime actress and she wrote these things in a play. We offer this speculation as a good working hypothesis to explain her popularity and the popularity and style of her work. We are certain that the authors of *Matthew* and *Mark* took a great deal of text about John the Baptist and changed it into text about Jesus. We are less certain, when we suggest that the author of *Mark* was a scribe and the author of *Matthew* was a wealthy landowner. The terse writing style of Mark and the number of parables involving wealthy landowners strongly suggest these things, but do not make them certain.

The reader should apply as much skepticism to this new *Non-Eusebean* history as we hope she/he will apply to Eusebius' older history. In some cases our conclusions undoubtedly overreached the evidence. However, the reader should also note that in some cases our conclusions fit the facts so well that no other case seems reasonable or coherent. Perhaps, instead of saying we are writing a true history we should say we are giving notes for an interesting back story to the *New Testament* texts. We only contend that these notes fit the known facts better than many previous attempts to reconstruct that history.

Narratological Archaeology Applied to Jesus' Mother

> The fact that so much that is widely believed is wrong is a great incentive for research. In this case the joys of discovery are increased by finding buried treasures under the accumulated rubbish of centuries[6].
>
> Walter Kaufman
> *Tragedy and Philosophy*

I am doing narratological archaeology. I am looking at narratives or stories as human constructions and analyzing them to see how they probably came together. I use the jumps, contradictions and unusual constructions in sections of the narrative to reconstruct the earlier layers of that narrative.

If I was practicing a science rather then an art, I would start by laying out a set of rules and principles. However, for the most part, I have only used ordinary extensive research and logical deduction to arrive at my propositions and conclusions.

Rather then lay out a set of rules, I will give an example of how this technigue works. We may take the character of Mary, the mother of Jesus, as an example. The question that we ask is what do the primary texts tell us about the relationship between Jesus and his mother.

The twenty-one canonical *Epistles* and *Revelation* tell us nothing about Mary the mother of Jesus. This is an interesting oversight in light of later interest in the character. It suggests that the character was developed later than these texts. There is one small reference at the beginning of *Acts* to Mary after Jesus ascends to Heaven:

> 13. and when they had entered, they went up to the upper room, where they were staying, Peter and John and James and Andrew, Philip and Thomas, Bartholomew and Matthew, James the son of Alphaeus and Simon the Zealot and Judas the son of James.
> 14: All these with one accord devoted themselves to prayer, together with the women and Mary the mother of Jesus, and with his brothers.

We may take it that the author of *Acts* wished to paint a picture of harmony between the family of Jesus and the Apostles after his death. The author is not interested in telling us what happened to Mary after Jesus' death. Does she remarry? Does she live a long life? Does she wash floors in the church? The author tells us nothing. The author is reassuring us that Mary associated with the

Apostles after Jesus' death. Why would the author want to tell us this and only this? Could the audience for this work have thought that perhaps Mary did not associate with the Apostles after Jesus' death?

To answer this question, we need to look carefully at all the references to Mary in the four canonical gospels.

In the *Gospel of Mark*, there is no mention of Mary by name, only this one reference (chapter 3):

> 31: And his *mother* and his brothers came; and standing outside they sent to him and called him.
> 32: And a crowd was sitting about him; and they said to him, "Your *mother* and your brothers are outside, asking for you."
> 33: And he replied, "Who are my *mother* and my brothers?"
> 34: And looking around on those who sat about him, he said, "Here are my *mother* and my brothers!
> 35: Whoever does the will of God is my brother, and sister, and *mother*."

Note that Jesus is denying his mother and family and refusing even to speak with them at their request. This indicates a sharp rift between Jesus and his mother.

It is important to note that Mark does not say anything else about Mary. Given the importance on family background in virtually all ancient biographical material, the best explanation for this is that there was a major division between Jesus and his family including his mother.

The Church Father Tertullian, writing circa 205 CE, confirms this division (*De Carne Christi*, chapter 7):

> "The Lord's brethren had not yet believed in Him." So is it contained in the Gospel which was published before Marcion's time; whilst there is at the same time a want of evidence of His mother's adherence to Him, although the Marthas and the other Maries were in constant attendance on Him. In this very passage indeed, their unbelief is evident. Jesus was teaching the way of life, preaching the kingdom of God *and* actively engaged in healing infirmities of body and soul; but all the while, whilst strangers were intent on Him, His very nearest relatives were absent. By and by they turn up, and keep outside; but they do not go in, because, forsooth, they set small store on that which was doing within; nor do they even wait, as if they had something which they could contribute more necessary than that which He was so earnestly doing; but they prefer to interrupt Him, and wish to call Him away from His great work

If any literature existed before the third century showing the adherence of Mary, Jesus' mother, to him or his cause, we should expect that Tertullian would know about it and mention it. He confirms what the text suggests: Jesus' mother was not a follower.

A rift between Jesus and his family would explain why there is only one nameless reference to Mary in the *Gospel of Mark*. It also explains why the *Gospel of John*, like *Mark*, does not mention Mary's name. The writer of *John* does give us three additional scenes where conflict between Jesus and his family is also evident. Here is the first (*John, 2*):

1: On the third day there was a marriage at Cana in Galilee, and the *mother* of Jesus was there;
2: Jesus also was invited to the marriage, with his disciples.
3: When the wine failed, the *mother* of Jesus said to him, "They have no wine."
4: And Jesus said to her, "O woman, what have you to do with me? My hour has not yet come."
5: His *mother* said to the servants, "Do whatever he tells you."

Note that the line "O woman, what have you to do with me?" indicates that there has been a serious rift between Jesus and his mother before this point in the story and that he is not speaking or associating with her. It is only because they are at a wedding that they are together.

The line "O woman, what have you to do with me?" echoes a line from the *Gospel of Luke*, where Jesus meets a man possessed by a demon at a place called Gerasenes (Luke 8.28): "What have you to do with me, Jesus, Son of the Most High God? I beseech you, do not torment me." The expression "What have you to do with me," is extremely rude. It denies any kinship or social connection. It is something a demon possessed man would say. The similarity of the speech here and what Jesus says to his mother may indicate that Jesus was under the possession of a (demon or angel) in an earlier narrative when he spoke to his mother in this tone.

His mother speaks to the servants and gives authority over them to Jesus. "Servants" is simply a modern euphemism for "slaves". This appears to indicate that she was the owner of the servants/slaves in an earlier narrative. If the mother was merely a guest, why would she have authority over the slaves at the wedding? Also, why should she go to Jesus instead of the wedding host to get something done about the wine situation? It only makes sense if Jesus, or she herself, is the wedding host. We may assume that in the original story, the wedding was either the wedding of Jesus or a member of his family. Likewise we may assume that Jesus came from a wealthy family that owned slaves. We also have to consider the fact that she has to tell the slaves to obey Jesus. The fact that Jesus does not have authority over the slaves before this point in the narrative suggests his lowly status in the family and his poor relationship to his mother.

The next reference is more oblique but adds more weight to the contention of a rift (John 6):

> 41. The Jews then murmured at him, because he said, "I am the bread which came down from heaven."
> 42: They said, "Is not this Jesus, the son of Joseph, whose father and *mother* we know? How does he now say, 'I have come down from heaven'?"

The Jews take it that Jesus is denying his family by saying that he came from heaven. Note that the Jews are not denying that Jesus came down from Heaven, but simply indicating that by saying he came down from heaven, he has denied the parentage of his father and mother. Also note that the Jews do not distinguish between his denying Joseph and his denying Mary. They take it that Jesus has denied not only Joseph as his father, but also Mary as his mother. The *Gospel of John* has no birth narrative. We may take it that the author did not expect his readers to consult other gospels for a birth narrative of Jesus. Rather, the author of John strongly suggests that Jesus was not human but divine. The expression "I have come down from heaven," appears to exclude earthly parentage and is quite different from saying "I have a heavenly father and earthly mother."

The one other reference to the mother of Jesus occurs at the crucifixion scene (John 19):

> 25: So the soldiers did this. But standing by the cross of Jesus were his *mother*, and his *mother*'s sister, Mary the wife of Clopas, and Mary Magdalene.
> 26: When Jesus saw his *mother*, and the disciple whom he loved standing near, he said to his *mother*, "Woman, behold, your son!"
> 27: Then he said to the disciple, "Behold, your *mother*!" And from that hour the disciple took her to his own home.

The scene is confusing as we have no idea why Jesus would say to his mother, "Woman, behold, your son" while he is on the cross. Also, as written, his statement to the disciple, "Behold your mother" is incoherent. Why is he calling his own mother "your mother?" One should expect the disciple to respond, "What do you mean my mother? She's your mother."

Further, there appears to be little need for Mary, wife of Clopas, to be in the scene. She does not speak or do any action. If the readers had thought that Jesus was the son of Mary, wife of Clopas, then it would have been important for the author to distinguish her from Mary, mother of Jesus. We may take this to be the case. In the original text Jesus had been identified as the son of Mary and Clopas. The text wants to set them straight on this issue: Jesus was not the son of Mary Clopas. This appears to be additional information added onto the original scene.

Robert Eisenman in *James the Brother of Jesus*[7] has associated the name Clopas as a transformation of the name of the Jewish high priest Caiaphas, the high priest who turned Jesus over to Pilote. Later, in examining the passion narratives, we will see that it makes sense for the wife of Caiaphas to be referred to as the mother of Jesus.

For the moment, let us assume that the scene was not incoherent to begin with. If we combine the Mother of Jesus with the *Mary Wife of Clopas/Caiaphas* and switch the speakers of the lines, we can get the scene to make sense.

Cross Scene Reconstruction:

25: So the soldiers did this. But standing by the cross of Jesus were his mother, Mary, wife of Caiaphas, and Mary Magdalene.
26: When Mary saw his mother, she said to his mother, "Woman, behold, your son!"
27: Then Jesus said to Mary, "Woman, behold, your mother!" And from that hour Mary took her to her own home.

This reconstruction solves the following problems:

1) There is no need for Mary, wife of Clopas, to be in the scene in the original except to tell the readers that she is not Jesus' mother. Now, as Jesus' mother and the wife of the person who betrayed him, it makes perfect sense for her to be at the scene.
2) Instead of being confusing, the line of Jesus, "Woman, behold your mother" now matches the sharp and witty repartee of Jesus generally found in John.
3) In the gospel text, there is no reason for Jesus to tell his mother to look at her son. In the reconstructed text, it makes perfect sense for Mary to be accusing Jesus' mother in some sense as being responsible for her son's being on the cross, and demanding that she look at the results of her actions. There were probably more explicit scenes involving her rejection of Jesus in the original text and/or her collabation with Caiaphas in turning him over to the Roman authorities. Whatever she has done, the reconstruction indicates that her actions towards her son were considered wrong by the character Mary Magdalene and probably the author, herself. This reconstruction makes these relationships more explicit.
4) *John's Gospel* is the only gospel to acknowledge that Jesus' mother was at the crucifixion. The other gospels directly deny this by leaving her out and

substituting another woman named Mary. From this reconstruction, it now seems apparent why they are changing the scene. They are trying to hide Mary Magdalene's dominant role in the scene, and her antagonistic relationship to Jesus' mother. This explains the strange appearance of other Marys at the scene in the other gospels.

5) By having Mary take his mother into her house, Jesus is demanding that Mary forgive and reconcile with his mother. Not only does the reconstructed scene make more sense than the original, but it gives us deeper insight into the characters and shows Jesus' forgiving nature.

It should be noted again that neither John nor Mark name Jesus' mother as Mary. They do seem to know that there was conflict between Jesus and his mother. Either they did not know her name, or more likely because of the conflict between Jesus and his mother, they were suppressing her name. Both texts refer to this conflict, but at the same time gloss over it. Either explanation, that they didn't know her name, or wanted to hide her name, would account for the extraordinary lapse of not naming the mother of the lead character in their narratives. The authors' failure to provide us with this elementary biographical information contrasts sharply with other biographical narratives of the period and cannot be considered normal or accidental.

The *Gospel of Matthew* does name Jesus' mother. However, like the other two gospels it has nothing positive to say about her. His first reference is in the very first chapter:

> 18: Now the birth of Jesus Christ took place in this way. When his *mother* Mary had been betrothed to Joseph, before they came together she was found to be with child of the Holy Spirit;
> 19: and her husband Joseph, being a just man and unwilling to put her to shame, resolved to divorce her quietly.
> 20: But as he considered this, behold, an angel of the Lord appeared to him in a dream, saying, "Joseph, son of David, do not fear to take Mary your wife, for that which is conceived in her is of the Holy Spirit;

Mary would be 12½ years old, the age when Jewish girls were ordinarily put under contract for marriage. Joseph could break the contract if he found that she was not a virgin on the wedding night. So the fact that he is willing to marry her and divorce her quietly later afterwards shows concern for her and/or her family.

Since Joseph has already resolved to take Mary as his wife, the angel saying "do not fear to take Mary your wife" is a little strange if interpreted as the angel saying that Joseph should marry Mary. Why is the angel telling him to do something he has already decided to do? Rather, the angel seems to be telling him to not be afraid to "take Mary," i.e., have sex with her. This interpretation is confirmed by the lines immediately following (24, 25):

> When Joseph woke from sleep, he did as the angel of the Lord commanded him; he took his wife, but knew her not until she had borne a son; and he called his name Jesus.

The writer probably means to indicate that Jesus' brothers and sisters were born naturally through intercourse between Mary and Joseph and that none of them were divine. This is why the angel instructs Joseph to not be afraid to "take Mary."

There is also the idea in the background that if he did take Mary (i.e. have sex with her) and she produced another son, the first son, Jesus, would have inheritance rights and the true son of Joseph would be disinherited. We may guess that in an earlier narrative, Jesus was an illegitimate first born son, and one or more of Joseph's later real sons came in conflict with him. The divine paternity of Jesus was invented to answer the question, "Why would Joseph have a real son with Mary if she first had an illegitimate son?" Apparently, this problem was serious enough in the original narrative that an author had to bring in an angel (the Jewish equivalent of a *Deus ex machina* to explain it).

It is ironic that Jesus' divine paternity comes out of a desire to make the earlier narrative more realistic and believable.

It is also noteworthy that the text does not deny Mary's pregnancy before marriage. This indicates that the story of Jesus' illegitimate paternity circulated before the story of his divine paternity. It is important that there is no denial of Jesus' illegitimate paternity as it indicates it was an essential part of an earlier story.

The next reference to Jesus' mother is oblique (Matthew, 10):

34: "Do not think that I have come to bring peace on earth; I have not come to bring peace, but a sword.
35: For I have come to set a man against his father, and a daughter against her *mother*, and a daughter-in-law against her *mother*-in-law;
36: and a man's foes will be those of his own household.
37: He who loves father or *mother* more than me is not worthy of me; and he who loves son or daughter more than me is not worthy of me;

This is a general anti-family message, but most possibly it was meant to apply directly to Jesus' family, especially "and a man's foes will be those of his own household." It seems that in the stories that Matthew heard, Jesus considered his family his enemy. This is more evidence of a deep conflict between Jesus and his family. In chapter 12, Matthew repeats the information contained in Mark, but makes the rift between Jesus and his family more explicit, saying it was because of "their unbelief:

> 54: and coming to his own country he taught them in their synagogue, so that they were astonished, and said, "Where did this man get this wisdom and these mighty works?
>
> 55: Is not this the carpenter's son? Is not his *mother* called Mary? And are not his brothers James and Joseph and Simon and Judas?
>
> 56: And are not all his sisters with us? Where then did this man get all this?"
>
> 57: And they took offense at him. But Jesus said to them, "A prophet is not without honor except in his own country and in his own house."
>
> 58: And he did not do many mighty works there, because of their unbelief.

The statement about a prophet not having honor in his own country and his own house appears to confirm the fact of major antagonism between Jesus and his family. His not being able to perform magic because of their unbelief clearly shows that his family, including his mother, did not believe he had supernatural powers.

This gospel (12:46-50) also repeats the tale in the *Gospel of Mark* of Jesus refusing to see his mother and brothers. Like *Mark*, it replaces Jesus' mother at the crucifixion scene with another woman named Mary (27.6)

We have four scenes in the gospel of *Matthew* which match quite well with *Mark* and *John*. They show Jesus' mother as a source of conflict. The one scene that appears to show some sympathy for Mary, an angel announcing her divine pregnancy to her husband Joseph is probably more concerned with establishing that Jesus was not an ordinary illegitimate child and that Joseph was not behaving unrealistically by having more children with her.

From the three gospels of *Mark, Matthew* and *John* we may conclude that Jesus in an earlier narrative was an illegitimate first child who was rejected by his mother and brothers. This family conflict appears to have been an important element in the earlier narratives, but has been largely erased.

As he does in *Acts*, the author of the *Gospel of Luke* seems intent on rehabilitating the relationship between Jesus and his mother. For example in retelling the scene of Jesus refusing to see his mother and brothers, he blames it on the crowds (Luke, 8):

> 19: Then his *mother* and his brothers came to him, but they could not reach him for the crowd.
>
> 20: And he was told, "Your *mother* and your brothers are standing outside, desiring to see you."
>
> 21: But he said to them, "My *mother* and my brothers are those who hear the word of God and do it."

The way the author has rewritten the scene, it appears that Jesus' family is trying to see him preaching. This is in contrast to the other gospels where they appear to be trying to stop his preaching[8]. The fact that Tertullian seems unaware of this interpretation of the scene would suggest that it was written at or after his time in the early third century.

Most of our information about Mary comes from the first two chapters of the *gospel of Luke*. The first chapter actually begins by telling a tale of the birth of John the Baptist. While he's burning incense in a temple, an angel tells Zachariah, John's father, that his wife Elizabeth will give birth. The text tells us that Zachariah does not believe it and the angel makes him mute as punishment. The text continues:

24: After these days his wife Elizabeth conceived, and for five months she hid herself, saying,

25: "Thus the Lord has done to me in the days when he looked on me, to take away my reproach among men."

26: In the sixth month the angel Gabriel was sent from God to a city of Galilee named Nazareth,

27: to a virgin betrothed to a man whose name was Joseph, of the house of David; and the virgin's name was Mary.

It appears strange that the text is measuring the time of Gabriel's visit to Mary by the time (six months) of the conception of Elizabeth. One may conclude that in the original text Gabriel made his visit to Elizabeth after six months to explain to her that she was carrying a divine child. It is not only the awkward introduction of the Mary material that indicates this, it is also the fact that Zachariah does not believe the angel while the woman who Gabriel visits afterward does believe him. The symmetrical logic here is that Zachariah did not believe the angel, while Elizabeth his wife, did believe the angel. With the sudden and awkward introduction and substitution of Mary, the text loses that symmetry.

If we assume that Gabriel first announced this coming conception and birth to Elizabeth, we have an explanation for why Elizabeth ran and hid for five months. We must assume that it was she and not her husband Zachariah who was burning incense in the temple when the angel first appeared to her. We also should assume that after six months the angel visited Zachariah

Additionally, Gabriel does not tell Mary (originally Elizabeth) that the baby will be supernatural. He simply pronounces that she will become pregnant.

28: And he came to her and said, "Hail, O favored one, the Lord is with you!"

29: But she was greatly troubled at the saying, and considered in her mind what sort of greeting this might be.

30: And the angel said to her, "Do not be afraid, Mary, for you have found favor with God.
31: And behold, you will conceive in your womb and bear a son, and you shall call his name Jesus.
32: He will be great, and will be called the Son of the Most High; and the Lord God will give to him the throne of his father David,
33: and he will reign over the house of Jacob for ever; and of his kingdom there will be no end."
34: And Mary said to the angel, "How shall this be, since I have no husband?"

The response of Mary makes no sense here. She was engaged to be married. Marriages took place six months after the wedding contract. All young girls knew the facts of life and sexual reproduction. Censorship of such things for children hardly existed at the time. Nude statues and pictures of intercourse were in practically every Non-Jewish home. Mary would have assumed that she would be made pregnant by her husband and she must have known that she was under contract for marriage and would soon have a husband. This line must have originally read:

And Elizabeth said to the angel, "How shall this be, since my husband is so old and I am barren?"

This explains the followings lines:

35: And the angel said to her, "The Holy Spirit will come upon you, and the power of the Most High will overshadow you; therefore the child to be born will be called holy, the Son of God.
36: And behold, your kinswoman Elizabeth in her old age has also conceived a son; and this is the sixth month with her who was called barren.
37: For with God nothing will be impossible."
38: And Mary said, "Behold, I am the handmaid of the Lord; let it be to me according to your word." And the angel departed from her.

There is an interesting theological distinction here as the Holy Spirit appears to be the cause of Mary's pregnancy as opposed to a/the God of the most high. The author seems to want to explain that the pregnancy was caused by a spirit as opposed to directly by intercourse with a God. Be that as it may, it is an interruption of the text, as we have reconstructed it, and therefore, may be considered an addition to the original text. The answer to Elizabeth's question and the original text can be found in the next line, which we may reconstruct as:

36: And behold, your kinswoman ___?___ who was called barren also conceived a son with her husband in his old age.

The following scene describes Mary visiting Elizabeth. While it must have been fun for the author to put the two together while both were pregnant with their extraordinary progeny, it is clear that in the original scene, the pregnant visitor was not visiting the home of another pregnant woman. The giveaway is this line:

56: And Mary remained with her about three months, and returned to her home.
57: Now the time came for Elizabeth to be delivered, and she gave birth to a son.

It is quite absurd that Mary would stay with Elizabeth through the last three months of her pregnancy and then suddenly leave the house, just as Elizabeth would be giving birth and needing her assistance. Of course the idea that a pregnant 12 year old Mary would leave her parent's house and go running off for an unannounced visit to her pregnant Aunt's house is a little hard to take in the first place. It is clear that the woman who traveled is Elizabeth (who was in hiding as the text tells us).

Who did Elizabeth visit? In the next chapter, the author of Luke is kind enough to tell us this:

36: And there was a prophetess, Anna, the daughter of Phanuel, of the tribe of Asher; she was of a great age, having lived with her husband seven years from her virginity,
37: and as a widow till she was eighty-four.
38: And coming up at that very hour she gave thanks to God, and spoke of him to all who were looking for the redemption of Jerusalem.

The text on its own makes little sense. We may take this scene as having originally been part of the Elizabeth-in-hiding scene. We may take it that Elizabeth visited Anna and stayed with her. We may reconstruct the original scene this way:

In those days Elizabeth arose and went with haste into the hill country, to Jerusalem a city of Judah,

And there was a prophetess, Anna, the daughter of Phanuel, of the tribe of Asher; she was of a great age, having lived with her husband seven years from her virginity, and as a widow till she was eighty-four. She did not depart from the temple, worshiping with fasting and prayer night and day.

> And coming up at that very hour she gave thanks to God when Elizabeth entered the house of Phanuel, and she greeted Elizabeth.
>
> And when Elizabeth heard the greeting of Anna, the babe leaped in her womb; and Elizabeth was filled with joy and Anna exclaimed with a loud cry, "Blessed are you among women, and blessed is the fruit of your womb!
>
> And blessed is she who believed that there would be a fulfillment of what was spoken to her from the Lord."
>
> And why is this granted me, that the mother of my Lord should come to me?
>
> And Elizabeth said: For behold, when the voice of your greeting came to my ears, the babe in my womb leaped for joy.
>
> And Anna said "My soul magnifies the Lord, and my spirit rejoices in God my Savior, for he has regarded the low estate of his handmaiden. For behold, henceforth all generations will call me blessed; for he who is mighty has done great things for me, and holy is his name.
>
> And his mercy is on those who fear him from generation to generation.
>
> He has shown strength with his arm, he has scattered the proud in the imagination of their hearts, he has put down the mighty from their thrones, and exalted those of low degree; he has filled the hungry with good things, and the rich he has sent empty away.
>
> He has helped his servant Israel, in remembrance of his mercy, as he spoke to our fathers, to Abraham and to his posterity for ever."
>
> And Elizabeth remained with her about three months, Now the time came for Elizabeth to be delivered, and she gave birth and returned to her home. and Anna spoke of him to all who were looking for the redemption of Jerusalem.
>
> And her neighbors and kinsfolk heard that the Lord had shown great mercy to her, and they rejoiced with her.

The lines of the prophetess Anna, known as *the Magnificat* are an adaptation of Hannah's speech in *1 Samuel 2*. The lines are appropriate for a prophetess who longed to see the savior of Israel and now finds that the savior in the womb of a relative has come into her home. An editor of *Luke* switches these lines quite inappropriately to 12 year old Mary, where they make no narrative sense.

Up to this point we only have a narrative of the birth of John the Baptist by Elizabeth. The author of Luke has changed it to give us information about Mary's pregnancy. Since there is no gap between the point where Elizabeth leaves Anna's house to presumably return to Zachariah and the time she goes to Nazareth to give birth, we must assume that we are still dealing with the birth-of-John-by-Elizabeth text at this point. Assuming the opposite we will have to account for the fact that the narrative tells us nothing about Mary in the last six months of her pregnancy from the time she supposedly leaves Elizabeth's house to the time she goes to Nazareth. We must also account for the fact that John's birth is not described. Instead of a missing later pregnancy and a missing birth, seeing the original material as one text about Elizabeth, we find it a full and coherent narrative describing quite well both the later pregnancy of Elizabeth and birth of John.

An additional bit of evidence that Luke has split and rewritten Elizabeth's birth narrative to cover both Mary and Elizabeth can be found at Mary's final line at the end of chapter two. This line contradicts much hollowed ideology (*Luke*, 2.48):

> **And when they saw him they were astonished; and his mother said to him, "Son, why have you treated us so? Behold, your father and I have been looking for you anxiously."**

Mary here pronounces Joseph as Jesus' father. If we take the text as authentic as originally written by Luke, we have to say that Mary is making quite an error about his paternity. Since she has been told directly by an angel that the Holy Spirit is Jesus' father, we must conclude that she has been lying to Jesus or that she disbelieved the angel who pronounced the holy spirit and not Jesus as his father. On the supposition that the text originally read Elizabeth at this point, we may only conclude that the editor suffered fatigue at this point and did not bother to change the text to fit the prior narrative he had created. He simply changed the name of the wayward child from John to Jesus.

In sum, we may conclude that the earliest layers of the gospel reflect the idea that Jesus did not get along with his mother and family and that in some very early stories there was a great deal of conflict between them. The idea of Jesus' divine birth through Mary and the Holy Spirit seems to be a late addition by the editor of the *gospel of Luke, occuring* in the third century. It is unknown to the writers of the gospels of John and Mark, although Matthew mentions it also in an offhanded fashion to resolve a problem with the narrative developing out of Jesus' illegitimacy.

Most importantly, while we have seen that Mary, the mother of Jesus, plays an antagonistic role towards Jesus in the early text, we have seen that Mary Magdalene plays the role of faithful and obedient lover. Even from this slight textual analysis and reconstruction, we can see that Mary Magdalene played a more significant role in the earlier narratives than the canonical gospel writers reveal to us. As we will see later, she is Jesus' "passion" in the *Passion story of Jesus the Christ*.

If this is correct there is a great deal of irony in the fact that Jesus' mother was changed into an obedient sexual virgin in the later narratives. We may take it that in the earliest narratives she had children by different lovers/husbands and was antagonist towards the work of Jesus. On the other side, Mary Magdalene, who was probably a sexual virgin and showed the greatest loyalty towards Jesus of any of his disciples seems to have ended up in later tales labeled as a demon possessed prostitute. We should keep this in mind when we later look more closer at her role in the gospels.

This is an illustration of my technique for analyzing the Christ narratives in the Bible. It uses a variety of techniques aimed at working out the development of the story. While we cannot expect to find all the changes that the narratives went through, I believe we can get a pretty good idea of most of them. The reconstructions are problematical because we have no outside evidence for them. However, if we do not assume that such earlier narratives existed, we are left with a multitude of narratological problems. For example, if the writer of *Luke* did not rewrite a narrative of John's birth, how do we account for the fact that none of the other text seems aware of the family relationship between John and Jesus? Why spend so much time describing the situation of John's parents and so little time describing the situation with Jesus' parents? Why should Zachariah's disbelieving attitude towards the angel not be contrasted with Elizabeth's attitude, but instead contrasted with Mary's attitude? A multitude of such problematical configurations disappear when we simply assume the writer has edited a pre-existing narrative of John's birth into the gospel. Similarly, one has to ask why Jesus tells his mother to look at him on the cross? One cannot possibly understand why he does this from the text as written. Why does the writer of *John* not tell us which disciple took the mother of Jesus in? Why do the other writers not even mention Jesus' mother being at the cross? These and many other obvious questions are answered by assuming an earlier text and reconstructing it along the lines I have indicated. While my reconstructions of scenes here and in later parts of this work are unlikely to be perfect copies of what the original narrative texts were, they may be taken as containing some important elements that the original narratives presented. These important elements were lost or suppressed by the later gospel writers.

All archaeological hypotheses involve painting pictures of what was in existence in the past from what has actually come down to us through time. The Christ narratives are no different than the ruins of other structures from Antiquity. We need to use deductive and inductive skills to recreate an image of what was there. Hopefully, we will find these original layers of text. Until we do, we may analyze all the texts we do have to suggest what we do not have.

Mosiac Christ as a Young Beardless Roman Soldier.

Archbishop Andrea's Palace Chapel, Ravenna, Italy, circa 500. Christ carries a wand-cross and stands on a Lion and Snake. The book he holds reads, "I am the way, the truth and the life."

Chapter 1

Eusebius the Master Forger

The History that is Not "a Perfect and Complete History"

> But at the outset I must crave for my work the indulgence of the wise, for I confess that it is beyond my power to produce a perfect and complete history[9] . . .
>
> Eusebius
> Pamphilius

In an extraordinary moment of extreme honesty, in his work *Theophania*, Eusebius Pamphilius, Bishop of the major city of Caesarea, and first Christian historian tells us that he finds the teachings of the apostles ridiculous. They are filled with contradictions. They are not something that he or any intelligent man could take seriously. He writes:

> But, let it be supposed that the persuasives now put forth were these, (viz.) that those who were His ambassadors, should at one time preach that He was God; that, in body, He was human; and that, in his nature, He was no other than The Word Of God: on which account also, He performed all these miracles, and (put forth these) powers: but, that at another time, He suffered reproach and infamy, and at last the capital and shameful punishment of the Cross; which is inflicted on those (only), who are in their deeds the worst of all men. Who then, would not (now) properly treat them with ridicule, as affirming things opposed to each other? And, Who is he, whose intellect would (partake) so much of stone, as readily to believe them, when they said that they saw Him after His death? that He rose from the dead?—Him (I say), who could

> not help Himself when among the living And (again), Who would ever be persuaded by men so illiterate and, deficient as these, when saying; You should despise the things of your own forefathers; charge as folly those of the wise of ancient times; suffer yourselves to be persuaded by us alone, and to be commanded by the precepts of Him who was crucified: for He only is the beloved, and only (begotten) of that God alone, who is over all?
>
> I myself however, investigating for myself with effort and in the love of truth, this same thing (singly), should perceive not one virtue in it (making it) credible, nor even any thing great, or worthy of faith, nor so persuasive, as adequate to the persuading of even one illiterate person, much less men wise and intellectual. Nevertheless, when again I view its power, and the result of its doings; how the many myriads have given their assent to it, and how Churches of tens of thousands of men have been brought together, by these very deficient and rustic persons;—nor that these were built in obscure places, nor in those which are unknown, but rather in the greatest cities, I say in the Imperial city of Rome itself, in Alexandria, in Antioch, in all Egypt, in Libya, in Europe, in Asia, both in the villages and (other) places, and among all nations; I am again compelled to recur to the question of (its) cause, and to confess, that they (the Disciples) could not otherwise have undertaken this enterprise, than by a Divine power which exceeds that of man, and by the assistance of Him who said to them, "Go, *and make Disciples of all nations in my name.*[10]"

The gospel texts of the apostles are not "credible" for Eusebius. They could not persuade "even one illiterate person, much less wise and intellectual." What is credible for Eusebius, and incredible too, is the power of the church that he sees before his own eyes, "I view its power and the results of its doings; how the many myriads have given their assent to it, and how Churches of tens of thousands have been brought together."

What has converted Eusebius to Christianity[11], is the rags to riches tale of the Roman Catholic Church. He is struck by how it has gone from one righteous man and a few poor followers to a world wide institution that brings tens of thousands of people together. Eusebius cannot explain this transformation except by supposing that it is a miracle from God. It is this thrilling tale of God's direct intervention in human history that Eusebius seeks to tell in his *Church History*.

In one sense his *History* acts as a supplement to the *Gospels*. While it basically starts from the canonical gospel stories, it mainly continues their theme of God's intervention in history showing that only the Roman Catholic Church faithfully followed in the footsteps of Jesus, with the Church being persecuted and triumphantly resurrected like Jesus. It suggests that the real fulfillment of the gospel story is occurring in his own time with the triumph of Constantine, the Catholic Church and Christianity in Rome. In another sense his *History* may be seen as a replacement or a substitution for the antiquated gospel narratives, generalizing and universalizing the rather provincial and time specific incidents found in them to give a more complex and complete picture of Christianity. To Eusebius, the gospel stories of Jesus were narratives of an archetypal event that preceded and predicted the historical story of the Church. The persecution and martyrdom of Jesus was repeated over and over again in the Church, until, like Jesus rising to serve at the right hand of the one true God, the Church rose to serve at the right hand of the one true Emperor of Rome.

This background ideology should be kept in mind when we examine the opening passages of the *History* where he states his methodology for carrying out his plan for the *History*. Here are the opening lines.

1. It is my purpose to write an account of the successions of the holy apostles, as well as of the times which have elapsed from the days of our Saviour to our own; and to relate the many important events which are said to have occurred in the history of the Church; and to mention those who have governed and presided over the Church in the most prominent parishes, and those who in each generation have proclaimed the divine word either orally or in writing.

2. It is my purpose also to give the names and number and times of those who through love of innovation have run into the greatest errors, and, proclaiming themselves discoverers of knowledge falsely so-called have like fierce wolves unmercifully devastated the flock of Christ.

3. It is my intention, moreover, to recount the misfortunes which immediately came upon the whole Jewish nation in consequence of their plots against our Saviour, and to record the ways and the times in which the divine word has been attacked by the Gentiles, and to describe the character of those who at various periods have contended for it in the face of blood and of tortures, as well as the confessions which have been made in our own days, and finally the gracious and kindly succor which our Saviour has afforded them all. Since I propose to write of all these things I shall commence my work with the beginning of the dispensation of our Saviour and Lord Jesus Christ[12].

Note in the first paragraph, the first thing he mentions is his plan to write about the "successions" of the holy apostles. He is starting at the starting point of the Acts of the Apostles. That work only shows the succession of Matthew to the position of Judas among the twelve apostles. He will show how James succeeded Jesus, Peter succeeded James and founded the Roman Church and Paul succeeded Peter in Rome.

This again suggests that he sees the *History* as a needed supplement, addition or correction to the now defective New Testament texts of which he has told us he "perceive not one virtue in it (making it) credible, nor even any thing great, or worthy of faith, nor so persuasive, as adequate to the persuading of even one illiterate person, much less men wise and intellectual." Eusebius intends to write something "credible," "great," "worthy of faith," and "persuasive." He intends his *History* to bring both illiterate and wise and intellectual people into the Church.

Each of the three paragraphs may be taken separately. In the first he tells us that he is going to write about the Church. In the second, he tells us that he is going to write about Christians who opposed the Church, (the inside enemies of the Church). In the third, he tells us that he is going to write about the Jewish and gentile opposition of the Church (the outside enemies of the Church), and the defenders of the church as well. The second two paragraphs may be taken as an expansion on what he tells us in the first paragraph. He merely tells us that he will name the bad guys as well as the good guys.

Focusing in on the first paragraph, we see that Eusebius intends to provide five types of information. He is going to tell us 1) the "successions of the holy apostles," to the leadership role in the Church, the order of the apostles—who came first, second, third and fourth, 2) an account of "the times which have elapsed," 3) relate the most important events in the development of the Church, 4) mention or give a list of the leading Bishops of the Roman and other main churches, and 5) mention or give a list of Church defenders. He does not tell us why he is selecting these types of information to put together. Unlike other ancient historians who explain why they are writing, Eusebius gives no explanation.

It is true he tells us he asks for God's help, "I pray that I may have God as my guide," that nobody has covered the material before, "I know of no ecclesiastical writer who has devoted himself to this subject," and he hopes it will be useful, "I hope that it will appear most useful to those who are fond of historical research." However, he gives no explicit statement of why he is writing this material in the way he is writing it.

Contrast this with, for example, Josephus who immediately tells us why he is writing his history.

> **Whereas the war which the Jews made with the Romans hath been the greatest of all those, not only that have been in our times, but, in a manner, of those that ever were heard of; both of those wherein cities have fought against cities, or nations against nations; while some men who were not concerned in the affairs themselves have gotten together vain and contradictory stories by hearsay, and have written them down**

after a sophistical manner; and while those that were there present have given false accounts of things, and this either out of a humor of flattery to the Romans, or of hatred towards the Jews; and while their writings contain sometimes accusations, and sometimes encomiums, but no where the accurate truth of the facts; I have proposed to myself, for the sake of such as live under the government of the Romans, to translate those books into the Greek tongue, which I formerly composed in the language of our country...

Josephus intends to give a more balanced and accurate account of the war: why he is writing is clear; however, Eusebius, in contrast, starts by telling us what he intends to do and not why. We can make some reasonable guesses of why he wrote based on the clues he gives us in his plan of writing. He begins with the succession of the Apostles. If we assume Eusebius wrote his opening around 310-315 C.E., this would be around the period of Constantine coming to power in the Western Empire (306 C.E. in Britain, Gaul, and Spain). By 310 there were actually five emperors vying for power and legitimacy over Rome—Constantine, Galerius, Maxentius, Maximinus II, and Licinius. The *Tetrarchy* that Diocletian had created just 17 years before in 293 to save the Roman Emperor was already falling apart. Henry Chadwick in his recent book *The Church in Ancient Society* reminds us that succession was an extremely important issue around this time for the first Christian Emperor Constantine:

> Until reluctantly recognized as a Caesar by Galerius he was actually a usurper without proper title to the authority claimed. In those circumstances it would have seemed desirable at least to have divine sanction, and not merely that of his legions[13].

Did Eusebius intend to give divine sanction to Constantine, to show him in a direct line of rulers from the Christian God to Jesus to the Apostles and the Bishops of Rome? It is probable that Eusebius was writing parts of his *History* before Constantine had obtained his victory in 312 over Maxentius. Timothy Barnes suggested that Eusebius worked on the *History* from before 300 to 325[14]. More likely Eusebius just wanted to show an orderly succession of divine sanction for the Church itself in contrast to the non-divine, non-sanction of the Roman emperors. Constantine does not become the hero of Eusebius's *History* until the later books, probably in a later revision. Actually, Eusebius shows no intention of making him the hero at this starting point. At best, helping the legitimacy of Constantine may have been a background consideration for Eusebius until he wrote the last books.

We may take it that Eusebius just wishes to teach a moral lesson by demonstrating the orderly and peaceful succession of the apostles in the Church in contrast to the disorderly and violent succession of Emperors of contemporary

Rome. This is his first goal. The second goal follows from this. He will give an account "of the times which have elapsed from the days of our Saviour to our own." The reason for this is easy to discern. It has been over two hundred years since the time of the Apostles. Eusebius has to explain why with an orderly and peaceful succession of Apostles it still took over two hundred years for the Church to reach its newly found prestige in the Roman Empire. In order to do this, Eusebius will do his third action of relating the major events in the History of the Church. These major events will be the persecutions and betrayals that the Church suffered from the time of the Apostles.

Fourth on his list of things to do is "to mention those who have governed and presided over the Church in the most prominent parishes." This is as astonishing for what Eusebius does not tell us as for what he does tell us. He does not tell us that he is going to give a Bishop's list for Rome and the other prominent parishes. This should be put in contrast with the first intention of Eusebius to give a list of the succession of the Apostles. Eusebius does not intend to give a list of the succession of Bishops at Rome at this point. He is just going to mention those who have "governed and presided over the most prominent parishes" It is astonishing that he intends to mention these people but unlike the Apostles he is not going to put them in chronological order and show their succession. One would expect that there would be debates over who ruled which parishes when and that it would be an important point for Eusebius to put them in order. This is what he actually does inside the text. However, it is apparent that his intention at this point is only to mention them and not give their succession as he will with the Apostles.

At this point in the writing of the text, Eusebius tells us he wants to make them known. One may take it that the heads of the churches were unknown, nameless administrators who did their job behind the scenes and avoided scandal and gossip as much as possible. This was the position of the Chairmen of the Boards of Directors of most major corporations in the nineteenth and early twentieth centuries. Although some, like Henry Ford, John D. Rockerfeller, Andrew Carnegie and Howard Hughes did attract enormous press attention due to their incredible and excessive wealth. We may suppose that most leaders of churches were quite unknown outside their local communities. Eusebius wishes to give them credit for the important role they have played in defending Christianity, at least the ones like himself from the more prominent churches.

Fifth, Eusebius tells us of his intention to mention "those who in each generation have proclaimed the divine word either orally or in writing." Beside the leaders of the Church, Eusebius wants to name the publicists and writers for the Church. Note that for Eusebius the category of proclaimer of the divine word is separate from the category of church leader. There were church leaders who did not proclaim the divine word and non-leaders who did. The phrase "in each generation" suggests that he does plan to put these writers and preachers in chronological order.

We can say that Eusebius started out with a plan to show the orderly succession of the apostles. We can derive this from it being the first intention he mentions, but also from this early statement in the *History* that he would be, "content if we preserve the memory of the successions of the apostles of our Saviour; if not indeed of all, yet of the most renowned of them in those churches which are the most noted, and which even to the present time are held in honor[15]." It is to create or collect these tales of apostolic origin for the major churches that is the first important task that Eusebius sets for himself. It is clear that Eusebius is intent on creating tales of divine origin for his churches from the language he uses when first describing the origin of the churches:

> Thus, under the influence of heavenly power, and with the divine co-operation, the doctrine of the Saviour, like the rays of the sun, quickly illumined the whole world, and straightway, in accordance with the divine Scriptures, the voice of the inspired evangelists and apostles went forth through all the earth, and their words to the end of the world.
>
> In every city and village, churches were quickly established, filled with multitudes of people like a replenished threshing-floor. And those whose minds, in consequence of errors which had descended to them from their forefathers, were fettered by the ancient disease of idolatrous superstition, were, by the power of Christ operating through the teaching and the wonderful works of his disciples, set free, as it were, from terrible masters, and found a release from the most cruel bondage. They renounced with abhorrence every species of demoniacal polytheism, and confessed that there was only one God, the creator of all things, and him they honored with the rites of true piety, through the inspired and rational worship which has been planted by our Saviour among men[16].

We should keep in mind that Eusebius is writing about events 250 years in his past. He cites no sources for this description. It is clear in these passages we are not dealing with writing that may in any meaningful sense be labeled history. Rather, it fits more easily into the category of apocalyptic writing, with the Roman Church of his time undergoing the apocalypse. To put it bluntly, Eusebius is not reporting history, he is telling us a fairy tale. Barnes has put it less bluntly but has indicated the non-historical nature of the work when he wrote:

> Eusebius was limited by more than his inability to date and evaluate all the evidence correctly. He projected the Chruch of the late third century back into the first two centuries and assumed that Christian churches had always been numerous, prosperous, and respectable. He thus could not perceive or document one of the crucial transitions in early Christianity. In 180 the Christians were an obscure sect, widely

believed to enjoy "Oedipodean incests and Thyestean banquets." Within a generation, however, there were Christians or Christian sympathizers at the imperial court and in the Roman Senate... [17]

Eusebius and the Miraculous Founding of Christian Churches

To understand the methods and motives of Eusebius better, we may look at how he treats the founding and history of three churches: Edessa, Jerusalem and Caesarea. I picked these churches for good reasons. Edessa is the first church he covers and he obviously has a lot of information about it from what he calls "public registers[18]," Jerusalem is an extremely important church and Caesarea being just a couple of days travel time from Jerusalem, he should be able to give us a lot of information about it, while the Church at Caesarea is his home base and logically, he should have the most easy access to historical information about it.

1. The Church at Edessa

As the succession of the apostles and a description of their founding of the churches is one of the primary intentions of Eusebius ("to mention those who have governed and presided over the Church in the most prominent parishes"), we should expect that he would put a great deal of energy to this portion of his narrative. Certainly, if the Churches had been refuting heretical Christians for hundreds of years, they must have pointed out repeatedly how they were founded by the actual apostles of the Christ himself in counter distinction to the heretics. One would expect that each church would have kept a detailed description of when and how each apostle founded it. Let us examine the information Eusebius gives us in this regard

Eusebius first tells us about the founding of the Christian Church in Edessa, present day Sanliurfa in Southeastern Turkey. Eusebius tells us a long story about the King of Edessa, Abgar, sending letters to Jesus to entreat him to come to Edessa and heal him. Jesus begs off but sends a follower named Thaudas (also called Addas) to heal and convert Abgarus and start the Church in Edessa Walter Bauer notes this about the text:

> The account of the conversion of Edessa, which we have just presented from Eusebius (EH 1.13; cf. 2.1.6-8), can in no way and to no extent be traced back as a report that is earlier than the beginning of the fourth century[19]...

Two texts may appear to controvert Bauer's assessment. There is a work called The *Doctrina Addai* from the early fifth century that includes and expands upon Eusebius's tale and there is a line in a fourth century work called the *Book of the Laws of the Countries* by the poet Bardasanes from Edessa, which includes a single line which may be taken as evidence of King Abgar's conversion. Bauer points out about the former work, *Doctrina Addai*, "In it the material known from Eusebius reappears, albeit to a considerable measure expanded, among other things, by a detailed account of the activity of the apostolic emissary in Edessa, who preaches, baptizes, and builds the first church." We are dealing with someone using the Abgarus story from Eusebius's History rather than someone using an independent source[20].

The second source is more interesting. Bauer tells us this about it:

> Chapter 45 reads: "In Syria and in Urhâi the men used to castrate themselves in honor of Taratha. But when King Abgar became a believer, he commanded that anyone who emasculated himself should have a hand cut off. And from that day to the present no one in Urhâi emasculates himself anymore." Thus we have reference to a Christian King Abgar by an Edessene author at the beginning of the third century. Since, on the basis of what is known, Abgar V does not qualify, one may now think of the ninth Abgar, who probably would have been an early contemporary of that author.
>
> But does a person use the expression "from this day down to mine" to speak of his contemporary? Is not one who speaks in this way looking back to a personality who lived much earlier? But this observation, which serves to shake the opinion that the text refers to Abgar IX, by no means leads to the view that one must now refer it to Abgar V and suppose that the Abgar legend already existed in some form at the time when the *Book of the Laws of the Countries* was written. For that book really offers no guarantee for the presence of Christianity within the Edessene royal household, be it earlier or later. The Syriac text from which we have proceeded can not be trusted. The earliest witness for the text of that ancient Syriac writing under consideration is not a codex in that language, but is Eusebius, who has copied the *Book of the Laws* n his *Preparation for the Gospel* (6.10.) When he comes to speak of the customs in Edessa, he is in close enough agreement, for the most part, with the Syriac text; but the explanation referring to the faith of the king—that is, the words "when he became a believer" in the passage cited above—cannot be found in Eusebius (6.10.44). But since he knew of a King Abgar of Edessa who had become a believer, as is clear from the *Ecclesiastical History* and since he had absolutely no reason to eliminate the words which would have been helpful to the Christian cause, the only remaining conclusion is that he did not find them in his source; and the Syriac text doubtless is indebted for them, as an appended postscript, to someone who knew the Abgar legend. If this sort of person heard of such a measure taken by a King Abgar, a measure

> which from his point of view must have seemed directed against paganism, to what else could he attribute it than the Christian faith of the famous prince Abgar? Actually the decisive stand of an ancient ruler against emasculation requires no Christian motivation. From the time of Domitian, the pagan emperors proceeded with ever sharper measures against this offense.

Bauer points out the Eusebean text which quotes Bardasanes does not have the phrase "when he became a believer" while the Syrian text does. Bauer simply concludes that it was not in the original text and was added post-Eusebius and therefore cannot be used as support that the story of Abgarus' conversion was known pre-Eusebius.

Now, if we look at the text Eusebius quotes in *Preparation for the Gospel*, we find that Bardasanes is arguing for the diversity of human laws. Suddenly at the very end, totally out of place, after the mention of King Abgarus, the text argues a different opinion that there is only one true law, the Christian law. We may take it that someone has forged a Eusebean position onto the original text by Bardasanes. That it was Eusebius himself who did it becomes clear when we consider that the King Abgarus passage includes the phrase "to the present time." We will demonstrate later that this phrase is Eusebius's tell, a phrase used repeatedly by Eusebius that gives him away when he is rewriting a text.

From this, and other examples I will give later, we may conjecture that Eusebius would take a text and copy it into a work he was writing. While rewriting into his text, he would change the text to include what he wishes to prove his argument (in this case that Christian law is universal). He then takes the original work and rewrites it (or has it rewritten) to reflect the changes he has made in his own work. While rewriting the original work, he again adds and changes it from his own work to sharpen his point. Most likely, he then destroys the copy of the original work he has changed. I will give more examples of his use of this methodology later[21].

To return to my main point in this section, Eusebius gives his source for the beginning of the Church in Edessa by Abgarus as "the archives of Edessa[22]." We have no evidence that this source existed or that anybody knew about this source before or after Eusebius.

One may wonder why Edessa was chosen as the first church to be mentioned by Eusebius. Actually, it seems reasonable that Eusebius wanted to show that a king and Jesus could/did get along. The idea that Christianity was anti-king or emperor was probably still strong, and Eusebius wanted to reassure the powerful that Jesus came to heal and help the powerful as well as the poor and weak. Secondly, we should note that it is Thaddeus, one of the seventy, rather than one of the twelve apostles who founds the Church. This would help to explain lapses in doctrine in Edessa. As Eusebius later explains, Jesus gave truth to James, John and Peter, and they gave it to the remaining

THE EVOLUTION OF CHRISTS AND CHRISTIANIES

Apostles, like Thomas, who in turn told the seventy like Thaddeus, the church starts off in a subordinate position to those church founded directly by the main Apostles, like the Church at Rome and Eusebius's church at Caesarea.

2. The Church of Jerusalem

The second Church that Eusebius covers is the Church of Jerusalem. Here, he informs us James the "so-called[23]" brother of Jesus became head after Jesus' death. He gets this from Acts of the Apostles. Eusebius has a problem with this. It appears that nepotism is involved with the selection of James. However Eusebius apparently wants us to believe that Mary remained a Virgin and thus was not James real mother, and naturally even if Joseph was his real father, this would not make James a real brother to Jesus who had God as a father. Eusebius wants to show it is not his sibling relationship to Jesus that got him the job, but his righteousness. He uses Clement of Alexandria as his source on this:

> But Clement in the sixth book of his Hypotyposes writes thus: "For they say that Peter and James and John after the ascension of our Saviour, as if also preferred by our Lord, strove not after honor, but chose James the Just bishop of Jerusalem." But the same writer, in the seventh book of the same work, relates also the following things concerning him: "The Lord after his resurrection imparted knowledge to James the Just and to John and Peter, and they imparted it to the rest of the apostles, and the rest of the apostles to the seventy, of whom Barnabas was one. But there were two Jameses: one called the Just, who was thrown from the pinnacle of the temple and was beaten to death with a club by a fuller, and another who was beheaded[24]. Paul also makes mention of the same James the Just, where he writes, "Other of the apostles saw I none, save James the Lord's brother."

Notice here the second statement that Eusebius alleges he found in Clement, "The Lord after his resurrection imparted knowledge to James the Just and to John and Peter, and they imparted it to the rest of the apostles, and the rest of the apostles to the seventy, of whom Barnabas was one." Compare this to what Eusebius himself has said in Book I.

> The names of the apostles of our Saviour are known to every one from the Gospels. But there exists no catalogue of the seventy disciples. Barnabas, indeed, is said to have been one of them, of whom the Acts of the apostles makes mention in various places, and especially Paul in his Epistle to the Galatians.

49

In book one, Eusebius has mentioned the seventy disciples and immediately identified Barnabas as one of them. In book two, Eusebius has quoted Clement mentioning the seventy disciples and immediately identified Barnabas as one of them. We may assume that Eusebius has gotten his information from Clement regarding Barnabas being one of the seventy. Indeed in the text that follows Eusebius gives us two more examples of Clement mentioning names of members of the seventy.

> They say that Sosthenes also, who wrote to the Corinthians with Paul, was one of them. This is the account of Clement in the fifth book of his Hypotyposes, in which he also says that Cephas was one of the seventy disciples, a man who bore the same name as the apostle Peter, and the one concerning whom Paul says, "When Cephas came to Antioch I withstood him to his face." Matthias, also, who was numbered with the apostles in the place of Judas, and the one who was honored by being made a candidate with him, are like-wise said to have been deemed worthy of the same calling with the seventy. They say that Thaddeus also was one of them, concerning whom I shall presently relate an account which has come down to us[25].

Eusebius tells us that Clement in his work Hypotyposes (Outlines) has told him that Sosthenes and Cephas were among the seventy. We may also suppose, since Eusebius shows us Clement saying that Barnabas was among the seventy (at 2:1.4), that he is getting his information about this too from Clement. Notice also that Eusebius mentions that Clement includes two men named Cephas among the seventy. Now, it is easy to believe that Clement identified Cephas as one of the seventy and separated him out from the tradition that identified him with Peter Simon. It is a little harder to believe that two books later, he does the same thing with James. According to Eusebius in the sixth book, Clement declares that James, John and Peter have elected James the Just. Then according to Eusebius in his seventh book, Clement explains that there are two Jameses. It is hard to imagine that Clement would have waited a whole book to clear up any confusion caused by talking about James electing James the Just.

Look again at the passage:

> "The Lord after his resurrection imparted knowledge to James the Just and to John and Peter, and they imparted it to the rest of the apostles, and the rest of the apostles to the seventy, of whom Barnabas was one. But there were two Jameses: one called the Just, who was thrown from the pinnacle of the temple and was beaten to death with a club by a fuller, and another who was beheaded. Paul also makes mention of the same James the Just, where he writes, "Other of the apostles saw I none, save James the Lord's brother."

Notice that the line referring to two "Jameses" is parenthetical. There is no reason for it. Clement has not mentioned two people named James, only one, James the Just. One would have expected him to explain about the two Jameses when mentioning that James elected James the Just, not here. Let us reconstruct the text by taking out this aside:

> "The Lord after his resurrection imparted knowledge to James the Just and to John and Peter, and they imparted it to the rest of the apostles, and the rest of the apostles to the seventy, of whom Barnabas was one. Paul also makes mention of the same James the Just, where he writes, "Other of the apostles saw I none, save James the Lord's brother."

Now the paragraph makes sense. Clement is not trying to distinguish two Jameses. This conjecture gets more evidence when we realize that Eusebius has only quoted Clement talking about the death of one John by beheading[26]. For Clement there are not two James, only one. We can see this from Clement's legitimate mentions of James in his Stromata: "Well, they preserving the tradition of the blessed doctrine derived directly from the holy apostles, Peter, James, John, and Paul, the sons receiving it from the father (but few were like the fathers), came by God's will to us also to deposit those ancestral and apostolic seeds[27]," and "For we now dare aver (for here is the faith that is characterized by knowledge) that such an one knows all things, and comprehends all things in the exercise of sure apprehension, respecting matters difficult for us, and really pertaining to the true *gnosis* such as were James, Peter, John, Paul, and the rest of the apostles[28]." It seems that the elderly Clement writing the *Stromata* has not even heard of James the Just. We may see the epithet "the Just" as another Eusebean addition. Taking them out, we get this as the original text of Clement:

> "The Lord after his resurrection imparted knowledge to James and to John and Peter, and they imparted it to the rest of the apostles, and the rest of the apostles to the seventy, of whom Barnabas was one. Paul also makes mention of the same James, where he writes, "Other of the apostles saw I none, save James the Lord's brother."

This matches the other statements we find in Clement. The statement "there were two Jameses: one called the Just, who was thrown from the pinnacle of the temple and was beaten to death with a club by a fuller, and another who was beheaded, is entirely an invention of Eusebius. He is inserting it in Clement to back up the description of James' death at the temple that he relates from the writings of Hegessipus.

We are actually dealing with two simultaneous inventions here. Eusebius has invented the character of James the Just, the lead character in the tale and he has invented the historian Hegessipus to tell the tale. The invention of James the Just reflects Eusebius's desire to rewrite the Acts of the Apostles, while the invention of Hegessipus reflects his desire to rewrite the history of Josephus.

When we analyze the character of James the Just, who exists nowhere before or after Eusebius, we find four clear sources. We may suppose that Eusebius began with the killing of the martyr Stephen in Acts. Eusebius liked the story of the heroic Stephen speaking out and being killed by a Jewish mob, but for Eusebius there are at least two major problems. Stephen is merely a lowly unknown disciple. He is selected "to wait on tables[29]" (arrange food distribution for widows) because the Apostles are too busy spreading the gospel to be bothered. For Eusebius, the first Christian Martyr should have been someone like himself, a Church Bishop known for his righteousness. Secondly, Acts tells us that "Stephen, full of grace and power, did great wonders and signs among the people[30]." Eusebius has been at pains in his other works to explain that Jesus was not a magician[31]. It is quite embarrassing to Eusebius to say that the first Christian martyr was a lowly table waiter whom the Apostles taught to do "wonders and signs." Eusebius found a reference to the killing of James, the brother of the High Priest, Jesus Damneus by an illegal Jewish council. It provided him with a way to change the story of the first Christian Martyr. He cut the name Damneus from the line at 20:9.1 and added the words "the so-called Christ." Voila. Now, with the erasing of one word and the substitution of three in its place, Josephus could testify that James was martyred.

The throwing off the roof of the temple motif also comes directly from Josephus. This time it is Josephus's *War* which has inspired Eusebius. Note these two passages from Josephus, both in book four, chapter five (paragraphs two and five). The first refers to the High Priest Ananus, the second refers to the eminent citizen Zacharias, the son of Baruch.

> But the rage of the Idumeans was not satiated by these slaughters; but they now betook themselves to the city, and plundered every house, and slew every one they met; and for the other multitude, they esteemed it needless to go on with killing them, but they sought for the high priests, and the generality went with the greatest zeal against them; and as soon as they caught them they slew them, and then standing upon their dead bodies, in way of jest, upbraided Ananus with his kindness to the people, and Jesus with his speech made to them from the wall. Nay, they proceeded to that degree of impiety, as to cast away their dead bodies without burial, although the Jews used to take so much care of the burial of men, that they took down those that were condemned and crucified, and buried them before the going down of the sun. I should not mistake if I said that the death of Ananus was the beginning of the destruction of the city, and that from this very day may be dated the overthrow of her wall, and the ruin of her affairs, whereon they saw their

THE EVOLUTION OF CHRISTS AND CHRISTIANIES

high priest, and the procurer of their preservation, slain in the midst of their city. He was on other accounts also a venerable, and a very just man[32]...

... So two of the boldest of them fell upon Zacharias in the middle of the temple, and slew him; and as he fell down dead, they bantered him, and said, "Thou hast also our verdict, and this will prove a more sure acquittal to thee than the other." They also threw him down from the temple immediately into the valley beneath it. Moreover, they struck the judges with the backs of their swords, by way of abuse[33]

Compare this with Eusebius's description of the death of James.

And they cried out, saying, 'Oh! oh! the just man is also in error.' And they fulfilled the Scripture written in Isaia 'Let us take away the just man, because he is troublesome to us: therefore they shall eat the fruit of their doings.' So they went up and threw down the just man, and said to each other, 'Let us stone James the Just.' And they began to stone him, for he was not killed by the fall; but he turned and knelt down and said, 'I entreat thee, Lord God our Father, forgive them, for they know not what they do.' And while they were thus stoning him one of the priests of the sons of Rechab, the son of the Rechabites, who are mentioned by Jeremiah the prophet, cried out, saying, 'Cease, what do ye? The just one prayeth for you.' And one of them, who was a fuller, took the club with which he beat out clothes and struck the just man on the head. And thus he suffered martyrdom. And they buried him on the spot, by the temple, and his monument still remains by the temple. He became a true witness, both to Jews and Greeks, that Jesus is the Christ. And immediately Vespasian besieged them." These things are related at length by Hegesippus, who is in agreement with Clement. James was so admirable a man and so celebrated among all for his justice, that the more sensible even of the Jews were of the opinion that this was the cause of the siege of Jerusalem, which happened to them immediately after his martyrdom for no other reason than their daring act against him. Josephus, at least, has not hesitated to testify this in his writings, where he says," These things happened to the Jews to avenge James the Just, who was a brother of Jesus, that is called the Christ. For the Jews slew him, although he was a most just man[34]."

There are a bunch of clues here that allow us to figure out how Eusebius has played around with Josephus to come up with his dramatic death of James scene. First note that the line in Eusebius, "And immediately Vespasian besieged them." It is

53

entirely out of place in his narrative. Eusebius tells us that the death of James happened just after Paul was sent to Rome and Festus had died[35]. This would be the year 62 C.E. Vespasian did not besiege the Jews until the year 69 C.E. To say that an event that happened seven years later happened "immediately" is certainly telescoping things. One may apologetically suggest that the Historian Hegessipus was just trying to show the connection between the death of James and the war. We now have to believe that two Jewish historians, Josephus and Hegessipus, from two different centuries explicitly connected the killing of the leader of the Christian Church and the brother of Jesus, James to the Roman War against the Jews. We also have to believe that the second one, ignored the nuanced and multiple reasons that the first historian gives for the war and chose instead to distort history and give a singular cause for the Roman-Jewish War, the Jewish murder of a Christian leader. While the statement, "And immediately Vespasian besieged them" makes no sense coming after the description of the death of James, it makes perfect sense coming just after Josephus's description of the murder of the High Priest Ananus. In fact, this murder did take place in 69 C.E. just before Vespasian attacked the Jews. In the very next chapter, Josephus talks about it. To sum up, the line should be in Josephus and it is not, while it should not be in Hegessipus and it is.

Our second clue is the burial and monument built to James next to the Temple. Why would the leaders of the Jews kill James and then immediately build a monument to him, a man who apparently led the Christian Church for some 32 years? It seems absurd. On the other hand, it makes perfect sense for the Jews to "bury him on the spot" and build a monument next to the temple for their leader Ananus, who had just been slain by Idumeans. Again we find the things described making no sense in the report by Hegessipus of James' death, but making perfect sense if they were in the report by Josephus.

Let us examine specifically the text of Josephus when he describes the killings by the Idumeans. He says they sought for the high priests, and "they generality went with the greatest zeal against them; and as soon as they caught them they slew them," The translation makes it seem as if they caught many high priests, but the next line makes it clear that they only sort and caught the two high priests Ananus and Jesus. Josephus writes, "then standing upon their dead bodies, in way of jest, upbraided Ananus with his kindness to the people, and Jesus with his speech made to them from the wall." It makes no sense to mock Ananus and Jesus when catching each high priest. It only makes sense to do this when catching the High Priests Ananus and Jesus. Josephus continues, "Nay, they proceeded to that degree of impiety, as to cast away their dead bodies without burial, although the Jews used to take so much care of the burial of men, that they took down those that were condemned and crucified, and buried them before the going down of the sun." It is at this point we should find the same kind of statement in Josephus, "And they buried *them* on the spot, by the temple, and *their* monument still remains by the temple."

THE EVOLUTION OF CHRISTS AND CHRISTIANIES

Two paragraphs later Josephus writes this on the killing of Zacharius, "So two of the boldest of them fell upon Zacharias in the middle of the temple, and slew him; and as he fell down dead, they bantered him, and said, "Thou hast also our verdict, and this will prove a more sure acquittal to thee than the other." They also threw him down from the temple immediately into the valley beneath it." Notice, the action of the Idumeans. They kill in the middle of the temple, they mock their victim, and they throw him from the temple. In the paragraph regarding Ananus and Jesus, the Idumeans kill them in the middle of the temple and mock them, but we are only told that they, "cast away their dead bodies without burial." Why should Josephus be so vague when describing the deaths of his most important characters Ananus and Jesus, and so specific about the death of the relatively minor character Zacharias? Also why would the Idumeans throw the ordinary citizen Zacharias down from the temple, but just cast out the bodies of their most hated enemies the High Priest Ananus and Jesus? It would make more sense from the point of view of symmetrical literary structure, from the literary dramatic point of view and from a psychological point of view that we should find the Idumeans casting the bodies of Ananus and Jesus down from the Temple.

We may add one more point here. The word "also" in the statement "They *also* threw him down from the temple" is ambiguous. Does it mean they threw him down as well as killing him, or does it mean they threw him down from the temple as well as others? As the text stands now, it must refer to the fact that the Idumeans killed Zacharius. Thus they killed him and "also" threw him from the temple. It means, "in addition." In addition to killing him they threw him from the temple. Because there is no other reference in the current state of the text of Josephus, the term "also" does not refer to a previous action of throwing someone from the temple. Now, Josephus, just two paragraphs before has contrasted the horrible treatment of the dead by the Idumeans with the good treatment of the dead by the Jews. One would expect that he would tie this new indignity to dead bodies in with that idea, saying something like, "This is another example of their disrespect for Jewish customs," but he does not do this. If the "also" referred back to the throwing of the bodies of Ananus and Jesus from the temple, then there would be no need to relate this new type of indignity back to the Idumean characteristic of disrespect for the dead. He would have already made the point that throwing dead bodies from the temple is part of their character. We may take it that the "also" probably did refer back to this earlier instance of Ananus and Jesus being thrown from the temple. It is another piece of circumstantial evidence.

Based on this circumstantial evidence, we may suppose that Eusebius has cut out the description of the death of Ananus from Josephus and used it for his death of James narrative. Upon this supposition, we can also explain why Eusebius says that Josephus wrote that the death of James was the cause of the Jewish downfall, when we, in fact, have Josephus saying it about the death of Ananus. Eusebius intended to rewrite Jospehus' *Wars* to show that it was the death of James not the death of Ananus that caused the downfall. Apparently at some point he found it troublesome rewriting

Josephus's report on Ananus as a report on James. Possibly, the relationship between the high priests Ananus and Jesus sounded too much like it was referring to the relationship of James and Jesus the Christ when he substituted James for Ananus into the text. He decided to move the report to his fictional historian Hegessipus[36] and just cut the killing scene from Jospehus' *Wars*, and transfer it to Hegessipus' account of James. One can conjecture that Eusebius found that the report in Josephus's *Antiquities* of the death of James, brother of Jesus Damneus was a much simpler target for fixing. It had the advantage of requiring that only one word be erased and three substituted. When he wrote in his *History* that Josephus blamed the Jesus disaster on the death of James, it was still while he was planning on changing Ananus to James in Josephus[37].

We can also make reasonable conjectures about Euebius' methodology based on his other choices for Jerusalem Church leaders. He tells us that after James, a cousin of Jesus named Symeon was elected leader. It seems that originally Eusebius had in mind to show a family dynasty in the church at Jerusalem, with Jesus's brother James and then his cousin Symeon taking over and ruling for some sixty years till the time of Hadrian circa 98 C.E. At some point and for some reason Eusebius nixed the idea of a brother relationship between Jesus and James, but did not change the original plan of making Symeon, an uncle next in line of succession[38]. The evidence for this is certain as Eusebius, has left in this statement in his third book:

> **At this time Ignatius was known as the second bishop of Antioch, Evodius having been the first. Symeon likewise was at that time the second ruler of the church of Jerusalem, the brother of our Saviour having been the first**[39].

After arguing that James was not the brother of Jesus, in book two[40], it is quite surprising to find Eusebius declaring in book three that he was the brother of Jesus. The most obvious explanation for this is that Eusebius first wrote that the brother of Jesus, James, was the first head of the church. He later added corrections based on objections to the idea of James being Jesus' brother. However he only corrected book two and forgot this earlier mention in book three. We would probably have to know the specific circumstances and issues involved with the succession of the emperors of Rome while he was writing and rewriting this text to understand why he made these specific decisions.

Another major piece of evidence that Eusebius is inventing his history of the Church of Jerusalem, not to mention Hegessipus, his historian of this Jerusalem Church, when we put the four quotes relating to Symeon in their most logical order:

> **"And after James the Just had suffered martyrdom, as the Lord had also on the same account, Symeon, the son of the Lord's uncle, Clopas, was**

appointed the next bishop. All proposed him as second bishop because he was a cousin of the Lord. "Therefore, they called the Church a virgin, for it was not yet corrupted by vain discourses. But Thebuthis, because he was not made bishop, began to corrupt it. He also was sprung from the seven sects among the people, like Simon, from whom came the Simonians, and Cleobius, from whom came the Cleobians, and Dositheus, from whom came the Dositheans, and Gorthaeus, from whom came the Goratheni, and Masbotheus, from whom came the Masbothaeans. From them sprang the Menandrianists, and Marcionists, and Carpocratians, and Valentinians, and Basilidians, and Saturnilians. Each introduced privately and separately his own peculiar opinion. From them came false Christs, false prophets, false apostles, who divided the unity of the Church by corrupt doctrines uttered against God and against his Christ." The same writer also records the ancient heresies which arose among the Jews, in the following words: "There were, moreover, various opinions in the circumcision, among the children of Israel. The following were those that were opposed to the tribe of Judah and the Christ: Essenes, Galileans, Hemerobaptists, Masbothaeans, Samaritans, Sadducees, Pharisees[41]." . . .

"Of the family of the Lord there were still living the grandchildren of Jude, who is said to have been the Lord's brother according to the flesh. Information was given that they belonged to the family of David, and they were brought to the Emperor Domitian by the Evocatus. For Domitian feared the coming of Christ as Herod also had feared it. And he asked them if they were descendants of David, and they confessed that they were. Then he asked them how much property they had, or how much money they owned. And both of them answered that they had only nine thousand denarii, half of which belonged to each of them; and this property did not consist of silver, but of a piece of land which contained only thirty-nine acres, and from which they raised their taxes and supported themselves by their own labor." 5 Then they showed their hands, exhibiting the hardness of their bodies and the callousness produced upon their hands by continuous toil as evidence of their own labor. And when they were asked concerning Christ and his kingdom, of what sort it was and where and when it was to appear, they answered that it was not a temporal nor an earthly kingdom, but a heavenly and angelic one, which would appear at the end of the world, when he should come in glory to judge the quick and the dead, and to give unto every one according to his works. Upon hearing this, Domitian did not pass judgment against them, but, despising them as of no account,

> he let them go, and by a decree put a stop to the persecution of the Church. But when they were released they ruled the churches because they were witnesses and were also relatives of the Lord. And peace being established, they lived until the time of Trajan[42]....
>
> "Certain of these heretics brought accusation against Symeon, the son of Clopas, on the ground that he was a descendant of David and a Christian; and thus he suffered martyrdom, at the age of one hundred and twenty years, while Trajan was emperor and Atticus governor[43]."...
>
> "They came, therefore, and took the lead of every church as witnesses and as relatives of the Lord. And profound peace being established in every church, they remained until the reign of the Emperor Trajan, and until the above-mentioned Symeon, son of Clopas, an uncle of the Lord, was informed against by the heretics, and was himself in like manner accused for the same cause before the governor Atticus And after being tortured for many days he suffered martyrdom, and all, including even the proconsul, marveled that, at the age of one hundred and twenty years, he could endure so much. And orders were given that he should be crucified[44]."

What is both astonishing and clear is that either quotes 3 or 4 can come after quote 2, but not both. They are clashing alternative developments of the narrative. They are both directly referring to the material on the heretical relatives of Jesus that has come before. One sees that quote 4 is actually a development of quote 3, adding information or quote 3 is a shortening of the original quote 4. One may try to fit multiple solutions of rearranging the text and adding text as much as one likes, but I have found it quite impossible to imagine how the two quotes can exist as they stand in a single narrative as Eusebius suggests. On the contrary, the obvious and most probable solution is that we are dealing with two drafts of the same text. One may defend Eusebius by saying that he had two versions of the work by Hegessipus and simply combined them, forgetting to mention this to his readers. In fact both versions show the text in a state of underdevelopment.

We may most easily explain these facts by proposing that Eusebius was in fact writing the Hegessipus material as an earlier draft of his history. Apparently, he never completed the work. We can tell a great deal from what he has incorporated into his *Church History*. This is the outline of the novel that Eusebius was writing. It was only later that he credited the unfinished material to the imaginary historian Hegessipus.

The first section was about James the Just. As noted, he took from Josephus's description of the death of the High Priest Ananus. From the quotes about his successor

Symeon, we may take it that this was the second second section. He then described how Thebutis a grandson of Jesus' brother Jude and his unnamed brother corrupted the Church and started heresies. They did this after Symeon, the elderly son of Joseph's brother, Clopas was chosen over them to lead the Church at Jerusalem. These poor relatives who had been arrested by Domitian and let go, betrayed the elderly Symeon, just as Judas had betrayed Jesus. The purpose of the novel would have been to explain how the Jerusalem Church and other Churches became corrupted and heretical though Jude, a brother of Jesus from Joseph's side of the family.

This hypothesis explains the draft state of the quotes from Hegessipus on Symeon that we find in Eusebius. It has the added benefit of explaining another interesting discrepancy in Eusebius' *History*. At one point Eusebius says that according to Hegessipus, Vespasian persecuted the Christians.

> **Hegesippus records that Clopas was a brother of Joseph. He also relates that Vespasian after the conquest of Jerusalem gave orders that all that belonged to the lineage of David should be sought out, in order that none of the royal race might be left among the Jews; and in consequence of this a most terrible persecution again hung over the Jews**[45].

Yet just five chapters later, Eusebius is telling us that no persecution took place under Vespasian. Instead, it is now his son Domitian who persecuted the relatives of Christ.

> **Domitian, having shown great cruelty toward many, and having unjustly put to death no small number of well-born and notable men at Rome, and having without cause exiled and confiscated the property of a great many other illustrious men, finally became a successor of Nero in his hatred and enmity toward God. He was in fact the second that stirred up a persecution against us, although his father Vespasian had undertaken nothing prejudicial to us**[46].

We also find that Hegessipus says nothing about Vespasian's persecution of the Jews as Eusebius has told us. Instead, he also now declares Domitian guilty. The solution is that in the original draft of his novel it was Vespasian who persecuted the Christian descendents of Jesus. He later changed it to his son Domitian[47]. Making Vespasian the culprit would have been more realistic since he was describing events that happened around the time of the war. We may guess that Eusebius thought about it and found that his claim that a popular Roman emperor attacked Christians on the basis of their lineage to Judaism was probably not a great idea as it attracted too much sympathy for Jews. He changed the persecutor from Vespasian to the less significant Domitian.

Eusebius mentions that someone named Justus was the third Bishop of Jerusalem. He tells us virtually nothing about further about Justus, noting only, "But when Symeon also had died in the manner described, a certain Jew by the name of Justus succeeded to the episcopal throne in Jerusalem. He was one of the many thousands of the circumcision who at that time believed in Christ[48]."

Eusebius wants to make the point that Jesus did not fail to convert Jews. Apparently it was a common and accepted notion of the time that Jesus had failed to convert his own people, the Jews and Eusebius wants to deny that this was the case.

He ends his discussion of the Jewish Church at Jerusalem by reiterating this point and giving a simple list of names.

> The chronology of the bishops of Jerusalem I have nowhere found preserved in writing; for tradition says that they were all short lived. But I have learned this much from writings, that until the siege of the Jews, which took place under Adrian, there were fifteen bishops in succession there. all of whom are said to have been of Hebrew descent, and to have received the knowledge of Christ in purity, so that they were approved by those who were able to judge of such matters, and were deemed worthy of the episcopate. For their whole church consisted then of believing Hebrews who continued from the days of the apostles until the siege which took place at this time; in which siege the Jews, having again rebelled against the Romans, were conquered after severe battles. But since the bishops of the circumcision ceased at this time, it is proper to give here a list of their names from the beginning. The first, then, was James, the so-called brother of the Lord; the second, Symeon; the third, Justus; the fourth, Zacchaeus; the fifth, Tobias; the sixth, Benjamin; the seventh, John; the eighth, Matthias; the ninth, Philip; the tenth, Seneca; the eleventh, Justus; the twelfth, Levi; the thirteenth, Ephres; the fourteenth, Joseph; and finally, the fifteenth, Judas. These are the bishops of Jerusalem that lived between the age of the apostles and the time referred to, all of them belonging to the circumcision[49].

We may note that the statement "they were all short lived" contradicts what Eusebius has told us about Symeon living to the age of 120. His statement that he has found "nowhere preserved" the chronology of the Bishops contradicts the fact that he has quoted Hegesippus preserving at least the chronology of the first three bishops. Notice that he refers here to James as "the so called brother of the Lord" but does not call him James the Just, and he simply says Symeon rather than Symeon, Son of Clopas, or cousin of the Lord. We may explain all these things by the suggestion that this passage was written before he started to write his novel on the early Jewish church.

Eusebius was being totally honest when he says he has found the chronology of the Bishops of Jerusalem nowhere written. The chronology was nowhere written because the Church never existed. The names he gives are fictious. Again, the point for Eusebius is not to reveal a true history, but to combat those who propagated the embarrassing fact that Jesus and his followers did not convert Jews. It is for this reason that he has invented his Christian Church at Jerusalem.

3. The Church at Caesarea

If he has invented the history of the Churches at Edessa and Jerusalem, we may still expect that Eusebius should have a pretty good idea of the history of his own church at Caesarea, and at least here, he may relay on good sources. With this in mind, we may be surprised about what he writes about the history of his own Caesarean Church. The first mention of the church is this:

> In the tenth year of the reign of Commodus, Victor succeeded Eleutherus, the latter having held the episcopate for thirteen years. In the same year, after Juliana had completed his tenth year, Demetrius received the charge of the parishes at Alexandria. At this time the above-mentioned Serapion, the eighth from the apostles, was still well known as bishop of the church at Antioch. Theophilus presided at Caesarea in Palestine; and Narcissus, whom we have mentioned before, still had charge of the church at Jerusalem. Bacchylus at the same time was bishop of Corinth in Greece, and Polycrates of the parish of Ephesus. And besides these a multitude of others, as is likely, were then prominent. But we have given the names of those alone, the soundness of whose faith has come down to us in writing[50].

Amazingly, when it comes to his own church, Eusebius gives no founding information and no bishops list. It is in a discussion of events concerning the year 190 C.E. that Eusebius first mentions a bishop at Caesarea. He does not even tell us what number Bishop it is to give us a clue how old the Church at Caesarea is, while he is careful to tell us in same sentence that the eight bishop rules in Antioch. One should suspect that even if Eusebius found no written information about the founding of his Church, the members of his church would be outraged that Eusebius did not even bother to write their own versions of the founding of the church. Once we realize that Eusebius has created fictional beginnings for other churches it becomes even more puzzling why he does not create anything for his own church.

Perhaps his Church was unimportant. Yet, immediately he tells us that at an important synod and meeting of Bishops that year, "There is still extant a writing of those who were then assembled in Palestine, over whom Theophilus, bishop of

Caesarea, and Narcissus, bishop of Jerusalem, presided[51]." Yet that is it. Theophilus, after another brief mention, immediately disappears from the story.

The next bishop Theocritus[52] gets mentioned briefly in passing in connection with the Alexandrian Christian writer Origen and events circa 215 C.E. We basically only find out that this Bishop Theocritus liked and supported Origen. Eusebius writes, "And Alexander, bishop of Jerusalem, and Theoctistus, bishop of Caesarea, attended on him constantly, as their only teacher, and allowed him to expound the Divine Scriptures, and to perform the other duties pertaining to ecclesiastical discourse[53]. Eusebius mentions too that the writer Dionysius invited him along with others to a synod against Novatus in Antioch[54]. Through another letter by Dionysius, just after the reign of Decian (251-253 C.E.) he tells us that Theoctistus has rejected the heretical views of Novatus.

Eusebius gives us more information about Theoctistus in referring to things that took place sometime after Gallienus became sole emperor (260-268 C.E.):

> At that time Xystus was still presiding over the church of Rome, and Demetrianus, successor of Fabius, over the church of Antioch, and Firmilianus over that of Caesarea in Cappadocia; and besides these, Gregory and his brother Athenodorus, friends of Origen, were presiding over the churches in Pontus; and Theoctistus of Caesarea in Palestine having died, Domnus received the episcopate there. He held it but a short time, and Theotecnus, our contemporary, succeeded him. He also was a member of Origen's school. But in Jerusalem, after the death of Mazabanes, Hymenaeus, who has been celebrated among us for a great many years, succeeded to his seat.

Eusebius tells us virtually nothing about Theotecnus. In discussing a writer, Anatolius, Eusebius tells us "Theotecnus, bishop of Caesarea in Palestine, first ordained him as bishop, designing to make him his successor in his own parish after his death. And for a short time both of them presided over the same church[55]." Finally, Eusebius gives us this information:

> In Caesarea in Palestine, Agapius succeeded Theotecnus, who had most zealously performed the duties of his episcopate. Him too we know to have labored diligently, and to have manifested most genuine providence in his oversight of the people, particularly caring for all the poor with liberal hand. In his time we became acquainted with Pamphilu,s that most eloquent man, of truly philosophical life, who was esteemed worthy of the office of presbyter in that parish.

He tells us nothing further about Agapius except that he died in the fourth year of the Diocletian persecution of Christians in (probably 306 C.E.)[56]. Actually, this is uncertain. He does not name him as a bishop when describing his persecution, but merely describes him as the second person arrested. We cannot even be sure that the martyr Agapius is the same man as the Bishop Agapius.

To sum up what Eusbius tells us of the history of his own Church in Caesaria: he gives us five names Theophilus, Theocritus, Domnus, Theoctistus, Agapius. He asserts that Theophilus was bishop around 190 C.E., and Agapius (apparently) died in 306. It is quite amazing that over a 116 year period there should be only five bishops in Caesarea. Yet, it is not impossible, during one period 1831-1958, there were only seven bishops of Rome. Still dividing the 265 popes by 1870 years gives us an average of just over 7 years per pope. Based on this, we should have expected that the Church at Caesarea should have had about 15 bishops over this period of time.

Eusebius gives us no firm dates for when these men took office or when they left office. He tells us virtually nothing of their practices or lives. He only claims that the bishop before him, Agapius was persecuted and martyred (although we cannot be certain that this is the claim he is making). This is surprising. Caesarea was perhaps the second largest city in Palestine.

One may come up with a number of reasons for Eusebius' lack of interest in displaying knowledge about the history of his own Church of Caesarea or in exploiting that history. Perhaps, he did not want to be accused of self promotion and glorification by the other churches, or perhaps there was something he considered shameful in the history of his Church that he preferred not to go into.

Still, if one looks at *Acts of the Apostles*, one finds lots of things happening at Caesarea. What is the relationship between between that material and Eusebius' silence about the early history of his church?

The Daughters of Philip and Caesarea and the ERA Hypothesis

In this section, I shall propose the hypothesis that Eusebius rewrote *Acts* (The ERA hypothesis). While the primary evidence I give here relates to Eusebius's relationship to Caesarea and the editor of *Acts* seeming to have a similar relationship to Caesarea, much other evidence can be found to support it.

Eusebius' first mention of Caesarea is in regards to the Apostle Philip and his daughters, four women prophetesses. In fact, this is the fourth mention by Eusebius of these four women, who are called prophetesses, although we are never told what they prophesized.

1. Clement, indeed, whose words we have just quoted, after the above-mentioned facts gives a statement, on account of those who rejected marriage, of the apostles that had wives. "Or will they," says he, "reject even the apostles? For Peter and Philip begat children; and Philip also gave his daughters in marriage[57] . . .

2. The time of John's death has also been given in a general way but his burial place is indicated by an epistle of Polycrates (who was bishop of the parish of Ephesus), addressed to Victor, bishop of Rome. In this epistle he mentions him together with the apostle Philip and his daughters in the following words: "For in Asia also great lights have fallen asleep, which shall rise again on the last day, at the coming of the Lord, when he shall come with glory from heaven and shall seek out all the saints. Among these are Philip, one of the twelve apostles, who sleeps in Hierapolis, and his two aged virgin daughters, and another daughter who lived in the Holy Spirit and now rests at Ephesus[58].

3. And in the Dialogue of Caius which we mentioned a little above, Proclus, against whom he directed his disputation, in agreement with what has been quoted, speaks thus concerning the death of Philip and his daughters: "After him there were four prophetesses, the daughters of Philip, at Hierapolis in Asia. Their tomb is there and the tomb of their father." Such is his statement.

4. But Luke, in the Acts of the Apostles, mentions the daughters of Philip who were at that time at Caesarea in Judea with their father, and were honored with the gift of prophecy. His words are as follows: "We came unto Caesarea; and entering into the house of Philip the evangelist, who was one of the seven, we abode with him. Now this man had four daughters, virgins, which did prophesy[59]."

We may note as an aside how much these early sources disagree. Clement (of Alexandria circa 200 C.E.) does not say how many daughters but knows they were married. Polycrates (in a letter to Pope Vitor, 189-199 C.E.) talks about three, two of whom were virgins. Caius ("a member of the Church, who arose under Zephyrinus[60], (Pope Zephyrinus, 199-217)" Proclus says four and does not say if married or not, while Acts gives us four as the number but in direct contradiction to the first two sources says they were all virgins. Apparently even basic information, such as how many daughters an important apostle had and if they were married was in short supply around the turn of the third century. It is also noteworthy that these three Christian sources directly contradict the Book of Acts. This would suggest that either the book of Acts was not canonical at that point and/or a different version of the Book of Acts was in existence at that time.

We will also note that the early third century sources say that Philip, the apostle had daughters. On the other hand *Acts* seems to be talking about Philip the evangelist, one of seven chosen by the twelve apostles: "And what they said pleased the whole multitude, and they chose Stephen, a man full of faith and of the Holy Spirit, and Philip, and Proch'orus, and Nica'nor, and Ti'mon, and Par'menas, and Nicola'us, a proselyte of Antioch[61]. These second-tier seven evangelist apostles may represent a different and probably earlier tradition of the Christ having seven apostles rather than twelve. Acts not only brings together stories from Pauline and Petrine traditions, but also seems to preserve pieces of stories from this seven apostle tradition. In any case, the early third century sources seem to know only the twelve apostle canonical gospel tradition which would again indicate that the text of *Acts* was not consulted as a primary historical source or was in a different state.

Two of the sources agree that Philip and his daughters died in Hierapolis in Asia (present day Turkey). Eusebius quotes *Acts*, that Philip and his daughters were in Caesarea. It is this last fact that is most interesting. Eusebius is talking about where the apostles died. Why does he suddenly say that *Acts* mentions that they were in Caesarea? It seems to be irrelevant to the point of where they died? Eusebius is, in effect, using *Acts* to impeach his own sources.

When we look at *Acts* we notice something strange. *Acts* gives credit to Philip for being the first Apostle to go to Samaria and convert the people there. He then converts an Ethiopian on the road to Gaza. God then wisks him away to the town of Azotus: "But Philip was found at Azo'tus, and passing on he preached the gospel to all the towns till he came to Caesare'a."

We never find out what he did at Caesarea. There was obviously a lot more to the story of Philip, but he suddenly disappears and the story becomes about Peter and later about Paul. Since the story has been edited, there is no reason to believe that the town of Caesarea was ever in the original story. It is more likely that the next story of Philip took place in Azotus rather than Caesarea. The story is being abruptly cut off at Azotus, and like God has just whisked Philip to Azotus, the editor is whisking him to Caesarea. However the editor has no story to tell of Philip in Caesarea. He just wants us to know that Philip was in Caesarea.

Much later, in Chapter 21, Philip reappears in Caesarea in a story about Paul.

> On the morrow we departed and came to Caesare'a; and we entered the house of Philip the evangelist, who was one of the seven, and stayed with him. And he had four unmarried daughters, who prophesied. While we were staying for some days, a prophet named Ag'abus came down from Judea. And coming to us he took Paul's girdle and bound his own feet and hands, and said, "Thus says the Holy Spirit, 'So shall the Jews at Jerusalem bind the man who owns this girdle and deliver him into the hands of the Gentiles.'" When we heard this, we and the people there begged him not to go up to Jerusalem[62].

It is text from this passage that Eusebius quotes. The passage reassures us that Philip is the later evangelist, one of the seven and not the apostle Philip. Note this absurdity in the narrative. Although Philip has four daughters who prophesize, yet

Agabus has to suddenly be brought in from Judea to prophesize about the coming arrest of Paul. Note also we are in the house of Philip, but the narrative has absolutely no action by Philip.

We can figure out what the editor has done to the scene by examining an earlier passage of the story where Philip was the central character:

> But Saul was ravaging the church, and entering house after house, he dragged off men and women and committed them to prison. Now those who were scattered went about preaching the word. Philip went down to a city of Sama'ria, and proclaimed to them the Christ. And the multitudes with one accord gave heed to what was said by Philip, when they heard him and saw the signs which he did[63].

If we combine the two stories of Saul "entering house after house" persecuting the Church while Philip is proclaiming the Christ to the people of Samaria, we can understand the original narrative. Saul/Paul must have come to Philip's home, probably in Azotus, to arrest Philip. As he binds Philip, one of the four daughters of Philip grabbed Saul's girdle and prophesized, "As you bind this man deliver him to the Jews at Jerusalem, so shall the Jews at Jerusalem bind the man who owns this girdle and deliver him into the hands of the gentiles. Thus says the Holy Spirit."

I suggest that the original story had just one rather than all four daughters of Philip prophesizing. Remember, what Polycrates letter, quoted by Eusebius says: Among these are Philip, one of the twelve apostles, who sleeps in Hierapolis, and his two aged virgin daughters, and another daughter who lived in the Holy Spirit and now rests at Ephesus[64]. The other daughters of Philip were probably added to make the one daughter seem less special.

We can be certain that this motif of "what you do shall be done onto you" ran through the earlier story by considering another passage that has been tampered with.

> When they arrived at Sal'amis, they proclaimed the word of God in the synagogues of the Jews. And they had John to assist them. When they had gone through the whole island as far as Paphos, they came upon a certain magician, a Jewish false prophet, named Bar-Jesus. He was with the proconsul, Sergius Paulus, a man of intelligence, who summoned Barnabas and Saul and sought to hear the word of God. But El'ymas the magician (for that is the meaning of his name) withstood them, seeking to turn away the proconsul from the faith. But Saul, who is also called Paul, filled with the Holy Spirit, looked intently at him and said, "You son of the devil, you enemy of all righteousness, full of all deceit and villainy, will you not stop making crooked the straight paths of the Lord? And now, behold, the hand of the Lord is upon you,

THE EVOLUTION OF CHRISTS AND CHRISTIANIES

> and you shall be blind and unable to see the sun for a time." Immediately mist and darkness fell upon him and he went about seeking people to lead him by the hand. Then the proconsul believed, when he saw what had occurred, for he was astonished at the teaching of the Lord[65].

The story as told here is mean spirited and ridiculous. If blinding El'ymas or Bar-Jesus (Son of Jesus) converts the the proconsul Paulus, why not just have Paul kill all his enemies with the magical powers he evidently possesses in the story. In fact, we can easily reconstruct that in the original story, it was Bar Jesus who accused Saul and prophesized, "You son of the devil, you enemy of all righteousness, full of all deceit and villainy, will you not stop making crooked the straight paths of the Lord? And now, behold, the hand of the Lord is upon you, and you shall be blind and unable to see the sun for a time."

> Now as he journeyed he approached Damascus, and suddenly a light from heaven flashed about him. And he fell to the ground and heard a voice saying to him, "Saul, Saul, why do you persecute me?" And he said, "Who are you, Lord?" And he said, "I am Jesus, whom you are persecuting; but rise and enter the city, and you will be told what you are to do." The men who were traveling with him stood speechless, hearing the voice but seeing no one. Saul arose from the ground; and when his eyes were opened, he could see nothing; so they led him by the hand and brought him into Damascus. And for three days he was without sight, and neither ate nor drank. Now there was a disciple at Damascus named Anani'as. The Lord said to him in a vision, "Anani'as." And he said, "Here I am, Lord." And the Lord said to him, "Rise and go to the street called Straight, and inquire in the house of Judas for a man of Tarsus named Saul; for behold, he is praying, and he has seen a man named Anani'as come in and lay his hands on him so that he might regain his sight." But Anani'as answered, "Lord, I have heard from many about this man, how much evil he has done to thy saints at Jerusalem; and here he has authority from the chief priests to bind all who call upon thy name."

Notice that the street where Ananias lives is called "Straight." In the original story, this was a direct reference to Bar Jesus' attack on Paul, "Will you not stop making crooked the straight paths of the Lord?" We may take it that Bar Jesus or El'ymas the Magician was Jesus and that Saul/Paul had just arrested him. The light from Heaven causing blindness and the voice are nice magic tricks.

In any case, it is hard to say if these specific changes were made by Eusebius or an earlier redactor. The circumstantial evidence suggests strongly that at the very least he moved this key scene to his hometown of Caesarea.

Two other key scenes in *Acts* take place in Caesarea. Peter converts his first Gentile Cornelius in Caesarea[66] and Paul's trial before going to Rome takes place in Caesarea. However, note that Cornelius sends messengers to the city of Joppa to the house of Simon, the tanner, looking for Peter. Joppa is in Samaria. Now, the text tells us that it was Philip who was converting in "a city of Samaria[67]" It also tells us that Philip converted a man named Simon (the magician) in the city. When God whisks Philip away after Baptizing a Eunuch from Ethiopia at the end of Chapter 8, he appears at Azotus. Now Azotus was only a few miles from Joppa. This can hardly be coincidental. Apparently, the original miracle in the story involved Philip being swept in the sea while baptizing several miles to the next town. It seems apparent that it was Philip, not Peter who was called to baptize Cornelius. Someone wanted to give Peter credit for the first baptism of the gentiles.

But if Philip was really in Joppa and not Peter, was Cornelius really from Caesarea? In the following chapter *Acts* reports this:

> Now those who were scattered because of the persecution that arose over Stephen traveled as far as Phoeni'cia and Cyprus and Antioch, speaking the word to none except Jews. But there were some of them, men of Cyprus and Cyre'ne, who on coming to Antioch spoke to the Greeks also, preaching the Lord Jesus[68].

It seems that despite what *Acts* has just told us about Peter converting Cornelius in Caesarea, *Acts* wants to tell us that the first non-Jewish converts were from Antioch. Since the narrative goes on to talk about the church at Antioch in Chapter 13, while telling us nothing about any church at Caesarea, we may be sure that originally Cornelius was from Antioch and have the strongest suspicions that an editor from the city of Caesarea switched his location to Caesarea to have Caesarea recognized as the first city where non-Jews were converted.

Finally, we find the suspicious fact that Paul is put on trial in Caesarea, a trial where he is found innocent by the good King Agrippa. Basically from the time Paul arrives in Jerusalem in chapter 21 to his departure in chapter 27, we are getting a text almost wholly in the same style as Eusebius' *Church History*. The period references are coming straight from Josephus. What we may suppose Eusebius has done is to rewrite the trial of Christ with a happy ending. Instead of crucifixion, the hero Paul gets to go to Rome and meet the Emperor. It is a wonderful fantasy reflecting both the life and desires of Eusebius. Just as Eusebius had Jesus converse with King Abgarus and show his good will, Eusebius has Paul converse with King Agrippa and convince him of his good will. Eusebius, in real life, it appears convinced the emperor Constantine of his good will.

From our reconstruction of the Saul story we can see that it involved an agent of the Jews who arrested Jewish Christians. No doubt, his Jewish bosses turned them over to the cruel Roman authorities who hanged the radical Christians. He gets warned that what he does will happen to him. Saul sees the light and hears the voice of Jesus. He goes blind. He converts to Christianity. In the end the same Jewish leaders that he worked for arrest him and turn him over to the Romans who kill him. This certainly takes place in Jerusalem. In the original story there is no point in him going to Caesarea or Rome. However the story of the villain-hero Saul/Paul was apparently quite appealing. Later Christians expanded the story of the converted Saul/Paul to include the story of the brave Christian woman Thecla.

The original story of Paul showed the betrayal and cruelty of the Jews towards the Christians, but it also showed the even deeper cruelty of the Romans towards the Jews. The revised version of the story we get in *Acts* actually has the Romans saving Paul from the Jews. Just as we get a near rescue of Jesus in the letter of Abagarus, we get a real rescue of Paul in this letter from a Roman Tribune:

> 25: And he wrote a letter to this effect: "Claudius Lys'ias to his Excellency the governor Felix, greeting. This man was seized by the Jews, and was about to be killed by them, when I came upon them with the soldiers and rescued him, having learned that he was a Roman citizen. And desiring to know the charge on which they accused him, I brought him down to their council. I found that he was accused about questions of their law, but charged with nothing deserving death or imprisonment. And when it was disclosed to me that there would be a plot against the man, I sent him to you at once, ordering his accusers also to state before you what they have against him." So the soldiers, according to their instructions, took Paul and brought him by night to Antipatris. And on the morrow they returned to the barracks, leaving the horsemen to go on with him. When they came to Caesare'a and delivered the letter to the governor, they presented Paul also before him[69].

We may suspect that Eusebius planned on showing the execution of Paul by the evil emperor Nero. Why did he not carry out his plan? Possibly he never found the time, or possibly he just was not satisfied with the drafts he came up with. It would have been difficult to portray an evil Nero without giving the impression that he thought all Roman emperors were like him. In any case, he just cut off the narrative in midstream to make it look like an incomplete ancient document that had only been preserved in part.

Our conclusion is that the evidence strongly indicates that Eusebius not only rewrote *Acts* in his *Church History*, he rewrote *Acts* in *Acts* itself. This explains why he did not need to promote his city of Caesarea in his *History*, he had already made it world famous by including it at important moments in *Acts*. Including these important moments in his history would only have drawn attention to his own role in creating them.

We may also note in support of *ERA*, that Paul's Epistle to the Romans is following the pre-Roman narrative in *Acts* when it says, "Through mighty signs and wonders, by the power of the Spirit of God; so that from Jerusalem, and round about unto Illyricum, I have fully preached the gospel[70]." Ilyricum would in this case be a reference to Corinth. The classicist editor of this letter is making a subtle comparison of Paul to Odysseus. Obviously, if the editor had read the later edition of Acts with Paul preaching in Rome, he would not have said that Paul fully preached the gospel from Jerusalem to Ilyricum, but from Jerusalem to Rome.

Also it is noteworthy that Origen also uses the phrase in his Commentaries on John's Gospel,

> But he who was made fit to be a minister of the New Covenant, not of the letter, but of the spirit, Paul, who fulfilled the Gospel from Jerusalem round about to Illyricum, did not write epistles to all the churches he taught, and to those to whom he did write he sent no more than a few lines.

Again Origen would not have used the expression "from Jerusalem round about to Illyricum" if he was aware of Paul's trip to Rome. Thus we may take it that the Rome addition was post mid-second century.

In examining the way Eusebius gives the history of three major Churches of his time, we have found how he uses his sources; historical, fictional and edited in whole and in part, to create his own unique history, reflecting his ideals, wishes and desires.

Saints Who Help Us Understand How Eusebius Worked

1. Gregory and Basil

In finding excuses for Eusebius, Barnes notes the misdating of a work by Maximus.

> The first historian of the early Church was confronted with a mass of letters, sermons, and documents of many types, which he needed to arrange in chronological order. How did Eusebius proceed? Clearly, he first looked for passages referring to emperors or bishops whose dates the Chronicle tabulated. Failing that, he sought vauer synchronisms, or even similarities of content. In every case error could arise through faulty reasoning or simple oversight. Eusebius knew a dialogue by one Maximus entitled *On Matter*, whose subject he describes as "on the origin of evil and that matter had a beginning." He dated the dialogue

to the reign of Septimius Severus. But it seems probable that Maximus' work is in fact the extant dialogue conventionally entitled *On Right Belief in God* and ascribed to an unknown "Adamantius," and that Maximus wrote it not long after the death of Origen[71].

First we should note that Eusebius himself tells us "Adamantius, for this also was a name of Origen[72]." So Adamantius is hardly unknown as Barnes states. But is this really just a simple case of misdating a document by 50 or 60 years as Barnes suggests?

In book seven of his *Praeparatio*, Eusebius quotes a long passage over 200 lines from someone he calls Maximus. He tells us "Maximus too, a man not undistinguished in the Christian life, has composed a special treatise *Concerning Matter;* from which I think it will be useful to quote some sentences of moderate length, for the accurate decision of the question before us[73]." In the *History*, Eusebius again refers to Maximus. Talking about the time of Commodus (circa 180-192) Eusebius writes, "Numerous memorials of the faithful zeal of the ancient ecclesiastical men of that time are still preserved by many. Of these we would note particularly the writings of Heraclitus *On the Apostle*, and those of Maximus on the question so much discussed among heretics, *the Origin of Evil, and on the Creation of Matter*[74]."

Around 360, Gregory of Nazianzus and Basil of Caesarea wrote "The Philocalia of Origen," a compilation of selected passages from Origen's works. In that work, they quote the same passage quoted by Eusebius and say, "The foregoing is taken from Book VII. of the *Praeparatio Evangelica* of Eusebius; being, as he says, the work of Maximus, a Christian writer of some distinction. But it has been discovered word for word in Origen's discussion with the Marcionites and other heretics, Eutropius defending, Megethius opposing[75]."

Thus we have a long passage that Eusebius assigns to somebody named Maximus, Two Christian writers Gregory and Basil come along twenty-five years or so after Eusebius's death and discover the same passage in a work they attribute to Origen. They include it in a work of passages composed by Origen, which would seem to indicate that they believe the work was not by Maximus but by Origen.

At first glance, it does not seem that important who actually wrote the material. Somebody has made a mistake, either Eusebius has or Gregory and Basil have credited the wrong person with the work. Nothing is amiss here. Pages become loose and fall out of manuscripts. A copyist mistakes the style for another. Perhaps a copyist changed the authorship from an old obscure writer whom he did not know to a more famous writer, thus increasing its value.

However, in this case there is strong evidence that these things did not happen. There is strong contextual evidence that Eusebius deliberately changed the name of the author.

First, we have to consider that Maximus is entirely unknown outside of these two references by Eusebius. Eusebius seems to have a very limited knowledge of him telling us only that he was a distinguished Christian writing towards the end of the second century. Eusebius does not tell us where he came from or why he was distinguished. He only names this one work by him. Yet he quotes this work extensively. Why give so much space to a writer who appears to have written only one work and to be entirely unknown to his audience?

Second, we have to consider that Eusebius was quite familiar with Origen's work. He devotes about half of book six of his ten book history to him. He claims to have composed a defense of him[76] and he writes

> But why should we give in this history an accurate catalogue of the man's works, which would require a separate treatise? we have furnished this also in our narrative of the life of Pamphilus, a holy martyr of our own time. After showing how great the diligence of Pamphilus was in divine things, we give in that a catalogue of the library which he collected of the works of Origen and of other ecclesiastical writers, Whoever desires may learn readily from this which of Origen's works have reached us. But we must proceed now with our history[77].

This would suggest that he should have known about the identical passage in Origen. Who should know a writer better than the cataloger of his works. Based on the fame of Origen versus Maximus, the interest of Eusebius in Origen versus Maximus, the extraordinary length of the passage (it takes up nearly a third of the book), we can say that it is surprising that Eusebius claims authorship for Maximus rather than Origen.

When we go to the text of Eusebius's *Praeparatio* we find structures in the text that point towards Origen as the author. Eusebius ends book six with a long quotation of over 200 lines from Origen, just as he ends book seven with the long quotation from Maximus. Here is his introduction to Origen:

> You would not, however, be able to understand the bare letter of the sacred oracles, since in most points they are obscurely expressed. And therefore I shall set before you their interpreter: and if you are not envious of stronger minds, you know perhaps the man, who to this present time still takes rank in the companies of Christ by the works which he has bequeathed, nor indeed is unknown even to those without for the zeal which he has displayed in their studies also. Consider then how many and how excellent determinations on the subject before us the admirable Origen has given in his *Commentaries on Genesis*, and how he traced out the argument concerning Fate[78].

Eusebius tells us that Origen is a great interpreter of obscure works and is famous for both Christian and non-Christian studies. This explains why he is using such a long quotation from his work.

THE EVOLUTION OF CHRISTS AND CHRISTIANIES

Towards the end of book seven, in chapter 20, he again quotes Origen, this time on the question of the creation of matter. He quotes about 25 lines from Origen. Then he quotes about 20 lines from Philo on the same subject. It is at this point that he places his long quotation by Maximus on the creation of matter which runs to the end of the book.

Now, even if we grant that Gregory and Basil somehow got it wrong and the work they attribute to Origen was really by Maximus, we have to account for the coincidence that Eusebius quotes a long passage from Origen to end book six just as he quotes a long passage to end book seven and that he quotes Origen on the same subject in book seven, just before his long quote. Incidentally these are the only two times he quotes Origen in the fourteen book *Praeparatio*. This quote from Maximus is the only quote he ever uses from Maximus. One would expect him to quote Origen whom he catalogued and wrote a defense of, and was world famous more, and Maximus who was unknown less.

The solution that best explains the coincidences is that Eusebius was embarrassed to have two long quotes from Origen ending books six and seven. It made him seem to be someone just regurgitating Origen's work rather than an independent thinker and writer. Eusebius's solution was to simply change the authorship to the fictitious Maximus. In this way he appeared to be using more sources than he had. This explains 1) why Eusebius tells us so little about Maximus and yet quotes him so extensively along with Philo and Origen, 2) why Maximus is otherwise unknown, 3) why Gregory and Basil find the identical material in Origen, 4) why book six should end with a long passage from Origen and book seven should end the same way, and 5) why Origen's writings on the same subject are mentioned in book seven just before the passage in question[79].

2. Jerome

In the year 397, a Church elder named Tyrannius Rufinus published a work by a Christian martyr named Pamphilus called "the Apology of Pamphilus for Origen." Shortly thereafter, another Christian intellectual, and an old friend of Rufinus, named Jerome declared the work a forgery. He declared that it had been taken directly from a six-book work called "Defense of Origen" by the student of Pamphilus, (and famous historian) Eusebius of Caesarea. This led to a series of books and letters between the two men filled with acrimony and mutual charges of deceit, betrayal, lies, forgery and heresy[80]. Both of these men went on to bigger and better things with Rufinus translating Eusebius's *Church History* into Latin and adding some of his own history to it, and Jerome translating Old and New Testament books into a Latin version Bible which became known as the *Vulgate*.

In looking at the claims of the two men over Rufinus' work, we can reconstruct a bit of the original work which is now missing. It is evident that Eusebius did not

73

include his own name in his work, *Defense of Origen*. Jerome never charges Rufinus with deleting the name, only with assigning the work to the wrong man. It seems highly unlikely that Rufinus would simply take a published work by Eusebius, the most famous Christian writer of the previous generation, cut out his self-references and publish it as a work by Pamphilus. Rufinus must have genuinely thought that the work was by Pamphilus. While we cannot be sure that Eusebius included passages in the original work to suggest that it was a work by Pamphilus, we can be sure that Eusebius hid the fact that he was the author by not including his name in it.

Rufinus does admit to making changes to the original work which must have been by Eusebius. Rufinus admits to cutting out quoted passages in his translation of the original work, but he insists that the passages he did not translate had been forged to make Origen look like a heretic. If Rufinus is correct, we must consider who could have forged these passages. Eusebius had the best motive and the best opportunity.

Today, certain writers claim that both Rufinus and Eusebius wrote apologies for Origen or that they collaborated in some way. The later suggest that the affair is just a simple case of misunderstanding on the part of Jerome and may cite Eusebius's *History* itself in this:

> **The elder brethren among us have handed down many other facts respecting Origen which I think proper to omit, as not pertaining to this work. But whatever it has seemed necessary to record about him can be found in the Apology in his behalf written by us and Pamphilus, the holy martyr of our day. We prepared this carefully and did the work jointly on account of faultfinders[81].**

Both of these claims (dual authors of two works or dual authorship of one work) Sharply contradict Jerome and seem improbable. On the contrary, it seems most probable Eusebius was the sole author of the work. Attacks against Origen came shortly before the time of the Nicene Council in 324 C.E, when he was associated with the Arian Heresy. Pamphilus had been dead a dozen years at this point. It is quite unbelievable that the one and only book Pamphilus supposedly wrote defended Origen against charges that Pamphilus could never have heard or known about. As Jerome points out, "The very name of an apology which the treatise bears implies a previous charge made; for nothing is defended that is not first attacked[82]." Should we accept the apologetic notion that Pamphilus did indeed write such a work, then we must find Eusebius guilty of stealing the work and publishing it without giving Pamphilus credit. Yet, giving credit to the famous martyr Pamphilus should have been the first thing Eusebius should have done to promote the work. Pamphilus lacked both motive and opportunity. It is evident that there was only ever one work in defense of Origen and it was by Eusebius. Jerome asserts it this way, attacking Rufinus directly.

> Your Preface tells us that you have also translated the work of Pamphilus the martyr in defence of Origen; and you strive with all your might to prevent the church from condemning a man whose faith the martyr attests. The real fact is that Eusebius Bishop of Caesarea, as I have already said before, who was in his day the standard bearer of the Arian faction, wrote a large and elaborate work in six books in defence of Origen, showing by many testimonies that Origen was in his sense a catholic, that is, in our sense, an Arian. The first of these six books you have translated and assigned it to the martyr. I must not wonder, therefore, that you wish to make me, a small man and of no account, appear as an admirer of Origen, when you bring the same calumny against the martyr. You change a few statements about the Son of God and the holy Spirit, which you knew would offend the Romans, and let the rest go unchanged from beginning to end; you did, in fact, in the case of this Apology of Pamphilus as you call it, just what you did in the translation of Origen's Peri 'Arxwn. If that book is Pamphilus's, which of the six books is Eusebius's first? In the very volume which you pretend to be Pamphilus's, mention is made of the later books. Also, in the second and following books, Eusebius says that he had said such and such things in the first book and excuses himself for repeating them. If the whole work is Pamphilus's, why do you not translate the remaining books? If it is the work of the other, why do you change the name? You cannot answer; but the facts make answer of themselves: You thought that men would believe the martyr, though they would have turned in abhorrence from the chief of the Arians[83].

Shortly after in the same work, Jerome cites two writings of Eusebius himself that contradict the idea that Pamphilus wrote an *Apology for Origen*, or any work at all. Again, he addresses Rufinus directly:

> I will not suppose that you are ignorant of Eusebius' Catalogue, which states the fact that the martyr Pamphilus never wrote a single book. Eusebius himself, the lover and companion of Pamphilus, and the herald of his praises, wrote three books in elegant language containing the life of Pamphilus. In these he extols other traits of his character with extraordinary encomiums, and praises to the sky his humility; but on his literary interests he writes as follows in the third book: "What lover of books was there who did not find a friend in Pamphilus? If he knew of any of them being in want of the necessaries of life, he helped them to the full extent of his power. He would not only lend them copies of the Holy Scriptures to read, but would give them most readily,

and that not only to men, but to women also if he saw that they were given to reading. He therefore kept a store of manuscripts, so that he might be able to give them to those who wished for them whenever occasion demanded. He himself however, wrote nothing whatever of his own, except private letters which he sent to his friends, so humble was his estimate of himself. But the treatises of the old writers he studied with the greatest diligence, and was constantly occupied in meditation upon them[84]."

It is hard to reconcile the statement Jerome finds in Eusebius's *Life of Pamphilus*, "He himself however, wrote nothing whatsoever of his own," with the statement in the *History*, "the Apology in his behalf written by us and Pamphilus, the holy martyr of our day. We prepared this carefully and did the work jointly on account of faultfinders."

Ironically, a later forger inserted into Jerome's book on "Illustrious Men," in the passage on Pamphilus, the assertion "He wrote an *Apology for Origen* before Eusebius had written his[85]." This contradicts what Jerome wrote about the affair, that only Eusebius wrote a defense of Origen. It makes Jerome look foolish, but it seemingly helps to exonerate Eusebius. Exonerate him from what?

At the very least, we can say that Eusebius published an anonymous work, attempting to deceive the public into believing that someone besides himself was defending Origen. At the most, we can say that Eusebius gave hints in the work to lead people to believe that his teacher, the Christian martyr Pamphilus, had written the work, and that he forged passages attributed to Origen to show support for the Arian views that Eusebius himself held. If the passage from the *History* is true, that Eusebius and Pamphilus wrote the book together, which seems extraordinarily unlikely, then Eusebius has lied in a rather strange manner in his Life of Pamphilus by claiming that Pamphilus wrote nothing.

I should note that none of the people involved in this controversy directly accused Eusebius of any deception in his writings. His *Ecclesiatical History* was the only one available at the time and had proved invaluable to the faithful and the growth of the Church. It would not have been prudent to suggest that the writer of this great work was involved in forgery or deception. One could be critical of the supposedly heretical views of Eusebius, but one had to stop at the borderline of criticizing his general writing methodology.

Doubts About Eusebius Suppressed

Many writers have been critical of Eusebius since ancient times. The nineteenth century Theosophist, H.P. Blavatsky called him "the Baron Munchausen of the patristic hierarchy[86]." However, while generally critical, writers have been critical in a modest, restricted way. For example, Eusebius tells us that Jesus wrote letters to a King Abgarus of Edessa. He even quotes from them. Everyone regards these letters as spurious with excellent reason: Jesus' literary talents are unsupported in the New Testament texts or any other early Christian texts. Eusebius is the first writer to assert that Jesus wrote letters. Still, few writers have asserted that Eusebius forged these letters[87]. They tend to portray Eusebius as a dupe who used bad judgment in his sources.

Eusebius makes even more historically outrageous claims than this. For example, he claims that the Third Roman Emperor, Tiberius Caesar, who lived in the time of Jesus Christ was pro-Christian[88] and that he attempted to have Jesus Christ declared a God by the Roman Senate. No Roman writer records any such thing about Tiberius. This incredible fable also does not seem to hurt his reputation for truth and honesty. Most writers again give him the benefit of the doubt and just believe he chose his sources poorly.

Timothy Barnes is a good example of this. In his *Constantine and Eusebius*, he notes carefully the obvious deceptions of Eusebius and then declares him otherwise honest:

> A close inspection of the text and a comparison of the History with the documents and writers employed as sources immediately discloses several grave deficiencies. When Eusebius parphrases, he feels free to rewrite, to omit or to expand passages, to alter the emphases of the original, and he often misreports, just as if he had composed his paraphrase from memory. When he quotes extant writers directly, Eusebius often truncates his source, beginning or ending a quotation in the middle of a sentence. As a result he sometimes misrepresents his authority or renders the mutilated sentence unintelligible. Sometimes too, Eusebius leaves out a section in the middle of an extract, with consequent alteration of its overall meaning. It must be inferred that the quotations of lost documents and lost writers have undergone similar alterations. The quotations, moreover, are often preceded by introductions or paraphrases which partially contradict or are contradicted by their contents. It seems probable, therefore, that Eusebius trusted a scribe or assistant to insert the quotations and neglected to remove the inconsistencies which he introduced. In any event, it is unwise to rely on Eusebius' reports as reproducing exactly the precise tenor, or even main purport, of lost evidence.
>
> That Eusebius sometimes used forged documents, that he could not detect Christian interpolations in Josephus, that he evinced bias towards heretics and persecutors, that he sometimes contradicted himself, that he tamely believed miracles which a less credulous age rejects will occasion no surprise. A danger exist, however, that the evident care and honesty of his scholarship may be assumed to guarantee the

> accuracy of his results. It is requisite, therefore, to ask how far Eusebius' interpretation of early Christian history corresponds with reality[89].

Despite finding that what we can readily check of the scholarship of Eusebius does not check out, and is fulled with carelessness and/or deception, Barnes finds that Eusebius' care and honesty is evident.

What we cannot readily check out also appears highly unlikely to check out. Eusebius often give us sources that nobody has even heard of or recorded before or since. For example, he states:

> It is worthy of note that Pilate himself, who was governor in the time of our Saviour, is reported to have fallen into such misfortunes under Caius, whose times we are recording, that he was forced to become his own murderer and executioner; and thus divine vengeance, as it seems, was not long in overtaking him. This is stated by those Greek historians who have recorded the Olympiads, together with the respective events which have taken place in each period[90].

Who are these Greek Historians that record this obviously important fact about Pilate demonstrating divine justice? Why does Eusebius not name them or give us the name of the book where we may find this fact? Did so many Greek historians write about Pilate that it was common knowledge?

The *Testimonium Flavianum* of Josephus, is another case where few writers have shown an understanding of the artificial nature of Eusebean History. The recent article by Ken Olson[91] which proved that Eusebius was the author of the *Testimonium Flavianum* is a recent turning point in New Testament Studies. Even after this, few writers have understood that the obvious forgeries found in Eusebeus are not accidents of erroneous transmission or due to his bad judgment in source selection. Creating and presenting fictitious documents and quotes is his *modus operandi*.

Olson demonstrated that the phrases and words in the *TF* reflected language Eusebius often uses but Josephus never or hardly ever does. For example, the phrases: "maker of many miracles," "tribe of Christians," and "until this day" are found throughout Eusebean texts and rarely in others. What Olson actually proved was not only did Eusebius write the *Testimonium*, but that he was a rather inept forger. Unlike good forgers with the ability to copy the language or voice of the works they interpolate into, Eusebius's text always sounds like Eusebius. It does not matter if he is quoting a first century Jewish Historian, a second century Christian Philosopher, or a third century group of Christian prisoners in Gaul, the voice is identical and identifiable as Eusebius's.

In spite of our knowing this, Eusebius' narrative remains credible for academicians throughout the world. As Everett Ferguson declares, "However one evaluates Eusebius's achievement, his work remains foundational for our knowledge of the church in its first three centuries. And this foundation stands firm despite noticeable crack.[92]"

Knowing this should drastically affect every aspect of New Testament Studies. For example, the work *Dialogue with Trypho* of Justin Martyr is often used for dating other documents and to assert an early date for the Gospel of Luke. Yet scholars base the dating of this work to Justin's references to the Bar Kochbar War of 132-135 C.E. We must consider that Eusebius himself is the first person to mention this text and the first person to mention this date within the text. We must consider the possibility that he wrote this text and/or inserted this date reference into the text specifically to support his own chronology and history. If this is the case, when we date other works, based on the date of Justin Martyr's *Dialogue*, we are following the chronology of Eusebius, whether scholars know it or not, or wish to acknowledge it or not. When we trace back almost all the certainties regarding the chronology of early Christian documents, we find that the certainties really are certainties because they match Eusebius's chronology and do not come from sources really independent of Eusebius. Eusebius provides the anchor for historical certainty for most scholars in the field.

Philosophy and Style

In reading several hundred philosophers over the past 35 years or so, I have noticed that it is quite easy to tell them apart and generally not difficult to place them chronologically. Philosophers have problematics, sets of problems they deal with, and they have their own methodologies or styles of argumentation. Also they develop their own central ideas and solutions to their problems. When we examine their problematics, methodologies and central ideas, we can distinguish between Philosophers and easily put them in chronological order, even when direct biographical or historical references are missing from their works, as is often the case when they deal in abstract concepts for long periods of time.

Occasionally, the problematics, methodologies and central ideas can be quite close. For example, there is a certain similarity in the writings of Epictetus and Marcus Aurelius, the Second Century Stoic Philosophers. Likewise, in the 17th Century, the early works of Baruch Spinoza might be mistaken for the works of René DesCartes. This rare similarity occurs when a talented young protégé comes under the influence of a great writer from the generation (20 or 30 years) before. Other than these cases, we find that philosophical writings reflect their time, place and the personality of their writer with a great deal of chronological precision. To the knowledgeable person, the texts of any two philosophers from different centuries are almost as different and easily detectible as two people's DNA.

The fact that we have so many problems distinquishing the chronology of Christian works may be considered as due to deliberate attempts by people in control of the works to create false chronological impressions.

Eusebius' Tell (*ET*)

The study of an author's literary style by examining the frequency of word usage is called stylometry. The field has had something of a breakthrough in recent years:

> The idea of using sets (at least 50 strong) of common high-frequency words and conducting what is essentially a principal components analysis on the data has been developed by Burrows (1987) and represents a landmark in the development of stylometry. The technique is very much in vogue now as a reliable stylometric procedure and Holmes and Forsyth (1995) have successfully applied it to the classic 'Federalist Papers' problem[93].

As far as I know, no recent stylometrical studies have been done in the field of Patristics, the study of the writings of the Church Fathers. I am eagerly awaiting the results of such a study by some bright young mathematician. In the meantime, there is another way of identifying a forgery without doing any precise mathematics. This is by spotting a "tell," or writer's trope, a habit that a writer has that is relatively unique to a writer and acts as a fingerprint in identifying that writer's work whenever it appears.

Ordinarily, this is an insecure method as one writer may pick up another writer's tell by studying their work. However, in the case of Eusebius, we have him in a single work quoting the works of no less than eight different writers, from eight different time periods, writing about eight different topics and each time we find the same telltale tell. The appearance of such a tell in one quotation might raise suspicions, the repeated use of the same tell in numerous quotations provides strong evidence of systematic change.

The key to seeing "Eusebius's Tell" (which I abbreviate as *ET*) is in his work called *The Theophonia*. It gives one of his most important central concepts:

> For, the miracles which were performed by Him may he divided into (two) periods; that, in which the conversations He made on earth are commemorated, and that which succeeded, and extends *to our times*. Those great acts then, which he formerly did when he was with the men who happened to exist at that time, it was in their power openly to view ; but to us, these were unseen; and they are laid down, (as) having been unseen. And thus again also, the things which have been fulfilled *in our times*,—in the order in which His words foretold them, and are *even to this present* witnessed by us in the very facts,—could not, to those of the times in which they were foretold, have yet been known as to their results; and they were, no doubt, considered by them, who believed not, as impossible[94].

Eusebius divides Jesus' miracles into those of Jesus' time and those that happen "in our times." His predictions are being fulfilled "in our times." We may witness this "even to this present" [day]. For Eusebius the proof of the truth of something is not only that it was seen by people in the past, but that it may be seen still in the present time. Note the phrases that he uses for this important concept, "to our times," "in our times," "Even to this present" [day]. Here is another quote from the same work, *Theophonia*:

> The Book of the Acts of the Apostles also attests, that there were many thousands of the Jews, who were persuaded that He was that Christ of God, who had been preached of by the Prophets. It is also on record, that there was a great Church of Christ at Jerusalem; which had been collected from among the Jews, *even to the times* of its reduction by Hadrian. The first Bishops too who were there, are said to have been, one after another, fifteen (in number), who were Jews; the names of whom are published to the men of that place, *even until now*[95].

Here he uses the term "even until now," to support his statement that a Christian Church that had fifteen Jewish Bishops existed in Jerusalem after Jesus Christ[96]. Eusebius gives no source for this Christian Church in Jerusalem after Christ.

The things of the present proving the things of the past is not a minor point for Eusebius. It is at the core of his belief in Christianity. He writes a reply to a follower of Apollonius[97], Hierocles in which he makes fun of Apollonius because his works are not seen in the present time:

> In what light then, this being so, do you envisage for us Apollonius, my good compiler? If as a divine being and superior to a philosopher, in a word as one superhuman in his nature, I would ask you to keep to this point of view throughout your history, and to point me out effects wrought by his divinity enduring *to this day*. For surely it is an absurdity that the works of carpenters and builders should last on ever so long after the craftsmen are dead, and raise as it were an immortal monument to the memory of their constructive ability; and yet that a human character claimed to be divine should, after shedding its glory upon mankind, finish in darkness its short-lived career, instead of displaying for ever its power and excellence. Instead of being so niggardly liberal to some one individual like Damis and to a few other short-lived men, it should surely make its coming among us the occasion of blessings, conferred on myriads not only of his contemporaries, but also of his posterity[98].

Apollonius cannot be Christ because his miracles do not endure "to this day." A divinity is a divinity, not only in the past, but in the present as well. For Eusebius, this is the mark of a true divinity. It shows itself not only in "its short-lived career" to a few other "short-lived men," but to the "myriads" of "his posterity."

I would suggest that the concept is not quite developed in Eusebius' mind when he writes this work on Apollonius. Only in thinking about the differences between Apollonius and Jesus does Eusebius develop his "continues into the present" criteria for distinguishing the true divine from the false.

Let us call this concept that a past divine miracle or miracle worker is only divine if it continues to the present *ET* (Eusebius' Tell). It is not that Eusebius is the first or only one to use the concept, but the way he uses it makes it a marker of his writing. He uses the concept as his ace up his sleeve, his irrefutable argument. It is his trademark secret ingredient. In short, it is his writer's trope. Here he is using it three more times in the same work, *Theophania*:

> Nor was it only, that He impressed on the souls of those who (immediately) followed Him such power, that when, having done nothing worthy of death, they willingly underwent every species of punishment and torment, for the sake of the righteousness of that God who is overall; but also, on those who received (it) from them; and so again, on those who came afterwards; and on those *even to this present*, and (who live) *in our own times*;—How does this not transcend every sort of miracle[99].
>
> For the army of the Romans came soon after, and took the city, and destroyed the Temple itself by fire. And, of Whom was it, except of Him who is King of all, God over all, that it was thus said, that *"the King shall send his army, and shall slay those murderers, and shall burn up their city?" To this very time indeed*, the remnants of the conflagration which took place in various parts of the city, are obvious to the sight of those who travel thither. But, how those murderers of the Apostles were taken in the reduction (of the city), and suffered the punishment which they deserved[100],
>
> Who is not also astonished at this, when he considers with himself, and feels satisfied, that this could not have been of man; that never at any former time, were the many nations of the whole creation subject to the one sovereign rule of the Romans, except only since the time of our Saviour? For it happened, immediately upon His passing about among men, that the affairs of the Romans became great; that, at that time, Augustus was primarily the sole Sovereign of many nations; and that in his time Cleopatra was inflamed with love; and the traditionary (kingdom) of the Ptolemies in Egypt was dissolved. For, *from that time, and until now*, that kingdom which was from ancient time; and of it, as one might say, the ancient germ of men which was established in Egypt, have been rooted up[101].

In the first passage, note the phrases "even to this present [day]" and "in our own time." In this case the sacrifices of the apostles are legitimized because people are still making the same sacrifices. In the second passage, Eusebius tells us that the miracle of the Romans avenging the deaths of Jesus and the Apostles can still be seen "to this very time indeed" in parts of Jerusalem. In the third passage, the miracle of Roman started in the time of Christ and continues to the present. Note that Eusebius puts Cleopatra in the time of Christ, compressing and merging Christian and Roman history.

At the very beginning of Eusebius's most important theoretical work, the *Demonstratio Evangelica*, (*Demonstration of the Gospels*) we again find this explicit use of the tell in this statement:

> I propose to use as witnesses those men, beloved by God, whose fame you know to be far-spread in the world: {2} Moses, I mean, and his successors, who shone forth with resplendent godliness, and the blessed prophets and sacred writers. I propose to show, by quotations from them, how they foretold events that came to the light long ages after their time, the actual circumstances of the Saviour's own presentment of the Gospel, and the things which *in our own day* are being fulfilled by the Holy Spirit before our very eyes[102].

Again, it is not only the men of Jesus' time that saw the fulfillment of prophecy, but "in our own day" we are seeing it. Note also that "seeing" with "our very eyes" is often associated with the truth of the divine. It also often appears in his tell.

Besides the beginning of this work, we encounter *ET* at the beginning of his *Ecclesiastical History*:

> It is my intention, moreover, to recount the misfortunes which immediately came upon the whole Jewish nation in consequence of their plots against our Saviour, and to record the ways and the times in which the divine word has been attacked by the Gentiles, and to describe the character of those who at various periods have contended for it in the face of blood and of tortures, as well as the confessions which have been made in *our own days*.

Eusebius intends to show us that the prophesies of the divine word came true not only in the past but also "in our days." Further, he tells us,

> Having gathered therefore from the matters mentioned here and there by them whatever we consider important for the present work, and having plucked like flowers from a meadow the appropriate passages

from ancient writers, we shall endeavor to embody the whole in an historical narrative, content if we preserve the memory of the successions of the apostles of our Saviour; if not indeed of all, yet of the most renowned of them in those churches which are the most noted, and which *even to the present time* are held in honor[103].

Note Eusebius's phrase "even to the present time." He is writing a history, but also reminding us that the work of the Apostles continues into the present. He uses it again when referring specifically to Jesus Christ:

But it is a great and convincing proof of his incorporeal and divine unction that he alone of all those who have ever existed is *even to the present day* called Christ by all men throughout the world, and is confessed and witnessed to under this name, and is commemorated both by Greeks and Barbarians and *even to this day* is honored as a King by his followers throughout the world, and is admired as more than a prophet, and is glorified as the true and only high priest of God[104].

For Eusebius, it is a "great and convincing proof," of his divinity that Jesus, "even to the present day" has the title of "Christ," and "even to this day" is honored as the only high priest. Not only when talking abstractly, but when talking about real historical events we find *ET*. At the end of his rather long discussion of the letters of Abgarus to Jesus, he tells the story of Thomas's disciple, Thaddeus, curing Abgarus. Then, he states

When he came to that place he healed Abgarus by the word of Christ; and after bringing all the people there into the right attitude of mind by means of his works, and leading them to adore the power of Christ, he made them disciples of the Saviour's teaching. And from that time *down to the present* the whole city of the Edessenes has been devoted to the name of Christ, offering no common proof of the beneficence of our Saviour toward them also[105].

The miracle of Jesus is still acknowledged "down to the present" in Edessa. Thus we find this concept of the present validating the past presented prominently in at least four different works of Eusebius: *History*, *Demonstratio*, *Theophania*, and *Treatise against Hierocles*. In none of these works does he seem to be getting the concept from another source.

At a certain point in his writing of his *History*, he begins to use this concept repeatedly and apparently unconsciously. It appears as a writer's trope, or nervous habit. He generally uses it almost to say "Isn't that right?" when he is finished with a

THE EVOLUTION OF CHRISTS AND CHRISTIANIES

topic and wants to move on. In addition to the ten previous examples, here are eight other examples of *ET* from his *History*:

This account of Peter and Paul is substantiated by the fact that their names are preserved in the cemeteries of that place *even to the present day*[106].

This shows that the statement of those is true, who say that there were two persons in Asia that bore the same name, and that there were two tombs in Ephesus, each of which, *even to the present day*, is called John's[107].

There is extant also another epistle written by Dionysius to the Romans, and addressed to Soter, who was bishop at that time. We cannot do better than to subjoin some passages from this epistle, in which he commends the practice of the Romans which has been retained *down to the persecution in our own days*[108].

After Trajan had reigned for nineteen and a half years Aelius Adrian became his successor in the empire. To him Quadratus addressed a discourse containing an apology for our religion, because certain wicked men had attempted to trouble the Christians. *The work is still in the hands of a great many of the brethren*, as also in our own, and furnishes clear proofs of the man's understanding and of his apostolic orthodox[109].

Aristides also, a believer earnestly devoted to our religion, left, like Quadratus, an apology for the faith, addressed to Adrian. His work, too, has been *preserved even to the present day* by a great many persons[110].

And that Theophilus also, with the others, contended against them, is manifest from a certain discourse of no common merit written by him against Marcion. This work too, with the others of which we have spoken, has been *preserved to the present day*[111].

But it was not the custom of the churches in the rest of the world to end it at this time, as they observed the practice which, from apostolic tradition, *has prevailed to the present time*, of terminating the fast on no other day than on that of the resurrection of our Saviour[112].

For there stands upon an elevated stone, by the gates of her house, a brazen image of a woman kneeling, with her hands stretched out, as if she were praying. Opposite this is another upright image of a man, made of the same material, clothed decently in a double cloak, and extending his hand toward the woman. At his feet, beside the statue itself, is a certain strange plant, which climbs up to the hem of the brazen cloak, and is a remedy for all kinds of diseases. They say that this statue is an image of Jesus. *It has remained to our day*, so that we ourselves also saw it when we were staying in the city[113].

> The chair of James, who first received the episcopate of the church at Jerusalem from the Saviour himself and the apostles, and who, as the divine records show, was called a brother of Christ, *has been preserved until now*, the brethren who have followed him in succession there exhibiting clearly to all the reverence which both those of old times *and those of our own day* maintained and do maintain for holy men on account of their piety[114].
>
> Zambdas received the episcopate of the church of Jerusalem after the bishop Hymenaeus, whom we mentioned a little above. He died in a short time, and Hermon, the last before the persecution in our day, succeeded to the apostolic chair, which *has been preserved there until the present time*[115].

In all of these cases, Eusebius is speaking in his own name. It should be remembered that the fifteen or so examples of this trope in the *History* take place over ten long books. While Eusebius probably uses this trope more than anybody else, still he only uses it relatively infrequently, about once in five hundred sentences in this work. Being a history book, one should expect to find comparisons between the past and present, and even the rhetorical style that marks this trope is not remarkable.

Now, one should not expect to find the trope used as much by writers whom Eusebius quotes. He generally quotes only bits and pieces from them and they have little reason to use the rhetorical and dramatic style of comparison that Eusebius typically uses. If Eusebius quotes texts from diverse earlier writers containing this concept of miracles continuing into the present in diverse contexts where this concept has no particular relevance to the argument being made, and these writers almost never use it except when Eusebius quotes them, we may suppose that Eusebius has put his own central concept into the mouths of earlier writers and that it is a proof of systematic forgery on his part. This is precisely what we do find in his *History*. We find he has used this trope when quoting Josephus, Justin Martyr, Hegesippus, Quadratus, Irenaeus, Christian Prisoners from Gaul, Tertullian, Dionysius and even the Emperor Augustus.

Eleven More Cases of Eusebius' Trope

Here are more instances of *ET* in his quotes from his *History*:

1. Quoting Josephus:

> And there lived at that time Jesus, a wise man, if indeed it be proper to call him a man. For he was a doer of wonderful works, and a teacher of such men as receive the truth in gladness. And he attached to himself many of the Jews, and many also of the Greeks. He was the Christ.

> When Pilate, on the accusation of our principal men, condemned him to the cross, those who had loved him in the beginning did not cease loving him. For he appeared unto them again alive on the third day, the divine prophets having told these and countless other wonderful things concerning him. Moreover, the race of Christians, named after him, *continues down to the present day*[116].

The miracles of Christians following Jesus "did not cease" after his death, but "continues down to the present day." It is nice of Josephus to adopt the central concept of Eusebius that Jesus' miracles continue into the present.

2. **Quoting Justin:**

> "We do not think it out of place to mention here Antinoüs also, *who lived in our day*, and whom all were driven by fear to worship as a god, although they knew who he was and whence he came."[117].

Here Eusebius uses the phrase "lived in our day" to point out that Antinoüs was living in the time of Justin Martyr. If the mark of a true God is that his works occur in the present, Eusebius would want his reader to be sure to place a false God like Antinoüs only in the present time of Justin. Justin, allegedly writing around 156 C.E. would have no need to remind his audience when Antinoüs lived as they would have been alive at that time.

3. **Quoting Hegesippus:**

> "To whom they erected cenotaphs and temples, *as is done to the present day*. Among whom is also Antinoüs, a slave of the Emperor Adrian, in whose honor are celebrated also the Antinoian games, which were instituted in our day. For he [i.e. Adrian] also founded a city named after Antinoüs, and appointed prophets[118]."

Here again we find *ET* in the phrase "as is done in the present day." Again it is to make sure that people realize that the false God Antinoüs was only worshipped in his own time, the time of Hegesippus (allegedly mid-second century). We should note that Eusebius introduces both quotes as a means of identifying the date of both authors. Quite fantastically, Justin has written a work to the Emperor as a real defense of Christians living in his time, and supposedly Hegesippus has written five books of "Memoirs," and yet the only way to identify the time period of these works is through their references to the same Antinoüs cult set up by the Emperor Hadrian. One would expect that Justin would write about some known persecution or event involving

Christians in his defense of Christianity to the Emperor, and one would expect Hegesippus in five books of memoirs to mention some person or event that took place in his time that would identify his time. Eusebius would have us believe that coincidentally both of these authors only date their works through the mention of the Antinoüs Cult. It is quite unlikely. This information itself would make one suspect the two quotes as forgeries, even if the tell was not present.

4. Quoting Hegesippus Again

> James, the brother of the Lord, succeeded to the government of the Church in conjunction with the apostles. He has been called the Just by all from the time of our Saviour *to the present day*; for there were many that bore the name of James[119].

The phrase "to the present day" is a bit odd here. Eusebius has just told us that Hegesippus lived "immediately after the apostles." This would suggest the later half of the First Century[120]. It is quite usual for nicknames to be applied to people after they die, so there is little point to saying it is still applied "to the present day." It is only later that Eusebius tells us that Hegesippus really lived in the late second century. Thus this qualifies as a writer's trope of Eusebius. Most likely James the Just and James, the brother of the Lord were two different characters bound into one here by Eusebius. Note that the reason that he was called James the Just "that there were many that bore the name of James" seems to suggest that the author knew of multiple James, but does not explain at all why he was given the name "the Just" instead of being called James, the brother of the Christ. Was being the brother of the Christ not enough to identify him?

5. Quoting Hegesippus A Third Time:

> And one of them, who was a fuller, took the club with which he beat out clothes and struck the just man on the head. And thus he suffered martyrdom. And they buried him on the spot, by the temple, and his monument *still remains by the temple*. He became a true witness, both to Jews and Greeks, that Jesus is the Christ. And immediately Vespasian besieged them."

This passage tells us "his monument still remains by the temple," which is a slight variation of "to the present day." Since the temple was destroyed in 70 C.E., it is difficult not to read this as meaning that Hegessipus wrote this before the temple's destruction in 70 C.E., in which case saying a monument built within the previous 30 years "still remains" seems absurd. On the other hand, we take this to mean after the

THE EVOLUTION OF CHRISTS AND CHRISTIANIES

destruction of the temple, it is hard to understand why the writer does not point out that the monument of the Christian James remains, while the Temple was destroyed. Also note that the sentence "He became a true witness, both to Jews and Greeks" matches the reference found in the *Testimonium Flavianum*, i.e., "He attached to himself many of the Jews and also many of the Greeks."

6. **Quoting Quadratus:**

> But the works of our Saviour were always present, for they were genuine:- those that were healed, and those that were raised from the dead, who were seen not only when they were healed and when they were raised, but were also always present; and not merely while the Saviour was on earth, but also after his death, they were alive for quite a while, so that some of them lived *even to our day*[121]."

After Jesus performed the miracle of raising the dead, the miracles themselves, the raised dead, are "seen" as proof, "some of them lived even to our day." Note that Quadratus, a supposed second century writer does not give the names of any of these miracle raised dead, although living in the present time with them, he must have known who they were and it would help his case to name them. This statement reflects Eusebius's central idea of true miracles lasting to the present.

7. **Quoting Irenaeus:**

> But Polycarp also was not only instructed by the apostles, and acquainted with many that had seen Christ, but was also appointed by apostles in Asia bishop of the church of Smyrna. We too saw him in our early youth; for he lived a long time, and died, when a very old man, a glorious and most illustrious martyr's death, having always taught the things which he had learned form the apostles, which the Church also hands down, and which alone are true. To these things all the Asiatic churches testify, as do also those who, *down to the present time*, have succeeded Polycarp, who was a much more trustworthy and certain witness of the truth than Valentinus and Marcion and the rest of the heretics[122].

In this case "down to the present time" would be to around the time of 190 C.E. when Irenaeus allegedly writes this. We might also point out that Eusebius's concept of "seeing" miracles in this case becomes the miracle of Irenaeus seeing Polycarp, a man who was instructed by the Apostles and "had seen Christ." Like, Hegessipus, Clement and others in Eusebius's tale Polycarp lived and worked after the age of one hundred.

8. Quoting Irenaeus Again:

"We are not bold enough to speak confidently of the name of Antichrist. For if it were necessary that his name should be declared clearly *at the present time*, it would have been announced by him who saw the revelation. For it was seen, not long ago, but almost in our generation, toward the end of the reign of Domitian[123].

This passage is slightly different than the others in that the author is declaring that a miracle (the coming of the antichrist) is not happening "at the present time." Apparently, the miracle of the antichrist was expected and declared around the year 200[124]. Obviously this turned out to be wrong. Eusebius has Irenaeus say that he cannot "speak confidently of the name of the Antichrist," to show that the Church did not really claim falsely that the Antichrist had come around the year 200. This leaves the fulfillment of the prophecy open to take place in Eusebius' time. This non-prediction of the Anti-Christ in the time of Irenaeus is an absurd thing for Irenaeus to say. Whoever heard of a preacher saying this is not the time of the antichrist? However, it is perfectly logical coming from Eusebius, who wants to prove that the prophecies are coming true in his own time and not in the prior times. Also, in this passage, Irenaeus dates the book of Revelations to the time of Domitian and attributes it to John the evangelist, something that Eusebius wishes to demonstrate and probably puts in the passage in the work.

9. Quoting an Unnamed Writer Against Artemon

I will remind many of the brethren of a fact which took place *in our time*, which, had it happened in Sodom, might, I think, have proved a warning to them. There was a certain confessor, Natalius, not long ago, but *in our own day*[125].

Here Eusebius repeats his usual trope twice.

Quoting Letters from Unnamed Christian Prisoners in Gaul to Churches in Asia and Phrygia:

It is reported that Marcus Aurelius Caesar, brother of Antoninus, being about to engage in battle with the Germans and Sarmatians, was in great trouble on account of his army suffering from thirst. But the soldiers of the so-called Melitene legion, through the faith which has given strength *from that time to the present*, when they were drawn up before the enemy, kneeled on the ground, as is our custom in prayer, and engaged in supplications to God[126].

THE EVOLUTION OF CHRISTS AND CHRISTIANIES

The battle took place in 175 C.E. and Cassius Dio tells us that the troops successfully supplicated the Roman God Mercury for help. The use of phrase "from that time to the present" certainly sounds like *ET*. However since "the present" would have to be only a few years later (since the prisoner-authors also wrote to Eleutherus the alleged Bishop from 175-192, the distant from that time to the present time is not very great. We may look at this passage in conjunction with the next use of the Tell regarding the same incident:

10. Quoting Tertullian's Apology:

> Tertullian is a trustworthy witness of these things. In the Apology for the Faith, which he addressed to the Roman Senate, and which work we have already mentioned that he confirms the history with greater and stronger proofs. He writes that *there are still extant letters* of the most intelligent Emperor Marcus in which he testifies that his army, being on the point of perishing with thirst in Germany, was saved by the prayers of the Christians[127].

The use of *ET* here is a little bit harder to detect, as Eusebius appears to have interpolated it into the original text, but only paraphrased it here in the phrase "still extant letters." It is a bit absurd to use the phrase when we consider that the "still extant" letters by Marcus Aurelius would have had to been written after 175 C.E. and Tertullian's *Apology* is a work around 200 C.E. Why would letters written so recently not be extant? It is like somebody in 2005 saying there are "still extant letters" from President Jimmy Carter. Why would letters of an emperor not be extant a few decades after his reign? On the other hand, Eusebius, writing 125 years later would find it important that these letters describing a miracle would be around 125 years later. We should digress a moment to look at the actual passage as it now appears in Tertullian's Apology

11. Directly in Tertullian's Apology

> Domitian, too, a man of Nero's type in cruelty, tried his hand at persecution; but as he had something of the human in him, he soon put an end to what he had begun, even restoring again those whom he had banished. Such as these have always been our persecutors,-men unjust, impious, base, of whom even you yourselves have no good to say, the sufferers under whose sentences you have been wont to restore. But among so many princes *from that time to the present day*, with anything of divine and human wisdom in them, point out a single persecutor of the Christian name. So far from that, we, on the contrary, bring before you

one who was their protector, as you will see by examining the letters of Marcus Aurelius, that most grave of emperors, in which he bears his testimony that that Germanic drought was removed by the rains obtained through the prayers of the Christians who chanced to be fighting under him[128].

Note the example of *ET* in "from that time to the present day." It is nearly identical to the phrase used by the Christian Prisoners from Gaul in their letter, "the faith which has given strength from that time to the present." This is the only time in Tertullian's *Apology* that we find *ET* and this is the only passage Eusebius quotes from the *Apology*. It suggests that chapter five in Tertullian's *Apology* is an interpolation. The material in this chapter involves fantastic claims that are out of place in the argument of this work and are never repeated in any other work of Tertullian.

Three Perhaps Coincidental Uses of Phrases Similar to Eusbebius' Trope

We cannot assume that every use of the term "in the present time," or similar terms, reveals the hand of Eusebius. There are contextual reasons for suggesting that these three uses may have been in the original quoted material.

1. Quoting From Dionysius

> But I will relate one occurrence as an example. Chaeremon, who was very old, was bishop of the city called Nilus. He fled with his wife to the Arabian mountain and did not return. And though the brethren searched diligently they could not find either them or their bodies. And many who fled to the same Arabian mountain were carried into slavery by the barbarian Saracens. Some of them were ransomed with difficulty and at a large price *others have not been to the present time*. I have related these things, my brother, not without an object, but that you may understand how many and great distresses came upon us[129].

2. Another Quote from Dionysius

> For as I have said before, *unto the present time* the governor continues to put to death in a cruel manner those who are brought to trial[130].

The phrases "have not been to the present time," and "unto the present time," do not quite fit the ordinary concept of Eusebius that miracles are continuing to the present time. Eusebius uses the letters of Dionysius quite differently from the way he uses most of the other writings in the *History*. He uses them in generally short quotes to suggest the attitudes of Dionysius on many subjects. It is almost as if he was writing a biography of Dionysius and not a book on Church History. It is possible that a large amount of material from books six and seven originally started out as a work on Dionysius. In contrast to the most of the other early material, these passages reflect an independent voice and ideology from Eusebius. One may suppose from this that Eusebius did not start out with the notion of fabricating a Church History filled with his inventions. Only when he found that he lacked any material from the first two centuries of Christianity to support his main points did he choose to create that material. Starting with the Dionysian material in the sixth book we seem to be getting a relatively honest History, while the first five books are filled mainly with inventions.

3. Quoting from the Emperor Constantine

> Since, therefore, we have commanded a number of bishops from a great many different places to assemble in the city of Arles, before the kalends of August, we have thought proper to write to thee also that thou shouldst secure from the most illustrious Latronianus, corrector of Sicily, a public vehicle, and that thou shouldst take with thee two others of the second rank whom thou thyself shalt choose, together with three servants who may serve you on the way, and betake thyself to the above-mentioned place before the appointed day; that by thy firmness, and by the wise unanimity and harmony of the others present, this dispute, which has *disgracefully continued until the present time*, in consequence of certain shameful strifes, after all has been heard which those have to say who are now at variance with one another, and whom we have likewise commanded to be present, may be settled in accordance with the proper faith, and that brotherly harmony, though it be but gradually, may be restored[131].

We find the phrase "until the present time" inserted here. It is surprising, but does not fit that closely the typical conceptual use of *ET*, where it is generally associated with seeing miracles. It is quite amazing to think that Eusebius forged edicts from the Emperor Constantine. I assume that if it is not a simple coincidence, Eusebius simply composed the edict in his own words with Constantine's approval.

The fourteen quotes from nine different sources all using a variant of *ET*, or at least the eleven quotes from seven different sources which I think are authentic cases of *ET*, presents I believe a significant case that the *History* is an untrustworthy document. At least when it comes to the first five books of the *History* and the first two and a half centuries of Christian History. However, while I want to prove this to the reader, I do

93

not want to give the impression that Eusebius was a pathological liar or morally deficient. In fact the existence of the ET, a rather noticeable act of nervousness, supports the idea that his actions may have been troubling to him. Then why did he do it?

In Defense of Eusebius

From his arguments in the *Theophania*, *Demonstratio* and the *History*, we can suspect that the *Testimonium* was an early forgery done by Eusebius, and we can get a pretty good idea of why he did it. In his *History* he writes:

> Accordingly the forgery of those who have recently given currency to acts against our Saviour is clearly proved. For the very date given in them shows the falsehood of their fabricators. For the things which they have dared to say concerning the passion of the Saviour are put into the fourth consulship of Tiberius, which occurred in the seventh year of his reign; at which time it is plain that Pilate was not yet ruling in Judea, if the testimony of Josephus is to be believed, who clearly shows in the above-mentioned work that Pilate was made procurator of Judea by Tiberius in the twelfth year of his reign[132].

First note the odd phrase "if the testimony of Josephus is to be believed." Why should the testimony not be believed? Usually when a writer quotes a source, it is because a writer presumes the source is telling the truth. Here, Eusebius himself raises the question of the truthfulness of the text. To be sure it is a rhetorical phrase for Eusebius. Josephus would not be doubted. Eusebius is telling us that we cannot doubt this text. Why should Eusebius be worried about us doubting this text? What about the text makes it something that might be doubted?

Apparently, a document called the *Acts of Pilate* had been circulating and causing much damage to Christian credibility. Eusebius talks about this important document again in his ninth book, where he blames the Emperor Maximinus for production and wide circulation of the document.

> Having therefore forged Acts of Pilate and our Saviour full of every kind of blasphemy against Christ, they sent them with the emperor's approval to the whole of the empire subject to him, with written commands that they should be openly posted to the view of all in every place, both in country and city, and that the schoolmasters should give them to their scholars, instead of their customary lessons, to be studied and learned by heart[133] ...

> The memorials against us and copies of the imperial edicts issued in reply to them were engraved and set up on brazen pillars in the midst of the cities, a course which had never been followed elsewhere. The children in the schools had daily in their mouths the names of Jesus and Pilate, and the Acts which had been forged in wanton insolence[134].

Based on his defense elsewhere of Christianity against pagan attacks[135], we can suppose the flavor of the "Acts of Pilate and Jesus." It denounced Jesus as a "magician, seducer, cunning deceiver, impostor and fabricator of magical rites and drugs[136]." His disciples were illiterate deceivers who spoke only Aramaic[137]. It also placed the crucifixion around the year 22 C.E., the seventh year of Pilate's reign. While Eusebius could scream, "forgery," it really did not do any good, as there were no independent or scientific bodies around at the time to prove it was a forgery. To counter the charges in the document, Eusebius had to use an unimpeachable and believable source. The only possible one that people would believe was Josephus. After all, Josephus was a Jewish historian. He would have no reason to lie. No doubt Eusebius could justify this as merely fighting fire with fire, a forgery for God to counter a forgery from the Devil. Changing the date of Pilate's arrival in Jerusalem from 22 to 27 C.E. was one change Pilate made to Josephus' work. However, this was insufficient and trivial. Josephus could have gotten the date wrong. This minor change would not discredit the charges made in the *Pilate* text. Thus Eusebius needed to create and add the *Testimonium Flavianum*, and probably make other changes as well.

The negative effects of the *Acts of Pilate* were neutralized. However, if one could justify such an action once, why not twice, three or more times? Eusebius took the same pragmatic approach when constructing his *History* of supplying texts needed to counter an opponent's arguments. One may find a multitude of other explanations in psychoanalyzing Eusebius. In the interest of not taxing the reader's patience, I will simply leave the evidence in this state.

Checking ET

Now, one can argue that *ET* is early Christian and not Eusebean. The argument can be made that early Christian writers used similar concepts and vocabulary with similar meanings and any random sampling of their work would include *ET* at approximately the same rate we find it in his *History*. As a check on this hypothesis, I examined all the extant works of Tertullian, who wrote circa 200-220. We have more of his works preserved than any other Christian writer. If Christians had picked up the trope from each other, we should find it in Tertullian.

In the ten books of the *History*, I found about 25 uses of the trope where the writer tries to surprise the reader by telling the reader that a great good or evil continues in the present day or time. I examined 38 books of 32 works[138] by Tertullian. These books are generally significantly shorter than the books of the *History*, but added together easily surpass double the length of the *History*. In all this material, I found five instances of what may be considered Eusebius's Tell:

1) One will even suffer for the sake of a man what he hesitates to undergo in the cause of God. On this point, indeed, *even the present times* may furnish us with proof, when so many persons of dignity are meeting with deaths never dreamt of for them in view of their family, rank, bodily condition and age—and all in the cause of a man, being punished either by himself if they have acted against him, or by his opponents if they have ranged themselves on his side[139].

2) In short, again, a throne "unto the age" is more suitable to Christ, God's Son, than to Solomon,—a temporal king, to wit, who reigned over Israel alone. *For at the present day* nations are invoking Christ which used not to know Him; and peoples at the present day are fleeing in a body to the Christ of whom in days bygone they were ignorant), you cannot contend that is future which you see taking place [14] Either deny that these events were prophesied, while they are seen before your eyes; or else have been fulfilled, while you hear them read: or, on the other hand, if you fail to deny each position, they will have their fulfilment in Him with respect to whom they were prophesied[140].

3) To the testimony of antiquity is added that of later games instituted in their turn, and betraying their origin from the titles which *they bear even at the present day*, in which it is imprinted as on their very face, for what idol and for what religious object games, whether of the one kind or the other, were designed[141].

4) So, too, righteousness—for the God of righteousness and of creation is the same—was first in a rudimentary state, having a natural fear of God: from that stage it advanced, through the Law and the Prophets, to infancy; from that stage it passed, through the Gospel, to the fervour of youth: now, through the Paraclete, it is settling into maturity. He will be, after Christ, the only one to be called and revered as Master; for He speaks not from Himself, but what is commanded by Christ. He is the only prelate, because He alone succeeds Christ. They who have received Him set truth before custom. They who have heard Him prophesying *even to the present time*, not of old, bid virgins be wholly covered[142].

5) But out of so many emperors who reigned *from that time to the present*, men versed in knowledge, human and divine, show us one who set himself to destroy the Christians[143].

We find that the trope appears in Eusebius' *History* at a rate some five times greater, 25-5, than Tertullian uses it throughout all his works. Since the size of Tertullian's works are double that of the *History*, we find that it is appearing 10 times more often. However one can suspect even this simple check is unbalanced. We have already noted that Eusebius quotes one of these passages containing the trope from Tertullian's *Apology* (#1 *above*). We have to suspect that Eusebius put it into Tertullian's *Apology* himself. This means, we really only find four uses in Tertullian. However, the uses in *Martyrs* (#2 above) and *Jews* (#3 above) are also quite suspect. *ET* comes at the very end of these very short works without dates, names or much style to identify their authors. There is no reason to believe that Eusebius only interpolated and forged works that he mentions in the *History*. One may suspect that Eusebius spent a few minutes adding his own new endings to these works by Tertullian. The remaining two (#'s 4 and 5 above) are borderline cases of *ET*. In *Spectacles*, Tertullian merely tells us that we may add the testimony of the present names of festivals to the old names. This is not meant to surprise us in the same way as Eusebius generally uses his trope. Likewise, in *Virgins*, Tertullian is not really surprising us but adding information about present conditions. The subtle difference is like the difference between saying "It snowed last Monday, and it is still snowing, today, Saturday," and "It snowed last Monday and it is snowing today, Saturday, again." The first emphasizes the extraordinary depth of the snowstorm, while the second simply indicates a coincidence of occurrences. In sum, while I would attribute the three uses in *Apology*, *Martyrs* and *Jews* to Eusebius, I would say that the uses in *Spectacles* and *Virgins* are just apparent but not actual example of *ET*. In sum, we cannot point to an authentic certain use of *ET* in all of Tertullian's work.

Even if we accept all five examples as legitimate, still one has to calculate the odds of Eusebius just picking one of the five to quote out of thousands of possible sentences in Tertullian's work. We also have to consider that the phrase "at the present time" is stylistic and irrelevant to the main contention in the sentence that most emperors did not support persecution of Christianity. Tertullian could easily have said something like "out of Rome's 22 emperors, only 2 have persecuted Christianity. The present one does not." In other words we need to consider not that we find the term in a text of Tertullian, but that Eusebius has picked out just this specific piece of text from Tertullian to quote. One may suppose Eusebius looked specifically for the phrase in Tertullian and other authors and then built his arguments around whatever ideas happened to be conjoined with it, but such a conjecture seems absurd. What if the passage with the phrase contained ideas that Eusebius disagreed with, would he suddenly change his position to agree with the ideas because the phrase "until the present time" was used.

For me, the next step forward is determining how much Eusebius has contributed to each work he mentions. For example, I believe, he has only interpolated the fifth paragraph into Tertullian's *Apology*, while I should be surprised to find out that he did not rewrite several paragraphs in both the *Apologies* of Justin Martyr[144]. Being precise in separating out Eusebius's changes to the works that came before him and assigning the texts he did write to him will help develop a Non-Eusebean view of History.

Did Eusebius Make Interpolations into Other People's Texts?

So far we have established a number of interpolations to documents mentioned within Eusebius's *History*. This has been relatively easy to do as Eusebius's methodology seems to have been for the most part rather ad hoc. He figures out a good rhetorical point and then changes or invents documents to support that point. There are also what appear to be Christian interpolations in important historical works outside Eusebius's *History*. It is difficult to establish that Eusebius is the man behind these textual manipulations. Still there is evidence supporting such a hypothesis.

Here we will try to establish that two early references to Christianity found in the historians Tacitus and Suetonius are likely from Eusebius. While the non-mention of both these references in his *History* would seem to indicate they could not have been done by Eusebius, we should keep in mind that Eusebius lived at least ten years after he finished his *History*. If anything, he would have had more access to these works during this part of his life. While it is fairly clear he would have included their mention in his *History* if he had done them prior to his *History*, we may suggest that he did them subsequent to his *History*.

The earliest reference to Christianity by a Roman historian comes from Cornelius Tacitus, writing circa 110-117. It is in his annals:

> But all human efforts, all the lavish gifts of the emperor, and the propitiations of the gods, did not banish the sinister belief that the conflagration was the result of an order. Consequently, to get rid of the report, Nero fastened the guilt and inflicted the most exquisite tortures on a class hated for their abominations, called Christians by the populace. Christus, from whom the name had its origin, suffered the extreme penalty during the reign of Tiberius at the hands of one of our procurators, Pontius Pilatus, and a most mischievous superstition, thus checked for the moment, again broke out not only in Judaea, the first source of the evil, but even in Rome, where all things hideous and shameful from every part of the world find their centre and become popular. Accordingly, an arrest was first made of all who pleaded guilty; then, upon their information, an immense multitude was convicted, not so much of the crime of firing the city, as of hatred against mankind. Mockery of every sort was added to their deaths. Covered with the skins of beasts, they were torn by dogs and perished, or were nailed to crosses, or were doomed to the flames and burnt, to serve as a nightly illumination, when daylight had expired[145].

THE EVOLUTION OF CHRISTS AND CHRISTIANIES

The next reference to Christianity appearing in a history book is in Gaius Suetonius's *Lives of the Twelve Caesars*, written circa 122-140 C.E.:

> He devised a new form for the buildings of the city and in front of the houses and apartments be erected porches, from the flat roofs of which fires could be fought [*This was undoubtedly after the great fire*]; and these he put up at his own cost. He had also planned to extend the walls as far as Ostia and to bring the sea from there to Rome by a canal. During his reign many abuses were severely punished and put down, and no fewer new laws were made: a limit was set to expenditures; the public banquets were confined to a distribution of food, the sale of any kind of cooked viands in the taverns was forbidden, with the exception of pulse and vegetables, whereas before every sort of dainty was exposed for sale. Punishment was inflicted on the Christians, a class of men given to a new and mischievous superstition. He put an end to the diversions of the chariot drivers, who from immunity of long standing claimed the right of ranging at large and amusing themselves by cheating and robbing the people. The pantomimic actors and their partisans were banished from the city [*Because of their disorderly conduct*][146].

What is most interesting is the context of these two passages. Neither Tacitus nor Suetonius refers to Christians before[147] or after this point in their works. If we allow that they are both working from a third source, we must allow that it is quite a fantastic coincidence that they both chose to include exactly the same incident and do not choose any other incidents involving Christians from any other sources. We also have to account for the fact that neither mentions this third source and nobody else mentions a third source regarding Nero and the fire. We may reject the third source hypothesis as unnecessary to explain the phenomena we are studying. Since Suetonius is writing after Tacitus, we may suppose that he found only this one reference to Christians in Tacitus and summarized that one incident. This argument is bolstered by the fact that they both use the same phrase "mischievous superstition" in reference to Christianity.

Actually there is an alternative to the hypothesis that the passage concerning Christianity was in Tacitus and Suetonius copied it. The alternative hypothesis is that someone interpolated the Christian reference into both works.

Now, Suetonius writing only a decade or so after Tacitus requires the reference in Tacitus to be authentic. Conversely, if the passage in Tacitus is fake, we may assume that the passage in Suetonius is as well. Anybody who knew the historian Tacitus, we may expect to also know the historian Suetonius. If we prove the Tacitus passage a forgery, we may assume that the same hand worked on both passages.

We will examine the passage in conjunction with Eusebius's Nero references in *Church History*. We will show how in these texts the relationship of Nero to the Christians was created and evolved. After demonstrating how the passage in Tacitus most likely came to be, we will show how the passage in Suetonius changed along with the Tacitus passage. Surprisingly, when properly understood, the Suetonius passage is not a witness to the existence of the Tacitus passage as we have received it, but a witness to the changes that the Tacitus text has undergone.

There are numerous reasons to suspect that the passage in Tacitus is a forgery. It goes unmentioned in antiquity until Sculpitius Severus[148] apparently quotes from it in his *Sacred History* circa 425 C.E. Both Tertullian and Eusebius talk about Nero but do not quote the text. It is a quite surprising that Tacitus refers incorrectly to Pontius Pilate by the title of procurator, instead of his correct title of prefect (*praefectus*), It is a bit like a historian of today confusing a general with a governor. It is also surprising that he gives us a title at this point at all. This indicates that he is mentioning him for the first time, by identifying him with his title—"in the hands of one of our procurators, Pontius Pilate." If Tacitus had already spoken about Pilate, we would already know that he was "one of our procurators" and there would be no need to repeat this information as if new.

One would have expected that he would have told us something about Pilate when discussing the reign of Tiberius. After all, Pilate ruled over the important Roman province of Judaea for at least ten years. Is it possible that nothing worthy of note happened in Judea during this time so that Tacitus would not even have recorded his name and title while writing about Tiberius in his Annals? Some of the most important Annals are missing, so we cannot be absolutely sure if Pilate was mentioned or not. Still it is odd that Tacitus mentions a personage like Pilate over twenty-five years after his rule and does not refer us back to any prior reference to him. Why mention his name now if he did nothing to merit mention before. If mentioned before why not refer us back to that mention with something like "Pilate whom I told you before served under Tiberius and was so cruel to the Jews."

While being suggestive and allowing us to be suspicious of the passage, none of these characteristics disqualify the reference from being authentic. Christians may have been hesitant to use a passage that referred negatively to Christianity. Eusebius may not have known Latin very well, and Tertullian may have been obliquely referring to it when he urged Romans to consult their records. Tacitus may have misheard and misunderstood a source about Pilate being a procurator. It is not necessary that Tacitus found anything interesting in Pilate during the time he lived to write about. Only in hindsight and because of his mention in the gospels does Pilate seem significant to us. Each of the objections to the passage has a plausible or at least possible counter.

Still, instead of creating plausible reasons/excuses for these oddities, we may try a different approach. Darrell Doughty has already done a deconstruction of the passage, taking out what he considers the interpolated material with the problems and restoring the original passage by Tacitus:

> "Therefore, to put an end to the rumor Nero created a diversion and subjected to the most extra-ordinary tortures those hated for their abominations by the common people. Nero had thrown open the gardens for the spectacle, and was exhibiting a show in the circus, while he mingled with the people in the dress of a charioteer or drove about in a chariot. Hence, even for criminals who deserved extreme and exemplary punishment there arose a feeling of compassion; for it was not, as it seemed, for the public good, but glut one man's cruelty, that they were being punished[149]."

This suggestion eliminates the numerous anomalies mentioned above. It explains all the anomalies. Nobody, including Eusebius and Tertullian, quotes the passage before 425 C.E. because there was originally no reference to Christians in it. Tacitus did not make the silly procurator-prefect mistake, and Tacitus did not refer to Pilate for the first time more than twenty-five years after he left office. We have to consider it a viable alternative hypothesis as it explains the anomalies as well as the plausible counter suggestions.

However, there are several problems with this reconstruction. Our current copy of the passage has this line: "a most mischievous superstition, thus checked for the moment, again broke out not only in Judaea, the first source of the evil, but even in Rome . . ." A Christian interpolator would not say that Christianity first broke out in Judaea, but would more likely claim Nazareth, Bethlehem or Galilee as the place where it started. This suggests that a Christian interpolator did not write this line but it was in the text prior to any interpolation. Secondly, the use of the term "procurator" was probably in the original as an interpolator would have checked Pontius Pilate's status first and would not have inserted it. The term makes perfect sense when referring to an appointment by Nero. It only does not make sense when referring to Tiberius. Thirdly, the term "extreme penalty" would not be a term a Christian would use for the crucifixion of Jesus. We may take it that this term too was part of the original text. Fourthly, and most importantly, we find that Tacitus (Histories, Book 5) later refers to Judaism repeatedly as a superstition: "King Antiochus strove to destroy the national superstition," "fostered the national superstition by appropriating the dignity of the priesthood as the support of their political power," "Prodigies had occurred, which this nation, prone to superstition . . ." We may conclude from this that reference in the original to a superstitious people from Judea was to Jews and not to Christians. We may reconstruct the original passage this way:

Reconstruction of Tacitus Christian Reference

> But all human efforts, all the lavish gifts of the emperor, and the propitiations of the gods, did not banish the sinister belief that the

conflagration was the result of an order. Consequently, to get rid of the report, Nero fastened the guilt and inflicted the most exquisite tortures on a class hated for their abominations, called Jews by the populace. Jews suffered extreme penalties[150] during the reign of Nero who sent the procurator Porcius Festus[151], and a most mischievous superstition, thus checked for the moment, again broke out not only in Judaea, the first source of the evil[152], but even in Rome, where all things hideous and shameful from every part of the world find their centre and become popular. Accordingly, an arrest was first made of all who pleaded guilty; then, upon their information, an immense multitude was convicted, not so much of the crime of firing the city, as of hatred against mankind. Mockery of every sort was added to their deaths. Covered with the skins of beasts, they were torn by dogs and perished, or were nailed to crosses, or were doomed to the flames and burnt, to serve as a nightly illumination, when daylight had expired.

As with Tacitus, Suetonius never mentions Christians, neither before nor after his one sentence, "Punishment was inflicted on the Christians, a class of men given to a new and mischievous superstition." He does mention Jews some four times before and four times after. As we noted before, if Tacitus is an interpolation than Suetonius must also be an interpolation. We may reconstruct the original sentence as "Punishment was inflicted on the Jews, a class of men given to an old and mischievous superstition."

Now, almost any Christian could have decided that these passages referring to Jews was probably a mistake and needed slight corrections. However not many Christians would have had the opportunity to make the corrections. Certainly, no one before the time of Eusebius would have had the necessary power and authority to do so. We may conclude from the fact that Eusebius did not quote the passages in his *History* that he had not done it before that point in time, but the way he handles the Nero material in his *History* may suggest that he did it afterwards.

There are two clues here that point towards Eusebius. First, while he does not quote Tacitus's fire report, he does suggest that "many have recorded his history" which seems to be a reference to Tacitus and Suetonius. Second, in the same passage, he paraphrases the passage in Tacitus that leads into the report on Nero and the fire. This makes it certain that Eusebius did know the Nero fire passage. Here is the passage in Tacitus's *Annals*, before the fire passage, and the relevant passage in Eusebius's *Church History*:

> For Nero's part, he wallowed in all sorts of defilements, natural and unnatural. He, in truth, had then left no kind of abomination untried, which could serve to finish his vileness, had he not, in a few days after, personated a woman, and been given in marriage, with all the forms and

solemnity of genuine nuptials, to one of this contaminated herd, a Pathic named Pythagoras: Over the Roman Emperor, as over a bride, was cast the sacred nuptial veil; the Augurs were seen in form solemnizing the espousals, the portion of the bride was openly paid, the bridal bed displayed, the nuptial torches kindled, and, in fine, to view was exposed whatever, even in natural commerce with women, is buried under the shades of night[153].

To describe the greatness of his depravity does not lie within the plan of the present work. As there are many indeed that have recorded his history in most accurate narratives, every one may at his pleasure learn from them the coarseness of the man's extraordinary madness, under the influence of which, after he had accomplished the destruction of so many myriads without any reason, he ran into such blood-guiltiness that he did not spare even his nearest relatives and dearest friends, but destroyed his mother and his brothers and his wife, with very many others of his own family as he would private and public enemies, with various kinds of deaths. But with all these things this particular in the catalogue of his crimes was still wanting, that he was the first of the emperors who showed himself an enemy of the divine religion[154].

For Tacitus, Nero had committed every kind of depravity, save one: his depravity was complete when he became a cross-gender homosexual and married a man. For Eusebius, Nero had only left one thing out of his "catalogue of crimes": his attack on the divine religion. Eusebius has copied the anti-Nero rhetoric of Tacitus, only changing the nature of the ultimate crime from becoming a wife to attacking Christians. This shows that Eusebius was familiar with the relevant section in Tacitus. We must conclude that he left out a direct reference to the following fire passage only because the passage in Tacitus did not contain a reference to Christians. While presenting a proof of Eusebius's involvement in the Tacitus/Suetonius interpolations lie outside the plan of the current work, we can at least put him down as a chief suspect in the case.

The Ending of Eusebean History:

We can debate how many changes to other historical texts both Christian and non-Christian Eusebius made. However, it is not debatable that much of the *History* that Eusebius did write is fiction to the point of being a religious fairy tale. For those not convinced that most of Eusebius's *History* is a fairy tale, we may simply reproduce his ending:

> Thus, suddenly, and sooner than can be told, those who yesterday and the day before breathed death and threatening were no more, and not

even their names were remembered, but their inscriptions and their honors suffered the merited disgrace. And the things which Licinius with his own eyes had seen come upon the former impious tyrants he himself likewise suffered, because he did not receive instruction nor learn wisdom from the chastisements of his neighbors, but followed the same path of impiety which they had trod, and was justly hurled over the same precipice. Thus he lay prostrate.

But Constantine, the mightiest victor, adorned with every virtue of piety, together with his son Crispus, a most God-beloved prince, and in all respects like his father, recovered the East which belonged to them; and they formed one united Roman empire as of old, bringing under their peaceful sway the whole world from the rising of the sun to the opposite quarter, both north and south, even to the extremities of the declining day.

All fear therefore of those who had formerly afflicted them was taken away from men, and they celebrated splendid and festive days. Everything was filled with light, and those who before were downcast beheld each other with smiling faces and beaming eyes. With dances and hymns, in city and country, they glorified first of all God the universal King, because they had been thus taught, and then the pious emperor with his God-beloved children.

There was oblivion of past evils and forgetfulness of every deed of impiety; there was enjoyment of present benefits and expectation of those yet to come. Edicts full of clemency and laws containing tokens of benevolence and true piety were issued in every place by the victorious emperor.

Thus after all tyranny had been purged away, the empire which belonged to them was preserved firm and without a rival for Constantine and his sons alone. And having obliterated the godlessness of their predecessors, recognizing the benefits conferred upon them by God, they exhibited their love of virtue and their love of God, and their piety and gratitude to the Deity, by the deeds which they performed in the sight of all men[155].

Like most fairy tales, Eusebius's *History* has a happy ending with good triumphant over evil.

The Evolution of Christianity

In Eusebius's fairy tale history, the church emerges pristine from the head of Christ. Its practices and ideology does not change. Instead it fights valiantly against the persecutions and tricks of the lying devil inspired Pagans, Jews, and Gnostics, and with the help of God and Constantine emerges triumphant.

In fact, Eusebius has just anachronized the practices and ideology of the fourth century Roman Church back in time. In actuality, churches evolved through trial and error of numerous and diverse ideologies and practices into the complex, modern ideological fighting machine that the Roman Catholic Church became in the Fourth Century.

The evolution of the ideologies and practices of the Early Church can be seen in a variety of adaptations to economic and social realities. One early, and perhaps for a while, dominant group of Christians were the Carpocratians. While their exact practices are hard to know, it was rumored that they engaged in incestuous orgies. They may have engaged in eating the babies or fetuses that resulted from these orgies in order to obtain eternal life, a literal rather than symbolic eating of the body and drinking the blood of Christ. For over 150 years Romans took Carpocratian Christianity very seriously. They defined Christianity by it and persecuted it. The Church Father Tertullian, at the beginning of the third century, still had to defend Christianity against such charges. We should not assume that the Romans were simply making up horrible tales to justify persecution. There seems to be no reason for the persecutions other than the belief in the practices. It is very possible that some forms of early Christianity did engage in these practices that so outraged Roman society. It is even possible that members of Carpocratian Christianity did for a short time abort the fetuses of the babies that resulted from their incestuous orgies and ritualistically feasted on them in order to gain eternal life. While an interesting scientific experiment, it did not work, and the Carpocratean Christians died out[156]. Ironically, stem cell research, a promising field for extending life today seems to be a more scientific version of this ancient notion of taking the life force of the newly born to extend an adult's life.

On the other hand, in opposition to the pro-sex Carpocrateans and other related Christian communities, certain Christian sects developed ideologies against sex, marriage and remarriage. It is counterintuitive to believe that such anti-sexual ideologies helped to spread Christianity rather than leading to its termination, but, in fact, it actually met certain social and personal needs of the populace during this time. First we should note that overpopulation was a problem in Rome where the means of food production barely ran ahead of the population and sometimes ran behind it leading to famines. With little real birth control, children were commonly exposed at birth, as poor parents realized they could not afford to feed them. The Christian policy of sexual abstinence was the only real form of birth control available. Giving birth was also a dangerous practice and commonly led to the death of the mother. The Christian churches that adopted a strict form of sexual control were more likely to have its members survive and continue. In churches and cults that did not control their members' sexuality, not only would the women die more frequently in childbirth, but even when the birth was successful, the women would use their money to raise their children rather than giving it to the Church. Thus both successful birth or unsuccessful birth (involving the death of the mother) could diminish Church resources. Thus the churches that adopted rebirth (usually through baptism) as an artificial substitute would be more successful. We also have to keep in mind the position of many women in Roman society at that time. Marriages were social contracts between families often arranged for the financial interests of the families. Women would marry around the age of thirteen to men often in their thirties or forties. The Husbands did not consider the women sex objects, they had concubines for that, but they did consider them baby producing machines. It was the duty of the wife to give birth to children and the marriage could be dissolved with negative consequences for the wife if she did not fulfill her duty. There were no "Joy of Sex" manuals for married couples. If men wanted pleasure from sex there were plenty of prostitutes for that. In fact, if a wife did enjoy sex, she would be under suspicion. If she enjoyed sex with her husband, might she not enjoy it with others? Sex was a duty for wives not a sport. For many women sexual encounters with their husbands would be nothing more than a series of quick brutal rapes. Undoubtedly, many wives learned to endure sex, but found it unpleasurable. The age difference in marriage, plus the short life expectancy in Roman society meant that large numbers of women became widows and inherited their husbands' wealthy estates, while in their twenties or thirties. Under Augustus's laws, women were penalized if they did not remarry within two years[157]. Christian groups opposed remarriage. Instead of remarriage, wealthy widows often decided to join their local Christian church. They would not have to lose control of their money to a new husband, and not have to endure loveless pro-creative sex with him. This was a positive and reasonable alternative for many women. When these widows died, and given the short life-expectancy, this would only be a matter of ten or twenty years, they would leave their inheritance to the Church. In addition to taking care of Widows, churches also welcomed orphans. The historian Robin Lane Fox notes this:

> Nor did the churches profit only from widows. They exalted virginity, and their young female membership actually practiced it, a point which greatly struck Galen in Rome. Again, these women grew up without any family, yet they were heiresses to parts of their fathers' and mothers' property. Bequests were antiquity's swiftest route to social advancement and the increase of personal capital. By idealizing virginity an frowning on second marriage, the Church was to become a force without equal in the race for inheritance[158].

Orphans, many wealthy, were encouraged not to marry in the first place, and thus they could donate all their time and money to the Church. When they too died, the Church was the only beneficiary. We might also look to the curious form of health care practiced by the Church called exorcism. This involved yelling, screaming at and torturing a sick person until the evil spirit causing the illness came out. One can imagine that this also caused the premature death of many Church members. This bad medical practice paradoxically also added to the church coffers. The Church also embraced slaves, not to free them, but to make them better slaves. Slaves were a way into the households of the wealthy and the elite of Roman society. The Church taught Christian slaves to obey and serve their masters with absolute obedience. This helped them win the trust of their masters and mistresses. The slaves with a well placed word here and there could lead their masters and mistresses into the magical secret world of Christianity. Slowly adapting to these economic realities and retrofitting their earlier texts to reflex these developments, certain Churches grew quite wealthy by helping the widow, orphans, slaves, and the sick. Charity never paid so well. Once wealthy, the churches gained rapid economic and social power.

Roman Christianity as it developed in the third century offered another advantage to the elite of Roman Society. Whereas it was expected that wealthy pagans would pay for the upkeep of the temples, statues, festivals and shrines of the Gods of the city, Christian had no such responsibilities for such civic duties. Pagans would often go bankrupt trying to fulfill their social obligations to their beloved cities. The Christians denied any social responsibility. They could be a nation onto themselves and thus destroy the fabric of Roman social society from within. As the elite of Roman society became Christianized, the Churches became more and more elite. This evolving form of ideological/economic social warfare on Roman Pagan Culture was not planned by Christians or their churches, but it did evolve over the centuries.

What it evolved from is the question we shall attempt to answer.

Sculpture. Jesus as Roman Emperor-God.

Sarcophagus of Junius Bassus, 359. Christ is beardless with short coiffed, curly hair. He stands on the head of the Roman God Jupiter.

Chapter 2

Non-Eusebean History

Over the last 200 years, Christian writers have tended to gain authority by secularizing their histories of Jesus and Christianity. They normally take the obviously mythological stuff about the God or Gods out, and present what is left over as history. It is like discounting all the Superman panels in the Superman Comic Books and proclaiming the Clark Kent panels to be an accurate history and biography.

What is left over is a mock naturalized Nicene Creed[159] that runs something like, "We believe that Jesus Christ was born to Mary in Nazareth at the beginning of the First Century, preached Christianity and was executed around the early 30's by Pontius Pilate." Only a few writers have challenged this by pointing out the lack of evidence for even this much history.

The official Eusebean-based history sees a "big bang" at the beginning of Christianity with the apostles including Paul preaching the words of Jesus Christ and spreading Christianity throughout the Roman Empire within a few decades. This alternative history sees a "Big Crunch" with many different Christianities falling together to produce the narratives in the New Testament. We can propose four distinct long stages to the evolution of Christianity:

Four Broad Stages of Early Christian History

1. First Century Jewish Christianities: Samaritan, Jewish and Galilean practices and stories are mixed together with Greek philosophical and theological ideas and mystery cult practices to form a number of local cults in the Roman Syria-Palestine region, spreading rapidly throughout the Roman empire.
2. Second Century Greek Christianities: After the Roman War (67-73) there is a split off of Christianity from Judaism. Jesus Cults spread throughout Asia Minor

and Greece and continue to diversify as they mix with more practices and theologies of Mystery Cults.
3. Third Century Roman Christianities: Christians grow to become a small but significant political force within the Roman Empire. There are still many diverse ideologies and practices which vary from city to city and region to region. Consolidation of power around the Church at Rome begins.
4. Fourth Century Imperial Roman Christianity: The Roman Catholic Church under the control of the Emperor Constantine becomes the most dominant political force in Roman History since Augustus Caesar. It centralizes all power and violently attempts to suppress all older Christianities as heterodox. It is at this time that the text based canon of the New Testament[160] and an official history are created.

The rest of this work will concentrate on the first two Christianities. It will develop alternative, Non-Eusebean based description of phenomena that hopefully makes more sense of the available data than the official version[161].

Not Starting with Paul

One might think to start our reconstruction with the letters of the Apostle Paul as they are commonly viewed as the oldest texts in the New Testament. However, there are good reasons why we should not. First, there is wide spread disagreement over the authenticity of the letters. Some consider all fourteen letters authentic, some thirteen, some seven letters, others consider no letters authentic. There are significant contradictions between letters, and within letters, which indicates heavy editing. The letters revolve around the central location of Ephesus in Asia Minor. They describe a fairly well developed system of established and interrelated churches. These things point to the second century, for the time of major editing, if not writing.

The first known publisher of many letters of Paul was Marcion and/or his Marcionite followers, around 175 C.E. Did he edit them? Did he write them? We rely on the African Roman-Christian writer Tertullian for our best information on Marcion and the Marcionites.

Tertullian the Master Rhetorician

Tertullian tells us, "it is evident that those men lived not so long ago,—in the reign of Antoninus for the most part,—and that they at first were believers in the doctrine of the Catholic Church, in the church of Rome under the episcopate of the blessed Eleutherus[162]." Eleutherus dates vary depending on the source, with 171-192 being the range. Antoninus ruled from 169 to 180. This suggests the 170's for the time Marcion came to Rome and published his letters of Paul. Since Tertullian gives us no date for a previous publication, we should probably assume the 170's as the first publication date of the letters of Paul. Tertullian claims Marcion edited an earlier publication, but gives no evidence. In fact, an examination of his treatment of the text reveals the rhetorical nature of his claim that Marcion edited a previous existing copy of the *Gospel of Luke*.

Tertullian tells us in that work Marcion "expressly and openly used the knife, not the pen, since he made such an excision of the Scriptures as suited his own subject-matter[163]." Tertullian also tells us, "Now, the garbled form in which we have found the heretic's Gospel will have already prepared us to expect to find the epistles also mutilated by him with like perverseness—and that even as respects their number[164]."

It is strange that he does not tell us what that number is. If he did we could tell if the early Roman Church included *Hebrews* or not. It is extremely bizarre that he tells us the number of letters were changed, but he does not mention the number of letters of Paul that was change, so that we do not know this fact for sure. Did Tertullian originally mention the number and was this number excised from the text because it did not match the fourteen letters of Paul that we now have in our New Testaments? This is most probable. We must assume that Catholic transmitters of the works of Tertullian have gone over most of his text and expunged embarrassing information like this.

Tertullian carefully goes over the Pauline letters of Marcion. At first we think he is going to point out the discrepancies between the authentic Church letters of Paul and the expunged letters of Marcion. In fact, he barely mentions the changes and instead spends most of the fifth book of his work against Marcion arguing the meaning of the text. It is worthwhile to take a moment to glance at the specific changes Tertullian finds between Marcion's version of Paul's letters and those allegedly accepted by his church.

1. In one sentence, he cut out the words "Though it be but a man's covenant, no man disannulleth, or addeth thereto[165]."
2. In another sentence Marcion changed "thy seed" to "his seeds[166]."
3. He expunged some part of Romans from 8.10-10.2[167]. Tertullian is vague here.
4. He changed title of an epistle from Ephesians to Laodicians[168].
5. He erased the prefix "in" from a word[169].
6. He left out the two epistles of Timothy and the Titus epistle[170].

The first five changes seem rather trivial and appear to hardly help promote Marcion's radically different Christian ideology. The sixth change, actually the most serious change, comes in the last paragraph of the work and offer no proof, but makes a joke out of it, "His aim, was, I suppose, to carry out his interpolating process even to the number of (St. Paul's) epistles." Again, the text makes the claim that the number of Paul's letters were changed, but does not tell us that extremely important number. We must assume that this last paragraph has again been toyed with. Since Tertullian only covers ten letters of Paul in Marcion's Gospel and says the two letters of Timothy and Titus were excluded, we should assume that the Letter to the Hebrews was not included in either Marcion or the Roman Church's official letters of Paul at this time.

We may go further and ask why Tertullian does not give us proof of his charges that Marcion made significant changes to the Letters of Paul for theological purposes. The key text to understand, perhaps, is this:

> But what serious gaps Marcion has made in this epistle especially, by withdrawing whole passages at his will, will be clear from the unmutilated text of our own copy. It is enough for my purpose to accept in evidence of its truth what he has seen fit to leave unerased, strange instances as they are also of his negligence and blindness[171].

Tertullian says he will show us the gaps by showing us his "unmutilated text of our own copy." However, in the next breathe so to speak, Tertullian says he will not show us the gaps, "it is enough for my purpose," to show "what he has seen fit to leave unerased." In other words, Tertullian says he will show the gaps in Marcion, and in the next sentence says he will not show the gaps in Marcion, but what Marcion has included. It is as if Tertullian is waving Marcion's book, and promises to show us evidence of Marcion's forgery by his own "unmutilated text." He reaches into his briefcase to pull out his book, suddenly stops and says, "No, it enough for my purpose just to read from Marcion's copy. The obvious conclusion one may draw from his halting action is that Marcion does not have a copy of Paul's unmutilated letters in his briefcase. There are no unmutilated letters because Tertullian and Roman Church have not made them up yet.

Thus we may suppose that our current versions of the Epistles of Paul have come by way of Marcion in the 170's. So too we must suggest comes our Gospel of Luke. The Gospel of Luke is addressed to someone named Theophilus. Eusebius, as I've mentioned named Theophilus as the earliest Bishop of Caesarea. However, he tells us nothing about this Theophilus beyond the name, suggesting that he is a fabrication. Eusebius does however tell us of a Bishop of Antioch named Theophilus, who lived around the 170's[172]. We may suppose that for a moment that Marcion addressed his original Lucan Gospel to this Theophilus (if he was a Bishop or not is another matter.) The current introduction makes the point that the narrative is being delivered "Even as they delivered them unto us, which from the beginning were eyewitnesses, and ministers of the word." This is the main ideological point of Tertullian's attack on Marcion. We may assume that Tertullian rewrote Marcion's Gospel, probably trying to show that Marcion's inscription to Theophilus was phony and an orthodox Churchman had written to Marcion years earlier. Tertullian intended Polycarp, the Bishop of Smyrna, to be the man delivering the Lucan Gospel to Theophilus. Tertullian writes this about Polycarp:

> But if there be any (heresies) which are bold enough to plant themselves in the midst of the apostolic age, that they may thereby seem to have been handed down by the apostles, because they existed in the time of the apostles, we can say: Let them produce the original records of their

churches; let them unfold the roll of their bishops, running down in due succession from the beginning in such a manner that [that first bishop of theirs bishop shall be able to show for his ordainer and predecessor some one of the apostles or of apostolic men,—a man, moreover, who continued steadfast with the apostles. For this is the manner in which the apostolic churches transmit their registers: as the church of Smyrna, which records that Polycarp was placed therein by John; as also the church of Rome, which makes Clement to have been ordained in like manner by Peter In exactly the same way the other churches likewise exhibit (their several worthies), whom, as having been appointed to their episcopal places by apostles, they regard as transmitters of the apostolic seed.

We should note that it appears that Marcion was also playing the authority game with his Gospel. Marcion placed it with the Epistles of Paul to suggest that his Gospel came directly from Paul. Tertullian came up with a perfect counter move by rewriting it as the Gospel of Luke. Tertullian explains what he's up to in book four of his work against Marcion:

That same authority of the apostolic churches will stand as witness also for the other gospels, which no less <than Luke's> we possess by their agency and according to their text—I mean John's and Matthew's, though that which Mark produced is stated to be Peter's, whose interpreter Mark was. Luke's narrative also they usually attribute to Paul[173].

Tertullian tells us that apostolic churches consider the gospel of Mark to be Peter's gospel and the gospel of Luke to be Paul's. Mark and Luke are merely scribal servants writing down the gospels of the original apostles.

In short, from among the apostles the faith is introduced to us by John and by Matthew, while from among apostolic men Luke and Mark give it renewal, ... For out of those authors whom we possess, Marcion is seen to have chosen. Luke as the one to mutilate. Now Luke was not an apostle but an apostolic man, not a master but a disciple, in any case less than his master, and assuredly even more of lesser account as being the follower of a later apostle, Paul, to be sure: so that even if Marcion had introduced his gospel under the name of Paul in person, that one single document would not be adequate for our faith, if destitute of the support of his predecessors. For we should demand the production of that gospel also which Paul found <in existence>, that to which he gave his assent, that with which shortly afterwards he was anxious that his own should

> agree: for his intention in going up to Jerusalem to know and to consult the apostles, was lest perchance he had run in vain.

Tertullian basically says that *Luke's Gospel* is inferior to the other gospels. This is a bizarre argument indeed, if Tertullian believed that *Luke's Gospel* was actually by Luke and not Marcion. Why argue that one gospel is inferior to another? Here's the reasoning— Tertullian tells us that his Church's four gospels are by two apostles and two apostlic men (assistant apostles). In this way, he orders their authority. He does this because he realizes there are major contradictions between them and he needs to explain this. For Tertullian, John is the most authoritative. It comes from a direct apostle (the beloved one) of Jesus. Next comes *Matthew's gospel*. Matthew gets only one brief mention in one gospel (Matthew 9.9), where a line has been inserted referring to him as a tax collector[174]. He gets mentioned in the apostle lists in *Matthew*, *Luke* and *Acts*[175]. He is certainly part of the outer circle of apostles, and has to be considered slightly inferior to John in authority. *The Gospel of Mark* is by Peter's assistant, Mark. He writes the story down for Peter, but he is certainly a less reliable writer than the genuine apostle John and the second string apostle Matthew. Finally we have *Luke's Gospel*. As Mark is inferior to Peter, Luke is inferior to Paul. Worse, Paul is not one of the twelve apostles, so Luke's text does not even have the backing of a genuine original apostle. It is the least reliable text. So, even if *Marcion's Gospel* is the real gospel produced by Luke, it is an inferior gospel.

It is a strange argument to make if he knew Marcion's *Gospel* was a fraud and his was the real thing. Tertullian is arguing that Marcion's *Gospel* is a fraud, but even if it is real, it is not as good as ours. This line of argument suggests that something else is going on. It appears to me to be this: Tertullian wants to convert the Marcionites by taking their main gospel and re-editing it, but he does not want his gospel recognized as equal to the others. So he attributes the source of Marcion's gospel to Luke, not an apostle, but an "apostolic man," i.e., servant, like Mark. This gospel gets its only authority from the born out of time, inferior apostle Paul. On this supposition, we may take the version of *Luke's Gospel* we now possess as Tertullian's rewrite of *Marcion's Gospel*.

What leads us to this idea among other things is that Tertullian's argument is too smooth. The names and authors of the gospels that Tertullian gives seems created specifically to be used against *Marcion's Gospel*. Tertullian tells us:

> Marcion, on the other hand, attaches to his gospel no author's name,[1]— as though he to whom it was no crime to overturn the whole body, might not assume permission to invent a title for it as well. At this point might have made a stand, arguing that no recognition is due to a work which cannot lift up its head, which makes no show of courage, which gives no promise of credibility by having a fully descriptive title and the requisite indication of the author's name. But I prefer to join issue on all points[176].

His claim of self-magnanimity aside, Eusebius tells us here that Marcion attached no name to his gospel. However, since he placed it with letters of Paul, it is apparent that he meant it to be taken as the Gospel of Paul. In effect Marcion has presented us with the Gospel of Paul. Tertullian claims he has made changes to his church's nearly identical gospel called the Gospel of Luke. Luke, Tertullian informs us was Paul's friend. It is quite evident that if his church had copied the work from Marcion it too would be claiming to hold Paul's Gospel and not a Gospel from the inferior helper of Paul, the "Apostolic Man" Luke. Therefore we can trust that Tertullian is telling the truth and Marcion has copied his gospel from the Gospel of Luke. This logic is quite reasonable. There is only one case where it would be wrong. It would be wrong in the case that Tertullian has invented the name of Luke for a revised copy of Marcion's Gospel and has given us the name of Luke specifically so he could make this argument—that nobody would claim a lesser authority for a copied gospel.

Tertullian does not want to make the claim that he, like Marcion, has the real *Gospel of Paul*. That would make him exactly equal to Marcion in his claim. Then, he can be accused of just copying Marcion. Tertullian is being extremely subtle in claiming that his gospel is by Luke, the companion of Paul, according to the epistles of Paul himself. In doing so, he knows that his audience will assume Marcion has copied from him. Like the master rhetoretician he is, he knows what his audience will believe.

It is most curious that outside of books four and five in *Against Marcion*, in over thirty preserved works, Tertullian never mentions the gospels of Mark or even John. He does make a single reference to the gospels of Matthew and Luke in *Against Praxeas*[177], and refers to Luke as the author of *Acts* in *On Fasting*[178]. He also makes a couple of references to Matthew in *On the Flesh of Christ*[179], another work aimed at Marcion. All of these works were written subsequent to *Against Marcion*. In the fifteen or so works written prior, Tertullian mentions the names of no gospels. Again, this suggests Tertullian is making up the names/authors of the gospels or at least attaching the name of Luke to the work that we refer to as the *Gospel of Luke* specifically to counter Marcion.

One could argue that Irenaeus talks about the gospels in his works before Tertullian. However, we must rely on Eusebius's word for the date of Irenaeus. As we have seen, his history is less than reliable. In fact, I hope to demonstrate in the future that the works Eusebius attributes to Irenaeus, were in fact composed by Tertullian, and Eusebius has simply added a bit of material to make it look like Irenaeus was the author. That requires a whole book to demonstrate, so I will leave it for the moment as a work for the future.

In any case, neither the *Gospel of Luke* nor *Epistles of Paul* are appropriate starting places to start our search for a Non-Eusebean alternative history of Christianity. Both are late rewrites of much different earlier material. The Marcion/Tertullian creation of the Gospel of Luke reflect their Roman mentalities and ideologies, far removed from the concerns of the three prior gospels. The *Epistles* make no direct quote of any of the gospels and possibly no references to a living man named Jesus[180]. The culture that produced the *Epistles* seems to be closely related to the culture that produced the letters of Ignatius, which are self proclaimed second century documents. The Epistles have little connection with the Jerusalem Syrian-Palestinian based culture that produced the *Gospels of John, Matthew* and *Mark*. It is true that the author of the *Gospel of Luke* in the *Acts of the Apostles* does attempt to bring the Jerusalem culture of Peter together with the Eastern Mediterranean Culture of Paul, but one can easily see how the author has woven two quite separate texts together. *Acts* can also be seen as a rather late, second century/early third century solution to bringing together two separate Christianities (Pauline and Petrine). Since, there is such evidence that the *Epistles of Paul* and the *Gospel of Luke* represents a later, at least second century Greco-Roman tradition, our reconstruction must start from the real center of the New Testament, the *Gospels of Mark, Matthew and John*.

Fresco. Christ and Woman at Well.

Wall Painting in Catacomb on the Via Latina, circa 350. Christ is beardless with short coiffed hair. Woman is well dressed and pretty.

Chapter 3

Mary, the Author of the Word Become Flesh

What are the Gospels?

Philosophers ask elementary questions, but not naively or rhetorically. They do it to encourage major shifts in common perspectives on subjects. It is in this spirit that I ask this question: "What are Gospels?"

Around 250 C.E. the Alexandrian Christian writer Origen tackled the same question:

> Now the Gospel is a discourse containing a promise of things which naturally, and on account of the benefits they bring, rejoice the hearer as soon as the promise is heard and believed. Nor is such a discourse any the less a Gospel that we define it with reference to the position of the hearer. A Gospel is either a word which implies the actual presence to the believer of something that is good, or a word promising the arrival of a good which is expected. Now all these definitions apply to those books which are named Gospels[181].

Origen may be right with this general definition of a gospel as any report of something good happening now or in the future to the listener or reader. However, his definition may be overly broad for our purposes. For example, it makes any report of stocks going up for an investor a gospel. I would try to narrow our understanding to the specifically materialistic understanding of Christian gospels of the first centuries.

THE EVOLUTION OF CHRISTS AND CHRISTIANIES

Perhaps we may begin by trying a *via negativa*, telling what the gospels are not. Gospels are not movies. Movies were invented in 1889. Gospels came before them. They are not television shows, videotapes or DVD's, these were invented in the second half of the twentieth century. They are not journalists' reports for newspapers of contemporary events. Newspapers are an eighteenth century invention, made possible only by the fifteenth century invention of the printing press.

This is a way of saying that the ability of a culture to record, preserve and distribute narratives of events is directly dependent on the technology of a culture. We commit an anachronistic error when we assume that this ability is innate or has remained fixed through history. In dealing with events occurring within the Roman empire some 2,000 years ago, we have to understand and remember the technology available and its function. Most events were communicated by individuals through speech, either to individuals or groups, some in letters, some in decrees, some in scrolls, and some in books. Most events became "mythologized" or filled with supernatural, dreamlike peoples and fantasies as they were transmitted throughout the empire.

The gospels were written texts. They played a social function of transmitting a series of stories between people. These narratives or tales seem to mainly involve one central character, as Plato's dialogues center around the character of Socrates, and like Plato's *Dialogues*, they give lots of information about the people who constructed and transmitted them.

Unlike Plato's *Dialogues* in which we seem to have one easily identifiable author and rarely more than one version of events and sayings, the gospels were written by a number of writers and contain multiple versions of events and sayings. The canonical gospels had at least four writers and many other gospels and Christ centered texts had numerous other authors.

Within each gospel we are dealing with a number of different narratives, some quite short, a single sentence and others a hundred sentences long. Some follow in a strict chronological order, many seem pasted together in no particular order. Some narratives are repeated in each of the canonical gospels and other gospels, while some narratives appear in only one gospel, either canonical or not.

The personalities and desires of the authors appear now and again either openly or through their style. Luke seems to see himself as a junior Josephus, a serious historian who has investigated the old stories of Jesus and has put together a true version. Matthew, seemingly a wealthy landowner, castigates the Jews for their rebellion against the Romans, making Jesus into a moralistic stoic prophet-politician who foresaw the disaster of the Jewish rebellions of the first and second centuries and forewarned the wayward Jews. He has Jesus giving long speeches to the masses on morality. Mark, seemingly a scribe, gives a bare bones, no frills narrative, just the facts, but not the well known stuff, only the juicy private stuff that the top echelon of Jesus' followers were privy to see and hear. John is seemingly the revolutionary in the bunch. His Jesus is the totally alienated outsider, a man from outer space/heaven that nobody understands at all.[182].

As literature, the Christian Gospels are *sui generis*. They seem to lie between the biographical holy-man narrative, like Philostratus's *Apollonius of Tyana* written around 200 C.E.(but based on the memoirs of the disciple Damis of Nineveh, written around 100 C.E.), and the more single narrative driven Roman novel of the period, like Apuleius *Metamorphoses* (AKA *The Golden Ass*). These works are helpful in understanding the popularity of the gospels, but neither of them attracted the attention of so many writers and their narratives were not changed multiple times, in multiple ways. This feature of narratives being rewritten and changed is perhaps the most significant feature of the Gospels. It indicates both the desire to preserve significant events in a stable way and the technical inability to do so. The need or desire to answer new questions involving the characters within the story caused repeated revisions. These constant updates and revisions show that the gospels belong to a significantly different genre then either the biography of Apollonius or the novel of Apuleius. It is impossible to understand the gospels without understanding the unusual nature of the rewrites of these narrative tales.

New Paradigms: Beginning Deconstruction

Throwing out Eusebean History, we are forced to begin reconstructing early Christian History from the gospel texts and other texts of the period. This actually works to our benefit in that we may apply a wealth of literary theory that has come forward only in the past several decades.

The most striking thing we notice about the canonical Gospel is the plethora of endings. We get a number of stopping points towards the end of all the Gospels which were obviously meant to be the ending and then we get revisions and additions to these endings. The two earliest endings are most probably found in Mark and John. These endings are simple, definite and clear. We should carefully notice who is at the center of action in these texts. Here is John followed by Mark

> 20.10. Then the disciples went back to their homes,
> 11. but Mary stood outside the tomb crying. As she wept, she bent over to look into the tomb
> 12. and saw two angels in white, seated where Jesus' body had been, one at the head and the other at the foot.
> 13. They asked her, Woman, why are you crying? They have taken my Lord away, she said, and I don't know where they have put him.
> 14. At this, she turned round and saw Jesus standing there, but she did not realise that it was Jesus.
> 15. Woman, he said, why are you crying? Who is it you are looking for? Thinking he was the gardener, she said, Sir, if you have carried him away, tell me where you have put him, and I will get him.

THE EVOLUTION OF CHRISTS AND CHRISTIANIES

16. Jesus said to her, Mary. She turned towards him and cried out in Aramaic, Rabboni! (which means Teacher).
17. Jesus said, Do not hold on to me, for I have not yet returned to the Father. Go instead to my brothers and tell them, 'I am returning to my Father and your Father, to my God and your God.'
18. Mary Magdalene went to the disciples with the news: I have seen the Lord! And she told them that he had said these things to her.

16.1 When the Sabbath was over, Mary Magdalene, Mary the mother of James, and Salome bought spices so that they might go to anoint Jesus' body.
2. Very early on the first day of the week, just after sunrise, they were on their way to the tomb
3. and they asked each other, Who will roll the stone away from the entrance of the tomb?
4. But when they looked up, they saw that the stone, which was very large, had been rolled away.
5. As they entered the tomb, they saw a young man dressed in a white robe sitting on the right side, and they were alarmed.
6. Don't be alarmed, he said. You are looking for Jesus the Nazarene, who was crucified. He has risen! He is not here. See the place where they laid him.
7. But go, tell his disciples and Peter, 'He is going ahead of you into Galilee. There you will see him, just as he told you.'
8. Trembling and bewildered, the women went out and fled from the tomb. They said nothing to anyone, because they were afraid.

The very next line in the Gospel of Mark is "When Jesus rose early on the first day of the week, he appeared first to Mary Magdalene, out of whom he had driven seven demons." If we take both John and Mark to be revisions of the original ending, it is apparent that we have an ending which focuses in on Mary Magdalene. We may say that the original ending was "Mary-centric". This Mary-centricity can also be found in the ending of the non-canonical Gospel of Mary:

1. When Mary had said this, she fell silent, since it was to this point that the Savior had spoken with her.
2. But Andrew answered and said to the brethren, Say what you wish to say about what she has said. I at least do not believe that the Savior said this. For certainly these teachings are strange ideas.
3. Peter answered and spoke concerning these same things.
4. He questioned them about the Savior: Did He really speak privately

with a woman and not openly to us? Are we to turn about and all listen to her? Did He prefer her to us?
5. Then Mary wept and said to Peter, My brother Peter, what do you think? Do you think that I have thought this up myself in my heart, or that I am lying about the Savior?
6. Levi answered and said to Peter, Peter you have always been hot tempered.
7. Now I see you contending against the woman like the adversaries.
8. But if the Savior made her worthy, who are you indeed to reject her? Surely the Savior knows her very well.
9. That is why He loved her more than us. Rather let us be ashamed and put on the perfect Man, and separate as He commanded us and preach the gospel, not laying down any other rule or other law beyond what the Savior said.
10. And when they heard this they began to go forth to proclaim and to preach.

The *Gospel of Luke* agrees with *Mark* in that Mary Magadalene and other women heard about Jesus. But it agrees with the *Gospel of Mary* in telling us that the disciples were skeptical of post-death communications by Jesus.

23.10. It was Mary Magdalene, Joanna, Mary the mother of James, and the others with them who told this to the apostles.
11. But they did not believe the women, because their words seemed to them like nonsense.

In looking at these endings, what is surprising is not the idea of Jesus being in some sense resurrected or communicating from beyond the grave to his disciples through Mary. This is a quite ordinary event for the time. At that time, it was the norm for relatives of the recently deceased to have dream visits from the departed as well as dream visits from Gods telling them what to do in life. This event, the dream visit of Jesus to Mary, may be seen as a necessary stage to the later, more bizarre idea that Jesus returned from the dead. Mary seeing Jesus after his death in a dream or vision involves no leap of credulity from the ordinary experiences and beliefs of that time. The idea of Jesus returning from the dead and acting like a living person with a material body, such as presented in *Acts of the Apostles* did involve a disbelief in ordinary experience of the time. This concept of Jesus returning from the dead is a later concept that develops out of Mary's encounter with Jesus.

What is extraordinary is that all these first gospel endings are Mary-centric, more about Mary than Jesus, and more about whether the disciples believe her or not than about anything Jesus does or says. Mary is an extremely minor character in the canonical gospels till this point, with the Gospels telling us virtually nothing about her. Why should the gospels suddenly switch to her as the main character at this point?

In another ending from the Gospel of John we are told this about the beloved disciple in the narrative:

> 21.20. Peter turned and saw that the disciple whom Jesus loved was following them ...
>
> 21.24. This is the disciple who testifies to these things and who wrote them down. We know that his testimony is true.

This passage tells us that the writer of the so-called *Gospel of John* was originally *The Beloved Disciple.* This passage suggests that there is debate over whether the things the writer or narrator of the story, the disciple whom Jesus loved, is telling the truth in her narration. We have to match this pronouncement about the beloved disciple with information from the *Gospel of Mary* which tells us decisively that Mary is the disciple whom Jesus loved. All of this suggests that the original debate after the death of Jesus was over a communication that Mary allegedly had from Jesus.

These early Mary-centric endings are also extraordinarily striking because the rest of the gospels are so extraordinarily Jesus-centric, where Jesus is at the center of virtually every scene, with a few important, but minor exceptions[183]. It is to me impossible to understand why this would be the ending point of the narrative of Jesus's life (or at least the events towards the end of his life) unless Mary was the narrator of the entire original gospel. Only then would it make sense to debate the truth or falsehood of Mary's extraordinary claim. If this was not the case, the claim that the female lover of Jesus heard from him or an angel after his death would not even be worth reporting, let alone debating. No one at this point in history would care that a woman reported an after death communication with her lover who suddenly died two days previously. It would be put down to normal female hysteria. It would never be included as the ending of narrative by a male writer. Only if she was the narrator/author of the entire narrative (as the *Gospel of Mary* portrays her to be and the *Gospel of John* suggests with a wink for the insiders) would the report become an issue. In this case, her ending would throw suspicion on the entire narrative and the community would have to debate it in order to maintain the truth or reality of the entire narrative.

An Example of the Erasing of Mary from the Narrative

> *Damnatio memoriae* (Latin for "damnation of memory", in the sense of *removed from the remembrance*) was a form of dishonor which could be passed by the Roman Senate upon traitors or others who brought discredit to the Roman Empire. The sense of the expression and of the sanction is to cancel every trace of the person from the life of Rome, as

if he had never existed, in order to preserve the honour of the *Urbs*; in a town that stressed the social appearance and respectability (and the pride of being a *civis romanus*) as a fundamental requirement of the citizen, it was perhaps the severest punishment[184].

After her death, many of her monuments were defaced or destroyed. Replacing the names on older monuments with one's own was a common practice of Egyptian Pharaohs, but in some cases it was an act of damnatio memoriae—condemning a person by erasing him or her from recorded existence. The traditional belief among historians is that Thutmose III was responsible; however, researchers such as Charles Nims and Peter Dorman have examined these erasures and found that those which can be dated were done after year 42 of Thutmose's reign. As with many details about Hatshepsut, historians have opposing views on who defaced her monuments. There is also much debate about Thutmose's motivation for removing her name from her the monuments: reasons include resentment for being denied the throne for so long, and/or the belief that a female Pharaoh was against Maat. Egyptologist Donald B. Redford suggests a more sympathetic—and complex—motivation, Thutmose's own need to demonstrate his legitimacy; Redford notes that "here and there, in the dark recesses of a shrine or tomb where no plebeian eye could see, the queen's cartouche and figure were left intact[185].

Was Mary Magdalene a *damnatio memoriae* for later Christian groups? Like Queen Hatshepsut was her name defaced and erased from her works? The works found at Nag Hammadi suggest great conflict and tension between her and the other disciples. Examining the gospels closely gives more evidence that this was/is the case.

Another scene gives an excellent example or proof of this fact. The scene where Jesus gets anointed with oil by a woman may be found in all four canonical gospels. In the Synoptic Gospels the woman is unnamed. Only in the Gospel of John do we find out that the woman was actually Mary Magdalene.

> Mk. 14.3 And while he was at Bethany in the house of Simon the leper, as he sat at table, a woman came with an alabaster flask of ointment of pure nard, very costly, and she broke the flask and poured it over his head. 4. But there were some who said to themselves indignantly, "Why was the ointment thus wasted?

> Mt. 26.7 a woman came up to him with an alabaster flask of very expensive ointment, and she poured it on his head, as he sat at table.

Lk. 7.26 And behold, a woman of the city, who was a sinner, when she learned that he was at table in the Pharisee's house, brought an alabaster flask of ointment

Jn. 12.1 Six days before the Passover, Jesus came to Bethany, where Laz'arus was, whom Jesus had raised from the dead.

2: There they made him a supper; Martha served, and Laz'arus was one of those at table with him.
3: Mary took a pound of costly ointment of pure nard and anointed the feet of Jesus and wiped his feet with her hair; and the house was filled with the fragrance of the ointment.

Mark and Matthew hide the identity of the woman by just associating her with an alabaster flask. Luke just calls her "a woman of the city, who was a sinner." Only John straight forwardly tells us that it was Mary of Bethany.

We may somehow imagine that John has mistakenly identified the nameless woman with Mary Magdalene based on Mark's identification of the woman as coming from Bethany. The ensuing argument recorded in all four gospels over the cost of the oil becomes absurd if we conclude that the woman was unknown and not Mary. If a strange woman has given some of her oil to Jesus, the disciples could not complain that the money should have gone to the poor. Only if the woman was a member of the group could they expect to control her purchases of expensive items. It is most probable that the *Gospel of John* is reporting the identity of the woman in the story honestly, while the synoptic authors are attempting to erase Mary from the original scene.

One might argue that the synoptic writers did not know the identity of the woman, but the importance of the action in the scene, the anointing of Jesus (remember "Christ" means "anointed one") belies that notion. At the end of the scene Mark writes,

6. But Jesus said, "Let her alone; why do you trouble her? She has done a beautiful thing to me.
7. For you always have the poor with you, and whenever you will, you can do good to them; but you will not always have me.
8. She has done what she could; she has anointed my body beforehand for burying.
9. And truly, I say to you, wherever the gospel is preached in the whole world, what she has done will be told in memory of her."

It is extremely ironic that Jesus predicts that the actions of the woman will be told "in the whole world," and that it "will be told in memory of her," and yet the synoptic gospels do not even name her. When we tell a tale in memory of someone, we always tell the person's name. Otherwise, the memory of the person is lost. There is no chance that the gospel writers did not know that it was Mary who anointed Jesus. The name of the person who anointed Jesus would be of inestimable importance and repeated with every telling of the incident. It is difficult to see any other explanation for its exclusion except that the synoptic writers did not want to give Mary the honor of being the person to anoint Jesus. These writers or their predecessors deliberately erased her name from this scene.

We should also note the action in the scene of pouring expensive oil on a person's feet and wiping the feet with hair until the whole room smells fragrant. Mary clearly did not intend for her action to be a ritual anointing of a dead body. She had no way of knowing that Jesus was going to die. Mary's intention was not to anoint a dead body, it was to pleasure a live one. Importantly, we learn three things about Mary from the scene; 1) she was wealthy, 2) she had erotic physical contact with Jesus in public, and 3) she had long hair.

One should also take note of the Jesus' expression, "She has done what she could. She has anointed my body beforehand for burial." This suggests that she could not anoint his body after his death, but only before death. This only makes sense if she was expected to anoint his body after death and could not for some reason do it after his death. Mark, through Jesus, is excusing Mary for not anointing Jesus' body after death. Why would Mary be expected to anoint Jesus' body after his death? Since she was not his sister or mother, one would not expect her to perform ritual anointing after his death, unless she was his wife or lover.

Finally and most importantly, notice that the scene is not Jesus-centric, but Mary—centric. The main actions are performed by Mary. The debate is over Mary and her actions in opposition to the disciples. Jesus honors Mary by saying that she will always be remembered wherever his own Gospel gets told. Metaphorically speaking, in this scene, it is Jesus who is carving Mary Magdalene's initials together with his own inside a heart.

This interpretation of the scene matches well the information about the relationship of Jesus, Mary and the disciples found in the Nag Hammadi texts; especially the *Gospels of Mary* and *Thomas*. The cutting out of Mary from this extremely important scene by the synoptic writers supports the idea that not just the ending, but a whole layer of early gospel material was Mary-centric. If the Mary-centric ending was part of an original Mary-centric gospel or at least a Mary/Jesus-centric gospel, we need to look for more clues. I will start looking for these clues in the *Gospel of Mark* because his gospel has been considered the earliest canonical gospel by most people for the last century. If we can identify motifs in Mark that are not in the other gospels, we can see what Mark added to his gospel. After this, we may subtract these motifs to get an idea of what the gospels about Jesus must have looked like before Mark.

Two Motifs of Mark that May Reflect the Life of Mark

There are two motifs in Mark that are almost obsessively repeated. Two themes are touched upon after every miracle 1) fear and 2) secrecy. While one gets touches of these in the other Gospels, they are so concentrated in Mark that we have to attribute them to his unique contributions to the story.

1. The Fear Factor in Mark

These are the fifteen passages in mark that reflect fear:

- 4.40. He said to his disciples, Why are you so afraid? Do you still have no faith?
- 41. They were terrified and asked each other, Who is this? Even the wind and the waves obey him!

- 5.15. When they came to Jesus, they saw the man who had been possessed by the legion of demons, sitting there, dressed and in his right mind; and they were afraid.
- 16. Those who had seen it told the people what had happened to the demon-possessed man—and told about the pigs as well.
- 17. Then the people began to plead with Jesus to leave their region.

- 5.30. At once Jesus realised that power had gone out from him. He turned around in the crowd and asked, Who touched my clothes?
- 31. You see the people crowding against you, his disciples answered, and yet you can ask, 'Who touched me?'
- 32. But Jesus kept looking around to see who had done it.
- 33. Then the woman, knowing what had happened to her, came and fell at his feet and, trembling with fear, told him the whole truth.
- 34. He said to her, Daughter, your faith has healed you. Go in peace and be freed from your suffering.
- 35. While Jesus was still speaking, some men came from the house of Jairus, the synagogue ruler. Your daughter is dead, they said. Why bother the teacher any more?
- 36. Ignoring what they said, Jesus told the synagogue ruler, Don't be afraid; just believe.

- 6.19. So Herodias nursed a grudge against John and wanted to kill him. But she was not able to,

20. because Herod feared John and protected him, knowing him to be a righteous and holy man.

6.48. He saw the disciples straining at the oars, because the wind was against them. About the fourth watch of the night he went out to them, walking on the lake. He was about to pass by them,
49. but when they saw him walking on the lake, they thought he was a ghost. They cried out,
50. because they all saw him and were terrified. Immediately he spoke to them and said, Take courage! It is I. Don't be afraid.
51. Then he climbed into the boat with them, and the wind died down. They were completely amazed,

9.5. Peter said to Jesus, Rabbi, it is good for us to be here. Let us put up three shelters—one for you, one for Moses and one for Elijah.
6. He did not know what to say, they were so frightened.

9.30. They left that place and passed through Galilee. Jesus did not want anyone to know where they were,
31. because he was teaching his disciples. He said to them, The Son of Man is going to be betrayed into the hands of men. They will kill him, and after three days he will rise.
32. But they did not understand what he meant and were afraid to ask him about it.

10.32. They were on their way up to Jerusalem, with Jesus leading the way, and the disciples were astonished, while those who followed were afraid. Again he took the Twelve aside and told them what was going to happen to him.
33. We are going up to Jerusalem, he said, and the Son of Man will be betrayed to the chief priests and teachers of the law. They will condemn him to death and will hand him over to the Gentiles,
34. who will mock him and spit on him, flog him and kill him. Three days later he will rise.

11.17 And as he taught them, he said, Is it not written:
'My house will be called a house of prayer for all nations'?
But you have made it 'a den of robbers'.
18. The chief priests and the teachers of the law heard this and

19. When evening came, they went out of the city.

11.29. Jesus replied, I will ask you one question. Answer me, and I will tell you by what authority I am doing these things.
30. John's baptism—was it from heaven, or from men? Tell me!
31. They discussed it among themselves and said, If we say, 'From heaven', he will ask, 'Then why didn't you believe him?'
32. But if we say, 'From men' (They feared the people, for everyone held that John really was a prophet.)
33. So they answered Jesus, We don't know. Jesus said, neither will I tell you by what authority I am doing these things.

12.9. What then will the owner of the vineyard do? He will come and kill those tenants and give the vineyard to others.
10. Haven't you read this scripture:
 'The stone the builders rejected has become the capstone;
11. the Lord has done this, and it is marvellous in our eyes'?
12. Then they looked for a way to arrest him because they knew he had spoken the parable against them. But they were afraid of the crowd; so they left him and went away.

12.33. To love him with all your heart, with all your understanding and with all your strength, and to love your neighbor as yourself is more important than all burnt offerings and sacrifices.
34. When Jesus saw that he had answered wisely, he said to him, You are not far from the kingdom of God. And from then on no-one dared ask him any more questions.

14.32. They went to a place called Gethsemane, and Jesus said to his disciples, Sit here while I pray.
33. He took Peter, James and John along with him, and he began to be deeply distressed and troubled.
34. My soul is overwhelmed with sorrow to the point of death, he said to them. Stay here and keep watch.
35. Going a little farther, he fell to the ground and prayed that if possible the hour might pass from him.
36. Abba, Father, he said, everything is possible for you. Take this cup from me. Yet not what I will, but what you will.

Note: The first line "began looking for a way to kill him, for they feared him, because the whole crowd was amazed at his teaching." precedes verse 19.

14.70. Again he denied it. After a little while, those standing near said to Peter, Surely you are one of them, for you are a Galilean.
71. He began to call down curses on himself, and he swore to them, I don't know this man you're talking about.
72. Immediately the cock crowed the second time. Then Peter remembered the word Jesus had spoken to him: Before the cock crows twice you will disown me three times. And he broke down and wept[186].

16.8. Trembling and bewildered, the women went out and fled from the tomb. They said nothing to anyone, because they were afraid.

The dominant ideology here is that God and his holy men cause fear. The antidote for this fear is belief. As Jesus tells Jairus, the head of the Synagogue, "Don't be afraid; just believe." As he tells the disciples, "Why are you so afraid? Do you still have no faith?" One may suggest that this motif reflects Mark's own transition from fear of Jesus to faith/belief.

One might also note that the fear is generally caused by Jesus and his miracles and not by the Jewish authorities. Mark (in the character of Jesus) seems only to fear that they will accuse him of not having authority. On the other hand, the Jewish people and the Jewish authorities are afraid of Jesus' magic. The Christians apparently claimed great magical powers. All peoples of this time being superstitious and believing in magic would naturally fear them. This fear by the Jewish masses of the Christians and their magical powers seems to be a motif added by Mark and reflecting the world he lives in.

The fear of the many characters in the Gospel can be seen as reflecting Mark's own fear. He was attacking the Jewish establishment. One may presume that he anticipated a counter-attack for his actions. He transfers to his Jesus character his own expectation that someone will ask him by what authority he does these things. Mark's short sentences and choppy narrative style suggests a copier of official documents rather than a professional story-teller. Tradition portrays Mark as a scribe. It is possible that those who started this tradition did not know the writer, but assumed he was a scribe based on his writing style. Assuming he was a scribe and not a priest, we may imagine that he did not have any authority to do midrash. After all, the scribe's job is to copy and preserve, not to teach and explain. He may have been afraid of being caught doing something illegal by writing this text. Perhaps, he put his own fear into the text.

Besides fear, there is also the need for secrecy, another motif that Mark probably brings to the story.

2. Secrecy in Mark: Spread the Word, But Don't Tell Anyone About Me!

Here are the seventeen passages that show Mark's evident desire/obsession for secrecy.

1.25. Be quiet! said Jesus sternly. Come out of him!
26. The evil spirit shook the man violently and came out of him with a shriek.
27. The people were all so amazed that they asked each other, What is this? A new teaching—and with authority! He even gives orders to evil spirits and they obey him.
28. News about him spread quickly over the whole region of Galilee.

1.34. and Jesus healed many who had various diseases. He also drove out many demons, but he would not let the demons speak because they knew who he was.

1.42. Immediately the leprosy left him and he was cured.
43. Jesus sent him away at once with a strong warning:
44. See that you don't tell this to anyone. But go, show yourself to the priest and offer the sacrifices that Moses commanded for your cleansing, as a testimony to them.
45. Instead he went out and began to talk freely, spreading the news. As a result, Jesus could no longer enter a town openly but stayed outside in lonely places. Yet the people still came to him from everywhere.

3.11. Whenever the evil spirits saw him, they fell down before him and cried out, You are the Son of God.
12. But he gave them strict orders not to tell who he was.

4.34. He did not say anything to them without using a parable. But when he was alone with his own disciples, he explained everything.

5.18. As Jesus was getting into the boat, the man who had been demon-possessed begged to go with him.
19. Jesus did not let him, but said, Go home to your family and tell them how much the Lord has done for you, and how he has had mercy on you.
20. So the man went away and began to tell in the Decapolis how much Jesus had done for him. And all the people were amazed[187].

5.37. He did not let anyone follow him except Peter, James and John the brother of James.
38. When they came to the home of the synagogue ruler, Jesus saw a commotion, with people crying and wailing loudly.

39. He went in and said to them, Why all this commotion and wailing? The child is not dead but asleep.
40. But they laughed at him. After he put them all out, he took the child's father and mother and the disciples who were with him, and went in where the child was.
41. He took her by the hand and said to her, Talitha koum! (which means, Little girl, I say to you, get up!).
42. Immediately the girl stood up and walked around (she was twelve years old). At this they were completely astonished.
43. He gave strict orders not to let anyone know about this, and told them to give her something to eat[188].

7.35 At this, the man's ears were opened, his tongue was loosened and he began to speak plainly.
36. Jesus commanded them not to tell anyone. But the more he did so, the more they kept talking about it.

8.11. The Pharisees came and began to question Jesus. To test him, they asked him for a sign from heaven.
12. He sighed deeply and said, Why does this generation ask for a miraculous sign? I tell you the truth, no sign will be given to it.
13. Then he left them, got back into the boat and crossed to the other side.

8.25. Once more Jesus put his hands on the man's eyes. Then his eyes were opened, his sight was restored, and he saw everything clearly.
26. Jesus sent him home, saying, "Don't go into the village."

8.29. But what about you? he asked. Who do you say I am? Peter answered, You are the Christ.
30. Jesus warned them not to tell anyone about him.

9.7. Then a cloud appeared and enveloped them, and a voice came from the cloud: This is my Son, whom I love. Listen to him!
8. Suddenly, when they looked round, they no longer saw anyone with them except Jesus.
9. As they were coming down the mountain, Jesus gave them orders not to tell anyone what they had seen until the Son of Man had risen from the dead.

14.67. When she saw Peter warming himself, she looked closely at him. You also were with that Nazarene, Jesus, she said.

68. But he denied it. I don't know or understand what you're talking about, he said, and went out into the entrance.

15.43. Joseph of Arimathea, a prominent member of the Council, who was himself waiting for the kingdom of God, went boldly to Pilate and asked for Jesus' body.
44. Pilate was surprised to hear that he was already dead. Summoning the centurion, he asked him if Jesus had already died[189].

15.36. One man ran, filled a sponge with wine vinegar, put it on a stick, and offered it to Jesus to drink. Now leave him alone. Let's see if Elijah comes to take him down, he said.
37. With a loud cry, Jesus breathed his last.
38. The curtain of the temple was torn in two from top to bottom.
39. And when the centurion, who stood there in front of Jesus, heard his cry and saw how he died, he said, Surely this man was the Son of God!
40. Some women were watching from a distance. Among them were Mary Magdalene, Mary the mother of James the younger and of Joses, and Salome[190].

15.46. So Joseph bought some linen cloth, took down the body, wrapped it in the linen, and placed it in a tomb cut out of rock. Then he rolled a stone against the entrance of the tomb.
47. Mary Magdalene and Mary the mother of Joses saw where he was laid[191].

16.5. As they entered the tomb, they saw a young man dressed in a white robe sitting on the right side, and they were alarmed.
6. Don't be alarmed, he said. You are looking for Jesus the Nazarene, who was crucified. He has risen! He is not here. See the place where they laid him.
7. But go, tell his disciples and Peter, 'He is going ahead of you into Galilee. There you will see him, just as he told you.'
8. Trembling and bewildered, the women went out and fled from the tomb. They said nothing to anyone, because they were afraid.

We may examine the ending in light of Mark's motifs of fear and secrecy. The women end up afraid, which indicates that they did not believe in Jesus, as their belief would have been the antidote to their fear. On the other hand, the fact that they are afraid would indicate in Mark's world that they have seen a miracle or magic of some kind.

The greatest irony here is that they are obeying Jesus by keeping silent. He has often repeated his desire for witnesses to miracles to remain silent. But now, instead of telling the witnesses to remain silent, he wants them to deliver his message. Mark's poor Jesus can't catch a break. When he wants the witnesses to shut up, they talk, and when he wants them to talk, they shut up.

If the secrecy, fear and belief motifs we see at the end of Mark are his own creation, we ask what the story of Jesus was like before Mark quietly added his fears and beliefs to it?

Guarding Jesus' Tomb

The development of the gospels was an interactive process. Not only did gospel writers take material directly from other gospels, but they changed their gospels based on critical reaction. In a way, it parallels the cinematic process of previewing movies before test audiences and making changes to the movie. This process can most readily be seen in the diverse endings where there was apparently lots of disagreement. The four canonical gospels show evidence of about a dozen different endings.

The changes to the text in response to criticism can be most easily shown by Matthew's insertion of a story about Jesus' tomb being guarded by Roman soldiers. This rather interesting plot point does not appear in Mark. Here it is in Matthew.

> 27.62. The next day, the one after Preparation Day, the chief priests and the Pharisees went to Pilate.
> 63. Sir, they said, we remember that while he was still alive that deceiver said, 'After three days I will rise again.'
> 64. So give the order for the tomb to be made secure until the third day. Otherwise, his disciples may come and steal the body and tell the people that he has been raised from the dead. This last deception will be worse than the first.
> 65. Take a guard, Pilate answered. Go, make the tomb as secure as you know how.
> 66. So they went and made the tomb secure by putting a seal on the stone and posting the guard.
>
> 28.11. While the women were on their way, some of the guards went into the city and reported to the chief priests everything that had happened.
> 12. When the chief priests had met with the elders and devised a plan, they gave the soldiers a large sum of money,
> 13. telling them, You are to say, 'His disciples came during the night and stole him away while we were asleep.'

14. If this report gets to the governor, we will satisfy him and keep you out of trouble.
15. So the soldiers took the money and did as they were instructed. And this story has been widely circulated among the Jews to this very day.

It is evident that at some point after Mark's Gospel came out, someone objected to the empty tomb ending, suggesting that the most logical explanation for the missing body was that the disciples themselves stole the body. The direct response to this argument from Matthew (or possibly a later reviser of Matthew) is to make up a fabulous story about a Roman guard being posted around Jesus' tomb.

The charge that the disciples stole the body logically follows the early gospel ending that Mary and possibly others found Jesus' tomb empty. The counterclaim that troops were placed around the tomb to prevent stealing the body is not the only answer Christians came up with to the charge of disciple body-snatching. In the work *Dialogue With Trypho* allegedly by Justin Martyr we get another response to the original empty tomb story.

> "And though all the men of your nation knew the incidents in the life of Jonah, and though Christ said amongst you that He would give the sign of Jonah, exhorting you to repent of your wicked deeds at least after He rose again from the dead, and to mourn before God as did the Ninevites, in order that your nation and city might not be taken and destroyed, as they have been destroyed; yet you not only have not repented, after you learned that He rose from the dead, but, as I said before you have sent chosen and ordained men throughout all the world to proclaim that a godless and lawless heresy had sprung from one Jesus, a Galilean deceiver, whom we crucified, but his disciples stole him by night from the tomb, where he was laid when unfastened from the cross, and now deceive men by asserting that he has risen from the dead and ascended to heaven[192].

Note that in *Trypho*, the Jews "chose and ordained men throughout the world" to say that the disciples stole the body. This is somewhat different than what the Gospel of Matthew text reports. It claims the Jews set up a body guard around the tomb. The guards fell asleep (explaining why they were not witnesses to the resurrection) and the Jews bribed them to say that they saw the disciples steal the body. Both the writers of this passage and the writer of *Trypho* trace the stolen body story to the Jews, but *Trypho* traces it to appointed anti-apostles, while Matthew traces it to roman soldiers bribed by Jews.

One could point out that the two stories do not directly contradict each other and both may describe two different events, bribing of guards and ordaining anti-apostles to spread the anti-gospel. However, speaking pragmatically, it seems likely that the charge of disciple body-snatching was current when the writer of *Trypho* wrote his work and he was not familiar with the appropriate guard bribery passages in the Gospel of Matthew. Dating-wise, it is highly likely these passages were inserted into Matthew slightly after the writing of the *Trypho*[193].

One may take this as the model for the creation of most events in the Gospels. Many events in the Gospels were created to answer objections to prior passages. By asking the simple question, "What objection does this passage get rid of?" we may discover why many passages in the Gospels were created and the state of the text before the new scene/s were added.

One should also note that the Gospel writers did not give objections along with their answers, they "intercut" their responses into the existing material. Matthew has broken his explanation for the "disciples stole the body" story into two parts. In the first part (27:62-67), he has the Jews going to Pilate and posting guards, this explains why the disciples could not have stolen the body. The second passage explains how this story that the Disciples stole the body circulated.

This dialectical procedure of re-editing the narrative in order to answer objections has an interesting effect. It adds realism to the narrative as objections are answered within the text itself. On the other hand it may leave obvious contradictions between earlier gospel text with unanswered objections and later gospel text with answers to unstated objections. It helps us enormously to understand the chronology of the writing.

Differences in the Endings of Mark and Matthew

Now the "Disciples stole the body" story is an objection to the ending of Mark's Gospel wherein the three women find only an empty tomb, so there are no eyewitnesses to Jesus' resurrection. Here is Mark's ending.

1. When the Sabbath was over, Mary Magdalene, Mary the mother of James, and Salome bought spices so that they might go to anoint Jesus' body.
2. Very early on the first day of the week, just after sunrise, they were on their way to the tomb
3. and they asked each other, Who will roll the stone away from the entrance of the tomb?
4. But when they looked up, they saw that the stone, which was very large, had been rolled away.
5. As they entered the tomb, they saw a young man dressed in a white robe sitting on the right side, and they were alarmed.
6. Don't be alarmed, he said. You are looking for Jesus the Nazarene,

THE EVOLUTION OF CHRISTS AND CHRISTIANIES

> who was crucified. He has risen! He is not here. See the place where they laid him.
>
> 7   But go, tell his disciples and Peter, 'He is going ahead of you into Galilee. There you will see him, just as he told you.'
>
> 8   Trembling and bewildered, the women went out and fled from the tomb. They said nothing to anyone, because they were afraid.

Here is Matthew's revision of Mark's text.

> 1   After the Sabbath, at dawn on the first day of the week, Mary Magdalene and the other Mary went to look at the tomb.
>
> 2   There was a violent earthquake, for an angel of the Lord came down from heaven and, going to the tomb, rolled back the stone and sat on it.
>
> 3   His appearance was like lightning, and his clothes were white as snow.
>
> 4   The guards were so afraid of him that they shook and became like dead men.
>
> 5   The angel said to the women, Do not be afraid, for I know that you are looking for Jesus, who was crucified.
>
> 6   He is not here; he has risen, just as he said. Come and see the place where he lay.
>
> 7   Then go quickly and tell his disciples: 'He has risen from the dead and is going ahead of you into Galilee. There you will see him.' Now I have told you.
>
> 8   So the women hurried away from the tomb, afraid yet filled with joy, and ran to tell his disciples.
>
> 9   Suddenly Jesus met them. Greetings, he said. They came to him, clasped his feet and worshipped him.
>
> 10 Then Jesus said to them, Do not be afraid. Go and tell my brothers to go to Galilee; there they will see me.

We can list the major changes that Matthew has made and the objections that they answer to Mark's original story and to Matthew's innovations.

1.   The women do not come to perform a cleansing ceremony on Jesus, but merely to look at the tomb. In Mark's version, the women forget that a stone has been placed in front of the tomb, and they can't get in to perform their ceremony. One may object that the women would never be so stupid as to forget that a stone is in front of the Tomb of their Lord. Matthew changes Mark to answer this objection. They were not going into the tomb to cleanse the body, but merely to look at the tomb.

137

2. Seeing a man dressed in a white robe would not have frightened the women as it does in Mark. The women would have taken his presence as merely proof that the disciples had rolled away the stone and had moved the body. Matthew puts in the special effect of an Earthquake and has the women witnessing the man (who is now explicitly an angel) rolling back the stone, proving the disciples did not do it.

3. The guards become frightened. Matthew foresees the objection that the guards would have stopped the women from going into the tomb to see that Jesus was not there and talking with the angel, so he freezes the guards with fear.

4. In Mark's version the women were frightened and told no-one, so nobody presumably knows about the resurrection outside of the three women. Matthew wants the women to be witnesses for Jesus' rising, so he cannot have them remain silent. Matthew agrees that they were frightened, but instead of saying that "they said nothing to anyone" he changes this to "they were filled with joy and ran to tell the disciples."

5. Finally, one could object to Mark's ending that the women never actually saw Jesus after he arose. Matthew answers that objection by having Jesus suddenly appear to them. Note that Jesus just repeats the message of the angel. Since the women were going to deliver the message anyway, Jesus' message to them is pointless. The writer only wanted the women to be eyewitnesses to Jesus' appearance and Matthew does not have anything new that he wants Jesus to say to them. Thus we get the pointless redundancy of the Jesus' message repeating the angel's message at this point.

Matthew adds the tomb scene and the surrounding guard scenes to defend against skeptical attacks. This suggests Mark's Gospel was in circulation and drawing criticism before Matthew wrote. Matthew is quite willing to make up and insert any detail that will make Mark's narrative more believable. Thus he improvises the reason for the women coming to the tomb (to see the tomb), the earthquake, the angel rolling the stone, the changing of the moods and intentions of the women afterwards, and the women meeting with Jesus. Note that neither the Jewish objections nor Matthew's counter-propositions are based on historical, oral or eyewitness testimony. Both the skeptical objectors and Matthew are discussing the logic of the narrative and if it is consistent. This is sometimes taken to mean that they both agree to the basic historical events. Quite the contrary, this means neither are looking at historical, oral or eyewitness testimony to create their material. It appears that neither the Christian nor the Jews have any evidence to support their claims of what happened to Jesus' body.

In any case, we can see here how gospel writers/editors introduced scenes for the specific purpose of answering critics of previous gospel versions. This is a good starting point for understanding how gospel scenes developed and changed. We may ask what problem a scene solves in order to understand why the scene has been included.

Time Out of Joint

Rather than looking at the contradictions between Matthew and Mark, we get a better understanding of the development of the gospels by looking at the contradictions between John and Mark. The contradicting chronologies hold the key.

The chronology of the Gospel of Mark in the end narrative is not easy to follow, but it appears that Jesus dies on the Passover Day of Friday (Thursday sunset to Friday sunset in the Jewish tradition of measuring a day from sunset to sunset). According to Mark, Passover fell on the Day before the Sabbath, Thursday sunset to Friday sunset (Mk. 15:42). The Gospel of John has Jesus die on the same day, but he tells us that this is not Passover, but the Day of Preparation before Passover (Jn. 19:14). For John, Passover falls on the same day as the Sabbath, Friday sunset to Saturday sunset. For Mark Passover falls on the previous day.

One can easily dismiss this as simple faulty memory. John remembered the Passover falling on Saturday (Friday sunset to Saturday sunset), while Mark remembered it falling on Friday (Thursday sunset to Friday sunset). One might suppose that John, writing last, as an old man, simply got it wrong, and Jesus died on Passover as Mark first wrote. The evidence, however, suggests that it was Mark who changed the death of Jesus from the day before Passover to Passover. Gerd Theissen brings up the relevant evidence:

> In my opinion, in Mark we can discern behind the text as we now have it a connected narrative that presupposes a certain chronology. According to Mark, Jesus died on the day of Passover, but the tradition supposes it was the preparation day before Passover: in 14:1-2 the Sanhedrin decided to kill Jesus before the feast in order to prevent unrest among the people on the day of the feast. This fits with the circumstance that in 15:21 Simon of Cyrene is coming in from the fields, which can be understood to mean he was coming from his work. It would be hard to imagine any author's using a formulation so subject to misunderstanding in an account that describes events on the day of Passover, since no work was done on that day. Moreover, in 15:42 Jesus' burial is said to be on the "preparation day," but a relative clause is added to make it the preparation day for the Sabbath. Originally, it was probably the preparation day for the Passover (cf. Jn 19:42). The motive for removing Jesus from the cross and burying him before sundown would probably have been to have this work done before the beginning of the feast day, which would not make sense if it were already the day of Passover. Finally, the "trial" before the Sanhedrin presupposes that this was not a feast day, since no judicial proceedings could be held on that day. It would have been a breach of the legal code that the narrator could

scarcely have ignored, because the point of the narrative is to represent the proceeding against Jesus as an unfair trial with contradictory witnesses and a verdict decided in advance by the high priests[194].

The question is why did Mark change the death and burial of Jesus from the day before Passover to the Day of Passover? What difference does it make? The answer is shocking. The answer is "None." There is no theological reason for this.

One might say that dying on the Passover, Jesus is no longer the Passover lamb which traditionally gets slaughtered on the day of Passover, but it is difficult to see why Mark should find that objectionable. If this was his intention to insist that Jesus was not the Passover Lamb who dies on the preparation day, one would expect that he would be a bit more explicit in pointing out why Jesus could not be the sacrificial Lamb. We are left with the question of why Mark changed the tradition found in John of Jesus' death from the day before Passover to Passover. Conversely, was it John that objected to Jesus' death on Passover, or wanted to show Jesus as the Passover sacrificial lamb? What is the real reason for the conflicting dates?

John Makes Jesus into the Sacrificial Lamb of God

Unlike the sharp pointed dialogue in much of the rest of the *Gospel of John*, Jesus' farewell speech to the disciples is long, unfocused and repetitious. It contains one primary idea that the character of Jesus seems to be working out on the spur of the moment, but probably reflects the author working it out on the spur of the moment. Jesus is trying to get across to the disciples that he came from the father and he is going back to the father. Towards the end, the disciples seem to finally understand him.

> 25: "I have said this to you in figures; the hour is coming when I shall no longer speak to you in figures but tell you plainly of the Father.
> 26: In that day you will ask in my name; and I do not say to you that I shall pray the Father for you;
> 27: for the Father himself loves you, because you have loved me and have believed that I came from the Father.
> 28: I came from the Father and have come into the world; again, I am leaving the world and going to the Father."
> 29: His disciples said, "Ah, now you are speaking plainly, not in any figure!
> 30: Now we know that you know all things, and need none to question you; by this we believe that you came from God."

We must assume that this is an ideal scene created by John. After three years of being with Jesus it seem absurd that a few hours before his arrest, Jesus finally says outright that he is a son and/or messenger from God and the disciples finally all get it and stop questioning it. It also contradicts and makes inexplicable Peter's denial a few scenes later.

We may assume that it is much more likely the disciples of Jesus were not clear about this issue. While John makes the point explicitly that Jesus is from "the Father" a reference to the Jewish creator God, the common opinion expressed in John by both disciples and Jews is that Jesus is an enigma: He is a man from outer space who has arrived on Earth and talks in obscure riddles.

We may that it that the alien nature of Jesus that we find in *John* comes partly from the character in the original story and partly from the author of *John* himself. The author seems to be giving a new interpretation to the Jesus tales. He is proposing that Jesus came as a fulfillment of Hebrew Prophecies and that he was the sacrificial Passover Lamb. This Jewish explanation of Jesus' teaching may have been quite alien to the followers of Jesus at this time. In fact the author of John may have felt like his character Jesus, a misunderstand man from outer space in proposing it.

John's *Preparation Day Gospel* seems to have been a direct revision of the earlier story that Jesus died on Passover. We take this from the fact that it makes little sense to move the death day from the Preparation day to the Passover day. It destroys the meaning of the references to Jesus' as the Sacrificial Passover Lamb. On the contrary, by moving the death day from Passover to the Preparation day, John turns Jesus into the Passover Lamb. This works well with the shepherd/sheep imagery/references in other parts of John. For example, the first time we meet Jesus in this gospel, John the Baptist refers to Jesus as the Lamb of God.

> *28:* This took place in Bethany beyond the Jordan, where John was baptizing.
> *29:* The next day he saw Jesus coming toward him, and said, "Behold, the Lamb of God, who takes away the sin of the world!

In the context of meeting someone, the reference to a man as a lamb seems quite out of place. It foreshadows Jesus as the sacrificial Passover lamb, but why foreshadow that so early? Originally, John merely predicted that Jesus would become Messiah (King), not that he would die tragically the day before Passover like a sacrificial lamb. Later in the story, Bethany is associated with Mary Magdalene. We may conjecture that the term was originally applied by Jesus to Mary Magdalene at Bethany in an early scene in the *Passover Day Gospel*. The author of John decided to rewrite the line showing Jesus' sexual attraction to Mary (calling her a lamb) and introduce the doctrinal point about Jesus being a type of sacrificial lamb.

We may propose that the shift in association of Mary and the lamb to Jesus and the lamb brought a certain subconscious uneasiness that certain readers of the text can sense. The relationship emerged nearly 1800 years later in the poem of the schoolteacher Sarah Josepha Hale[195]:

> Mary had a little lamb
> Its fleece was white as snow,
> And everywhere that Mary went
> The lamb was sure to go.
>
> It followed her to school one day,
> That was against the rule;
> It made the children laugh and play
> To see a lamb at school.
>
> And so the Teacher turned him out,
> But still he lingered near,
> And waited patiently about
> Till Mary did appear:
>
> And then he ran to her, and laid
> His head upon her arm,
> As if he said, "I'm not afraid,
> You'll save me from all harm."
>
> "What makes the lamb love Mary so?"
> The little children cry-
> "O Mary loves the lamb, you know,"
> The teacher did reply:
>
> "And you each gentle animal
> In confidence may bind,
> And make them follow at your call,
> If you are always kind."

In any case, whether there was an original reference to Mary as the lamb or not, John follows up the lamb reference with shepherd imagery:

> 11: I am the good shepherd. The good shepherd lays down his life for the sheep.
> 12: He who is a hireling and not a shepherd, whose own the sheep are not, sees the wolf coming and leaves the sheep and flees; and the wolf snatches them and scatters them.

13: He flees because he is a hireling and cares nothing for the sheep.
14: I am the good shepherd; I know my own and my own know me,
15: as the Father knows me and I know the Father; and I lay down my life for the sheep.
16: And I have other sheep, that are not of this fold; I must bring them also, and they will heed my voice. So there shall be one flock, one shepherd.

We may take it that the author is not only envisioning Jesus here, but himself as well. The author of *John* is trying to unite sheep "that are not of this fold." He wants to be the one shepherd of this one flock and he is willing to give up his life to do it. We may take it that the author of John sees himself as the Paraclete or Counselor that Jesus promises to send to the disciples (15:26):

> But when the Counselor comes, whom I shall send to you from the Father, even the Spirit of truth, who proceeds from the Father, he will bear witness to me;

The author's interpretation of the Jesus tale(s) of miracles and strange paradoxical sayings as fulfillment of Hebrew Scriptures must have seemed an odd interpretation to the Jesus community "who was not of this fold." Ultimately he was successful as Mark, Matthew and Luke followed suit and interpreted the tales in the same way. To a generation brought up on the image of Jesus as a mystical magician, the image we find in the *Gospel of Thomas*, the interpretation of the sayings and events of Jesus' life as fulfillment of Jewish omens must have seemed the wild and crazy rantings of an alien man from outer space. This may be one reason Mark chose to write his gospel. He wanted to clarify and support John's Jewish interpretation of Jesus.

Why did the three Women Come to the Tomb?

Let us step back for a moment. The changes that Mark made in the earlier tomb story are important. These changes present some serious difficulties to plausibility. I find two major problems that tell us that Mark's text could not have been the original story. The first problem is the unanointed body of Jesus lying in the tomb throughout the Sabbath Day and the second problem is the women going to the tomb but not seeing/meeting Jesus. Here is Mark's version.

15.45. When he learned from the centurion that it was so, he gave the body to Joseph.
46. So Joseph bought some linen cloth, took down the body, wrapped it in the linen, and placed it in a tomb cut out of rock. Then he rolled a stone against the entrance of the tomb.

143

> 47. Mary Magdalene and Mary the mother of Joses saw where he was laid.
> 16.1. When the Sabbath was over, Mary Magdalene, Mary the mother of James, and Salome bought spices so that they might go to anoint Jesus' body.
> 2. Very early on the first day of the week, just after sunrise, they were on their way to the tomb and they asked each other, Who will roll the stone away from the entrance of the tomb?

In relation to the first problem, we may ask why the women did not anoint Jesus with spices before his entombment. If Joseph had time to buy linen ("Joseph bought some linen"), why did the women not have time to buy spices to anoint the body? It seems that the three women were rather thoughtless in not having prepared this while Jesus was on the Cross. Again, if Joseph could buy linen, could not the women buy spices? Are we to assume that linen stores were open during the day of Passover ("Joseph bought some linen cloth."), and spice stores were not, so Joseph could buy his linen on Friday afternoon, while the women had to wait till Saturday night to buy their spices?

Logically, they should have performed the ritual cleaning of the body before the burial of Jesus. One could argue that there was no time and the body needed to be buried before nightfall and the beginning of Passover. However, the applicable Jewish law merely says:

> [23] you must not leave his body on the tree overnight. Be sure to bury him that same day, because anyone who is hung on a tree is under God's curse[196].

Jesus' body had been taken down before nightfall, or shortly thereafter, depending on the textual reading. He would not be hanging from a tree overnight, so that part of the command had been fulfilled. Now he just needed to be buried because he was under a curse. The anointing of the body with spices could not have been a long process, especially if three women participated. In the *Gospel of John*, Nicodemus puts spices by himself in the tomb with the body of Jesus, presumably taking only a few minutes. If we consider this an earlier gospel, we have to explain why Mark would cut this out. The answer is not obvious. Probably, by eliminating Nicodemus and his putting spices in the tomb with Jesus, Mark provided a reason for the women to return to the tomb.

As for the second problem, the intention of the scene is clearly to have the women testify to the rising of Jesus. Having the women just witness an empty tomb does not even tell us that Jesus came back to life. Joseph or anyone else could have easily come back to the tomb Saturday night and moved the body[197]. Mark gives us only the angel's testimony that Jesus has risen. But the angel could have appeared to anyone at anytime and told them Jesus had risen. Why does the angel instruct the women to tell the disciples that Jesus had risen? Why can't the angel do this himself? This is indeed a lazy angel who does not deliver messages in person, but trusts human women to deliver them? But why does Mark not have the women themselves see Jesus rise and testify to it? Why bring them all the way to the Tomb and then tell them they are too late for the climax of the story? The scene, as played out now is ridiculous, with the women not testifying that they saw Jesus resurrected, but merely testifying that they saw an angel who told them Jesus had been resurrected.

Mark, being a typical male of the time would be distrustful of the women's testimony, or at least would realize that most male listeners would be distrustful. If the women testified they saw Jesus rise, the male listener to the story would conclude that the women fabricated the story of Jesus' resurrection from the dead, and that the women moved the body themselves. To overcome this objection, Mark places a stone in front of the Tomb and does not allow the women to perform the cleaning ceremony. This answers the charge that the women moved the body. How could they, they could not even get into the tomb—but this solution creates a bigger problem. We now have no witnesses that Jesus rose. Mark has put out one fire, only to see a bigger one blaze up. The stone stops the women from taking the body, but it also stops them from being witnesses to the rising. The solution that Mark arrives at is the one we now find in the text. Like every Greek playwright who called upon a God to come down and set things straight when his plot got too tangled to be repaired, Mark calls on a *deus ex machina*, or the Jewish equivalent in this case, an angel, to help him fix the scene. The women are now not eyewitnesses to Jesus' rising but merely to an angel (perhaps Jesus himself in a truer form) who tells them that he has risen. But angels in Jewish tales were as common as superheroes are in comic books. Testimony that an angel has told someone something is worth only slightly more than the testimony of three women. Matthew evidently realized this and so restored a meeting between Jesus and the women ("And behold Jesus met them[198].").

In Mark's case, since the women are not eyewitnesses any longer in the scene, Mark just has them shut up and not say anything. The scene ends by negating its own function in the narrative. Apparently Mark thought that the women's testimony was worthless anyway, so he just has them shut up altogether and lets an angel tell us what happened. For Mark, an ending of having an angel testifying to Jesus rising is better than an ending in which women are testifying to Jesus' rising. Mark's community might believe a story in which an angel testifies to a miracle, but they would not believe a story in which women testify to a miracle.

However, replacing the women's testimony with an angel is not the only or most serious change that Mark has made. We must notice that a ceremony is missing. The women should have anointed Jesus' body before he was buried. This ceremony does not take place. The women should have anointed Jesus' body when they hurried to the tomb. This ceremony again does not take place. Mark has perhaps suggested that the women missed their first appointment to perform a ceremony with Jesus' dead body, due to the coming of the Sabbath and the need to quickly bury Jesus. They missed their second appointment because they arrived too late at the tomb and Jesus had already risen. Mark has insisted that the women had missed two appointments and never got their chance to perform their ceremony with Jesus' dead body[199].

"The Time is out of Joint, O cursed spite" said Hamlet[200].

It seems Mark does not want the women seeing and testifying to Jesus' resurrection. It also seems Mark does not want the women cleaning Jesus' dead body. We may suspect that in an earlier story, Jesus' body was cleaned, probably by Mary. We may also suspect the women did keep their appointment to see the resurrected Jesus, or at least Mary did. This is exactly what we find in the *Gospel of John*.

A Symbolic Change: Death on the Preparation Day for Passover

We are fortunate in that the Gospel of John has preserved a good deal of the earlier tomb narrative, which takes place in John after Jesus died on the Preparation Day before Passover.

19.38. Later, Joseph of Arimathea asked Pilate for the body of Jesus. Now Joseph was a disciple of Jesus, but secretly because he feared the Jews. With Pilate's permission, he came and took the body away.

39. He was accompanied by Nicodemus, the man who earlier had visited Jesus at night. Nicodemus brought a mixture of myrrh and aloes, about seventy-five pounds.

40. Taking Jesus' body, the two of them wrapped it, with the spices, in strips of linen. This was in accordance with Jewish burial customs.

41. At the place where Jesus was crucified, there was a garden, and in the garden a new tomb, in which no-one had ever been laid.

42. Because it was the Jewish day of Preparation and since the tomb was near by, they laid Jesus there.

20.1. Early on the first day of the week, while it was still dark, Mary Magdalene went to the tomb and saw that the stone had been removed from the entrance.

2. So she came running to Simon Peter and the other disciple, the one Jesus loved, and said, They have taken the Lord out of the tomb, and we don't know where they have put him!

3. So Peter and the other disciple started for the tomb.

4. Both were running, but the other disciple outran Peter and reached the tomb first.

5. He bent over and looked in at the strips of linen lying there but did not go in.

THE EVOLUTION OF CHRISTS AND CHRISTIANIES

6. Then Simon Peter, who was behind him, arrived and went into the tomb. He saw the strips of linen lying there,
7. as well as the burial cloth that had been around Jesus' head. The cloth was folded up by itself, separate from the linen.
8. Finally the other disciple, who had reached the tomb first, also went inside. He saw and believed.
9. (They still did not understand from Scripture that Jesus had to rise from the dead.)
10. Then the disciples went back to their homes,
11. but Mary stood outside the tomb crying. As she wept, she bent over to look into the tomb
12. and saw two angels in white, seated where Jesus' body had been, one at the head and the other at the foot.
13. They asked her, Woman, why are you crying? They have taken my Lord away, she said, and I don't know where they have put him.
14. At this, she turned round and saw Jesus standing there, but she did not realise that it was Jesus.
15. Woman, he said, why are you crying? Who is it you are looking for? Thinking he was the gardener, she said, Sir, if you have carried him away, tell me where you have put him, and I will get him.
16. Jesus said to her, Mary. She turned towards him and cried out in Aramaic, Rabboni! (which means Teacher).
17. Jesus said, Do not hold on to me, for I have not yet returned to the Father. Go instead to my brothers and tell them, 'I am returning to my Father and your Father, to my God and your God.'
18. Mary Magdalene went to the disciples with the news: I have seen the Lord! And she told them that he had said these things to her.

Notice the incompleteness of this narrative. Here are four immediate problems: 1) Mary does not have a reason for going to the tomb and how does she know where the tomb is? 2) She sees that the stone has been removed from the entrance, but how did she know that there was a stone in the first place. 3) She says, "They have taken the Lord out of the tomb and we don't know where they have put them." How does Mary immediately know that the Lord's body is not in the tomb without going inside. 4) Why does she use the pronoun "we" when she was alone in seeing the tomb?

In order for the narrative to make sense we have to go back to the Gospel of Mark and add the parts that answer these questions. We also have to adjust for the changes that John made to the narrative. Here is a reconstruction of the original that John and Mark worked from, the *UrTomb Story*. We have put what Mark preserves in bold:

John 19.38. Later, Joseph of Arimathea asked Pilate for the body of Jesus. Now Joseph was a disciple of Jesus, but secretly because he feared the Jews. With Pilate's permission, he came and took the body away.

39. He was accompanied by Nicodemus, the man who earlier had visited Jesus at night. Nicodemus brought a mixture of myrrh and aloes, about seventy-five pounds.
40. Taking Jesus' body, the two of them wrapped it, with the spices, in strips of linen. This was in accordance with Jewish burial customs.
41. At the place where Jesus was crucified, there was a garden, and in the garden a new tomb, in which no-one had ever been laid.
42. Because it was the Jewish day of Preparation and since the tomb was near by, they laid Jesus there ... Then they rolled a stone against the entrance of the tomb.

Mark 15.47. Mary Magdalene and Mary the mother of Joses saw where he was laid.
16.1. Mary Magdalene, Mary the mother of James, and Salome bought spices so that they might go to anoint Jesus' body.
2. just after sunrise, they were on their way to the tomb and they asked each other[201], Who will roll the stone away from the entrance of the tomb?

John 20.1. Mary Magdalene went to the tomb and saw that the stone had been removed from the entrance.
2. So she came running to Mary and the other disciple, the one Jesus loved, and said, "They have taken my Lord away, and I don't know where they have put him[202]."
3. So Mary and the other disciple started for the tomb.
4. Both were running, but the other disciple outran Mary and reached the tomb first.
5. She bent over and looked in at the strips of linen lying there but did not go in.
6. Then Mary, who was behind her, arrived and went into the tomb. She saw the strips of linen lying there,
7. as well as the burial cloth that had been around Jesus' head. The cloth was folded up by itself, separate from the linen.
8. Finally the other disciple, who had reached the tomb first, also went inside. She saw and believed.
10. Then the disciples went back to their homes,

11. but Mary stood outside the tomb crying. As she wept, she bent over to look into the tomb
12. and saw two angels in white, seated where Jesus' body had been, one at the head and the other at the foot.
13. They asked her, Woman, why are you crying? They have taken my Lord away, she said, and I don't know where they have put him.
14. At this, she turned round and saw Jesus standing there, but she did not realise that it was Jesus.
15. Woman, he said, why are you crying? Who is it you are looking for? Thinking he was the gardener, she said, Sir, if you have carried him away, tell me where you have put him, and I will get him.
16. Jesus said to her, Mary. She turned towards him and cried out in Aramaic, Rabboni! (which means Teacher).
17. Jesus said, Do not hold on to me, for I have not yet returned to the Father. Go instead to my brothers and tell them, 'I am returning to my Father and your Father, to my God and your God.'
18. Mary Magdalene went to the disciples with the news: I have seen the Lord! And she told them that he had said these things to her.

We should notice how well the text from Mark fits within the text of John at this point. This could hardly be accidental. The way they fit helps us to understand how both the Gospel of John and Mark developed.

The Modus Operandi of Mark and the Earlier Gospel of John

Mark has the stone being placed in front of Jesus' tomb, but does not have the spices being placed with Jesus. John has the spices being placed with Jesus but does not have the stone. It would seem that both would be necessary in both stories. Mark would not want us to think of Jesus' body stinking without spices and John needs the stone placed in front of the tomb so Mary can see it missing. There is one explanation for two such enormous lapses and for the pieces in Mark fitting so well into John. Originally the two texts were one and contained both bits of important information. We may deduce that Mark was literally cutting out the text from a manuscript to create his new manuscript. Whoever published John must have had the very same manuscript with the holes that Mark had left in it.

We may contrast Mark's procedure with Eusebius. To my knowledge none of the original texts that Eusebius altered have been found in their original state. This would suggest that Eusebius gathered and destroyed all the original works after he had made copies with alterations in them. On the other hand, Mark preserved the original manuscript to the point that others could come along years later and make the *Gospel of John* out of it. This means that we are getting some of the earlier manuscript from the text of Mark and some of the earlier manuscript preserved in John. This earlier manuscript which we may be able to reconstruct, at least in part, we may call the *Preparation Day Gospel,* as Jesus dies on the day before Passover in this, whereas Mark has Jesus dying on Passover. We may suppose that the same community that edited the *Gospel of Mark,* later edited the *Gospel of John.* This probably explains why our version of John is so different from the synoptic gospels and yet was included with them. For the most part, our present Gospel of John contains the material that Mark chose not to use.

Thus chronologically, the *Passover Day Gospel of Mary* comes first, the *Preparation Day Gospel* of John comes next, and the mixed *Gospel of Mark* comes third. However, it appears that we have a mutilated version of *John.* Therefore, some of the narratological material in Mark that comes from the *Passover Day Gospel of Mary* actually predates the material in *John.*

Our reconstruction of this part of the *Preparation Day Gospel* still can be examined to find out more on the thought and operating procedure of the gospel writers. Two important points we need to examine are 1) the number of women at the tomb and 2) the precise ending.

The Number of Women at the Tomb

It is a little difficult to know how many women Mark places at the scene of the crucifixion. It is possibly two, Mary Magdalene and the mother of James, Joses and Salome, or it is three, Mary Magdalene, the mother of James, Joses, and a third woman named Salome. Again at the crucifixion scene it is either these two or three women. However, Mark has only two women witnessing the burial, Mary Magdalene and Mary, Mother of Joses. Since he writes that only two women witnessed where Jesus was buried (15:47), it seems that we should probably read the text as saying that Salome was the sister of James (and therefore a sister of Jesus) and not place her in the crucifixion or tomb scenes. Otherwise we should have to imagine that Mark wanted us to believe that Salome hung around for the crucifixion, but did not bother to go see the burial. That would indeed be strange. If this was the case, one would think that the writer would at least give us a clue as to why Salome who "followed him and ministered to him in Galilee" (Mk15:41) did not stick around to see the burying of Jesus. Besides this, there is really no need for a third person to be in the two scenes. The third person says nothing and takes no role in the action. Finally, it seems most probable that Matthew and Mark agree with the proposition that there are two women at the tomb. Mark tries to make her identity fuzzy by calling her Mary, the mother of James, Joses and Salome, and Matthew tries to make it fuzzier still by just calling her the "other Mary." (Mt 27:61). Luke not only misreads Mark by thinking Salome is a third woman in the scenes, but changes her name to Jo-anne for some reason.

The Original Ending

The Gospel of John has Mary at the tomb. We may take this as the earlier version. It is quite impossible to believe that John would cut out Mary, the mother of James, Joses and Salome, and possibly the mother of Jesus, and just leave Mary Magdalene. We have to assume that Mark is adding the mother as a chaperon form Mary Magadelene in the scene. Possibly he is inventing it, but as likely there is already another source that has already placed her on the scene.

We next have to note a couple of small changes that John and Mark made to the ending. John at 20:7 has Jesus say, "Do not hold on to me, for I have not yet returned to the Father." He has cut out the action of Mary just before this, which Matthew preserves for us (Mt 28:9) "They came to him, clasped his feet and worshipped him." A reconstruction would be, "Mary came to him, clasped his feet and worshipped him." John cuts out her action, while Matthew changes it to two women (Mary and the "Other Mary") and just cuts out Jesus' "don't-hold-me" reaction. We can simply restore the original dramatic scene:

> Mary came to him, clasped his feet and worshipped him. "Jesus said, "Do not hold on to me, for I have not yet returned to the father."

However, Mark has given us a strange arrest scene in which Judas sees Jesus and kisses him (Mark 14:45), "Going at once to Jesus, Judas said, Rabbi! and kissed him." I am going to guess that Christian men greeting each other with a kiss was not the custom at the beginning of Christianity. Mark has taken this line from the tomb greeting of Mary to Jesus. A reconstruction would be, "Going at once to Jesus, Mary said, Rabbi! and kissed him." Combining these bits of John, Mark and Matthew, we get as our best reconstruction,

> "She turned towards him and cried out in Aramaic, Rabboni! (which means "Teacher,") She ran to him and kissed him, clasped his feet and worshipped him."

Also Mark has the women too frightened to say anything to the disciples. John preserves the original ending (John 20:18), "Mary Magdalene went to the disciples with the news: I have seen the Lord! And she told them that he had said these things to her."

It is possible that he has cut out the disciples' response. Both the longer version of Mark and Luke give the disciple's negative response to Mary.

> **Mark 16:10. She went and told those who had been with him and who were mourning and weeping.**

> 11. When they heard that Jesus was alive and that she had seen him, they did not believe it.

> Luke: 24:11. And their words seemed to them as idle tales, and they believed them not.

This ending matches the scene at the end of the *Gospel of Mary*, and may be derived from it. Here are the relevant lines:

> 2) But Andrew answered and said to the brethren, Say what you wish to say about what she has said. I at least do not believe that the Savior said this. For certainly these teachings are strange ideas.
> 3) Peter answered and spoke concerning these same things.
> 4) He questioned them about the Savior: Did He really speak privately with a woman and not openly to us? Are we to turn about and all listen to her? Did He prefer her to us?
> 5) Then Mary wept and said to Peter, My brother Peter, what do you think? Do you think that I have thought this up myself in my heart, or that I am lying about the Savior?

The earlier ending in the *Preparation Day Gospel*, probably had the disciples matching this skepticism towards Mary. The line, "Did he really speak privately with a woman and not openly to us," matches the skeptical attitude that each of the four canonical gospels contains towards Mary's encounter with Jesus at the tomb. However note that the disciples are not surprised in the *Gospel of Mary* about the Savior being alive or coming back from the dead. They show not the least skepticism about this. What they are skeptical about is that Jesus would speak in private with a woman. The issue here is Jesus' relationship to Mary, not if he was alive after crucifixion.

Changes in the Preparation Day Gospel of John

While the mixed *Gospel of Mark* made changes to the material, we should not forget that the earlier Preparation Day *Gospel of John* also made significant changes. For example, John writes this:

> 38 And after this Joseph of Arimathaea, being a disciple of Jesus, but secretly for fear of the Jews, besought Pilate that he might take away the body of Jesus: and Pilate gave him leave. He came therefore, and took the body of Jesus.

39 And there came also Nicodemus, which at the first came to Jesus by night, and brought a mixture of myrrh and aloes, about an hundred pound weight.
40 Then took they the body of Jesus, and wound it in linen clothes with the spices, as the manner of the Jews is to bury.

It is doubtful that Pilate would release the body to an unknown disciple. Why would Pilate even meet with a disciple of Jesus? Instead, he would release the body to Jesus' father Joseph. Originally, this more likely read "Joseph of Arimathaea, being the father of Jesus, besought Pilate that he might take away the body of Jesus"

Nicodemus also is out of place. There is no indication that he has anything to do with spices, and for the most part plays no role in the story that would entitle him to this important action. The only character who has been introduced who has been associated with spices is Mary Magdalene. We read in chapter 12, "Then took Mary a pound of ointment of spikenard, very costly, and anointed the feet of Jesus, and wiped his feet with her hair: and the house was filled with the odour of the ointment[203]." Preparation of the dead was woman's work.

Also, unless she buries Jesus, she cannot know where Jesus is buried to find him in the next scene. For these three reasons: 1) Nicodemus is a minor character, without reason for burying Jesus, 2) Women are associated with preparing corpses for burial, and 3) Mary is associated in a previous scene with costly ointments. We can be fairly certain that the original John-Mark scene included Mary, not Nicodemus.

When we take all these changes into account, we get this reconstruction of the UrTomb Scene:

First Reconstruction of UrTomb Scene

John 19.38. Later, Joseph of Arimathea asked Pilate for the body of Jesus. Now Joseph was the father of Jesus, but he asked secretly because he feared the Jews. With Pilate's permission, he came and took the body away.

39. He was accompanied by Mary, the woman who earlier had visited Jesus at night[204]. Mary brought a mixture of myrrh and aloes, about seventy-five pounds.

40. Taking Jesus' body, the two of them wrapped it, with the spices, in strips of linen. This was in accordance with Jewish burial customs.

41. At the place where Jesus was crucified, there was a garden, and in the garden a new tomb, in which no-one had ever been laid.

42. Because it was the Jewish Passover and since the tomb was near by, they laid Jesus there. Then they rolled a stone against the entrance of the tomb.

Mark 15.47. Mary Magdalene and _____ saw where he was laid.

16.1. Mary Magdalene and _____ bought spices so that they might go to anoint Jesus' body

2. just after sunrise, they were on their way to the tomb and they asked each other, Who will roll the stone away from the entrance of the tomb?

John 20.1. Mary Magdalene went to the tomb and saw that the stone had been removed from the entrance.

2. So Mary, the one whom Jesus loved, came running to the other disciple, and said, "They have taken my Lord away, and I don't know where they have put him."
3. So Mary and _____ started for the tomb.
4. Both were running, but _____ outran Mary and reached the tomb first.
5. She bent over and looked in at the strips of linen lying there but did not go in.
6. Then Mary, who was behind her, arrived and went into the tomb. She saw the strips of linen lying there,
7. as well as the burial cloth that had been around Jesus' head. The cloth was folded up by itself, separate from the linen.
8. Finally, _____ who had reached the tomb first, also went inside. She saw and believed.
10. Then the disciple went back to her home,
11. but Mary stood outside the tomb crying. As she wept, she bent over to look into the tomb
12. and saw two angels in white, seated where Jesus' body had been, one at the head and the other at the foot.
13. They asked her, "Woman, why are you crying?"

    "They have taken my Lord away," she said, and "I don't know where they have put him."
14. At this, she turned round and saw Jesus standing there, but she did not realise that it was Jesus.
15. Woman, he said, why are you crying? Who is it you are looking for? Thinking he was the gardener, she said, Sir, if you have carried him away, tell me where you have put him, and I will get him.
16. Jesus said to her, Mary. She turned towards him and cried out in Aramaic, Rabboni! (which means "Teacher"). She ran to him and kissed him clasped his feet and worshipped him.
17. Jesus said, Do not hold on to me, for I have not yet returned to the Father. Go instead to my brothers and tell them, 'I am returning to my Father and your Father, to my God and your God.'

> 18. Mary Magdalene went to the disciples with the news: I have seen the
> Lord! And she told them that he had said these things to her.
> Mark 16.11. When they heard that Jesus was alive and that she had seen
> him, they did not believe it.

Later, we will discover who the second person with Mary Magdalene at the tomb is and be able to fill in the blanks. In the last chapter of this book we will give a Second Reconstruction. This is good enough for the moment.

How can we be certain? What proof do we have that this was the original or close to the original ending of the Mary narrative? Fortunately, we have the Jewish response to this ending. Tertullian gives it. He mentions the earlier ending while mocking the Jews on a hypothetical Judgement Day:

> 'This is He,' I will say, 'the son of the carpenter and the harlot, the sabbath-breaker, the Samaritan who had a devil. This is He whom you purchased from Judas, this is He who was struck with reed and fist, defiled with spittle, given gall and vinegar to drink. This is He whom the disciples secretly stole away to spread the story of His resurrection, or whom the gardener removed lest his lettuces be trampled by the throng of curious idlers.'[205]!

The Jewish response to this ending was that Mary had mistook the Gardener for Jesus. He took the body away himself because he did not want the visitors to trample his lettuces. Such a response would not have made sense unless the original version of the tale contained this scene. After the other gospel endings came out, it would have been a meaningless response for Jews to make. The meetings between Jesus and the disciples were themselves later inventions designed to off-set the objection that the resurrected Jesus was only seen by a woman or two women. So we can consider that this reconstructed ending, with Mary alone meeting Jesus, and the disciples rejecting her testimony, or something close to it, was very early. It was widely circulated, enough to draw a Jewish response. In response Christians added women and had Jesus seen by the disciples as well.

Another source that confirms this earlier reconstruction comes from Egypt. In *The Book of the Resurrection of Christ by Bartholomew the Apostle*, we find:

> Early in the morning of the Lord's day the women went to the tomb. They were Mary Magdalene, Mary the mother of James whom Jesus delivered out of the hand of Satan, Salome who tempted him, Mary who ministered to him and Martha her sister, Joanna (al. Susanna) the wife of Chuza who had renounced the marriage bed, Berenice who was healed of an issue of blood in Capernaum, Lia (Leah) the widow whose

son he raised at Nain, and the woman to whom he said, 'Thy sins which are many are forgiven thee'.

These were all in the garden of Philogenes, whose son Simeon Jesus healed when he came down from the Mount of Olives with the apostles (probably the lunatic boy at the Mount of Transfiguration).

Mary said to Philogenes: If thou art indeed he, I know thee. Philogenes said: Thou art Mary the mother of Thalkamarimath, which means joy, blessing, and gladness. Mary said: If thou have borne him away, tell me where thou hast laid him and I will take him away: fear not. Philogenes told how the Jews sought a safe tomb for Jesus that the body might not be stolen, and he offered to place it in a tomb in his own garden and watch over it: and they sealed it and departed. At midnight he rose and went out and found all the orders of angels: Cherubim Seraphim, Powers, and Virgins. Heaven opened, and the Father raised Jesus. Peter, too, was there and supported Philogenes, or he would have died.

The Saviour then appeared to them on the chariot of the Father and said to Mary: Mari Khar Mariath (Mary the mother of the Son of God). Mary answered: Rabbouni Kathiathari Mioth (The Son of God the Almighty, my Lord, and my Son[206].)

This text mixes and elaborates characters and incidents from different gospels in an imaginative way. However, it does list Mary Magdalene, Mary—the Mother of James, and Salome as the first three women who visit the tomb, which agree somewhat with Mark. It does contain an important role for the Gardener, and it does offer an alternative to Matthew's version of the Jews posting a guard around the tomb. This would indicate that it was written without knowledge of Matthew's version, and most probably before Matthew's version with the Roman tomb guards. It says nothing about "Peter and the Beloved Disciple" visiting the tomb which we find in our current text of *John*, so it was probably written before the later version of *John*. It is evidence that the gardener talking to Mary tale (found in John's Gospel only) was a very early part of the story

After reconstructing the original (or at least earlier ending) we can now go back to our original question of why Mark changed the death of Jesus from the Preparation day to the actual day of Passover. Notice that in this reconstruction, there is no mention of three days passing. Mary goes to the tomb the following morning after Jesus gets buried.

Mark's change of the text from the preparation day to Passover is not motivated by theological reasons, it is motivated by his function as a scribe. If Mark did make the change, it would have necessitated some comment or theological reason, and would have entailed an answer to the readers of the John Gospel who thought Jesus died on the preparation day.

If Mark did not change Jesus' death day to Passover, then we must conclude that it was a tradition before him. It seems logical to conclude that Mark had two texts before him. In one text Jesus dies on the Preparation Day for Passover, Friday (Thursday sunset to Friday sunset), and a second text where Jesus dies on again on Friday, but it is called the Passover Day. The first text, the *Preparation Day Gospel*, we find Jesus killed as a Passover sacrifice, and has a coda attached in which Jesus rises on Passover, less than twelve hours after being put in the tomb. The second text has Jesus simply dying on Passover. We have called this second source *the Passover Gospel of Mary*.

Mark solves the problem of the conflicting text by combining the resurrection coda from the *Preparation Day Gospel of John* with the Passover death day chronology from *the Passover Gospel of Mary*.

The question is why does Mark have Jesus rise on Sunday, the third day (day one is Friday, day two is Saturday and day three is Sunday), instead of the next day as he does in the *Preparation Day Gospel*? For the probable answer to this we have to look to an earlier failed prediction by Jesus.

Why Mark made Jesus Dead for Three Days

Mark tells us that Jesus said that he would rebuild a destroyed Jewish Temple in three days[207]. Mark tells us that Jesus meant his body, not the actual Jerusalem Temple. The Jews thought he meant that he was actually going to rebuild the temple in three days. We may take the Jewish understanding as the original understanding and meaning of the line. My best guess is that in the original text, the three days simply signified a fast time. God took six days to create the world and everything in it, a fantastically small amount of time for a big job. Rebuilding the temple in three days just seems to mean that he will do this big job in half the time that God took to create the world, in other words quite rapidly[208]. A day was often considered to be equal to seven years, so the line probably came to connote the idea that the Christians/Jews would rebuild the Temple twenty-one years after its destruction. This suggest the saying developed or at least became popular sometime within twenty-one years of the destruction of the temple. One might guess that after the Emperor Titus died in 81 C.E., the Jews had some real hope of rebuilding the temple under Domitian. So between 81 C.E. and 88 C.E. would probably be a good guess for when this saying of Jesus developed or became popular. For Mark, presumably writing after the 21 years had elapsed, it would be necessary for him to revise this failed prophesy. He would have to have the prophesy refer to Jesus' body being underground three days and then rising. It was a good way of saving the prophesy, which must have disheartened many Christians and Jews when it did not come true in 91 C.E.

One may suppose that Jews accused zealous Christians after the temple was destroyed. If the Christians participated in the fighting, which I think is likely, or if they sat out the conflict, the Jews could blame the destruction of the temple on them for introducing a false deity and dividing the strength of the Jews. Christians would have responded by saying that Jesus had predicted the destruction of the temple and (when it looked like the temple would be rebuilt) that he also predicted that he would rebuild the temple in 21 years. However the year 91 C.E. came and went and the temple was not rebuilt. Mark found a wonderful way to neutralize this failed prediction. Jesus did not mean the actual temple but really meant himself. Jesus was underground and dead for three days.

Mark is so proud of his solution that he indicates it three times in the text (8:31, 9:31, 10:34). However Mark certainly was adopting this concept from Greek mythology, as there is nothing in Hebrew Scripture about a God dying and rising in three days[209].

The Second Death of Jesus Story: On the Passover Day

Mark had a text of Jesus dying on the Preparation Day before him. He also had a text of Jesus eating a Passover Meal on Passover Eve and being betrayed, arrested, tried and executed on Passover.

Mark tells us very straightforwardly that Jesus eats the Passover Meal.

> 14.12. On the first day of the Feast of Unleavened Bread, when it was customary to sacrifice the Passover lamb, Jesus' disciples asked him, Where do you want us to go and make preparations for you to eat the Passover?
> 13. So he sent two of his disciples, telling them, Go into the city, and a man carrying a jar of water will meet you. Follow him.
> 14. Say to the owner of the house he enters, 'The Teacher asks: Where is my guest room, where I may eat the Passover with my disciples?'
> 15. He will show you a large upper room, furnished and ready. Make preparations for us there.
> 16. The disciples left, went into the city and found things just as Jesus had told them. So they prepared the Passover.
> 17. When evening came, Jesus arrived with the Twelve.
> 18. While they were reclining at the table eating, he said, I tell you the truth, one of you will betray me—one who is eating with me.

By using this text from the *Passover Gospel* which takes place on Passover, it became necessary for Mark to change the death day of Jesus to Passover day as well. Obviously Mark could not have Jesus and the disciples eat the Passover Meal and then be killed the day before on the Passover Preparation Day. Mark wanted Jesus to have his Passover Meal and not to die before eating it.

A later editor of *John* recognizes that Mark has mixed this *Passover Gospel* narrative with the *Preparation Day Gospel* narrative. He does not disagree with Mark mixing the two narratives, but decides to take the opposite path and change the Passover meal to a pre-Passover meal, rather and keep Jesus' death on the Preparation day.

> 13.1 It was just before the Passover Feast. Jesus knew that the time had come for him to leave this world and go to the Father. Having loved his own who were in the world, he now showed them the full extent of his love.
> 2. The evening meal was being served, and the devil had already prompted Judas Iscariot, son of Simon, to betray Jesus.

How can we tell that the two narratives were originally separate? How do we know that Mark or John was not just copying from one narrative, where both meal and death was pre-Passover, or meal and death was on the Passover? The scenario does not work because there are major clues that the two texts were quite separate and telling separate tales. Three clues are 1) The chief priests plan to kill Jesus before Passover, 2) Judas' pointing out the famous Jesus with a kiss, although he was well known and 3) Jesus' contrasting moods towards Peter on Mount Gazin and the Mount of Olives.

First, in Mark's Gospel, This bit of information greets us before Judas arrives to offer his service to the Chief Priests:

> **Now the Passover and the Feast of Unleavened Bread were only two days away, and the chief priests and the teachers of the law were looking for some sly way to arrest Jesus and kill him. ²"But not during the Feast," they said, "or the people may riot**[210]**.**

The writer of this text is aware of the story of Jesus dying on Passover. He is also aware of an objection to the story that the people would have rioted if Jesus was killed on Passover. The writer is explaining why Jesus died on the preparation day and not Passover. However, the writer of these lines cannot be Mark. Mark tells us the contrary—that Jesus does die on Passover Day. Mark must have copied this scene before he had decided to have Jesus die on Passover Day. If Mark had bothered to reread his work, he would have realized immediately that this pronouncement that Jesus was not to die on Passover day is pointless if Jesus does die on Passover. This indicates two things. First that the *Preparation Day Gospel*, actually came after the other *Passover Gospel* and was written in conscious opposition to it and second that Mark did not write either the *Preparation Day Gospel* or the *Passover Gospel*. We know the *Preparation Day Gospel* comes before the *Passover Gospel* because the text is trying to give an explanation for why Jesus did not die on Passover (i.e. the chief priests were afraid the people would riot). We know Mark did not write this, but only copied it, because he, in fact, does have Jesus dying on Passover, but does not show any riot by the people.

Second, Jesus himself points out the ridiculousness of the Priests depending on Judas for the identification of Jesus. Mark has him say:

> "Am I leading a rebellion, said Jesus, that you have come out with swords and clubs to capture me? Every day I was with you, teaching in the temple courts, and you did not arrest me[211]."

Mark recognizes that his putting together the two tales has created an absurdity. In Mark's Gospel, it is Jesus' preaching in the Temple that arouses the Priests against him. They obviously knew where he was and did not need Judas to find, identify and arrest him. The line is certainly not based on any sayings of Jesus and contains a criticism of the very narrative that Mark is recording. We can therefore attribute the line to Mark himself. Mark wants to explain the narrative inconsistency of an elaborate secret raid on an open target by blaming it on the Jewish Priests' excessive fear of Jesus. It is a narrative inconsistency he has created himself by mixing a narrative where Jesus speaks in the open with a narrative where he is captured on the run.

The Gospel of John has preserved the other story in the *Passover Gospel* where Jesus does not preach in the open, but hides, so the priests did need Judas or someone to help them find and identify Jesus. This passage occurs in the Gospel of John after he describes Jesus raising Lazarus from the dead:

> 45. Therefore many of the Jews who had come to visit Mary, and had seen what Jesus did, put their faith in him.
> 46. But some of them went to the Pharisees and told them what Jesus had done.
> 47. Then the chief priests and the Pharisees called a meeting of the Sanhedrin. What are we accomplishing? they asked. Here is this man performing many miraculous signs.
> 48. If we let him go on like this, everyone will believe in him, and then the Romans will come and take away both our place and our nation.
> 49. Then one of them, named Caiaphas, who was high priest that year, spoke up, You know nothing at all!
> 50. You do not realise that it is better for you that one man die for the people than that the whole nation perish.
> 51. He did not say this on his own, but as high priest that year he prophesied that Jesus would die for the Jewish nation,
> 52. and not only for that nation but also for the scattered children of God, to bring them together and make them one.
> 53. So from that day on they plotted to take his life.
> 54. Therefore Jesus no longer moved about publicly among the Jews.

Instead he withdrew to a region near the desert, to a village called Ephraim, where he stayed with his disciples.

55. When it was almost time for the Jewish Passover, many went up from the country to Jerusalem for their ceremonial cleansing before the Passover.
56. They kept looking for Jesus, and as they stood in the temple area they asked one another, What do you think? Isn't he coming to the Feast at all?
57. But the chief priests and Pharisees had given orders that if anyone found out where Jesus was, he should report it so that they might arrest him.

In this narrative, which is not in Mark, Jesus is in hiding when he goes to Jerusalem for Passover. In this narrative, it makes sense that the Chief Priests and Pharisees depend on Judas, or someone, to locate and identify him. However, note that there is a jump in the logic between lines 53 and 54. Caiaphas starts to plot against Jesus and Jesus starts to hide. But how does Jesus know that Caiaphas is out to get him? This indicates that John too is condensing the original story.

A third piece of evidence that Mark is working from two different texts is the two moods of Jesus before his arrest. Let us take a moment to study this.

The Schizoid Jesus

> On this Mount of Olives, vigil is futile, the mind recalls and approves the sleeping Apostles. Were they really wrong? They nonetheless had their revelation.
>
> Albert Camus[212]

The two different texts that Mark used for the last section of his narrative are evident in the two different moods of Jesus—calm in some scenes and wildly emotional in others. Note how calm and controlled Jesus is with Peter at the Mount of Olives and how emotional he is with Peter at Gethsemane. First, here is the Mount of Olives scene:

14:22. While they were eating, Jesus took bread, gave thanks and broke it, and gave it to his disciples, saying, Take it; this is my body.
23. Then he took the cup, gave thanks and offered it to them, and they all drank from it.
24. This is my blood of the covenant, which is poured out for many, he said to them.

25. I tell you the truth, I will not drink again of the fruit of the vine until that day when I drink it anew in the kingdom of God.
26. When they had sung a hymn, they went out to the Mount of Olives.
27. You will all fall away, Jesus told them, for it is written: 'I will strike the shepherd, and the sheep will be scattered.'
28. But after I have risen, I will go ahead of you into Galilee.
29. Peter declared, Even if all fall away, I will not.
30. I tell you the truth, Jesus answered, today—yes, tonight—before the cock crows twice you yourself will disown me three times.
31. But Peter insisted emphatically, Even if I have to die with you, I will never disown you. And all the others said the same.

This is a Philosophical, Zen Jesus totally accepting of his fate. Contrast this with the hysterical Jesus at Gethsemane:

14:32. They went to a place called Gethsemane, and Jesus said to his disciples, Sit here while I pray.
33. He took Peter, James and John along with him, and he began to be deeply distressed and troubled.
34. My soul is overwhelmed with sorrow to the point of death, he said to them. Stay here and keep watch.
35. Going a little farther, he fell to the ground and prayed that if possible the hour might pass from him.
36. Abba, Father, he said, everything is possible for you. Take this cup from me. Yet not what I will, but what you will.
37. Then he returned to his disciples and found them sleeping. Simon, he said to Peter, are you asleep? Could you not keep watch for one hour?
38. Watch and pray so that you will not fall into temptation. The spirit is willing, but the body is weak.
39. Once more he went away and prayed the same thing.
40. When he came back, he again found them sleeping, because their eyes were heavy. They did not know what to say to him.
41. Returning the third time, he said to them, Are you still sleeping and resting? Enough! The hour has come. Look, the Son of Man is betrayed into the hands of sinners.
42. Rise! Let us go! Here comes my betrayer!

One might say that Jesus was drunk from the wine and that explains his schizophrenic behavior, calm and accepting at one moment, scared and angry the next. The Zen Jesus suddenly turns into the Passionate Jesus. The simpler explanation is that the two different Jesus characters in these two scenes belong to two different texts that Mark has patched together.

Notice that the scene on the Mount of Olives and the scene at Gethsemane[213] are fragments of two longer scenes. Mark tells us nothing about Jesus at the Mount of Olives. The exchange he has with Peter could just as well have taken place at the Passover supper or at Gethsemane. There was seemingly a text with something happening at the Mount of Olives at this point, but Mark has cut the action there entirely. The scene at Gethsemane comes from a different text and has also been edited by Mark. Notice that Jesus takes Peter, James and John with him to go pray away from the disciples, and then returns to his disciples. He finds Peter sleeping with the disciples. Did Peter slip away without telling Jesus and rejoin the snoozing disciples? There was some deeper interaction in the text between Jesus and his three top disciples that has been cut. While we cannot be sure that Mark, and not some later editor, was the one that cut it, it seems the best guess at the moment. We can, at least for the moment, give Mark the credit for the ragged editing of the second scene at Gethsemane and the complete censoring of the first scene on the Mount of Olives. Mark himself probably introduced the disciples sleeping motif. It is related to the "too late" motif which we find in other places in Mark (e.g. Jesus' visit to the temple and the women's late visit to the tomb).

In any case, Mark has apparently cut material between the top disciples and Jesus from the Gethsemane scene which indicates that the scene must have existed in some form before him. He has also cut out entirely the action in the Mount of Olives scene. But the fact that he mentions it strongly suggests that it was included in other material. One senses that Mark wrote by going between the two texts, taking just what he wanted from one, and then the other. He made changes to both, thus creating his own narrative.

Crowing Cocks

Mark's handling of the material has to be seen in contrast with John and what he has preserved of the original material. Jesus' prediction of Peter's betrayal differs significantly in the two texts. Here is Mark's handling:

> 14:30. I tell you the truth, Jesus answered, today—yes, tonight—before the cock crows twice you yourself will disown me three times.
> 31. But Peter insisted emphatically, Even if I have to die with you, I will never disown you. And all the others said the same.

John has:

> 13:36. Simon Peter asked him, Lord, where are you going? Jesus replied, Where I am going, you cannot follow now, but you will follow later.

37. Peter asked, Lord, why can't I follow you now? I will lay down my life for you.
38. Then Jesus answered, Will you really lay down your life for me? I tell you the truth, before the cock crows, you will disown me three times!

John has the cock crowing once and Mark has the cock crowing twice. This may not seem like a big change, but it really is. In John's text the phrase "before the cock crows" is a poetical way of saying "Night." Peter will betray Jesus three times before the night is over. Mark is referring to the specific scene which he will introduce later in which a real living cock crows twice and Peter disowns him three times in the space of the two cock crows. In other words, the cock is a metaphorical expression in John for the "morning" and a metaphorical expression in Mark meaning "a very short period of time".

Now, in Mark, Peter disowns Jesus three times. Here they are:

14.53. They took Jesus to the high priest, and all the chief priests, elders and teachers of the law came together.
54. Peter followed him at a distance, right into the courtyard of the high priest. There he sat with the guards and warmed himself at the fire . . .

14.66. While Peter was below in the courtyard, one of the servant girls of the high priest came by.
67. When she saw Peter warming himself, she looked closely at him. You also were with that Nazarene, Jesus, she said.
68. But he denied it. I don't know or understand what you're talking about, he said, and went out into the entrance.
69. When the servant girl saw him there, she said again to those standing around, This fellow is one of them.
70. Again he denied it. After a little while, those standing near said to Peter, Surely you are one of them, for you are a Galilean.
71. He began to call down curses on himself, and he swore to them, I don't know this man you're talking about.
72. Immediately the cock crowed the second time. Then Peter remembered the word Jesus had spoken to him: Before the cock crows twice you will disown me three times. And he broke down and wept.

We have the second cock crow in this narrative but not the first. It is evident that the first cock crow took place at the time the servant girl of the High Priest came by at the beginning of the scene.

The three betrayals in Mark are 1) in the courtyard of the high priest, a servant girl says he was with "that Nazarene," 2) at the entrance, the servant girl repeats to others the charge, and 3) again at the entrance, others ask him because he is a Galilean. Notice the movement here of Peter is from inside the palace (in the courtyard) to outside by the entrance.

Here is the version of the denial in *John*:

> 18:15. Simon Peter and another disciple were following Jesus. Because this disciple was known to the high priest, he went with Jesus into the high priest's courtyard,
>
> 16. but Peter had to wait outside at the door. The other disciple, who was known to the high priest, came back, spoke to the girl on duty there and brought Peter in.
>
> 17. You are not one of his disciples, are you? the girl at the door asked Peter. He replied, I am not.
>
> 18. It was cold, and the servants and officials stood round a fire they had made to keep warm. Peter also was standing with them, warming himself...
>
> 18:25. As Simon Peter stood warming himself, he was asked, You are not one of his disciples, are you? He denied it, saying, I am not.
>
> 26. One of the high priest's servants, a relative of the man whose ear Peter had cut off, challenged him, Didn't I see you with him in the olive grove?
>
> 27. Again Peter denied it, and at that moment a cock[214] began to crow.

First we must note that the cock crowing here in John is out of place. As mentioned before, in John's Gospel, the phrase "cock crow" just means "sunrise" It is not a literal cock crow. It was just an idiom that Jesus used.

In Mark, it makes sense. Peter starts to weep when he hears the cock crow, so the cock crow brings about a realization on Peter's part that he has betrayed Jesus. Here there is no reaction by Peter to the cock crow. The cock crow here serves no narrative function. The listener already understands that it is night and Peter has betrayed Jesus. The cock crowing is superfluous and adds nothing to our understanding. Whoever added it was just trying to harmonize the two gospels.

Note how the cock only crows once here. Here are the three denials in John: 1) ambiguous location, probably at the door but possibly inside: the girl at the door asks if he is a disciple, 2) inside by fire of servant or official: someone asks if he is a disciple, 3) same place: someone who saw Peter in the Olive Grove asks if Peter was with him.

Notice the reversals. Mark has the servant girl ask twice and a presumably male bystander ask once. John has the servant girl ask once and the bystanders ask twice.

Mark has Peter asked first inside the courtyard once and outside at the gate twice. John has Peter asked outside once, and then asked twice inside.

In Mark, Peter denies three times that he is a Nazarene. This is slightly different than denying Jesus. It indicates that Mark sees Jesus as a Nazarene. For Mark, if you are a follower of Jesus, you are a Nazarene (a specific Jesus sect). It seems that John has more closely observed the actual disowning of Jesus.

Now, note that the last disowning in John is of a completely different sort. Peter disowns being on the Mount of Olives. This is not a disowning of Jesus. It is simply saying that a bystander did not see him with Jesus. If I say that you did not see me with Gandhi in Cleveland, then I am certainly not disowning Gandhi, but simply saying I was not with him on a specific occasion.

Also, why is the relative of the servant with the ear cut off merely asking "Didn't I see you with him in the olive grove?" Should he not be saying, "Didn't I see you cutting off the ear of my relative?" How could this man be there at the capture of Jesus and not notice that his relative's ear had been cut off?

But we know that there has to be three disownings in John for the prophesy of Jesus to come true. Where is the third disowning in John?

The fact that Mark has the serving girl accuse Peter twice is the key. This should actually count as one disowning. It is really just him repeating twice to the servant girl that he is not a Nazarene. John only has two disownings to the girl servant and the bystander. The conversation with the servant is a denial and not a disowning.

What seems to have happened is that John has two very casual disownings. Mark has changed them into three. We may note that Mark's statement that Peter will disown Jesus three times before the cock crows twice is also curious. It would make more dramatic sense for Peter to disown Jesus three time before the cock crows three times, with the cock crowing each time for dramatic effect. What explains all these curiosities?

Apparently, in the original text, we have Jesus saying to Peter that he will disown him twice before the cock crows (i.e "sunrise"). Since there are only two actual disownings in the text, we can be sure that originally Jesus just said that Peter would disown him twice before the cock crows. Mark is establishing his Jesus-rose-on-the-third-day motif in order to explain the line about Jesus rebuilding the temple on the third day and make it refer to the rising of Jesus. Mark is trying to tell us that Jesus had some kind of preference for the number three. Therefore he changes the number of disownings by Peter from two to three by repeating the first disowning twice. That is why we find three disownings in Mark and only two disownings in John, which follows the original.

Mark has in fact made two changes to the text that was before him. He has changed the two disownings into three and the one cock crows into two. We may examine these changes more closely. The difference between how Mark uses the term "cock crows twice" (a very short difference of time) and the original use of the term "cock crows" (sunrise) in the original text is unusual. One may suspect that Mark was changing the meaning of Jesus' words from "you will betray me very soon," to "you will betray me very quickly." But it is hard to see what Mark really gains by doing this. Telling someone that they will soon disown you makes sense, telling someone that they will disown you rapidly makes almost no sense. Conceivably, twenty years later, Peter could have heard the cock crow, disowned Jesus three times, and heard the cock crow again. This would have fulfilled the prophecy. For Mark, the fact that the disownings happen the same night is entirely coincidental. However, in the original, it must happen the same night in order for the prediction to come true. The change is not one that anyone would consciously make and it drastically weakens the dramatic and immediate nature of the prediction. It seems most likely that Mark did not make this change deliberately.

This leaves us with only one explanation for the change: Mark was translating. This tale must have been in another language and Mark did not understand the cock crow idiom as meaning "sunrise". As often happens when a person translates from another language the idiomatic use of the term is mistaken for a literal use. Mark mistook the idiomatic use of cock crowing ("sunrise") for a real cock crowing. He translated as best he could. He supposed somehow that the two disownings somehow meant two cock crows.

We know that Mark wrote in Greek. This means the text that he was translating was almost certainly in Aramaic, the other major language in the region at the time. Since John includes the prediction of Peter's denial in a long Passover Supper Speech, it is evident that this comes from what we have been calling the *Passover Gospel*. It seems most probable that the *Passover Gospel* was originally written in Aramaic and Mark was translating it into his Gospel.

This allows us some conjectural insights into Mark and his community. It was a primarily Greek speaking community that knew little Aramaic. The Greek *Preparation Day Gospel* was the Gospel they knew, possibly written by their founder, but they were aware of the Aramaic *Passover Gospel* used by the Nazarenes. Mark was ordered (or perhaps paid) to do a translation that combined the two. It must have been clear to Mark that the *Preparation Day Gospel* contradicted the *Passover Gospel*, and was probably written in opposition to it. He also knew that his translating abilities were not that great. The secrecy motifs probably reflect the fact that Mark was working secretly on writing the text, possibly at night, and like Jesus' disciples having difficulty staying awake. The fear motifs also reflect his fear of failure, or of being found out as a fraud in his translation work. The scene that Mark apparently made up of Jesus wishing that he did not have to drink from the cup perhaps reflected his own feelings about his assignment, "Father, if thou are willing, remove this cup from me."

Why is Mary in the Courtyard of the High Priest?

As presented in *John*, Peter's disownings are not real disownings of Jesus. These are charade disownings of Jesus so that Peter can get into Annas' courtyard, go to the fire, and keep from freezing to death. But in Mark, Peter leaves the courtyard, so it seems like a real disowning. John's text with its faux disownings must be the original. After all, Peter has seen Jesus talking with Moses and Elijah. It is unthinkable that he would disown Jesus after seeing him talk with Moses and Elijah. It would especially be inappropriate for Peter to disown him just a few minutes after swearing he would never do it. In fact, it appears that Peter defended Jesus with a sword at his arrest, so why would he be disowning him now, a few moments later? There is nothing that accounts for Peter's change of heart towards Jesus. It is true that Jesus has been arrested, but Peter left his former life to follow Jesus wherever he might go, braving thirst, hunger, poverty and hostile crowds for Jesus. It cannot be imagined that his sudden arrest would affect Peter's love for Jesus.

If we take Peter's disownings as simply being his way of getting into the courtyard, we see the beauty of the original writing. This is a wonderfully clever way of getting Peter to fulfill the prophecy (disowning Jesus) without him even realizing that he has fulfilled it. Only the audience realizes that Jesus knew that Peter would say the words disowning him. This scene displays wit, cleverness and style. But there is something else about this scene even more important to notice. It is this line from John:

> Simon Peter and another disciple were following Jesus. Because this disciple was known to the high priest, she went with Jesus into the high priest's courtyard, but Peter had to wait outside at the door.

At this point, Simon Peter and Mary are following Jesus and according to the Gospels of Mark and John, Jesus is under arrest. But compare the two Gospels of Mark and John on this point.

> Mark 14.53. They took Jesus to the high priest, and all the chief priests, elders and teachers of the law came together.
> 54. Peter followed him at a distance, right into the courtyard of the high priest. There he sat with the guards and warmed himself at the fire....

> John 18:15. Simon Peter and another disciple were following Jesus. Because this disciple was known to the high priest, he went with Jesus into the high priest's courtyard,
> 16. but Peter had to wait outside at the door. The other disciple, who was known to the high priest, came back, spoke to the girl on duty there and brought Peter in.

THE EVOLUTION OF CHRISTS AND CHRISTIANIES

Mark has eliminated John's "other disciple." John says, "He went with Jesus into the high priest's courtyard. If Jesus was under arrest why would they let "the other disciple" into the courtyard with him?

Mark just has Peter waltz right into the courtyard. He sits with the guards. But what are the guards there for if not to keep out potential terrorists like Peter? Mark has to allow Mark to walk in by himself because he has eliminated the "other disciple" from the text. In John, the "other disciple" functions to let Mark into the courtyard of the high priest.

Who is John's "other disciple?" We can immediately eliminate the poor Galilean fishermen like Andrew, James and John. They would hardly have influence at the home of the high priest. Also John has no reason not to name them. John tells us who this "other disciple" with Peter was in another scene where he mentions "the other disciple."

1. Early on the first day of the week, while it was still dark, Mary Magdalene went to the tomb and saw that the stone had been removed from the entrance.
2. So she came running to Simon Peter and the other disciple, the one Jesus loved, and said, They have taken the Lord out of the tomb, and we don't know where they have put him!
3. So Peter and the other disciple started for the tomb.

It seems that there are three people in this scene, Mary, Peter and "the other disciple." This is due to the punctuation. When we put in a period where it naturally belongs, and change the "we" to "I," we find only two characters[215].

1. Early on the first day of the week, while it was still dark, Mary Magdalene went to the tomb and saw that the stone had been removed from the entrance.
2. So she came running to Simon Peter. And the other disciple, the one Jesus loved, and said, They have taken the Lord out of the tomb, and I don't know where they have put him!
3. So Peter and the other disciple started for the tomb.

The problem in the text of Mark of having an unguarded guarded courtyard results from his eliminating "the other disciple," Mary, from the scene.

John might change the identity of Mary, but he at lest keeps her function of getting Peter through the gate intact. This tells us that John is closer to the original text here, and the statement "he went with Jesus" into the high priest's courtyard was in the original, only it read, "*she* went with Jesus."

The text indicates that unlike Peter who was following, Mary went at the same time with Jesus into the courtyard. Why would she just accompany the arrested Jesus into the courtyard? How could Jesus be under arrest and Mary be walking alongside him?

There is a scene at the end of John that has never made any sense. Understanding this scene, we can now unravel the mystery of why Mary accompanies Jesus into the high priest's courtyard.

> 21.15. When they had finished eating, Jesus said to Simon Peter, "Simon son of John, do you truly love me more than these?"
> "Yes, Lord," he said, "you know that I love you."
> Jesus said, "Feed my lambs."
>
> 16. Again Jesus said, "Simon son of John, do you truly love me?"
> He answered, "Yes, Lord, you know that I love you."
> Jesus said, "Take care of my sheep."
>
> 17. The third time he said to him, "Simon son of John, do you love me?" Peter was hurt because Jesus asked him the third time, "Do you love me?" He said, "Lord, you know all things; you know that I love you."
>
> 18. Jesus said, "Feed my sheep. I tell you the truth, when you were younger you dressed yourself and went where you wanted; but when you are old you will stretch out your hands, and someone else will dress you and lead you where you do not want to go."
>
> 19. Jesus said this to indicate the kind of death by which Peter would glorify God. Then he said to him, "Follow me!"
>
> 20. Peter turned and saw that the disciple whom Jesus loved was following them. (This was the one who had leaned back against Jesus at the supper and had said, "Lord, who is going to betray you?")
>
> 21. When Peter saw him, he asked, "Lord, what about him?"
>
> 22 Jesus answered, "If I want him to remain alive[216] until I return, what is that to you? You must follow me."

For John, who was probably gay, the rewriting of the scene this way made sense. He gets to have a love scene between two men. He does this by making the scene take place outside any story context, as just a visit by the ghostly Jesus and his Earthly lover and disciple Peter. But for us trying to get to the original, it is perfectly obvious that this scene is a farewell between two very living lovers. It is a scene that fits perfectly as a farewell speech between Jesus and Mary before his arrest.

Reconstruction of Farewell Scene

> When they had finished eating,
> Jesus said to Mary, "Mary daughter of _____[217], do you truly love me more than these?"

"Yes, Lord," she said, "you know that I love you."

Jesus said, "Feed my lambs."

Again Jesus said, "Mary, daughter of _____, do you truly love me?"

She answered, "Yes, Lord, you know that I love you."

Jesus said, "Take care of my sheep."

The third time he said to her, "Mary, daughter of _____, do you love me?"

Mary was hurt because Jesus asked her the third time, "Do you love me?" She said, "Lord, you know all things; you know that I love you."

Jesus said, "Feed my sheep. I tell you the truth, when you were younger you dressed yourself and went where you wanted; but when you are old you will stretch out your hands, and someone else will dress you and lead you where you do not want to go."

Jesus said this to indicate the kind of death by which he would glorify God. Then he said to her, "Follow me!"

Mary, the disciple whom Jesus loved, turned and saw Peter was following them. Mary was the one whose breast Jesus had leaned back against,[218] at the supper when Peter said, "Lord, who is going to betray you?"

When Peter saw her, he asked, "Lord, what about her?"

Jesus answered, "If I want her to follow me and you to remain until I return, what is that to you? Don't follow me[219].

Simon Peter followed Mary and Jesus. Because this disciple was known to the high priest, she went with Jesus into the high priest's courtyard, but Peter had to wait outside at the door.

As we reconstruct this scene, we have to add the material Mark has inserted arbitrarily at the Mount of Olives of Jesus telling Peter that he will disown him. Here is the scene from book 13.

36. Simon Peter asked him, Lord, where are you going? Jesus replied, Where I am going, you cannot follow now, but you will follow later.
37. Peter asked, Lord, why can't I follow you now? I will lay down my life for you.
38. Then Jesus answered, Will you really lay down your life for me? I tell you the truth, before the cock crows, you will disown me three times!

This text certainly belongs to the beginning of the courtyard scene which is actually the scene in which Peter disowns Jesus three times. Inserting it into the scene, we get this reconstruction:

Reconstruction of Farewell Scene #2

When they had finished eating,

Jesus said to Mary, "Mary daughter of _____[220], do you truly love me more than these?"

"Yes, Lord," she said, "you know that I love you."

Jesus said, "Feed my lambs."

Again Jesus said, "Mary, daughter of _____, do you truly love me?"

She answered, "Yes, Lord, you know that I love you."

Jesus said, "Take care of my sheep."

The third time he said to her, "Mary, daughter of _____, do you love me?"

Mary was hurt because Jesus asked her the third time, "Do you love me?" She said, "Lord, you know all things; you know that I love you."

Jesus said, "Feed my sheep.

He said to her, "Follow me!"

Mary, the disciple whom Jesus loved, turned and saw Peter was following them. Mary was the one whose breast Jesus had leaned back against, at the supper when she asked, "Lord, who is going to betray you?"

When Peter saw Mary, he asked Jesus, "Lord, where are you going?"

Jesus replied, "Where I am going, you cannot follow now, but you will follow later.

Peter asked, "Lord, why can't I follow you now."

Jesus said, "I tell you the truth, when I was younger I dressed myself and went where I wanted; but now that I am old I will stretch out my hands, and someone else will dress me and lead me where I do not want to go[221]."

Jesus said this to indicate the kind of death by which he would glorify God.

Peter said, "I will lay down my life for you."

Then Jesus answered, Will you really lay down your life for me? I tell you the truth, before the cock crows, you will disown me three times!

Peter asked, "Lord, what about her?"

Jesus answered, "If I want her to follow me and you to remain until I return, what is that to you? Don't follow me.

Simon Peter followed Mary and Jesus.

Because this disciple was known to the high priest, she went with Jesus into the high priest's courtyard, but Peter had to wait outside at the door.

Peter Gets an Earful

The Gospel of John has Mary, Peter and Jesus entering the Palace of Annas, the father-in-law of the Chief Priest Caiaphas (John 18:13). Annas then binds Jesus and sends him to Caiaphas. Mark, on the other hand has Jesus led directly to the house of the High Priest, whom we may assume is Caiaphas. There is no meeting with Annas in Mark.

This makes sense in Mark, as Jesus would be taken to Caiaphas, and not his father-in-law, Annas. The meeting with Annas makes no sense if Jesus was under arrest. They would have taken him directly to the Chief Priest Caiaphas and the other officials. Annas, as father-in-law of the Chief Priest had no judicial function. When we tie this fact to the fact of Mary accompanying Jesus into the courtyard, we understand that Jesus was not under arrest when he went to see Annas. It is Annas who arrests Jesus, binds him and brings him to Caiaphas. *The Passover Gospel* had quite a different story than we find in John's revised version.

What we are getting here in the *Gospel of John* is a suggestion of a much more intricate plot against Jesus. This is not just a simple case of Judas leading a pact of troops and officials to his secret hiding place in a garden on Mount Olive. What has happened apparently in this narrative is that a free Jesus goes willingly to Annas, the father-in-law of the High Priest Caiaphas.

But the evidence we have so far for this earlier tale of Jesus is 1) the perfect fit for the Mary and Jesus farewell scene before going to Annas, 2) the senselessness of the arrested Jesus being brought to Annas and 3) the out of place line preserved by John of Mary entering Annas' courtyard with Jesus. Can we find more evidence? Let's examine John's text again:

> 18.10. Then Simon Peter, who had a sword, drew it and struck the high priest's servant, cutting off his right ear. (The servant's name was Malchus.)
>
> 11. Jesus commanded Peter, Put your sword away! Shall I not drink the cup the Father has given me?
>
> 12. Then the detachment of soldiers with its commander and the Jewish officials arrested Jesus. They bound him
>
> 13. and brought him first to Annas, who was the father-in-law of Caiaphas, the high priest that year.
>
> 14. Caiaphas was the one who had advised the Jews that it would be good if one man died for the people.
>
> 15. Simon Peter and another disciple were following Jesus. Because this disciple was known to the high priest, he went with Jesus into the high priest's courtyard,

The flow seems natural. But we must examine the scene more closely. Peter has just cut off the ear of the High Priest's servant. What is the reaction? Jesus commands him to put away his sword. The soldiers arrest Jesus and Peter follows him. What is wrong with this scene? We are so use to hearing this scene that we do not even think twice about the incredibility of it. Peter has just "cut off the ear" of the High Priest's servant, Malchus. Hello, excuse me, but is this not a crime? How can Peter remain free and follow Jesus after this? So we may add this fourth point to our list of indicators of a changed text. We now have 1) farewell scene fits, 2) pointlessness of bringing Jesus to Annas, 3) Mary or "the other disciple" enters courtyard unchecked with the arrested Jesus, and 4) Peter slices an ear and nobody stops him. We may add a fifth. Why does Peter pick on the poor servant of the High Priest? I mean with dozens and perhaps hundreds of soldiers around, why does Peter attack an unarmed slave? What did the unlucky fellow do to deserve it?

We may answer this by remembering our reconstructed scene in Annas' courtyard. Here's John's take on it:

> 18. 26. One of the high priest's servants, a relative of the man whose ear Peter had cut off, challenged him, Didn't I see you with him in the olive grove?
> 27. Again Peter denied it,

It seems a bit of a coincidence that Peter meets two of the high priests servants in the same night and they are relatives. Here is Mark's take on it:

> 14.70. After a little while, those standing near said to Peter, Surely you are one of them, for you are a Galilean.
> 71. He began to call down curses on himself, and he swore to them, I don't know this man you're talking about.

We can combine these two accounts with Peter's swordplay we get the original version of the scene, as it takes place in the courtyard of the high priest.

Reconstruction of Ear Cutting Scene

> One of the high priest's servants said, "Didn't I see you with him in the olive grove. Again Peter denied it, "I don't know this man you're talking about." The Servant began to call down curses on him. Then Simon Peter, who had a sword, drew it and struck the high priest's servant, cutting off his right ear. The servant's name was Malchus[222]. 18:11. Jesus commanded Peter, Put your sword away! Shall I not drink the cup the Father has given me?

The reconstruction fits perfectly with the actions of both Peter and the servant now making sense. But what is Jesus doing here? This seems to interrupt the action. Here is John's description of the arrest scene on Mount Olive before this point.

18.4. Jesus, knowing all that was going to happen to him, went out and asked them, Who is it you want?

5. Jesus of Nazareth, they replied. I am he, Jesus said. (And Judas the traitor was standing there with them.)

6. When Jesus said, I am he, they drew back and fell to the ground.

7. Again he asked them, Who is it you want? And they said, Jesus of Nazareth.

8. I told you that I am he, Jesus answered. If you are looking for me, then let these men go.

9. This happened so that the words he had spoken would be fulfilled: I have not lost one of those you gave me.

Notice the slight contradiction between the last lines. Jesus says, "If you are looking for me, then let these men go," but the words of the prophecy are "I have not lost one of those you gave me." The use of the plural "men" and the singular "one of these" is enough of a contradiction, for us to seek a better fit for the lines. We saw before, in the tomb scene, that someone had changed Mary's singular "I" to the plural "we." Perhaps, this is another case of turning the singular to the plural to obscure the meaning. Jesus did not say "men," but "man." Jesus said, "If you are looking for me, then let this man go." If this was the original line, it would come just after the cutting off of the servant's ear by Peter. The "man" refers to Peter. Thus we may reconstruct the scene in Annas' courtyard this way:

Reconstruction of Courtyard Scene

One of the high priest's servants said, "Didn't I see you with him in the olive grove. Again Peter denied it, "I don't know this man you're talking about." The Servant began to call down curses on him. Then Simon Peter, who had a sword, drew it and struck the high priest's servant, cutting off his right ear. The servant's name was Malchus[223]. Jesus went out and commanded Peter, "Put your sword away! Shall I not drink the cup the Father has given me? If you are looking for me, then let this man go." This happened so that the words he had spoken would be fulfilled: I have not lost one of those you gave me[224].

And Judas the traitor was standing there with them.
Jesus asked them, "Who is it you want?"
"Jesus of Nazareth," they replied.
"I am he," Jesus said
When Jesus said, "I am he," they drew back and fell to the ground.
Again he asked them, "Who is it you want?"
And they said, "Jesus of Nazareth."
"I told you that I am he,"

The last part of this does not quite work. The mention of Judas the traitor is pointless here. It does make a point if Jesus is addressing him. Therefore, we may change this to:

> And Judas the traitor was standing there with them
> Jesus, asked him, "Who is it you want?" "Jesus of Nazareth," He replied.
> "I am he," Jesus said.
> When Jesus said, "I am he," he drew back and fell to the ground.
> Again he asked officials and servants "Who is it you want?"
> And they said, "Jesus of Nazareth."
> "I am he,"
> They drew back and fell to the ground.

Now we can see the parallelism in the scene. Peter disowns being a follower of Jesus two times by saying, "I am not he[225]." Jesus admits to being Jesus by saying "I am he." two times.

There is still one minor problem with the reconstruction. The name Jesus of Nazareth would not have the power to make people fall to the ground. The only name that would have that power would be Jesus, the Christ. We may assume that John and Mark were trying to associate Jesus of Nazareth with Jesus the Christ when they made the name change. We may change the name back and reconstruct the whole scene.

Reconstruction of Jesus's Capture

> Simon Peter and Mary were following Jesus. Because this disciple was known to the high priest, she went with Jesus into the high priest's courtyard, but Peter had to wait outside at the door. It was cold, and the servants and officials stood round a fire they had made to keep warm. Mary, who was known to the high priest, came back, spoke to the girl on duty there.
> "You are his disciple, aren't you?" the girl at the door asked Peter.
> He replied, "I am not he."
> As Simon Peter stood warming himself, he was asked, "You are not his disciple, are you not?"
> He denied it, saying, "I am not he."
> One of the high priest's servants said, "Didn't I see you with him in the olive grove." Again Peter denied it, "I don't know this man you're talking about." The Servant began to call down curses on him. Then Simon Peter, who had a sword, drew it and struck the high priest's servant, cutting off his right ear.

> Jesus went out and commanded, "Peter, Put your sword away! Shall I not drink the cup the Father has given me?
>
> He said to the soldiers, "If you are looking for me, then let this man go."
>
> And Judas was standing there with them. Jesus asked him, "Who is it you want?" "Jesus the Christ," He replied.
>
> "I am he," Jesus said.
>
> When Jesus said, "I am he," he drew back and fell to the ground.,
>
> Again he asked them, "Who is it you want? And they said, Jesus the Christ."
>
> "I told you that I am he,"
>
> They drew back and fell to the ground.

I think the reconstruction really works because of the parallelism between Peter's rejection of Jesus and Jesus of Nazareth's contrastingly strong acceptance of his role as Jesus Christ. When asked if he is a disciple, Peter says, "I am not he." When asked if he is Jesus the Christ, Jesus answers, "I am he." One may ask why John would break up such a powerful scene in Annas' courtyard and move the second half to Mount Olive. I will give an answer in a moment, but first we need to complete, the reconstruction of this original arrest of Jesus. There is a problem in this reconstruction in that at the beginning we are twice told that the "other disciple" (Mary) was known to the high priest.

> **John 18:15. Simon Peter and another disciple were following Jesus. Because this disciple was known to the high priest, he went with Jesus into the high priest's courtyard,**
> 16. **but Peter had to wait outside at the door. The other disciple, who was known to the high priest, came back, spoke to the girl on duty there and brought Peter in.**

This information may be repeated, but it would not be repeated so quickly. Another scene would logically intervene. This would be the interrogation of Jesus scene that we find preserved in both Mark and John.

> 18:19. Meanwhile, the high priest questioned Jesus about his disciples and his teaching.
> 20. I have spoken openly to the world, Jesus replied. I always taught in synagogues or at the temple, where all the Jews come together. I said nothing in secret.
> 21. Why question me? Ask those who heard me. Surely they know what I said.
> 22. When Jesus said this, one of the officials near by struck him in the face. Is this the way you answer the high priest? he demanded.

> 23. If I said something wrong, Jesus replied, testify as to what is wrong. But if I spoke the truth, why did you strike me?

We may note that Mark has placed a summary of these lines (Mark 14:49) at the time of Jesus' arrest on Mount Olive:

> 14.46. The men seized Jesus and arrested him.
> 47. Then one of those standing near drew his sword and struck the servant of the high priest, cutting off his ear.
> 48. Am I leading a rebellion, said Jesus, that you have come out with swords and clubs to capture me?
> 49. Every day I was with you, teaching in the temple courts, and you did not arrest me. But the Scriptures must be fulfilled.
> 50. Then everyone deserted him and fled.

Jesus' protestation that he taught in the temple without being arrested is quite out of place here. Mark must have realized that an arrest in public would have caused a scandal, while an arrest in Jesus' hiding place would be quite different. Mark wants to make the point that Jesus was not afraid of arrest, but since he has eliminated the arrest scene at Annas' house, the line just becomes silly and inappropriate.

On the other hand, where John has the line, as a response to Annas' questioning on his teachings, the point is well taken and important. Jesus made no secret of his teachings and was a public figure. We may assume that this was in the original *Passover Gospel*. We may add this to our reconstruction:

Reconstruction of Jesus's Capture #2

> Simon Peter was following Mary and Jesus. Because this disciple was known to the high priest, she went with Jesus into the high priest's courtyard, but Peter had to wait outside at the door. Meanwhile, the high priest questioned Jesus about his disciples and his teaching.
>
> "I have spoken openly to the world, "Jesus replied. "I always taught in synagogues or at the temple, where all the Jews come together. I said nothing in secret. Why question me? Ask those who heard me. Surely they know what I said."
>
> When Jesus said this, one of the officials near by struck him in the face. "Is this the way you answer the high priest?" he demanded.
>
> "If I said something wrong, "Jesus replied, "testify as to what is wrong. But if I spoke the truth, why did you strike me?"
>
> It was cold, and the servants and officials stood round a fire they had made to keep warm. Mary, who was known to the high priest,

came back, spoke to the girl on duty there. She went out to bring Peter in.

"You are not his disciple, are you?" the girl at the door asked Peter.

He replied, "I am not he."

As Simon Peter stood warming himself, he was asked, "You are his disciple, are you?"

He denied it, saying, "I am not he."

One of the high priest's servants said, "Didn't I see you with him in the olive grove." Again Peter denied it, "I don't know this man you're talking about."

The Servant began to call down curses on him. Then Simon Peter, who had a sword, drew it and struck the high priest's servant, cutting off his right ear. Jesus went out and commanded, "Peter, Put your sword away! Shall I not drink the cup the Father has given me?"

Turning to the soldiers he said, "If you are looking for me, then let this man go."

And Judas was standing there with them. Jesus asked him, "Who is it you want?" "Jesus the Christ," He replied.

"I am he," Jesus said. When Jesus said, "I am he," he drew back and fell to the ground.,

Again he asked the soldiers, official and servants, "Who is it you want?"

And they said, "Jesus the Christ."

"I told you that I am he."

They drew back and fell to the ground.

The Appearance of Judas and Caiaphas

There are still a number of problems with the scene that suggest a number of changes that still need to be made. We have to figure out how Judas got there. We also have to figure out who came with Judas. Once we figure these out, we will see that perhaps Judas was not in the *Passover Gospel* at all.

Judas' arrival is missing from our reconstruction of the courtyard scene. John's description of the arrival of Judas on the Mount of Olives seems to fit perfectly:

> Now Judas, who betrayed him, knew the place, because Jesus had often met there with his disciples. Judas came to the grove, guiding a detachment of soldiers and some officials from the chief priests and Pharisees. They were carrying torches, lanterns and weapons.

Besides adding Judas, we still have to make a number of changes for the scene to make sense. First we have to make the word "grove" into "house." The description of

Judas as the one "who betrayed him" is unnecessary as it has not happened yet in the story. Thus we get, "Judas knew the place because Jesus had often met there with his disciples." But this seems ridiculous. Why would Jesus be meeting with his disciples at Annas' house. We know that John uses the euphemism "other disciple" for Mary. Perhaps he is using the euphemism "other disciples here for Mary and someone else. The text makes sense if Jesus met there with Mary or Mary and Salome. Mary must be known to the house of Annas. That is what gives her ready access with Jesus. Since John has used the plural (disciples), it is slightly more likely that "Mary and Salome," or Mary and Martha, rather than "Mary" was in the original. But since we do not know who the other disciple might be, we might as well just leave it with him meeting with "Mary."

The scene has another big problem. Who exactly does arrive with Judas. A detachment of soldier appears out of nowhere in the Mount of Olives arrest scene. This means that Jesus was a rebel being hunted. This is not the case in this scene where Jesus has come voluntarily to Annas' house and has taught openly in the Temple. We cannot expect that a Jew, even the High Priests Annas or Caiaphas could just summons a detachment of Roman soldiers at will. Also, they hardly could obey Jesus and refuse to arrest Peter when he cuts off the servant's ear. We can drop them from the scene. The real question is did Judas come with officials from the High Priests and Pharisees or did he come with officials from the High Priests and Servants? One has to ask why the Pharisees would build a fire and not enter. It is more likely we had just "servants" and not "Pharisees" in the original. Mark preserves this fact that the Pharisees were not involved in this scene by saying that a "detachment of soldiers with its commander and the Jewish officials arrested Jesus[226]." It is possible that the writer of *John* was an Essene and anti-Pharisee and added this, but it just as well could have come later.

But why is Judas arriving with a detachment of soldiers, officials and servants? Why would these important people be following Judas who is simply one of the disciples. The answer is they wouldn't. The leader of the pack could only be the High Priest Caiaphas. Caiaphas is the betrayer in this early gospel.

Reconstruction of Jesus's Capture #3

(The lines in bold are text added to make sense.)

> Simon Peter and Mary were following Jesus. Because this disciple was known to the high priest, she went with Jesus into the high priest's courtyard, but Peter had to wait outside at the door. **Jesus went inside the house.**
>
> Caiaphas knew the place because Jesus had often met there with Mary. Caiaphas came to the **house**, guiding a detachment of soldiers

THE EVOLUTION OF CHRISTS AND CHRISTIANIES

and some officials from the chief priests and Servants. They were carrying torches, lanterns and weapons. **The Officials went inside the house**.

Meanwhile, the high priest questioned Jesus about his disciples and his teaching. "I have spoken openly to the world," Jesus replied, "I always taught in synagogues or at the temple, where all the Jews come together. I said nothing in secret. Why question me? Ask those who heard me. Surely they know what I said." When Jesus said this, one of the officials near by struck him in the face. "Is this the way you answer the high priest?" he demanded. "If I said something wrong," Jesus replied, "testify as to what is wrong. But if I spoke the truth, why did you strike me?"

It was cold, and the servants and officials stood round a fire they had made to keep warm. Mary, who was known to the high priest, came back; spoke to the girl on duty there. She brought Peter in.

"You are not his disciple, are you?" the girl at the door asked Peter.

He replied, "I am not he."

As Simon Peter stood warming himself, he was asked, "You are not his disciple, are you?"

He denied it, saying, "I am not he."

One of the high priest's servants said, "Didn't I see you with him in the olive grove." Again Peter denied it, "I don't know this man you're talking about."

The Servant began to call down curses on him. Then Simon Peter, who had a sword, drew it and struck the high priest's servant, cutting off his right ear.

Jesus went out and commanded, "Peter, "Put your sword away! Shall I not drink the cup the Father has given me?

"If you are looking for me, then let this man go."

And Caiaphas the traitor was standing there with them. Jesus asked him, "Who is it you want?"

"Jesus the Christ," he replied.

"I am he," Jesus said.

When Jesus said, "I am he," he drew back and fell to the ground.

Again, he asked the officials, "Who is it you want?"

And they said, "Jesus the Christ."

"I told you that I am he,"

They drew back and fell to the ground.

It is surprising to find that Judas does not arrest or betray Jesus in the *Passover Gospel*. We can understand the logic by which Judas, a disciple of Jesus replaced Caiaphas, who is not even named in Mark. It must have been people with ties to the Jerusalem establishment who rejected the idea of Caiaphas betraying Jesus and named one of Jesus' own disciples as the traitor. Judas does not have any role in any Jesus story, except as a betrayer, so one must assume that he was a purely made up figure. One can imagine that Caiaphas who was high priest for some twenty years still had many supporters in the decades following Jesus' death. Thus it would have been politically expedient to drop the charges of betrayal against Caiaphas and to denounce an unknown disciple as the betrayer.

But the term "betrayer" is especially interesting when used in reference to Caiaphas. It really implies that Caiaphas and Jesus must have had a close relationship at some point. If they had not known each other and agreed on some things, it would have been inappropriate to say that Caiaphas betrayed Jesus. Note in the scene that when asked who it is that he wants, he answers Jesus the Christ. This might suggest that the Jewish High Priest Caiaphas was some sort of proto-Christian. He is stunned when Jesus says that he is the Christ. This would imply that he knew Jesus before hand, but did not know that he was the man called Jesus, the Christ. Caiaphas is looking for Jesus the Christ, He does not suspect the man called Jesus that he knows is the man called Jesus the Christ. How could Caiaphas know Jesus, but not know that he was the man he was looking for called Jesus, the Christ?

Mary, Daughter of Annas, Wife of Caiaphas

I would like to draw attention to two little bits of information in this reconstruction. The first is the statement that Mary was known by the high priest. At first, one may imagine that this is innocent enough. Mary, shown pouring oil on Jesus in one scene, was perhaps a prostitute or concubine. We should remember that this occupation did not have the overwhelmingly negative connotations that we find in large segments of society today. It could indicate an independent, strong and free woman. However, it is another reference that moves me away from that idea. It is the statement that Judas knew Annas' house because Jesus often met there with Mary (*disciples*, in the gospel). It is impossible to imagine Mary as a prostitute meeting a lover in the home of the father-in-law of the High Priest. The suggestion of this line is that Mary lives in the home of Annas and Jesus often visited her there.

But if she lives in the home of Annas, could she be a servant? Possibly. But note that she has the power to go to the girl at the door and have Peter brought in. This would indicate that she is of higher rank than the girl. Let us look at the original lines in John again"

> 18:16. but Peter had to wait outside at the door. The other disciple, who was known to the high priest, came back, spoke to the girl on duty there and brought Peter in.
> 17. You are not one of his disciples, are you? the girl at the door asked Peter. He replied, I am not.

We are given no information about how it was that this disciple was known to the high priest in such a way as to gain entry to his guarded house on the night before Passover. This is extremely strange. How does a newly arrived disciple from Galilee gain such immediate authority in Jerusalem. Might not John want to tell us a bit more about this relationship between the leading Jewish family and the disciples of Jesus. But, in his own way, John does reveal everything to us.

John tells us Annas was the father-in-law of the High Priest Joseph Caiaphas (John 18:13). This is the key to how "the other disciple" can enter the courtyard with Jesus the renegade, the dangerous rebel who is arousing the people of Judea. It is the key to how she could often meet Jesus there. She could go with Jesus into the courtyard because she lived there. Mary, "The other disciple" could only be the daughter of Annas. Joseph Caiaphas married her and thus became the son-in-law of Annas. Mary could not very well meet Jesus at her home, but she could arrange meetings with him at the home of her father-in-law Annas.

The line "Because this disciple was known to the high priest, she went with Jesus into the high priest's courtyard," was originally "Because Mary was the Daughter of the high priest, she went with Jesus into the high priest's courtyard. We can now fill in the blank we had left open, when Jesus addresses Mary in his farewell love speech about taking care of his lambs, He asks, "Mary, daughter of Annas, do you love me?"

Reconstruction of Mary's Identity

> When they had finished eating,
> Jesus said to Mary, "Mary daughter, of Annas, do you truly love me more than these?"
> "Yes, Lord," she said, "you know that I love you."

The Secret Identity of Jesus

The identification of Mary as the daughter of the High Priest Annas and wife of High Priest Caiaphas, forces us to draw a certain conclusion about an identity of Jesus. Let us first review some of the evidence about Mary.

We have a several documents found at Nag Hammadi that expressly claim that she is "the beloved disciple." In the canonical gospels, John is never named as the beloved disciple. The term appears in several scenes involving Mary. Mary is the only disciple to anoint Jesus, literally turn him into the Christ, and the only character to be first at the tomb of Jesus or to see Jesus in all four Gospels. On the other hand, the disciple John is not singled out in any way in any gospel to indicate that he has any special relationship with Jesus. We know that one scene involving the beloved disciple involves a breast which is almost always a sign of femaleness. While Eusebean history offers testimony that John was the beloved disciple, and divides Mary into two characters: whore and mother, none of this testimony can really be reliably traced to much before the third century. In short, all the early evidence, in both canonical and non-canonical gospels point towards Mary as the beloved disciple and none points towards John.

Now, we know that in the Gospel of John, the "beloved disciple" is also referred to as the "other disciple." We are told quite directly that this 'other disciple" has access to the High Priest Annan's Courtyard, can order the gatekeeper to let her friends in, and frequently meets Jesus there for rendezvous that are known to Annan's son-in-law Caiaphas. Our conclusion from this evidence is that Mary can only be Annan's daughter in the original text that the Gospel of John bases itself on.

Now, logically, if Jesus is meeting his beloved Mary, Caiaphas' wife, how can the text say that Caiaphas is a betrayer for arresting Jesus. There is only one circumstance in which this action can be seen as a betrayal. Only if Jesus is the son of Caiaphas can we say that Caiaphas has betrayed him. This explains why Caiaphas faints when he hears that the man he has been looking for, Jesus the Christ, is actually his son.

Let us look more closely at the reconstruction of the courtyard scene.

> Jesus went out and commanded, "Peter, "Put your sword away! Shall I not drink the cup the Father has given me?
> "If you are looking for me, then let this man go."
> And Caiaphas the traitor was standing there with them. Jesus asked him, "Who is it you want?"
> "Jesus, the Christ," he replied.
> "I am he," Jesus said.
> When Jesus said, "I am he," he drew back and fell to the ground.

Note the line, "Shall I not drink the cup the Father has given me," We may see the line as a direct reference to Jesus' father Caiaphas who is standing right there. The term "Father" is not a theological reference to "God," in this context it is a direct reference to Caiaphas who has come to arrest Jesus, the Christ, who happens to be his son. We may suppose it was originally "my father" and was later changed to the rather odd, "the father."

We should note at this point that this is not the first time we have reconstructed the text to eliminate contradictions and found Caiaphas to be the father of Jesus. Recall our reconstruction of the Marys at the Cross scene in the Introduction to this work:

> 25: So the soldiers did this. But standing by the cross of Jesus were his mother, Mary, wife of Caiaphas, and Mary Magdalene.
> 26: When Mary saw his mother, she said to his mother, "Woman, behold, your son!"

27: Then Jesus said to Mary, "Woman, behold, your mother!" And from that hour Mary took her to her own home.

Here too we found Jesus to be the son of Caiaphas. The reconstruction of both the arrest scene and the Marys at the Cross scene were done to resolve certain obvious contradictions in the texts of the two scenes. It was quite accidental and unforeseeable that in the resolving of these contradictions in both cases, it would appear that in each scene, Jesus turns out to be the son of the High Priest Caiaphas. Based on this I am certain that in the original text, the Jesus Christ character was the son of the High Priest Caiaphas.

Summary of Passover Gospel Reconstruction: Mark is Third Generation

From the reconstruction of the courtyard arrest scene, we can see that the Jesus story underwent quite a bit of change before getting to Mark. We may see the change of betrayer from Caiaphas-father of Jesus to Judas disciple of Jesus as indicative of this change. I do not think that Mark made this change but he found it already made in his *Preparation Day Gospel*.

The idea that the high priest arrested Jesus is in some sense an attack on the institution of the high priest. On the other hand the idea that Judas, a member of Jesus' inner circle arrested him is an attack on the followers of Jesus. We may assume that the writers of the *Preparation Gospel* were defenders of the high priest and Jewish institutions.

Now Mark associates Jesus with a group called the Nazarenes in his revised courtyard scene in his gospel. It is hard to know if he put that in or found it there in the *Preparation Gospel*. In any case this association was not in the earlier *Passover Gospel*. From what we know about the Nazarenes from other sources, they were pretty orthodox Jews who adopted Jesus as their Christ at an early stage of the development of Christianities. It is quite probable that the Nazarenes wrote the *Preparation Gospel* in opposition to the group that wrote the Passover Gospel.

It should be noted that the idea of Jesus coming from the originally fictional town of Nazareth postdates Mark. Only the opening line of Mark declares that Jesus was from Nazareth and this is not in all the early manuscripts. Also the early manuscripts vary in their opening line. Because there is no other reference in Mark to Jesus being from Nazareth, we may take this as a second century idea that post dates Mark and derives from an earlier association of Jesus with the Nazarene group.

There is no indication that Mark was part of this Nazarene group and his portrayal of Jesus flouting Jewish laws and customs would suggest that he was not. We may take Mark's gospel as being a third generation Jesus production, coming after the *Passover Gospel* and the *Preparation Day Gospel*. Mark and his gospel represents another group entirely who were revising both texts to meet their own special ideological needs and desires.

Historical Analysis of Joseph Caiaphas and Mary

The evidence so far leads us to a story where Mary and Jesus are lovers. Mary is the wife of Joseph Caiaphas, while Jesus is his son. We may be sure that Mary Magdalene is not Jesus' biological mother in this story, as such an incestuous relationship would have horrified people in the Jewish community. A solution is that Caiaphas was married to a woman named Mary and had a son. Caiaphas later married Annas' daughter named Mary (Magdalene). At this point the son fell in love with the step-mother Mary. The antagonism between Mary (first wife of Caiaphas and mother of the son) and Mary, daughter of Annas, second wife of Caiaphas and lover of the son) must have been intense. This would have made the reconciliation scene between the two of them at the cross infinitely more dramatic than it now appears.

This might seem unbelievable that the early *Passover Gospel* text had Jesus having an affair with his step-mother Mary; however, we have to look more closely at the facts. First, there is no mention of the name of Jesus' mother in the text of *John* and there is no indication that Jesus has a biological mother named Mary. This suggests that the author is hiding the name. Second, remember that according to Jewish customs of the period, high priests married virgins (young girls) who were just around the age of thirteen. The High Priests themselves were often much older. Caiaphas became High Priest sometime between 18 and 26 C.E.[227]. It is possible that he married Mary, the daughter of Annas as a condition of his priesthood. This marriage would cement his position with the powerful family of Annas[228] (Josephus tells us that Annas was the only person to have five sons as High Priests). The *Gospel of Luke* has Jesus born during the census of 6 C.E. Since this directly contradicts the story that King Herod who died in 4 B.C. tried to kill Jesus, we can take this date as coming from another tradition about Jesus. This means that he would be about 13 in 18 C.E. If we assume that Caiaphas got his position as high priest immediately after marrying into Annas' family, this means Jesus was about the same age as Mary when she marries Caiaphas. Caiaphas was probably in his forties by this time, as it is unlikely a much younger man would be considered for the position of high priest. The young Mary would possibly have more in common with Jesus than with Caiaphas.

We have no direct evidence that Caiaphas was married before he married Annas' daughter. But ambitious men often rose in rank at this time by marrying upward. If his first wife did not die, he could easily have divorced her to marry into the family of the Annas, which was the leading Jewish family in Jerusalem outside of King Herod's family. Now, we are not arguing that any of this is real, only that a story involving a step-mother and son relationship and the high priest would be considered plausible at that time, and perhaps not quite so shocking as it appears now.

It is strongly suspected that Caiaphas had a son named Elionaeus who became High Priest in 44-46 C.E. We actually may have his ossuary[229]. We have no way of knowing if he is the son referred to in the *Passover Gospel* text, but it is possible.

Was Mary a Stepmother and Lover of Jesus?

The genealogy of Matthew (1.16) has this line "*16:* And Jacob begat Joseph the husband of Mary, of whom was born Jesus, who is called Christ." Paul David Younan has argued that in the original Aramic, *Orbg*, the word used for husband meant "father," or "male head of the household[230]." Chris Weimer, using very different arguments has suggested that the Greek word for husband *áíänä* had been changed from the Greek word for father *ðáôÝñáò*. Regardless of whether the word was changed from the Greek or Aramaic, we have to consider the real possibility that Joseph was not the husband, but the father of Mary.

There is also the problem that the geneaology which consistently uses the word "beget," *ää ååååíí̧óåí* for sons suddenly switches and says "of whom was born," *åî ç̣ò ååååíí̧çåç ẹ̀ç̣óïûò*. It is possible that this was changed from "Mary whom was married to Jesus." Both Younan and Weimer suggest that Mary was the 6th sixth (#36) in a line from Abraham. But Younan points to three Jewish medieval Hebrew manuscripts which has the name "Avner" inserted between "Abiud" and "Eliachim" in the genealogy. If we assume Mary as the daughter of Joseph, then she is the 42nd or 6th seventh. She would be the end of the 6th seven generations from Abraham and their children. Her child would presumably be the beginning of the seventh generation from Abraham. Obviously the number seven associated in Jewish numerology with the seventh day would have great significance. In this case, we can surmise that the genealogy was developed not to put forward the claim that Jesus was the king (anointed one) of Israel, but that the son of Mary should be.

If the high priest Elionaeus was the son of Mary and Caiaphas, the establishment of Mary from the line of Abraham and David would be necessary to establish his claim to the kingship. Establishing the bloodline of Mary from David would have been especially important in 44 to 46 C.E., when Elionaeus became High Priest because the Jewish King Agrippa had just died.

Josephus describes the death of the new Jewish King Agrippa during this time:

> Now when Agrippa had reigned three years over all Judea, he came to the city Caesarea [. . .] There he exhibited shows in honor of the emperor [. . .] On the second day of the festival, Herod put on a garment made wholly of silver, and of a truly wonderful contexture, and came into the theater early in the morning; at which time the silver of his garment was illuminated by the fresh reflection of the sun's rays upon it. It shone out after a surprising manner, and was so resplendent as to

spread a horror over those that looked intently upon him. At that moment, his flatterers cried out [. . .] that he was a god; and they added, 'Be thou merciful to us; for although we have hitherto reverenced thee only as a man, yet shall we henceforth own thee as superior to mortal nature.'

Upon this the king did neither rebuke them, nor reject their impious flattery. But as he presently afterward looked up, he saw an owl sitting on a certain rope over his head, and immediately understood that this bird was the messenger of ill tidings, as it had once been the messenger of good tidings to him; and he fell into the deepest sorrow. A severe pain also arose in his belly, and began in a most violent manner. He therefore looked upon his friends, and said, 'I, whom you call a god, am commanded presently to depart this life; while Providence thus reproves the lying words you just now said to me; and I, who was by you called immortal, am immediately to be hurried away by death. But I am bound to accept of what Providence allots, as it pleases God; for we have by no means lived ill, but in a splendid and happy manner.'

After he said this, his pain was become violent. Accordingly he was carried into the palace, and the rumor went abroad that he would certainly die in a little time. But the multitude presently sat in sackcloth, with their wives and children, after the law of their country, and besought God for the king's recovery. All places were also full of mourning and lamentation. Now the king rested in a high chamber, and as he saw them below lying prostrate on the ground, he could not himself forbear weeping. And when he had been quite worn out by the pain in his belly for five days, he departed this life, being in the fifty-fourth year of his age, and in the seventh year of his reign[231].

Shortly before he died in 44, King Agrippa had appointed "Elioneus, the son of Cantheras[232]" high priest[233]. Now if Elioneus is the son of Caiaphas, not Cantheras, we can imagine that his situation was not very secure when his benefactor Agrippa suddenly died.

But when it was known that Agrippa was departed this life, the inhabitants of Cesarea and of Sebaste forgot the kindnesses he had bestowed on them, and acted the part of the bitterest enemies; for they cast such reproaches upon the deceased as are not fit to be spoken of; and so many of them as were then soldiers, which were a great number, went to his house, and hastily carried off the statues of this king's daughters, and all at once carried them into the brothel-houses, and when they had set them on the tops of those houses, they abused them to the utmost of their power, and did such things to them as are too indecent to be related. They also laid themselves down in public places, and celebrated general feastings, with garlands on their heads, and with ointments and libations to Charon, and drinking to one another for joy that the king was expired[234].

He was, in fact, directly replaced when Herod, Agrippa's brother, took power[235]. Before he was replaced, it would have been a good time to make his claim for kingship helped by Mary's genealogy.

We also know that the Simon and James, sons of the notorious rebel, Judas the Galilean, were gaining power around this time. According to Josephus, they would shortly be crucified. Also the Magician Theudas gets crucified around this time. Elioneus, Theuda, Simon and James may all have been looked upon as Messiah/King material. In the mid 40's we have some of the key elements that conceptually form the bases for the gospels. We have a God or Son of a God-King of the Jews dying in the person of Agrippa, and an outlaw son, Simon, with a brother, James, probably claiming to be the Messiah[236]. What we are getting here in Jospehus' history is a confluence of events and social attitudes that matches the confluence of events and social attitudes in parts of the gospel texts. This tells us not when the death of Jesus occurred, but when the story of the death of Jesus was most likely written. We have a terminus a quo of 45 C.E for the writing of this text, which probably could not have been written before the death of the son of God /King of Israel Agrippa. John's change in the arrest scene to the Mount of Olives could not have happened until after the arrest of the prophet called the Egyptian on the Mount of Olives probably in the mid 50's. This is an extremely important point for dating the writing of the earliest Jesus arrest narrative. Let us pause for moment.

Felix the Egyptian and the Capture on the Mount of Olives

Mark (and Matthew following him) has Jesus arrested at a place called Gethsemane. But notice the tag line to Mark's scene before Jesus' arrest, "Rise' Let us go! Here comes my betrayer[237]." This is a scared Jesus fleeing from his betrayer. We must assume that this scene is an interpolation by Mark in this position in the text. He has taken a scene that comes earlier in the story, where Jesus flees from "my betrayer" or someone and escapes, and he sets it as the arrest scene. This material belongs with the other Peter-James-John material (1:29-30, 5:35-43, 9:2-8, 10:35-45, 13:3-32, 14:33-42).

Luke has Jesus arrested on the Mount of Olives. John strongly suggests the Mount of Olives but does not specifically say that it was:

> When he had finished praying, Jesus left with his disciples and crossed the Kidron Valley. On the other side there was an olive grove, and he and his disciples went into it.

Jesus prays after he has a last supper on the Passover Preparation Day (John 13:29-30). We do not know where he is when he has the Last Supper. John has simply told us that he is in hiding (John 12:36) The Kidron Valley separates Jerusalem from the Mount of Olives. The reference to the olive grove strongly suggests that Jesus has left Jerusalem where he was in hiding and gone to the Mount of Olives.

The most probable historical personage that may be a referent to this action of moving in hiding from Jerusalem to the Mount of Olives is a Prophet known as "The Egyptian." In his *War*, After talking about robbers whom he calls Sicarri, (referred to in the following quoted paragraph as "these murders,") Josephus talks about two groups, one who leads people into the Wilderness (John the Baptist?) and another led by a prophet called "The Egyptian."

> 4. There was also another body of wicked men gotten together, not so impure in their actions, but more wicked in their intentions, which laid waste the happy state of the city no less than did these murderers. These were such men as deceived and deluded the people under pretense of Divine inspiration, but were for procuring innovations and changes of the government; and these prevailed with the multitude to act like madmen, and went before them into the wilderness, as pretending that God would there show them the signals of liberty. But Felix thought this procedure was to be the beginning of a revolt; so he sent some horsemen and footmen both armed, who destroyed a great number of them.
>
> 5. But there was an Egyptian false prophet that did the Jews more mischief than the former; for he was a cheat, and pretended to be a prophet also, and got together thirty thousand men that were deluded by him; these he led round about from the wilderness to the mount which was called the Mount of Olives, and was ready to break into Jerusalem by force from that place; and if he could but once conquer the Roman garrison and the people, he intended to domineer over them by the assistance of those guards of his that were to break into the city with him. But Felix prevented his attempt, and met him with his Roman soldiers, while all the people assisted him in his attack upon them, insomuch that when it came to a battle, the Egyptian ran away, with a few others, while the greatest part of those that were with him were either destroyed or taken alive; but the rest of the multitude were dispersed every one to their own homes, and there concealed themselves[238].

Some twenty years later, around 93 C.E., Josephus wrote again about "The Egyptian" in his *Antiquities*.

> These works, that were done by the robbers, filled the city with all sorts of impiety. And now these impostors and deceivers persuaded the multitude to follow them into the wilderness, and pretended that they would exhibit manifest wonders and signs, that should be performed by the providence of God. And many that were prevailed on by them suffered the punishments of their folly; for Felix brought them back, and then punished them. Moreover, there came out of Eygpt about this time to Jerusalem one that said he was a prophet, and advised the multitude of the common people to go along with him to the Mount of Olives, as it was called, which lay over against the city, and at the distance of five furlongs. He said further, that he would show them from hence how, at his command, the walls of Jerusalem would fall down; and he promised them that he would procure them an entrance into the city through those walls, when they were fallen down. Now when Felix was informed of these things, he ordered his soldiers to take their weapons, and came against them with a great number of horsemen and footmen from Jerusalem, and attacked the Egyptian and the people that were with him. He also slew four hundred of them, and took two hundred alive. But the Egyptian himself escaped out of the fight, but did not appear any more. And again the robbers stirred up the people to make war with the Romans, and said they ought not to obey them at all; and when any persons would not comply with them, they set fire to their villages, and plundered them[239].

Felix ruled over Judea from 52 to 59. Tacitas reports that "Felix stimulated outbreaks by injudicious disciplinary measures[240]." Josephus also notes that "The bandits whom he crucified, and the local inhabitants in league with them whom he caught and punished, were too many to count[241]" and "Not a day passed, however, but that Felix captured and put to death many of these impostors and brigands[242]." This may give us our *terminus a quo* for John's text which includes lots of references to bandits and most significantly the arrest on Mount Olive story. We may put it after 55 C.E. for this reason. John wrote his text after the arrest of the Egyptian, but certainly before the War in 66 C.E. There is no hint of war or mention of the Destruction of the Temple in John.

However the use of the name Jesus gives us another clue. Josephus tells us that there was a High Priest named Jesus Damneus[243] or (more likely) Jesus Gamaliel[244], probably starting around 62 C.E. It seems a strange coincidence that John would name his character Jesus and then a High Priest named Jesus would appear on the scene a few years later. There was no High Priest named Jesus in the previous hundred years. More likely the High Priest Jesus appeared on the scene first and the Savior character was named after him.

We also have Josephus talking about the adventures during this time period of the bandit Jesus, son of Sapphias, apparently a leader from Tiberius in Galilee[245].

> So Jesus the son of Sapphias, one of those whom we have already mentioned as the leader of a seditious tumult of mariners and poor people, prevented us . . .

While this Jesus from Galilee, leading fishermen and poor people is not the crucified Samaritan man whom Mary wrote about, John possibly used him as a model and possibly named his lead character Jesus after him. This limits John's novel to the window period from the High Priest Jesus/Galilean Bandit Jesus of Sapphias period after 62 C.E. and before the war in 66 C.E.

While this date I take to be highly probable, I am going to be quite speculative in developing my scenario for why the text was written and by whom. I could be entirely wrong on this speculation, but I think the dating is still a good bet and the logic behind it gives a better date than I have seen anyone else develop.

Scenario Behind the First Gospel Text:

Let us suppose that the Son of Caiaphas, Elioneus (disposed from the High Priesthood in 46 C.E.) was trying to make a political comeback, offering himself as the new Messiah. Let us suppose he married his stepmother Mary after the death of Caiaphas. Let us suppose that she wrote the "Tale of the Crucified Messiah," in response to the deaths of Simon and Theudas and the cults that formed around him[246]. She was trying to show how Caiaphas and his son Elioneus had tricked Pilate into fulfilling the prophesy for killing the Messiah who had to die in his first lowly incarnation. Since the Messiah does not really die, but he is revived in the tomb, the implication is that Elioneus is the real Messiah who died/didn't die. The message of the story is that Elioneus, the son of the High Priest Caiaphas is the real messiah and put to death once, he now comes back in glory to save Israel.

I suggest that the writer is Mary for several reasons. First the romantic attachment subplot between Jesus and Mary is just too strong and passionate for a man of that time to write. Very few Jewish women would have the background, time, and intellectual training to actually write a story that would be put into circulation. However, an extraordinary woman who was both the daughter and wife of Jewish high priests might. The fact that she gives herself nearly equal status to Jesus, the son of a high priest in the story, also points towards a woman of extraordinarily high social status as the author of the original story.

Our conclusion is that the original passion narrative was written by a woman, probably named Mary. If the story is true, she was the daughter of the Jewish high priest Annas. She married Caiaphas the Jewish High Priest. She fell in love with the son of Caiaphas. He was the son of Caiaphas and Caiaphas' first wife, also named Mary. This first wife Mary was the daughter of Joseph. This son claimed to be Jesus the Christ. The son was betrayed by Caiaphas to the Romans. At this point he underwent a mock, but legal coronation ceremony. The Romans then crucified him. However, apparently there was some kind of trick involved and he was revived after his death, and thus he was not only available to become the new King of the Jews, but had already gone through a coronation ceremony, and so in fact, was already King of the Jews.

This is the original plot of the original gospel story. The question is, "Is any of this plot true?"

The Real Name of the Real Man that was Crucified in Mary's tale

Elioneus son of Caiaphas is one name we can point to as the possible source for the original passion of Jesus story. Yet there is a second, even more probable name that fits in here perfectly. The name is Simeon bar Cleophas. In most texts he is referred to as a cousin of Jesus. However, if the writer of *John* has changed Jesus' mother, Mary Caiaphas, into Jesus' aunt, Mary Clopas, may we not change back to Mary Caiaphas, mother of Jesus. Since her son is Jesus and her son is Simeon bar Caiaphas, by simple logic this means Jesus was Simeon bar Caiaphas.

This deduction that the man on the cross was supposed to be Simeon bar Caiaphas has been made extremely simple by the extraordinary work of Robert Eisenman. In his monumental work, *James the Brother of Jesus*, he comes within a hair's breadth of making the right connection. He is puzzled by a line in the *Second Apocalypse of James*. He correctly identifies the stoning of James scene and then finds the line "And I was with the Priests, but I did not reveal our kinship." Eisenman asks exactly the right question. Who is speaking this line?

> It is difficult to understand who this narrator can be other than Simeon bar Cleophas, the witness to the stoning of James in Epiphanius' version of Hegesippus, either him or a reference of some kind to the 'kindship' of James and Jesus.
>
> The mention of 'Priests', again here, is, of course, interesting in view of the reference to James' Disciple 'Mareim' at the beginning of the Apocalypse as being 'one of the Priests' and the whole issue of the relationship of 'Rechabite'/'Nazirite'/'Essen Priests' to those in the Temple generally. It also links up with the peculiar notice of the Book of Acts of a large number of 'Priests' having made their conversion that we noted above.
>
> The 'kinship', then, is either between James and Jesus or Simeon bar Cleophas and James—it is difficult to decide which from the context[247].

Eisenman is exactly right in that we cannot decide between Jesus or Simeon bar Cleophas in this context. We cannot decide because there is no difference. The brother of James in this context is Simeon bar Cleophas AKA Simeon bar Caiaphas AKA the Lord Jesus.

Eusebius makes Simeon bar Cleophas into the successor of James as the leader of the Church of God[248],"

> And after James the Just had suffered martyrdom, as the Lord had also on the same account, Symeon, the son of the Lord's uncle, Clopas, was appointed the next bishop. All proposed him as second bishop because he was a cousin of the Lord. "Therefore, they called the Church a virgin, for it was not yet corrupted by vain discourses.

He also tells us that "he suffered a death similar to that of our Lord in the time of Trajan[249]" (98 to 117). He also quotes Hegessipus that he died at the age of 120 years, the same age that Moses died non-coincidentally. The story that he died on the cross in the time of Trajan told by Eusebius is almost certainly apocryphal. It is probably a response to the story by Mary that he suffered a fake crucifixion in the time of Tiberius. We may also suggest that the same two brothers James and Simon are involved in a story told by Josephus. Josephus relates that Simon and James were the sons of the rebel Judas of Galilee and that Josephus' relative Alexander the Alabarch of Alexandria[250] crucified them in 45 CE.

At the moment, we do not need to separate out the truth from these three tales about Simon Ben Caiaphas AKA Jesus Christ. Instead we'll use our new found knowledge to reconstruct one more scene, the strange ending of the Gospel of Luke:

The Original Ending of the *Gospel of Luke*

Here is the original text of the ending from the King James Bible:

> 24:10 It was Mary Magdalene and Joanna, and Mary the mother of James, and other women that were with them, which told these things unto the apostles.
> 24:11 And their words seemed to them as idle tales, and they believed them not.
> 24:12 Then arose Peter, and ran unto the sepulchre; and stooping down, he beheld the linen clothes laid by themselves, and departed, wondering in himself at that which was come to pass.
> 24:13 And, behold, two of them went that same day to a village called Emmaus, which was from Jerusalem about threescore furlongs.
> 24:14 And they talked together of all these things which had happened.

24:15 And it came to pass, that, while they communed together and reasoned, Jesus himself drew near, and went with them.

24:16 But their eyes were holden that they should not know him.

24:17 And he said unto them, What manner of communications are these that ye have one to another, as ye walk, and are sad?

24:18 And the one of them, whose name was Cleopas, answering said unto him, Art thou only a stranger in Jerusalem, and hast not known the things which are come to pass there in these days?

24:19 And he said unto them, What things? And they said unto him, Concerning Jesus of Nazareth, which was a prophet mighty in deed and word before God and all the people:

24:20 And how the chief priests and our rulers delivered him to be condemned to death, and have crucified him.

24:21 But we trusted that it had been he which should have redeemed Israel: and beside all this, to day is the third day since these things were done.

24:22 Yea, and certain women also of our company made us astonished, which were early at the sepulchre;

24:23 And when they found not his body, they came, saying, that they had also seen a vision of angels, which said that he was alive.

24:24 And certain of them which were with us went to the sepulchre, and found it even so as the women had said: but him they saw not.

24:25 Then he said unto them, O fools, and slow of heart to believe all that the prophets have spoken:

24:26 Ought not Christ to have suffered these things, and to enter into his glory?

24:27 And beginning at Moses and all the prophets, he expounded unto them in all the scriptures the things concerning himself.

24:28 And they drew nigh unto the village, whither they went: and he made as though he would have gone further.

24:29 But they constrained him, saying, Abide with us: for it is toward evening, and the day is far spent. And he went in to tarry with them.

24:30 And it came to pass, as he sat at meat with them, he took bread, and blessed it, and brake, and gave to them.

24:31 And their eyes were opened, and they knew him; and he vanished out of their sight.

24:32 And they said one to another, Did not our heart burn within us, while he talked with us by the way, and while he opened to us the scriptures?

24:33	And they rose up the same hour, and returned to Jerusalem, and found the eleven gathered together, and them that were with them,
24:34	Saying, The Lord is risen indeed, and hath appeared to Simon.
24:35	And they told what things were done in the way, and how he was known of them in breaking of bread.
24:36	And as they thus spake, Jesus himself stood in the midst of them, and saith unto them, Peace be unto you.
24:37	But they were terrified and affrighted, and supposed that they had seen a spirit.
24:38	And he said unto them, Why are ye troubled? and why do thoughts arise in your hearts?
24:39	Behold my hands and my feet, that it is I myself: handle me, and see; for a spirit hath not flesh and bones, as ye see me have.
24:40	And when he had thus spoken, he shewed them his hands and his feet.
24:41	And while they yet believed not for joy, and wondered, he said unto them, Have ye here any meat?
24:42	And they gave him a piece of a broiled fish, and of an honeycomb.
24:43	And he took it, and did eat before them.
24:44	And he said unto them, These are the words which I spake unto you, while I was yet with you, that all things must be fulfilled, which were written in the law of Moses, and in the prophets, and in the psalms, concerning me.
24:45	Then opened he their understanding, that they might understand the scriptures,
24:46	And said unto them, Thus it is written, and thus it behoved Christ to suffer, and to rise from the dead the third day:
24:47	And that repentance and remission of sins should be preached in his name among all nations, beginning at Jerusalem.
24:48	And ye are witnesses of these things.
24:49	And, behold, I send the promise of my Father upon you: but tarry ye in the city of Jerusalem, until ye be endued with power from on high.
24:50	And he led them out as far as to Bethany, and he lifted up his hands, and blessed them.
24:51	And it came to pass, while he blessed them, he was parted from them, and carried up into heaven.
24:52	And they worshipped him, and returned to Jerusalem with great joy:
24:53	And were continually in the temple, praising and blessing God. Amen.

THE EVOLUTION OF CHRISTS AND CHRISTIANIES

Note that as written we are faced with a number of puzzles. The two "men" on the road call themselves apostles of Jesus, but they go to the eleven apostles (twelve minus Judas) with their story of meeting Jesus on the road. This would indicate that neither of them is one of the eleven apostles. One of the men on the road is called Cleopas, but we have not met anybody named Cleopas except for Mary Cleopas.

The story makes sense only if Cleopas/Caiaphas is the mother of Jesus and the other person is Mary Magadalene. Recall that in our earlier reconstruction, Jesus reconciled the two at the tomb. The fact that Jesus escorts them to Bethany, Mary's hometown, indicates further that Mary Magdalene and Mary Caiaphas are the two unnamed "men" whom Jesus meets going to Emmaus.

Also the text moves back and forth between the disciples and the scene on the road in an uneasy intercut manner. Jesus and the women interact, then the women go retell the story, but add new information that we did not get before. We may conclude that this new information actually took place within the original scene. There was no need for the women to repeat information that the audience already received. We may assume that the entire scene on the road took place before the scene with the apostles.

Lastly, the sudden vanishing and reappearance of Jesus before the women currently makes little sense. It is as if he forgot something. We have to assume that when the Christ vanishes it is for good. We can easily fix all these editor's mistake to get the narrative back to its original form.

We must assume that the *Gospel of Mark's* strange ending with the frightened women telling nobody what happened at the tomb was the original ending. Obviously someone asked how the disciples found out about the tomb if they were not told. This new ending was created to provide the answer.

Reconstruction of the Final Scene in the Gospel of Luke

It was Mary Magdalene and Mary the mother of Cleopas which told these things unto the apostles. The two of them went that same day to a village called Emmaus, which was from Jerusalem about threescore furlongs. And they talked together of all these things which had happened. And it came to pass, that, while they communed together and reasoned, Simon himself drew near, and went with them. But their eyes were holden that they should not know him.

And he said unto them, "What manner of communications are these that ye have one to another, as ye walk, and are sad?"

And the one of them, Cleopas, answering said unto him, "Art thou only a stranger in Jerusalem, and hast not known the things which are come to pass there in these days?"

And he said unto them, "What things?"

And they said unto him, "Concerning Simon which was a prophet mighty in deed and word before God and all the people: And how the chief priests and our rulers delivered him to be condemned to death, and have crucified him.

But we trusted that it had been he which should have redeemed Israel: and beside all this, today is the third day since these things were done. Yea, we women went to the sepulchre where we found not his body but we saw a vision of angels and, they came, saying, he was alive, which made us astonished but him we saw not."

Then he said unto them, "O foolish women, and slow of heart to believe all that the prophets have spoken: Ought not Christ to have suffered these things, and to enter into his glory?" And beginning at Moses and all the prophets, he expounded unto them in all the scriptures the things concerning himself.

And they drew nigh unto the village, whither they went: and he made as though he would have gone further. But they constrained him, saying, "Abide with us: for it is toward evening, and the day is far spent. And he went in to tarry with them."

And it came to pass, as he sat at meat with them, he took bread, and blessed it, and brake, and gave to them. And their eyes were opened, and they knew him;

And he said unto them, "Why are ye troubled? And why do thoughts arise in your hearts? Behold my hands and my feet, that it is I myself: handle me, and see; for a spirit hath not flesh and bones, as ye see me have."

And when he had thus spoken, he shewed them his hands and his feet.

And while they yet believed not for joy, and wondered, he said unto them, "Have ye here any meat?"

And they gave him a piece of a broiled fish, and of an honeycomb. And he took it, and did eat before them.

And he said unto them, "These are the words which I spake unto you, while I was yet with you, that all things must be fulfilled, which were written in the law of Moses, and in the prophets, and in the psalms, concerning me."

Then opened he their understanding, that they might understand the scriptures,

And said unto them, "Thus it is written, and thus it behoved Christ to suffer, and to rise from the dead the third day: And that repentance and remission of sins should be preached in his name among all nations, beginning at Jerusalem. And ye are witnesses of these things. And, behold, I send the promise of my Father upon you: but tarry ye in the city of Jerusalem, until ye be endued with power from on high.

And he led them out as far as to Bethany, and he lifted up his hands, and blessed them. And it came to pass, while he blessed them, he was parted from them, and carried up into heaven.

And they worshipped him, and returned to Jerusalem with great joy:

And were continually in the temple, praising and blessing God.

And they said one to another, "Did not our heart burn within us, while he talked with us by the way, and while he opened to us the scriptures?"

And they rose up the same hour, and returned to Jerusalem, and found the eleven gathered together, and them that were with them, saying, "The Lord is risen indeed, and Simon hath appeared."

And they told what things were done in the way, and how he was known of them in breaking of bread. They told these things unto the apostles.

And their words seemed to them as idle tales, and they believed them not.

And as they thus spake, Jesus himself stood in the midst of them, and saith unto them, Peace be unto you." and he vanished out of their sight.

Then arose Peter, and ran unto the sepulchre; and stooping down, he beheld the linen clothes laid by themselves, and departed, wondering in himself at that which was come to pass.

Note that the text probably reflects the fact that the first Christian eating ceremony involved simply breaking bread and blessing it. I tend to think that this ending was not written by a woman. Still it is quite early and before the Mary loathing gospel writers took over.

Fresco. Christ Healing Woman.

Catacombs, Rome, before 300. This appears to be the miracle of healing the menustrating woman on his way to raising Jairus' sick/dead daughter. As Jairus' daughter was 12 and the text tells us implausibly that the woman had menustrated for 12 years, we may suggest that the original story involved only the single healing of a 12 year old girl who was menustrating for the first time. The fact that Jesus calls the healed woman "Daughter" (MK 5:34) supports this contention. The author of *Mark* broke the story up into two different miracles[251].

Chapter 4

A New Feminist Paradigm for Understanding the Evolution of the Gospels

Our reconstructions have been based on correcting illogical and ill-fitting points in narrative passages in the canonical gospels. We have filled in the most probable alternative constructions based on information from other canonical and non-canonical texts. It has led us to the conclusion that a very early non-gospel text written by a woman named Mary formed the basis for the present canonical gospels.

If this is in fact the case, we can best understand the gospels and the early development of Christianity by looking at other paradigmatic cases where innovative textual works originated by women became popular, went through textual mutations, and had enormous influence in other fields. We should also look for cases where the fact that a woman created the innovation was suppressed or forgotten. The 1905 adventure novel and play, *The Scarlet Pimpernel,* The 1920 play "The Bat" by Mary Roberts Rinehart, The 1818 novel, *Frankenstein,* and the 1927 play *Chicago* are our paradigmatic cases.

Secret Identities and Jesus

> We seek him here, we seek him there,
> Those Frenchies seek him everywhere.
> Is he in heaven?—Is he in hell?
> That damned elusive Pimpernel[252]?

> Then sought they for Jesus, and spake among themselves, as they stood in the temple, What think ye, that he will not come to the feast? Now both the chief priests and the Pharisees had given a commandment, that, if any man knew where he were, he should shew it, that they might take him[253].

The reconstruction we have done suggests that a woman wrote an important source for the trial, death and resurrection of Jesus. It also suggests that Jesus, the Christ had a secret identity as the son of the High Priest Caiaphas or rather, the son of the High Priest Caiaphas has a secret identity as Jesus, the Christ in this original work. All of the canonical Gospels to a certain degree maintain a certain secret identity for Jesus, however there is no logical reason for it in these narratives. It is just a left-over tradition. On the other hand, we can see that Jesus as the son of Caiaphas would be challenging his own father's authority by proclaiming himself the Christ and therefore it is part of the central conflict in the story.

We may suggest both the Genesis story of Moses and Sophocles's *Oedipus Rex* really contains early secret identity stories. The Pharaoh's daughter raises Moses, but his identity as a Jew is unknown to her. King Oedipus searches for the man who killed the prior king, unaware both that he is the killer and that the King was his father.

Would and could a woman make up such a tale of Jesus having an identity he must keep secret from his father? In the twentieth century, secret identities abound. We have adventure stories with heroes with secret identities like Zorro (1919), The Shadow (1931), Superman, (1938) Batman (1939), Spiderman 1962) and the Hulk (1962) being the most popular tales in diverse media like comic strips, comic books, movies and television. In most cases these heroes and their secret identities are associated with men and action entertainment primarily aimed at men.

However, it is somewhat surprising to find the first popular adventure hero with a secret identity was created by a woman. In 1903, Emmuska Magdalena Rosalia Maria Josefa Barbara Orczy, a baroness, co-authored a stage play with her husband called *The Scarlet Pimpernel*. In 1905, Emmuska Orczy published her novel *The Scarlet Pimpernel*. The play was produced in London the same year.

The Scarlet Pimpernel takes place at the time of the French Revolution. It is all about identities, lost identities and secret identities. In the very first chapter, the book tells us this:

> Every afternoon before the gates closed and the market carts went out in procession by the various barricades, some fool of an aristo endeavoured to evade the clutches of the Committee of Public Safety. In various disguises, under various pretexts, they tried to slip through the barriers, which were so well guarded by citizen soldiers of the Republic. Men in women's clothes, women in male attire, children

THE EVOLUTION OF CHRISTS AND CHRISTIANIES

disguised in beggars' rags: there were some of all sorts: *ci-devant* counts, marquises, even dukes, who wanted to fly from France, reach England or some other equally accursed country, and there try to rouse foreign feelings against the glorious Revolution, or to raise an army in order to liberate the wretched prisoners in the Temple, who had once called themselves sovereigns of France[254].

It is also about secret sexual identities. The very first time we see the hero, the Scarlet Pimpernel, he is disguised as an old lady. He is driving a cart with hidden aristocratic within escaping from the Revolutionary Guards in Paris.

The story is about a wealthy British aristocrat actually named Percy Blakeney who creates the identity of The Scarlet Pimpernel, a hero who rescues French Noblemen condemned to the guillotine by the French Revolutionary Government. However, the central character is his wife, Lady Blakeney. She is really an actress named Marguerite St. Just. Orczy seems to have based her character on the title character from the popular 1856 novel Madame Bovary by Gustave Flaubert[255]. She faces the dilemma of having to discover and reveal the identity of the Scarlet Pimpernel to the French Government in order to save the life of her brother. She is unaware that the Pimpernel is actually her new husband Percy Blakeney.

> She despised her husband for his inanities and vulgar, unintellectual occupations; and he, she felt, would despise her still worse, because she had not been strong enough to do right for right's sake, and to sacrifice her brother to the dictates of her conscience.

While she loves her husband the dandy Blakeney only a little, she idolizes the dashing heroic Pimpernel passionately. Ironically, not only is Lady Blakeney the central character, but she is also the hero. It is she who solves the puzzle of the Scarlet Pimpernel's identity and it is she who rushes off to rescue him from the clutches of the villain Chauvelin. Again the genders are mixed.

> "But, Lady Blakeney," said the young man, touched by the gentle earnestness of this exquisitely beautiful woman, "do you know that what you propose doing is man's work?—you cannot possibly journey to Calais alone.

However, the ending is quite conventional. her courage proves less than helpful, and in the end, Percy Blakeney needs to disguise himself as a "dirty old Jew," named Reuben Goldstein to save himself, and his wife, his and rescue more "aristos." In this disguise, he does suffer a severe beating, while saving Lady Blakeney.

203

Perhaps, we should distinguish between a "disguise" and a "secret identity." Reuben Goldstein is just a disguise that the character briefly assumes. Sherlock Holmes and previous detectives often went around in disguise, as James Bond and his competitors in the spy genre later did. A secret identity is a far more elaborate disguise. It involves one person leading two lives. For the most part the people who exist in one world of the character do not know that the same character has the other identity in the other world. This always leads to conflict as to which character is real and which the mask.

In the *Scarlet Pimpernel*, Lady Blakeney falls in love with Percy/Pimpernel only when she realizes that the dandy Percy is really the heroic Pimpernel and that he is only playing a part as Percy. For her, the Pimpernel is the real character, albeit necessarily secret.

We can see the emphasis on secret identity growing out of her life experience. Her own identity was as a baroness. However, this meant nothing to the readers of the popular detective fiction stories she started writing in 1901. To her circle of friends she was the Baroness Orczy, but to her readers she was just an anonymous woman writer of pulp fiction. Apparently she did not try to conceal her aristocratic background.

> When Baroness Orczy (pronounced "OR-see") created the gallant and beautiful aristocrats of The Scarlet Pimpernel, she was writing partly out of her own experience. Born in 1865, the only child of a Hungarian baron, she was herself an aristocrat. And although unrest in Hungary made her father give up the family's holding and leave the country when she was just a little girl, all her life she proudly used her title. When she began writing her novels, she signed them not "Emmuska" (or more properly, "Emma Magdalena Rosalia Maria Josefa Barbara Orczy"), but "Baroness Orczy"[256].

In fact, as her secret identity as a lowly writer of pulp fiction, the Baroness Orczy could fight for her aristocratic class as surely as Percy Blakeney fought for the aristocracy in the fifteen novels she ended up writing about the character. It is interesting to note that she often used the names and positions of real characters in her historical fictions. For example, in the novels Lady Blakeney (Marguerite St. Just) is a cousin to Louis-Antoine St. Just. In the novels and in history he was actually a close friend of the revolutionary leader Maximillian Robespierre[257]. It is probable that she took her work quite seriously as a way of influencing the sympathies of the masses and rewriting history in the popular imagination to portray the French aristocracy as the victims and heroes of the French Revolution and the democratic revolutionaries as bands of evil villains and terrorists[258].

We should consider that like Madame Orczy, Mary Magdalene could have used her fiction to make significant political points. It seems probable that she was from a faction that opposed Caiaphas, since it is he who betrays his son Jesus to the Romans. We should also consider that like Madame Orczy, Mary belonged to the upper class in society. We may gather this from the fact that her main character Mary appears as the daughter and wife of a high priest. Also it would be necessary for her to be from the upper classes for her to learn to read and write and to gather an audience for her productions.

In any case, the important thing here is that a woman's innovative work, based on events in her own background was immediately successful as a novel and play, and her device of the hero with a secret identity went on to play an important part in other areas of culture over the next century.

Batman Begins as Jesus Begins

Emmuska's character was the basis for the character of Zorro. In 1919, Pulp fiction writer Johnston McCulley first wrote the dual identity swashbuckling hero Zorro/*Don Diego de la Vega* as a serialized novel for *The Curse of Capistrano* for the magazine *All-Story Weekly*. The popularity of this character rivaled the Scarlett Pimpernel in a series of movies and books in the 1920's and 1930's.

Bob Kane, the creator of the comic-book character, Batman, has said that "his inspiration came from three basic sources—Zorro, a Leonardo da Vinci sketch of a man trying to fly with attached bat-like wings and a silent mystery movie titled 'The Bat.'"[259] It is this third source for the Batman character that we turn to—"The Bat." We find behind it another woman author who can be created with creating a character that has had extraordinary popular appeal.

Mary Roberts Rinehart was the undisputed Queen of Detective fiction in the first half of the twentieth century. One of her biographers, Charlotte Macleod, one of the great mystery writers of the last half of the twentieth century, compared her talent to Mozart's[260]:

> Nowadays we hear a fair amount about right-brain and left-brain characteristics. The general idea seems to be that the creative side of the brain feeds on honeydew and drinks the milk of paradise while the stodgy old other half is the dependable drudge that remembers to clean the cat box and pay the light bill. By now it must be clear to us that Mary Roberts Rinehart had a brain half that worked much like Mozart's, whizzing out new plots and dialogue even faster than her well-trained hand could write them down.

Her writing career spanned nearly fifty years. She was perhaps the highest paid writer in the world for the first half of the twentieth century. She was a 31 year old nurse, married to a doctor, when she published her first detective novel, *The Circular Staircase* in 1907.

> The Circular Staircase was first published as a serial in All-Story Magazine from November 1907-March 1908. Rinehart revised it for publication in book form by Bobbs-Merrill in 1908, her first book pubication. It was adapted and released in 1915 as a silent film by Selig (VLSE), directed by Edward J. LeSaint, starring Eugenie Besserer, Stella Razeto, Guy Oliver, Edith Johnson, William Howard, and Anna Dodge. In her autobiography, Rinehart said of The Circular Staircase: "And strange to relate *The Circular Staircase* was intended to be a semi-satire on the usual pompous self-important crime story. When later on as a book it was taken seriously and the reviews began to come in, I was almost overwhelmed... *The Circular Staircase*... had made a huge success. The notices were excellent, laying great stress on the relief of humor in a crime story, and so I kept to myself the deadly secret that the book had been written as a semi-satire.... But also to my astonishment I read that I had developed a new technique of the crime novel; that I had made the first advance in the technique of the crime story since Edgar Allan Poe! I was stunned[261]."

From 1917-1920, she worked on adopting her first novel, *The Circular Staircase* into a play. It opened with the title of *The Bat*. The play was extremely successful, opening August 23, 1920, it ran for 867 performances, the second longest running show in Broadway history at the time. In 1926, Stephen Vincent Benet wrote the novel *The Bat* based on the play. Two more extremely successful movie versions, *The Bat* (West, 1926), a silent film, and *The Bat Whispers* (West 1930), the sound remake followed. It was apparently the last two that had a lasting effect on Bob Kane, the creator of the comic-book Batman. At the age of 22, he produced the comic-book story of *the Bat-Man* in 1939.

He credits his inspiration to three sources[262].

> There were three major influences on Batman. The first was Zorro. As a kid, I was a movie buff. One of my favorites was The Mark of Zorro, with Douglas Fairbanks Sr. Zorro had the dual identity. By day, like Bruce Wayne, he feigned being a bored, foppish count, the son of one of the richest families in Mexico. By night, he became a vigilante. He would disguise himself, wearing a handkerchief mask with the eyes slit out. He exited on a black horse from a cave underneath his home, and that's the inspiration for the Batcave and the Batmobile.'

THE EVOLUTION OF CHRISTS AND CHRISTIANIES

'The second influence was a Leonardo da Vinci book I had seen. The book had a lot of inventions, including a flying machine. It was a man on a sledlike contraption with huge bat wings. Da Vinci had a quote that went something like, "Your bird will have no model but that of a bat." There it was—from a book 500 years old!'

'The third inspiration was a silent mystery movie called *The Bat*, in which the bat was a villain. They had a searchlight in the movie with a bat in the middle, just like my Batsignal.'

The second inspiration source, Da Vinci was simply a look for the character's costume. Eliminating him from the mix, we see that the character of Batman was conceived as a combination of Zorro, himself inspired by Baroness Orczy's Scarlet Pimpernel, and "The Bat" created by Mary Roberts Rinehart.

The evolution of the bat character before Kane is quite interesting. He does not appear in her original novel *the Circular Staircase*. The original novel takes place in a mansion in Pittsburgh. A wealthy woman, Miss Rachel Innes and her maid Liddy have rented the mansion for the summer. The plot involves the murder of the owner of the house and a robbery of the local bank. The original novel presents us with at least half a dozen plausible suspects for the crimes. These include a butler, a gardener, a doctor, a bank clerk and Rachel's niece and nephew Halsey and Gertrude. The ending contains a fabulous twist, in which a little suspected character turns out to be the main culprit.

The 1920 play has the same setting but takes place in a single night as opposed to the several week period that the novel covers. The names of the heroines have been changed to Cordelia Van Gorder and Lizzie Allen. Cordelia was Rinehart's mother's name. Several of the suspects, for example, the nephew, have been eliminated. One important suspect has been added, a notorious super-criminal nicknamed "The Bat."

If Rinehart had done a faithful adaptation of her novel, the audience, already knowing the surprise ending would have been bored. It would have been a mystery without mystery for them. Instead, she came up with an entirely new plot twist at the end that is different but equally surprising and clever as the original.

In the novel Rinehart has her heroine Rachel Innes gives a formula that seems to reflect her own formula for mystery writing:

> At this point in my story, Halsey always says: "Trust a woman to add two and two together, and make six." To which I retort that if two and two plus X make six, then to discover the unknown quantity is the simplest thing in the world. That a houseful of detectives missed it entirely was because they were busy trying to prove that two and two make four[263].

Male mystery writers of the time were interested in making sure that the suspects they added to the plot were plausible. Trying to be realistic, it was difficult for them to come up with four people who could be suspected of the same crime. Because she does not take the story seriously, Rinehart easily comes up with more than four plausible suspects. In fact, she can give us six suspects and kill off two, as if giving the reader a generous present. With suspects eliminated, the reader feels they should easily be able to guess the criminal. It adds to the novel's playfulness that even with this gift the ending comes as a complete surprise.

Rinehart brought a quality of lightness of touch to the field. Other women soon followed suit in the field. Apparently, this lightness of touch to the manly field of crime detection was not appreciated by all men. A period of censorship in the field of detective fiction followed shortly after her success. Michael Grost notes:

> There have been moments of backsliding in which women were excluded from some branches of mystery fiction. Women mystery writers were prominent in the early pulp magazines. These included such general purpose pulps such as Argosy and All-Story, which published Mary Roberts Rinehart from 1905 on, and the first specialized mystery pulp, Street and Smith's Detective Story Magazine, founded in 1915, which often featured Carolyn Wells and Isabel Ostrander. But with the rise of the "hard-boiled" pulp Black Mask in the early 1920's, women found themselves systematically excluded from the pulps. It is hard to believe that the near absence of women from the "tough" detective pulps of the 1920's and 30's is the result of anything but discrimination. Black Mask used to bill itself as the "he-man magazine". Similarly, historian Anthony Slide has documented how in the rough and ready, pioneer film industry of the 1910's, one out of every ten film directors in the US was a woman. His *Early Women Film Directors* documents the careers of 22 women directors, out of an industry that contained roughly 200 directors all told. After Wall Street started investing big money in the film industry in 1922, the careers of almost all these women came to an abrupt end. The profession of film director became almost all male, and remained so until modern times (roughly the mid 1970's). The rise of Black Mask and its exclusion of women took place virtually simultaneously, c1923. This should sound a cautionary note for feminists: history is not always full of "progress", in which people gradually learn to be less discriminatory. Instead, history shows that women can be excluded from a field in which they previously have had great success. While women writers disappeared from the pulps during the 1920's and 30's, they were flourishing among book publishers, and among the better paying "slick magazines". Huge numbers of women published in both media, often with works of the highest quality[264].

THE EVOLUTION OF CHRISTS AND CHRISTIANIES

Women won the right to vote in the United States with the passage of the 19th Amendment to the constitution in the United States in 1920. The immediate attack against women in many fields may be seen as a reaction against this victory. As often happens, a public political victory by a group leads to an increase of oppression of that group in other private areas.

One may note here that the time of the setting of the Christ stories, the time of Augustus and Tiberius, was a time of great progress for women. Livia, wife of Augustus (AKA Julia Augusta) advised her husband Augustus for 51 years and she advised her son Tiberius for 15 years. Probably through her prodding, progressive laws were passed regarding divorce and property rights.

In any case, when first introduced in the play of 1920, the bat character is little more than a plot device. In the first act of the play, we only get this information about him read by Cornelia from a newspaper:

> Cornelia. Police again baffled by the Bat! This unique criminal, known to the underworld as 'The Bat,' has long baffled the Police. The record of his crimes shows him to be endowed with almost diabolical ingenuity. So far there is no clue to his identity—but Anderson, City Detective, today said—'We must cease combing the criminal world for The Bat and look higher. He may be a merchant—a lawyer—a doctor, honored in his community by day—and at night a blood-thirsty assassin[265].'"

Later in the first act, a detective gives us this further information about the character:

> Detective. . . . The newspapers named him "The Bat" because he moved with incredible rapidity—always at night—and he seemed to be able to see in the dark. Cornelia. I wish I could. These country lights are always going out.
>
> Detective. Within the last six months, he's taken up the name himself—pure bravado—Sometimes he draws the outline of a bat, at the scene of the crime. Once, in some way, he got hold of a real bat and nailed it to the wall. He seems to have imagination.

"The Bat" seems to be partly a stereotype borrowed from the Rogue[266] school of Detective fiction. Michael Grost tells us this about that genre.

> The Rogue school, such writers as Guy N. Boothby, *Max Pemberton*, Maurice Leblanc, and E.W. Hornung, wrote tales about clever thieves and swindlers, that were at one time immensely popular with Late Victorian readers. The stories were comic and cheery in tone, and treated the crook protagonist as a hero. This thief only stole from the very rich,

and never committed murder, rarely used violence, and never did anything to harm anyone except the very wealthy. He often outwitted policemen who were trying to catch him. Many of their works involve impersonation, one of the key elements of the Rogue writers. The rogue would often impersonate well to do members of the upper classes. Oftentimes the crook is dressed as a very rich man.

The Bat does kill his victims, so technically he is not a rogue. Still, the fact that he is not connected to the underworld, impersonates a member of the upper classes, and that he's extremely clever puts him on the edge of Rogue fiction world of villain-heroes.

The play was a huge success and when the first silent movie version came out along with Stephen Benet's new novelization in 1926, the bat character changed. He had acquired a supernatural grandeur. Here is the description of him in the novel.

Columnists took him up, played with the name and the terror, used the name and the terror as a starting point from which to exhibit their own particular opinions on everything and anything. Ministers mentioned him in sermons; cranks wrote fanatic letters denouncing him as one of the even-headed beasts of the Apocalypse and a forerunner of the end of the world; a popular revue put on a special Bat number wherein eighteen beautiful chorus girls appeared masked and black-winged in costumes of Brazilian bat fur; there were Bat club sandwiches, Bat cigarettes, and a new shade of hosiery called simply and succinctly Bat. He became a fad—a catchword—a national figure. And yet—he was walking Death—cold—remorseless. But Death itself had become a toy of publicity in these days of limelight and jazz[267].

In the time between the writing of the play and the writing of the novel, 1920 to 1926, the play "the Bat" and its lead character had become famous. The role of the character changed. In the play the Bat is merely a clever plot device to provide a sense of danger and add mystery to the play. By the time of the novel, he is becoming the antagonist and a central character. The play had run for 867 performances, the second longest running play in Broadway history up until that time. It is almost as if Rinehart, always a self conscience author, decided to transfer the notoriety and fame of the play to the character.

Both the play and the silent movie end with an amazingly ironic line by the heroine Cornelia. The Bat finds a gun and orders everybody to put up their hands. Cornelia calmly continues her knitting. She explains that she removed the bullets from the gun earlier. The other characters quickly arrest the Bat. Cornelia says, "The first lie of an otherwise stainless life." We may consider that Mary Rinehart was sarcastically referring to her first novel which launched her career as a novelist: "The first lie in an otherwise stainless life."

The 1930 movie version, *the Bat Whispers*, adds an epilogue to this in which the Bat menacingly promises that he will return. The shift away from Cornelia and towards the Bat as the central character in this version is obvious. One can say that the originator of the story, Mary Roberts Rinehart put herself in her novel as the hero. It was a woman's wit and ingenuity that was the center of the original novel. When the novel became popular, men took over and pushed her to the side. Eventually men substituted the plot device that she had invented as the central theme. Today, nobody gives her the least credit for the invention of one of the most popular literary characters of the 20th century.

The parallels with the earliest layers of the gospel texts are many. We'll briefly look at one: the adding of a light touch to a traditionally serious man dominated field of fiction—prophesy writing.

In fact, we find a great deal of humor in the earliest layers of the gospel text. For example, the scenes at the well and the wedding are quite light. It is not surprising that the opening early scenes of a tragedy are filled with humor. What is surprising is that even in the tragic ending, we find the same light humor. How can we explain this?

He Who Gets Slapped: the Crucifixion as Plot Device

Literary critic Northrop Frye notes this

> ... A king of Babylon, we are told, such as Nebuchadnezzar, would have to go through a ceremony of ritual humiliation at each new year, with his face slapped by the high priest, in order to renew his title to the kingdom[268] ... The greatest triumph of David's reign, from the Biblical point of view, was his bringing of the "ark of the covenat" into the newly captured Jerusalem; and David showed his sense of the importance of the occasion by dancing in front of it "with all his might." His wife Michal, Saul's daughter, watched him and sneered at him as having made an exhibitionistic fool of himself in front of the servants. David's reply was: And I will yet be more vile than thus, and will be base in mine own sight: and of the maidservants which thou hast spoken of, of them shall I be had in honour. (11 Samuel 6:22)"

Frye also notes:

> ... What associations there are with royalty, including the crown of thorns and the inscription "King of the Jews" over the cross, are in a context of mockery and torture[269].

Frye appreciates that ceremonial humiliation was tied to kingship, but does not catch that this is exactly the kind of ceremony that the character of Jesus does undergo. A people accustomed to freedom would consider humility and reluctance to serve as necessary qualities required in a king. Therefore, a ceremony showing that the king was being forced to serve against his will would be essential.

Before his death on the cross, Jesus goes through such a humiliating coronation ceremony. Mary anoints him and he rides to his coronation on an ass (John 12), Jesus washes the feet of others (John 13), he marches with soldiers carrying swords and clubs at his arrest, again indicating humility and reluctance to serve (John, 18), his own chief guard/military officer (Peter) rejects him (John 18), A high priest slaps him (John 18), the old chief of state (Pilate) ignores him and will have nothing to do with him (John 18), he loses an election running against a criminal (John 19), he wears a crown of thorns, (John 19), people put him on a cross like a rebellious slave, (John 19), and his old clothes are distributed (John 19,) finally his mother and wife walk off (John 19).

What we are getting here is not the description of a man undergoing arrest, trial and execution, but a description of a man undergoing a humiliating coronation ceremony. His coronation ceremony takes place accidentally and coincidentally while he is being arrested, tried and executed. This is not tragedy. This is wit and humor.

What we see here is that the Passion of Christ is really not about the arrest and execution of Christ. The Passion of Christ is about the coronation of Christ. The crucifixion is merely the plot device used to achieve the goal. One can compare it to what happened with Rinehart's "Bat" character. It starts off as merely a clever plot device, but it works so well that it moves to the center of later stories. Likewise, the crucifixion starts off as merely a plot device to get help get Christ coroneted, but it ends up becoming the centerpiece of later tellings of the tale.

The original author is not telling us the story of Christ's crucifixion, she is telling us the story of how the Jews and Romans made someone king without knowing it. This is not meant to be a tragedy. This is meant to be a witty comedy.

Based on Herod's surprise at Jesus' quick death (Mark 15) and the fact that his legs are not broken[270] (John 19), we may assume in the original that the Christ did not die on the cross. Neither of these elements have any meaning in a story about a real death. They are dramatic elements in a tale where the main character narrowly escapes death.

Besides the coronation ceremony, the quick death and the rescue from broken bones evidence, one also has to consider the logic of the tone of the story. Would someone have inserted the comical incidents of a man accidentally being made king into a serious story about a man's crucifixion? The reverse seems more likely, the crucifixion has been turned into the main element out of a comical tale involving a man's accidental coronation. The crucifixion is merely a plot device to aid in explaining how the man was crucified.

Because the crucifixion is merely a plot device in a comic tale, may we assume that the Christ character did not exist? Not necessarily. It appears that some people were attacking someone as a demon-possessed, drunken and whoring prophet. Were people saying this about John or someone else? In any case, a story where the Jews accidentally made this man into their king would be hilarious. The person who wrote it could demonstrate her/his wit and that "I too, have a little imagination."

If this is the case it is entirely possible that the first version of the play was written in 35 or 36 before the death of John or whoever was the model for the executed Savior character.

Walter Kaufmann notes in *Tragedy and Philosophy* that there is an apparent contradiction in what Aristotle writes in chapters 13 and 14 in his *Poetics*[271]. In chapter 13, Aristotle tells us that plays like Oedipus are the most tragic, but in chapter 14, he suggests that plays with happy endings like *Iphigenia in Taurus* are the best. There is nothing to indicate that the original writer had an essentially tragic view of life. In fact, everything leading up to the ending indicates that the writer was happy and enjoyed verbal jousting as a sport. Just as Iphigenia rescues Orestes at the last moment, in the tomb sequence we seem to have had a case of Mary rescuing Jesus at the last moment. One can well imagine that the original story ended with Mary kissing a revived and living Jesus, as opposed to the revised ending where his ghost tells her not to touch him before he goes to heaven.

Incidentally, if this is the case, we must give the writer of the gospel of John, (possibly in the mid-late 50's) the credit for transforming a comedy into a tragedy. John's other great contribution (ignoring his covering up of Mary's identity as author) is the Eucharist ceremony and Jesus' farewell speech. This speech sounds very much like a soldier going off to war. These two things suggests that John was aiming his writing at a Mithraic audience of soldiers. Since Mithra had a large following in Tarsus, it is possible that John was writing from there. The theme of a God sacrificing his life would have appealed to these soldiers who sacrificed their lives all the time. A romantic comedy written by a woman would not have had much appeal to them.

Frankenstein and Jesus

Another case we may examine where a story narrated by a woman in a patriarchal society became a cause célèbre is the case of Mary Shelley who wrote the novel *Frankenstein* around 1817. Parallels between this event and the writing of the original gospel tale by Mary Magdalene are numerous and extraordinary and work at a number of levels. For example, the identity of the author was kept secret when the novel *Frankenstein* came out. It was thought that the identification of the gender of the author would keep the work from being taken seriously as literature. In a similar fashion, we can surmise that later Christians thought to hide the author's gender by changing the gender of the beloved disciple of Jesus and thus the gender of the author from female to male.

We caught Emmuska Orczy borrowing from Flaubert's *Madame Bovary* for her French actress, heroine Marguerite St. Just; so we can catch Mary Shelley borrowing from the German Romanticist writer Johann Goethe the character of the emotionally distraught Young Werther for her model of her hero, Victor Frankenstein. However, unlike *Scarlet Pimpernel* and "The Bat" where the central characters are woman, the central characters in *Frankenstein* are men, Victor Frankenstein and his monster. Still, the action is frequently driven by unseen women. For example, the entire novel is a series of letter from Captain Walton to a woman, his sister, Mrs. Saville. Other, little seen, women characters continually influence the action of the men, for example, the false accusation and trial of the servant Justine, the desire of the monster to have a female mate, and the wedding of Victor Frankenstein to Elizabeth.

Comparison of *Frankenstein* to the *Passover Gospel* by Mary Magdalene

The first adaptation of Mary Shelley's novel was a three-act opera by R. B. Peake titled *Presumption; or, The Fate of Frankenstein* in 1823. There was a second adaptation the same year, and a trio of comedic versions. By 1826, new versions were staged in London and Paris. Thomas Edison's company, Biograph, produced a filmed version in 1910 and James Whale's 1931 version for Universal Pictures brought it renewed fame and interest. We may consider the numerous versions of the gospels and adaptations and permutations in numerous books, theater pieces and films as all coming from the original work of Mary Magdalene.

As with the gospels, the original story of *Frankenstein* has been buried under the mass of texts that has grown from it. This has led to much confusion. We have confusion over names and bodies. First, we have the popular confusion of the monster's name with his creator, Victor Frankenstein. In the popular vocabulary they are called by the same name. In fact, the monster has no name in the novel. In the same way, there is popular confusion over the title Christ (meaning Savior) and it has been taken as the actual name of Jesus. In fact, Jesus of Nazareth would be the character's name and Christ an epitaph. In the Gospel of Mary, he is called Savior or the Blessed One or Son of Man. It is possible that in the original material, like Frankenstein's monster, the Savior did not have a name. There is also popular identity confusion regarding John the Baptist and Jesus, Simon and Peter, Simon and Simon Magus, Jesus and Simon Magus; as well as, John the Baptist, John the Disciple and John, the Gospel Writer.

Letters of Mary

Like the four gospels, we find complex structures. There are four narrators in Mary Shelley's book. On the first level we have Mary herself, (if we consider her 1831 introduction for the novel as part of the narrative, or if we consider the book's author as the "real" narrator). On the second level is the narrative of the Sea Captain Walton. Much of his narrative is part of the third level narrative of Victor Frankenstein, and even within the third level narrative, we get a fourth level narrative by the Monster himself. Thus at one point in the novel, we have Shelley telling a story about Walton telling a story about Victor Frankenstein telling a story about his Monster telling a story about a family he met and that family bears more than a passing resemblance to the real family of Mary Shelley. In each case the narrator describes a character who has tried to do something great and has suffered greatly for it. In each narration, we seem to be getting a story that reflects Mary's self image.

In the canonical gospels, we do not get this simple embedding of narrative, but in the *Gospel of Mary* recovered from Nag Hammadi, we do have the author telling a story of Mary telling a story to the disciples of Jesus telling a story to Mary. So we are at least getting a three level narrative and in each case the lead character is Mary. It is apparent that there is tremendous friction between other disciples and Mary

At one point in the embedded narrative in *Frankenstein*, the Monster tries to convince Frankenstein of the truth of what he is saying:

> "During the ensuing days, while the preparations were going forward for the escape of the merchant, the zeal of Felix was warmed by several letters that he received from this lovely girl, who found means to express her thoughts in the language of her lover by the aid of an old man, a servant of her father, who understood French. She thanked him in the most ardent terms for his intended services towards her parent; and at the same time she gently deplored her own fate.
>
> "I have copies of these letters; for I found means, during my residence in the hovel, to procure the implements of writing; and the letters were often in the hands of Felix or Agatha. Before I depart, I will give them to you, they will prove the truth of my tale . . ."

Even in the fourth and last level of the embedded narrative the story is of a woman writing to her lover deploring her fate. It is interesting that the Monster wishes to present these letters as evidence for the truth of his tale. In fact the entire narrative of Frankenstein is presented in the form of letters from Sea Captain Walton to his sister Mrs. Saville. If we follow the Monster's logic that letters equal authenticity then we have to accept Frankenstein as an authentic tale.

In the New Testament Canon we also find letters. Interestingly, we find no letters written by Luke, Mark or Matthew, but we do find letters attributed to the author of the Gospel of John. The style and thought patterns certainly match the writer of the Gospel of John and bind the works together.

In the three letters of John in the New Testament, we have letters I would conjecture are written by Mary[272]. One proof that the three canonical letters from John were written by a woman comes from the second letter, called 2 John:

1. The elder,
   To the chosen lady and her children, whom I love in the truth—and not I only, but also all who know the truth&—
2. because of the truth, which lives in us and will be with us for ever:
3. Grace, mercy and peace from God the Father and from Jesus Christ, the Father's Son, will be with us in truth and love.
4. It has given me great joy to find some of your children walking in the truth, just as the Father commanded us.
5. And now, dear lady, I am not writing you a new command but one we have had from the beginning. I ask that we love one another.
6. And this is love: that we walk in obedience to his commands. As you have heard from the beginning, his command is that you walk in love.
7. Many deceivers, who do not acknowledge Jesus Christ as coming in the flesh, have gone out into the world. Any such person is the deceiver and the antichrist.
8. Watch out that you do not lose what you have worked for, but that you may be rewarded fully.
9. Anyone who runs ahead and does not continue in the teaching of Christ does not have God; whoever continues in the teaching has both the Father and the Son.
10. If anyone comes to you and does not bring this teaching, do not take him into your house or welcome him.
11. Anyone who welcomes him shares in his wicked work.
12. I have much to write to you, but I do not want to use paper and ink. Instead, I hope to visit you and talk with you face to face, so that our joy may be complete.
13. The children of your chosen sister send their greetings.

Notice the beginning and closing lines:

"The Elder, To the chosen lady and her children."

"The children of your chosen sister send their greetings."

Notice how balanced the lines are. The opening is a greeting from the writer "to the chosen lady and her children." The closing line is a greeting from "the children of your chosen sister." Basically, the writer is saying in the first line, "I greet you" and in the last line "my children greet you." We may take "chosen sister" as a term of self reference. The letter is "to the chosen lady," from the "chosen sister." A "chosen sister" can only refer to a woman. Only by treating the last line as trivial and ignoring its poetical structural function in the work, can we come to the conclusion that the writer is a man.

In *Frankenstein*, the reader is reading a letter addressed to a sister and when we read it, we are put into the position, in some sense, of being the writer's sister and feeling towards the writer a sisterly sense of sympathy. In the second letter of John, it seems apparent that the author/authoress has done the same. Also, if the letters in Frankenstein present us with a tale of woe and despair over the falling apart of grandiose humanitarian plans, we get exactly the same type of tale in the letters of John. The letter writer has apparently lost a power struggle with other disciples of Jesus, ones who do not believe that Jesus was the Christ. This is reflected in the first letter.

15. Do not love the world or anything in the world. If anyone loves the world, the love of the Father is not in him.
16. For everything in the world—the cravings of sinful man, the lust of his eyes and the boasting of what he has and does—comes not from the Father but from the world.
17. The world and its desires pass away, but the man who does the will of God lives for ever.
18. Dear children, this is the last hour; and as you have heard that the antichrist is coming, even now many antichrists have come. This is how we know it is the last hour.
19. They went out from us, but they did not really belong to us. For if they had belonged to us, they would have remained with us; but their going showed that none of them belonged to us.
20. But you have an anointing from the Holy One, and all of you know the truth.
21. I do not write to you because you do not know the truth, but because you do know it and because no lie comes from the truth.
22. Who is the liar? It is the man who denies that Jesus is the Christ. Such a man is the antichrist—he denies the Father and the Son.
23. No-one who denies the Son has the Father; whoever acknowledges the Son has the Father also.
24. See that what you have heard from the beginning remains in you. If it does, you also will remain in the Son and in the Father.
25. And this is what he promised us—even eternal life.
26. I am writing these things to you about those who are trying to lead you astray.

Notice the mixing of themes here: the world is bad, evil has triumphed, the world is ending, we've been betrayed, I am telling the truth, they are liars. The writer is a poet, not schooled in rhetoric. She cannot marshal any witnesses in her defense. She is only able to appeal to the heart. Apparently she belongs at this time to a minority (perhaps just herself) in the Christian movement who believe Jesus is the Christ. We must assume that others who became leaders of the movement at this time did not believe that "Jesus is the Christ."

The theme of betrayal is picked up and made explicit in the third epistle.

1. The elder, To my dear friend Gaius, whom I love in the truth.
2. Dear friend, I pray that you may enjoy good health and that all may go well with you, even as your soul is getting along well.
3. It gave me great joy to have some brothers come and tell about your faithfulness to the truth and how you continue to walk in the truth.
4. I have no greater joy than to hear that my children are walking in the truth.
5. Dear friend, you are faithful in what you are doing for the brothers, even though they are strangers to you.
6. They have told the church about your love. You will do well to send them on their way in a manner worthy of God.
7. It was for the sake of the Name that they went out, receiving no help from the pagans.
8. We ought therefore to show hospitality to such men so that we may work together for the truth.
9. I wrote to the church, but Diotrephes, who loves to be first, will have nothing to do with us.
10. So if I come, I will call attention to what he is doing, gossiping maliciously about us. Not satisfied with that, he refuses to welcome the brothers. He also stops those who want to do so and puts them out of the church.
11. Dear friend, do not imitate what is evil but what is good. Anyone who does what is good is from God. Anyone who does what is evil has not seen God.
12. Demetrius is well spoken of by everyone—and even by the truth itself. We also speak well of him, and you know that our testimony is true.
13. I have much to write to you, but I do not want to do so with pen and ink.
14. I hope to see you soon, and we will talk face to face.
    Peace to you. The friends here send their greetings. Greet the friends there by name.

THE EVOLUTION OF CHRISTS AND CHRISTIANIES

Notice that Mary accuses Diotrephes of loving to be first. This theme is brought out in the *Gospel of Mary*, where an apostle named Levi points this out about Peter:

8. But if the Savior made her worthy, who are you indeed to reject her? Surely the Savior knows her very well.
9. That is why He loved her more than us. Rather let us be ashamed and put on the perfect Man, and separate as He commanded us and preach the gospel, not laying down any other rule or other law beyond what the Savior said.

In the *Gospel of Mary*, Mary has Levi accuse her rival of jealousy. In 3:John, Mary herself accuses her rival Diotrephes of jealousy, or at least a desire to place himself first. One may conjecture that Diotrephes is another name for Peter. Mary seems to state explicitly here that he represents a faction that does not believe that Jesus is the Christ. We may conjecture that Mark was well aware that Peter did not believe in the Christhood of Jesus and to counter this idea placed this passage in his Gospel[273]:

> Jesus and his disciples went on to the villages around Caesarea Philippi. On the way he asked them, Who do people say I am?
> They replied, Some say John the Baptist; others say Elijah; and still others, one of the prophets.
> But what about you? he asked. Who do you say I am? Peter answered, You are the Christ.

Peter may, in fact, have been one of those who said that John the Baptist was the Christ. There is some evidence he was originally a disciple of John the Baptist.

In fact, by the importance she places on the concept of Jesus being the Christ, we may suggest that it is Mary's idea alone. The disciples might have been willing to believe her when she said that she had seen a vision of Jesus after his death, but her absurd notion that Jesus is the Christ crossed the line. Despite her obviously close relationship to Jesus and her brilliant writing, the more sober minded apostles could not tolerate her blasphemous and weird notion that "Jesus is the Christ." It is ironic that this strange notion that Mary invented, along with her invented tale of Jesus' return from the dead actually became the litmus tests of truth and orthodoxy for the Christian movement. This is exactly what she wanted them to be. Unfortunately, her idea that this would return her to a position of power in the movement seems to have failed. It is a testament to the woman's great persuasive ability and her exalted status in the Jesus circles that she was able to get these notions accepted.

In any case, the association of letters with a sort of honesty and truth is probably the reason that the New Testament Canon contains so many of them. Mary Shelley reminds us that letters may easily be presented to give veracity to a false tale. Mary Magdalene may have understood the same.

Jesus and *All That Jazz*

Understanding how and why these multiple gospel narratives came about is not an easy task. We simply do not have a parallel situation in the First and Second Centuries[274] that we can look at and analyze to help our understanding. We have no first hand accounts of a trial and later mythologized versions of events surrounding that trial. We do have texts relating to trials but these texts were not mythologized and rewritten by different authors in different editions, or if they were, only one version quickly became recognized as standard. It is not just the numerous rewrites, but the fact that we are getting numerous mythologized rewrites of a text with a centralized event—the trial of Jesus—that is important. While this is highly suggestive that the event was real or at least meant to be taken as real by the author, we have no real trustworthy eyewitness narrative of the event.

However, there is a modern transformation of events-narratives that parallels closely some of these unusual features of the production of the Gospel texts, especially the numerous rewritings by different authors over a hundred year period of the initial text. This triggering event/narratives relationship can be used as a paradigm to understand the original event and the transformations of the narratives (gospel texts) resulting from it. This set of triggering event/narratives starts from a real historical event that occurred April 3, 1924 in Chicago, Illinois. It led to a play called *Chicago*.

Maurine Watkins, the writer of the play *Chicago* was the daughter of a Pastor from Louisville, Kentucky. She was beautiful, attended the most prestigious Woman's College in the country at the time, Radcliffe, and developed a relationship with a Professor George Pierce Baker, who taught English and playwriting classes.

Chicago as a Paradigm Text for the Gospels

> "If Jesus Christ had lived in Chicago, and if he'd had $5,000, and had come to me, things would have turned out differently[275]."

Beulah Sheriff was born in 1901[276] in Kentucky, USA. About age 15, She married Perry Stephans and soon gave birth to a son. She divorced him and married Albert Annan an auto mechanic and moved to Chicago, Illinois. They went shopping for a car, and met salesman Harry Kalstedt in the process. Beulah and Harry began a secret love affair. On April 3, 1924, Beulah Sheriff Stephans Annan shot Harry Kalstedt. This was a real event in our space and time.

THE EVOLUTION OF CHRISTS AND CHRISTIANIES

The narrative stories associated with this event have changed repeatedly over time. Very few people have read about the actual events, but millions of people are aware of the narratives this event generated.

The first narrative came quickly. Beulah called her husband Harry at work and told him that she had killed a man who "tried to make love to her"[277] Her husband rushed home and called the police, although she begged him not to. She grabbed the phone and told the police, "I've just killed my husband[278]."

Under police interrogation, she admitted that she had been having an affair with Harry. She shot him when he said that he wanted to break off their affair. After shooting him, she had listened to a phonograph record for the next four hours until her husband came.

The next day, in the presence of her new lawyer, W.W. O'Brien, she told the coroner's jury a different narrative. They had quarreled. They both reached for the gun. She shot him in self defense.

Chicago Newspapers repeated these narratives, labeling her "the prettiest murderess," The prosecution and defense attorneys at her trial also repeated these narratives with variations. She was found innocent by a jury on May 24, 1924.

At this point, the event and the narratives were really quite ordinary. Very probably hundreds of similar shootings and narratives were repeated that year. Something quite remarkable happened two years later. The reporter covering the story for the Chicago Tribune, Maurine Watkins, wrote a comical play based on the events. At first called "Play Ball," it opened under the title "Chicago" in Chicago, in September of 1927. The lead character's name was changed to Roxie Hart. Maurine Watkins used the name Mary Sunshine for the reporter character in the play modeled on herself. The play made fun of the newspaper industry and the justice system of Chicago. It was quite successful. It spawned other plays about the newspaper industry including *The Front Page*. A movie version soon followed. Millions of people now saw and heard the fictionalized story of Beulah Annan/Roxie Hart. Only a small number probably knew or cared that it was a highly fictionalized version of a true story.

In 1942, the movie was remade by William Wellman (director) and Nunnally Johnson (producer and writer). Ginger Rodgers, best known as the dance partner of Fred Astaire, played Roxie Hart. At this time, the Hays Moral Code was in effect in Hollywood. It did not allow a murderess to get off for her crimes. The writer, Nunnally Johnson changed the narrative. Instead of Roxie Hart/Annan Beulah killing the man, her husband kills him. She takes the blame for the publicity it will bring her. Ginger Rodgers also added two short dance numbers that were not in the original play or movie. She noted in her 1991 autobiography later that the film became popular many years later:

> Roxie hart has become a cult film in recent years. I know of one theater in Philadelphia that runs it frequently. The manager told a friend of mine, Sidney Luce, "We practically sell out the house for the entire run." Not bad for a film released in 1942[279].

In 1975, in New York, the play became the basis for *Chicago, A Musical Vaudeville*. It was directed by one of the most influential choreographers of the late 20th century, Bob Fosse[280]. It was only moderately successful, having the misfortune of opening the same year as the more popular musical *A Chorus Line*. Not having to worry about the Hays Moral Code, Fosse again portrayed Roxie Hart as a real murderess. Her rivalry and relationship with another murderess, Belle Gaertner (named Velma Kelly in the play) became a focal point of the new musical. Whereas the original play emphasized the similarity of newspapers and the legal system to show business, Fosse seemed to go further and emphasize the intertwined nature of life itself and show business.

In 1997, the play was revived by a protégé of Fosse's, Ann Reinking[281]. She won a Tony Award for directing and choreographing the musical. In 2002, Chicago again became a movie, this time as a musical, starring Renée Zellweger, Catherine Zeta-Jones, and Richard Gere. It received an Academy Award that year for best picture.

They Both Reached for the Gun

It may be helpful in understanding the development of Gospel scenes, to follow the evolution of just one narrative associated with the texts. Soon after being arrested, reporters interviewed Beulah Annan. We may follow this narrative report as it evolves. We can see the scene as it was reported in a newspaper article the next day written by Maurine Watkins, a play two years after written by the same woman, a movie written and acted 15 years later and as a scene in the musical play by Bob Fosse some 33 years after that.

Here is a part of the newspaper article:

BEULAH ANNAN SOBS REGRET FOR LIFE SHE TOOK

Lives Through Crime Again as She Awaits Trial
April 6 1924, p.4

By Maurine Watkins

"Of course I'm sorry! I'd give my life to have Harry Kolstedt alive again! And I never said I was glad. Why, I couldn't. Why—" and tears filled the eyes of Mrs. Beulah May Annan, the "prettiest murderess," held to the grand jury for shooting her sweetheart in a drunken quarrel at her apartment on Thursday.

Thursday night, a mad, hysterical frenzy, when she babbled conflicting accounts of the murder. Friday, a daze that left her cold and unmoved at the inquest. But yesterday afternoon in the county jail, where she awaits indictment for murder, she began to realize what it means to kill.

And the music changed, too. ""Hula Lou," on the phonograph while the lover she shot lay dying; a funeral song in the chapel, when she awaited the inquest, and yesterday "Bring them in from the fields of sin!" sung by prisoners indicted or sentenced for robbery, prostitution and murder.

It jars on her horribly—the laughter of the girls, their constant talking, the music. "How can they!" she said, shivering.

She posed for her picture with Mrs. Belva Gaertner, whose trial for the shooting of Law, the young auto salesman, begins on April 21, but as yet the two have not talked over their common interests.

A man, a woman, liquor, and a gun—

But unlike Mrs. Gaertner, who waits cheerfully and philosophically, protesting her innocence and disclaiming all recollection of the killing, Mrs. Annan remembers.

"Never Forget It"

"I'll never forget it." She shuddered, "That white silk shirt—all covered with blood! He never spoke or moved, just lay there—I know he died as soon as he fell. And I was with him—dead," her eyes widened in horror, "for two or three hours. I never thought of a doctor until the policemen came, and when they said he might be alive—O, it was the happiest moment in my life!"

She remembers, too, just how it happened.

I had learned that morning—just before I came home—that he had been in the penitentiary, and I accused him of it. And he grew angry and—but it wouldn't have happened if we both hadn't been drinking; and he had had quite a lot before he came over. We both lost our heads, saw the revolver lying there uncovered by the pillow, for I hadn't made the bed that morning, and grabbed for it. I can see him now—that look in his eyes! He was perfectly wild, and I know he would have killed me if I hadn't reached it first."

We have a relatively "straight" and "objective" account here. Watkins has prefaced Annan's narrative of the events with some humor, calling her the "prettiest murderess" and relating her case to the then more famous case of Belva Gaertner. She observes a possible relationship developing between Belva Gaertner and Beulah Annan. Ironically, this relationship, portrayed develops into a central theme of the movie *Chicago*, with Roxie Hart and Velma Kelly competing for fame some 78 years later[282].

Note that Beulah's speech becomes confused when describing the shooting. She blames it on drinking, especially his drinking, "he had quite a lot before he came over." (How would she know this? Why would she give him more?) Was she saying this to please the newspapers and the leading Chicago citizens who favored prohibition against alcohol at this time? This statement is suspect.

We also have to suspect her next statement, "We both lost our heads, saw the revolver lying there uncovered by the pillow, for I hadn't made the bed that morning, and grabbed for it." She had just left a gun lying by the pillow? She knew that her boyfriend was coming over and she knew that they were going to have sex as they usually did. It is doubtful that she did not make the bed, or at least put away the gun, knowing that he was coming over. The bed was most likely unmade because they were using it. The close proximity of the pillow to the gun is striking. What was a gun doing next to the pillow. The most probable answer is that Beulah had placed it there. This suggests that she planned on shooting Harry before he came over. It appears probable that her murder was not a spur of the moment accident due to over consumption of alcohol, but an act of premeditation on her part. It is probable that she was the one who was drinking "quite a lot before he came over." She probably killed him as revenge for trying to leave her.

As part of her confession, she said that she played the song "Hula Lou" for two hours after she shot him, before calling her husband. This too is almost certainly a lie. It is most probable that she had sex with Harry for two hours before shooting him. Beulah did not mind being considered a murderer, but was probably more ashamed about letting it be known that she had killed her lover just after they had made love.

Her original story that he said that he was leaving her and that triggered the shooting makes much more sense than her revised version here that they quarreled about his having been in the penitentiary. One can guess that she was also ashamed and angry at being in a jail and that she transferred her feelings back into the story of the killing of Harry. These points suggest that her narratives about the events were filled with lies, evasions and deceptions at the first telling, before it became a play.

It is surprising that only the 1975 Fred Ebb and Bob Fosse musical presents this hard fact that Roxie Hart did murder her lover in cold blood after making love.

> Roxie.   So that's final, huh Fred? (Fred stands, puts on his jacket, and straightens his tie. Roxie gets the gun, from under the pillow.)
> Fred.   Yeah, I'm afraid so, Roxie.
> Girls.   (Calling.) Oh, Fred . . .
> Fred   (Turning back to ROXIE) Yeah?
> ROXIE.   (Pointing gun at him.) Nobody walks out on me. (She shoots him.)
> FRED.   (As he falls, clutching stomach.) Sweetheart . . .
> ROXIE.   Don't "sweetheart me, you son-of-a-bitch! (She shoots him again. He dies . . . [283]

The 2002 movie shows the lovemaking and shooting, but softens our shock by first showing Fred mistreating Roxie. He lies to her about helping with her show business career, shoves her and threatens her. In the same way that her lawyer got sympathy from a jury by adding details to the narrative, the filmmakers get the audience's sympathy by inventing details.

The historical accuracy that Ebb and Fosse brought to the murder scene is quite surprising. They seem to care nothing about any real history in the narratives in the rest of the play. For example, Velma Kelly based on Belvah Gaertna, not only kills her boyfriend in the play, but her sister as well. Yet, small details, such as the fact that Velma/Belvah did not remember the shooting are kept. We should keep in mind that they are turning it from an historical-news event into a show. They are primarily interested in adding "show business" to the narratives not in generating accurate historical narratives.

Comparison of the Interview Scenes

Maurine Watkins, the writer of the Chicago Tribune article controls Beulah's narratives in the Chicago Tribune article. She selects the sentences and details she wants people to know. We should also keep in mind that her editors to a large degree controlled what she wrote, and these editors themselves faced social pressures and constraints.

In the article, she portrays only a mild sense of fear and desperation on the part of Beulah. Watkins adds some subtle humor in her observations, for example her observation about what Beulah and Belvah have in common. It is interesting to see how this key scene which brings forward Beulah's narratives to a mass audience, itself becomes part of a changing narrative.

In looking at the stage play that Watkins wrote two years later, we see that she brings even more satirical humor to the narrative in a jailhouse reporters-interview scene. Much of the humor comes from the lead character's bungling attempts to follow her lawyer's instructions. She becomes artificial trying to imitate him too closely. Part of this previous scene needs to be read in order to understand how and why Watkins changes the interview-confession narrative. This part of the scene comes just after Roxie's lawyer Flynn has told Roxie that a reporter named Mary Sunshine and others are going to interview her:

> Roxie: I won't see her
> Flynn: You've talked so much, you can't stop now. [Grimly.] If you tell enough lies they're bound to forget a few!
> Roxie: But not her—I'll be damned if I do!
> Flynn [Pleasantly]: You'll be hanged if you don't.... And by the way, pipe down on that swearing. What we've got to do now is go out for sympathy through the press. The story of your life starts tomorrow in the Star: "From Convent to Jail."
> Roxie: What?

225

Flynn: My secretary's writing it this afternoon—signed with your name, of course.
Roxie: Gee, an authoress!
Flynn: Beautiful southern home, every luxury and refinement, [she listens with interest] parents dead, educated at the Sacred Heart, fortune swept away, runaway marriage . . . [Severely] You're a lovely, innocent child bewildered by what has happened. Young, full of life, lonely, you were caught up by the mad whirl of a great city—she gives a red-hot picture of cabaret life—that jazz stuff is always good . . . . And you were drawn inevitably like a butterfly crushed on the wheel . . . And you sob with remorse for the life you have taken—
Roxie: O God!
Flynn: Cut out "God"-stay where you're better acquainted. . . . And don't overdo it. Go as far as you like with Mary Sunshine—she'll swallow hook, line, and sinker, for it's what she wants, but easy with the Ledger woman. The important thing is regret. You're sorry-sorry: you'd give your life gladly to bring him back.
Roxie: [drops pose]: Say, why did I do it? What's my defense? Was I drunk or crazy?"
Flynn [shakes head]: Nobody cares about a lunatic unless they've got money. Whenever they ask "why," all you remember is a fearful quarrel, he threatened to kill you. You can see him coming toward you with that awful look in his eyes— that wild look! And—get this now: you both grabbed for the gun. See? Self-defense. Whatever else we weave in afterwards, that's there from the start . . . You've spent a sleepless night.—tossing about—

The scene comically emphasizes the amorality of the lawyer who basically makes up a narrative that sounds plausible and does not care if it is true or not. This theme is repeated and emphasized with the reporters who also are not interested in the facts in the case, but only expressing their point of view. Watkins, the playwright, even satirizes her old self as the newspaper woman Mary Sunshine in the interview scene:

Sunshine: My dear, O my dear, what is it?
Roxie [lifts sweet tragic face]: I've given all—all that a woman can give . . .

THE EVOLUTION OF CHRISTS AND CHRISTIANIES

Sunshine [grabs notebook]: Yes—yes: you've given your all . . .
Roxie: And now the mad whirl is over—a butterfly crushed on the wheel—you know: a butterfly . . . moth and the flame . . . [with that lovely wistful smile.]
Sunshine [scribbles]: And what caused you to—
Roxie [sadly, with Liz' mystic intonation]: It might have been different once . . . but dancing feet find sorrow . . .
Sunshine: "Dancing." Er—jazz? The Charleston? Shall we say the Charleston, Mrs Hart? And er—drink—you had been drinking?
Roxie [with Velma's ease]: O yes, I was drunk, my dear, dead drunk!
Sunshine: O lovely, lovely—my paper's dry, you know! . . . So you would advise girls to avoid jazz and drink. What else, Mrs. Hart? How did you happen to . . . just why did you . . . shoot . . .
Roxie {grows dramatic]: I was mad—crazy—insane!'
Sunshine: O dear!
Roxie [hastily]: Not enough for the asylum, you know—over with right away.
Sunsine [nods]: Temporary insanity.
Roxie: For I really have the tenderest heart in the world—wouldn't hurt a worm . . . not even [with Velma's tremolo] a worm . . . .
Sunshine [sympathetically]: And what brought it on?
Roxie [her eyes grow dark and her emotion rises]: He—threatened my life . . .
Sunshine: What a terrible man!
Roxie: O he was! Very terrible!
Matron: [enters with two monstruous baskets, one tied with pink ribbon, which she places on the table and examines]: It's your supper—two of 'em.
Roxie [looks blank]: Two?
Matron: One from Woosters' and a fancy chicken dinner from someplace, with a note.
Roxie [opens and reads]:

> "My heart and hand are at your feet,
> With you my life would be complete.
> >Yours, with pleasure—
> >An Unknown Admirer."

>   Poetry! Ain't that romantic!
> Sunshine [takes note]: I'll thank you for you through the paper.
> Roxie [arranges food]: You might tell him, too, that I like Russian dressing.... Shortcake—say, he's a regular guy!
> [Matron disappears with other basket. Roxie falls to eating heartily, and Sunshine watches fascinated.]
> Sunshine: They'll all be so glad to know you can eat.
> Roxie [stops short and resumes "character"]: It's choking me, every mouthful.... but I feel its my duty....
> Sunshine: O it is! You must keep your strength!
> Roxie [forces herself to a more languid pace]: The first bite I've tasted since.... he went to his reward.... [Presses handkerchief to her eyes.]
> Sunshine [pats her hand]: Dear Mrs. Hart!
> Roxie: O, if I could only bring him back! How gladly.... how gladly I'd give my own life! [Chokes with emotion, takes a few healthy bites.] And sleep—I can't sleep either.... All night I walked about—tossing the floor....
> Sunshine: O my dear.
> Roxie [in hollow tone]: Always his face coming toward me... [her emotion rises as she lives through it all] with that terrible look—that wild look—in his eyes... We both grabbed for the gun! [She reaches forth her hand and clasps a roll of bread.]—And I shot [dramatic pause]—to save my honor!
> [The Salvation Army starts up again:]
>   "In the sweet by-and-bye,
>   We shall meet on that beautiful shore;
>   In the sweet bye-and-bye...."
>   Ain't it grand—the Salvation Army! I love to hear 'em: I'm awful refined.... You see, I was born in a convent.... [Continues talking and eating, while Sunshine writes, as The Curtain Falls

The narrative of events of the night of the murder in this scene are close to what we get in the newspaper article interview. They had been drinking, a quarrel, the shooting and the remorse, but important subtle changes have been made. Now the lead character does say, "We both grabbed for the gun!" The statement in the original article is far less definite, "We both lost our heads, saw the revolver lying there uncovered by the pillow, for I hadn't made the bed that morning, and grabbed for it." The subject pronoun "I" is most closer to the verb "grabbed" in the sentence than the

THE EVOLUTION OF CHRISTS AND CHRISTIANIES

subject pronoun "we" Perhaps the original sentence in her confession was closer to "I grabbed for the gun which I had placed under the pillow when I made the bed that morning." Having to integrate the new story from her lawyer that they both grabbed for the gun, with the story she had rehearsed, she came up with the garbled complex sentence structure we now have.

When we get to the 1942 *Roxie Hart*, we find the scene following pretty closely to the play with some interesting additions. The writer/director Nunally Johnson worked as a newspaper reporter in the 1920's. He has shifted the narrative so that a male newspaper reporter (presumably representing himself) is the narrator and the story is told in flashbacks. In this particular scene, a reporter named Jake tries to get more specific information about the shooting. Roxie says that she can't remember specifically what happened. Interestingly, Johnson has shifted Watkins' report of Belva Gaertner not remembering her shooting onto the Beulah/Roxie character. The most interesting change, perhaps, is the scene's ending. Roxie again warns against the deadly combination of alcohol and jazz. Jake asks her for a demonstration of her dancing to jazz. This leads to a brief, but extraordinary musical number called "the Black Bottom." Almost falling out of character, Ginger Rodgers, well known at the time for her extraordinary dancing in a series of movies with Fred Astaire asks if it would be "out of place." The Jake character, seeming to speak directly for the writer/director Nunally Johnson, reassures her, "Certainly not, do you think we'd ask you if it would be?"

Hermes[284] Panagiotopoulos, more commonly known as Hermes Pan, choreographed the exuberant dance number that follows. He was perhaps the most important choreographer of the time, having choreographed most of the dance numbers in the Fred Astaire/Ginger Rodgers musicals. One may suggest that Bob Fosse who would have been 15 when the movie came out in 1942, saw the movie, and appreciated the possibility of mixing dance into the witty story narratives, based primarily on this dance number.

He attempted to turn the play into a musical throughout the 1950's but only obtained the rights after the playwright, Maurine Watkins, died[285]. In the 1975 musical, the jailhouse interview scene becomes a surrealistic vaudeville number, "the Press conference Rag," in which Roxie and the reporters are literally puppets being manipulated by the lawyer Billie Flynn. The major emphasis of the play on the cynical manipulation of narratives by lawyers remains intact. It is now shown literally. This entails a subtle shift in emphasis. The newspaper professionals are no longer the manipulators as in the play, they are now the manipulated, just puppet conduits of the legal profession. This manner of presentation also emphasizes another theme, that life is theater. While Watkins suggests this to some degree, Bob Fosse makes it a central concept. If for Watkins, it is a revelation and novelty, for Fosse it is dogma. Ironically, the song which repeats the phrase "They both reached for the gun" as a refrain over and over, has elements of Negro gospel hymns in it.

229

A Good Model

The original event was probably one of individual horror and terror for young Beulah Annan. At 23 years old, she had already been divorced and lost custody of her seven year old son. Now she was facing the death penalty for killing her lover. It must have been an emotionally devastating time for her. The plays and movie largely gloss over this[286] and produce laughs by showing her clever manipulation of the narratives within the narratives of her crime and trial. For example, in real life and in the plays and movies, she announces that she is pregnant to gain sympathy from the press and public. It is difficult to know how much she invented on her own and how much was her lawyer's idea.

Beulah actually died of Tuberculosis in a Sanitarium three years after her trial. Roxie Hart has happier endings in her plays and movies. In the 1942 movie version, she ends up married to a newspaperman. In the 2002 movie version, she ends up becoming a star nightclub performer.

We do not have the original records of the events of the Jesus Christ story. We do have the original events in the story of Beulah Annan/Roxie Hart. We can use this to see just how great are the transformations of narratives from the original events that trigger them.

What if we did not have the earliest narratives? We have to imagine that we have the later narratives of the Beulah Annan/Roxie Hart story. Could we work our way back to the original historical events? Could we find the hidden real life incidents that triggered the popular narrative tales?

Some parallels are quite direct, for example, both start from an ordinary criminal event of its time (a shooting involving liquor and Jazz, and a Jewish Messianic Rebellion against Roman Authority. Both move immediately towards a climatic trial[287]. In the beginning, at least, there appeared to be little interest in Jesus' life before his arrest and execution, as there is little interest in Beulah Annan's life before her crime, although we find in the later case fictitious details, such as her ambition to be a dancer, are being added. I believe censorship of sordid details appears early in the transformation of each narrative. It is likely that Beulah Annan lied when she said that she listened to a phonograph record for hours after shooting her lover, more likely she was having sex with him during this time period, and shot him afterwards. In the Jesus story, it is likely the love affair between Jesus and Mary Magdalene was similarly quickly covered up. In the Gospel of John, the "beloved disciple" and author, Mary, is changed into a man (the disciple John). In the Ebb and Fosse musical, the reporter Mary Sunshine, who represents the author Watkins, also changes into a man[288].

The popularity of the subsequent narratives in each case could never have been predicted based on the ordinariness of the events that triggered it. Thousands of women were arrested and acquitted of killing their lovers in the twentieth century, and thousands of Jews and rebels were crucified by Romans in the first Century, with few people weaving tales around these events[289] and none of them becoming as popular as the Roxie Hart and Jesus Christ tales.

The biggest disanalogy is that no religion developed out of the play *Chicago*. However, we should not confuse religion, a particular mode of human cultural expression, with the development of shifting narratives from events. The understanding of the development and production of events-narratives is independent of their use as religious texts. It is this development of events-narratives phenomena that we seek to understand before the incidental development of specific religions

The *Chicago Paradigm* warns us especially about one feature we need to keep in mind. Once we find the material that the gospels are based on, we still have no guarantee of finding a simple truth. Even more basic primary narratives are likely to be filled with lies, deceptions and contradictions.

In *Scarlett Pimpernel*, Baroness Orczy's love for the aristocracy was true. In *The Bat*, Mary Roberts Rinehart's equal cleverness to men was true. In Frankenstein, Mary Shelley's sadness and alienation was true. In *Chicago*, it was true that Maurine Watkins reported on a murder, arrest, trial and acquittal.

And Harry Potter Too!

I have written about four modern women over the last two centuries who have created extraordinarily popular fictional characters. As I write in the present time, the most popular international fiction character is a young wizard named Harry Potter. He too is the creation of a woman—J.K. Rowling. She got the idea for Harry Potter at the age of 25 in 1990, while riding on a train from Manchester to London. She started writing that evening, although she notes that "those first few pages bear no resemblance at all to anything in the finished book[290]." She notes in her biography that the death of her own mother made "Harry's feelings about his dead parents ... more real." While Harry Potter is quite fantastic, apparently the writer has drawn on real life events to help create the impression of reality.

An important part of the success of Harry Potter may come from the odd sounding names she uses for characters and places. They seem to delight readers as if casting a spell:

> As early as 1983 Rowling was collecting obscure old English words and odd or unusual names from maps and towns in England. These names began to find their purpose in 1990 when she conceived of and began work on a book about an orphaned boy, mistreated by his custodial aunt and uncle, who doesn't yet realize he is a wizard[291].

I must admit to being a bit disappointed that my accidental chain of name coincidences for women writers of famous fictional characters came to an end with J.K.

Rowling. The other four women all had names derived from Mary. In this case, we have a woman named Joanne. However a quick name search did establish that the name Joanne means the same as in Hebrew as Joanna: God is Gracious. Coincidentally, Joanna is a biblical character associated with Mary. From Luke (8.2-3) we get, "and also some women who had been healed of evil spirits and infirmities: Mary, called Magdalene, from whom seven demons had gone out, and Joanna, the wife of Chuza, Herod's steward, and Susanna, and many others, who provided for them out of their means." Later in Luke we find, "Now it was Mary Magdalene and Joanna and Mary the mother of James and the other women with them who told this to the apostles; but these words seemed to them an idle tale, and they did not believe them." Like our other four Marys, our Joanna, J.K. Rowling, appears to be a teller of idle tales.

Jesus the Anti-Christ

> The gospels have been read as a *book of innocence*... surely no small indication of the high skill with which the trick has been done[292].
> Friedrich Nietzsche

One mark of a good theory is that it leads to new understanding of phenomena. Understanding that a woman poet wrote the original material that the canonical gospels are based on allows us to have new insights into the meaning of the texts. For example, let us go back over some passages from the *Second Epistle of John*, which on our hypothesis was written by Mary.

> 19. They went out from us, but they did not really belong to us. For if they had belonged to us, they would have remained with us; but their going showed that none of them belonged to us.
> 20. But you have an anointing from the Holy One, and all of you know the truth.
> 21. I do not write to you because you do not know the truth, but because you do know it and because no lie comes from the truth.
> 22. Who is the liar? It is the man who denies that Jesus is the Christ. Such a man is the antichrist—he denies the Father and the Son.
> 23. No-one who denies the Son has the Father; whoever acknowledges the Son has the Father also.
> 24. See that what you have heard from the beginning remains in you. If it does, you also will remain in the Son and in the Father.
> 25. And this is what he promised us—even eternal life.
> 26. I am writing these things to you about those who are trying to lead you astray.

THE EVOLUTION OF CHRISTS AND CHRISTIANIES

Notice that the terms "son" and "father" are used metaphorically. Denying that Jesus is the Christ is like denying a son has a father. For Mary, Jesus is not the Son of God, he is the Christ (Savior). The father in this relationship is the concept of eternal life, the son is the concept of Jesus being the Christ. You cannot have the father, eternal life, unless you acknowledge the son, Jesus is the Christ.

Does this mean that the disciples saw Jesus as the Messiah, or Jesus saw himself as the Christ (Messiah). On the contrary, we can surmise that both Jesus and his disciples regarded the coming of a Christ with skepticism. To arrive at this position we have to ask why does Mary use the term "Christ" in reference to Jesus here?

If there had been discussion of Jesus being the Christ, Mary could point to Jesus' pronouncements on the topic to either assert or deny it. She does not do this. There is a reason this would not be a live question among the disciples. Neither the disciples nor Jesus had any belief in a coming Messiah at all. After his sudden and tragic death, apparently Peter (or the new leaders of the group) started looking for the Christ, adopting a normal Jewish position. If Mary just reiterates Jesus' position that there is no Christ coming, Peter can just say, "Hey, Jesus did not believe in a Christ. Look what happened to him. He was an anti-Christ and God punished him for it." Mary's response is to basically say, "There are no Christs coming from Heaven, but Jesus was the closest thing to a Christ, we are ever going to get, so he was in effect the Christ and you guys are antichrists to be still looking for Christs." For Mary, Jesus was the Christ by default, in a negative metaphorical sense. The later Church co-opted her original idea of Jesus being the Christ, but turned it into a positive attribute) and combined it with Peter's Jewish expectation of a later coming Messiah.

This passage tells us that Jesus the Christ is an invention of Mary. It also tells us that the "father" concept or primary teaching of Jesus was "eternal life." This coincides well with the opening of the *Gospel of Thomas* which also gives this concept a position of prominence in the first saying of Jesus: "'And,' he said, 'Whoever discovers the interpretation of these sayings will not taste death.'"

While there are many sayings in *Thomas* referring to the Kingdom of God, the conception of the Kingdom of God is quite different than its portrayal in the Gospels. It is not a coming event but a state of being.

> Jesus said, "If your leaders say to you, 'Look, the (Father's) kingdom is in the sky,' then the birds of the sky will precede you. If they say to you, 'It is in the sea,' then the fish will precede you. Rather, the Kingdom is within you and it is outside you[293].

On the other hand, the *Gospel of Mark* does not begin with a discussion of Jesus' primary doctrine of eternal life, but with his pronouncement of a coming Kingdom of God.

> After John was put in prison, Jesus went into Galilee, proclaiming the good news of God. The time has come, he said. The kingdom of God is near. Repent and believe the good news[294]!

We may take this as a revision of the image of Jesus. Mary and Thomas portray Jesus as a teacher of mysteries of eternal life. Mark takes Jesus as a clone of John the Baptist, a sin-forgiving prophet pronouncing the future Kingdom of God.

Thomas Doubts Mary

We can find another proof of Mary's original authorship of the primary Jesus tale in the *Gospel of John*. All the canonical gospels speak of Jesus being crucified, which may have entailed either Jesus being tied to a cross or nailed to one. This is the only gospel that speaks of Jesus being "pierced," Ironically, this is in reference to his being pierced by a soldier in the side, not the piercing by nails of crucifixion. How can we know this? Look at the piercing scene:

> 19.33. But when they came to Jesus, and saw that he was dead already, they brake not his legs: 34. But one of the soldiers with a spear pierced his side, and forthwith came there out blood and water. 35. And he that saw it bare record, and his record is true: and he knoweth that he saith true, that ye might believe. 36. For these things were done, that the scripture should be fulfilled, A bone of him shall not be broken. 37. And again another scripture saith, They shall look on him whom they pierced.

Obviously if Jesus had been pierced during the crucifixion, the piercing of Jesus' side would not have been needed to fulfill the Hebrew scripture. The writer who added the soldier piercing Jesus' side did not know or believe that Jesus' hands and feet had been pierced. If the writer had known, the writer could/would not have declared this piercing was in fulfillment of the piercing prophesy. It seems probable that the writer thought Jesus had been bound by rope, most common in crucifixion cases, and that the only piercing that took place was the piercing of Jesus' side.

However, this does not mean that the piercing tradition was later than the hanging/bound tradition. The Doubting Thomas story in the same Gospel indicates that there was an early tradition of Jesus being nailed to the cross. Look at these scenes

> 20:24. But Thomas, one of the twelve, called Didymus, was not with them when Jesus came. 25. The other disciples therefore said unto him, We have seen the LORD. But he said unto them, Except I shall see in his hands the print of the nails, and put my finger into the print of the nails, and thrust my hand into his

> side, I will not believe. 26. And after eight days again his disciples were within, and Thomas with them: then came Jesus, the doors being shut, and stood in the midst, and said, Peace be unto you. 27. Then saith he to Thomas, Reach hither thy finger, and behold my hands; and reach hither thy hand, and thrust it into my side: and be not faithless, but believing.

Now, we have to wonder about the description of this scene. It appears quite disgusting, with Thomas actually placing his hand inside a cavity in Jesus' body and apparently feeling his internal organs. It is quite gross when thought of this way. However, recall that Thomas was not there when the soldier pierced Jesus, so he could not verify it was Jesus from this action. How could Thomas know that the report of Jesus' wounding was real? People get wounded all the time. Not only would this action not identify Jesus, this would actually prove nothing about Jesus being alive or dead. Both then and now physicians place their hands inside the wounds of both living and dead men. Could we be missing something here?

Since we know that the piercing of the side (not the hands) and the piercing of the hands were two separate traditions, we have to ask how Thomas knows about both of them? If he was reading the other three gospels, he certainly could not have known about the side wound. If he was reading this gospel before the second author put in the scene, he also would not have known about it.

The answer is he does not know about the side wound. Thomas puts his hand through Jesus' side, not to prove Jesus is alive, but to prove that he is a ghost. In other words there is no wound in Jesus' side, but only a wound/nailmark in Jesus' hand. Thomas puts his hand in Jesus' side to prove that he is an immaterial ghost. The writer who added the soldier piercing Jesus put the hole in Jesus' side precisely to make Jesus' post-death appearance a fleshy one, rather than a ghostly one.

Assuming the opposite, that Thomas somehow knew about Jesus' pierced side, we are left with the problem of why the writer would ignore the pierced hands and feet of Jesus and say that the piercing of the side was in fulfillment of prophecy. The understanding that Thomas was testing for Jesus' ghostliness and the piercing of Jesus' side was added to the text afterwards, gets rid of this textual problem.

Origen a mid-third century Christian writer gives us more evidence regarding this. In his work *Contra Celsus*, he argues against a mid-second century Pagan writer named Celsus. Apparently Celsus was reading an earlier edition of one of the gospels. Origen writes:

> Speaking next of the statements in the Gospels, that after His resurrection He showed the marks of His punishment, and how His hands had been pierced, he asks, "Who beheld this?" And discrediting the narrative of Mary Magdalene, who is related to have seen Him, he replies, "A half-frantic woman, as ye state." And because she is not the only one who is

recorded to have seen the Saviour after His resurrection, but others also are mentioned, this Jew of Celsus calumniates these statements also in adding, "And some one else of those engaged in the same system of deception![295]"

In the version of the gospel that Celsus read, Jesus shows the marks of his punishment and how "his hands had been pierced" to a half-frantic woman. First note that there is no reference to the side wound, but only his hands being pierced. Second note that it is to Mary, not Thomas that Jesus shows his wounds. Third, the reference to "some one else of those engaged in the same system of deception" may refer to Thomas, but most probably refers to the tomb version of Matthew, when both Mary Magdalene and "the other Mary" encounter Jesus[296]. Celsus draws the obvious conclusions about the incident, as Origen reports:

> In the next place, as if this were possible, viz., that the image of a man who was dead could appear to another as if he were still living, he adopts this opinion as an Epicurean, and says, "That some one having so dreamed owing to a peculiar state of mind, or having, under the influence of a perverted imagination, formed such an appearance as he himself desired, reported that such had been seen; and this," he continues, "has been the case with numberless individuals[297]."

We know that the incorporeal nature of Jesus after his return was a problem for the later orthodox Church. Eusebius quotes this passage, which Jerome attributes to the Gospel of the Hebrews and Origin attributes to the Teaching of Peter.

> "But I know and believe that he was in the flesh after the resurrection. And when he came to Peter and his companions he said to them, Take, handle me, and see that I am not an incorporeal spirit. And immediately they touched him and believed[298]."

It is evident from this that there was a real question about the corporality of Jesus. The name of Ignatius was invoked to give credibility to the corporeal side.

This analysis just tells us what the scene was originally about, the ghostly appearance of Jesus after his death. We can use the tool of psychoanalysis to go further in understanding this scene. In 1900 Freud published his essay *The Interpretation of Dreams*, in which he examined the transference of conscious meanings and values to symbols in dreams. While many of Freud's other theories and practices have withered under criticism, this methodology has been expanded to the field of literary criticism, where it has been used to produce interesting results in by both critics and authors.

How might the author have fictionalized (changed the values and symbols) in her real life to come up with this scene?

The poetical style of the writing tells us immediately that the scene is authentically by Mary. The line, "Have you believed because you have seen me? Blessed are those that have not seen and yet believe me," is typical of that style where an element in the first proposition is negated to produce a new meaning in the second proposition.

We have to think about the meaning of the text in relationship to the Gospel of Thomas and Mary texts. We know that the question of belief is Mary's problem. The disciples do not believe her tale of a ghostly Jesus appearance.

The nature of the proof that Thomas wants is purely physical. He does not want Jesus to answer questions like where were you on the night of the 24th or what city were you born. He does not want Jesus to produce 500 more witnesses to his resurrection. He wants to touch the mark of the nail and put his hand inside of Jesus. We are talking about touching and penetrating the body here. We should remember Mary is always associated with physicality and sexuality in the Gospels. Whether it is washing his feet with her hair, leaning on his breast (or him leaning on her breast which is more likely) or going to embrace him after seeing him in the tomb.

Subjecting the text to the most simple psychoanalysis possible, we may say that the ghost of Jesus represents Mary herself. The scene reflects Thomas offering to believe Mary if he can touch and penetrate her. Mary not only agrees but erotically instructs him on how to do it.

The final lines in the scene can easily be translated from their present form into their original sense:

> 20:27. Then he said to Thomas, Put your finger here; see my hands. Reach out your hand and put it into my side. Stop doubting and believe.
> 28. Thomas said to him, My Lord and my God!
> 29. Then Jesus told him, Because you have seen me, you have believed; blessed are those who have not seen and yet have believed.

Psychoanalytical Reconstruction of Thomas' Doubts

> Then she said to Thomas, Put your finger here, see my hands. Reach out your hand and put it into my Vagina. Stop doubting and believe.
> Thomas said to her. My lord and my Goddess.
> Then Mary told him, because you have penetrated me, you have believed; blessed are those who have not penetrated and yet have believed.

This is not a textual reconstruction. Mary never wrote such a text. It is a psychoanalytical reconstruction of a probable original meaning that has been sublimated and transformed symbolically in turning the event portrayed into literature. To get it, we take what we know about the author's life situation (the disciples did not believe her about her dream of Jesus' appearance[299]) and what we know about the scene (a wish fulfillment that Jesus would appear and the disciples would believe her) and asking how she could have derived that scene from a real incident in her life.

The information about Jesus in the canonical gospels is generally taken as truthful and reasonably accurate. Before deconstructing them to show that this may not be the case, we should begin by asking a more basic question about them.

Part II: What is the Gospel?

Besides finding a parallel in a modern events-narratives phenomenon, it will also help us to understand the *genre* of the *Gospels*. In her recent book, Reading *Roman Women: Sources, Genres and Real Life*, Suzanne Dixon notes:

> It should be stated from the outset that ancient authors sometimes perceived *genre* in more formal terms than moderns, always allowing for continuing debates about the boundaries... But there is nonetheless a connection in ancient terms between content and genre. It happens, for example, that references to the female body and female sexualities are concentrated in satire and elegy... Economic activity generally had no place in the more esteemed ancient literary *genres* but women's economic roles do figure in certain non-literary sources and in law-court speeches[300].

As she suggests, certain genres allowed certain things to be portrayed in certain ways and others did not. She writes, "Unhappy marriages, for example, have no place in epitaphs, happy marriages have none on the comic stage, and marriage does not fit into the formulaic narrative of illicit love promoted in elegy[301]."

It is quite fantastic that the literary category *Gospel* should be invented magically from nothing. By figuring out how it evolved, and out of what *genre*, we should get a better understanding of the evolution of the events-narratives phenomenon. In this respect the rigidity of Roman written *genres* helps us enormously.

The Gospels That are Not Gospels

Gospels (*euangelion*) in the first century C.E. were short announcements of happy news about events of empire-wide or cosmic significance. Craig A. Evans gives these examples of its usages[302]:

> The emperor's reign or victory was announced as 'gospel' or 'good news' (εὐαγγελιον or εὐαγγελίζετααι). The good news was celebrated as a

religious event. For example, cities rejoiced and offered sacrifices to the gods upon receiving the good news (ευαγγελίζεται) of the royal heir's coming of age. The calendrical inscription from Priene, mentioned above, describes the birthday of Augustus 'the beginning of the good news for the world'. Plutarch says that 'a number of people sailed for Lesbos, wishing to announce to Cornelia the good news [ευαγγελζόμενοι] that the war was over' (*Pomp*. 66.3).8 Jews also understood and employed this terminology. When word spread of Vespasian's accession to the throne, 'every city celebrated the good news [ευαγγελια] and offered sacrifices on his behalf' (Josephus, *War* 4.10.6 §618). Josephus later relates: 'On reaching Alexandria Vespasian was greeted by the good news [ευαγγελια] from Rome and by embassies of congratulation from every quarter of the world, now his own . . . The whole empire being now secured and the Roman state saved [σωζειν] beyond expectation, Vespasian turned his thoughts to what remained in Judaea' (*War* 4.11.5 §§656-657).

Here is an example of a "gospel" of the period, the announcement of Nero Caesar's ascension to the throne:

> The one who was owed to the ancestors, and god-made-manifest, Caesar, has gone to join them. And the Emperor whom the world anticipated and hoped for has been proclaimed; the good spirit of the inhabited world and source of all goodness, Nero Caesar, has been proclaimed. Consequently, we should all wear garlands and with sacrifices of oxen give thanks to all the gods. (Year) one of Nero Claudius Caesar Augustus Germanicus, the twenty-first of the month Neus Sabastus[303].

Note that in response to the gospel of Nero, people are told to do two things: 1) wear garlands and 2) sacrifice oxen. The use of the term "gospel" within the Gospel of Mark refers to the good news that "The Kingdom of God is at hand[304]." Again in response to the gospel of the Kingdom at God, people are told to do two things, 1) repent and 2) believe.

> After John was put in prison, Jesus went into Galilee, proclaiming the good news of God. The time has come, he said. The kingdom of God is near. Repent and believe the good news[305]!

At this stage, Jesus is simply carrying on the work of John in announcing the gospel (good news) that the Kingdom of God is at hand. This usage of the term contradicts the usage at the beginning of this text: "The beginning of the Gospel of Jesus the Christ." We may take this line as a much later textual marker, where the whole text itself has become "the gospel." Note the slide in meaning of the term "gospel," from something within the text to the text itself. The gospel of John/Jesus is originally the announcement that the kingdom of God is at hand. Later, the text in which Jesus appears to announce this gospel becomes "the gospel." In the 1960's, 1970's and 1980's, car chase scenes appearing in "action movies" became quite popular. Variations on these scenes appeared using trucks, skies, boats, spaceships and almost any other transportation vehicle the screenwriters could imagine. In the 1990's, critics started to term such movies themselves as "rides." It was a way of labeling and classifying movies through one of the elements they had in common. In effect, by changing the word "Gospel" to refer to these texts while retaining its old meaning of a happy announcement of events, ancient critics were being labeling and classifying them in a particular way to draw together their commonality.

Once this labeling and classification was done by using the word "ride" in reference to action movies, screenwriters consciously sought even more ways to include "rides" (transportation vehicles) in their "rides." (movies)[306]. Likewise, once the genre was labeled as "Gospel" specific "Gospels" elements were added. "Gospels" (birth announcements) were added to the text of Matthew and Luke. We can see in all three different gospel elements that developed in these texts:

1) the gospel pronounced by John announcing that the Kingdom of God is near, After John's death, the character of Jesus continues to pronounce this gospel.
2) the gospel pronounced by John announcing that the messiah is coming.
3) the gospel announcing the birth of Jesus in Matthew.
4) the gospel announcing the birth of John in Luke.

The last two can be seen as a conscious attempt by the writers to add more gospel elements to the gospels after the texts themselves had acquired the name gospel.

The Memoirs That are Not Memoirs

While others used the term "gospel" to apply to their works, the authors of Mark and John certainly could not have thought of their works in such terms because their works had not come into existence yet. If they could not have thought that they were writing Gospels, then what did they think they were doing? The introduction in the **New Oxford Annotated Bible with the Apocrypha: New Revised Standard Version** is quite helpful here.

> Second-century CE authors, on the other hand, both adherents of Christianity like Justin Martyr and opponents like Celsus, presumed that the evangelists intended to provided information. Justin Martyr's designation of the Gospels as "memoirs" (Gk "hypomnemata"; *1 Apology*

1.67.3) suggests something less than the full literary biography, and something more like a gathering of notes about the subject and his teaching. This perception may have been enhanced by the fact that early Christians disseminated their writings using the codex (similar to a bound book) rather than the scroll. Though modern readers often think of the codex as a technological advance over the scroll, the ancients did not. Serious literary works were copied onto scrolls. Notes, primarily drafts, and all sorts of records were kept in codices. Thus their physical appearance would suggest to an ancient reader that the Gospels were something like educational handbooks or pamphlets, not examples of high literary art. Papias's comment that Mark is "not in order" (Eusebius, *History of the Church* 3.39.5) shows that even some Christian readers considered it n unfinished composition. Papias also noted that Matthew was a more polished work (Eusebius, *History of the Church* 3.39.16). Luke's prologue states that he intends to correct the deficiencies in earlier accounts (1.1-4). Such concerns indicate that Mark's earliest readers treated the Gospel as a rough life of Jesus. Such a biography invited the expansions in content and revisions of style that Matthew and Luke subsequently undertook[307].

I would like to make two points. First, the designation of the gospels as memoirs is quite inaccurate. Second, the unfinished quality of the *Gospel of Mark* is especially important to understanding the wild and ragtag nature of the development of all the Gospels.

Justin Martyr's designation of the gospels as "memoirs" probably shows some confusion over how to categorize the text, and indeed, which text to accept as authoritative. In actual "memoirs" (both ancient and modern) we always get a high degree of subjectivity expressed, at the very least, in a frame surrounding the recalled incidents. For example, note the beginning and end of Xenophon's Memorabilia, his memoirs of his teacher, Socrates. This is the beginning:

> I have often wondered by what arguments those who indicted Socrates could have persuaded the Athenians that his life was justly forfeit to the state. The indictment was to this effect: "Socrates is guilty of crime in refusing to recognise the gods acknowledged by the state, and importing strange divinities of his own; he is further guilty of corrupting the young." In the first place, what evidence did they produce that Socrates refused to recognise the gods acknowledged by the state? Was it that he did not sacrifice? or that he dispensed with divination? On the contrary, he was often to be seen engaged in sacrifice, at home or at the common altars of the state. Nor was his dependence on divination less manifest. Indeed that saying of his, "A divinity gives me a sign,"

was on everybody's lips. So much so that, if I am not mistaken, it lay at the root of the imputation that he imported novel divinities; though there was no greater novelty in his case than in that of other believers in oracular help, who commonly rely on omens of all sorts: the flight or cry of birds, the utterances of man, chance meetings, or a victim's entrails[308].

Notice the subjectivity. "I have often wondered," "If I am not mistaken." This subjectivity appears sporadically throughout the work and again in the ending:

> ... Such are the words which he spoke in conversation with Hermogenes and the rest. But amongst those who knew Socrates and recognised what manner of man he was, all who make virtue and perfection their pursuit still to this day cease not to lament his loss with bitterest regret, as for one who helped them in the pursuit of virtue as none else could.
>
> To me, personally, he was what I have myself endeavoured to describe: so pious and devoutly religious[13] that he would take no step apart from the will of heaven; so just and upright that he never did even a trifling injury to any living soul; so self-controlled, so temperate, that he never at any time chose the sweeter in place of the better; so sensible, and wise, and prudent that in distinguishing the better from the worse he never erred; nor had he need of any helper, but for the knowledge of these matters, his judgment was at once infallible and self-sufficing. Capable of reasonably setting forth and defining moral questions,[14] he was also able to test others, and where they erred, to cross-examine and convict them, and so to impel and guide them in the path of virtue and noble manhood. With these characteristics, he seemed to be the very impersonation of human perfection and happiness[309].

Compare this beginning and ending with the beginning and ending of the Gospel of John:

> In the beginning was the Word, and the Word was with God, and the Word was God. He was with God in the beginning[310] ...

There is no hint of subjectivity here. The author is doing a dramatic poetic exposition of the book of Genesis. The ending is totally different.

> ... Peter turned and saw that the disciple whom Jesus loved was following them. (This was the one who had leaned back against Jesus at the supper and had said, Lord, who is going to betray you?)

> When Peter saw him, he asked, Lord, what about him?
>
> Jesus answered, If I want him to remain alive until I return, what is that to you? You must follow me. Because of this, the rumour spread among the brothers that this disciple would not die. But Jesus did not say that he would not die; he only said, If I want him to remain alive until I return, what is that to you?
>
> This is the disciple who testifies to these things and who wrote them down. We know that his testimony is true.
>
> Jesus did many other things as well. If every one of them were written down, I suppose that even the whole world would not have room for the books that would be written[311].

Only at the very end of the work do we get the subjectivity that could mark the work as a set of memoirs. But the last lines function in quite a different way within the text. The writer does not say "I am the disciple who testifies to these things." On the contrary, he writes, "This is the disciple who testifies to these things and who wrote them down." This is merely an identification of the beloved disciple character in the story as the source for the editor's material. In other words, the editor reveals himself as not the person who testifies and wrote these things down. The editor belongs to the other group "we" in "We know that his testimony is true."

In fact, we are getting the editor's testimony that the beloved disciple (writer/testifier) was telling the truth when she wrote these things (stories) down. However, note, immediately, the editor tells us that the writer/testifier has only included a small portion of the truth. Even more, when we understand that the beloved disciple and writer was Mary, the last two lines may be read with a sarcastic and bitter tone. The line "We know that his testimony is true," means "We know what a liar that Mary is." The last line about the many things that Jesus did, can be read as meaning "We know that loudmouth Mary makes up such a number of stories about Jesus, the world can't hold them all."

What we are getting in this work is not "memoirs" but edited testimony of the beloved disciple of Jesus. This work is quite unique in this respect, the synoptic gospels do not claim to be to testimonies by anyone, although the anonymous author of Luke does claim in his prologue that he "carefully investigated everything from the beginning," quite categorically denying denying that he is writing memoirs. Who needs to investigate their own memories? At least in the ancient world nobody did.

Now, regarding the observation that the technological development of the codex around the time of the beginning of Christianity was an important influence on the development of the gospels, we should be careful to note exactly how this took place. Note the expressions "Matthew was a more polished work" and "expansions in content and revisions of style that Matthew and Luke subsequently undertook." We have to be careful here not to lump the production of all these texts together and assume that they were all produced in the same fashion. Only Mark really gives us the impression of coming from the codex. Like cinema in the 20th century, the codex was a fairly new invention in the first and second centuries, making note-taking, editing and textual expansion much easier. John's work, like Matthew and Luke's, is a "polished" work. It is the only work which someone deemed important enough to write a commentary on as early as the middle of the Second Century. The teacher of the Christian movement of Valentinus, Ptolemy, wrote a commentary, at least on the Prologue of John, and Herakleon, a student of Valentinus wrote a commentary on the entire work. This indicates that the text we now call the Gospel of John was considered a complete work by the middle of the Second Century.

The Testimony That is a Play

At the end of the Gospel of John, the editor has thrown in a piece of a scene from earlier in the play, just before Jesus gets arrested. This is a scene where Jesus says goodbye to Mary and asks her to feed his sheep. I will show how I deconstructed this scene to arrive at this proposition later. For the moment, I would like to examine the last three lines at the end of this scene that do not belong to the feeding the sheep farewell scene that currently precedes it.

> 24. This is the disciple which testifieth of these things, and wrote these things: and we know that his testimony is true.
> 25. And there are also many other things which Jesus did, the which, if they should be written every one, I suppose that even the world itself could not contain the books that should be written. Amen.

The last line is just a joke that subverts the idea that the gospel is true. It points up the human ability to infinitely create stories. Textually, the line is suspect. Our best ancient manuscript of the text, the Codex Sinaiticus from the fourth century contains it only as a later addition. It originally ended at John 21:24:

> The last verse of the Gospel according to John (21:25) is another passage where the use of ultra-violet light has confirmed Tischendorf's surmise as to the original reading. It is now known that the scribe for some reason finished the Gospel with verse 24, adding a subscription and drawing, as usual, a *coronis* (tail-piece) in the left-hand margin between the text and the subscription. Later, however, the same scribe washed the vellum clean of the coronis and subscription and added the concluding verse, repeating the coronis and subscription in a correspondingly lower position[312].

We can see 21:24 as the true ending of the narrative. However it certainly did not come after the discussion about feeding sheep and following and remaining[313]. It came after the concluding verse at 20:30:

> Jesus did many other miraculous signs in the presence of his disciples, which are not recorded in this book. [31]But these are written that you may[1] believe that Jesus is the Christ, the Son of God, and that by believing you may have life in his name.

At this point we may add 21:25, but at this point, there is no reason for the original author to speak of herself in the third person. The concluding verse we can reconstruct as:

> I am the disciple who testifies to these things and wrote these things and my testimony is true.

The phrase "son of God" shows a later Christology, as it does in the opening verse of Mark. The phrase "in this book" is also suspect to me. The term "book" probably had not even been invented yet. The latin "scripta" (vulgate) and the Greek "γεγραπται" can better be translated as referring to a writing or written work.

> "Jesus did many other miraculous signs in the presence of his disciples, which are not in this writing, But these are written that you may believe that Jesus is the Christ, and that by believing you may have life in his name.
> I am the disciple who testifies to these things and wrote these things and my testimony is true.

In this context, the disciple is testifying specifically to the miracles in this work. She is allowing that other disciples may have experienced other miracles, but the miracles described in this work are the miracles that she is testifying about.

Note that the beginning of the Gospel of Thomas seems to be a continuation with these opening lines tied in to the closing lines of the Gospel of John:

> These are the sayings of the living Jesus, which the Didymos Judas Thomas wrote down. And he said, "Whoever finds the meaning of these sayings will not experience death.

Chronologically speaking, Thomas seems to be following at the heels of this gospel. While this gospel gives the signs of Jesus, Thomas gives the sayings. The

Gospel of John seems to be indicating that other miracle gospels exist, by saying that other disciples experienced other miracles in the presence of Jesus. The Gospel of Thomas seems to be acknowledging that other sayings gospels exist by saying that these are just the sayings that Didymos Judas Thomas wrote down. From this it appears that very early we have miracle stories and sayings, but that the two genres are separate. Only later, it seems we get a combination of the two genres, as reflected in the synoptic gospels.

In any case, we should note the essentially poetical character of the writing. Compare the beginning and ending of this text:

> 1. **In the beginning was the Word, and the Word was with God, and the Word was God. 2. He was with God in the beginning.**

> "Jesus did many other miraculous signs in the presence of his disciples, which are not in this writing, But these are written that you may believe that Jesus is the Christ, and that by believing you may have life in his name.
> I am the disciple who testifies to these things and wrote these things and my testimony is true.

What we are getting here is not prose, but a very definite chiasmic structure of ABBA, not on the concept level, but on the immediate symbol or word level. So

- ➤ A) Beginning-word, B) Word-God, B) Word-God A) God-Beginning
- ➤ A) I-disciple, B) testify-things B) wrote-things A) testimony-true

We may reconstruct the original last line as saying "I am the *true* disciple," based on this chiasmic structure. What is important is the poetical quality of the writing. The poetical quality limits the genre that the author is working in. For example, nobody wrote biographies or legal testimonies in poetical verse. We have eliminated the categories of gospels, (a later invention) and memoirs (no frame at the beginning, besides no examples in poetical verse). History certainly was not written in poetical verse.

What kind of poetry could this work be? The nature of the narrative, a description of a recent historical event, a political execution of a messiah figure, excludes it from being lyrical, elegiac, bucolic or epic poetry. There is only one genre that the style and substance of the work fits. The only genre that would be appropriate for this type of mixing of poetry and narrative would be a theater play. When we ask what genre of poetry this writing belongs to, the startling answer is *Drama*[314].

The Mime Play:

As we noted before Jesus was the lover of Mary, the wife of Caiaphas. The relationship of Jesus to Mary in the *Passover Gospel* text would seem to indicate support for an hypothesis that the gospels came from the script of a mime play. Writing on mime plays, Michael Jones notes:

> The *mima* was also quite often called upon to play the part of an adulterous *matrona*, trapped between the affections of a paramour and the demands of a husband (Reynolds 1946, McKeown 1979). As it turns out, this transformation of *matrona* into *meretrix* figures in at least two fragments from mime-scripts of the late Republic (Laberius fr. 33R, Publilius *ad Petr. Sat.* 55)[315].

The reconstructed ending, the line "I am the disciple who testifies to these things and wrote these things and my testimony is true," suggests that the author herself was onstage and that she testified that she was the disciple in the play. A quick glance at the Roman plays of Terence show that the author (or author representative) addressing the audience directly at the end of the play was a feature of these works:

> Chremes: All right, I'll let him off.
> (Ambivius reappears)
> And we'll let you off now,
> Because,
> You see, that's how it was!
> Do we hear your applause[316]?

> Davus: I'm going.
> (To the audience) Don't you just sit there,'
> Waiting for them to come out here again.
> The ceremeonies all take place inside,
> And whatever little settlements are left
> To work out with the property.
> Well now, it's all worked out quite properly, don't you think?
> Let's see: two husbands, two wives, two fathers,
> Probably a little property clause
> For Crito. Makes you pause
> And think. I think it's pretty nice.
> Love and marriage in a good cause.
> And you might want to add to it the spice
> Of a good round of applause[317].

To counter that this pre-gospel gospel was originally a play, one can make the gross generalization that new plays were not being performed and/or presented at this time. Yet we have the works of Seneca and the author of the *Octavia* to counter this. The circumstances of performance, whether just a simple read-through by the author or a full scale production in one of the theaters built in Jerusalem or Caesarea[318], in the Middle of the First Century, may be a matter for debate, but these questions are secondary to the question of the genre of material that the Gospels evolved out from.

One may also deny that Jews would be involved in plays, a specifically Greek and Roman literary form. However Josephus mentions a Jewish actor who was instrumental in helping him release Jewish Priests from captivity.

> I became acquainted with Aliturius, an actor of plays, and much beloved by Nero, but a Jew by birth; and through his interest became known to Poppea, Caesar's wife, and took care, as soon as possible, to entreat her to procure that the priests might be set at liberty. And when, besides this favor, I had obtained many presents from Poppea, I returned home again[319].

Since I will propose later that the author, producer and star of this work was a woman, I should mention a bit about the role of women in ancient theater. We have to again be very careful about gross generalizations that women were kept locked away in Rome, or women did not attend theater, or that women did not act in plays. The period just after Augustus Caesar seems to have been a sort of Golden age for women. They attained quite a bit of power and influence.

> All cultures evolve and in the long evolution of Rome from Republic to Empire towards decline, the positions of all citizens continued to change as the times changed them. Yet, for Roman women, it is arguable that no changes in how society viewed them matched the dislocations and opportunities of the period between Cornelia and Agrippina[320]. Although Augustus attempted to legislate a return to the older, restrictive morality, women were never again as invisible or as voiceless in the Empire as they had been in the Republic. Restrictions once removed were not effectively reimposed.
>
> The older customs requiring a guardian or tutor for women who wished to transact business were frequently ignored from the first century AD and after. Women could now frequently participate in commerce or become patronesses of craft or professional guilds. Loopholes in inheritance laws permitted them, increasingly, to build up independent fortunes. Building on Livia's example, later Empresses frequently governed in the Emperor's absence and wielded genuine power, more or less overtly. Their images were frequently shown on the Imperial coinage,

individually or side by side with the Emperor. Their idealized images, as his, were distributed throughout an interconnected Empire. They were frequently deified with their husbands and shown ascending with him to the gods[321].

Combining the concept that the original gospel text was a play with the understanding that the "beloved disciple" was Mary and she both wrote and appeared in the play, we can now name the genre of this work: a Mime Play.

Mime Actresses and Mime Plays

Today, the word mime is associated with the pantomime, the clowns of the medieval *commedia dell'arte*, or the white faced street performers who imitate Marcel Marceau. When thinking about Roman Mime theater, we should not think about silent performances, or Pantomimes (all mime) who came later, but rather about the Platonic concept of *mimesis*, or imitation. The mimes of the Roman theater were interested in copying the gestures as well as the words of their characters. It was performed without masks, or slight masks, so the facial expressions could be seen. It was far more naturalistic than the highly stylized Greek theater. One might compare it to the naturalistic style of method acting that gripped Hollywood movies in the 1950's and 60's.

We know that while men only acted in ancient Greek theater, women did perform in Roman Mime theater. As Giusto Traina notes in a recent article[322], "Long barred from serious theater, women acted in mime performances from the very beginning, as was the Greek practice. Their presence was fundamental, for they lightened the tone of the performance and made it more sensual, if not openly erotic." We have significant information about one Mime Actress, from the Mid-Late First Century B.C.

> Cytheris/Lycoris was a *mima*, an actress specialized in the art of mime, a semiliterary genre of the theater, which in that era reached the height of its popularity and was appreciated by the ruling classes. The brief mention of Lycoris in *De viris illustribus* clearly defines her role in Roman society: an actress-courtesan. All of her lovers were key figures in the Roman revolutions: Gallus, Brutus, Mark Anthony[323].

Michael Jones reminds us, "Only in the mime, and in no other type of ancient dramatic performance, were female roles played by performers who were actually women. In other words, person and persona fit perfectly[324]." He further notes that the identity of the mime "is an identity in flux, an identity in a state of perpetual motion, continually made and unmade by the gendered gaze of the spectators. On the one hand, the *mima* was figured as *meretrix*, both by the nature and by the very fact of her performance. But hers was a theatrical prostitution, just as her body was a theatricalized body: costume-as-costume gives way to the body-as-costume."

The observation that the mime was an "identity in flux" applies quite literally to the actors and actresses who would play multiple parts from everyday life, political life and from mythology. We can suspect that this had a tremendous effect on the actors and actresses themselves. It may be seen as a culture in itself.

The important text found at Nag Hamadi in 1948, "The Thunder, Perfect Mind" may have been a Mime Song. Its meter is quite similar to the poetical meter found at the beginning of the Gospel of John. The original song at the beginning of the Gospel of John may have come from the same woman who wrote "The Thunder, Perfect Mind." These are the opening lines, which so clearly reflect "the identity in flux" life of the Mime Performer.

> I was sent forth from the power,
> and I have come to those who reflect upon me,
> and I have been found among those who seek after me.
> Look upon me, you who reflect upon me,
> and you hearers, hear me.
> You who are waiting for me, take me to yourselves.
> And do not banish me from your sight.
> And do not make your voice hate me, nor your hearing.
> Do not be ignorant of me anywhere or any time. Be on your guard!
> Do not be ignorant of me.
> For I am the first and the last.
> I am the honored one and the scorned one.
> I am the whore and the holy one.
> I am the wife and the virgin.
> I am <the mother> and the daughter.
> I am the members of my mother.
> I am the barren one and many are her sons.
> I am she whose wedding is great, and I have not taken a husband.
> I am the midwife and she who does not bear.
> I am the solace of my labor pains.
> I am the bride and the bridegroom,
> and it is my husband who begot me.
> I am the mother of my father
> and the sister of my husband and he is my offspring.
> I am the slave of him who prepared me.
> I am the ruler of my offspring.
> But he is the one who begot me before the time on a birthday.
> And he is my offspring in (due) time,

and my power is from him.
I am the staff of his power in his youth,
and he is the rod of my old age.
And whatever he wills happens to me.
I am the silence that is incomprehensible
and the idea whose remembrance is frequent.
I am the voice whose sound is manifold
and the word whose appearance is multiple.
I am the utterance of my name[325] ...

We cannot directly link this to a mime actress. However, we should take note that the author, a women poet, not only openly and boldly questions all sexual identities and roles, but places herself at the center of the controversy. We should also keep in mind that her followers honored and preserved this work for hundreds of years after it was written. Its discovery at Nag Hammadi is one of the greatest fortunate accidents in history.

We should note that its ideology fits in with the ideology of the pre-canonical *Gospel of Thomas*. Compare these lines from that gospel and *Thunder*

> 89. Jesus said, "Why do you wash the outside of the cup? Don't you understand that the one who made the inside is also the one who made the outside?"
>
> For what is inside of you is what is outside of you, and the one who fashions you on the outside is the one who shaped the inside of you.
> And what you see outside of you, you see inside of you; it is visible and it is your garment.

The concept of the outside and inside being made by the same thing is too unusual to be mere coincidence. The writer of *Thomas* and the woman writer of *Thunder* were listening to someone expressing the same concepts. It is no coincidence either that the ending of the Gospel of Thomas is also Mary-centric.

> 114. Simon Peter said to them, "Make Mary leave us, for females don't deserve life."
> Jesus said, "Look, I will guide her to make her male, so that she too may become a living spirit resembling you males. For every female who makes herself male will enter the kingdom of Heaven."

Suzanne Dixon makes the general point that all literary genres were under the control of men in Ancient Rome. All references to women are from a male point of view. She puts forward the proposition that these references:

Amount to male-centered fantasies and moral statements of what women should or should not be, whether they are nominally attached to individuals, to fictitious characters or to groups of women. What has been labeled women's history is largely history of male-female relations or of men's musings about women, usually in terms of women's sexual and reproductive rules and with more moralizing than observation[326].

However, I would suggest that the centrality of women to mime theater should not be underestimated, and that this directly contradicts the patristic norms of Roman society. Not only were women performers, but they seem to have been a major part of the audience. In his defense "Of Pantomine," Lucian's hater of the Pantomimic Art, Crato, declares it ridiculous to think he would attend a performance, "that I should show my long beard and white hairs amid that throng of women and lunatics; and clap and yell in unseemly rapture over the vile contortions of an abandoned buffoon[327]."

Between the female courtesan mimes on stage and the women and lunatics in the audience, we may have the only opportunity to hear authentic females speaking in their own voice in the mime theater. The mime theater may have provided a real arena for power struggles against Roman sexual and class oppression. It is perhaps for that very reason that the vocal mime theater evolved into the silent pantomime theater. We know that starting with Tiberius Caesar laws were passed to weaken the strong appeal of Mime Theater. Its oppositional voice was literally taken away from it.

The popularity of Mime theater may be suggested by the deathbed question of Augustus Caesar, "Have I played my part well in the mime of life?[328]" Its widespread influence and popularity is unquestionable:

> Such performers were not only powerful. In Rome they and their supporters caused theatre riots, in fact the most disruptive known in classical times. This led to their frequent banishment and eventual recall in the first and second centuries. The reasons are not entirely clear. There is no doubt that they appeared in competitions, which exacerbated fan rivalry. Equally clear is that their connections with the upper classes gave them an assurance that could lead to provocations. We know of decrees of the senate under Tiberius that were directed at the pantomimes, until finally they were banished in 23. This is probably to be connected with the fact that Drusus, son of Tiberius, was their sponsor. But the senate sought to prevent contact between the upper classes and these performers. Therefore it ruled that pantomimes were not to perform in private houses, i.e. in the private theatres of the wealthy Romans; and that members of the upper orders were not to process with these artists in the street. Twice it sought by legislation to prevent younger members of the upper orders, both male and female, from performing professionally as pantomimes, something that would

normally have led to their removal from these orders. The penalty was probably exile. It seems clear that the attraction was both the great financial rewards and also the popular acclaim. Though the usual venue for the great spectacles was the theatre, the pantomime is found adapted to private houses and to the amphitheatre and stadium as well[329].

A century ago, Frank Frost noted that the Roman orator Cicero felt "the public opinon found true expression only at the theatrical performances and gladiatorial contests.[330]" He writes further:

> That writers of mimes occupied themselves with political matters may also be inferred from other statements in the Letters of Cicero. In one of these he hint of passages descriptive of Caesar's exploits in the plays which Laberius and Publilius Syrus brought out at the dramatic festival given by the dictator to celebrate his victory at Thapsus. Speaking of his own philosophical acceptance of the political situation, he says, "In fact, I have already become so callous that at the games given by our friend Caesar, with perfect equanimity, I gazed upon Titus Plancus and listened to the production of Laberius and publilius. In another letter he remarks to atticus, "You will write to me if you have anything of practical importance,; if not, describe tome fully the attitudes of the people [in the theatre] and the local hits in the mimes[331]."

Mimes wore tunics and *ricinium* (hoods/veils). Mime plays were known as *fibula riciniata*, stories of the hooded ones. There may be a reference to this in the New Testament work 2 Peter.

> non enim doctas fabulas secuti notam fecimus vobis Domini nostri Iesu Christi virtutem et praesentiam sed speculatores facti illius magnitudinis[332].

It is possible that the depictions of Mary Magdalene and Mary, Mother of Jesus, in veiled tunics, as well as monk's cowls come from the costumes of the mimes. Although, I am conjecturing wildly here.

We are left at this point with questions. Was the writer of the *Passover Gospel*, the primary story from which the gospels evolved a mime actress or the daughter/wife of the High Priest Caiaphas? According to the storyline she is the daughter/wife of Caiaphas. How true is the story? I confess at this point I have no idea. It is improbable, but not impossible.

We have dated the original theater piece/gospel by Mary to the late 40's and a revision close to the gospel of John which we now possess to the 60's. Can we learn anything more precise about the dating of events in these works.

Ivory. Jesus Healing Blindman or Is It Mary?

Murano Diptych, 4th century. If this is the Christ then the feminization of the figure is noteworthy, intentional and puzzling. Could it be Mary performing miracles?

Chapter 5

Dating the Death of an Unknown Man More Precisely

The Missing Interrogation/Trial scene in John

> 18:12. Then the detachment of soldiers with its commander and the Jewish officials arrested Jesus. They bound him
>
> 13 and brought him first to Annas, who was the father-in-law of Caiaphas, the high priest that year.
>
> 18:24. Then Annas sent him, still bound, to Caiaphas the high priest.
>
> 18.28. Then the Jews led Jesus from Caiaphas to the palace of the Roman governor.

John leaves out the trial/interrogation scene in Caiaphas' house that Mark and the Synoptics include. One may interpret this as John just being lazy and not including the scene which he already finds in three gospels. In our reconstruction of the scene, we saw that Jesus did not go to Caiaphas' house, but went to the courtyard and protected Peter and pronounced himself Jesus Christ. Leaving out a dramatic confrontation scene with Caiaphas, the man John has told us is behind the crucifixion of Jesus is absurd[333]. Our *Narrative Sense Tool* tells us we cannot accept such a gap in the text as being naturally created by John.

Rather then hypothesizing that John cut the pivotal scene in Caiaphas' house that he found in the Synoptics, we must postulate that Mark added the scene in Caiaphas' house. Someone added to John the footnote that Jesus was led bound to Caiaphas' House, and changed the text at 18:28 to read "from Caiaphas' house," whereas it originally read "from Annas' house."

We can find more evidence for this important point by looking at the scene in Caiaphas' house in Mark. It is significant that Mark never mentions Caiaphas as the High Priest who interrogates Jesus. It is difficult to imagine why, if Caiaphas is doing the interrogating, Mark never mentions his name. On the other hand, if Mark knows two texts, one with Caiaphas interrogating Jesus and the other with only Annas interrogating, it makes sense for him to split the difference, and just call the man doing the interrogation "The High Priest." Also, if Mark himself is inventing the scene, he also might not want to say definitively that Caiaphas was doing the interrogation; less other texts falsify his claim. Mark could always say, No, I did not say Caiaphas was the interrogater, I said "High Priest." Annas was also High Priest from about 8-16 C.E. before Caiaphas.

A third point, if Caiaphas does interrogate Jesus why does he not appear in the next scene with Pilate? Would Pilate not want to consult with the man who conducted the interrogation/trial. We cannot know for sure, but we may assume John and Mary's text never had a Caiaphas interrogation scene to cut.

Fourth, the decision that Jesus dies before Passover already has been made. It is ridiculous for the High Priest to hold a mock trial on the Night of the Preparation Day of Passover. How busy must the High Priest and other officials must have been taking care of the problems of tens of thousands, or possibly hundreds of thousands of Jewish Pilgrims to Jerusalem?

Fifth, In Mark's Gospel, witnesses are brought in to testify. These people would quickly spread the word around of what was going to happen. This would certainly arouse Jesus' many followers who just a few days before had proclaimed him King. This is exactly what they are trying to avoid.

Sixth, the Jewish Officials in the next scene in the Gospel of John know nothing about any trial[334].

Also, On the assumption that Jesus is Caiaphas' son, it makes little sense for the High Priest Caiaphas to be interrogating his own son and then going into the Palace of Herod with his own son to get him crucified. In John's Gospel and I believe in the original text, it is Annas, the father-in-law who takes Jesus to Caiaphas. Using our Narrative Sense Rule, we can say here that this is most probably the case.

It is most probable that the Caiaphas trial scene is an invention of Mark. In blaming the Jews for Jesus' death, Mark had to find something that he was guilty of doing for which the Jews could blame him. He came up with the prophesy about the "destruction of the temple and rebuilding of the temple in three days." While this prophesy was in a different text and created years later after the destruction of the temple to explain the destruction of the temple, Mark wanted badly to use it to explain why the Jews put

Jesus to death. He therefore created the trial scene at Caiaphas' house to insert this passage into the story.

Note also in the passage in John that Jesus is led by Jewish Officials to Pilate. Caiaphas is nowhere in sight and Jesus is not bound. Jesus is going of his own free will to Pilate's house, just as he went of his own free will to Annas' house.

An Interesting Discovery about Barabas

If we examine the scene of Pilate's interrogation of Jesus in the Gospel of John, we discover many amazing things.

> 18:28. Then the Jews led Jesus from Caiaphas to the palace of the Roman governor. By now it was early morning, and to avoid ceremonial uncleanness the Jews did not enter the palace; they wanted to be able to eat the Passover.
> 29. So Pilate came out to them and asked, What charges are you bringing against this man?
> 30. If he were not a criminal, they replied, we would not have handed him over to you.
> 31. Pilate said, Take him yourselves and judge him by your own law. But we have no right to execute anyone, the Jews objected.

First note that the Jewish officials do not bring Jesus into the palace. They do not go into the Palace because this would make them unclean. This tells us a great deal about the relationship of Jews and Romans. The Jews thought just going into the home of a Roman on the day before Passover would make them unclean. Pilate has to come out to them to ask the charges against Jesus.

Note carefully the general response of the Jews. They do not say that they have had a trial and convicted him of anything. They just say that he is a criminal. They say nothing about him wanting to destroy the temple. These ideas are later additions to the text found later in the Synoptic Gospels. Instead of specific charges, the Jews just tell Pilate generally that he is a criminal.

Pilate is quite disinterested. He wants them to deal with it as a purely Jewish matter. They then tell him that they cannot do that because they do not have the "right to execute anyone." The next line is out of place.

> 18:32. This happened so that the words Jesus had spoken indicating the kind of death he was going to die would be fulfilled.

We'll see later that it does belong at another point in the scene. For the moment note what happens next.

> Pilate then went back inside the palace, summoned Jesus and asked him, Are you the king of the Jews?
>
> Is that your own idea, Jesus asked, or did others talk to you about me?
>
> Am I a Jew? Pilate replied. It was your people and your chief priests who handed you over to me. What is it you have done?
>
> Jesus said, My kingdom is not of this world. If it were, my servants would fight to prevent my arrest by the Jews. But now my kingdom is from another place.
>
> You are a king, then! said Pilate. Jesus answered, You are right in saying I am a king. In fact, for this reason I was born, and for this I came into the world, to testify to the truth. Everyone on the side of truth listens to me.
>
> What is truth? Pilate asked. With this he went out again to the Jews and said, I find no basis for a charge against him.

What we are getting here is intercutting between two scenes. Pilate outside speaking to the Jewish Officials, Pilate inside speaking to Jesus, then Pilate outside again speaking to the Jewish Officials. It is likely that the intercut scene has been put in the middle of the Pilate addressing the Officials scene to cover up something. Let us reconstruct the scene without the interrupting intercut. Here is Pilate's full private interview with Jesus.

> 18:28. Then the Jews led Jesus from Caiaphas to the palace of the Roman governor. By now it was early morning, and to avoid ceremonial uncleanness the Jews did not enter the palace; they wanted to be able to eat the Passover.
> 29. So Pilate came out to them and asked, What charges are you bringing against this man?
> 30. If he were not a criminal, they replied, we would not have handed him over to you.
> 31. Pilate said, Take him yourselves and judge him by your own law. But we have no right to execute anyone, the Jews objected.
> 18:39. But it is your custom for me to release to you one prisoner at the time of the Passover. Do you want me to release 'the king of the Jews'?
> 40. They shouted back, No, not him! Give us Barabbas! Now Barabbas had taken part in a rebellion.

Notice that we now have a logical flow. Pilate wants the Jews to judge Jesus. The Jews say that only Pilate can put him to death. Pilate is now allowing the Jews to judge

Jesus and agreeing to put him to death for them. But something is very wrong with the text. Pilate has been asked to execute a man by the Jews. Pilate is responding that he will "release" one man. This is exactly the opposite of what the Jews request. This makes no sense. The scene would only make sense if Pilate offers to execute one man. Here is the reconstructed original

Pilate and the King of the Jews Reconstruction

> Pilate said, Take him yourselves and judge him by your own law. But we have no right to execute anyone, the Jews objected.
> But it is your custom for me to execute for you one prisoner at the time of the Passover. Do you want me to execute 'the King of the Jews'?
> They shouted back, No, not him! Give us Barabbas!

Barabbas means "Son of the Father." The Jews are not asking for the "Son of the Father" to be set free, they are asking for Barabbas, the "Son of the Father" to be executed! The "King of the Jews" was a different prisoner. The King of the Jews is the one who did not get executed. For a text being written in the mid 40's to mid-50's the term "King of the Jews" may have a real reference—Herod Agrippa. Given the choice between the King of the Jews, Herod Agrippa, or the son of the father (the high priest, Calaiphas), the Jews call for the execution of the son of the father. This line also gives us an exact dating for the setting of the original story—the year when Herod Agrippa was in prison.

History, Josephus and the Death of a Leader of a Samaritan-Jewish Revolution

At this moment we have to pause in our reconstruction. If I have properly understood the term "King of the Jews" as a reference to Herod Agrippa many consequences fall from this. Not the least important of which is that we can gather the specific date for the story of the crucifixion.

We know that Tiberius Caesar died on March 16, 37 C.E.[335]. Herod Agrippa went up to Rome around March of 36 C.E. and was imprisoned around September of 36 C.E.[336]

Now Josephus does not tell us how soon after Tiberius' death Agrippa was released from prison. He only tells us:

> Now, as soon as Caius was come to Rome, and had brought Tiberius's dead body with him, and had made a sumptuous funeral for him, according to the laws of his country, he was much disposed to set Agrippa at liberty that very day; but Antonia hindered him, not out of any ill-will to the prisoner, but out of regard to decency in Caius, lest that should

> make men believe that he received the death of Tiberius with pleasure, when he loosed one whom he had bound immediately. However, there did not many days pass ere he sent for him to his house, and had him shaved, and made him change his raiment; after which he put a diadem upon his head, and appointed him to be king of the tetrarchy of Philip[337].

While it is uncertain how many days after the death of Tiberius (March 16, 37 C.E.) it took for Caius to release Agrippa, it certainly must have been near the time of Passover in 37 C.E. We can assume the date of Passover to be close to the Vernal Equinox on March 21st, but it may well have been in April.

> In ancient times... Passover was set by actual observations of the Moon and of the vernal equinox. However, after Hillel II standardized the Hebrew calendar in the 4th century, actual observations of celestial events no longer played a part in the determination of the date of Passover[338].

The important thing here is not when Tiberius died and when Agrippa was released from prison, but when Pilate would have heard about it. The distance from Rome to Jerusalem is 1428 miles (2298 km).[1] Pliny brags in his Natural History, writing around 75 C.E., that "It was only this very last summer, that Valerius Marianus, a senator of prætorian rank, reached Alexandria from Puteoli in eight days[339]." Puteoli, the port at Naples is 1094 miles (1761 km) from Alexandria, Egypt. It is 119 miles (192 km) from Rome. Alexandria, Egypt is 314 miles (506 km) from Jerusalem. Recognizing that eight days was probably a record circa 75 C.E. due to advanced technology, we can assume in 37 C.E. the news of Tiberius' death took at most three weeks to reach Alexandria and another week to reach Jerusalem, or a total time of one month[340].

> The Roman Empire had a postal service that would be unequalled until the 19th century, the *cursus publicus*. Through this system, riders on a relay could carry a letter as many as 170 miles in 24 hours[341].

Tacitus tells us that in 47 C.E., "Vardanes traversed 375 miles in two days, and drove before him the surprised and terrified Gotarzes." In this case, Tacitus is talking about transportating a whole army and not just a letter[342].

If Pilate was in Jerusalem for Passover, the news of Herod's death and Agrippa's subsequent release from prison would not have reached him before Passover. One might object that Agrippa, the King of the Jews, was in prison in Rome and Pilate would have no way to execute Agrippa. However, Pilate, being egotistical, could feel that he had the power to persuade Tiberius to get rid of Agrippa. In having him offer this to the Jews, the text may be indicating this egotistical side of his nature.

The real problem with the idea that Pilate is talking about Agrippa and his imprisonment in 37 C.E. is the fact that Pilate seems to have been removed from office in 36 C.E. However a careful study of Josephus reveals fuzziness and ambiguity on this point to such a degree that one may conclude that later day Christians changed the text of Josephus to give this impression.

How History was Changed to Get Rid of Pilate a Year Earlier

There is no problem with Josephus' *War*. The relevant text does not indicate when Pilate went out of office, but it does suggest it was not much before Tiberius died. The text talks about Pilate brutally suppressing a disturbance by Jews against his use of money from the Temple to build aqueducts[343]. It then says, "In the meantime Agrippa . . . came to Tiberius to accuse Herod the Tetrarch[344]. This would tend to imply that Pilate was still in office when Agrippa came to Rome around 36 C.E, "a year before Tiberius died[345]."

When we examine Josephus' *Antiquities* we find all sorts of problems and contradictions. What is clear is that Pilate brutally suppresses a Samaritan revolt led by a man he says "professed to instruct men in the wisdom of the laws of Moses[346]." The man had tricked Fulvia "a woman of great dignity" into sending him "purple and gold" at the Temple in Jerusalem. Josephus tells us that the Emperor Tiberius expelled the Jews from Rome because of the "wickedness of four men[347]," The Samaritan instructor and three of his friends. This man was apparently preparing to lead an armed revolt from Mount Gerizzim in Samaria when Pilate attacked and slew him and a great many others. While not stated, this Samaritan was almost certainly considered a Christ (an anointed king) or a Jesus (Joshua—the anointed one of Moses who liberated the Holy Land for the Jews). The text describes Pilate's attack on the movement this way, "when they came to an action, some them they slew, and others of them they put to flight and took a great many alive, the principal of whom, and also the most potent of those that fled away, Pilate ordered to be slain." It is quite possible that Pilate had this Samaritan Christ figure and other leaders crucified.

The text at this point in Josephus has been rearranged in such a way as to create confusion about the order and time of the events associated with the leader of the Samaritan rebellion as the end of Pilate's career. As the text stands now, we have this order of events.

1. Samaritan Christ leads people to Mount Gerizzin to show them the sacred vessels (clothes) of the Priests and Moses. Pilate puts down Samaritan Uprising[348].
2. Samaritans complain to the Syrian Legate Vitellius. He sends Marcellus to control Judea and sends Pilate to Rome. The text tells us "So Pilate, when he

had tarried ten years in Judea, made haste to Rome, and this in obedience to the orders of Vitellius, which he dare not contradict; but before he could get to Rome, Tiberius was dead[349].

3. Vitellius went to Passover in Jerusalem[350]. He found the Priest's vestments in the Tower in Antonia and gave them back to the high priest. He removed Caiaphas from office and appointed Jonathan, his brother in law High Priest and "took his journey back to Antioch[351].

4. Tiberius orders Vitellius to make peace with Artabanus. He goes to a bridge and makes peace with him. He writes to Tiberius. Tiberius receives the letter and sends him a letter telling him that he has already received the news from Herod[352].

5. Tiberius orders Vitellius to avenge the defeat of Herod by Aretas[353].

6. Vitellius leads his army through Judea and goes to Jerusalem "to offer sacrifice to God, an ancient festival of the Jews being then just approaching. After three days he removes Jonathan from office as High Priest and puts in brother Theophilus in his place. He hears the news that Tiberius has died and makes the people swear an oath to the new emperor Caius. He disbands his army and "retired back to Antioch[354]."

The first problem is when we see Tiberius, already several weeks dead ordering Vitellius to make peace with Artabanus. This is possible, but that he should carry out these orders, send correspondence to Tiberius saying he had carried out these orders, and receive yet another reply from Tiberius who has been dead several months at this point is impossible. We may take these sections of Josephus (18:4.4 and 5) out of the mix. They interrupt the narrative flow where they presently occur. It is most probable they originally occurred directly after chapter 18:2.4, where Josephus begins his discussion of Artabanus, King of the Parthians. These two paragraphs (18:4.4 and 5) simply continue the story of Artabanus, which Josephus begins at 18:2.4. There is simply no reason for Josephus to break up this narrative into two separate parts.

The two passages 18:4.4 and 18:4.5 have been torn from their natural place and inserted between Vitellius' trip to Jerusalem and his trip Jerusalem for the "ancient festival".

Tacitus tells us that the Parthian affair started "In the consulship of Caius Cestius and Marcus Servilius, some Parthian nobles came to Rome without the knowledge of their king Artabanus[355]." This is 35 C.E. Tacitus then tells about the whole Artabanus affair. When he finishes, he says, "I have related in sequence the events of two summer-campaigns, as a relief to the reader's mind from our miseries at home[356]." Thus we may assume that the affair ended with a peace treaty between Vitellius and Artabanus in the Summer of 36 C.E[357]. It appears that whoever cut and repasted the text of Josephus 18:4.4 and 5, wanted us to believe that Vitellius had gone up to Jerusalem at Passover of 36, and had removed Pilate just before this time. This appears to be the reason for taking the events of 36 out of their natural order following 18:2.4 and placing them in this spot of the text.

The problem here is that the text tells us that before going to Passover Festival, Vitellius removed Pilate from office and he sailed for Rome. It seems impossible that Pilate could have left before Passover in 36, made "haste" to go to get to Rome and not arrived by the death of Tiberius in March of 37. Pilate was traveling to Rome on a matter that concerned his whole career. It is most likely that the trip would take one to two months. This places Vitellius' trip to Jerusalem at Passover 37.

The movement of the two Vitellius-Artabanus passages (18:4.4 and 5) to their present position from their original position after 18:2.4 seemed designed to tell us that Vitellius replaced Pilate before 36. The statement that Pilate did not reach Tiberius before his death is a time marker and only a time marker. We are never told the consequences of Pilate not reaching Tiberius before his death. It is a time marker designed to tell us that Pilate was removed just before the Passover of 37. The text as it stands now, contradicts itself by trying to get us to believe first that Vitellius removed Pilate just before Passover of 37 and then suggesting it was before Passover of 36.

Passover 36 or 37 or Not Passover at All

Obviously, Vitellius could not have given back the sacred vestments to the Jews in both 36 and 37, so it must have been in one of those years. Now, this issue is so important that Josephus actually mentions it two other times, in book 15 and book 20. Here is the mention in book 20. After the Roman Prefect Fadus has taken away the priestly vestments from them, the Jews send a delegation to Claudius in 50.

> 2. Hereupon Claudius called for the ambassadors; and told them that he granted their request; and bade them to return their thanks to Agrippa for this favor, which had been bestowed on them upon his entreaty. And besides these answers of his, he sent the following letter by them: "Claudius Caesar Germanicus, tribune of the people the fifth time, and designed consul the fourth time, and imperator the tenth time, the father of his country, to the magistrates, senate, and people, and the whole nation of the Jews, sendeth greeting. Upon the presentation of your ambassadors to me by Agrippa, my friend, whom I have brought up, and have now with me, and who is a person of very great piety, who are come to give me thanks for the care I have taken of your nation, and to entreat me, in an earnest and obliging manner, that they may have the holy vestments, with the crown belonging to them, under their power,—I grant their request, as that excellent person Vitellius, who is very dear to me, had done before me. And I have complied with your desire, in the

first place, out of regard to that piety which I profess, and because I would have every one worship God according to the laws of their own country; and this I do also because I shall hereby highly gratify king Herod, and Agrippa, junior, whose sacred regards to me, and earnest good-will to you, I am well acquainted with, and with whom I have the greatest friendship, and whom I highly esteem, and look on as persons of the best character. Now I have written about these affairs to Cuspius Fadus, my procurator. The names of those that brought me your letter are Cornelius, the son of Cero, Trypho, the son of Theudio, Dorotheus, the son of Nathaniel, and John, the son of Jotre. This letter is dated before the fourth of the calends of July, when Ruffis and Pompeius Sylvanus are consuls."

Claudius became imperator first on August 24th, 41 C.E. His statement that this is the Tenth time he is imperator, plus the date of July fourth in the consulship of Ruffis and Sylvanus gives us the exact date of July 4th 50 C.E. for the return of the vestments. Unfortunately, he is not as specific about the date when Vitellius granted the request before him.

The first mention that Josephus makes of the vestments and Vitellius is in the fifteenth chapter:

4. Now on the north side [of the temple] was built a citadel, whose walls were square, and strong, and of extraordinary firmness. This citadel was built by the kings of the Asamonean race, who were also high priests before Herod, and they called it the Tower, in which were reposited the vestments of the high priest, which the high priest only put on at the time when he was to offer sacrifice. These vestments king Herod kept in that place; and after his death they were under the power of the Romans, until the time of Tiberius Caesar; under whose reign Vitellius, the president of Syria, when he once came to Jerusalem, and had been most magnificently received by the multitude, he had a mind to make them some requital for the kindness they had shewn him; so, upon their petition to have those holy vestments in their own power, he wrote about them to Tiberius Caesar, who granted his request: and this their power over the sacerdotal vestments continued with the Jews till the death of king Agrippa; but after that, Cassius Longinus, who was president of Syria, and Cuspius Fadus, who was procurator of Judea, enjoined the Jews to reposit those vestments in the tower of Antonia, for that they ought to have them in their power, as they formerly had. However, the Jews sent ambassadors to Claudius

Caesar, to intercede with him for them; upon whose coming, king Agrippa, junior, being then at Rome, asked for and obtained the power over them from the emperor, who gave command to Vitellius, who was then commander in Syria, to give it them accordingly. Before that time they were kept under the seal of the high priest, and of the treasurers of the temple; which treasurers, the day before a festival, went up to the Roman captain of the temple guards, and viewed their own seal, and received the vestments; and again, when the festival was over, they brought it to the same place, and showed the captain of the temple guards their seal, which corresponded with his seal, and reposited them there. And that these things were so, the afflictions that happened to us afterwards [about them] are sufficient evidence. But for the tower itself, when Herod the king of the Jews had fortified it more firmly than before, in order to secure and guard the temple, he gratified Antonius, who was his friend, and the Roman ruler, and then gave it the name of the Tower of Antonia[358].

As presented the narrative is confusing, it moves from the time of the first King Herod to the time of Tiberius to the time of Claudius, then back to the time of Tiberius and back to the time of Herod. We can take out the relevant portions involving the time of Tiberius and Claudius and see the three sections.

These vestments king Herod kept in that place; and after his death they were under the power of the Romans, until the time of Tiberius Caesar; under whose reign Vitellius, the president of Syria, when he once came to Jerusalem, and had been most magnificently received by the multitude, he had a mind to make them some requital for the kindness they had shewn him; so, upon their petition to have those holy vestments in their own power, he wrote about them to Tiberius Caesar, who granted his request: and this their power over the sacerdotal vestments continued with the Jews till the death of king Agrippa; but after that, Cassius Longinus, who was president of Syria, and Cuspius Fadus, who was procurator of Judea, enjoined the Jews to reposit those vestments in the tower of Antonia, for that they ought to have them in their power, as they formerly had. However, the Jews sent ambassadors to Claudius Caesar, to intercede with him for them; upon whose coming, king Agrippa, junior, being then at Rome, asked for and obtained the power over them from the emperor, who gave command to Vitellius, who was then commander in Syria, to give it them accordingly. Before that time they were kept under the seal of the high priest, and of the treasurers of the

temple; which treasurers, the day before a festival, went up to the Roman captain of the temple

We can put the two sections relating to Vitellius together and place the discussion of the second return of the vestments in 50 right after it, where it logically (and I believe, originally) belonged:

Reconstruction of Vestment Passage in Josephus:

These vestments king Herod kept in that place; and after his death they were under the power of the Romans, until the time of Tiberius Caesar; under whose reign Vitellius, the president of Syria, when he once came to Jerusalem, and had been most magnificently received by the multitude, he had a mind to make them some requital for the kindness they had shewn him; so, upon their petition to have those holy vestments in their own power, he wrote about them to Tiberius Caesar, who granted his request: who gave command to Vitellius, who was then commander in Syria, to give it them accordingly. Before that time they were kept under the seal of the high priest, and of the treasurers of the temple; which treasurers, the day before a festival, went up to the Roman captain of the temple.

And this their power over the sacerdotal vestments continued with the Jews till the death of king Agrippa; but after that, Cassius Longinus, who was president of Syria, and Cuspius Fadus, who was procurator of Judea, enjoined the Jews to reposit those vestments in the tower of Antonia, for that they ought to have them in their power, as they formerly had. However, the Jews sent ambassadors to Claudius Caesar, to intercede with him for them; upon whose coming, king Agrippa, junior, being then at Rome, asked for and obtained the power over them from the emperor,

The reconstruction, by simply switching the middle and end parts according to their natural and logical chronological order makes things a great deal clearer. First note that we are told that Vitellius came to Jerusalem and was magnificently received. It says nothing about Passover or the removal of Pilate. We are not given the date, but note that Vitellius writes to Tiberius and gets an answer. This means it could not have been at Passover in 37, which took place weeks after Tiberius died.

This is by far the more reasonable account. The account in chapter 18 has Vitellius giving the vestments without any consultation or correspondence with Tiberius. It is hardly believable that he would have acted alone on an administrative matter of such importance when he had no authority in Judea. But if we place Vitellius' Passover visit back to 36 C.E. we are faced with the same problem of Pilate's previous removal before Vitellius' visit and his one year travel in haste to Rome. We are left with three choices:

a. Vitellius attended Passover 36, and Pilate took a year to reach Rome.
b. Vitellius attended Passover 37, and Vitellius corresponded with a dead man.
c. It was not at the Passover Festival that Vitellius was magnificently received.

Dating Vitellius' Second Visit

The second visit of Vitellius seemed to follow closely after the first visit. Since he arrived to sacrifice at an ancient festival, we might assume that festival was Shavuot which occurs 50 days after the start of Passover. Since Vitellius hears of the news of Tiberius' death after he arrives in Jerusalem a little before the start of this festival. This means that the news of Tiberius' death had taken over a month to reach him. This seems a long time, but is plausible. However, let us look more closely at what happens after the news of Tiberius' death:

> But when on the fourth day letters came to him, which informed him of the death of Tiberius, he obliged the multitude to take an oath of fidelity to Caius; he also recalled his army, and made them every one go home, and take their winter quarters there, since, upon the devolution of the empire upon Caius, he had not the like authority of making this war which he had before. It was also reported, that when Aretas heard of the coming of Vitellius to fight him, he said, upon his consulting the diviners, that it was impossible that this army of Vitellius's could enter Petra; for that one of the rulers would die, either he that gave orders for the war, or he that was marching at the other's desire, in order to be subservient to his will, or else he against whom this army is prepared. So Vitellius truly retired to Antioch; but Agrippa, the son of Aristobulus, went up to Rome, a year before the death of Tiberius, in order to treat of some affairs with the emperor, if he might be permitted so to do.

The text tells us that Tiberius dies. Vitellius makes his army go home to "winter quarters" and retires to Antioch. Agrippa then goes up to Rome a year before the death of Tiberius." This makes no sense. Agrippa is leaving after Tiberius' death to arrive in Rome a year before Agrippa's death.

Let us review the facts. Tiberius is preparing for war. He goes up to Jerusalem for a festival. He hears reports of a death on the fourth day. He disbands his army. Agrippa goes to Rome about a year before the death of Tiberius.

What if the festival was in 36 a year before Tiberius' death and it was the death of somebody else that caused the disbanding of Vitellius' army? But who?

Who Died in 36?

Since the easy and apparent solutions do not work, but lead to intolerable contradictions, we have to try more drastic ones. We have to assume that editors of Josephus have had a more hands-on approach, the type that the gospel writers had. We must deconstruct and reconstruct using the same methods.

Let us look again at the passage regarding the war between Aretas and Herod.

> So they raised armies on both sides, and prepared for war, and sent their generals to fight instead of themselves; and when they had joined battle, all Herod's army was destroyed by the treachery of some fugitives, who, though they were of the tetrarchy of Philip, joined with Aretas's army. So Herod wrote about these affairs to Tiberius, who being very angry at the attempt made by Aretas, wrote to Vitellius to make war upon him, and either to take him alive, and bring him to him in bonds, or to kill him, and send him his head. This was the charge that Tiberius gave to the president of Syria[359].

Herod Antipas lost the war because of the "treachery of some fugitives, who, though they were of the tetrarchy of Philip joined Aretas's army." One could say that Philip was at fault for the lose because he failed to apprehend the fugitives. Now one could easily imagine Herod writing to Philip and blaming him for his defeat. However, the text tells us that he wrote to Tiberius instead. Now the war had been a family squabble between Herod and his father-in-law Aretas, brought about by Herod marrying his brother Philip's wife Herodias, which was an insult to Herod's earlier wife—Aretas' daughter. Why write to Tiberius about this family affair? It was Philip's wife, Herodias, who caused the war. It was Philip's fugitives who caused Herod's defeat. It makes sense to write to him, not Tiberius. We read that Tiberias was "very angry at the attempt made by Aretas." But why should Tiberias be upset? This was a family affair involving a point of family honor. It seems to have involved no conquest of land or interference with Roman interests whatsoever. It would again be more logical for Philip to be angry with Aretas. After all, it was Aretas' daughter who could not accept an inferior position to his wife, Herodias.

Philip would not be in any position to help his brother militarily, but he could rely on his friendly neighbor to the North, Vitellius to help him. When did this occur? Vitellius was council in Rome in 34[360]. He came in 35 to Syria. So this gives us our *terminus a quo*. At the end of this affair, Josephus tells us that two things happened, 1) Vitellius sent his troops to Winter quarters and 2) Agrippa went up to Rome:

> [Vitellius] he also recalled his army, and made them every one go home, and take their winter quarters ... Agrippa, the son of Aristobulus, went up to Rome, a year before the death of Tiberius.

THE EVOLUTION OF CHRISTS AND CHRISTIANIES

This means that it must have been winter or near the winter at the end of 35 and beginning of 36 when Vitellius attended the festival. The only two possible festivals are the ten days of Rosh Hashana and Yom Kippur in September and October or Channukah in December. The clue that Agrippa went up to Rome "a year before the death of Tiberius" (who died March, 37) makes it most likely that the festival is Channukah, and Agrippa arrived in Rome around January of 36 C.E. This gives us a date of October/December 35 for the death of Philip, and Vitellius sending his troops into winter quarters. This means that the war between Aretas and Herod must have occurred in Summer/Fall of 35, as we may assume Vitellius was acting quickly at the end of it.

This is on the supposition that it was Philip, not Tiberius who died and cut off the need for the war. If it was Tiberius who died and stopped the war, then we have to explain how Agrippa could have flew back in time a year to go up to Rome when the incident ended.

The Double Date Switch Hypothesis

We have to consider why the editors would want us to believe that the war between Aretas and Herod took place in 36 (in the year before Tiberius' death) instead of in 35. The clearest answer is that the editors needed it to match the Synoptic Gospels in which John dies in the same year as Jesus. We have to assume that the Christian editors found the death of Jesus to be at Passover in 37 in Josephus. They tried to make it look like the incidents between Aretas and Herod took place in 36, in order to have it look like John the Baptist died in 36, within a year of Jesus. At a later point, the editors decided that Jesus could not die at Passover in 37. They therefore changed the text again and had Pilate sailing off to Rome before Passover of 37. This created even more confusion in the chronological narrative, but this would not necessarily be considered a bad thing for the editors, who would certainly prefer that people believe that Josephus was confused than that Josephus clearly contradicted the synoptic gospels by having the death of Jesus at Passover in 37 and the only possible time for Aretas-Herod War post death of John to be in 35.

It seems to me almost certain that the passages about Tiberius ordering the death of Aretas and Tiberius dying before the orders arrived originally read "Philip" instead of "Tiberius." It is also probable that the passages about Vitellius removing Pilate and Pilate not arriving before Herod's death in March, 37 are interpolations.

Is there any more evidence for this double switch—making events of 35 to appear to happen in 36 and changing events of 37 (post Tiberius) to sometime before 37? I believe there is more such evidence.

Look at passages in "Wars[361]" regarding Pontius Pilate:

> 4. After this he raised another disturbance, by expending that sacred treasure which is called Corban (10) upon aqueducts, whereby he

269

> brought water from the distance of four hundred furlongs. At this the multitude had indignation; and when Pilate was come to Jerusalem, they came about his tribunal, and made a clamor at it. Now when he was apprized aforehand of this disturbance, he mixed his own soldiers in their armor with the multitude, and ordered them to conceal themselves under the habits of private men, and not indeed to use their swords, but with their staves to beat those that made the clamor. He then gave the signal from his tribunal [to do as he had bidden them]. Now the Jews were so sadly beaten, that many of them perished by the stripes they received, and many of them perished as trodden to death by themselves; by which means the multitude was astonished at the calamity of those that were slain, and held their peace.
> 5. In the mean time Agrippa, the son of that Aristobulus who had been slain by his father Herod, came to Tiberius, to accuse Herod the tetrarch; who not admitting of his accusation, he staid at Rome, and cultivated a friendship with others of the men of note, but principally with Caius the son of Germanicus, who was then but a private person.

We can coordinate Agrippa going up to Rome which Josephus tells us in *Antiquities* happened in the year before Tiberius' death (in March, 37) with Pilate's massacre of Jews over the Corban money. So this massacre probably happened in early 36 C.E.

In both *Wars* and *Antiquities*, Josephus directly preceeds this story with the story of Pilate bringing ensigns with forbidden images on them into Jerusalem[362]. In his "Embassy to Gaius," Philo also notes this incident, quoting from a letter by Agrippa to Gaius, about Pilate putting "Gilt shields in the palace of Herod[363]. In Josephus' version, Pilate seems to show compassion and back down, but in the Philo/Agrippa version, Tiberius commands Pilate to back off. Since Agrippa was writing within a few years of the actual event, we may take his version as the more likely. Like the two versions of the High Priest's vestment story, the one that involved writing to Tiberius for instructions seems more truthful.

Philo does not date the gilt shields story. However, he does say that Pilate was afraid of a Jewish embassy because of the things he had done:

> he feared least they might in reality go on an embassy to the emperor, and might impeach him with respect to other particulars of his government, in respect of his corruption, and his acts of insolence, and his rapine, and his habit of insulting people, and his cruelty, and his continual murders of people untried and uncondemned, and his never ending, and gratuitous, and most grievous inhumanity[364].

THE EVOLUTION OF CHRISTS AND CHRISTIANIES

This certainly implies that Pilate had been on the job a long time. We cannot get a specific date for the incident, but it does seem to have happened more towards the end of Pilate's career than the beginning. The event is harder to place chronologically in *Wars*. Here is the paragraph leading up to it and the first sentence:

1. And now as the ethnarchy of Archelaus was fallen into a Roman province, the other sons of Herod, Philip, and that Herod who was called Antipas, each of them took upon them the administration of their own tetrarchies; for when Salome died, she bequeathed to Julia, the wife of Augustus, both her toparchy, and Jamriga, as also her plantation of palm trees that were in Phasaelis. But when the Roman empire was translated to Tiberius, the son of Julia, upon the death of Augustus, who had reigned fifty-seven years, six months, and two days, both Herod and Philip continued in their tetrarchies; and the latter of them built the city Cesarea, at the fountains of Jordan, and in the region of Paneas; as also the city Julias, in the lower Gaulonitis. Herod also built the city Tiberius in Galilee, and in Perea another that was also called Julias.
2. Now Pilate, who was sent as procurator into Judea by Tiberius, sent by night those images of Caesar that are called ensigns into Jerusalem[365].

The movement between paragraphs seems jerky with no obvious connection. Josephus talks about the administrative status of parts of Judea and creation of cities. He suddenly moves to an incident of Jewish defense of their traditions. It is improbable that Josephus would not try to make some kind of logical connection in his material. Also, in *Antiquities*, Josephus is careful to enumerate the procurators (actually prefects) who came to Judea before Pilate. Here, the casual reader would get the impression that Pilate was the first procurator sent by Tiberius to govern Judea and the events Josephus is relating in this section happened soon after Tiberius took power around 16 C.E. Josephus could not have wanted to give this impression. This suggests to me that material has been deleted.

However *Wars* does help us to date the incidents in one respect. After relating the ensign incident, Josephus goes directly into the Corban money incident, saying, "After this, he raised another disturbance[366]." This implies that the two incidents happened pretty close together. The next paragraph begins, "In the mean time Agrippa, the son of that Aristobulus who had been slain by his father Herod, came to Tiberius . . ." This would be Agrippa's famous visit a year before Tiberius' death. This suggests late 35 or early 36 for the Corban Money incident and possibly early 35 for the Forbidden Ensigns incident.

Likewise, in *Antiquities,* the two events of the Forbidden Ensigns and the Corban Money occur one after the other without a break.

> and when the Jews petitioned him again, he gave a signal to the soldiers to encompass them routed, and threatened that their punishment should be no less than immediate death, unless they would leave off disturbing him, and go their ways home. But they threw themselves upon the ground, and laid their necks bare, and said they would take their death very willingly, rather than the wisdom of their laws should be transgressed; upon which Pilate was deeply affected with their firm resolution to keep their laws inviolable, and presently commanded the images to be carried back from Jerusalem to Cesarea. But Pilate undertook to bring a current of water to Jerusalem, and did it with the sacred money, and derived the origin of the stream from the distance of two hundred furlongs. However, the Jews were not pleased with what had been done about this water; and many ten thousands of the people got together, and made a clamor against him, and insisted that he should leave off that design[367].

Again, there is not a hint of a gap between the two events. The description of these two events are immediately followed by the *Testimonium* and two related events, the expulsion of the Isis cult and the Jews from Rome. According to Cassius Dio. The expulsion of the Jews from Rome happened during the consulship of Marcus Junius and Lucius Norbanus (19 C.E.). Dio says, "As the Jews flocked to Rome in great numbers and were converting many of the natives to their ways, he banished most of them[368]." This contradicts the reason Josephus gives for the expulsion of the Jews that it was as a result of a Jewish teacher tricking a Roman woman into giving him money and clothes. These two passages may be as spurious as the Testimonium, or, more likely, they are simply from an earlier chapter that has been rearranged.

The purpose for these two passages being in their position appears to be to date the death of Jesus to the year 19 C.E. This means that whoever did the interpolation did not know that Pilate was appointed in 26 C.E. and could not have killed Jesus or anyone in 19 C.E. The interpolators may very well have been anti-Christians trying to mess up the gospel chronology.

The Man Executed by Pilate

There is only one messianic figure whom Josephus suggests died just before Pilate was recalled. Josephus devotes two paragraphs to him.

THE EVOLUTION OF CHRISTS AND CHRISTIANIES

There was a man who was a Jew, but had been driven away from his own country by an accusation laid against him for transgressing their laws, and by the fear he was under of punishment for the same; but in all respects a wicked man. He, then living at Rome, professed to instruct men in the wisdom of the laws of Moses. He procured also three other men, entirely of the same character with himself, to be his partners. These men persuaded Fulvia, a woman of great dignity, and one that had embraced the Jewish religion, to send purple and gold to the temple at Jerusalem; and when they had gotten them, they employed them for their own uses, and spent the money themselves, on which account it was that they at first required it of her. Whereupon Tiberius, who had been informed of the thing by Saturninus, the husband of Fulvia, who desired inquiry might be made about it, ordered all the Jews to be banished out of Rome; at which time the consuls listed four thousand men out of them, and sent them to the island Sardinia; but punished a greater number of them, who were unwilling to become soldiers, on account of keeping the laws of their forefathers. Thus were these Jews banished out of the city by the wickedness of four men.

But the nation of the Samaritans did not escape without tumults. The man who excited them to it was one who thought lying a thing of little consequence, and who contrived every thing so that the multitude might be pleased; so he bid them to get together upon Mount Gerizzim, which is by them looked upon as the most holy of all mountains, and assured them, that when they were come thither, he would show them those sacred vessels which were laid under that place, because Moses put them there. So they came thither armed, and thought the discourse of the man probable; and as they abode at a certain village, which was called Tirathaba, they got the rest together to them, and desired to go up the mountain in a great multitude together; but Pilate prevented their going up, by seizing upon file roads with a great band of horsemen and foot-men, who fell upon those that were gotten together in the village; and when it came to an action, some of them they slew, and others of them they put to flight, and took a great many alive, the principal of which, and also the most potent of those that fled away, Pilate ordered to be slain[369].

It is hard to tell if Josephus is talking about two men or one here. Is the man who gathered people together upon Mount Gerizzim the same man driven away from his own country to Rome? It is hard to believe that both the scheme in Rome and the scheme in Samaria were the scheme of one man, yet this is what the text seems to suggest. The man in Rome "professed to instruct men in the wisdom of the laws of Moses," while the Samaritan man knows the place of the sacred vessels because "Moses put them there."

It is clear that the second event took place in the last year of Pilate's rule as Josephus tells us in the very next paragraph that he was removed from office over this incident.

> **But when this tumult was appeased, the Samaritan senate sent an embassy to Vitellius, a man that had been consul, and who was now president of Syria, and accused Pilate of the murder of those that were killed; for that they did not go to Tirathaba in order to revolt from the Romans, but to escape the violence of Pilate. So Vitellius sent Marcellus, a friend of his, to take care of the affairs of Judea, and ordered Pilate to go to Rome, to answer before the emperor to the accusations of the Jews. So Pilate, when he had tarried ten years in Judea, made haste to Rome, and this in obedience to the orders of Vitellius, which he durst not contradict; but before he could get to Rome Tiberius was dead**[370].

The fact that the deaths of people over the Mount Gerizzim revolt led to the removal of Pilate is important. It is the type of incident that could be expected to be talked about throughout Judea for a long time. It is the type of triggering incident that could form the basis of dramatic retellings over a period of years.

Josephus does not really tell us a great deal about the main figure involved. He was a teacher of the laws of Moses. He was kicked out of his own country (Judea?) for transgressing laws. He had a shady deal with the wife of a high Roman official. This would indicate that he was part of the ruling class of Judea, as an ordinary person would be unlikely to travel to Rome and have access to the wife of a friend of Caesar. He knew the secret location of sacred vessels from Moses. He led an armed revolt of Samaritans at Mount Gerizzim. It is a bit odd that Josephus does not name him but calls him "a wicked man" and "the one who thought lying of no consequence." It seems nearly sixty years after his death, Josephus was still angry at him.

Now surprisingly, Josephus does not tell us what happened to this "wicked man," "teacher of the laws of Moses." This is surprising because all of Josephus is intended to show the mysterious workings of God and how the wicked get punished sooner or later. Looking at the structure of the text, we get several paragraphs primarily about foreign affairs, the Artabanus, King of Parthia, and Vitellius President of Syria, the death of Philip, the brother of Herod Antipas the Tetrarch, and the war between Philip King Aretas of Petras and Herod Antipas. Then we have this paragraph.

> 2. Now some of the Jews thought that the destruction of Herod's army came from God, and that very justly, as a punishment of what he did against John, that was called the Baptist: for Herod slew him, who was a good man, and commanded the Jews to exercise virtue, both as to righteousness towards one another, and piety towards God, and so to come to baptism; for that the washing [with water] would be acceptable to him, if they made use of it, not in order to the putting away [or the remission] of some sins [only], but for the purification of the body; supposing still that the soul was thoroughly purified beforehand by righteousness. Now when [many] others came in crowds about him, for they were very greatly moved [or pleased] by hearing his words, Herod, who feared lest the great influence John had over the people might put it into his power and inclination to raise a rebellion, (for they seemed ready to do any thing he should advise,) thought it best, by putting him to death, to prevent any mischief he might cause, and not bring himself into difficulties, by sparing a man who might make him repent of it when it would be too late. Accordingly he was sent a prisoner, out of Herod's suspicious temper, to Macherus, the castle I before mentioned, and was there put to death. Now the Jews had an opinion that the destruction of this army was sent as a punishment upon Herod, and a mark of God's displeasure to him.

Something does not make sense here. Why does Herod fear that John will raise a rebellion? Josephus gives us a rather sharp observation that John's baptism was for the purification of the body and not the remission of sins, a minor detail more of interest no doubt to a fourth century bishop than a first century general Roman audience. Yet, he does not tell us any specific reason for Herod arresting John. Of course a fourth century Christian audience would know that John opposed Herod's marriage from reading the book of *Acts*, but a first century general audience would have no way of knowing this. Thus it appears that Herod just arrests anyone who tells people to do good and becomes popular.

Let us assume that Eusebius has played around a bit with this passage. It is possible that Josephus had already named the wicked man as John. Thus we can suppose that the reader will know Josephus is referring back to the man who led the Samaritan revolt when he mentions John. We may reconstruct the passage this way with the additions by Eusebius in normal text:

Reconstruction of Original Josephus Passage on John

> Now some of the Jews thought that the destruction of Herod's army came from God, and that very justly, as a punishment of what he did against John, that was called the Baptist: for Herod slew him, who was a good man, and commanded the Jews to exercise virtue, both as to righteousness towards one another, and piety towards God, and so to come to baptism; for that the washing [with water] would be acceptable to him, if they made use of it, not in order to the putting away [or the remission] of some sins [only], but for the purification of the body; supposing still that the soul was thoroughly purified beforehand by righteousness.
>
> Now when [many] others came in crowds about him, for they were very greatly moved [or pleased] by hearing his words, Herod, who feared lest the great influence John had over the people might put it into his power and inclination to raise a rebellion, (for they seemed ready to do any thing he should advise,) thought it best, by putting him to death, to prevent any mischief he might cause, and not bring himself into difficulties, by sparing a man who might make him repent of it when it would be too late. Accordingly he was sent a prisoner, out of Herod's suspicious temper, to Macherus, the castle I before mentioned, and was there put to death. Now the Jews had an opinion that the destruction of this army was sent as a punishment upon Herod, and a mark of God's displeasure to him.

Reconstructed in this way, the passage now makes sense, with Herod fearing the leader of the rebellion's popularity, instead of fearing a harmless baptizing preacher telling people to do good.

Now we can go back and examine Eusebius's *Testimonium*.

> 3. Now there was about this time Jesus, a wise man, if it be lawful to call him a man; for he was a doer of wonderful works, a teacher of such men as receive the truth with pleasure. He drew over to him both many of the Jews and many of the Gentiles. He was [the] Christ. And when Pilate, at the suggestion of the principal men amongst us, had condemned him to the cross, those that loved him at the first did not forsake him; for he appeared to them alive again the third day; as the divine prophets had foretold these and ten thousand other wonderful things concerning him. And the tribe of Christians, so named from him, are not extinct at this day.

THE EVOLUTION OF CHRISTS AND CHRISTIANIES

Some writers have proposed that Eusebius rewrote this text from a more neutral reference to Jesus. I would like to propose that he rewrote it from a completely negative reference to John. We may turn the phrases inside out so to speak:

- Jesus a wise man, if it be lawful to call him a man
  John a demon possessed man, if it be lawful to call him a man

- For he was a doer of wonderful works.
  For he was a doer of terrible works

- A teacher of such men as receive the truth with pleasure
  A teacher of such men as receive lies with pleasure.

- He drew over to him both many of the Jews and many of the Gentiles

- He was [the] Christ. And when Pilate, at the suggestion of the principal men amongst us, had condemned him to the cross, those that loved him at the first did not forsake him;
  He pretended to be the Christ. And when Pilate at the suggestion of the principal men amongst us, had arrested him, those that loved him at the first did not forsake him.

- for he appeared to them alive again the third day; as the divine prophets had foretold these and ten thousand other wonderful things concerning him.
  for he appeared to them to be a prophet and foretold ten thousand wonderful things.

- And the tribe of Christians, so named from him, are not extinct at this day.
  And the tribe of Nazarenes, so named from him, are not extinct at this day.

If this is correct we may reconstruct the original *testimonium* of Josephus this way:

> Now some of the Jews thought that the destruction of Herod's army came from God, and that very justly, as a punishment of what he did against John, a demon possessed man, if it be lawful to call him a man for he was a doer of terrible works, a teacher of such men as receive lies with pleasure. He drew over to him both many of the Jews and many of the Gentiles. He pretended to be the Christ. And when Pilate at the suggestion of the principal men amongst us, had arrested him, those that loved him at the first did not forsake him for he appeared to them to be a prophet and foretold ten thousand wonderful things. And the tribe of Nazarenes, so named from him, are not extinct at this day. Now when others came in crowds about him, for they were very greatly moved by

277

hearing his words, Herod, who feared lest the great influence John had over the people might put it into his power and inclination to raise a rebellion, for they seemed ready to do any thing he should advise, thought it best, by putting him to death, to prevent any mischief he might cause, and not bring himself into difficulties, by sparing a man who might make him repent of it when it would be too late. Accordingly he was sent a prisoner, out of Herod's suspicious temper, to Macherus, the castle I before mentioned, and was there put to death. Now the Jews had an opinion that the destruction of this army was sent as a punishment upon Herod, and a mark of God's displeasure to him.

Summary of Years 36-37 Investigation Results

At this point we can summarize the results of our investigation in this section. In the year 37, Pontius Pilate arrested a man leading a revolt in Samaria on Mount Gerizzim. Herod Agrippa had him put to death in Macherus. The incident happened near the time of Tiberius's death and Pilate's recall to Rome. The Jews may have connected the events. They may have felt that the sacrificial execution led to the hated Pilate's removal. In about a decade, a woman wrote a play about the incident in which Pilate executed the son of the High Priest on Passover. Perhaps the most controversial part of the play was the woman's claim that she saw the son alive after the execution. In the play, the son may have been seen as the incarnation of the word of God.

Probably in the early 60's, another tale incorporating references to later historical messianic characters circulated. In this newer version the character died on the day before Passover.

These tales of the brave holy Jew who sacrificed his life against the Romans no doubt inspired many of the fighters in the Roman-Jewish War of 66-73. After the losing war, we may assume that a backlash took place and people blamed the popularity of the character for the war and the destruction of the temple. Others, however, defended the character and blamed the defeat in the war on the Jewish leadership and their compromising attitude towards the Romans.

It is at this point that we find the writers of the canonical Mark and Matthew gospels going to work.

Mosaic. Baptism of Young Hermaphrodite Jesus

Arian Baptistery, Ravenna, Italy, circa 500. Note feminine breasts and wide hips on Christ. A Neptune-life God figure apparently declares Jesus his son.

Chapter 6

Deconstructing the Gospel of Mark

In this chapter, I will discuss structures in the *Gospel of Mark* and indicate how they were constructed. From this we can understand what he thought he was doing and what he was trying to accomplish with this work.

The Dating Game

I have spent a lot of time thinking about the dating of the gospel of Mark. I have been all over the map with the problem, thinking that I detected dates in the 70's all the way to the 140's. I include some of my meditations and attempts at deconstruction on this difficult problem. I admit in this case to being less successful than I would have hoped.

In order to deconstruct a text we must use certain tools or principles. These tools are not foolproof, but they can help us to understand what went on if applied with discretion and sensitivity. This actually is the case in all historical fields. For example, in understanding manuscript evolution, we use the principle *lectio difficilior lectio potior* ("the more difficult reading is the more probable reading") and *lectio brevior lectio potior* ("the shorter reading is the more probable reading")[371]. This rule hardly is ironclad, but it works enough to make it a useful starting point.

The deconstruction and interpretation of a text is only as good as the tools used to deconstruct. The main tool that I use here, we might call the *Dramatic and Cinematic Quality of Ancient Narrative*. For the most part using this tool involves merely imagining the creation of an ancient textual narrative as a movie being shot and edited. It allows us to see that most likely when different narrative scenes are intercut, and each scene has a separate point without any real connection between them, each scene existed as part of a separate storyline. By separating the intercut scenes, one may discover the earlier versions of the two storylines. Those who have studied the early history of cinema and the pioneering editing techniques of D.W. Griffith will understand how useful it is to uncut and reconstruct intercut scenes to see how they were really filmed. Like all rules of textual analysis this technique should not be applied mechanically, but can be enormously useful when used in conjunction with other evidence.

First, we should consider what justifies our application of cinematic principles to narrative textual principles. We have little, but some, knowledge of how authors/editors worked in ancient times. We have much more knowledge and many more descriptions of how narrative film production started and developed in the late nineteenth and early twentieth centuries. We can see a certain parallel development that allows us to transfer principles from early corporate narrative movie production to Christian narrative textual production in ancient times. For example the early epistle writing stage in Christian narrative production may be compared to the early documentary stage that prevailed from 1894-1903. The early sayings gospels and magical tale gospels may be compared to the theatrical stage of cinematic narrative and trick film productions that dominated from 1903-1910 and the highly advanced mixed sayings/miracle/stories stage may be compared with the sophisticated silent films produced 1912-1927.

Early movies were produced by individuals and small groups of self-trained people possessing a severely limited amount of resources and limited amount of distribution opportunities. In ancient times, the writers of the scriptures also apparently faced analogous problems. The ability to read and write, to obtain writing material, and to distribute it was severely limited. Based on this analogous situation, and the results that we find in each, we may assume that the development in narrative cinema and the development of narrative gospels went through a certain parallel processes of development.

We take certain habitual processes as easy and natural because we are exposed to them often. In driving a car or riding a bicycle, it is only because we do it so often that we forget the multiple steps we had to be taught or discover before the trick could be accomplished. We are exposed to narratives so often today on television, in books and in movies that we hardly notice how producers deal with specific production problems in narrative itself. Only when we read an ancient text where specific problems are handled quite differently do we take note of them. For example, in Hebrew Scriptures, we often find two quite different versions of the same story put forward one after the other (e.g. two creations at the beginning of *Genesis*). The meaning of this technique was quite clear to the original editors and readers, something along the lines of "Here are two stories about the same event that we have heard. We do not know which is true. You decide." We are so accustomed to reading narratives, as processed and filtered, that we become confused by seeing the stories presented in a much more natural fashion as simply "heard and retold" stories. In a sense the ancient editors were being much more truthful by presenting heard and retold stories as heard and retold stories in their entirety and not bothering to exclude the contradictions or edit them into one single narrative. We take for granted that a modern story-teller would bother to eliminate the contradictions and give us one tale. It is as if ancient story-tellers held up a sign saying, "Here is a story I have heard" at the beginning of every tale, while modern story tellers hold up a sign saying "Here is a story I have made up."

One important feature of cinematic narrative that we take for granted is inter-cutting between scenes and shots. When the camera goes from face A to face B back to face A, we generally do not notice that this means two different shots have been separately constructed and put together at some point in the editing process. When the scene switches between the bomb about to go off and the shots of the hero/heroine racing to the scene, or when we cut from the young lovers to the old lovers and back to the young lovers, we often fail to notice that each scene had to be produced separately and spliced together. We may apply this insight to ancient narrative generally. Likewise, when there is intercutting between scenes in textual narratives, we hardly take note.

Cinematic narrative started off in a childlike narrative fashion in 1895, with discreet linear scenes following each other. A single event would be shown in a single shot, followed discreetly by another event in another shot. By 1899, George Méliès was playing around in his films with some trick shots, as a child might do a trick to illustrate a narrative point. In 1903, Edwin S. Porter started with the *Life of an American Fireman* and *The Great Train Robbery* experiment with inter-cutting shots within a scene and perhaps iinter-cutting between scenes. By 1908, we see this intercutting technique starting to be used more frequently in films like D.W. Griffith's *The Adventures of Dollie*, although it would still be five years more before it became the norm in narrative story telling.

In the gospels, we also see both linear and intercut narratives. Using our *Dramatic and Cinematic Quality of Ancient Narrative Rule* we can separate them out. We can see the linear narrative materials side by side before they were intercut. By looking at the changes that the intercutting produces, we can understand the dialectical (or dialogical) process involved with the development of the narrative. This tool is vitally important for a true deconstruction of the Gospels. It is like a screw driver opening the back of the toy to see what is inside. Without it, we can only guess wildly as to the construction of the toy. With it, we can see at once how it was put together.

Our second important tool is the *Gospel Separation Rule*. Many commentators interpret one gospel through the other gospels in order to harmonize them. This throws everything into confusion. For example, Mark writes:

> 12. Jesus replied, To be sure, Elijah does come first, and restores all things. Why then is it written that the Son of Man must suffer much and be rejected?

13. But I tell you, Elijah has come, and they have done to him everything they wished, just as it is written about him[372].

Matthew takes the same passage and significantly changes it.

10. The disciples asked him, Why then do the teachers of the law say that Elijah must come first?
11. Jesus replied, To be sure, Elijah comes and will restore all things.
12. But I tell you, Elijah has already come, and they did not recognise him, but have done to him everything they wished. In the same way the Son of Man is going to suffer at their hands.
13. Then the disciples understood that he was talking to them about John the Baptist.

Matthew adds the sentence "they did not recognize him" and "Then the disciples understood that he was talking to them about John the Baptist. There is nothing in Mark to suggest that he associated the coming of Elijah with the coming of John the Baptist. In fact in the previous scene[373] Elijah, Moses and Jesus have appeared together. Since the disciples presumably knew how John the Baptist looked and not how Elijah looked, should they not have identified "John the Baptist" as being with Moses and Jesus in the previous scene? In other words, since they knew how John the Baptist looked when they saw Jesus with Moses and Elijah, and Elijah looked exactly as John looked, why would they identifiy him as Elijah and not John? To get around this objection, we have to adopt a John the Baptist-as-Elijah-reincarnated-in-a-different body thesis. Howver, Jesus surely would have explained to his disciples about the body switching deal.

Also, we may assume that Mark would have said that Jesus was referring to John the Baptist when he was speaking about Elijah coming and not leave it to Matthew to explain. I will get back to this important passage later, but for the moment we may suggest that Matthew has given a quite new and different meaning to the text with his additions. He has taken what is a general statement by Mark that something expected has happened and made it into a specific statement that the expected thing has happened in a specific way. It certainly makes a big difference if I say generally, "John has been in a bank before," or I specify, "John was in a bank in disguise at 2 P.M., yesterday when the bank was robbed."

Those who simply assume that one gospel has made explicit a detail another gospel writer has left out are unconsciously harmonizing. We may assume that the gospel writers meant what they said, and said what they meant to say, and later gospel writers changed the text to make their own meanings. In short, the Christologies of the four gospel writers are very different and only by separating them can we understand the historical development of the Gospel narrative. When Matthew expands on Mark we get clues to Mark's original meaning, but only by asking what did Matthew find so wrong in Mark that he needed to change it. Matthew does not tell us what Mark meant, but only what he wants us to believe Mark meant. When I emphasize the absolute differences in the Gospel text, I call this approach *the Separation Tool*.

Our third tool is the *Narrrative Sense Rule*. We must assume that the gospel writers were at least of average intelligence for their time and not stupid or drunk when they wrote. Scenes should make sense. If a character is following Jesus (for example, John 21:20-25) it is ridiculous for Jesus to turn and say "I want you to remain alive until I return for the Apocalypse." What makes sense in this situation is for Jesus to say, "I want you to remain here until I return alive." Where a theological point subverts a plot point, we may put the obvious plot point back in and assume some later writer has fiddled with it.

Two Problems That are Really One

In investigating the history of the gospels, one finds two questions of extreme importance. First is dating the Gospels. This has been declared solved and resolved by consensus, but remains highly problematic. The second problem is discovering how the history of Jesus got into the gospel form. Why do we not have a simple single text biography of Jesus, the way we have a simple and singular biography of the traveling God/Man healer/magician Apollonius of Tyana, written by Philostratus around 100 CE[374]? Instead we have a series of documents written by authors who do not name themselves at an unspecified time. Usually, the explanation of this involves some babbling about the humility of the authors (as if spreading the gospel of a God was a humble thing) and the gospel authors' reliance on the concept of oral history. Oral history is a catch-all phrase which explains every textual change without providing us with a paper trail.

In any case, dating Christian documents from the early period is quite difficult. When one actually looks at how first and second century sources for Christianity gets dated, it usually turns out to depend on accepting the date suggested by a Church Father like Tertullian (circa 200-210 CE) or Eusebius (circa 320 CE). It is difficult to know if these Church Fathers themselves knew the date for much of the material that is actually dated through them. So Eusebius gives us the date for Papias, but the works of Papias mysteriously disappear after him. How much may we trust Eusebius in dating Papias to the time Eusebius (and solely Eusebius) gives to him? Often two or more shakey dates (e.g. letters of Clement and Paul) are put together to claim that dating evidence is clear. But when we look at each one, we find that they are dependent on an arbitrary determination for one of them. We constantly get cases of circular dating: Text **A** is dated by text **B** which is dated by text **C** which is dated by Text **A** . . . .

In the case of *Mark*, theologians, theologian/historians, and some historians tell us that we have the happy circumstance of internal evidence that gives us a small timeframe. *Mark* can be dated by Jesus' prediction of the fall of the Jerusalem Temple in 70 CE. This prediction has to be after the event, (except for believers in the supernatural power of prophesy) so Mark has to be post 70 CE. On the other side, we have Jesus' prediction at Mark (9.1) that he will return before all his followers died, "And he said to them, "Truly, I say to you, there are some standing here who will not taste death before they see that the kingdom of God has come with power." A similar statement is made later (Mk 13:30), "Truly, I say to you, this generation will not pass away before all these things take place." The writer would not have had Jesus make a false prediction, so it is a safe bet that the writer was writing fifty years or less from the time of Jesus' appearance in circa 35 CE. So we have circa 85 CE as the latest date for Mark's Gospel.

This reasoning is brilliant. It is straight as an arrow and clear and accepted by the overwhelming majority of scholars. The dating of Mark's text to this time has a repercussion effect on the secondary question of the historical Jesus. Mark could never have gotten away with writing about a fictional character set just 50 years in the past. Too many people would have been alive from the time to contradict him. Therefore this dating assures us with certainty that Jesus was an historical character. Let us call this the *First Century Mark Proof*.

However, there is also significant evidence pointing to a later date for Mark. The apocalyptic predictions he makes in chapter 13 would seem to describe the time of the Bar Kochba War from 132-135 as well as the war of 70 CE. For example a mention of "the abomination that causes desolation standing where it does not belong" (13.14) would appear to match Dio Cassius' description of a Roman Temple built on the site of the Jewish Temple around 132 C.E.[375] Church Father Jerome in the Fourth Century talks about a statue of Hadrian still found in Jerusalem in his time. This was likely to have been put there during the time of the Bar Kochba War or shortly thereafter[376]. There is no equivalent object from the Roman-Jewish War of 66-73 C.E that fits the reference to *the abomination of desolation*.

Adela Yarbro Collins in an article entitled *The Apocalyptic Rhetoric of Mark 13 in Historical Context* suggests a slightly pre-70 date for the speech. Collins makes this point:

> It is sometimes claimed that the prediction of vs 2 corresponds to what actually happened and thus is prophecy *ex evenu*. Rudolg Pesch and others have referred to Josephus' report ... But Josephus goes on to say that Titus deliberately left the three great towers standing, as well as the part of the city on the west. Thus the prophecy of 13:2 does not correspond to what actually happened, since the western wall is, in effect, part of the foundation of the temple and still stands today[377].

The contradiction between the text and Josephus does suggest a difficulty in attributing this speech as referring to the first century Roman-Jewish War, but Collins solution of attributing this discrepancy to Mark writing pre-70 is not the only one. In fact she notes this:

> According to the eschatological scenario presupposed by the speech, the second stage of the end-time, the θλῖψις, will be triggered by a sacrilegious deed of the Romans at the climax of the war. When they set up a statue in the temple, a divine intervention analogous to the destruction of Sodom will occur and the elect will flee to the mountains[378].

Collins suggests that the *Abomination of Desolation* does refer to a statue, which would make the Bar Kochba War the setting and the statue of Hadrian the *Abomination*, unless we want to give Mark prophetic powers of seeing some 60 years into the future.

Pieter J.J. Botha, in an article entitled *The Historical Setting of Mark's Gospel: Problems and Possibilities* makes this observation:

> Mark is simply unconcerned with constructing a narrative which flows smoothly from a geographical point of view. The text—when seen in terms of tradition plus redaction—provides evidence for editorial arbitrariness. These are the real data that need to be accounted for.
>
> The conclusion thus far is that we cannot deduce from Mark itself where and when it was written. If the destruction of the temple was important to Mark, or the communities in Galilee, he has failed quite spectacularly to communicate these concerns[379].

The generally supposed date of just after 70 C.E., or 80 C.E. would suggest that the question how Jews should live after the catastrophe of losing the war and the temple would be a central concern of the text. This does not appear to be the case in the text.

Another serious problem with the 70-90 dating of Mark is that many texts written in the second century seem unfamiliar with the text. Only when we get to the alleged Bishop Irenaeus circa 180 C.E. do we find somebody familiar enough with the writings of Mark to cite him. Yet, even here we are relying on Eusebius, a century and a half later for our information about Irenaeus. The writings of Irenaeus may very well be later than 180 C.E. If Eusebius has credited Ireneaus with works by Tertullian, as I suspect, then the first citation of Mark may be 200 C.E. or even later.

Assuming a date of 70-80 C.E., one would expect that in the period of over one century between the time of its alleged composition and the time of its first being cited as a source, someone would have written something about at least one of its passages. Even if we do not have that source, we should have some later source that quotes it. Why were Christians not writing about the gospel of Mark for more than a century after its alleged composition date?

Still does not the fact of Jesus walking through through temple and predicting its destruction suggest a date shortly after the temple's destruction?

Imagine a story written today in 2005, in which the Messiah appears with his disciples in front of the World Trade Center. The disciples declare the World Trade Center an archetectural marvel. The Messiah responds that soon they will see it turned to dust. Obviously, the point of story is not that the Messiah appeared prior to 2001. The point of the story is that nothing man builds lasts and the Messiah knows this. It would be ludicrous to say that the author actually believes his story and is relating a history of the Messiah at some time between the 1960's and 2001 when the World Trade Center stood. Likewise in the scene of Jesus and disciples outside the Jerusalem Temple in chapter 13 of Mark, we are not getting an historical tale, but an allegorical one. The reference to the temple's destruction does assure us that the writer is writing post temple destruction (post 70 C.E.). This gives us our *terminus a quo*.

Now, we have to look at the other half of the question, our *terminus ad quem*. The allegorical point of Jesus predicting the temple's destruction could have been written a few years after the temple's destruction, but not necessarily, It could have been written many decades later. However, there are some statements about "this generation" that appear to limit the text to the first century (9.1 and 13.30). However, we know that taking statements out of context and putting them together may be misleading. It is a form of editing and can lead us astray as to meaning. We have to be sure that this was not the case with this proof. We must ask if the statement about the destruction of buildings at Mark 13.2 really belong with the "generation" statements at 9:1 and 13:30. It is now that we need to do some conscious reconstruction work.

Let us put the text around 13:2 under the microscope.

1. As he was leaving the temple, one of his disciples said to him, Look, Teacher! What massive stones! What magnificent buildings!
2. Do you see all these great buildings? replied Jesus. Not one stone here will be left on another; every one will be thrown down.
3. As Jesus was sitting on the Mount of Olives opposite the temple, Peter, James, John and Andrew asked him privately,
4. Tell us, when will these things happen? And what will be the sign that they are all about to be fulfilled?
5. Jesus said to them: Watch out that no-one deceives you.
6. Many will come in my name, claiming, 'I am he,' and will deceive many.
7. When you hear of wars and rumours of wars, do not be alarmed. Such things must happen, but the end is still to come.

Note that there is an incredibly quick scene shift here between 1-2 and 3-7. Jesus is leaving the temple and "one of his disciples" asks him a question. Jesus answers.

We are suddenly transported to a new location, sitting on the Mount of Olives and Jesus is alone with Peter, James, John and Andrew. What happened? Weren't there more disciples with Jesus? Just previously, in chapter 12, Jesus seemed to be with a whole bunch of disciples:

> 41. Jesus sat down opposite the place where the offerings were put and watched the crowd putting their money into the temple treasury. Many rich people threw in large amounts.
> 42. But a poor widow came and put in two very small copper coins, worth only a fraction of a penny.
> 43. Calling his disciples to him, Jesus said, I tell you the truth, this poor widow has put more into the treasury than all the others.
> 44. They all gave out of their wealth; but she, out of her poverty, put in everything—all she had to live on.

Note how the scenes change. Jesus is with a group of disciples opposite the temple courtyard. Next he is seemingly walking out of the temple, presumably with his disciples following. Finally, he is on the Mount of Olives opposite the Temple alone with Peter, James, John and Andrew. The disciples have dropped away. But think about what Jesus has just told the disciples upon coming out of the Temple. He has told them that all the buildings they see will be destroyed. The other disciples must have been incredibly perplexed by that. The disciples upon hearing that must think something like "Does he mean that all things are temporal so that even the greatest buildings are destroyed in the sea of time, or is he making a specific prediction that say next month there will be an earthquake and all the buildings will be destroyed?" With this reading of the scenes, we get the impression that Mark felt that Jesus said bizarre and incomprehensible things to his disciples, but only told Peter, James and John what they meant. We may assume that Mark held a Gnostic position that Jesus gave secret knowledge to some of his disciples.

We can try to fix this impression by supposing that either Peter, James, or John was the "one of the disciples" who mentioned the beauty of the buildings. Perhaps these three were the only three disciples that followed him outside the temple. But then we would expect Mark to have stated such information that only these three disciples were with him when he made the remark about the building. No, it seems unmistakable that Mark is giving us secret Gnostic-like information here, meant for the inner circle only.

Besides the rapid shift of scene and sudden shift from private to secret information, or from all disciples to a few special disciples, we should note a curious shift from the singular to the plural in the text. Jesus has described one event, the destruction of all the great buildings either in or around the temple. Yet note the four disciple's question, "Tell us when will these *things* happen?" But Jesus has not been talking about "things" happening, but only one event the destruction of the buildings. While Jesus has spoken of "stones" of "buildings," he has not indicated "things" will happen, only one *thing*, the destruction of the buildings.

In film/video editing, we often find mismatches like this. Shots and scenes that are contiguous in the finished product are often created days, weeks or months apart, so a special person, the Continuity Person has the task of seeing that mismatches do not occur. Still mismatches do occur and they indicate that the shots and scenes were created separately

Further, note that Jesus never mentions the destruction of the buildings again. He talks about the endtime and signs of the end time when these "things" (plural) will happen but he never mentions when the buildings will come down. If the disciples are referring to the coming down of the buildings that Jesus has mentioned in the previous scene, then the answer does not match the question.

It seems that the short scene of Jesus walking out of the temple with his disciples and predicting the buildings will fall has been created specifically to attach the following scene regarding Jesus' prediction of an end time to this point in the text. It is a bridge. It does not belong with the original apocalypse prediction text.

One can also take the first lines of this apocalypse prediction scene "As Jesus was sitting on the Mount of Olives opposite the temple," to be part of the bridge. It matches the previous scene where "Jesus sat down opposite the place where the offerings were put." The actions in the setting of the scenes binds them together, 1. Jesus sits opposite, 2. Jesus walks outside, and 3. Jesus sits opposite again. The transition scenes are put together flawlessly to get Jesus from the temple to a mountain.

Now, note carefully the disciples' opening line, "Tell us, when will these things happen? And what will be the sign that they are all about to be fulfilled?" Jesus has been discussing things happening and the disciples want to know when all the things will happen and what sign will occur to indicate that all these things are about to take place. Since this is a mismatch with the scene before, we can ask if there is any other text to be found in Mark which might have come before when the scene was originally shot, or rather when the text was in its original position. We need only look to the end of the previous scene in chapter 9 where Jesus is alone with Peter, James and John to see the answer.

9.2. After six days Jesus took Peter, James and John with him and led them up a high mountain, where they were all alone. There he was transfigured before them.

3. His clothes became dazzling white, whiter than anyone in the world could bleach them.

4. And there appeared before them Elijah and Moses, who were talking with Jesus.

5. Peter said to Jesus, Rabbi, it is good for us to be here. Let us put up three shelters—one for you, one for Moses and one for Elijah.

6. (He did not know what to say, they were so frightened.)
7. Then a cloud appeared and enveloped them, and a voice came from the cloud: This is my Son, whom I love. Listen to him!
8. Suddenly, when they looked round, they no longer saw anyone with them except Jesus.
9. As they were coming down the mountain, Jesus gave them orders not to tell anyone what they had seen until the Son of Man had risen from the dead.
10. They kept the matter to themselves, discussing what rising from the dead meant.
11. And they asked him, Why do the teachers of the law say that Elijah must come first?
12. Jesus replied, To be sure, Elijah does come first, and restores all things. Why then is it written that the Son of Man must suffer much and be rejected?
13. But I tell you, Elijah has come, and they have done to him everything they wished, just as it is written about him.

Now all we have to do is put the opening line from 13:4 in at this point:

12.4 Tell us, when will these things happen? And what will be the sign that they are all about to be fulfilled?

The match here is flawless. The *Jesus Apocalyptic Prophesy* scene, which is sometimes called the Little Apcoalypse, appeared after the *Transfiguration* scene in the original material. When we deconstruct Mark this way, we see that this material is quite different from much of Mark and has its own distinctive style and point of view.

Most importantly it appears that Jesus' appearance in the Jerusalem Temple and the Apocalyptic Prediction are two quite separate texts. The text in which the "Generation Statements" are made appears to be an Apocalyptic text that Mark inserted into his Gospel. But the Gnostic Apocalyptic text 8:27-9:13 and 13:4-37 merely sets a time limit of a generation (40 years?) for the Apocalypse.

What Mark has done is clear. He has reworked the apocalyptic material by inserting temple reference. Thus it appears that Jesus's "this generation shall not pass" refers to the time of the Roman-Jewish War and not to the Apocalypse. Mark has found that Jesus's prediction of the time of the apocalypse in one generation was wrong. More than one generation has passed and no apocalypse has taken place. Mark fixes this problem by having Jesus seem to predict the fall of the temple and the Roman-Jewish War. He cleverly slides the two together so one is unsure if Jesus is talking about the apocalypse or the Roman Jewish War.

THE EVOLUTION OF CHRISTS AND CHRISTIANIES

Here is the original question and answer with the Marcan material taken out.

13.4. Tell us, when will these things happen? And what will be the sign that they are all about to be fulfilled?
23. I have told you everything ahead of time.
24. But in those days, following that distress[380], 'the sun will be darkened, and the moon will not give its light;
25. the stars will fall from the sky, and the heavenly bodies will be shaken.'
26. At that time men will see the Son of Man coming in clouds with great power and glory.
27. And he will send his angels and gather his elect from the four winds, from the ends of the earth to the ends of the heavens ...
30. I tell you the truth, this generation will certainly not pass away until all these things have happened.
31. Heaven and earth will pass away, but my words will never pass away.

Note that this original prediction puts the Apocalypse at the time of the death of the Son of Man. This would tend to indicate that in the original *Gnostic Apocalyptic Work* that Mark uses here, Jesus does not regard himself as the Son of Man.

This leads us to the question, if Jesus is not the Son of Man, who exactly is making the prediction about the son of man. When we put the text leading up to the prediction under the microscope, we get our answer. He are the relevant clues:

1. And he said to them, "Truly, I say to you, there are some standing here who will not taste death before they see that the kingdom of God has come with power."
2. And after six days Jesus took with him Peter and James and John, and led them up a high mountain apart by themselves; and he was transfigured before them,
3. and his garments became glistening, intensely white, as no fuller on earth could bleach them.
4. And there appeared to them Eli'jah with Moses; and they were talking to Jesus.
5. And Peter said to Jesus, "Master, it is well that we are here; let us make three booths, one for you and one for Moses and one for Eli'jah."
6. For he did not know what to say, for they were exceedingly afraid.
7. And a cloud overshadowed them, and a voice came out of the cloud, "This is my beloved Son; listen to him."

8. And suddenly looking around they no longer saw any one with them but Jesus only.
9. And as they were coming down the mountain, he charged them to tell no one what they had seen, until the Son of man should have risen from the dead.
10. So they kept the matter to themselves, questioning what the rising from the dead meant.
11. And they asked him, "Why do the scribes say that first Eli'jah must come?"
12. And he said to them, "Eli'jah does come first to restore all things; and how is it written of the Son of man, that he should suffer many things and be treated with contempt?

Note that the main character is predicting the coming of the Kingdom of God. This is the motif of John the Baptist. We should expect that it would be John the Baptist speaking this line. Now compare the preceding passage with this:

1. Then after fourteen years I went up again to Jerusalem with Barnabas, taking Titus along with me.
2. I went up by revelation; and I laid before them (but privately before those who were of repute) the gospel which I preach among the Gentiles, lest somehow I should be running or had run in vain.
3. But even Titus, who was with me, was not compelled to be circumcised, though he was a Greek.
4. But because of false brethren secretly brought in, who slipped in to spy out our freedom which we have in Christ Jesus, that they might bring us into bondage—
5. to them we did not yield submission even for a moment, that the truth of the gospel might be preserved for you.
6. And from those who were reputed to be something (what they were makes no difference to me; God shows no partiality)—those, I say, who were of repute added nothing to me;
7. but on the contrary, when they saw that I had been entrusted with the gospel to the uncircumcised, just as Peter had been entrusted with the gospel to the circumcised
8. (for he who worked through Peter for the mission to the circumcised worked through me also for the Gentiles),
9. and when they perceived the grace that was given to me, James and Cephas and John, who were reputed to be pillars, gave to me and Barnabas the right hand of fellowship, that we should go to the Gentiles and they to the circumcised;

The three pillars of the church are James and Cephas and John. Cephas is just Aramaic for Peter, so we have the same characters, James, Peter and John here. Note that James is not put with John. We have Peter with John. We may take it that the writer of this part of Paul's Ephesians did not know of any special connection between James and John. Note also that three people, Paul, Barnabas, and Titus are visiting the three pillars.

Now, if we go back to *Mark's* text we also have a visit. The three pillars Peter, James and John are going to visit three people on a mountain Moses, Elijah and Jesus. Only, Mark has changed the equation. Jesus is added at the beginning, so we get the three pillars plus Jesus visiting Moses and Elijah. Now Jesus gets transformed and suddenly he is with Moses and Elijah. Jesus has a double role here as the visitor and the visited. As Mark slid the Roman-Jewish War into the prediction of the Apocalypse, here he slides Jesus into the role of the visitor. We may reconstruct the original scene this way

Reconstruction of Original Tranfiguration Scene

1. And he said to them, "Truly, I say to you, there are some standing here who will not taste death before they see that the kingdom of God has come with power."
2. And after six days John took with him Peter and James and led them up a high mountain apart by themselves;
3. and his garments became glistening, intensely white, as no fuller on earth could bleach them.
4. And there appeared to them Eli'jah with Moses; and they were talking to Jesus.
5. And Peter said to John, "Master, it is well that we are here; let us make three booths, one for Jesus and one for Moses and one for Eli'jah."
6. For he did not know what to say, for they were exceedingly afraid.
7. And a cloud overshadowed them, and a voice came out of the cloud, "This is my beloved Son; listen to him."
8. And suddenly looking around they no longer saw any one with them but John only.
9. And as they were coming down the mountain, he charged them to tell no one what they had seen, until the Son of man should have risen from the dead.
10. So they kept the matter to themselves, questioning what the rising from the dead meant.
11. And they asked him, "Why do the scribes say that first Eli'jah must come?"
12. And he said to them, "Eli'jah does come first to restore all things; and how is it written of the Son of man, that he should suffer many things and be treated with contempt?

The original scene is simply John (the Baptist) taking his disciples Peter and James to the mountain where they encounter Moses, Elijah and Jesus (Joshua). This solution avoids the jump of Jesus's clothes turning super white and then all of a sudden having Elijah and Moses talking with him. In the original scene, John's clothes simply illuminate the presence of the three living dead spirits. The phrase "and he was transfigured before them" is an addition by Mark and was not in the original. Note how much smoother the passage runs without it.

This gives us a clue to what Mark is all about. He is taking material about John the Baptist, changing it to be about Jesus and adding it to Mary's play about the coming of the Word of God-Christ. We may take it that Mark got the idea for the transformation scene from watching a performance of Euripides' Bacchae at the theater in Caesarea. This is the scene that may have influenced him:

> DIONYSUS: Yes, I am Dionysus, son of Zeus.
> You see me now before you as a god.
> You Thebans learned about my powers too late.
> Dishonouring me, you earn the penalty.
> You refused my rites. Now you must leave—
> abandon your city for barbarian lands.
> Agave, too, that polluted creature,
> must go into perpetual banishment.
> And Cadmus, you too must endure your lot.
> Your form will change, so you become a dragon.
> Your wife, Harmonia, Ares' daughter,
> whom you, though mortal, took in marriage,
> will be transformed, changing to a snake.
> As Zeus' oracle declares, you and she
> will drive a chariot drawn by heifers.
> You'll rule barbarians. With your armies,
> too large to count, you'll raze many cities.
> Once they despoil Apollo's oracle,
> they'll have a painful journey back again.
> But Ares will guard you and Harmonia.
> In lands of the blessed he'll transform your lives.
> That's what I proclaim—I, Dionysus,
> born from no mortal father, but from Zeus.

It seems certain that Mark was trying to rewrite Mary's play. It also seems cetain that he is not a professional playwrite. His scenes are impossible to perform. One may take Mark's gospel as a botched play. His problem comes from what he is trying to do. Essentially he is trying to slide John the Baptist material into Mary's play. He's giving the good lines of John the Baptist to Jesus, but he's creating ideological havoc by having Jesus as his own prophet, predicting his own coming.

Mark is writing post war, although it is hard to say if it is post first or second Jewish War. He is combining two narratives from before the war, the Mary play narrative, where the son/word of God comes and gets executed by Pilate with a narrative of John the Baptist predicting the apocalyptic coming of the son of man. The result dramatically is a confused and absurdist mess.

This idea that Mark is rewriting a John as Christ text will be one of the primary ones investigated in the rest of this work. One should note that the author of the *Clementine Recognitions* was quite aware of a group that had suggested John as Christ.

> The scribes also, and Pharisees, are led away into another schism; but these, being baptized by John, and holding the word of truth received from the tradition of Moses as the key of the kingdom of heaven, have hid it from the hearing of the people. Yea, some even of the disciples of John, who seemed to be great ones, have separated themselves from the people, and proclaimed their own master as the Christ[381].

The people who proclaimed John as Christ wrote the original material that Mark worked from. Mark's task and purpose in writing his gospel was to change John the Christ back into Jesus the Christ.

The Apocalyptic Material and Mark's additions

Mark has changed an old general prediction about the Apocalypse to fit his own time and situation. It is not hard to separate the original apocalyptic material from his additions. I have put Mark's additions in bold.

5: And Jesus began to say to them,
Take heed that no one leads you astray.
6: Many will come in my name, saying, 'I am he!' and they will lead many astray.
7: And when you hear of wars and rumors of wars, do not be alarmed; this must take place, but the end is not yet.
8: For nation will rise against nation, and kingdom against kingdom; there will be earthquakes in various places, there will be famines; this is but the beginning of the birth-pangs.
9: "But take heed to yourselves; for they will deliver you up to councils; and you will be beaten in synagogues; and you will stand before governors and kings for my sake, to bear testimony before them.
10: And the gospel must first be preached to all nations.

11: And when they bring you to trial and deliver you up, do not be anxious beforehand what you are to say; but say whatever is given you in that hour, for it is not you who speak, but the Holy Spirit.
12: And brother will deliver up brother to death, and the father his child, and children will rise against parents and have them put to death;
13: and you will be hated by all for my name's sake. But he who endures to the end will be saved.
14: "But when you see the desolating sacrilege set up where it ought not to be (let the reader understand), then let those who are in Judea flee to the mountains;
15: let him who is on the housetop not go down, nor enter his house, to take anything away;
16: and let him who is in the field not turn back to take his mantle.
17: And alas for those who are with child and for those who give suck in those days!
18: Pray that it may not happen in winter.
19: For in those days there will be such tribulation as has not been from the beginning of the creation which God created until now, and never will be.
20: And if the Lord had not shortened the days, no human being would be saved; but for the sake of the elect, whom he chose, he shortened the days.
21: And then if any one says to you, 'Look, here is the Christ!' or 'Look, there he is!' do not believe it.
22: False Christs and false prophets will arise and show signs and wonders, to lead astray, if possible, the elect.
23: But take heed; I have told you all things beforehand.
24: "But in those days, after that tribulation, the sun will be darkened, and the moon will not give its light,
25: and the stars will be falling from heaven, and the powers in the heavens will be shaken.
26: And then they will see the Son of man coming in clouds with great power and glory.
27: And then he will send out the angels, and gather his elect from the four winds, from the ends of the earth to the ends of heaven.
28: "From the fig tree learn its lesson: as soon as its branch becomes tender and puts forth its leaves, you know that summer is near.
29: So also, when you see these things taking place, you know that he is near, at the very gates.

30: Truly, I say to you, this generation will not pass away before all these things take place.
31: Heaven and earth will pass away, but my words will not pass away.
32: "But of that day or that hour no one knows, not even the angels in heaven, nor the Son, but only the Father.
33: Take heed, watch; for you do not know when the time will come.
34: It is like a man going on a journey, when he leaves home and puts his servants in charge, each with his work, and commands the doorkeeper to be on the watch.
35: Watch therefore—for you do not know when the master of the house will come, in the evening, or at midnight, or at cockcrow, or in the morning—
36: lest he come suddenly and find you asleep.
37: And what I say to you I say to all: Watch."

Here is the original prediction of the coming of man material separated from Mark's additions:

Reconstruction of the Original Coming of Christ Predictions

7: And when you hear of wars and rumors of wars, do not be alarmed; this must take place, but the end is not yet.
8: For nation will rise against nation, and kingdom against kingdom; there will be earthquakes in various places, there will be famines; this is but the beginning of the birth-pangs.
12: And brother will deliver up brother to death, and the father his child, and children will rise against parents and have them put to death;
14: "But when you see the desolating sacrilege set up where it ought not to be, then let those who are in Judea flee to the mountains;
15: let him who is on the housetop not go down, nor enter his house, to take anything away;
16: and let him who is in the field not turn back to take his mantle.
17: And alas for those who are with child and for those who give suck in those days!
18: Pray that it may not happen in winter.
19: For in those days there will be such tribulation as has not been from the beginning of the creation which God created until now, and never will be.
20: And if the Lord had not shortened[382] the days, no human being would be saved;

24: "But in those days, after that tribulation, the sun will be darkened, and the moon will not give its light,
25: and the stars will be falling from heaven, and the powers in the heavens will be shaken.
26: And then they will see the Son of man coming in clouds with great power and glory.
27: And then he will send out the angels, and gather his elect from the four winds, from the ends of the earth to the ends of heaven.
30: Truly, I say to you, this generation will not pass away before all these things take place.
31: Heaven and earth will pass away, but my words will not pass away.

Note how smoothly the text now flows as it describes the coming of the "Son of Man."

Let us go back and examine the material that Mark has added to the apocalyptic John material to make it appear to be about the current period and his Christian movement. The following is the material that Mark added:

12.5. Jesus said to them: Watch out that no-one deceives you.
6. Many will come in my name, claiming, 'I am he,' and will deceive many.
9. You must be on your guard. You will be handed over to the local councils and flogged in the synagogues. On account of me you will stand before governors and kings as witnesses to them.
10. And the gospel must first be preached to all nations.
11. Whenever you are arrested and brought to trial, do not worry beforehand about what to say. Just say whatever is given you at the time, for it is not you speaking, but the Holy Spirit.
13. All men will hate you because of me, but he who stands firm to the end will be saved.
21. At that time if anyone says to you, 'Look, here is the Christ!' or, 'Look, there he is!' do not believe it.
22. For false Christs and false prophets will appear and perform signs and miracles to deceive the elect—if that were possible.
23. So be on your guard;
28. Now learn this lesson from the fig-tree: As soon as its twigs get tender and its leaves come out, you know that summer is near.
29. Even so, when you see these things happening, you know that it is near, right at the door.
32. No-one knows about that day or hour, not even the angels in heaven, nor the Son, but only the Father.

33. Be on guard! Be alert! You do not know when that time will come.
34. It's like a man going away: He leaves his house and puts his servants in charge, each with his assigned task, and tells the one at the door to keep watch.
35. Therefore keep watch because you do not know when the owner of the house will come back—whether in the evening, or at midnight, or when the cock crows, or at dawn.
36. If he comes suddenly, do not let him find you sleeping.
37. What I say to you, I say to everyone: 'Watch!'

Note first how Mark changes the time of the coming of the Apocalypse from the time immediately following the death and resurrection of the Son of Man when cataclysmic events are taking place to a time describing his own concrete situation: "You will be handed over to local councils" etc. Also note, he adds a weak apology at the end that nobody knows when the Messiah is coming. He is undermining the idea of the apocalypse in this generation, saying nobody knows when it will be.

A bit earlier in his text (Mark 8.31), we find, "He then began to teach them that the Son of Man must suffer many things and be rejected by the elders, chief priests and teachers of the law, and that he must be killed and after three days rise again." There is no mention here of Pontius Pilate, Romans, Herod, trials, Passover or crucifixion. One may argue that Jesus is just talking about what will happen in a general way, but it is just as likely that what gets described in the passion narrative gets developed out of the general notion expressed here that the Son of Man will suffer get rejected and come back in three days.

Does Mark Use the Temple as an Historical Marker?

We have to again go back to how Mark uses the temple to see if he uses it for its function as a temporal marker or for its symbolic function. We should take careful note of the fact that Mark never places the temple in history. He does not tell us how many years before its destruction Jesus visited the temple, nor who the chief priests were at the time. Mark's Jesus does not oppose the temple cult of sacrifice, but only opposes the commercialization of the temple. But opposition to commercialization of the sacred is a traditional theme in Jewish religious texts: From chapter three of Micah, we read

10. who build Zion with bloodshed,
 and Jerusalem with wickedness.
11. Her leaders judge for a bribe,
 her priests teach for a price,
 and her prophets tell fortunes for money.
 Yet they lean upon the LORD and say,

>   "Is not the LORD among us?
>   No disaster will come upon us."
> 12. Therefore because of you,
>   Zion will be plowed like a field,
>   Jerusalem will become a heap of rubble,
>   the temple hill a mound overgrown with thickets.

Rather than pinpointing Jesus' visit to a time in history, Mark seems to be using it to connect Jesus to Hebrew Scriptures. We may examine all six scenes that Mark places at the temple to be certain of this.

Six Scenes in the Temple

1. First Visit: Late Arrival

> 7. When they brought the colt to Jesus and threw their cloaks over it, he sat on it.
> 8. Many people spread their cloaks on the road, while others spread branches they had cut in the fields.
> 9. Those who went ahead and those who followed shouted, Hosanna! Blessed is he who comes in the name of the Lord!
> 10. Blessed is the coming kingdom of our father David! Hosanna in the highest!
> 11. Jesus entered Jerusalem and went to the temple. He looked around at everything, but since it was already late, he went out to Bethany with the Twelve.
> 12. The next day as they were leaving Bethany, Jesus was hungry.
> 13. Seeing in the distance a fig-tree in leaf, he went to find out if it had any fruit. When he reached it, he found nothing but leaves, because it was not the season for figs.
> 14. Then he said to the tree, May no-one ever eat fruit from you again. And his disciples heard him say it.

This first visit is a bit baffling as Jesus does not do anything in the temple except look around. The visit seems pointless. We may get a clue for the reason it is here by the simple fact that Mark makes him arrive late. Back in Chapter 6, we also find the "late" motif. People are late to come see Jesus:

> [35] By this time it was late in the day, so his disciples came to him. This is a remote place, they said, and it's already very late.

36 Send the people away so that they can go to the surrounding countryside and villages and buy themselves something to eat.
37 But he answered, You give them something to eat. They said to him, That would take eight months of a man's wages! Are we to go and spend that much on bread and give it to them to eat?

Mark uses the lateness of the hour to allow Jesus to perform a miracle. It is quite probable that Mark is working from a list of miracles he want/needs his Jesus character to perform. Jesus arriving late allows Mark to take Jesus back to Bethany and perform his miracle/cursing of the fig tree. It is hard to say why Mark did not just have the cursing of the fig tree earlier. It could just be that the entry on a donkey was on his "miracles to do" list before "cursing a fig tree." Or it could be that he left it out by mistake and decided to put it back in when he remembered it at this point. In any case, it seems clear that the first visit to the temple has no temporal or historical significance.

2. Second Visit: Overturning the Merchants

15. On reaching Jerusalem, Jesus entered the temple area and began driving out those who were buying and selling there. He overturned the tables of the money-changers and the benches of those selling doves,
16. and would not allow anyone to carry merchandise through the temple courts.
17. And as he taught them, he said, Is it not written:
    'My house will be called a house of prayer for all nations'?
    But you have made it 'a den of robbers'.
18. The chief priests and the teachers of the law heard this and began looking for a way to kill him, for they feared him, because the whole crowd was amazed at his teaching.
19. When evening came, they went out of the city.

Mark has juxtaposed Isaiah 56:7 with Jeremiah 7:11 here.

Their burnt offerings and their sacrifices will be acceptable on My altar; for My house will be called a house of prayer for all the peoples.

Will you steal, murder and commit adultery, and swear falsely, and offer sacrifices to Baal, and walk after other gods that you have not known, then come and stand before Me in this house which is called by My name, and say, 'We are delivered!'—that you may do all these abominations? Has this house, which is called by My name, become a den of robbers in your sight? Behold, I, even I, have seen it . . . . But go now to My place which was in Shiloh, where I made My name dwell at the first, and see what I did to it because of the wickedness of my people Israel . . . I will do to the house which is called by My name, in which you trust, and to the place which I gave you and your fathers, as I did in Shiloh."

In the Hebrew Scriptures, Shiloh ended up being destroyed, because it had become a "Den of Thieves." What Mark is actually doing here, through Jesus, is giving his opinion of why the temple was destroyed. He is alleging that God destroyed the temple due to the corruption that was taking place in the temple. The scene is not in any way meant to be historical. There is nothing about the reaction of the hundreds of merchants who made their living from the exchanging in the temple. It is impossible to believe that Jesus and his followers would not have been immediately arrested and executed for putting a stop to an activity that supported the livelihood of hundreds of merchants, thousands of Jewish priests, and brought in a large amount of money to Rome. It is clear that Mark is not writing history here, but writing allegorically. He is explaining why God destroyed the temple.

Hundreds or perhaps thousands of Priests and Merchants and virtually the whole economy of Jerusalem depended on the religious trade in the temple. It is hard to imagine the centralization of an economy like this in the age of economic diversity that we live in. A very rough modern analogy would be a band of communists coming to Wall Street and shutting it down.

While we have no historical record of any such incident in Jewish history, Josephus does talk of groups of radicals taking over the temple during the Roman-Jewish War:

> These men made the temple of God a strong hold for them, and a place whither they might resort, in order to avoid the troubles they feared from the people; the sanctuary was now become a refuge, and a shop of tyranny. They also mixed jesting among the miseries they introduced, which was more intolerable than what they did; for in order to try what surprise the people would be under, and how far their own power extended, they undertook to dispose of the high priesthood by casting lots for it, whereas, as we have said already, it was to descend by succession in a family. The pretense they made for this strange attempt was an ancient practice, while they said that of old it was determined by lot; but in truth, it was no better than a dissolution of an undeniable law, and a cunning contrivance to seize upon the government, derived from those that presumed to appoint governors as they themselves pleased[383].

Now the bandits who took over the temple in 69 C.E., did not turn it into an international House of Prayer, as Jesus seems to intend, but rather, democratized the selection of Priests. Rather than make it into an international House of Prayer, the rebels intended to do the exact opposite, make it more exclusively Jewish. Josephus has the High Priest Ananus give a speech talking about how good the Romans behaved in respecting the temple customs as opposed to the Jewish nationalist rebels:

> How then can we avoid shedding of tears, when we see the Roman donations in our temple, while we withal see those of our own nation taking our spoils, and plundering our glorious metropolis, and slaughtering our men, from which enormities those Romans themselves would have abstained? to see those Romans never going beyond the bounds allotted to profane persons, nor venturing to break in upon any of our sacred customs; nay, having a horror on their minds when they view at a distance those sacred walls; while some that have been born in this very country, and brought up in our customs, and called Jews, do walk about in the midst of the holy places, at the very time when their hands are still warm with the slaughter of their own countrymen. Besides, can any one be afraid of a war abroad, and that with such as will have comparatively much greater moderation than our own people have? For truly, if we may suit our words to the things they represent, it is probable one may hereafter find the Romans to be the supporters of our laws, and those within ourselves the subverters of them[384].

If Mark is referring to the actual historical event of the Zealots taking over the Temple, it is unlikely he could have recast the nationalist Zealots into the role of internationalists immediately after the event. If it is an historical reference to this event, we must imagine it coming many years afterwards, and meant to show a contrast between the purposes of the Zealots in taking over the temple and the purposes of Jesus taking over the temple. On the other hand, it is almost as likely that the whole scene is allegorical and not meant to recall the Zealot takeover in the late 60's.

3. Third Visit: Wrestling with the Authorities

11, 27. They arrived again in Jerusalem, and while Jesus was walking in the temple courts, the chief priests, the teachers of the law and the elders came to him.

28. By what authority are you doing these things? they asked. And who gave you authority to do this?

29. Jesus replied, I will ask you one question. Answer me, and I will tell you by what authority I am doing these things.

30. John's baptism—was it from heaven, or from men? Tell me!

12.1 He then began to speak to them in parables: A man planted a vineyard. He put a wall around it, dug a pit for the winepress and built a watchtower. Then he rented the vineyard to some farmers and went away on a journey.

2. At harvest time he sent a servant to the tenants to collect from them some of the fruit of the vineyard.

3. But they seized him, beat him and sent him away empty-handed.

4. Then he sent another servant to them; they struck this man on the head and treated him shamefully.

5. He sent still another, and that one they killed. He sent many others; some of them they beat, others they killed.

6. He had one left to send, a son, whom he loved. He sent him last of all, saying, 'They will respect my son.'

7. But the tenants said to one another, 'This is the heir. Come, let's kill him, and the inheritance will be ours.'

8. So they took him and killed him, and threw him out of the vineyard.

9. What then will the owner of the vineyard do? He will come and kill those tenants and give the vineyard to others.

10. Haven't you read this scripture:
'The stone the builders rejected has become the capstone;

11. the Lord has done this, and it is marvellous in our eyes'?

12. Then they looked for a way to arrest him because they knew he had spoken the parable against them. But they were afraid of the crowd; so they left him and went away.

13. Later they sent some of the Pharisees and Herodians to Jesus to catch him in his words.

14. They came to him and said, Teacher, we know you are a man of integrity. You aren't swayed by men, because you pay no attention to who they are; but you teach the way of God in accordance with the truth. Is it right to pay taxes to Caesar or not?

15. Should we pay or shouldn't we? But Jesus knew their hypocrisy. Why are you trying to trap me? he asked. Bring me a denarius and let me look at it.

16. They brought the coin, and he asked them, Whose portrait is this? And whose inscription? Caesar's, they replied.

17. Then Jesus said to them, Give to Caesar what is Caesar's and to God what is God's. And they were amazed at him.

18. Then the Sadducees, who say there is no resurrection, came to him with a question.

19. Teacher, they said, Moses wrote for us that if a man's brother dies and leaves a wife but no children, the man must marry the widow and have children for his brother.
20. Now there were seven brothers. The first one married and died without leaving any children.
21. The second one married the widow, but he also died, leaving no child. It was the same with the third.
22. In fact, none of the seven left any children. Last of all, the woman died too.
23. At the resurrection whose wife will she be, since the seven were married to her?
24. Jesus replied, Are you not in error because you do not know the Scriptures or the power of God?
25. When the dead rise, they will neither marry nor be given in marriage; they will be like the angels in heaven.
26. Now about the dead rising—have you not read in the book of Moses, in the account of the bush, how God said to him, 'I am the God of Abraham, the God of Isaac, and the God of Jacob'?
27. He is not the God of the dead, but of the living. You are badly mistaken!
28. One of the teachers of the law came and heard them debating. Noticing that Jesus had given them a good answer, he asked him, Of all the commandments, which is the most important?
29. The most important one, answered Jesus, is this: 'Hear, O Israel, the Lord our God, the Lord is one.
30. Love the Lord your God with all your heart and with all your soul and with all your mind and with all your strength.'
31. The second is this: 'Love your neighbour as yourself.' There is no commandment greater than these....
32. Well said, teacher, the man replied. You are right in saying that God is one and there is no other but him.
33. To love him with all your heart, with all your understanding and with all your strength, and to love your neighbour as yourself is more important than all burnt offerings and sacrifices.
34. When Jesus saw that he had answered wisely, he said to him, You are not far from the kingdom of God. And from then on no-one dared ask him any more questions.

On this third visit to the temple, Mark has Jesus fight the whole Jewish establishment: Priests, Elders, Saducees, Scribes, Pharisees, and Herodians. It would certainly help us if we could pinpoint a date for any of these groups. We cannot definitely say that any of them disappeared before the second century. Passages in this texts discusses authority (Jesus' authority is like John the Baptist's), legitimacy (vineyard tenants parable: The Jewish authorities are only squatter's on God's territory), paying taxes to Rome (no problem), resurrection (angelic, apparently not bodily), and top commandments (simply the basics, One God, love God, and love thy neighbor).

The important thing here to note is that none of these issues would be of any significance just after the destruction of the temple and a war in which possibly hundreds of thousands of Jews were killed and enslaved. The calm, joking manner in which the establishment comes under attack suggests that it was written a long time after the temple's destruction, when Jews were again firmly in control of Judea. It would be pointless to attack Jewish authority just after the war when Rome was in control of every aspect of life in Judea. It also makes no sense to attack these things before the war. Why attack the Jewish authorities for not universalizing the temple when the Jewish Authorities were under attack by Zealots for doing exactly that.

The ending of this third visit to the temple appears to me to be the original ending of *Mark's Gospel*. It is a happy ending with a scribe (perhaps intended to represent Mark himself) going over to the side of Jesus. It matches the ending at 16:8, where the three women are afraid. Here all the authorities are afraid of Jesus. It is a natural ending point as Jesus has shown himself a great debater, given the three most important commandments, and now there are no more questions for Jesus to answer. This scene begs for a "The End" title to put after it.

4. Fourth Visit: Odds and Ends

35. While Jesus was teaching in the temple courts, he asked, How is it that the teachers of the law say that the Christ is the son of David?
36. David himself, speaking by the Holy Spirit, declared:
'The Lord said to my Lord: Sit at my right hand until I put your enemies under your feet.'
37. David himself calls him 'Lord'. How then can he be his son? The large crowd listened to him with delight.
38. As he taught, Jesus said, Watch out for the teachers of the law. They like to walk around in flowing robes and be greeted in the market-places,
39. and have the most important seats in the synagogues and the places of honour at banquets.
40. They devour widows' houses and for a show make lengthy prayers. Such men will be punished most severely.

Jesus here argues a rather obscure theological point about the Christ. This attack on the teachers of the law seems an afterthought, but it does follow the motif of attacking the Jewish authorities in Jerusalem. This is another example where we get the absurdity of Jesus talking about himself. We must assume that these passages too originally involved John the Baptist and Mark has simply shifted them to Jesus.

5. Fifth Temple Scene: A Simple Economics Lesson

41. Jesus sat down opposite the place where the offerings were put and watched the crowd putting their money into the temple treasury. Many rich people threw in large amounts.
42. But a poor widow came and put in two very small copper coins, worth only a fraction of a penny.
43. Calling his disciples to him, Jesus said, I tell you the truth, this poor widow has put more into the treasury than all the others.
44. They all gave out of their wealth; but she, out of her poverty, put in everything—all she had to live on.

This scene seems to make no point. It is perfectly obvious that money is dearer to a poorer person. The throwing in of coins would suggest a fountain or pool. This may have been the original location of the scene.

The point of the scene must be the setting. Jesus is sitting "opposite" the temple treasury. The scene is there just to form a bridge connection with the upcoming prophesy scene where Jesus sits opposite the temple. A character at the end of a movie scene may sit in a certain position, just so a connection is made with the next scene where the character sits in the same position in another place. This is just a transition scene. The only other thing it tells us is that the Mark was most likely poor (preseuming the scene was self-referential) and could not afford to give much to the treasury.

6. Sixth Temple Scene—Leaving Temple Scene

13.1. As he was leaving the temple, one of his disciples said to him, Look, Teacher! What massive stones! What magnificent buildings!
2. Do you see all these great buildings? replied Jesus. Not one stone here will be left on another; every one will be thrown down.

As in the last scene, this is intended simply as a bridge to the prophesy material that Mark has decided to add. It is hard to determine why the location had to be the temple rather than any place in Jerusalem. We can not even be sure that the reference is to temple buildings rather than other buildings in Jerusalem.

Looking over the six temple scenes, we see that there is no narrative flow. The temple is only used as a background with the exception of the attack on the merchants where the temple seems to be only an allegorical symbol. There is nothing here that indicates an actual visit to the temple by Jesus or that the author Mark has even been to the temple for that matter. Most people are eager to show knowledge of a place they have been to in talking about it. They describe the uniqueness, or beauty of it or at least the relationships and distances between parts. The temple was the largest building in the Ancient World. Mark shows no knowledge whatsoever that it was anything but an ordinary temple.

As our review has shown, there is nothing about the temple setting that ties any of the scenes to a first century date. Mark uses the temple as scenery for Jesus to make general observations about Judaism. There is nothing that dates the writing to the first century rather than the second century. None of the issues raised are particularly relevant to the first dentury. Even the criticism of the money-changers could easily represent a second century criticism of Judaism.

The temple scenes function as transition scenes. They bring Jesus from his wandering preaching/healing stories to his arrest and execution. They solve a technical problem in the narrative. How do we get our Jesus from wandering around Galilee to being executed in Jerusalem by the Romans? Answer, let's have him wander into the Jerusalem temple and start preaching there. This so offends the Jewish authorities that they turn him over to the Romans.

Two Questions: Which buildings and Which War?

The text of chapter 13 of Mark is ambiguous on two important points. First, does he refer to the temple buildings or the buildings of Jerusalem when he exits the temple. Second, does he describe the Roman-Jewish War of 66-73 or 132-135?

The bridge scene at 13:1-2 is ambiguous. Is the reference to the destruction of the temple buildings or to the destruction of the city buildings? The text reads, "As he was leaving the temple, one of his disciples said to him, Look, Teacher! What massive stones! What magnificent buildings!" One clue that the reference is not to the buildings of the temple is the statement that "he was leaving the temple." The time to notice the great buildings of the temple would have been when he entered the temple. The text has Jesus going into the temple immediately upon his arrival in Jerusalem. Presumably, he has not seen any other part of the city. Therefore, it seems logical that by introducing the remark on "he was leaving the Temple," Mark may mean to indicate the disciples were seeing the buildings of the city for the first time. The buildings of the temple would have been visible from the temple courtyard, so there was no need to exit the temple to see the temple buildings. He would have to exit the temple to see the city buildings. While ambiguous, it seems more likely, the disciple refers to the buildings of Jerusalem rather than just the Temple buildings.

Jesus' answer is also ambiguous, "'Do you see all these great buildings? replied Jesus. Not one stone here will be left on another; every one will be thrown down.'" The destruction of a single temple complex even one as large as the ancient Jerusalem temple would have been unbelievable and fantastic, but to add that not one stone here will be left on another would not add to the level of destruction. The fact that a building or complex gets destroyed is the important thing, the fact that not one stone will be left on another hardly adds to the fact of a building's destruction. Most of the time when a building gets destroyed today, nothing is left. That would be the case in ancient times too. Why leave a part of a building standing? Usually you destroy a building to replace it with something, so naturally you remove every bit of the old building. One assumes that when you talk about a building being gone that it is gone completely. What would the difference be if there were a few stones left on top of each other? It is the norm when buildings are destroyed for them to be totally destroyed. Only when we are talking about the buildings of an entire city would one need to add that not one stone would be left on another to give the impression of enormous and catastrophic destruction. It is never the norm for all the buildings of a city to disappear at once completely. This indicates a real apocalyptic event.

So, from the scenic description and from the use of the phrase "not one stone here will be left on another" we have significant evidence that the reference is to the destruction of the buildings of the city of Jerusalem and not to just the temple. This is important in dating the description. We have to compare this description of a city which no buildings have a stone on stone with this description of Jerusalem from Josephus[385].

> **Now when Titus was come into this [upper] city, he admired not only some other places of strength in it, but particularly those strong towers which the tyrants in their mad conduct had relinquished; for when he saw their solid altitude, and the largeness of their several stones, and the exactness of their joints, as also how great was their breadth, and how extensive their length, he expressed himself after the manner following: "We have certainly had God for our assistant in this war, and it was no other than God who ejected the Jews out of these fortifications; for what could the hands of men or any machines do towards overthrowing these towers?" At which time he had many such discourses to his friends; he also let such go free as had been bound by the tyrants, and were left in the prisons. To conclude, when he entirely demolished the rest of the city, and overthrew its walls, he left these towers as a monument of his good fortune, which had proved his auxiliaries, and enabled him to take what could not otherwise have been taken by him.**

Not only does Josephus not say that all the buildings were completely destroyed, but he says that three of the most impressive towers were kept intact. Josephus again repeats this information that buildings were kept intact[386].

> Caesar gave orders that they should now demolish the entire city and temple, but should leave as many of the towers standing as were of the greatest eminency; that is, Phasaelus, and Hippicus, and Mariamne; and so much of the wall as enclosed the city on the west side.

One can hardly imagine that Josephus could be mistaken that the three most eminent towers remained standing after the siege of Jerusalem in 70 C.E. On the other hand, we have this testimony from Epiphanius

> Therefore, Hadrian made up his mind to rebuild the city, but not the temple. And he took the Aquila mentioned above, who was a Greek interpreter. Now Aquila was related to the emperor by marriage and was from Sinope in Pontus. Hadrian established him there in Jerusalem as overseer of the work of building the city

In building a new city it would make sense that you would level all the buildings before beginning new construction. This would include the three towers which would be 65 years older at this point. They would also be less stable and probably not as impressive as they had been to Trajan who preserved them. This again points to the Bar Kochba War as the period of the reference of this prophesy.

Counter-Evidence: Jesus' Destruction of the Temple

We have determined that Mark may be referring to the city buildings of Jerusalem being destroyed and the siege during the second century Bar Kochba War, rather than the first century War.

There is only one line in Mark that seems to directly point to the destruction of the Temple in 70 CE as the reference of Jesus' prophesy outside the Temple. This is the line of the witnesses against Jesus at his trial.

> We heard him say, 'I will destroy this man-made temple and in three days will build another, not made by man.[387]'

There is a similar reference while Jesus is on the cross.

> Those who passed by hurled insults at him, shaking their heads and saying, So! You who are going to destroy the temple and build it in three days, come down from the cross and save yourself![388]

At this point we can take out our *separation tool* and compare it to Matthew's version. He twice brings up this point at the same points, first at the trial and then at the crucifixion.

> Finally two came forward and declared, This fellow said, 'I am able to destroy the temple of God and rebuild it in three days.[389]

> Those who passed by hurled insults at him, shaking their heads and saying, You who are going to destroy the temple and build it in three days, save yourself! Come down from the cross, if you are the Son of God[390]!

The second references are virtually identical in the crucifixion scene. Matthew has simply changed "save yourself" to "if you are the Son of God," implying that the Jews knew that Jesus was the Son of God, a concept not found in Mark.

However, notice the subtle change Matthew has made in the first trial scene text. In Mark's text, the witnesses claim that Jesus said that he would destroy the man-made temple and replace it with a non-man made one. Matthew has the witness say that Jesus said that he is *able* to destroy the Temple and to rebuild it.

Now for a moment assume that the witnesses are telling the truth. In the case of Mark, Jesus has made a promise and fulfilled it. The temple has been destroyed and a different type of temple, not by human hands, a Christian one, has come into existence to replace it. In the case of Matthew, Jesus only claims to have the power to do it. No promise is made. No play, no foul. Matthew also now makes Jesus claim to have the power to rebuild the temple presumably as the man built temple as it stood before. Since the temple has not been rebuilt, it is clear that Jesus never exercised his prerogative to destroy and rebuild the temple.

We may presume that in the original text, early Christians had Jesus proclaiming that he would destroy the Jewish Temple and build a Christian non-human one in three days. We can now see the irony in the scene on the cross where the Jews passing by tease Jesus about it. In fact, when he gets down from the cross he does destroy the temple. Thus the witnesses against Jesus are telling the truth and the destruction of the temple in the original text was something that Jesus caused and Christians seemed to accept.

Note how the text almost stutters and how clumsy the editing becomes when Mark tries to tell this story.

> The chief priests and the whole Sanhedrin were looking for evidence against Jesus so that they could put him to death, but they did not find any.
>
> Many testified falsely against him, but their statements did not agree.
>
> Then some stood up and gave this false testimony against him:
>
> We heard him say, 'I will destroy this man-made temple and in three days will build another, not made by man.'

> Yet even then their testimony did not agree.
> Then the high priest stood up before them and asked Jesus, Are you not going to answer? What is this testimony that these men are bringing against you?
> But Jesus remained silent and gave no answer[391].

First there is the needless repetition of the line their testimony did not agree. The text has just quoted these men. It is perfectly silly to say that they did not agree when Mark has just quoted them agreeing, "We heard him say." Second, note that "Many testified falsely against him". We may interpret this as meaning either there were many (a large number) of people testifying against him, or as many (most but not all) testified falsely against him. The separation of the many who falsely testified from the final testifiers by the phrase "Then some stood up" indicates that we should not put them in the same category as the many who falsely testified. The repetition of the word "false" in front of the word testimony later in that sentence emphasizes the connection between the previous false testifiers and these final testifiers, yet the structural separation of them from the previous testifiers in a category by themselves would indicate that their testimony is not the same as the false testifiers. The solution is that the word "false" was added later. We may reconstruct the original text this way.

> The chief priests and the whole Sanhedrin were looking for evidence against Jesus so that they could put him to death, but they did not find any.
> Many testified falsely against him, but their statements did not agree.
> Then some stood up and gave this testimony against him:
> We heard him say, 'I will destroy this man-made temple and in three days will build another, not made by man.'
> Then the high priest stood up before them and asked Jesus, Are you not going to answer? What is this testimony that these men are bringing against you?
> But Jesus remained silent and gave no answer.

Jesus could not answer truthfully without incriminating himself so he had to remain silent. Matthew found the idea of Jesus destroying the Temple so disturbing, that he changed the text of Jesus' statement to say merely that he had the power to destroy the Temple, not that he would.

Apparently, the writer of John's gospel was even more disturbed by the idea still hinted at in Mark that Jesus destroyed the Temple. He turns the thing into a hilarious Jewish misunderstanding:

> Then the Jews demanded of him, What miraculous sign can you show us to prove your authority to do all this?
>
> Jesus answered them, Destroy this temple, and I will raise it again in three days.
>
> The Jews replied, It has taken forty-six years to build this temple, and you are going to raise it in three days?
>
> But the temple he had spoken of was his body.
>
> After he was raised from the dead, his disciples recalled what he had said. Then they believed the Scripture and the words that Jesus had spoken[392].

If the original story was about Jesus' destruction of the temple, then the lines in chapter 13 of Mark about the destroyed buildings may be directed at the temple building. In fact, it seems assured that it would be. We may read Jesus' sentence, "Not one stone here will be left on another; every one will be thrown down," as Jesus gloating about what he is going to do. But we have to be careful here before jumping to conclusions.

Let us call the results of this deconstruction the *Jesus Destroyed the Jerusalem Temple (JDJT) Hypothesis*.

The JDJT Hypothesis

> The instantaneous perfection of art, the necessity for its renewal—this is true only through a preconceived notion. For the work of art likewise is a construction and everyone knows how monotonous the great creators can be. For the same reason as the thinker, the artist commits himself and becomes himself in his work[393].
>
> Albert Camus

The *JDJT Hypothesis* seems to be a basic layer of story text that Mark used. The story ran something like this: the Jerusalem temple was destroyed because the Messiah had come and the Jews did not recognize him, but instead put him to death. He rose up from the dead and destroyed the temple. This is a Jewish Midrash story. It explains an event in Jewish history by interpreting various sections of their sacred texts. Date wise, all we can say for sure is that it was produced post 70 C.E.

But Mark is not telling this story, he is using it, and revising it in his own time for his own purposes. The story is no longer an explanation of why the temple is destroyed as a result of the Jews killing the Messiah, it is now about the Messiah's self sacrifice in allowing himself to become human and to be killed. As Mark puts it, "For even the Son of Man did not come to be served, but to serve, and to give his life as a ransom for many.[394]" Apparently, the Jesus—Destroying-the-Jerusalem-Temple story had become so widely known that Mark is writing a Midrash on it and does not even have to mention how Jesus destroyed the temple.

Even more interesting is the association of the death of Jesus with the destruction of the temple. We apparently have two different stories in Mark with three-day motifs. In one, Jesus dies and rises from the dead in three days[395]. In the other, Jesus destroys the temple and rebuilds a different non man-made one in three days[396]. We may suppose that both stories developed out of the original story that the Jewish High Priests killed Jesus/the Messiah and three days later the temple was destroyed. The first story uses the Jesus dying part, but softens the temple destruction to Jesus rising (and a hint of him coming on clouds to take revenge. The second story preserves the temple destruction latter part, but then softens it by having Jesus build another Temple. Mark uses both of these softened verses from the original *JDJT* story.

The Logic of First Century Christianity

"What's in a name? That which we call a rose by any other name would smell as sweet[397]".

—William Shakespeare
Romeo and Juliet
Act II, Scene II

Mark used the formula of adding John the Baptist material under the name of Jesus Christ to Mary's *Passion Play* about the Word of God. As we have seen, Mary's play was probably loosely based on a recent historical incident. Could John the Baptist have been a real person?

Let us also look more closely at the logic displayed in Mark when he uses both of the softened versions of the Jews killed Jesus/Jesus destroyed the temple concept.

In the first century, Jews considered themselves oppressed and enslaved by the Romans. Their God was the creator and most powerful God, so how could he let this happen. Their holy scriptures explained the situation to them. God chastised them with enslavement for worshipping other/false Gods. This happened in Egypt. Yahweh then sent a savior in the form of Moses to lead them out of Egypt. He taught Moses magic tricks and he single handedly, with God's power, defeated the powerful Egyptians. But the Jews were disobedient again and looked to false Gods, so he made them wander as stateless/homeless nomads in the dessert for forty years. God then had Joshua Nun (Jesus the Fish) anointed as the leader and savior (Christ) to militarily take the land of Israel from its inhabitants.

In the first century, the Jews again looked to God to send a magician and a military leader to save them. This was not an act of faith, but a scientific calculation on the part of the Jewish High Priests. The world for them, as for all ancient peoples around them, was cyclical in nature. The Sun went round the Earth daily, the phases of the moon repeated monthly, and the seasons changed annually. The moods of Yahweh and his relationship with his people was cyclical too. By consulting the Holy Scriptures, you learned what Yahweh had done in the past and what he would do in the future in any given situation. Yahweh's future actions could be forecast as clearly as the motion of the stars.

But the first century situation was not identical to the time of Moses when the Jews were enslaved in Egypt. Now they were nominally under self rule in their own homeland, but their Herodian leadership were wicked collaborators, puppets of the unholy foreign people who worshipped other Gods. The radical Priests looked to a closer situation in the Holy Scriptures. They looked to the time of Ahab.

> **In the thirty-eighth year of Asa king of Judah, Ahab son of Omri became king of Israel, and he reigned in Samaria over Israel twenty-two years. [30] Ahab son of Omri did more evil in the eyes of the LORD than any of those before him. [31] He not only considered it trivial to commit the sins of Jeroboam son of Nebat, but he also married Jezebel daughter of Ethbaal king of the Sidonians, and began to serve Baal and worship him. [32] He set up an altar for Baal in the temple of Baal that he built in Samaria. [33] Ahab also made an Asherah pole and did more to provoke the LORD, the God of Israel, to anger than did all the kings of Israel before him.**

The analogy of this past time to the present day situation was perfect for the priests who studied it. Like in the time of Ahab, the Herodian leadership were serving foreign Gods and provoking the wrath of Yahweh. Yahweh did not abandon his people in the time of Ahab. Instead he selected Elijah the Tishbite, from Tishbe in Gilead[398] (next to Galilee) to be their magician-savior (Christ).

> **Then the word of the LORD came to him: "Go at once to Zarephath of Sidon and stay there. I have commanded a widow in that place to supply you with food." [10] So he went to Zarephath. When he came to the town gate, a widow was there gathering sticks. He called to her and asked, "Would you bring me a little water in a jar so I may have a drink?" [11] As she was going to get it, he called, "And bring me, please, a piece of bread."**
>
> **"As surely as the LORD your God lives," she replied, "I don't have any bread-only a handful of flour in a jar and a little oil in a jug. I am gathering a few sticks to take home and make a meal for myself and my son, that we may eat it-and die." Elijah said to her, "Don't be afraid. Go home and do as you have said. But first make a small cake of bread for**

> me from what you have and bring it to me, and then make something for yourself and your son. For this is what the LORD, the God of Israel, says: 'The jar of flour will not be used up and the jug of oil will not run dry until the day the LORD gives rain on the land.'"
>
> She went away and did as Elijah had told her. So there was food every day for Elijah and for the woman and her family. [16] For the jar of flour was not used up and the jug of oil did not run dry, in keeping with the word of the LORD spoken by Elijah.

Note how this closely matches the Jesus of the Gospel of John, the meeting of a widow and asking her for water, the unlimited water miracle and the unlimited food miracle[399]. Elijah begins his miracle/magician career with a water and feeding miracle[400]. He soon graduates to returning the dead to life[401]:

> Some time later the son of the woman who owned the house became ill. He grew worse and worse, and finally stopped breathing. [18] She said to Elijah, "What do you have against me, man of God? Did you come to remind me of my sin and kill my son?"
>
> "Give me your son," Elijah replied. He took him from her arms, carried him to the upper room where he was staying, and laid him on his bed. Then he cried out to the LORD, "O LORD my God, have you brought tragedy also upon this widow I am staying with, by causing her son to die?" Then he stretched himself out on the boy three times and cried to the LORD, "O LORD my God, let this boy's life return to him!" The LORD heard Elijah's cry, and the boy's life returned to him, and he lived. Elijah picked up the child and carried him down from the room into the house. He gave him to his mother and said, "Look, your son is alive!"
>
> Then the woman said to Elijah, "Now I know that you are a man of God and that the word of the LORD from your mouth is the truth."

The gospel of John gives the raising of a sick son at the point of death as the second miracle of Jesus[402]. Matthew changes the miracle to a Roman centurion's servant[403]. There is also a centurion at the death of Jesus, who exclaims "Truly, this was the Son of God.[404]" We may suppose that the exclamation originally belonged with the raising the dead son and is an echo of the Sidonian Woman's exclamation of "Now I know that you are a man of God.

However, Elijah does not get to take revenge on the evil Ahab. Instead, he finds a disciple Elisha from Gilgal whom he calls in a scene that reminds one of Jesus calling his disciples:

THE EVOLUTION OF CHRISTS AND CHRISTIANIES

> So Elijah went from there and found Elisha son of Shaphat. He was plowing with twelve yoke of oxen, and he himself was driving the twelfth pair. Elijah went up to him and threw his cloak around him. ²⁰ Elisha then left his oxen and ran after Elijah. "Let me kiss my father and mother good-by," he said, "and then I will come with you.[405]"

As John the Baptist will pass his power to Jesus at the Jordan River, step aside, and bow out in later versions of the tale, Elijah passes his power to Elisha at the Jordan River.

> 6. Then Elijah said to him, "Stay here; the LORD has sent me to the Jordan." And he replied, "As surely as the LORD lives and as you live, I will not leave you." So the two of them walked on.
> 7. Fifty men of the company of the prophets went and stood at a distance, facing the place where Elijah and Elisha had stopped at the Jordan.
> 8. Elijah took his cloak, rolled it up and struck the water with it. The water divided to the right and to the left, and the two of them crossed over on dry ground.
> 9. When they had crossed, Elijah said to Elisha, "Tell me, what can I do for you before I am taken from you?" "Let me inherit a double portion of your spirit," Elisha replied.
> 10. "You have asked a difficult thing," Elijah said, "yet if you see me when I am taken from you, it will be yours-otherwise not."
> 11. As they were walking along and talking together, suddenly a chariot of fire and horses of fire appeared and separated the two of them, and Elijah went up to heaven in a whirlwind.
> 12. Elisha saw this and cried out, "My father! My father! The chariots and horsemen of Israel!" And Elisha saw him no more. Then he took hold of his own clothes and tore them apart.
> 13. He picked up the cloak that had fallen from Elijah and went back and stood on the bank of the Jordan. ¹⁴ Then he took the cloak that had fallen from him and struck the water with it. "Where now is the LORD, the God of Elijah?" he asked. When he struck the water, it divided to the right and to the left, and he crossed over.

Quite literally, Elisha receives the mantle of Elijah with double the power to do the miracles of God. The relationship between Elijah and Elisha is summed up in the next chapter:

11. But Jehoshaphat asked, "Is there no prophet of the LORD here, that we may inquire of the LORD through him?"
    An officer of the king of Israel answered, "Elisha son of Shaphat is here. He used to pour water on the hands of Elijah[406].

Elisha now performs more miracles than Elijah. John Dart, in his book *Decoding Mark*, notes some evidence that Elisha performed sixteen miracles to Elijah's eight. He suggests that Mark had Jesus perform twenty-four miracles to top both of them[407].

Now, the really interesting thing is that Elisha is not the Christ/Savior in the story either. He just continues on Elijah's legacy of prophesy and miracles. He does anoint a real Christ/Savior by the name of Jehu.

1. The prophet Elisha summoned a man from the company of the prophets and said to him, "Tuck your cloak into your belt, take this flask of oil with you and go to Ramoth Gilead.
2. When you get there, look for Jehu son of Jehoshaphat, the son of Nimshi. Go to him, get him away from his companions and take him into an inner room.
3. Then take the flask and pour the oil on his head and declare, 'This is what the LORD says: I anoint you king over Israel.' Then open the door and run; don't delay!"
4. So the young man, the prophet, went to Ramoth Gilead.
5. When he arrived, he found the army officers sitting together. "I have a message for you, commander," he said.
   "For which of us?" asked Jehu.
   "For you, commander," he replied.
6. Jehu got up and went into the house. Then the prophet poured the oil on Jehu's head and declared, "This is what the LORD, the God of Israel, says: 'I anoint you king over the LORD's people Israel.
7. You are to destroy the house of Ahab your master, and I will avenge the blood of my servants the prophets and the blood of all the LORD's servants shed by Jezebel. 8. The whole house of Ahab will perish. I will cut off from Ahab every last male in Israel-slave or free.
9. I will make the house of Ahab like the house of Jeroboam son of Nebat and like the house of Baasha son of Ahijah.
10. As for Jezebel, dogs will devour her on the plot of ground at Jezreel, and no one will bury her.' " Then he opened the door and ran.
11. When Jehu went out to his fellow officers, one of them asked him, "Is everything all right? Why did this madman come to you?"
    "You know the man and the sort of things he says," Jehu replied.

12. "That's not true!" they said. "Tell us."
    Jehu said, "Here is what he told me:'This is what the LORD says: I anoint you king over Israel.'"
13. They hurried and took their cloaks and spread them under him on the bare steps. Then they blew the trumpet and shouted, "Jehu is king!"

The newly anointed Jehu does indeed execute the children of the traitor king Ahab and his wife Jezebel[408]. The text tells us, "When Jehu came to Samaria, he killed all who were left there of Ahab's family; he destroyed them, according to the word of the LORD spoken to Elijah[409]." Thus Jehu ends up a Christ, an anointed King who delivers Israel from the wickedness of Ahab.

30. The LORD said to Jehu, "Because you have done well in accomplishing what is right in my eyes and have done to the house of Ahab all I had in mind to do, your descendants will sit on the throne of Israel to the fourth generation."

However, this being a Jerusalem-biased narrative, Jeru too ends up doing things that God does not like[410]. Regardless, we have found our pattern. A prophet/magician, Elijah, gives power to a prophet/magician, Elisha, who anoints a Messiah who avenges Yahweh by killing the children and wife of the traitor-King Ahab. This is our plot-pattern: prophet/magician gives power to a more powerful prophet/magician, who anoints a Military Messiah.

We should also mention that the middle prophet/magician, Elisha, performs a resurrection miracle after he dies:

20. Elisha died and was buried. Now Moabite raiders used to enter the country every spring.
21. Once while some Israelites were burying a man, suddenly they saw a band of raiders; so they threw the man's body into Elisha's tomb. When the body touched Elisha's bones, the man came to life and stood up on his feet[411].

Now, when we last saw Elijah he was swooped up in a fiery chariot and brought to Heaven. The prophet Malachi, in Book of Malachi, tells us that he is coming back.

1. "Surely the day is coming; it will burn like a furnace. All the arrogant and every evildoer will be stubble, and that day that is coming will set them on fire," says the LORD Almighty. "Not a root or a branch will be left to them.

2. But for you who revere my name, the sun of righteousness will rise with healing in its wings. And you will go out and leap like calves released from the stall.
3. Then you will trample down the wicked; they will be ashes under the soles of your feet on the day when I do these things," says the LORD Almighty.
4. "Remember the law of my servant Moses, the decrees and laws I gave him at Horeb for all Israel.
5. "See, I will send you the prophet Elijah before that great and dreadful day of the LORD comes.
6. He will turn the hearts of the fathers to their children, and the hearts of the children to their fathers; or else I will come and strike the land with a curse."

With this context in mind, we can now point again to Jesus' (originally John) reference to Elijah:

11 And they asked him, Why do the teachers of the law say that Elijah must come first?
12 Jesus replied, To be sure, Elijah does come first, and restores all things. Why then is it written that the Son of Man must suffer much and be rejected?
13 But I tell you, Elijah has come, and they have done to him everything they wished, just as it is written about him.

From Malachi, we get that the coming of Elijah is a last chance for the arrogant and evil. If the father's hearts are turned to the children and the children's hearts are turn to the fathers (returning all things to normal) then God will not need to come. Jesus claims that Elijah came and instead of doing what he wished, the evil and arrogant did to him what they wished. Thus the time is ready for God to come and curse the evil and arrogant.

The writer works backwards here. He does not relate Jesus to the Son of Man or Elijah. He relates the Son of Man to Elijah. There are two endtime passages being mixed here, a Son of Man passage from Daniel 7 and the Elijah Passage from Malachi. Here is the passage from Daniel 7.

13. As I watched the night visions, I saw one like a son of man coming with the clouds of heaven. He went to the Ancient of Days and was presented to him. 14. To him was given dominion, glory, and kingship. All people, nations, and languages would serve him. His

dominion would be an everlasting dominion that would not disappear. His kingship would never be destroyed.

So the writer gets the "Son of Man coming on clouds" in the endtime reference from Daniel and the "Elijah coming first" reference from Malachi. Daniel was apparently written during the time of the rule of the Seleucid Greek King Antiochus IV (175-164 B.C.E. over Israel[412]. It refers to the Maccabean revolt in these terms:

12. 1. At that time Michael, the great prince who protects your people, will arise. There will be a time of distress such as has not happened from the beginning of nations until then. But at that time your people—everyone whose name is found written in the book—will be delivered.
2. Multitudes who sleep in the dust of the earth will awake: some to everlasting life, others to shame and everlasting contempt.
3. Those who are wise will shine like the brightness of the heavens, and those who lead many to righteousness, like the stars for ever and ever.
4. But you, Daniel, close up and seal the words of the scroll until the time of the end. Many will go here and there to increase knowledge.
5. Then I, Daniel, looked, and there before me stood two others, one on this bank of the river and one on the opposite bank.
6. One of them said to the man clothed in linen, who was above the waters of the river, How long will it be before these astonishing things are fulfilled?
7. The man clothed in linen, who was above the waters of the river, lifted his right hand and his left hand towards heaven, and I heard him swear by him who lives for ever, saying, It will be for a time, times and half a time. When the power of the holy people has been finally broken, all these things will be completed.
8. I heard, but I did not understand. So I asked, My lord, what will the outcome of all this be?
9. He replied, Go your way, Daniel, because the words are closed up and sealed until the time of the end.
10. Many will be purified, made spotless and refined, but the wicked will continue to be wicked. None of the wicked will understand, but those who are wise will understand.
11. From the time that the daily sacrifice is abolished and the abomination that causes desolation is set up, there will be 1,290 days.
12. Blessed is the one who waits for and reaches the end of the 1,335 days.

13. As for you, go your way till the end. You will rest, and then at the end of the days you will rise to receive your allotted inheritance.

Now we compare this to the Prophesy of Jesus in *Mark*:

3. As Jesus was sitting on the Mount of Olives opposite the temple, Peter, James, John and Andrew asked him privately,
4. Tell us, when will these things happen? And what will be the sign that they are all about to be fulfilled?
5. Jesus said to them: Watch out that no-one deceives you.
6. Many will come in my name, claiming, 'I am he,' and will deceive many.
7. When you hear of wars and rumours of wars, do not be alarmed. Such things must happen, but the end is still to come.
8. Nation will rise against nation, and kingdom against kingdom. There will be earthquakes in various places, and famines. These are the beginning of birth-pains.
9. You must be on your guard. You will be handed over to the local councils and flogged in the synagogues. On account of me you will stand before governors and kings as witnesses to them.
10. And the gospel must first be preached to all nations.
11. Whenever you are arrested and brought to trial, do not worry beforehand about what to say. Just say whatever is given you at the time, for it is not you speaking, but the Holy Spirit.
12. Brother will betray brother to death, and a father his child. Children will rebel against their parents and have them put to death.
13. All men will hate you because of me, but he who stands firm to the end will be saved.
14. When you see 'the abomination that causes desolation' standing where it does not belong—let the reader understand&—then let those who are in Judea flee to the mountains.
15. Let no-one on the roof of his house go down or enter the house to take anything out.
16. Let no-one in the field go back to get his cloak.
17. How dreadful it will be in those days for pregnant women and nursing mothers!
18. Pray that this will not take place in winter,
19. because those will be days of distress unequalled from the beginning, when God created the world, until now—and never to be equalled again.

THE EVOLUTION OF CHRISTS AND CHRISTIANIES

20. If the Lord had not cut short those days, no-one would survive. But for the sake of the elect, whom he has chosen, he has shortened them.
21. At that time if anyone says to you, 'Look, here is the Christ!' or, 'Look, there he is!' do not believe it.
22. For false Christs and false prophets will appear and perform signs and miracles to deceive the elect—if that were possible.

First, we note that the writer has taken whole lines from Daniel, "because those will be days of distress unequalled from the beginning, when God created the world until now" matches "There will be a time of distress such as has not happened from the beginning of nations until then."

He has changed, "But at that time your people—everyone whose name is found written in the book—will be delivered." to the general phrase, "and never to be equalled again." We may assume that the Jews realized that the Prophesy of Daniel applied to the Maccabean War. If this is the case then the writer is simply shifting the Prophesy from a definite time in the past to an indefinite time in the future.

Most of the rest of Mark's additions have to do with staying away from false Christs and undergoing specific persecutions for being Christian. The false Christs and the persecutions of Christians may be referring to any time in the first or second century. It fits 50 C.E. or 150 C.E., or anytime in between quite nicely, and may even fit pre-50 or post 150.

The description of signs matches the description of Dio Cassius of the Second Century Bar Kochba War, Josephus of the First Century Roman-Jewish War. It also fits writer of 1 Maccabees in his first chapter:

41: Then the king wrote to his whole kingdom that all should be one people,
42: and that each should give up his customs.
43: All the Gentiles accepted the command of the king. Many even from Israel gladly adopted his religion; they sacrificed to idols and profaned the sabbath.
44: And the king sent letters by messengers to Jerusalem and the cities of Judah; he directed them to follow customs strange to the land,
45: to forbid burnt offerings and sacrifices and drink offerings in the sanctuary, to profane sabbaths and feasts,
46: to defile the sanctuary and the priests,
47: to build altars and sacred precincts and shrines for idols, to sacrifice swine and unclean animals,

48: and to leave their sons uncircumcised. They were to make themselves abominable by everything unclean and profane,
49: so that they should forget the law and change all the ordinances.
50: "And whoever does not obey the command of the king shall die."
51: In such words he wrote to his whole kingdom. And he appointed inspectors over all the people and commanded the cities of Judah to offer sacrifice, city by city.
52: Many of the people, every one who forsook the law, joined them, and they did evil in the land;
53: they drove Israel into hiding in every place of refuge they had.
54: Now on the fifteenth day of Chislev, in the one hundred and forty-fifth year, they erected a desolating sacrilege upon the altar of burnt offering. They also built altars in the surrounding cities of Judah,
55: and burned incense at the doors of the houses and in the streets.
56: The books of the law which they found they tore to pieces and burned with fire.
57: Where the book of the covenant was found in the possession of any one, or if any one adhered to the law, the decree of the king condemned him to death.
58: They kept using violence against Israel, against those found month after month in the cities.
59: And on the twenty-fifth day of the month they offered sacrifice on the altar which was upon the altar of burnt offering.
60: According to the decree, they put to death the women who had their children circumcised,
61: and their families and those who circumcised them; and they hung the infants from their mothers' necks.
62: But many in Israel stood firm and were resolved in their hearts not to eat unclean food.
63: They chose to die rather than to be defiled by food or to profane the holy covenant; and they did die.
64: And very great wrath came upon Israel.

What we can conclude from this is that the text does not present us with an historical marker that can determine a *terminus ad quem* for the text. There is nothing to suggest he had an historical setting in mind for Jesus. The prophecy is in the present time. It is "now" but Mark does not tell us the date of that "now."

One part of the text does appear to match the First Century Roman-Jewish War and cannot be found in Daniel or Maccabees. This is the astrological portion of the text.

THE EVOLUTION OF CHRISTS AND CHRISTIANIES

13.24. But in those days, following that distress, 'the sun will be darkened, and the moon will not give its light;
25. the stars will fall from the sky, and the heavenly bodies will be shaken.'
26. At that time men will see the Son of Man coming in clouds with great power and glory.
27. And he will send his angels and gather his elect from the four winds, from the ends of the earth to the ends of the heavens.

This matches a passage in Josephus' Jewish Wars:

3. Thus were the miserable people persuaded by these deceivers, and such as belied God himself; while they did not attend nor give credit to the signs that were so evident, and did so plainly foretell their future desolation, but, like men infatuated, without either eyes to see or minds to consider, did not regard the denunciations that God made to them. Thus there was a star resembling a sword, which stood over the city, and a comet, that continued a whole year. Thus also before the Jews' rebellion, and before those commotions which preceded the war, when the people were come in great crowds to the feast of unleavened bread, on the eighth day of the month Xanthicus, [Nisan,] and at the ninth hour of the night, so great a light shone round the altar and the holy house, that it appeared to be bright day time; which lasted for half an hour.

As one can readily see, the match here is extremely poor. Mark's text describes darkness in the skies with a darkened sun, lightless moon, falling stars. Josephus does not describe a darkening, but adds more light to the heavens in his description of an extra sword-like star, a comet remaining for a year, and a bright light around the holy house. One might suggest that Josephus is hinting that the Jews missed the signs because they were looking for darkness instead of light, but such a leap really does not help us to place the prediction in Mark to any specific time period. We do not know when astrological signs became part of disaster/endtime prophecies in Jewish culture.

Again, our conclusion is that Mark was writing after 70 C.E., but there is no real internal evidence that tells us how far after 70 C.E. Rhetorically, the purpose of the whole Prophesy is to support the reliability and operability of the Hebrew Scriptures, and specifically the coming of God/Son of Man expressed in the Book of Daniel. The attitude of the author is nicely summed up this way:

32. No-one knows about that day or hour, not even the angels in heaven, nor the Son[413], but only the Father.

33. Be on guard! Be alert! You do not know when that time will come.
34. It's like a man going away: He leaves his house and puts his servants in charge, each with his assigned task, and tells the one at the door to keep watch.
35. Therefore keep watch because you do not know when the owner of the house will come back—whether in the evening, or at midnight, or when the cock crows, or at dawn.
36. If he comes suddenly, do not let him find you sleeping.
37. What I say to you, I say to everyone: 'Watch!'

This writing suggests that Mark was a workman afraid that his absentee boss will come at any time to check his work. Unlike the confident John/Jesus who predicted the Apocalypse directly, Mark is not taking any bets on when the Apocalypse is coming, but he has faith that it will come.

Going back to our question of the historicity of John the Baptist, we find that John the Baptist seems to a first century character based upon the Elijah character. We can now make sense of these lines form Mark.

14. King Herod heard of it; for Jesus' name had become known. Some said, "John the baptizer has been raised from the dead; that is why these powers are at work in him."
15. But others said, "It is Eli'jah." And others said, "It is a prophet, like one of the prophets of old."
16. But when Herod heard of it he said, "John, whom I beheaded, has been raised."

Herod's definite answer really has to do with Mark's action of reincarnating John the Baptist as Jesus in his text. We may take it that the original question was "Is John Elijah reincarnated or a prophet like the prophets of old?" We may suppose that the original John the Baptist tales had several different writers. In some of them he was portrayed as Elijah and in some of them as an ordinary prophet of old. We cannot exclude the possibility that at some point in the first century C.E., a man named John did declare himself to be "Elijah reincarnated" or "a prophet of old." What we can be sure of is that Mark felt perfectly fine changing these John stories into stories about Jesus the Messiah. It seems Mark knew he was writing a novel, not a history.

Did John Baptize with Water or Holy Spirit?

Our reconstruction of Josephus' *Testimonium* indicates that Josephus thought of John as a real person, but curiously he does not mention anything about John baptizing.

THE EVOLUTION OF CHRISTS AND CHRISTIANIES

The ease with which the gospel writers are willing to turn John's words into Jesus' also should make us ask what is going on here?

We have to remember the setting of events and place John in his historical context whether he existed or not. The question of Roman domination was prime at this time. We should remember that Roman domination represented an alternative way of life and threat or potential threat to Jewish self definition. This domination took many forms. One form was architectural. Where-ever Rome conquered they built public bath houses. Daniel Boorstin gives us a glimpse into these Roman inventions

> Some historians count these among "the fairest creations of the Roman Empire." During the second century B.C. they multiplied at a great rate in Rome. It became common for a public-spirited citizen to make a gift of a public bath building to his neighborhood. Others were built commercially by contractors who hoped to make a profit from admission fees. Agrippa's census (33 B.C.) counted 170 such establishments in Rome, and a century later Pliny the Elder (2379) had to give up counting. Soon there were nearly a thousand. When Pliny the Younger arrived for a brief stay at his contry villa near Ostia, and did not want to fuel his own furnaces, he found "a great convenience" in the three public baths in the neighboring village.
>
> The essentials of a public bath were quite the same everywhere— a changing room, a sweating room heated by hot-air passages under the floor or in the wall, a large vaulted hall gently heated with intermediate temperatures, an unheated frigidarium partly open to the sky with a cold plunge, and a rotunda heated by circulating vapor, open at the top to admit sunlight at noon and in the afternoon. In addition, there were swimming pools. Nearby areas provided for strolling, for conversation, for sunning, for exercise, for various kinds of handball, hoop-rolling, and wrestling. Attached were concert halls, libraries, and gardens. The baths at their best were public art museums and museums of contemporary art. To them we owe the preservation of some of our best copies of Greek sculpture and our great treasures of Roman sculpture. Th Farnese Bull, the Hercules, and the Belvedere Torso survived in the remains of the baths of Caracalla and the famous Laocoön group was found in the baths of Trajan[414].

David Zimet, in an article entitled "Jewish Magic in the Roman Bathhouse," also notes the importance of Roman bathhouses to everyday life in the Roman empire[415]:

> Because the bathhouse was so universally used, it came to serve as a sort of gathering place, and a place to socialize with one's fellows.

Martial's accounts of Roman life paint the bathhouse as a place to drink, socialize, pursue members of the opposite gender, and generally indulge in social intercourse. The availability of alcoholic drinks and food in the bath, as well as sexual activity in the bathhouses, is corroborated in graffiti found in the various thermae. Additionally, several of the thermae offered various other forms of entertainment, including, "... gardens, conference halls, lectures and even libraries." The bathhouse, then, was in many cases a very important source of entertainment for citizens of the Roman empire.

Zimet notes the participation of even anti-Roman Rabbis in the custom of Roman Bathhouses.

Why, one might ask, would the Jews be willing to consent to participate in this characteristically Roman cultural tradition? The answer is that most likely the assimilation of the bathhouse into Jewish life took place through a filtered absorption, so that the Jews became acclimated to the concept of this cultural phenomenon while at the same time modifying it to suit their manner of living... the Jews tended to exclude statuary that would commonly be found in bathhouses in primarily non-Jewish cities. Also, the segregation of men and women, and deprecation of nude bathing, were Jewish customs that were most likely practiced more thoroughly in the bathhouses of predominantly Jewish neighborhoods, so that naked bathing and mixed-gender bathing were uncommon in these places.

If most Jews accepted Roman Bathhouses, at least in limited ways, we may assume that there were Jews who thought the bathhouses should be avoided altogether. They urged spiritual bathing in the Lord rather than physical bathing in water. We get this impression from *Oxyrhynchus 840 Gospel*:

"... earlier, before doing wrong, he slyly reasons everything out. Be careful that you do not end up suffering the same fate as them. For the evil-doers of humanity receive retribution not only among the living, but they will also undergo punishment and much torture later."
Taking them along, he went into the place of purification itself and wandered around in the temple. Then a certain high priest of the Pharisees named Levi came toward them and said to the savior, "Who permitted you to wander in this place of purification and to see these holy vessels, even though you have not bathed and the feet of your disciples have not been washed? And now that you have defiled it, you

walk around in this pure area of the temple where only a person who has bathed and changed his clothes can walk, and even such a person does not dare to look upon these holy vessels."

Standing nearby with his disciples, the savior replied, "Since you are here in the temple too, are you clean?"

The Pharisee said to him, "I am clean. For I bathed in the pool of David. I went down into the pool by one set of stairs and came back out by another. Then I put on white clothes and they were clean. And then I came and looked at these holy vessels."

Replying to him, the savior said, "Woe to blind people who do not see! You have washed in the gushing waters that dogs and pigs are thrown into day and night. And when you washed yourself, you scrubbed the outer layer of skin, the layer of skin that prostitutes and flute-girls anoint and wash and scrub when they put on make up to become the desire of the men. But inside they are filled with scorpions and all unrighteousness. But my disciples and I, whom you say have not washed, we have washed in waters of eternal life that come from the God of heaven. But woe to those . . . "

Note that there is no mention of Jesus here. Instead, we find the term "Savior" used as it is in the *Gospel of Mary*. Also, Levi is not a disciple of Jesus but a Pharisee. We may take it that this is a very early text. The Savior's attack on the idea of ritual bathing would apply to the type of ritual bathing associated with John the Baptist, so we may assume that the text comes before the canonical gospels which have Jesus becoming the Christ through ritual bathing. We may assign the text to the 40's.

The key phrase here is "we have washed in waters of eternal life that come from the God of Heaven" It is a reminiscent of Jesus offering "living water" in John (4:10) and his claim (7:38) "He who believes in me, as the scripture has said, 'Out of his heart shall flow rivers of living water.'" The phrase "living water" probably comes from Jeremiah (2:13), "for my people have committed two evils: they have forsaken me, the fountain of living waters, and hewed out cisterns for themselves, broken cisterns, that can hold no water." The language is metaphorical but it has a natural sense too, in that God (as creator of the world) obviously made the flowing (living) sources of water, the rivers, streams and oceans.

Faced with the problem of Jews losing their identities by going to Roman bathhouses on possibly a daily basis, we may imagine that the idea of bathing outdoors in naturally (God made) living (flowing) water would be put forward as an alternative for Jews to keep their identities separate from the Romans and to reaffirm their faith in the creator God.

The word baptism comes from the Greek verb, *baptizein* (βάπτειν), *to dip or immerse in water*. Baptism can also mean a ritual cleaning as it seems to in Luke (11:38) "wash before dinner," and Mark ((7:3-4) "when they come from the marketplace, they do not eat unless they *wash themselves*."

The canonical gospel speak of two types of baptism, the one by John involving water and the other by Jesus involving Holy Spirit. *Oxyrhynchus 80* suggests a stage where Baptism (ritual dipping or immersion) of spirit is put in opposition to dipping or immersion in water.

The canonical gospels do not describe a baptism ritual. The lack of description suggests that simply going in and out of the water was the ritual itself. We may see this as a kind of protest against the Roman bathhouses. By bathing or taking a dip in outdoor water sources the Jews were effectively protesting against Roman culture. One may see it as a symbolic boycott form of protest. For more militant Jews such symbolic protests would be rather tame. One may suggest that they felt that immersion in the holy spirit, talking about and reciting Jewish scriptural texts, was the answer.

Both of these antidotes to Roman culture were probably suggested about the same time. Eventually a combination of the two, immersion/dipping in holy spirit and water, became part of Christian initiation ceremonies as noted in later text like the *Didache*. However, there is no reason to believe baptism was an initiation ceremony to begin with. John was a prophet preaching the coming kingdom of God, what would he be initiating people into? Prophets were not organizational recruiters.

Also John comes from the desert. This could be a clue that he was originally of Nabatean origin. His death involving a war between the Nabatean King Aretas and Antipas would seem to suggest this. In any case, there is no water in the desert, so we have to be suspicious about the idea of John baptizing people with water. It is more likely that people trying to boost Jesus above John are putting John down by assigning him to the inferior status of water baptizer. We may take it that John actually baptized with the Holy Spirit before the Jesus spiritualists relegated him to this inferior physical area of activity.

How do we account for a lack of protest on behalf of the followers of John over this slighting? We may suppose that they were happy that the Jesus followers had made Jesus into a follower of John and his Kingdom of God movement. They did not care that much about the inferior baptizing proposition. We may suppose that the people who did practice baptism or cleaning themselves in outdoor water to protest the Roman bathhouses were not so upset to hear that the recent prophet John (the Nazarene?) was the founder of their practice. These Baptists may have actually been flattered to be associated with John, assuming he had a widespread group of admirers and was known for his righteousness.

The original stories of John baptizing (swimming in natural water sources outdoors to get clean) may have come from the Baptists themselves. The Baptists could have easily written texts to prove that baptism was an ancient practice that an ancient prophet had endorsed. I think it points towards John being a real and important historical personage that they would accept him as the modern founder of their practice. However, we cannot be sure that John himself is not just a modernized construction built from ancient prophetic texts to lend credence to the Kingdom of God ideology.

While some Jesus followers turned John into John the Baptist in some stories and made Jesus into his leading disciple, in other stories they changed him into a leading disciple of Jesus and made him the brother of James the Just. Eventually in other stories they made him take over Mary's role as the beloved disciple. This seems to have been his reward for the later gospel writers changing his words into Jesus' words and taking away his Christ title.

In any case, I think the evidence points towards an historical John, but not one who baptized anybody in water. My best guess is that Baptism or ritual cleaning in naturally flowing water may have started at this time as an anti-Roman protest practice and a means of reaffirming a Jewish identity in this time period. Because certain people wanted to suggest that John anointed Jesus as King, the term *Baptism* took on the meaning of anointing and became an initiation ritual in the Jesus cult.

Who is The Son of Man?

We have suggested that in the prophecy scenes in the *Gospel of Mark*, the original character making the prophesies about the coming messiah, the son of man, was John the Baptist, and not Jesus the Christ. We need to look at what the phrase "son of man" meant to better understand why it is a term natural for the John the Baptist character, but inappropriate for the Jesus the Christ character.

In Mark's Gospel the Jesus character constantly refers to himself as the "Son of Man." He refers this way to himself thirteen times[416]. He refers to himself in no other way. This seems to be the character's self description.

He is referred to as son of God, twice by demons and once by an unknown Roman Centurion[417]. Only once in the whole Gospel of Mark does Jesus seem to unambiguously say that he is the Christ:

> Then the high priest stood up before them and asked Jesus, "Are you not going to answer? What is this testimony that these men are bringing against you?" But Jesus remained silent and gave no answer.
>
> Again the high priest asked him, "Are you the Christ, the Son of the Blessed One?"
>
> "I am," said Jesus. "And you will see the Son of Man sitting at the right hand of the Mighty One and coming on the clouds of heaven[418]."

Matthew has Jesus's response "You have said so." Luke too gives ""You say that I am." This seems to indicate that different traditions. Why does Jesus give a straightforward answer in Mark but ambiguous answers in Matthew and Luke. Even here, the answer is not straightforward as it seems.

Jesus does not answer the charges against himself at first. He suddenly changes and answers. What causes this sudden change? We have to answer this question in light of the alternative (Matthew and Luke) tradition that he did not answer these charges directly. The key is in the question asked by the high Priest, "Are you the Christ, the Son of the Blessed One?" The phrase "Son of the Blessed One" here has to be taken as a title or name. Jesus' response "and you will see the Son of Man . . ." indicates that it is equivalent to the Son of Man. In magical folklore of the period when a demon or angel is addressed directly by name, the demon or angel must answer truthfully whatever you ask it. In this case, The High Priest compels Jesus to answer that he is the Christ because he has addressed him directly by Name "Son of the Blessed One." So while Jesus does identify himself here as the Christ (the anointed one) here, he is identifying himself more strongly as the "Son of Man" and "Son of the Blessed One." In other words, his identity is "Son of Man" or "Son of the Blessed One" and "the Christ" (savior) is a position he has been appointed to fulfill.

Logically, it would have been simple for Mark to go at this point from Christ to Son of God. At least two Hebrew Scriptures mention that the Christ (Messiah) will be a son of God: in 11 Samuel, 7:14 God prophesizes to Nathan about Solomon "I will be his father, and he shall be my son," and in Psalms. 2:7, we have the Lord saying to his Messiah "You are my son, today I have begotten you." However, Mark does not go from "Christ" to the title "Son of God," but to the title "Son of Man." We might stop at this point to consider who or what is the "Son of God" and who/what is the "Son of Man."

First, we should consider this important observation by Morton Smith:

> **In Hebrew and Aramaic "son of" is commonly used to mean "member of the class of"; hence, "the sons of god" is a regular way of saying "the gods," just as "the sons of men" (commonly translated "the children of men") is a regular way of saying "men." Thus in Genesis 6.2—"the sons of god saw the daughters of man" means "the gods saw women," A few other examples are scattered throughout the Old Testament. Isolated survivors of monotheistic censorship, they indicate the popular basis of the usage and justify us in supposing that when a Palestinian demoniac said "Jesus, son of god" he meant "Jesus, god." The evangelists took such expressions of Semitic paganism as portents and adjusted them to their own monotheistic belief: this is why Jesus moves through the gospels as a deity doing miracles by his own divine power, but in the synoptics is never explicitly called a god. It also explains why the title "Son of God" appears before and independently of the legends of divine paternity. The legends were apologetic, but the title preceded the apology and determined the line it was to take**[419].

"Son of God" is originally a phrase meaning no more than "a god" as "Son of Man" is originally a phrase meaning "a man." Smith notes that the canonical gospel writers "adjusted them to their own monothestic beliefs. Some people do not think they were adjusted.

In contrast to this answer, in a recent book, Walter Wink suggests:

> "The son of the man" is the expression Jesus almost exclusively used to describe himself. In Hebrew the phrase simply means "a human being." The implication seems to be that Jesus intentionally avoided honorific titles, and preferred to be known simply as "the man," or "the human being[420]."

In defense of this view, one can point to the "Testament of Solomon," although found only in Medieval copies it appears evidently to contain quite early and important material. In it, at one point King Solomon reports a conversation with the demon Asmodeus:

> And I said to him: "Thus punished as thou art, answerest thou me?" But he, with rage, said to me: "But how shall I answer thee, for thou art a son of man; whereas I was born an angel's seed by a daughter of man, so that no word of our heavenly kind addressed to the earth-born can be overweening[421].

At least some of this document which catalogues demons in heaven and how to get rid of them was possibly used by the writers of the earliest miracle stories about Jesus. This text has King Solomon being not only a son of man, but also "Christ," "Wisdom" and "Son of David," other terms applied to Jesus in the Gospels. It is possible the Gospel of Mark refers to this text in the passage: "While Jesus was teaching in the temple courts, he asked, "How is it that the teachers of the law say that the Christ is the son of David?[422]" The term "son of man" can also be found used in this way in very early in Daniel (7.13-14):

> In my vision at night I looked, and there before me was one like a son of man, coming with the clouds of heaven. He approached the Ancient of Days and was led into his presence.[14] He was given authority, glory and sovereign power; all peoples, nations and men of every language worshipped him. His dominion is an everlasting dominion that will not pass away, and his kingdom is one that will never be destroyed.

Thus, in the *Book of Daniel*, the term "Son of Man" is used metaphorically, "like a son of man." So there is evidence to support Wink's contention that references to a "son of man" in the gospels do have the meaning of "a son of a human" or more simply "a human being." However there is strong evidence that many references in the gospel have a different, more specific reference. Alan F. Segal responds this way to the idea that all references to the "son of man" are just to emphasize Jesus' human nature:

> This is a modern de-mythologization and re-mythologization of the figure of the Son of Man. There is nothing in the ancient world to suggest that anyone thought of the Son of Man in this particular way. Indeed, the Son of Man was a figure of vengeance, someone who was going to even the score between Israel and her enemies in the ancient period. Wink is using the historical record to display and expose his theology of Christianity[423].

Delbert Burkett in *The Son of Man Debate: A History and Evaluation* agrees that this and other theories which see a nontitular (not as a title or official position) explanation for the term are not tenable:

> The scholars who have investigated the nontitular explanation have performed a service for the scholarly community. It was a possibility that had to be explored and has been well explored. The time has come, however, to take stock and recognize that this line of research has not led to a convincing solution. Future research will make progress only with the recognition that "Son of Man" in the bulk of its occurrences is a title rather than a nontitular idiom[424].

While Walter Wink is correct in that the original usage of the term "son of man" in Jewish scripture was nontitular and merely a poetic synonym for "human being," it does seem that the writers of the canonical gospels are using the term differently. In later Jewish literature it does become a title or job description. We may assume it has the more concrete reference that it does in 1 Enoch 42:

> 1   And there I saw One who had a head of days,
>   And His head was white like wool,
>   And with Him was another being whose countenance had the appearance of a man,
>   And his face was full of graciousness, like one of the holy angels.
> 2   And I asked the angel who went with me and showed me all the hidden things, concerning that
> 3   Son of Man, who he was, and whence he was, (and) why he went with the Head of Days? And he answered and said unto me:

> This is the son of Man who hath righteousness,
> With whom dwelleth righteousness,
> And who revealeth all the treasures of that which is hidden,
> Because the Lord of Spirits hath chosen him,
> And whose lot hath the pre-eminence before the Lord of Spirits in uprightness for ever.
>
> 4 And this Son of Man whom thou hast seen
> Shall raise up the kings and the mighty from their seats,
> [And the strong from their thrones]
> And shall loosen the reins of the strong,
> And break the teeth of the sinners.
>
> 5 [And he shall put down the kings from their thrones and kingdoms]
> Because they do not extol and praise Him,
> Nor humbly acknowledge whence the kingdom was bestowed upon them.
>
> 6 And he shall put down the countenance of the strong,
> And shall fill them with shame.
> And darkness shall be their dwelling,
> And worms shall be their bed,
> And they shall have no hope of rising from their beds,
> Because they do not extol the name of the Lord of Spirits.
>
> 7 And these are they who judge the stars of heaven,
> [And raise their hands against the Most High],
> And tread upon the earth and dwell upon it.
> And all their deeds manifest unrighteousness,
> And their power rests upon their riches,
> And their faith is in the gods which they have made with their hands,
> And they deny the name of the Lord of Spirits,

Besides the term being used throughout 1 Enoch 37-70, 71, it is also used in 4 Ezra (13.1-13). Burkett notes differences between the figures portrayed in all these texts[425]:

> As a reference to the Messiah, Daniel 7.13 becomes one element incorporated into a variety of portraits of the Messiah. These various messianic figures differ in both their nature and their function. In 1 Enoch 37-70 an angelic/human Messiah is pictured who is created before the world and hidden in heaven until he sits as judge at the last judgment. The passage draws on Daniel 7.9-14 to describe the enthronement of this Messiah. In 1 Enoch 71 the same Danielic enthronement scene is used for Enoch, a human Messiah who neither

has pre-existence in heaven nor functions as judge. The Messiah in 4 Ezra 13.1-13, as in Daniel 7.13, looks like the figure of a man, but nothing in the vision suggests that he is pre-existent or heavenly or a judge. He arises on earth at the endtime and destroys an army that attacks Jerusalem. For the author of 4 Ezra, the Messiah, though hidden for ages, is a mortal human who will die after reigning over a temporary messianic kingdom for four hundred years.

Thus we see quite diverse interpretations of the "Son of Man" as some kind of avenging angel. These considerations lead Burkett to conclude[426]:

> Thus we cannot speak of a unified "Son of Man" tradition in ancient Judaism—either a common model of a transcendent deliverer or a common interpretation of Daniel 7.13. What we see instead is a shared set of messianic and messianically interpreted scriptural texts that exegetes combined and interpreted in various ways to produce a variety of portraits of the Messiah . . . Therefore, as Perrin recognized, when we come to the New Testament Son of Man passages we cannot presume that they reflect a unified pre-Christian tradition about a transcendent judge or a unified pre-Christian interpretation of Daniel 7.13.

Crispin H. T. Fletcher-Louis suggests that the figure of "Son of Man" should be put in a category of semi-divine creatures prevalent in first century C.E. Jewish thought[427]:

> Jewish belief in figures who mediate between the human and divine whilst possessing characteristics of both. This includes the following figures: the Son of Man; the Logos; the angel of the LORD; Wisdom; and various human beings who were believed to possess a more than human, transcendent identity such as Noah, Enoch, Adam, Moses, Israel, Melchizedek.

Daniel Boyarin also associates the concepts of Logos, Wisdom and Son of Man[428], "It is at least possible that the beginning of trinitarian reflection was precisely in non-Christian Jewish accounts of the second and visible God, variously, the Logos (Memra), Wisdom, or even perhaps the Son of God." The term "Logos" is most associated with the first century Jewish-Egyptian writer Philo. Boyarin notes, "it can hardly be doubted that for Philo the Logos is both a part of God and also a separate being, the Word that God created in the beginning in order to create everything else: the Word that both is God, therefore, and is with God." Philo calls the Logos the Divine Word and shows that it is derived from Wisdom[429]:

> The Divine Word descends from the fountain of wisdom like a river to lave and water the olympian and celestial shoots and plants of virtue-loving souls which are as a garden. And this Holy Word is separated into four heads, which means that it is split up into the four virtues.... It is this Word which one of Moses' company compared to a river, when he said in the Psalms: the river of God is full of water (Ps 65:10); where surely it were absurd to use that word literally with reference to rivers of the earth. Instead, as it seems, he represents the Divine Word as full of the stream of wisdom, with no part empty or devoid of itself.

Boyarin further emphasizes this point between the close association of the divine entity "Wisdom" and Philo's "logos," "In Philo, as well as in others, Sophia and the Logos are identified as a single entity. Indeed, we find God's Wisdom and his Word already as parallels in the Hebrew itself." Wisdom itself is described in the text *Wisdom of Solomon*:

> *9:* With thee is wisdom, who knows thy works and was present when thou didst make the world, and who understand what is pleasing in thy sight and what is right according to thy commandments. *10:* Send her forth from the holy heavens, and from the throne of thy glory send her, that she may be with me and toil, and that I may learn what is pleasing to thee. *11:* For she knows and understands all things, and she will guide me wisely in my actions and guard me with her glory. *12:* Then my works will be acceptable, and I shall judge thy people justly, and shall be worthy of the throne of my father. *13:* For what man can learn the counsel of God? Or who can discern what the Lord wills? *14:* For the reasoning of mortals is worthless, and our designs are likely to fail, *15:* for a perishable body weighs down the soul, and this earthy tent burdens the thoughtful mind. *16:* We can hardly guess at what is on earth, and what is at hand we find with labor; but who has traced out what is in the heavens? *17:* Who has learned thy counsel, unless thou hast given wisdom and sent thy holy Spirit from on high? *18:* And thus the paths of those on earth were set right, and men were taught what pleases thee, and were saved by wisdom."

Wisdom is portrayed here as a savior. The concept may be considered a Hellenization of the older concept of angels. The Jewish Encyclopedia says this about angels[430]:

> The Biblical name for angel... meaning, according to derivation, simply "messenger," obtained the further signification of "angel" only

> through the addition of God's name, as . . . ("angel of the Lord," or "angel of God" Zech. xii. 8). Other appellations are . . . ("Sons of God," Gen. vi. 4; Job, i. 6 [R. V. v. 1]; Ps. xxix. 1 [R. V. margin]); and . . . ("the Holy Ones").

Note especially the notion of angels being "Sons of God." If Jewish monotheists under the influence of Platonism made Gods into one God, then we can readily understand how some Jews could assume that the Sons of God (Angels) were all actually just one Son of God. The rather abstract question of whether this one son of God was an angel (a faithful messenger of God) or demon (unfaithful messenger of God) would blow apart the Judeo-Christian communities of the Second Century.

One can hardly go a few pages in the Hebrew Scriptures without encountering angels, these supernatural beings from the court of the Heavenly King Yaweh or Elohim. For our purposes we do not have to go into their complex development. It is enough that we see them at the base of a category of supernatural beings appearing in the literature of the First Century C.E.

We can see the evolution of the terms here. The "angels" named in the Book of Daniel, probably in the Second Century B.C.E., become the God/Goddess "Wisdom" in the Book of Solomon in the First Century B.C.E. Soon that figure gets transformed into the "Logos" by Philo in the First Century C.E., and in Enoch, late First Century C.E., we get "Wisdom" along with the Daniel-derived final judge/avenging angel "The Son of Man." We also get the forerunner of the Holy Ghost called the "Lord of Spirits."

The writers of the gospel epistles seem more influenced by Philo. The Son of God in all these epistles, the son of God (angel) named Jesus Christ is closer to Philo's "Logos" conception. These writers do not know the "Son of Man[431]" title for Jesus at all. Both Paul and *Revelation* use similar expressions to describe Jesus Christ, Paul has[432] "he is the beginning and the firstborn from among the dead, so that in everything he might have the supremacy," and *Revelation*, "from Jesus Christ, who is the faithful witness, the firstborn from the dead, and the ruler of the kings of the earth." The phrases "firstborn from among the dead," or firstborn from the dead" does not mean the first born from the underworld Sheol or Hades, instead the passage refers to the lifeless chaos in primordial times as in *Proverbs* (8):

> Proverbs 8:22-30 The LORD possessed me in the beginning of his way, before his works of old. I was set up from everlasting, from the beginning, or ever the earth was. When there were no depths, I was brought forth; when there were no fountains abounding with water. Before the mountains were settled, before the hills was I brought forth: While as yet he had not made the earth, nor the fields, nor the highest part of the dust of the world[433].

In fact it is pretty clear that Paul is getting his conception of Jesus Christ in *Corinthians* directly from Jewish wisdom literature such as the *Wisdom of Solomon*[434] and *Ecclesiasticus or Wisdom of Sirach*. Doing a quick comparison between Corinthians and the later book reveals the dependence:

- ❑ Wisdom 1:4: Wisdom existed before all things....
- ❑ 1 Corinthians 2:7: ... wisdom that God predestined before the ages....

- ❑ Wisdom 1:6: To whom has the root of wisdom been revealed?
- ❑ 1 Corinthians 2:10: God revealed these things to us....

- ❑ Wisdom 1:10: ... he has given [wisdom] to those who love him.
- ❑ 1 Corinthians 2:9:.. which God has prepared for those who love him.

- ❑ Wisdom 1:15: [Wisdom] has built an eternal foundation among men....
- ❑ 1 Corinthians 3:10: ... as a wise architect I laid down a foundation....

- ❑ Wisdom 2:5: Gold is tested in the fire....
- ❑ 1 Corinthians 3:12-13: And if any man builds upon the foundation with gold or silver or precious stones..., it is to be revealed in fire.

Here is a typical passage from *The Wisdom of Sirach*:

> My child, if you come to serve the Lord,
> Prepare yourself to be tried,
> Set your heart right and be firm,
> And do not be hasty when things go against you;
> Hold fast to him, and do not forsake him,
> So that you may be honored when your life ends.
> Accept whatever happens to you,
> And be patient in humiliating vicissitudes.
> For gold is tested with fire,
> And men who are approved must be tested in the furnace of humiliation [435].

Paul and the writer of *Revelation* are using the older conception of "Wisdom" to derive their god Jesus Christ. Mark uses Enoch's "Son of Man" final judge and Avenging Angel conception. In a sense he makes this the secret alter ego of the character Jesus.

Now, one fascinating aspect to this is that the middle of the *Book of Enoch*, sometimes called *the Similitudes' of Enoch* (chapters 37-71), the section that discusses the Son of Man, is missing from the Dead Sea Scrolls version of Enoch. I would conjecture that this may be a clue to the differences between John's Gospel and the Synoptic Gospels. The Marcan community had this important section so they know exactly what the reference is when Mark uses the phrase "Son of Man." There is no problem for this community. You want to know about the supernatural spirit that possesses Jesus, the one he calls "Son of Man," just read Enoch. The Johannine community, like the Paulist community does not have Enoch, or at least the similitudes of Enoch. They therefore have to explain the supernatural character of Jesus in the older Wisdom literature. They go back to the older Logos and Wisdom literature and take concepts directly from them. This is one explanation why the supernatural character of Jesus is so different from the Synoptics and John's gospel.

There were certainly groups within the Jewish community who thought the Christ would come as a warrior avenging angel either in human or supernatural form, and also groups who believed he would come bringing peace, possessed with the Spirit of Wisdom like Solomon. This split can be seen in Gospel of Thomas (16): "Jesus said, Men think, perhaps, that it is peace which I have come to cast upon the world. They do not know that it is dissension which I have come to cast upon the earth: fire, sword, and war." Both concepts of Christ make it into the canonical gospels.

In any case, we have shown the general development of the Divine nature of Jesus Christ. Now no one would argue that there was actually an angelic being called Wisdom and she got transformed into a being called Logos, who got transformed into a being called Jesus Christ, the Son of God, who was actually an angelic being called the Son of Man. One quickly and easily sees that these are literary transformations. They are the results of narrative changes in texts due to ideological, textural, social, linguistic and political considerations.

Now in the canonical text, we can see a dispute over when did this supernatural deity, "Son of Man" became human. The canonical texts preserve three viewpoints. They preserve the viewpoint of some Ebionites who saw the Jesus as purely human, and adopted after death to the status of Son of God. They also preserve the viewpoint that it happened at the time of baptism from John. Finally, they preserve the viewpoint that the deity was born into the host body as a result of some kind of asexual intercourse between a Virgin named Mary and the Jewish God.

At what point did the avenging spirit "Son of Man" become "Jesus, the Christ" and at what point did "Jesus, the Christ" become "Jesus of Nazareth?"

An Experiment

> **The blithe complacence with which Christian scholars have credited Jesus with such a huge store of wise sayings only reveals anew the**

implicit theological bias of supposedly critical scholars. They have just assumed that Jesus was Wisdom incarnate, and that therefore an infinite number of wise and pithy sayings might be attributed to him, while only one or two came from mere mortals like the rabbis or the Greek philosophers[436].

Robert M. Price
Deconstructing Jesus

For now it is enough to see that the gospel was not signed by its author. This agrees with what we know about all of the gospels. Writing one was a communal process in which stories were told, polished, changed, and rearranged many times in the course of several generations[437].

Burton Mack
Who Wrote the New Testament

If we compare the *Gospel of Thomas* to the *Gospel of Mark* we see that they are quite different. For example, in the *Gospel of Mark*, Jesus gets baptized by John, performs miracles, interacts with a Jewish community, and ends up being arrested, tried, and crucified, but these things are never suggested in the Gospel of Thomas. In Mark, the short perky, mysterious sayings found in Thomas are explained and amplified, often put into an anecdotal or story form very similar to stories we find in the *Talmud*.

One might suppose that the question of which came first is a chicken or egg type question, but it is quite the opposite. One can hardly suppose that the writer of *Thomas* went around collecting dozens or hundreds of stories about Jesus and then stripped off the context, time and place of the stories to just give us only the sayings. If he had acted this way, one would expect to find at least a few sayings that were taken directly from the canonical gospels exactly without being changed. In fact there is not a single one. We have to assume that the writer took a number of different sources and attributed the sayings in them to Jesus Christ.

The *gospel of Q* is a reconstructed sayings gospel similar to *Thomas*. It has been reconstructed from the common sayings in the gospels of *Matthew* and *Luke*. When we examine *Mark*, we also see that many scenes are built around sayings of Jesus where literally the scene ends with a wisdom pronouncement by Jesus. We may therefore assume that some such sayings gospel was a source for *Mark*.

Now, it is a generally accepted recent dogma within the field of gospel studies that *Mark* is the first gospel. They generally grant that sayings gospels (with the words of Jesus, real or imaginary) may have circulated earlier. For people with this position, I would like to ask the question how Mark could have made so many drastic changes to this type of gospel? If he started from a sayings gospel, he expanded them into anecdotes, added miracle stories, and the baptism at the beginning, and added the arrest, trial, crucifixion and resurrection scenes at the end.

It is especially hard to understand why Mark would both add the chronological narrative and expand sayings into anecdotal forms, but not do it consistently. The current gospel includes both chronological/narrative material at the beginning of chapter one and throughout chapters fourteen through sixteen. Chapter one begins by telling the chronological narrative of the baptism of Jesus by John the Baptist. Chapters fourteen through sixteen tell the chronological narrative about the arrest, trial and death of Jesus. But take practically any incident from the later part of chapter one all the way through chapter twelve, and changing its order changes nothing.

Here is the puzzle. Mark puts in narrative material in strict and clear chronological form in the first part of chapter one and throughout chapters fourteen through sixteen, but he does not do this in the rest of his material. One could easily imagine Mark giving a chronological presentation throughout: in January, Jesus did this, the next month he did this, then a week later he did this again. This is not the form that Mark follows. It is as if the author proposed, "I will tell you the beginning of a tale about Jesus, then I will give you a series of anecdotes, then I will tell you the ending of the tale."

Besides all the sayings material being in no real chronological order, we get no order for the miracles. They do not move from small to big, Spring to Winter or from one North to South. They can be rearranged in any order without any drastic effect, as the other gospel writers have done.

We may assume three source materials for Mark: chronological story material, sayings material and miracle material. We should look at all three types of material.

Regarding the chronological story material, we should be careful as even here we have a duality. There is the John the Baptist story which we find at the beginning of the text and there is the Mary-executed man story that we find at the end of the text. As noted before we have John as John at the beginning of the text, but we also have a sequence of John going to Mount Gerizzim and God claiming him as a son. God makes the same appearance in the opening baptism scene. We may assume that the two scenes are coming from the same source. We may assume that the original text that Mark was working from was about John the Baptist and started with the baptism of John the Baptist, wherein, a voice from heaven proclaimed John as his son and someone we should listen to. We may assume that there was no Jesus in the original story except for his appearance with Moses and Elijah on the mountain. So one source story that Mark works from is a story about John and his disciples and his prediction of the coming of the avenging "Son of Man." The other story that Mark works from is the Mary story of the incarnation of the word of God. In effect, Mark is fusing together these two disparate narratives and trying to make them seem like one story. He has a story of John the Baptist who predicts a Christ and he has another story of a Christ. This primary task of combining the two narratives explains the lapse in chronology in the gospel. He is not interested in maintaining the narrative chronology of either story. Rather, he must destroy both narrative chronologies in order to fit the two stories together.

THE EVOLUTION OF CHRISTS AND CHRISTIANIES

We may suppose that the book on John that Mark started from was called "The Gospel of John, the Nazarene." We may reconstruct the beginning this way:

Reconstruction of Ur-John Gospel That Mark Worked From

The beginning of the gospel of John, the Christ

As it is written in Isaiah the prophet, "Behold, I send my messenger before thy face, who shall prepare thy way; the voice of one crying in the wilderness: Prepare the way of the Lord, make his paths straight—"

John the Nazarene appeared in the wilderness, preaching a baptism of repentance for the forgiveness of sins.

And there went out to him all the country of Judea, and all the people of Jerusalem; and they were baptized by him in the river Jordan, confessing their sins.

Now John was clothed with camel's hair, and had a leather girdle around his waist, and ate locusts and wild honey.

In those days John the Nazarene bathed in the Jordan.

And when he came up out of the water, immediately he saw the heavens opened and the Spirit descending upon him like a dove; and a voice came from heaven, "Thou art my beloved Son; with thee I am well pleased."

The Spirit immediately drove him out into the wilderness.

And he was in the wilderness forty days, tempted by Satan; and he was with the wild beasts; and the angels ministered to him.

Now before John was arrested, John came into Galilee, preaching the gospel of God, and saying, "The time is fulfilled, and the kingdom of God is at hand; repent, and believe in the gospel."

And passing along by the Sea of Galilee, he saw Simon the brother of James casting a net in the sea; for they were fishermen. 19: And going on a little farther, he saw James the son of Zeb'edee who was in their boat mending the nets.

And immediately he called them, "Follow me and I will make you become fishers of men." And immediately they left their nets and they left their father Zeb'edee in the boat with the hired servants, and followed him.

And they went into Capernaum; and immediately on the sabbath he entered the synagogue and taught.

And they were astonished at his teaching, for he taught them as one who had authority, and not as the scribes.

And immediately there was in their synagogue a man with an unclean spirit; and he cried out, "What have you to do with us, John the Nazarene? Have you come to destroy us? I know who you are, the Holy One of God."

> But John rebuked him, saying, "Be silent, and come out of him!"
>
> And the unclean spirit, convulsing him and crying with a loud voice, came out of him.
>
> And they were all amazed, so that they questioned among themselves, saying, "What is this? A new teaching! With authority he commands even the unclean spirits, and they obey him."
>
> And at once his fame spread everywhere throughout all the surrounding region of Galilee.

We may take it that John was not known as the Baptist, but as a Nazarene. Mark is playing with the text, calling John—the Baptist—specifically because his function in the story is to baptize Jesus. At the same time he makes Jesus come from the town of Nazareth, playing cutely on the word Nazarene[438].

Also, note how this reconstruction eliminates the awkward movement we find in the beginning of the gospel of Mark with John the Baptist going out of the desert to the Jordan, then Jesus being baptized and going into the desert and then coming out of the desert. In the much simpler original, it is just John going into the desert for forty days. Note also that John is not just a prophet, but he has magical powers like Elijah. This is the explanation of the statement Jesus makes later on, "He is more than a prophet."

Robert M. Price notes that "Two pieces of New Testament evidence seem to attest an early stage of belief when Jesus was simply not remembered/regarded as a wonder-worker.[439]" The first is 1 Corinthians 22-25:

> **Jews demand miraculous signs and Greeks look for wisdom, but we preach Christ crucified: a stumbling block to Jews and foolishness to Gentiles, but to those whom God has called, both Jews and Greeks, Christ the power of God and the wisdom of God. For the foolishness of God is wiser than man's wisdom, and the weakness of God is stronger than man's strength.**

God demonstrates his power through miraculous signs. If God (and/or Jesus) had done miracles, this would have shown his strength, but the statement "the weakness of God is stronger than man's strength" indicates that the writer of this letter could point to no miracle performed by the Christ. It is the crucifixion of the Christ alone[440] that replaces the miracles the Jews demand.

Another passage in Mark expressed clearly indicates that Jesus worship contained a miracle-less Jesus stage:

> 11 The Pharisees came and began to question Jesus. To test him, they asked him for a sign from heaven. 12He sighed deeply and said, "Why does this generation ask for a miraculous sign? I tell you the

truth, no sign will be given to it." ¹³Then he left them, got back into the boat and crossed to the other side[441].

One could read this as a refusal to give the Pharisees alone a sign, but the statement of Jesus, "Why does this generation ask for a miraculous sign? I tell you the truth, no sign will be given to it," is perfectly clear. Jesus himself tells us that Jesus will not perform any miracles. If the writer of this statement had known of any miracle that Jesus had performed, s/he would never have made such a blanket statement. It seems that most of Jesus' miracles are being imported by way of John.the Nazarene material.

The UrMark Gospel

If we take out this miracle material and the chronological material (neither of which really contain snappy or memorable "sayings") and just include all passages with simple sayings and sayings with anecdotes, we get a gospel text much closer in style and characterization to the *Gospel of Thomas* and the *Q Sayings Gospel*. Like those gospels, this gospel within the writings attributed to Mark, seems not to know that Jesus performed miracles or that he was crucified. We may take this as the earliest stage or layer of the material. Mark may have been working on these expansion of sayings into anecdotal stories before he decided to combine the John the Nazarene material with Mary's passion play material.

These sayings seem to form a third separate layer that Mark worked from. I call this material "UrMark." Separating and examining this material will give us some exciting results.

Eliminating chronological and miracle elements, we get about sixty pericopes (sayings and sayings with anecdotes). It is difficult to give a precise number of pericopes because some of the sayings are difficult to know where to parse. Take for example these:

> And if your hand causes you to sin, cut it off; it is better for you to enter life maimed than with two hands to go to hell, to the unquenchable fire. And if your foot causes you to sin, cut it off; it is better for you to enter life lame than with two feet to be thrown into hell. And if your eye causes you to sin, pluck it out; it is better for you to enter the kingdom of God with one eye than with two eyes to be thrown into hell, where their worm does not die, and the fire is not quenched.

One can see this as one original saying, "And if your hand causes you to sin cut it off." With the rest elaboration from one or more writers, or one original saying, "And if your hand causes you to sin, cut it off; it is better for you to enter life maimed than with two hands to go to hell" with the rest later elaboration. Or the first two lines about the sinning hand and foot may be considered the original with the sinning eye a later addition. We may also consider the whole as one saying.

I wrestled with these problems in every case and decided that I needed to ask the following questions: "When did we reach a complete single thought?" and "Is there a significant difference in meaning when the second thought is added?"

Doing this with the sayings material, I arrive at a document I call "UrMark." It is completely contained within chapters 1-12 of Mark.

For the source of the sayings of UrMark, I found a pure sayings gospel even closer to Thomas, which I call "MQ[442]." Going further, it became fairly obvious that *MQ* itself has a clear source. I call this source "*MQQ*" containing half the sayings found in *MQ*. Breaking up the material along the lines discussed, and along lines I will discuss later, we get ten major stages in the development of the Gospel of Mark:

Here is UrMark, or the saying anecdotes that I believe Mark constructed out of a sayings of John the Nazarene Gospel. It is also possible that Mark wrote the saying-anecdotes originally with John as the central figure and only later changed the name to Jesus. I have put in bold lettering things which might have been in this first draft before John changed into Jesus. Note that in most cases the sayings might make better sense coming from John than Jesus. In all these 60 or so saying-anecdotes in Mark, there is nothing specific to Jesus that would not be just as appropriate coming from John. Looking at this material, one sees how easily John could be turned into Jesus.

1.14   Jesus **(John)** came into Galilee, preaching the gospel of God, 115 and saying, "The time is fulfilled, and the kingdom of God is at hand; repent, and believe in the gospel."

1.16   And passing along by the Sea of Galilee, he saw Simon and Andrew the brother of Simon casting a net in the sea; for they were fishermen. 1.17 And Jesus **(John)** said to them, "Follow me and I will make you become fishers of men."

2.1   And when he returned to Caper'na-um after some days, it was reported that he was at home. 2.2 And many were gathered together, so that there was no longer room for them, not even about the door; and he was preaching the word to them. 2.3 And they came, bringing to him a paralytic carried by four men. 2.4 And when they could not get near him because of the crowd, they removed the roof above him; and when they had made an opening, they let down the pallet on which the paralytic lay. 2.5 And when Jesus saw their faith, he said to the paralytic, "My son, your sins are forgiven." 2.6 Now some of the scribes were sitting there, questioning in their hearts, 2.7 "Why does this man speak thus? It is blasphemy! Who can forgive sins but God alone?" 2.8 And immediately Jesus **(John)**, perceiving in his spirit that they thus questioned within themselves, said to them, "Why do you question thus in your hearts? 2.9 Which is easier, to say to the paralytic, 'Your sins are forgiven,' or to say, 'Rise, take up your pallet and walk'?

THE EVOLUTION OF CHRISTS AND CHRISTIANIES

2.15 And as he sat at table in his house, many tax collectors and sinners were sitting with Jesus (John) and his disciples; for there were many who followed him. 2.16 And the scribes of the Pharisees, when they saw that he was eating with sinners and tax collectors, said to his disciples, "Why does he eat with tax collectors and sinners?" 2.17 And when Jesus (John) heard it, he said to them, "Those who are well have no need of a physician, but those who are sick; I came not to call the righteous, but sinners."

2.18 Now John's disciples and the Pharisees were fasting; and people came and said to him, "Why do John's disciples and the disciples of the Pharisees fast, but your disciples do not fast?" 2.19 And Jesus said to them, "Can the wedding guests fast while the bridegroom is with them? As long as they have the bridegroom with them, they cannot fast. 2.20 The days will come, when the bridegroom is taken away from them, and then they will fast in that day.

(Now the Scribes and Pharisees were fasting; and people came and said to him, "Why do the disciples of the Scribes and Pharisees fast, but your disciples do not fast?" And John said to them, "Can the wedding guests fast while the bridegroom is with them? As long as they have the bridegroom with them, they cannot fast. The days will come, when the bridegroom is taken away from them, and then they will fast in that day.)

2.21 No one sews a piece of unshrunk cloth on an old garment; if he does, the patch tears away from it, the new from the old, and a worse tear is made.

2.22 And no one puts new wine into old wineskins; if he does, the wine will burst the skins, and the wine is lost, and so are the skins; but new wine is for fresh skins."

2.23 One sabbath he was going through the grainfields; and as they made their way his disciples began to pluck heads of grain. 2.24 And the Pharisees said to him, "Look, why are they doing what is not lawful on the sabbath?" 2.25 And he said to them, "Have you never read what David did, when he was in need and was hungry, he and those who were with him: 2.26 how he entered the house of God, when Abi'athar was high priest, and ate the bread of the Presence, which it is not lawful for any but the priests to eat, and also gave it to those who were with him?" 2.27 And he said to them, "The sabbath was made for man, not man for the sabbath;

3.1 Again he entered the synagogue, and a man was there who had a withered hand. 3.2 And they watched him, to see whether he would heal him on the sabbath, so that they might accuse him. 3.3 And he said to the man who had the withered hand, "Come here." 3.4 And he said to them, "Is it lawful on the sabbath to do good or to do harm, to save life or to kill?" **12.12 Of how much more value is a man than a sheep! So it is lawful to do good on the sabbath."]**

3.19	Then he went home; 3.20 and the crowd came together again, so that they could not even eat. 3.21And when his family heard it, they went out to seize him, for people were saying, "He is beside himself." 3.23 And he called them to him, and said to them in parables, "How can Satan cast out Satan? 3.24 If a kingdom is divided against itself, that kingdom cannot stand. 3.25 And if a house is divided against itself, that house will not be able to stand. 3.26 And if Satan has risen up against himself and is divided, he cannot stand, but is coming to an end. 3.27 But no one can enter a strong man's house and plunder his goods, unless he first binds the strong man; then indeed he may plunder his house. 3.28 "Truly, I say to you, all sins will be forgiven the sons of men, and whatever blasphemies they utter; 3.29 but whoever blasphemes against the Holy Spirit never has forgiveness, but is guilty of an eternal sin" [A saying that probably belongs here is preserved at this point in Matthew 12.30 **"He who is not with me is against me, and he who does not gather with me scatters.**]
3.28	Truly, I say to you, all sins will be forgiven the sons of men, and whatever blasphemies they utter;
3.31	And his mother and his brothers came; and standing outside they sent to him and called him. 3.32 And a crowd was sitting about him; and they said to him, "Your mother and your brothers are outside, asking for you." 3.33 And he replied, "Who are my mother and my brothers?" 3.34 And looking around on those who sat about him, he said, "Here are my mother and my brothers! 3.35 Whoever does the will of God is my brother, and sister, and mother."
4.1	Again he began to teach beside the sea. And a very large crowd gathered about him, so that he got into a boat and sat in it on the sea; and the whole crowd was beside the sea on the land. 4.2 And he taught them many things in parables, and in his teaching he said to them: 4.3 Listen! A sower went out to sow. 4.4 And as he sowed, some seed fell along the path, and the birds came and devoured it. 4.5 Other seed fell on rocky ground, where it had not much soil, and immediately it sprang up, since it had no depth of soil; 4.6 and when the sun rose it was scorched, and since it had no root it withered away. 4.7 Other seed fell among thorns and the thorns grew up and choked it, and it yielded no grain. 4.8 And other seeds fell into good soil and brought forth grain, growing up and increasing and yielding thirtyfold and sixtyfold and a hundredfold." 4.9 And he said, "He who has ears to hear, let him hear."
4.10	And when he was alone, those who were about him with the twelve asked him concerning the parables. 4.11 And he said to them, "To you has been given the secret of the kingdom of God, but for those outside everything is

in parables; 4.12 so that they may indeed see but not perceive, and may indeed hear but not understand; lest they should turn again, and be forgiven."

4.13 And he said to them, "Do you not understand this parable? How then will you understand all the parables? 4.14 The sower sows the word. 4.15 And these are the ones along the path, where the word is sown; when they hear, Satan immediately comes and takes away the word which is sown in them. 4.16 And these in like manner are the ones sown upon rocky ground, who, when they hear the word, immediately receive it with joy; 4.17 and they have no root in themselves, but endure for a while; then, when tribulation or persecution arises on account of the word, immediately they fall away. 4.18 And others are the ones sown among thorns; they are those who hear the word, 4.19 but the cares of the world, and the delight in riches, and the desire for other things, enter in and choke the word, and it proves unfruitful. 4.20 But those that were sown upon the good soil are the ones who hear the word and accept it and bear fruit, thirtyfold and sixtyfold and a hundredfold."

4.21 And he said to them, "Is a lamp brought in to be put under a bushel, or under a bed, and not on a stand? 4.22 For there is nothing hid, except to be made manifest; nor is anything secret, except to come to light. 4.23 If any man has ears to hear, let him hear."

4.24 And he said to them, "Take heed what you hear; the measure you give will be the measure you get, and still more will be given you. 4.25 For to him who has will more be given; and from him who has not, even what he has will be taken away." 4.26 And he said, "The kingdom of God is as if a man should scatter seed upon the ground, 4.27 and should sleep and rise night and day, and the seed should sprout and grow, he knows not how. 4.28 The earth produces of itself, first the blade, then the ear, then the full grain in the ear. 4.29 But when the grain is ripe, at once he puts in the sickle, because the harvest has come." 4.30 And he said, "With what can we compare the kingdom of God, or what parable shall we use for it? 4.31 It is like a grain of mustard seed, which, when sown upon the ground, is the smallest of all the seeds on earth; 4.32 yet when it is sown it grows up and becomes the greatest of all shrubs, and puts forth large branches, so that the birds of the air can make nests in its shade."

6.1 He went away from there and came to his own country; and his disciples followed him. 6.2 And on the sabbath he began to teach in the synagogue; and many who heard him were astonished, saying, "Where did this man get all this? What is the wisdom given to him? What mighty works are wrought by his hands! 6.3 Is not this the carpenter, the son of Mary and brother of James and Joses and Judas and Simon, and are not his sisters here with us?" And they took offense at him. 6.4 And Jesus (John) said to them, "A prophet is not without honor, except in his own country, and among his own kin, and in his own house."

6.6 And he marveled because of their unbelief. And he went about among the villages teaching. 6.7 And he called to him the twelve, and began to send them out two by two, and gave them authority over the unclean spirits. 6.8 He charged them to take nothing for their journey except a staff; no bread, no bag, no money in their belts; 6.9 but to wear sandals and not put on two tunics. 6.10 And he said to them, "Where you enter a house, stay there until you leave the place. 6.11 And if any place will not receive you and they refuse to hear you, when you leave, shake off the dust that is on your feet for a testimony against them." 6.12 So they went out and preached that men should repent. 6.13 And they cast out many demons, and anointed with oil many that were sick and healed them

7.1 Now when the Pharisees gathered together to him, with some of the scribes, who had come from Jerusalem, 7.2 they saw that some of his disciples ate with hands defiled, that is, unwashed. 7.3 (For the Pharisees, and all the Jews, do not eat unless they wash their hands, observing the tradition of the elders; 7.4 and when they come from the market place, they do not eat unless they purify themselves; and there are many other traditions which they observe, the washing of cups and pots and vessels of bronze.) 7.5 And the Pharisees and the scribes asked him, "Why do your disciples not live according to the tradition of the elders, but eat with hands defiled?" 7.6 And he said to them, "Well did Isaiah prophesy of you hypocrites, as it is written, 'This people honors me with their lips, but their heart is far from me; 7.7 in vain do they worship me, teaching as doctrines the precepts of men.' 7.8 You leave the commandment of God, and hold fast the tradition of men." 7.9 And he said to them, "You have a fine way of rejecting the commandment of God, in order to keep your tradition! 7.10 For Moses said, 'Honor your father and your mother'; and, 'He who speaks evil of father or mother, let him surely die'; 7.11 but you say, 'If a man tells his father or his mother, What you would have gained from me is Corban' (that is, given to God)—7.12 then you no longer permit him to do anything for his father or mother, 7.13 thus making void the word of God through your tradition which you hand on. And many such things you do."

7.14 And he called the people to him again, and said to them, "Hear me, all of you, and understand: 7.15 there is nothing outside a man which by going into him can defile him; but the things which come out of a man are what defile him."

7.17 And when he had entered the house, and left the people, his disciples asked him about the parable. 7.18 And he said to them, "Then are you also without understanding? Do you not see that whatever goes into a man from outside cannot defile him, 7.19 since it enters, not his heart but his stomach, and so

THE EVOLUTION OF CHRISTS AND CHRISTIANIES

passes on?" (Thus he declared all foods clean.) 7.20 And he said, "What comes out of a man is what defiles a man. 7.21 For from within, out of the heart of man, come evil thoughts, fornication, theft, murder, adultery, 7.22 coveting, wickedness, deceit, licentiousness, envy, slander, pride, foolishness. 7.23 All these evil things come from within, and they defile a man."

8.11 The Pharisees came and began to argue with him, seeking from him a sign from heaven, to test him. 8.12 And he sighed deeply in his spirit, and said, "Why does this generation seek a sign? Truly, I say to you, no sign shall be given to this generation."

8.14 Now they had forgotten to bring bread; and they had only one loaf with them in the boat. 8.15 And he cautioned them, saying, "Take heed, beware of the leaven of the Pharisees and the leaven of Herod." 8.17 Jesus **(John)** said to them, "Why do you discuss the fact that you have no bread? Do you not yet perceive or understand? Are your hearts hardened? 8.18 Having eyes do you not see, and having ears do you not hear?

8.18 And do you not remember? 8.19 When I broke the five loaves for the five thousand, how many baskets full of broken pieces did you take up?" They said to him, "Twelve." 8.20 "And the seven for the four thousand, how many baskets full of broken pieces did you take up?" And they said to him, "Seven." 8.21 And he said to them, "Do you not yet understand?"

8:27 And Jesus **(John)** went on with his disciples, to the villages of Caesarea Philippi; and on the way he asked his disciples, "Who do men say that I am?" And they told him, "John the Baptist; and others say, Elijah; and others one of the prophets." And he asked them, "But who do you say that I am?" Peter answered him, "You are the Christ Peter answered him, and said, "Get behind me, Satan! For you are not on the side of God, but of men." Turning and seeing his disciples, he charged them to tell no one. And he would not have any one know it

9.30 They went on from there and passed through Galilee.; 9.33 And they came to Capernaum; and when he was in the house he asked them, "What were you discussing on the way?" 9.34 But they were silent; for on the way they had discussed with one another who was the greatest. 9.35 And he sat down and called the twelve; and he said to them, "If any one would be first, he must be last of all and servant of all."

9.36 And he took a child, and put him in the midst of them; and taking him in his arms, he said to them, 9.37 "Whoever receives one such child in my name receives me; and whoever receives me, receives not me but him who sent me."

9.38 John said to him, "Teacher, we saw a man casting out demons in your name, and we forbade him, because he was not following us." 9.39 But Jesus said, "Do not forbid him; for no one who does a mighty work in my name will be able soon after to speak evil of me. 9.40 For he that is not against us is for us.

James said to him, "Teacher, we saw a man casting out demons in your name, and we forbade him, because he was not following us. But John said," Do not forbid him…

9.41 For truly, I say to you, whoever gives you a cup of water to drink because you bear the name of Christ, will by no means lose his reward

9.42 "Whoever causes one of these little ones who believe in me to sin, it would be better for him if a great millstone were hung round his neck and he were thrown into the sea.

9.43 And if your hand causes you to sin, cut it off; it is better for you to enter life maimed than with two hands to go to hell, to the unquenchable fire. 9.44 9.45 And if your foot causes you to sin, cut it off; it is better for you to enter life lame than with two feet to be thrown into hell.

9.46 9.47 And if your eye causes you to sin, pluck it out; it is better for you to enter the kingdom of God with one eye than with two eyes to be thrown into hell, 9.48 where their worm does not die, and the fire is not quenched.

9.49 For every one will be salted with fire. 9.50 Salt is good; but if the salt has lost its saltiness, how will you season it? Have salt in yourselves, and be at peace with one another."

10.1 And he left there and went to the region of Judea and beyond the Jordan, and crowds gathered to him again; and again, as his custom was, he taught them. 10.2 And Pharisees came up and in order to test him asked, "Is it lawful for a man to divorce his wife?" 10.3 He answered them, "What did Moses command you?" 10.4 They said, "Moses allowed a man to write a certificate of divorce, and to put her away." 10.5 But Jesus (John) said to them, "For your hardness of heart he wrote you this commandment.

10.6 But from the beginning of creation, 'God made them male and female.' 10.7 'For this reason a man shall leave his father and mother and be joined to his wife, 10.8 and the two shall become one flesh.' So they are no longer two but one flesh.

10.9 What therefore God has joined together, let not man put asunder."

10.10 And in the house the disciples asked him again about this matter.

10.11 And he said to them, "Whoever divorces his wife and marries another, commits adultery against her;

10.12 and if she divorces her husband and marries another, she commits adultery."

10.13 And they were bringing children to him, that he might touch them; and the disciples rebuked them. 10.14 But when Jesus **(John)** saw it he was indignant, and said to them, "Let the children come to me, do not hinder them; for to such belongs the kingdom of God. 10.15 Truly, I say to you, whoever does not receive the kingdom of God like a child shall not enter it."

10.17 And as he was setting out on his journey, a man ran up and knelt before him, and asked him, "Good Teacher, what must I do to inherit eternal life?"

THE EVOLUTION OF CHRISTS AND CHRISTIANIES

10.18 And Jesus (John) said to him, "Why do you call me good? No one is good but God alone. 10.19 You know the commandments: 'Do not kill, Do not commit adultery, Do not steal, Do not bear false witness, Do not defraud, Honor your father and mother.'" 10.20 And he said to him, "Teacher, all these I have observed from my youth." 10.21 And Jesus looking upon him loved him, and said to him, "You lack one thing; go, sell what you have, and give to the poor, and you will have treasure in heaven; and come, follow me."

10.22 At that saying his countenance fell, and he went away sorrowful; for he had great possessions. 10.23 And Jesus (John) looked around and said to his disciples, "How hard it will be for those who have riches to enter the kingdom of God!"

10.24 And the disciples were amazed at his words. But Jesus (John) said to them again, "Children, how hard it is to enter the kingdom of God! 10.25 It is easier for a camel to go through the eye of a needle than for a rich man to enter the kingdom of God." 10.26 And they were exceedingly astonished, and said to him, "Then who can be saved?" 10.27 Jesus (**John**) looked at them and said, "With men it is impossible, but not with God; for all things are possible with God."

10.28 Peter began to say to him, "Lo, we have left everything and followed you." 10.29 Jesus (John) said, "Truly, I say to you, there is no one who has left house or brothers or sisters or mother or father or children or lands, for my sake and for the gospel, 10.30 who will not receive a hundredfold now in this time, houses and brothers and sisters and mothers and children and lands, with persecutions, and in the age to come eternal life. 10.31 But many that are first will be last, and the last first."

10.35 And James and John, (James and Peter) the sons of Zebedee, came forward to him, and said to him, "Teacher, we want you to do for us whatever we ask of you." 10.36 And he said to them, "What do you want me to do for you?" 10.37 And they said to him, "Grant us to sit, one at your right hand and one at your left, in your glory." 10.38 But Jesus (John) said to them, "You do not know what you are asking. Are you able to drink the cup that I drink, or to be baptized with the baptism with which I am baptized?" 10.39 And they said to him, "We are able." And Jesus (John) said to them, "The cup that I drink you will drink; and with the baptism with which I am baptized, you will be baptized; 10.40 but to sit at my right hand or at my left is not mine to grant, but it is for those for whom it has been prepared."

10.41 And when the ten heard it, they began to be indignant at James and John. 10.42 And Jesus (John) called them to him and said to them, "You know that those who are supposed to rule over the Gentiles lord it over them, and their great men exercise authority over them. 10.43 But it shall not be so among you; but whoever would be great among you must be your servant,

	10.44 and whoever would be first among you must be slave of all. 10:45 For the Son of man also came not to be served but to serve, and to give his life as a ransom for many."
11.15	And they came to Jerusalem. And he entered the temple and began to drive out those who sold and those who bought in the temple, and he overturned the tables of the money-changers and the seats of those who sold pigeons; 11.16 and he would not allow any one to carry anything through the temple. 11.17 And he taught, and said to them, "Is it not written, 'My house shall be called a house of prayer for all the nations'? But you have made it a den of robbers."
11.22	And Jesus (John) answered them, "Have faith in God. 11.23 Truly, I say to you, whoever says to this mountain, 'Be taken up and cast into the sea,' and does not doubt in his heart, but believes that what he says will come to pass, it will be done for him. 11.24 Therefore I tell you, whatever you ask in prayer, believe that you have received it, and it will be yours. 11.25 And whenever you stand praying, forgive, if you have anything against any one; so that your Father also who is in heaven may forgive you your trespasses." 11.26 But if you do not forgive, neither will your Father who is in heaven forgive your sins.
12.10	Have you not read this scripture: 'The very stone which the builders rejected has become the head of the corner; 12.11this was the Lord's doing, and it is marvelous in our eyes'?" Matthew preserves the rest of the saying. **12.11 He said to them, "What man of you, if he has one sheep and it falls into a pit on the sabbath, will not lay hold of it and lift it out**
12.13	And they sent to him some of the Pharisees and some of the Herodians, to entrap him in his talk. 12.14 And they came and said to him, "Teacher, we know that you are true, and care for no man; for you do not regard the position of men, but truly teach the way of God. Is it lawful to pay taxes to Caesar, or not? 12.15 Should we pay them, or should we not?" But knowing their hypocrisy, he said to them, "Why put me to the test? Bring me a coin, and let me look at it." 12.16 And they brought one. And he said to them, "Whose likeness and inscription is this?" They said to him, "Caesar's." 12.17 Jesus said to them, "Render to Caesar the things that are Caesar's, and to God the things that are God's."
12.18	And Sadducees came to him, who say that there is no resurrection; and they asked him a question, saying, 12.19 "Teacher, Moses wrote for us that if a man's brother dies and leaves a wife, but leaves no child, the man must take the wife, and raise up children for his brother. 12.20 There were seven brothers; the first took a wife, and when he died left no children; 12.21 and the second took her, and died, leaving no children; and the third likewise; 12.22and the seven left no children. Last of all the woman also died. 12.23

THE EVOLUTION OF CHRISTS AND CHRISTIANIES

> In the resurrection whose wife will she be? For the seven had her as wife." 12.24 Jesus (John) said to them, "Is not this why you are wrong, that you know neither the scriptures nor the power of God? 12.25 For when they rise from the dead, they neither marry nor are given in marriage, but are like angels in heaven.
>
> 12.26 And as for the dead being raised, have you not read in the book of Moses, in the passage about the bush, how God said to him, 'I am the God of Abraham, and the God of Isaac, and the God of Jacob'? 12.27 He is not God of the dead, but of the living; you are quite wrong."
>
> 12.28 And one of the scribes came up and heard them disputing with one another, and seeing that he answered them well, asked him, "Which commandment is the first of all?" 12.29 Jesus (John) answered, "The first is, 'Hear, O Israel: The Lord our God, the Lord is one; 12.30 and you shall love the Lord your God with all your heart, and with all your soul, and with all your mind, and with all your strength.' 12.31 The second is this, 'You shall love your neighbor as yourself.' There is no other commandment greater than these."
>
> 12.32 And the scribe said to him, "You are right, Teacher; you have truly said that he is one, and there is no other but he; 12.33 and to love him with all the heart, and with all the understanding, and with all the strength, and to love one's neighbor as oneself, is much more than all whole burnt offerings and sacrifices." 12.34 And when Jesus saw that he answered wisely, he said to him, "You are not far from the kingdom of God."

MQ

The author of UrMark did a fantastic job of creating a realistic narrative based on the sayings of Jesus. It is doubtful he came up with these sayings. They hardly ever really match the anecdotes he tells. For example take this one

> 10.13 And they were bringing children to him, that he might touch them; and the disciples rebuked them. 10.14 But when Jesus saw it he was indignant, and said to them, "Let the children come to me, do not hinder them; for to such belongs the kingdom of God. 10.15 Truly, I say to you, whoever does not receive the kingdom of God like a child shall not enter it."

The statement "let the children come to me, do not hinder them; for to such belongs the kingdom of God," does not match the anecdotal information "he was indignant." When someone is indignant, they do not make a commandment ("let the children come to me") followed by a doctrinal pronouncement about the Kingdom of

God ("to such belong the Kingdom of God"). The second statement, "whoever does not receive the kingdom of God like a child shall not enter it" has nothing to do with the situation." This can be seen by how the Gospel of Thomas makes the same suggestion in a completely different situation.

> Jesus saw infants being suckled. He said to His disciples, "These infants being suckled are like those who enter the Kingdom[443]."

One would have assumed that the writer would take sayings from somewhere that illustrated his story points. It is surprising to find that he worked off the sayings to build the anecdotes for his story. Still, once we recognize this, another intriguing idea pops up. Could the author have taken the sayings from just one document? We can easily see if this might have been the case. All we have to do is strip off the anecdotal material and leave the sayings. What I found when I did this simple experiment was even more amazing than UrMark. What I found was a sayings gospel more primitive than the *Gospel of Thomas* and *Q*. I called it *MQ*.

One feature is striking: the sayings are ordered in couplets. Each two sayings seem to be about the same subject.

Among other scholars Burton Mack has noticed this feature and attempted to explain it. Mack calls sayings or pronouncements by the Greek term *Chreia*:

> One learned in school how to turn a *chreia* into the story of a little debate between the protagonist and his challengers. One also learned how to "elaborate" the point of a *chreia* by providing a coherent set of arguments in its favor. In this case, the argument were one's own, not those of the protagonist of the *chreia*. As the Jesus people developed *chreiai* into more elaborate argumentations, however, they chose not to take the credit for the arguments they had found. Instead, just as with the attribution of new teachings to the founder of a school, they let Jesus take the credit both for the *chreia* and for the arguments in its favor. And it so happened that the standard outline for the elaboration of a *chreia* ended with an authoritative pronouncement (Mack and Robbin 1989). This resulted in giving Jesus two prominent pronouncements in each elaborated *chreaia*, with with the last statement invariably making a pronouncement on the correctness of his own views[444].

This would explain why we find pronouncements and elaborations attributed to Jesus, but it does not explain why we find two sets of either sayings or elaborations on the sayings for each topic. My first thought was that the author of UrMark collected two sayings and/or elaborations this way from a larger group of sayings. This led to the question of why just two for each subject. We would expect that the writer would find a number of subjects where there were many sayings of Jesus and other subjects where there was only one saying. Why restrict yourself to two on each subject?

Examining the sayings led to the answer. The sayings themselves were intertexual. They seemed to follow a saying and counter responsorial saying pattern. The best example is perhaps these:

> 2.21   No one sews a piece of unshrunk cloth on an old garment; if he does, the patch tears away from it, the new from the old, and a worse tear is made.
>
> 2.22   And no one puts new wine into old wineskins; if he does, the wine will burst the skins, and the wine is lost, and so are the skins; but new wine is for fresh skins."

The first sentence talks about combining something good and new—unshrunk cloth—with something old and bad—an old garment. The second sentence reverses this formula. It talks about something bad and new—new wine—combining with something good and old—old wineskins. Both statements agree that the new and the old cannot combine, but they have exactly opposite opinions about which is the good and which is the bad.

Here is another example:

> 4.24   Jesus said: Take heed what you hear; the measure you give will be the measure you get, and still more will be given you.
>
> 4.25   For to him who has will more be given; and from him who has not, even what he has will be taken away."

In the first saying the more you give the more you will have. In the second saying, the more you have the more you will be given. These are completely opposite. The first says that how much you get will be based on how much you contribute to the group. They second saying says that how much you get will be based on how much you already have.

For the author to find these contradictory sayings by chance would be quite difficult. But why would he put them together and make a story out of them? One has to consider that the author of UrMark did not go out and gather these sayings to be used in his construction project. He found these sayings already at hand. The fact that he used clearly contradictory ones without suppressing one or even changing their order in some way meant that he was using the text as he found it. It was even possible he was using all the sayings in the exact order he found them in a separate and complete text.

Analysis of MQ: The Prophet Versus Christ Hypothesis

In looking at MQ, the sayings document that the author of UrMark used, it appeared that it involved two groups with very different positions on a number of issues. Basically one group gives a saying of Jesus and the other group gives a counter saying either contradicting or elaborating on a saying by the first group.

This appears to me true in general. We are certainly dealing with two groups of sayings, and it seems again generally the second group is responding to the first. However, what the meaning of each individual saying might be depends on an exact knowledge of the circumstances of their production. This we do not have yet.

Therefore, the following interpretations are simply my guesses and any one or all may be quite wrong. I believe that the way the sayings are put together tells us what the groups thought of each other. Most importantly it indicates that the sayings are not necessarily coming from an oral tradition but are being made up for the immediate political purposes of attacking/debating another group.

In figuring out what is going on, I think we should take the Clementine Recognitions statement about the followers of John seriously:

> but these, being baptized by John, and holding the word of truth received from the tradition of Moses as the key of the kingdom of heaven, have hid it from the hearing of the people. Yea, some even of the disciples of John, who seemed to be great ones, have separated themselves from the people, and proclaimed their own master as the Christ[445].

This suggests a split in the John the Baptist movement between those that saw John as a prophet and those who "proclaimed their own master as the Christ." While the Clementine Recognitions is a literary novel, it has no reason to lie about this division in the movement.

Let us assume two John the Baptist groups involved in writing the texts. The first statement always comes from the P group (**P** for prophet) and the response, usually sarcastic and bitter, but sometimes just elaborating, comes from the C group (**C** for Christ).

When divided this way, the flow of the argument makes a great deal of sense. This is hard to imagine happening by coincidence. Therefore, I believe the writer of Urmark respected the sayings text to a great degree. He might combine two sayings of Jesus into one, or intersperse text between them if necessary to get the meaning he wanted, but I doubt if he left much out or changed the order of the sayings. He seems to have respected the text, treating the sayings not quite as sacrosanct, but more like a rule in

THE EVOLUTION OF CHRISTS AND CHRISTIANIES

a game where you're not allowed to cut your opponent's saying, but may counter it in other ways.

In reading the following, please keep in mind the "Jesus said," was probably "John said" in the original.

> P (Scribe): 1.15 Jesus said: "The time is fulfilled, and the kingdom of God is at hand; repent, and believe in the gospel."
>
> C (John): 1.17 Jesus said: "Follow me and I will make you become fishers of men."

P begins with this powerful announcement: The time is fulfilled, and the kingdom of God is at hand is the gospel (i.e. good news announcement).
C emphasizes his roll gathering men together.

> P: 2.9 Jesus said: Which is easier, to say to the paralytic, 'Your sins are forgiven,' or to say, 'Rise, take up your pallet and walk'?
>
> C: 2.17 Jesus said: Those who are well have no need of a physician, but those who are sick; I came not to call the righteous, but sinners."

P is making a point about healing verses forgiving. I tend to assume the correct answer is that it is harder to say 'Rise, take up your pallet and walk' as this would tend to indicate that Jesus' healings were harder than John the Baptist' forgiving of sins.
C talks about calling sinners. Are these supposed to be the Apostles, those who Jesus are making into fishers of men?

> P: 2.19 Jesus said: Can the wedding guests fast while the bridegroom is with them? As long as they have the bridegroom with them, they cannot fast.
>
> C: 2:20 [I've had to break up this saying which traditionally has been seen as going together to get it to fit the pattern.] The days will come, when the bridegroom is taken away from them, and then they will fast in that day.

P: explains that the followers of Jesus do not fast because we're happy as brides getting married to Jesus. Our lives are a continuous wedding feast.
C responds that they'll fast when the party's over. This is a direct response to S. This is important, as it shows P actually is responding to C, and the two texts are not being put together arbitrarily. An alternative explanation is that 2:19 and 2:20 are one saying. But if written about Jesus it does not make sense, as eating and not fasting distinguishes Jesus' followers from John. This could be one saying if it is referring to followers of John the Baptist not fasting in his lifetime.

P: 2.21 No one sews a piece of unshrunk cloth on an old garment; if he does, the patch tears away from it, the new from the old, and a worse tear is made.

C: 2.22 And no one puts new wine into old wineskins; if he does, the wine will burst the skins, and the wine is lost, and so are the skins; but new wine is for fresh skins."

P says the new ideas (unshrunk cloth) of Jesus do not fit with the old ideas (old garment) of Judaism. This tends to indicate that S sees his movement as more or less a new and better version of Judaism.
C agrees the new ideas (wine) ruins both the new and old. He adds new wine (bad wine—the ideas of Jesus) is for fresh skins (kids).

P: 2.25 Jesus said: Have you never read what David did, when he was in need and was hungry, he and those who were with him: how he entered the house of God, when Abi'athar was high priest, and ate the bread of the Presence, which it is not lawful for any but the priests to eat, and also gave it to those who were with him? The sabbath was made for man, not man for the Sabbath.

C: 3.4 Jesus said: Is it lawful on the sabbath to do good or to do harm, to save life or to kill? Matthew 12.11 He said to them, "If any of you has a sheep and it falls into a pit on the Sabbath, will you not take hold of it and lift it out? 12How much more valuable is a man than a sheep! Therefore it is lawful to do good on the Sabbath."

[The Gospel of Matthew preserves this second saying.]

P is attacking the privileges of the priests to eat on the Sabbath.
C is giving a more general rule that it is lawful to do good on the Sabbath

P 3.23 And he said to them in parables "How can Satan cast out Satan? 3.24 If a kingdom is divided against itself, that kingdom cannot stand. 3.25 And if a house is divided against itself, that house will not be able to stand. 3.26 And if Satan has risen up against himself and is divided, he cannot stand, but is coming to an end. 3.27 But no one can enter a strong man's house and plunder his goods unless he first binds the strong man; then indeed he may plunder his house 3.28" Truly, I say to you, all sins will be forgiven the sons of men, and whatever blasphemies they utter; 3.29 but whoever blasphemes against the Holy Spirit never has forgiveness, but is guilty of an eternal sin"[Matthew 12.30 preserves the next

THE EVOLUTION OF CHRISTS AND CHRISTIANIES

line.] "He who is not with me is against me, and he who does not gather with me scatters.

C: 3.34 And looking around on those who sat about him, he said, "Here are my mother and my brothers! 3.35 Whoever does the will of God is my brother, and sister, and mother."

P defines the strength and commitment of the movement in its solidarity
C says the movement is like a family.

P: 4.3 Jesus said: Listen! A sower went out to sow. 4.4 And as he sowed, some seed fell along the path, and the birds came and devoured it. Other seed fell on rocky ground, where it had not much soil, and immediately it sprang up, since it had no depth of soil; and when the sun rose it was scorched, and since it had no root it withered away. Other seed fell among thorns and the thorns grew up and choked it, and it yielded no grain. And other seeds fell into good soil and brought forth grain, growing up and increasing and yielding thirtyfold and sixtyfold and a hundredfold." 4.9 And he said, "He who has ears to hear, let him hear."

C: 4.10 And when he was alone, those who were about him with the twelve asked him cncerning the parables. 4.11 And he said to them, "To you has been given the secret of the kingdom of God, but for those outside everything is in parables; [Possibly Matthew 13:12 continues correctly "Whoever has will be given more, and he will have an abundance. Whoever does not have, even what he has will be taken from him."]

P is explaining why Jesus has such few followers and how they will be abundantly rewarded
C suggests that not only followers will be rewarded but outsiders will lose everything.

P: 4.9 Jesus said: He who has ears to hear, let him hear. 4.21 Jesus said: Is a lamp brought in to be put under a bushel, or under a bed, and not on a stand?

C: 4.22 Jesus said: For there is nothing hid, except to be made manifest; nor is anything secret, except to come to light. 4.23 Jesus said: If any man has ears to hear, let him hear.

This is interesting because of the statements that Matthew preserves in Matthew 5:14, "You are the light of the world. A city on a hill cannot be hidden." The first "P" saying about a lamp

361

elaborates on the first Matthew saying "You are the light of the world," while the "C" saying elaborates on the second Matthew saying about hidden things in the second saying "A city on a hill cannot be hidden." This suggests that the hypothesis that we have been following, that each saying represents an opposing writer may not be the case. Instead, the two writers may be elaborating different original sayings. It suggests that what we are getting here in Mark is not original sayings, but explanations of original sayings. For the moment, we'll just consider this an anomaly.

P suggest that a light/lamp (probably meaning group) should be in the open.
C may be attacking the secret teachings of the S group.

> P: 4.24 Jesus said: Take heed what you hear; the measure you give will be the measure you get, and still more will be given you.
>
> C: 4.25 For to him who has will more be given; and from him who has not, even what he has will be taken away."

P is calling for equality.
C is for maintaining their higher social position and increasing it.

> P: 4.26 Jesus said: The kingdom of God is as if a man should scatter seed upon the ground, and should sleep and rise night and day, and the seed should sprout and grow, he knows not how. The earth produces of itself, first the blade, then the ear, then the full grain in the ear. But when the grain is ripe, at once he puts in the sickle, because the harvest has come.
>
> C: 4.30 Jesus said: With what can we compare the kingdom of God, or what parable shall we use for it? It is like a grain of mustard seed, which, when sown upon the ground, is the smallest of all the seeds on earth; yet when it is sown it grows up and becomes the greatest of all shrubs, and puts forth large branches, so that the birds of the air can make nests in its shade."

P says don't worry about work, God will take care of us.
C talks about the greatness of the Kingdom of God movement.

> P: 6.4 Jesus said: A prophet is not without honor, except in his own country, and among his own kin, and in his own house.
>
> C: 6.10 And he said to them, "Where you enter a house, stay there until you leave the place. 6.11 And if any place will not receive you and they refuse to hear you, when you leave, shake off the dust that is on your feet for a testimony against them."

We seem to have very personal sayings being exchanged here.
P says he is a prophet that is unwelcome in his own house.
C seems to be saying "please leave," you're not welcome.

> P: 7.6 Jesus said: Well did Isaiah prophesy of you hypocrites, as it is written, 'This people honors me with their lips, but their heart is far from me; in vain do they worship me, teaching as doctrines the precepts of men. S: You leave the commandment of God, and hold fast the tradition of men.
>
> C: 7.9 You have a fine way of rejecting the commandment of God, in order to keep your tradition! For Moses said, 'Honor your father and your mother'; and, 'He who speaks evil of father or mother, let him surely die'; but you say, 'If a man tells his father or his mother, What you would have gained from me is Corban' (that is, given to God)—then you no longer permit him to do anything for his father or mother, thus making void the word of God through your tradition which you hand on.

P quotes Isaiah to show that the people have actually turned from God and embraced human traditions.
C attacks the P group for breaking up families and teaching disrespect, the opposite of Moses.

> P: 7.14 Jesus said: "Hear me, all of you, and understand: there is nothing outside a man which by going into him can defile him; but the things which come out of a man are what defile him.
>
> C: 7.18 Do you not see that whatever goes into a man from outside cannot defile him, since it enters, not his heart but his stomach, and so passes on? What comes out of a man is what defiles a man. For from within, out of the heart of man, come evil thoughts, fornication, theft, murder, adultery, coveting, wickedness, deceit, licentiousness, envy, slander, pride, foolishness. All these evil things come from within, and they defile a man."

P is attacking dietary restrictions. The things which come out of a man may be a reference to urine, excrement, vomit, etc.
C is making a more general attack on all of society.

> P: 8.11 Jesus said: Why does this generation seek a sign? Truly, I say to you, no sign shall be given to this generation.
>
> C: . . . (The response may be preserved in Matthew 12:41 The men of Nineveh will stand up at the judgment with this generation and

condemn it; for they repented at the preaching of Jonah, and now one greater than Jonah is here. The Queen of the South will rise at the judgment with this generation and condemn it; for she came from the ends of the earth to listen to Solomon's wisdom, and now one greater than Solomon is here.)

P says Jesus refuses to give a sign, which may indicate disbelief in the miracle stories.
C talks about the importance of the preachings of Jesus. There is no contradiction here, only an elaboration.

> P: 8.5 And he cautioned them, saying, "Take heed, beware of the leaven of the Pharisees and the leaven of Herod."
> C: 8.17 Jesus said to them, "Why do you discuss the fact that you have no bread? Do you not yet perceive or understand? Are your hearts hardened?

P seems to suggest that the Pharisess control people through bread
C minimizes the importance of bread, perhaps feeling that discussing bread instead of the coming of the Messiah is ridiculous.

> P: 8.21 And he said to them, "Do you not yet understand?" 8.33 "Get behind me, Satan! For you are not on the side of God, but of men."
> C: 9.35 Jesus said: If any one would be first, he must be last of all and servant of all.

P is still attacking the Pharisees and the leaven of Herod
C emphasizes the roll of serving and renouncing privileges. There does not seem to be a contradiction here, unless P is insinuating that C does not act like a servant. This seems to be an elaboration of P.

> P. 9.35 Jesus said: Whoever receives one child in my name receives me; and whoever receives me, receives not me but him who sent me.
> C. 9.42 Jesus said: Whoever causes one of these little ones who believes in me to sin, it would be better for him if a great millstone were hung round his neck and he were thrown into the sea.

P talks about receiving children.
C may be accusing P of causing children to sin.

> P: 9.43 Jesus said: And if your hand causes you to sin, cut it off; it is better for you to enter life maimed than with two hands to go to

THE EVOLUTION OF CHRISTS AND CHRISTIANIES

      hell, to the unquenchable fire. And if your foot causes you to sin, cut it off; it is better for you to enter life lame than with two feet to be thrown into hell.

C: 9.46 Jesus said: And if your eye causes you to sin, pluck it out; it is better for you to enter the kingdom of God with one eye than with two eyes to be thrown into hell, where their worm does not die, and the fire is not quenched.

P talks about cutting off limbs to avoid hell.
C responds that a person should blind himself rather than seeing things wrongly.

    P: 9.49 Jesus said: For every one will be salted with fire.
    C: 9.50 Jesus said: Salt is good; but if the salt has lost its saltiness, how will you season it? Have salt in yourselves, and be at peace with one another."

P says they're going to be tested.
C plays off the word salt. He probably means it as having a fiery attitude. His talking about being at peace with one another seems quite different from what S is saying.

    P: 10.5 Jesus said: For your hardness of heart he wrote you this commandment. But from the beginning of creation, 'God made them male and female.' 10.7 'For this reason a man shall leave his father and mother and be joined to his wife, and the two shall become one flesh.' So they are no longer two but one flesh. 10.9 What therefore God has joined together, let not man put asunder."
    C: 10.12 Jesus said: Whoever divorces his wife and marries another, commits adultery against her; and if she divorces her husband and marries another, she commits adultery.

P emphasizes that this is for the hard hearted.
C counters by saying both men and wives should not be allowed to divorce and get new husbands.

    P: 10.14 Jesus said: Let the children come to me, do not hinder them; for to such belongs the kingdom of God.
    C: 10.15 Truly, I say to you, whoever does not receive the kingdom of God like a child shall not enter it.

P says don't stop the children from becoming followers of the Jesus movement.
C says the movement is childish or should be childlike.

> P: 10.17 Jesus said: Why do you call me good? No one is good but God alone. 10.19 You know the commandments: 'Do not kill, Do not commit adultery, Do not steal, Do not bear false witness, Do not defraud, Honor your father and mother.'"
>
> C: 10.18 Jesus said: You know the commandments: 'Do not kill, Do not commit adultery, Do not steal, Do not bear false witness, Do not defraud, Honor your father and mother. You lack one thing, go, sell what you have, and give to the poor, and you will have treasure in heaven; and come, follow me

P is urging obedience to the commandments as the way to God.
C ells him to sell everything and give to the poor if he wants to be good. There is some similarity in structure but the meanings of S and P are quite different. It is important to note that both of these statements leave out and 'love your neighbor as yourself,' which Matthew 19.19 includes. It is hard to believe they both would take that out. The line is probably an addition by Matthew or later.

> P 10.23 Jesus said: "How hard it will be for those who have riches to enter the kingdom of God!"
>
> C 10:24 "Children, how hard it is to enter the kingdom of God! It is easier for a camel to go through the eye of a needle than for a rich man to enter the kingdom of God. With men it is impossible, but not with God; for all things are possible with God.

P is attacking the rich.
C is agreeing, but adding an escape clause.

> P: 10.29 Jesus said, Truly, I say to you, there is no one who has left house or brothers or sisters or mother or father or children or lands, for my sake and for the gospel, who will not receive a hundredfold now in this time, houses and brothers and sisters and mothers and children and lands, with persecutions, and in the age to come eternal life.
>
> C: 10:31 But many that are first will be last, and the last first."

P makes promises of good things for those who join.
C comes back with the saying about first being last, and last first. It simply suggests that conditions will change. P may not have liked the radical line about leaving houses, brothers, sisters etc. It simply says that all things change.

> P: "The cup that I drink you will drink; and with the baptism with which I am baptized, you will be baptized;

C: 10.42 Jesus said, You know that those who are supposed to rule over the Gentiles lord it over them, and their great men exercise authority over them. 10.43 But it shall not be so among you; but whoever would be great among you must be your servant.

P says we're in this thing together.
C suggests a criterion of equality to distinguish themselves from the Gentiles.

P: 11.17 Jesus said: "Is it not written, 'My house shall be called a house of prayer for all the nations'? But you have made it a den of robbers."

C: 11.22 And Jesus said 11.23 Truly, I say to you, whoever says to this mountain, 'Be taken up and cast into the sea,' and does not doubt in his heart, but believes that what he says will come to pass, it will be done for him. 11.24 Therefore I tell you, whatever you ask in prayer, believe that you have received it, and it will be yours.

P attacks the present state of things.
C calls for faith.

P: 11.25 And whenever you stand praying, forgive, if you have anything against any one; so that your Father also who is in heaven may forgive you your trespasses."

C: 11:26 But if you do not forgive, neither will your Father who is in heaven forgive your sins.

C says to pray for forgiveness.
P tells you what will happen if you do not.

P: 12.1 And he began to speak to them in parables. "A man planted a vineyard, and set a hedge around it, and dug a pit for the wine press, and built a tower, and let it out to tenants, and went into another country. 12.2 When the time came, he sent a servant to the tenants, to get from them some of the fruit of the vineyard. 12.3 And they took him and beat him, and sent him away empty-handed. 12.4 Again he sent to them another servant, and they wounded him in the head, and treated him shamefully. 12.5 And he sent another, and him they killed; and so with many others, some they beat and some they killed. 12.6 He had still one other, a beloved son; finally he sent him to them, saying, 'They will respect my son.' 12.7 But those tenants said to one another, 'This is the heir; come, let us kill him, and the inheritance will be ours.' 12.8 And they took him and killed him, and cast him out of the vineyard. 12.9 What will the owner of the vineyard do? He will come and destroy the tenants, and give the vineyard to others.

C: 12.10 Jesus said: Have you not read this scripture: 'The very stone which the builders rejected has become the head of the corner; this was the Lord's doing, and it is marvelous in our eyes'?"

P says the rightful owner will come back to the Vineyard and take over.
C answers by quoting scripture that the rejected stone has already been put in place by God

P: 12.17 Jesus Said: Render to Caesar the things that are Caesar's, 12:17 and to God the things that are God's.

C: 12.26 Jesus Said: For when they rise from the dead, they neither marry nor are given in marriage, but are like angels in heaven. 12.27 Jesus said: And as for the dead being raised, have you not read in the book of Moses, in the passage about the bush, how God said to him, 'I am the God of Abraham, and the God of Isaac, and the God of Jacob'? He is not God of the dead, but of the living."

P says do your bit for society.
C talks about the afterlife as a way of explanation of why we should render to Caesar and God their proper things.

P: 12.29 Jesus said: "The first is, 'Hear, O Israel: The Lord our God, the Lord is one; and you shall love the Lord your God with all your heart, and with all your soul, and with all your mind, and with all your strength.' The second is this, 'You shall love your neighbor as yourself.' There is no other commandment greater than these.

C: 12.32 Jesus said: He is one, and there is no other but he; and to love him with all the heart, and with all the understanding, and with all the strength, and to love one's neighbor as oneself, is much more than all whole burnt offerings and sacrifices."

P put forward love of God and neighbor as the two greatest commandments.
C here echoes S, but adds an attack on burnt offerings and sacrifices.

P 12.34 Jesus said: You are not far from the kingdom of God.

C 12.38 Jesus said: Beware of the scribes, who like to go about in long robes, and to have salutations in the market places and the best seats in the synagogues and the places of honor at feasts, who devour widows' houses and for a pretense make long prayers. They will receive the greater condemnation.

P ends on an optimistic note.
C ends with an attack on the Scribes.

Conclusions from *MQ*

I am not at all certain about individual interpretations. In fact, I am sure that I am interpreting them wrongly in some cases. However I think the *Prophet Versus Christ* hypothesis offers a reasonable explanation for the couplets. Before rejecting it, one must try to come up with a better explanation for the couplet phenomenon. I know of no better one.

The relationship between the two groups is both complimentary and antagonistic. We are dealing with an ideological struggle within two similar communities. This may be why the author of *UrMark* has to incorporate the contradictory material into his anecdotal gospel. He is still bound in some way to observe group protocols. One of these protocols may be that you cannot ignore the comments of a superior or equal in your writings, but must incorporate them into any text you develop for group instruction.

The author of *UrMark* is creating a coherent narrative. This narrative could very well be descriptive of the author's own life. We might even consider the main character of the stories, to be only a fictionalized version of the author. This might explain why people believe in the reality of Jesus Christ despite the fantastic mythological stories associated with him. One senses a real personality being described in the self description in the UrMark text which is at the core of the *Gospel of Mark* and exists in its synoptic revisions.

Albert Schweitzer has noted this[446]:

> Thus investigations which have been carried out by individuals substantiate the general and immediate impression that the teaching of Jesus must somehow go back to a historical personality of late Judaism.

The total surprise provided by this deconstruction is that part of the historical personality seems to be so closely tied to the author of *UrMark* and the relationships he creates in his narrative. It has nothing to do with the sayings which the author finds ready made.

MQQ

We can take the sayings in MQ by the prophet John faction as the basic source document for UrMark. We simply erase the responses by the Christ John faction to arrive at this possible sayings gospel. This is what we get:

1.15   Jesus /John said: "The time is fulfilled, and the kingdom of God is at hand; repent, and believe in the gospel."

2.9   Jesus/John said: Which is easier, to say to the paralytic, 'Your sins are forgiven,' or to say, 'Rise, take up your pallet and walk'?

2.19   Jesus/John said: Can the wedding guests fast while the bridegroom is with them? As long as they have the bridegroom with them, they cannot fast.

2.21   No one sews a piece of unshrunk cloth on an old garment; if he does, the patch tears away from it, the new from the old, and a worse tear is made.

2.25   Jesu/John s said: Have you never read what David did, when he was in need and was hungry, he and those who were with him: how he entered the house of God, when Abiathar was high priest, and ate the bread of the Presence, which it is not lawful for any but the priests to eat, and also gave it to those who were with him? The Sabbath was made for man, not man for the Sabbath.

3.23   And he said to them in parables "How can Satan cast out Satan? 3.24 If a kingdom is divided against itself, that kingdom cannot stand. And if a house is divided against itself, that house will not be able to stand. 3.26 And if Satan has risen up against himself and is divided, he cannot stand, but is coming to an end.

[A saying that may have originally gone here is preserved in Matthew 12.30 "He who is not with me is against me, and he who does not gather with me scatters.]

3.34   He said, "Here are my mother and my brothers!"

4.3   Jesus/John said: Listen! A sower went out to sow. 4.4 And as he sowed, some seed fell along the path, and the birds came and devoured it. Other seed fell on rocky ground, where it had not much soil, and immediately it sprang up, since it had no depth of soil; and when the sun rose it was scorched, and since it had no root it withered away. Other seed fell among thorns and the thorns grew up and choked it, and it yielded no grain. And other seeds fell into good soil and brought forth grain, growing up and increasing and yielding thirtyfold and sixtyfold and a hundredfold

4.9   Jesus/John said: He who has ears to hear, let him hear. 4.21 Jesus said: Is a lamp brought in to be put under a bushel, or under a bed, and not on a stand?

THE EVOLUTION OF CHRISTS AND CHRISTIANIES

4.24 Jesu/John s said: Take heed what you hear; the measure you give will be the measure you get, and still more will be given you.

4.26 Jesus/John said: The kingdom of God is as if a man should scatter seed upon the ground, and should sleep and rise night and day, and the seed should sprout and grow, he knows not how. But when the grain is ripe, at once he puts in the sickle, because the harvest has come.

6.4 Jesu/John s said: A prophet is not without honor, except in his own country, and among his own kin, and in his own house.

7.6 Jesu/John s said: Well did Isaiah prophesy of you hypocrites, as it is written, 'This people honors me with their lips, but their heart is far from me; in vain do they worship me, teaching as doctrines the precepts of men.

7.9 You leave the commandment of God, and hold fast the tradition of men.

7.14 Jesus/John said: "Hear me, all of you, and understand: there is nothing outside a man which by going into him can defile him; but the things which come out of a man are what defile him.

8.11 Jesus/John said: Why does this generation seek a sign? Truly, I say to you, no sign shall be given to this generation.

8.5 And he cautioned them, saying, "Take heed, beware of the leaven of the Pharisees and the leaven of Herod."

8.21 He said to them, "Do you not yet understand?" "Get behind me, Satan! For you are not on the side of God, but of men."

9.35 Jesus/John said: Whoever receives one child in my name receives me; and whoever receives me, receives not me but him who sent me.

.9.43 Jesus said: And if your hand causes you to sin, cut it off; it is better for you to enter life maimed than with two hands to go to hell, to the unquenchable fire. And if your foot causes you to sin, cut it off; it is better for you to enter life lame than with two feet to be thrown into hell.

9.49 Jesus/John said: For every one will be salted with fire.

10.5 Jesu/John s said: For your hardness of heart he wrote you this commandment. But from the beginning of creation, 'God made them male and female.' 10.7 'For this reason a man shall leave his father and mother and be joined to his wife, and the two shall become one flesh.' So they are no longer two but one flesh. 10.9 What therefore God has joined together, let not man put asunder."

10.14   Jesus/John said: Let the children come to me, do not hinder them; for to such belongs the kingdom of God.

10.17   Jesu/John s said: Why do you call me good? No one is good but God alone. 10.19 You know the commandments: 'Do not kill, Do not commit adultery, Do not steal, Do not bear false witness, Do not defraud, Honor your father and mother.'

10.23   Jesus/John said: "How hard it will be for those who have riches to enter the kingdom of God!"

10.29   Jesus/John said, Truly, I say to you, there is no one who has left house or brothers or sisters or mother or father or children or lands, for my sake and for the gospel, who will not receive a hundredfold now in this time, houses and brothers and sisters and mothers and children and lands, with persecutions, and in the age to come eternal life.

10.42   Jesu/John s said, You know that those who are supposed to rule over the Gentiles lord it over them, and their great men exercise authority over them. 10.43 But it shall not be so among you; but whoever would be great among you must be your servant.

11.22   And Jesus/John s said 11.23 Truly, I say to you, whoever says to this mountain, 'Be taken up and cast into the sea,' and does not doubt in his heart, but believes that what he says will come to pass, it will be done for him. 11.24 Therefore I tell you, whatever you ask in prayer, believe that you have received it, and it will be yours.

11.30   Jesus/John said: "Was the baptism of John from heaven or from men?[447]"

12.1   Jesus/John said: A man planted a vineyard, and set a hedge around it, and dug a pit for the wine press, and built a tower, and let it out to tenants, and went into another country. 12.2 When the time came, he sent a servant to the tenants, to get from them some of the fruit of the vineyard. 12.3 And they took him and beat him, and sent him away empty-handed. 12.4 Again he sent to them another servant, and they wounded him in the head, and treated him shamefully. 12.5 And he sent another, and him they killed; and so with many others, some they beat and some they killed. 12.6 He had still one other, a beloved son; finally he sent him to them, saying, 'They will respect my son.' 12.7 But those tenants said to one another, 'This is the heir; come, let us kill him, and the inheritance will be ours.' 12.8 And they took him and killed him, and cast him out of the vineyard. 12.9 What will the owner of the vineyard do? He will come and destroy the tenants, and give the vineyard to others.

THE EVOLUTION OF CHRISTS AND CHRISTIANIES

- 12.17 Jesus/John Said: Render to Caesar the things that are Caesar's, 12:17 and to God the things that are God's.
- 12.29 Jesus/John said: "The first is, 'Hear, O Israel: The Lord our God, the Lord is one; and you shall love the Lord your God with all your heart, and with all your soul, and with all your mind, and with all your strength.' The second is this, 'You shall love your neighbor as yourself.' There is no other commandment greater than these.
- 12.34 Jesus/John said: You are not far from the kingdom of God.

About 17 of these 33 sayings are matched in the *Gospel of Thomas*[448]. *MQQ* may be slightly earlier, as Thomas has 114 sayings, more than three times as many.

Thirty Questions: the John/Jesus FAQ sheet

The Gospel MQQ seems almost to be designed as the answer part to a FAQ (frequently asked questions) sheet. The questions can be reconstructed from the answers.

1. Are you a healer?
   Answer: 2.9. Jesus said: Which is easier, to say to the paralytic, 'Your sins are forgiven,' or to say, 'Rise, take up your pallet and walk'?

2. Why don't you fast like the Pharisees do?
   Answer: 2.19 Jesus said: Can the wedding guests fast while the bridegroom is with them? As long as they have the bridegroom with them, they cannot fast.

3. Why not just conform and be normal?
   Answer: 2:21 No one sews a piece of unshrunk cloth on an old garment; if he does, the patch tears away from it, the new from the old, and a worse tear is made.

4. Why don't you follow the Sabbath laws?
   Answer: 2.25 Jesus said: Have you never read what David did, when he was in need and was hungry, he and those who were with him: how he entered the house of God, when Abiathar was high priest, and ate the bread of the Presence, which it is not lawful for any but the priests to eat, and also gave it to those who were with him? The Sabbath was made for man, not man for the Sabbath.

5. Why do your family say you are possessed by an unclean spirit?
   Answer: 3.23 And he said to them in parables "How can Satan cast out Satan? 3.24 If a kingdom is divided against itself, that kingdom cannot stand. And if a

373

house is divided against itself, that house will not be able to stand. 3.26 And if Satan has risen up against himself and is divided, he cannot stand, but is coming to an end. 3.27 But no one can enter a strong man's house and plunder his goods, unless he first binds the strong man; then indeed he may plunder his house. 3.28 "Truly, I say to you, all sins will be forgiven the sons of men, and whatever blasphemies they utter; 3.29 but whoever blasphemes against the Holy Spirit never has forgiveness, but is guilty of an eternal sin"

6. What will we get if we follow you?
Answer: 4.3 Jesus said: Listen! A sower went out to sow. 4.4And as he sowed, some seed fell along the path, and the birds came and devoured it. Other seed fell on rocky ground, where it had not much soil, and immediately it sprang up, since it had no depth of soil; and when the sun rose it was scorched, and since it had no root it withered away. Other seed fell among thorns and the thorns grew up and choked it, and it yielded no grain. And other seeds fell into good soil and brought forth grain, growing up and increasing and yielding thirtyfold and sixtyfold and a hundredfold.

7. Why are you so open about your views?
Answer: 4.9 Jesus said: He who has ears to hear, let him hear. 4.21 Jesus said: Is a lamp brought in to be put under a bushel, or under a bed, and not on a stand?

8. How will the goods be distributed in your Kingdom of God?
Answer: 4.24 Jesus said: Take heed what you hear; the measure you give will be the measure you get, and still more will be given you.

9. What will your kingdom of God be like?
Answer: 4.26 Jesus said: The kingdom of God is as if a man should scatter seed upon the ground, and should sleep and rise night and day, and the seed should sprout and grow, he knows not how. The earth produces of itself, first the blade, then the ear, then the full grain in the ear. But when the grain is ripe, at once he puts in the sickle, because the harvest has come.

1. Why is it reported you were kicked out of your home?
Answer: 6.4 Jesus said: A prophet is not without honor, except in his own country, and among his own kin, and in his own house.

2. Why is your group's tradition so different from others?
Answer: 7.6 Jesus said: Well did Isaiah prophesy of you hypocrites, as it is written, 'This people honors me with their lips, but their heart is far from me; in

THE EVOLUTION OF CHRISTS AND CHRISTIANIES

vain do they worship me, teaching as doctrines the precepts of men. S: You leave the commandment of God, and hold fast the tradition of men

3. Why do you eat any food you want?
Answer: 7.14 Jesus said: "Hear me, all of you, and understand: there is nothing outside a man which by going into him can defile him; but the things which come out of a man are what defile him.

4. What is the sign that you are really from God?
Answer: 8.11 Jesus said: Why does this generation seek a sign? Truly, I say to you, no sign shall be given to this generation.

5. Why do the Pharisees and Herodians say you are hungry and without bread?
Answer: 8.5 And he cautioned them, saying, "Take heed, beware of the leaven of the Pharisees and the leaven of Herod

6. But why are they high and rich and you're poor and lowly?
Answer: 8.21 And he said to them, "Do you not yet understand?" 8.33 "Get behind me, Satan! For you are not on the side of God, but of men."

7. Why do you baptize children?
Answer: 9.35 Jesus said: Whoever receives one child in my name receives me; and whoever receives me, receives not me but him who sent me.

8. Why do you mutilate those who leave your group?
Answer: 9.43 Jesus said: And if your hand causes you to sin, cut it off; it is better for you to enter life maimed than with two hands to go to hell, to the unquenchable fire. And if your foot causes you to sin, cut it off; it is better for you to enter life lame than with two feet to be thrown into hell.

9. Why are you so salted (angry)?
Answer: 9.49 Jesus said: For every one will be salted with fire.

10. What about divorce?
Answer: 10.5 Jesus said: For your hardness of heart he wrote you this commandment. But from the beginning of creation, 'God made them male and female.' 10.7 'For this reason a man shall leave his father and mother and be joined to his wife, and the two shall become one flesh.' So they are no longer two but one flesh. 10.9 What therefore God has joined together, let not man put asunder."

11. What about the children after a divorce. Who gets them?
    Answer: 10.14 Jesus said: Let the children come to me, do not hinder them; for to such belongs the kingdom of God.

12. How can we be good like you?
    Answer: 10.17 Jesus said: Why do you call me good? No one is good but God alone. 10.19 You know the commandments: 'Do not kill, Do not commit adultery, Do not steal, Do not bear false witness, Do not defraud, Honor your father and mother.'"

13. What about the rich in your Kingdom of God?
    Answer: 10.23 Jesus said: "How hard it will be for those who have riches to enter the kingdom of God!"

14. If I leave my family for you, what will I get?
    Answer: 10.29 Jesus said, Truly, I say to you, there is no one who has left house or brothers or sisters or mother or father or children or lands, for my sake and for the gospel, who will not receive a hundredfold now in this time, houses and brothers and sisters and mothers and children and lands, with persecutions, and in the age to come eternal life.

15. How do you differ from the Roman's rule?
    Answer: 10.42 Jesus said, You know that those who are supposed to rule over the Gentiles lord it over them, and their great men exercise authority over them. 10.43 But it shall not be so among you; but whoever would be great among you must be your servant.

25. Where are you getting your authority for this?
    Answer: 11.30. Was the Baptism of John from Heaven or men[449]?

26. What happens if I pray to your God?
    Answer: 11.22 And Jesus said 11.23 Truly, I say to you, whoever says to this mountain, 'Be taken up and cast into the sea,' and does not doubt in his heart, but believes that what he says will come to pass, it will be done for him. 11.24 Therefore I tell you

27. How did your group inherit the Kingdom of God?
    Answer: 12.1 Jesus said: A man planted a vineyard, and set a hedge around it, and dug a pit for the wine press, and built a tower, and let it out to tenants, and went into another country. 12.2 When the time came, he sent a servant to the tenants, to get from them some of the fruit of the vineyard. 12.3 And they took him and beat him, and sent him away empty-handed. 12.4 Again he sent to them another servant, and they wounded him in the head, and treated him shamefully. 12.5 And he sent another,

and him they killed; and so with many others, some they beat and some they killed. 12.6 He had still one other, a beloved son; finally he sent him to them, saying, 'They will respect my son.' 12.7 But those tenants said to one another, 'This is the heir; come, let us kill him, and the inheritance will be ours.' 12.8 And they took him and killed him, and cast him out of the vineyard. 12.9 What will the owner of the vineyard do? He will come and destroy the tenants, and give the vineyard to others.

28. Can I go on praying to the Gods of Rome if I pray to your God?
    Answer: 12.17 Jesus Said: Render to Caesar the things that are Caesar's, 12:17 and to God the things that are God's.

29. What are the greatest commandments of your God?
    Answer: 12.29 Jesus said: "The first is, 'Hear, O Israel: The Lord our God, the Lord is one; and you shall love the Lord your God with all your heart, and with all your soul, and with all your mind, and with all your strength.' The second is this, 'You shall love your neighbor as yourself.' There is no other commandment greater than these.

30. Isn't the Kingdom of God pretty unrealistic.
    Answer: 12.34 Jesus said: You are not far from the kingdom of God.

One can also see pretty easily that the second set of answers, what I have called the C (Christ) text also answers these questions, but are dependent on a knowledge of the P (Prophet) text or earlier answers. For example:

21. How can I be good like you?
P: 10.17 Why do you call me good? No one is good but God alone. 10.19 You know the commandments: 'Do not kill, Do not commit adultery, Do not steal, Do not bear false witness, Do not defraud, Honor your father and mother.'"
C: 10.18 You know the commandments: 'Do not kill, Do not commit adultery, Do not steal, Do not bear falsewitness, Do not defraud, Honor your father and mother. You lack one thing, go, sell what you have, and give to the poor, and you will have treasure in heaven; and come, follow me

The first answer has Jesus denying his divinity ("No one is good but God alone") and basically saying follow the Mosaic Law. The second answer takes out the denial of Jesus' divinity and adds the idea of giving all worldly goods to the poor and joining the group. It is easy to imagine the second answer correcting the first, but difficult to see the first as correcting the second. It is fantastic to assume that such similar answers would be given independently, so we have to suppose that *MQ* is designed as a corrective or response to *MQQ*.

Mosaic. Baptism of Old Jesus.

Ravenna, Italy, Orthodox Baptistry Ceiling, 450[450]. Jesus has a balding head and pigtails. Notice that John with trimmed beard and mustache looks like Jesus. Just as the words of John the Baptist were appropriated in the second century and given to Jesus, in the fifth century, this look of John the Baptist became the look of Jesus in Byzantine imagery around the sixth century.

Chapter 7

Deconstructing the Gospel of Matthew

How Matthew Changed a Single Long Speech by John the Baptist into Multiple Jesus Speeches

First Evidence of Speeches from a John the Baptist Text

> What we see so clearly in the work of the school of Matthew is a simple fact. The work of making up exegeses of scripture, selecting the appropriate ones and saying important things about them, and the labor of collecting and compiling these exegeses of scripture into a larger composite together express a single principle, make a single statement, carry out the purposes of a single polemic... That is the fact of Matthew. It is true of sifra, Genesis Rabbah and Leviticus Rabbah and most, though not all, rabbinic midrash compilations.
>
> Jacob Neusner[451]

The fact that Mark seems not to have changed the order of sayings even when confronted with contradictory ones is important. We can follow that clue and apply it to the sayings *Gospel of Q*. Let us assume that Matthew working from a *Q* sayings document did not change the order of the sayings. This goes against the hypothesis that suggests Luke preserved *Q* in the correct order.

Still, when we put *Q* together mainly in the order we find it in Matthew and continue the text of *Q* wherever we do not get a clear and artificial break, we get a quite coherent text. We also see the breaking points where Matthew inserted other material. Additionally we see that Luke not only cut *Q* into smaller chunks, but rearranged the order, and in so doing, lost much of the coherence the material we have in Matthew. Taken together, the hints in the text and the simple reconstruction procedure by which we arrive at what I call UrMatthew, I believe, will make a strong case for the hypothesis that Matthew preserved the original sayings text order and not Luke.

Now, breaking up Mark into its parts was a rather simple affair, we simply assumed that the anecdotal material was separate from the miracle and other materials. This is also the case with Matthew, but he has connected his material quite smoothly and we have to examine the cutting points closely for clues.

It may seem in the following discussion that I have artificially broken the text apart to prove a pre-determined agenda. In fact I have merely identified some seventeen cut points in a long text that makes up about half of the Gospel of Matthew. Instead of keeping large chunks of it in precisely the order he found it, Matthew could have taken the path of Luke and cut the material into dozens of smaller pieces and rearranged them so the original text could never have been put together. Fortunately, Matthew seems only to have been concerned with intergrating different texts and not concerned with hiding the original texts. I will start from the beginning and show how I found the cut points[452].

It was looking at a small section of *Q*, Luke 24-35, that I found the clues that led me to my reconstruction; I will simply go over this section to demonstrate the kinds of clues and hints in the text that troubled me and ultimately led me to this discovery. I am sure now that other people are aware of it, it will seem amazing that no one detected it before and that other people will discover other points in the text where similar problems suggest the solution I have found.

Let us start by examining the middle of a bit of text. Luke 7.28-31:

> For I say unto you, Among those that are born of women there is not a greater prophet than John the Baptist: but he that is least in the kingdom of God is greater than he. 29 And all the people that heard him, and the publicans, justified God, being baptized with the baptism of John. 30. But the Pharisees and lawyers rejected the counsel of God against themselves, being not baptized of him. 31.And the Lord said, Whereunto then shall I liken the men of this generation? and to what are they like?[453]

Jesus is talking to an ordinary crowd of people. Jesus has just pronounced John the Baptist the greatest human being born of woman. That would mean John the Baptist was greater than Abraham or Moses. The writer tells us about the mixed response of the crowd. Then Jesus starts talking about a description of this generation. Stop. We need to freeze frame to discover what is wrong with this picture? First, why does John the Baptist rate so highly? He baptized a few people including Jesus, protested a remarriage by Herod and got executed. Why does Jesus consider him so great?

This major ideological problem is often considered. What is not considered is that it covers a seemingly slight, but perhaps more important narrational problem. The crowd is described as being two types of people, the majority and the publicans being baptized by John, and the minority—the Pharisees and lawyers—being unbaptized. How does the author know this? How does he know that baptism status of all the people watching Jesus's speech? Did the author attend all of John's baptisms and remember all the people baptized. Did Jesus ask for a show of hands of those baptized by John? Did he give an opinion survey to the crowd? The author doesn't tell us. He just accepts it as natural that we readers accept it as natural that he knows the baptized from the unbaptized.

There is another circumstance in which the author would know who was baptized by John and who not, and would not need to tell us how he found this out. The author would know about the baptism status of everybody hearing the speech, if the speech was being given at a baptism event just after the crowd was baptized. He would know who was and who was not baptized if this speech about John the Baptist was immediately after a baptizing event. He would know that the Pharisees and lawyers refused to participate because he would have seen it with his own eyes. Everyone else had participated in the baptism ceremony.

Neither Luke nor Matthew tells us this. In fact, neither tells us anything about the event. Both just say Jesus is addressing people or crowds. They tell us nothing about where or when. They have decontextualized the speech.

We can see that this speech does have a specific context clearly by examining the text just before this and just after, Luke (7:24-28):

> **When John's disciples left, Jesus began to speak to the crowds about John: "What did you go out into the wilderness to see? A reed shaking in the wind? Then tell me what you went out to see. A man in soft clothes? Look, those who wear soft clothes live in palaces. So what did you expect? A prophet? Yes, of course, and much more than a prophet. "This is the one referred to in the writings, 'Look, I am sending my messenger before you. He will prepare your path ahead of you.' I am telling you, no one born of a woman is greater than John; yet the least in God's realm is greater than he."**

Note that the speaker tells us that the crowd has gone "out into the wilderness" to see something. One might see this as a general statement aimed at the many people who went out to see John the Baptist. But, as noted, the author knows that the audience is made up of people who got baptized and those who did not. If Jesus was addressing a general audience, the odds are certain that Jesus should be addressing both people who were and were not baptized by John. Jesus should say 'some of you' or 'most of you' went out into the wilderness. But the address is to the whole crowd(s). The whole crowd has gone out to the wilderness, including the Pharisees and lawyers who did not get baptized. The question "So what did you expect? A prophet?" implies that the crowd specifically went out all expecting to see a prophet, John the Baptist. This was a one time event. Again, we must ask how the speaker knows the expectations of all the people he is talking to. If we place this speech at a baptizing event of John it makes sense. Outside one, it does not.

We have at least four clues: 1) the writer has knowledge of who was baptized by John, 2) the speaker knows everyone in the crowd went out to the wilderness which is associated with John, 3) the speaker has knowledge of the attitude of the crowd towards John, and 4) the speaker gives extravagant praise of John the Baptist and we are not told why the speaker would praise John if the people had gone out to see someone else. All of this makes sense if we assume a speech being given at a baptism event.

Now remember the split in the John community between those who thought John was a prophet and the later members of the community who thought he was Christ.

> When John's disciples left, Jesus began to speak to the crowds about John: "What did you go out into the wilderness to see? A reed shaking in the wind? Then tell me what you went out to see. A man in soft clothes? Look, those who wear soft clothes live in palaces. So what did you expect? A prophet? Yes, of course, *and much more than a prophet.* "This is the one referred to in the writings, 'Look, I am sending my messenger before you. He will prepare your path ahead of you.' I am telling you, no one born of a woman is greater than John; yet the least in God's realm is greater than he."

The phrase "and much more than a prophet" indicate that the writer considers John a Christ figure and not a prophet. He belongs to the Christ-John faction. Now look at the very next lines of Luke (7:31-35):

> "To what shall I compare this generation? It is like children sitting in the marketplace and calling to each other: 'We played the pipes for you and you did not dance.' 'We sang a dirge and you did not wail.' *For John did not come eating or drinking, and they are saying,* 'He is demon possessed.' The son of man has come eating and drinking, and they say, 'Look at him, a glutton and a drunkard, a friend of tax collectors and sinners.' But in spite of what they say, wisdom's children show that she is right.

Note, the original writer is also describing a split in Jewish society, the cheerful ones who play pipes and want to see John dancing, and the sad ones who sing a dirge

THE EVOLUTION OF CHRISTS AND CHRISTIANIES

and want to hear him wailing. Since the people are demanding that a prophet come dancing and singing, the next line should read John did not come "dancing and singing and they say he has a demon." The editor has changed this dancing and singing to "eating and drinking" The original thought was that some people wanted John to dance and some people wanted John to sing, he did not dance or sing so the people called him crazy. A later editor has ruined the answer by changing this to eating and drinking.

We can easily reconstruct the original

> "To what shall I compare this generation? It is like children sitting in the marketplace and calling to each other: 'We played the pipes for you and you did not dance.' 'We sang a dirge and you did not wail.' For John did not come dancing and singing. They are saying, 'He is demon possessed.'
>
> The son of man has come eating and drinking, and they say, 'Look at him, a glutton and a drunkard, a friend of tax collectors and sinners.' But in spite of what they say, wisdom's children show that she is right.

Probably the term "son of man" meant just "a man" in this context as it matches the thought "one born of woman" in the first previous passage, which also just means simply "a man"

We can actually see two transitions in the passages. We can reconstruct the first writing by the "John is a Prophet" people.

> "What did you go out into the wilderness to see? A reed shaking in the wind? Then tell me what you went out to see. A man in soft clothes? Look, those who wear soft clothes live in palaces. So what did you expect? A prophet? Yes, of course, "This is the one referred to in the writings, 'Look, I am sending my messenger before you. He will prepare your path ahead of you.'
>
> "To what shall I compare this generation? It is like children sitting in the marketplace and calling to each other: 'We played the pipes for you and you did not dance.' 'We sang a dirge and you did not wail.' For John did not come dancing and singing. They are saying, 'He is demon possessed.'

The "John is Christ" people added the rest of the lines about "more than a prophet," "born of woman" and "son of man." The later editors just had to change *John said* to *Jesus said*.

Thus far we have been looking at Luke, but Matthew preserves another section for us.

> *12:* From the days of John the Baptist until now the kingdom of heaven has suffered violence, and men of violence take it by force.
> *13:* For all the prophets and the law prophesied until John;
> *14:* and if you are willing to accept it, he is Eli'jah who is to come.
> *15:* He who has ears to hear, let him hear.

This makes no sense at all coming from Jesus, as the "days of John the Baptist" are the days of Jesus. Also, to say "until now" is strange as John is still alive, just in jail as Matthew (11.2) has just told us. One could suppose that Matthew or the last editor just made this up, but there is a jump in the original material between what the people went out to the wilderness to see and John talking about comparing this generation.

In the first passage, John is saying that he is not soft, that he is preparing the path
The second passage, the one Luke cuts out, talks about violence.

The third passage talks derisively about singing and dancing prophets. This attack on softness and pleasing the people with singing and dancing and this pronouncement that the kingdom of heaven is suffering violence, seems to indicate that John was calling for some kind of military action.

The second passage here is more difficult to reconstruct. We can guess what has been changed by taking out the phrases that do not make sense if John is speaking::

> *12:* From the days of _____ until now the kingdom of heaven has suffered violence, and men of violence take it by force.
> *13:* For all the prophets and the law prophesied until _____;
> *14:* and if you are willing to accept it, _____ Eli'jah who is to come.
> *15:* He who has ears to hear, let him hear.

The mention of Elijah is our clue. We look in Malachi (4:1-5) to find:

> 1: "For behold, the day comes, burning like an oven, when all the arrogant and all evildoers will be stubble; the day that comes shall burn them up, says the LORD of hosts, so that it will leave them neither root nor branch.
> 2: But for you who fear my name the sun of righteousness shall rise, with healing in its wings. You shall go forth leaping like calves from the stall.
> 3: And you shall tread down the wicked, for they will be ashes under the soles of your feet, on the day when I act, says the LORD of hosts.
> 4: "Remember the law of my servant Moses, the statutes and ordinances that I commanded him at Horeb for all Israel.
> 5: "Behold, I will send you Eli'jah the prophet before the great and terrible day of the LORD comes.

THE EVOLUTION OF CHRISTS AND CHRISTIANIES

We may take it that the original writer had this passage in mind when he was talking about violence and Elijah. We can now fill in the blanks:

> From the days of Moses until now the kingdom of heaven has suffered violence, and men of violence take it by force.
> 13: For all the prophets and the law prophesied until now;
> 14: and if you are willing to accept it, I am Eli'jah who is to come.

This speech explains why John the Baptist gets mistaken for Elijah in Mark (6:14-15), "Some said, 'John the baptizer has been raised from the dead; that is why these powers are at work in him.' But others said, 'It is Eli'jah.' And others said, 'It is a prophet, like one of the prophets of old.'" Also again in Mark (8.27-28), "he asked his disciples, 'Who do men say that I am?" And they told him, 'John the Baptist; and others say, Elijah and others one of the prophets.'

The fact that John advocates a violent rebellion here matches him with the unnamed figure in Josephus (Ant, 18:4.1) leading an armed rebellion of the Samaritans on Mount Gerizzam circa 37 C.E. One cannot expect too many prophetic-messianic figures being involved in leading armed struggle against Pilate and the Romans.

This suggests another motivation for changing John the Nazarene into Jesus the Christ. John was associated with a violent revolution against Rome. In the second century, it became a political necessity to disassociate the Christ from anti-Roman political activity. Thus John the Nazarene had to be turned into Jesus of Nazareth.

Second Evidence of Jesus' Speeches from a John the Baptist Text

Noticing that Matthew preserves more of the original speech of John than Luke, allows us to figure out another puzzle. John's speech does not just start at "What did you come out to the wilderness to see? It also does not stop at "We sang a dirge and you did not wail." By following this speech both backwards and forwards as it appears in Matthew, and using *Q* material as a guide, we can get an idea of what the speech by John originally looked like. Incidentally, if this is correct, it suggests that *Q* was originally a speech mainly by John the Nazarene. This may explain why we do not find *Q* in circulation. It was a document only in circulation in a small Mandean-like community. Once the sect switched allegiance to Jesus of Nazareth it would have suppressed past copies of John's speech/sayings.

We can trace John's speech both backwards and forwards from this point and what we get is an UrMatthew text.

In the Gospel of Matthew we read this about Jesus:

> "21.45 When the chief priests and the Pharisees heard his parables, they perceived that he was speaking about them. 22.46 But when they tried to arrest him, they feared the multitudes, because they held him to be a prophet.

Jewish leaders are afraid to act against Jesus because the common people believe him to be a prophet. Isn't it extraordinary that after all the miracles, the common people still consider Jesus just a prophet here and not the messiah. Compare this with the saying about John the Baptist which comes only a few sentences before (21:24-27):

> 21.24 Jesus answered them, "I also will ask you a question; and if you tell me the answer, then I also will tell you by what authority I do these things. The baptism of John, whence was it? From heaven or from men?" And they argued with one another, "If we say, 'From heaven,' he will say to us, 'Why then did you not believe him?' But if we say, 'From men,' we are afraid of the multitude; for all hold that John was a prophet."

Here Jewish leaders are afraid to act against John the Baptist because the common people believe him to be a prophet. Before this, Matthew has once before mentioned the idea of a Jewish leader being afraid because the masses regarded John as a prophet (14.3-5):

> For Herod had seized John and bound him and put him in prison, for the sake of Hero'di-as, his brother Philip's wife; because John said to him, "It is not lawful for you to have her." And though he wanted to put him to death, he feared the people, because they held him to be a prophet.

Thus we have Matthew telling us twice that the Jewish leaders are afraid to punish John because the people regard John as a prophet, and then telling us the exact same thing about Jesus. The thought involves a complex triadic relationship. The leader(s) is/are afraid to do something to "X" because the people think "X" is a prophet. Matthew uses John twice in the position of "X" and then suddenly switches to Jesus without explanation.

One could postulate that this was done consciously and Matthew was going for an effect. But if this was done consciously, what kind of effect was he going for? Is he promoting the idea of Jesus as John come back to life? Is Jesus just John *redividus* as some people apparently believed? This is Herod's claim. Does Matthew believe it too? Given the rest of the narrative, especially that Jesus meets John, making his reincarnation as Jesus impossible, this seems a long shot. We may assume that this material comes from the earliest layer of material written by the John community that considered him only a prophet.

Both the editors of Mark and Luke have caught the mistake of blatantly comparing John the Baptist and Jesus by having the common people regard them both as prophets, and they have cut out the reference to John the Baptist. Mark (12.12) has "And they tried to arrest him, but feared the multitude, for they perceived that he had told the parable against them; so they left him and went away." Luke (20.19) has "The scribes and the chief priests tried to lay hands on him at that very hour, but they feared the people; for they perceived that he had told this parable against them."

Mark and Luke have taken out this line out as it is certainly embarrassing. After performing all his miracles and even sending his followers out to perform miracles, his supporters in Jerusalem believe him to be merely a prophet like John. Since Jesus has already called John the Baptist more than a prophet, this is really putting Jesus beneath John the Baptist.

Why would Matthew say that the multitudes only regarded Jesus as a prophet? Remember, this is after he has portrayed scenes with Jesus performing miracles for thousands of people. This is not the only time we find this puzzling jump in narrative logic in Matthew where Jesus is simply called a "prophet" by the multitude. It happens just after Jesus comes to Jerusalem, (Matt, 21:6-11)

> The disciples went and did as Jesus had directed them; they brought the ass and the colt, and put their garments on them, and he sat thereon. Most of the crowd spread their garments on the road, and others cut branches from the trees and spread them on the road. And the crowds that went before him and that followed him shouted, "Hosanna to the Son of David! Blessed is he who comes in the name of the Lord! Hosanna in the highest!
> And when he entered Jerusalem, all the city was stirred, saying, "Who is this?" And the crowds said, "This is the prophet Jesus from Nazareth of Galilee.

Mark and Luke contain the story, but neither contain the last lines answering the all important question "Who is this, "and showing the people believing him to be a prophet. The author of the Gospel of John gives us a different version of the scene and changes the answer into what we would expect.

> 12.12   The next day a great crowd who had come to the feast heard that Jesus was coming to Jerusalem. 12.13 So they took branches of palm trees and went out to meet him, crying, "Hosanna! Blessed is he who comes in the name of the Lord, even the King of Israel!" 12.14 And Jesus found a young ass and sat upon it; as it is written, 12.15 "Fear not, daughter of Zion; behold, your king

> is coming, sitting on an ass's colt!" 12.16 His disciples did not understand this at first; but when Jesus was glorified, then they remembered that this had been written of him and had been done to him. 12.17 The crowd that had been with him when he called Laz'arus out of the tomb and raised him from the dead bore witness. 12.18 The reason why the crowd went to meet him was that they heard he had done this sign. 12.19 The Pharisees then said to one another, "You see that you can do nothing; look, the world has gone after him."

Note the last line, "You see that you can do nothing; look, the world has gone after him," According to this text, the crowd, after witnessing the miracle of Lazarus coming back to life, regard Jesus as a miracle worker and their king (Christ?). They passionately love him. There is no mention of him being a prophet. Prophets are generally not all that welcome

One could perhaps develop a sophisticated ideological explanation for this prophet reference being in the text of Matthew. Perhaps Matthew wanted to emphasize the humanness of Jesus by having the crowd regard him as a prophet. Looking at it from a narrator's point of view, it is simply a mistake. It confuses the reader as to the identity of Jesus and John the Baptist, making them equal.

But this mistake tells us a great deal about the conditions of construction of the text. Matthew could not have made such a big ideological mistake of saying that Jesus was regarded as a prophet unless he was putting together a variety of texts[454].

This suggests that he was working rapidly and being quite careless. One can easily see this from the fact that he has Jesus riding both the colt from Mark and the ass from John. But thankfully he has also preserved the "prophet" reference that Mark leaves out. We may easily reconstruct the original:

> And when he entered Jerusalem, all the city was stirred, saying, "Who is this?" And the crowds said, "This is the prophet John, the Nazarene of Galilee.

One should also note that we are back to the identity problem with people asking "Who is this?" Recall Mark (8:27-29):

> And Jesus went on with his disciples, to the villages of Caesare'a Philip'pi; and on the way he asked his disciples, "Who do men say that I am?" And they told him, "John the Baptist; and others say, Eli'jah; and others one of the prophets."
>
> And he asked them, "But who do you say that I am?" Peter answered him, "You are the Christ."

The slip that Matthew has made of leaving in material that has the masses calling Jesus a prophet (just like they call John) we may take as further evidence of the transition of John from prophet to reincarnated Elijah to Christ and then to Jesus the Christ and John the Baptist.

Third Evidence of Jesus Speeches from a John the Baptist Text

Matthew opens his third chapter with John the Baptist speaking and then breaks away (3.12), after announcing the coming of a messianic figure. But Luke gives us a bit of the speech that Matthew apparently left out. This bit fits perfectly as the continuation of John the Baptist's speech after the announcement of the Messiah, "What should we do then the crowd asked?" It does not fit in anywhere else. This passage continues the speech by John the Baptist until (Luke 3.14) John says to some soldiers, "Rob no one by violence or by false accusation, and be content with your wages."

How strange it is to end a speech here which begins with "Repent, for the kingdom of heaven is near." It is rather pedestrian advice, "rob no-one, be content with your wages." If it ended there, John's speech would have to be considered one of the poorest examples of ancient rhetoric in history. Why would anybody follow him at all after he gives advice that anybody might give. His popularity would be a real mystery if this was an actual indication of his speech-making ability. We must assume there is more to the speech. After all, would you make a long trip of hours or days in the desert to hear someone say, "The Kingdom of God is a hand, a messiah is coming, you soldiers, do not rob or ask for pay increases." We really have to assume there is more to John's Speech

Now, instead of continuing with John's speech, Matthew gives us another speech, Jesus' Sermon on the Mount. Matthew forgets to tell us where this Mountain is. It is by far the longest speech he gives to Jesus, but Matthew does not tell us the location. Fortunately, we can look in Mark and find out that it is happening on the Lake outside Jesus' home in Capernaum. To be fair Matthew does tell us that Jesus went back to his home in Capernaum after the speech[455]. This indicates that both he and Mark are on the same page as far as the location of the speech is concerned.

Now, Mark has great crowds coming to a lake to see Jesus and great crowds following him to a mountain[456]. But Jesus says nothing to them. We are just told about the popularity of his healings. Mark's Jesus turns out to be a failed public speaker. We are not given one public speech by Jesus in Mark. It is Matthew who makes Jesus into an orator. But how can he give such a great speech to Jesus (i.e. the Sermon on the Mount) and give such a pathetic speech to John. Maybe because John is a minor character or he wants to show the inferiority of John. This is certainly true. But let us consider another possibility.

Let us consider that Matthew finds himself with no speech by Jesus, but he possesses a beautiful long speech by John. Might not he be tempted to appropriate the speech by John. He might have John start the speech, but then after about 10 lines, he leaves out a passage and gives the rest of the speech to Jesus. The trick would be virtually undetectable, except that, our friend Luke has let the cat out of the bag by continuing with the part of the speech that Matthew took out. He provides us with the missing passages (Luke 3:10-14). It is easy to see how these lines logically flow into the beginning of the Sermon on the Mount. Read them straight through:

> (Luke 3:10) What should we do then? the crowd asked. 11. John answered, The man with two tunics should share with him who has none, and the one who has food should do the same. 12. Tax collectors also came to be baptised. Teacher, they asked, what should we do? 13. Don't collect any more than you are required to, he told them. 14. Then some soldiers asked him, And what should we do? He replied, Don't extort money and don't accuse people falsely—be content with your pay.
>
> (Matthew 5.3). Blessed are the poor in spirit, for theirs is the kingdom of heaven. 4. Blessed are those who mourn, for they will be comforted. 5. Blessed are the meek, for they will inherit the earth. 6. Blessed are those who hunger and thirst for righteousness, for they will be filled. 7. Blessed are the merciful, for they will be shown mercy.

There is no break between John's speech in Luke (3:14) and Matthew's Sermon on the Mount (Matt. 5.3): "Then some Soldiers asked him, and what should we do? He replied, "Don't extort money and don't accuse people falsely—be content with your pay. Blessed are the poor in spirit for theirs is the kingdom of heaven." The line said to the soldier, "be content with your pay" leads directly into the line "Blessed are the poor in spirit for theirs is the kingdom of heaven."

We have found our unfinished speech by John. Now that we know how Matthew has constructed it we may continue with it until we find its natural ending, no matter how Matthew and Luke have cut it up.

Matthew 3:1 is probably the start of the speech and the start of a text that Matthew used, an "UrMatthew." text.

An UrMatthew Document: The Teachings of John the Nazarene

When we put together all the anecdotal sayings in Mark, we discovered *MQ* and *MQQ*, which appear to be sayings documents that he worked from. When we put together all the speech material in Mathew in the order in which he has it, we get a document that he apparently worked from. It is obviously one speech given on a single day by John.

All the ideas reflect the speech of a Jewish prophet announcing the coming Kingdom of God. We have nothing that reflects the ideas of a Christ (Savior) or God/Son of God. Here is the reconstruction:

> 3.1. In those days John the Baptist came, preaching in the Desert of Judea. 2. and saying, Repent, for the kingdom of heaven is near. 3. This is he who was spoken of through the prophet Isaiah: A voice of one calling in the desert, 'Prepare the way for the Lord, make straight paths for him.' 4. John's clothes were made of camel's hair, and he had a leather belt round his waist. His food was locusts and wild honey. 5. People went out to him from Jerusalem and all Judea and the whole region of the Jordan. 6. Confessing their sins, they were baptised by him in the Jordan River. 7. But when he saw many of the Pharisees and Sadducees coming to where he was baptising, he said to them: You brood of vipers! Who warned you to flee from the coming wrath? 8. Produce fruit in keeping with repentance. 9. And do not think you can say to yourselves, 'We have Abraham as our father.' I tell you that out of these stones God can raise up children for Abraham. 10. The axe is already at the root of the trees, and every tree that does not produce good fruit will be cut down and thrown into the fire. 11. I baptise you with water for repentance. But after me will come one who is more powerful than I, whose sandals I am not fit to carry. He will baptise you with the Holy Spirit and with fire. 12. His winnowing fork is in his hand, and he will clear his threshing-floor, gathering his wheat into the barn and burning up the chaff with unquenchable fire[457].

[Luke 3.10-14 preserves the next part]

> 10. What should we do then? the crowd asked. 11. John answered, The man with two tunics should share with him who has none, and the one who has food should do the same. 12. Tax collectors also came to be baptised. Teacher, they asked, what should we do? 13. Don't collect any more than you are required to, he told them. 14. Then some soldiers asked him, And what should we do? He replied, Don't extort money and don't accuse people falsely—be content with your pay.

[Matthew 5, 6 and 7 continues the original.]

> 5.1 Now when he saw the crowds, he went up on a mountainside and sat down. His disciples came to him, 2. and he began to teach them, saying: 3. Blessed are the poor in spirit, for theirs is the

kingdom of heaven. 4. Blessed are those who mourn, for they will be comforted. 5. Blessed are the meek, for they will inherit the earth. 6. Blessed are those who hunger and thirst for righteousness, for they will be filled. 7. Blessed are the merciful, for they will be shown mercy. 8. Blessed are the pure in heart, for they will see God. 9. Blessed are the peacemakers, for they will be called sons of God. 10. Blessed are those who are persecuted because of righteousness, for theirs is the kingdom of heaven. 11. Blessed are you when people insult you, persecute you and falsely say all kinds of evil against you because of me. 12. Rejoice and be glad, because great is your reward in heaven, for in the same way they persecuted the prophets who were before you. 13. You are the salt of the earth. But if the salt loses its saltiness, how can it be made salty again? It is no longer good for anything, except to be thrown out and trampled by men. 14. You are the light of the world. A city on a hill cannot be hidden. 15. Neither do people light a lamp and put it under a bowl. Instead they put it on its stand, and it gives light to everyone in the house. 16. In the same way, let your light shine before men, that they may see your good deeds and praise your Father in heaven. 17. Do not think that I have come to abolish the Law or the Prophets; I have not come to abolish them but to fulfil them. 18. I tell you the truth, until heaven and earth disappear, not the smallest letter, not the least stroke of a pen, will by any means disappear from the Law until everything is accomplished. 19. Anyone who breaks one of the least of these commandments and teaches others to do the same will be called least in the kingdom of heaven, but whoever practises and teaches these commands will be called great in the kingdom of heaven. 20. For I tell you that unless your righteousness surpasses that of the Pharisees and the teachers of the law, you will certainly not enter the kingdom of heaven. 21. You have heard that it was said to the people long ago, 'Do not murder, and anyone who murders will be subject to judgment.' 22. But I tell you that anyone who is angry with his brother will be subject to judgment. Again, anyone who says to his brother, 'Raca,' is answerable to the Sanhedrin. But anyone who says, 'You fool!' will be in danger of the fire of hell. 23. Therefore, if you are offering your gift at the altar and there remember that your brother has something against you, 24. Leave your gift there in front of the altar. First go and be reconciled to your brother; then come and offer your gift. 25. Settle matters quickly with your adversary who is taking you to court. Do it while you are still with him on the way, or he may hand you over

THE EVOLUTION OF CHRISTS AND CHRISTIANIES

to the judge, and the judge may hand you over to the officer, and you may be thrown into prison. 26. I tell you the truth, you will not get out until you have paid the last penny. 27. You have heard that it was said, 'Do not commit adultery.' 28. But I tell you that anyone who looks at a woman lustfully has already committed adultery with her in his heart. 29. If your right eye causes you to sin, gouge it out and throw it away. It is better for you to lose one part of your body than for your whole body to be thrown into hell. 30. And if your right hand causes you to sin, cut it off and throw it away. It is better for you to lose one part of your body than for your whole body to go into hell. 31. It has been said, 'Anyone who divorces his wife must give her a certificate of divorce.' 32. But I tell you that anyone who divorces his wife, except for marital unfaithfulness, causes her to become an adulteress, and anyone who marries the divorced woman commits adultery. 33. Again, you have heard that it was said to the people long ago, 'Do not break your oath, but keep the oaths you have made to the Lord.' 34. But I tell you, Do not swear at all: either by heaven, for it is God's throne; 35. or by the earth, for it is his footstool; or by Jerusalem, for it is the city of the Great King. 36. And do not swear by your head, for you cannot make even one hair white or black. 37. Simply let your 'Yes' be 'Yes', and your 'No', 'No'; anything beyond this comes from the evil one.

6.1. Be careful not to do your 'acts of righteousness' before men, to be seen by them. If you do, you will have no reward from your Father in heaven. 2. So when you give to the needy, do not announce it with trumpets, as the hypocrites do in the synagogues and on the streets, to be honoured by men. I tell you the truth, they have received their reward in full. 3. But when you give to the needy, do not let your left hand know what your right hand is doing, 4. so that your giving may be in secret. Then your Father, who sees what is done in secret, will reward you. 5. And when you pray, do not be like the hypocrites, for they love to pray standing in the synagogues and on the street corners to be seen by men. I tell you the truth, they have received their reward in full. 6. But when you pray, go into your room, close the door and pray to your Father, who is unseen. Then your Father, who sees what is done in secret, will reward you. 7. And when you pray, do not keep on babbling like pagans, for they think they will be heard because of their many words. 8. Do not be like them, for your Father knows what you need before you ask him. 9. This, then, is how you should pray[458]: 'Our Father in heaven, hallowed be your name, 10. your kingdom come, your will be done on earth as it is in heaven. 11. Give us today our daily bread. 12. Forgive us our debts, as we also have forgiven our debtors. 13. And lead us not into temptation, but deliver us from the evil one.' 14. For if you forgive men when they sin against you, your heavenly Father will also forgive you. 15. But if you do not forgive men their sins, your Father will not forgive your sins. 16. When you fast, do not look sombre as the hypocrites do, for they disfigure their faces to show men they are fasting. I tell you the truth, they have received their reward in full. 17. But when you fast, put oil on your head and wash your face, 18. so that it will not be obvious to men that you are fasting, but only to your Father, who is unseen; and your Father, who sees what is done in secret, will reward you. 19. Do not store up for yourselves treasures on earth, where moth and rust destroy, and where thieves break in and steal. 20. But store up for yourselves treasures in heaven, where moth and rust do not destroy, and where thieves do not break in and steal. 21. For where your treasure is, there your heart will be also. 22. The eye is the lamp of the body. If your eyes are good, your whole body will be full of light. 23. But if your eyes are bad, your whole body will be full of darkness. If then the light within you is darkness, how great is that darkness! 24. No-one can serve two masters. Either he will hate the one and love the other, or he will be devoted to the one and despise the other. You cannot serve both God and Money. 25. Therefore I tell you, do not worry about your life, what you will eat or drink; or about your body, what you will wear. Is not life more important than food, and the body more important than clothes? 26. Look at the birds of the air; they do not sow or reap or store away in barns, and yet your heavenly Father feeds them. Are you not much more valuable than they? 27. Who of you by worrying can add a single hour to his life? 28. And why do you worry about clothes? See how the lilies of the field grow. They do not labour or spin. 29. Yet I tell you that not even Solomon in all his splendour was dressed like one of these. 30. If that is how God clothes the grass of the field, which is here today and tomorrow is thrown into the fire, will he not much more clothe you, O you of little faith? 31. So do not worry, saying, 'What shall we eat?' or 'What shall we drink?' or 'What shall we wear?' 32. For the pagans run after all these things, and your heavenly Father knows that you need them. 33. But seek first his kingdom and his righteousness, and all these things will be given to you as well. 34. Therefore do not worry about tomorrow, for tomorrow will worry about itself. Each day has enough trouble of its own.

7.1. Do not judge, or you too will be judged. 2. For in the same way as you judge others, you will be judged, and with the measure you use, it will be measured to you. 3. Why do you look at the speck of sawdust in your brother's eye and pay no attention to the plank in your own eye? 4. How can you say to your brother, 'Let me take the speck out of your eye,' when all the time there is a plank in your own eye? 5. You hypocrite, first take the plank out of your own eye, and then you will see clearly to remove the speck from your brother's eye. 6. Do not give dogs what is sacred; do not throw your pearls to pigs. If you do, they may trample them under their feet, and then turn and tear you to pieces. 7. Ask and it will be given to you; seek and you will find; knock and the door will be opened to you. 8. For everyone who asks receives; he who seeks finds; and to him who knocks, the door will be opened. 9. Which of you, if his son asks for bread, will give him a stone? 10. Or if he asks for a fish, will give him a snake? 11. If you, then, though you are evil, know how to give good gifts to your children, how much more will your Father in heaven give good gifts to those who ask him! 12. So in everything, do to others what you would have them do to you, for this sums up the Law and the Prophets. 13. Enter through the narrow gate. For wide is the gate and broad is the road that leads to destruction, and many enter through it. 14. But small is the gate and narrow the road that leads to life, and only a few find it. 15. Watch out for false prophets. They come to you in sheep's clothing, but inwardly they are ferocious wolves. 16. By their fruit you will recognise them. Do people pick grapes from thornbushes, or figs from thistles? 17. Likewise every good tree bears good fruit, but a bad tree bears bad fruit. 18. A good tree cannot bear bad fruit, and a bad tree cannot bear good fruit. 19. Every tree that does not bear good fruit is cut down and thrown into the fire. 20. Thus, by their fruit you will recognise them. 21. Not everyone who says to me, 'Lord, Lord,' will enter the kingdom of heaven, but only he who does the will of my Father who is in heaven. 22. Many will say to me on that day, 'Lord, Lord, did we not prophesy in your name, and in your name drive out demons and perform many miracles?' 23. Then I will tell them plainly, 'I never knew you. Away from me, you evildoers!' 24. Therefore everyone who hears these words of mine and puts them into practice is like a wise man who built his house on the rock. 25. The rain came down, the streams rose, and the winds blew and beat against that house; yet it did not fall, because it had its foundation on the rock. 26. But everyone who hears these words of mine and does not put them into practice is like a foolish man who built his house on sand. 27. The rain came down, the streams rose, and the winds blew and beat against that house, and it fell with a great crash.

[Matthew 8.1 ends this section]

> 8.1. When he came down from the mountainside, large crowds followed him.

[Matthew 9.36 resumes]

> 9.36. When he saw the crowds, he had compassion for them, because they were harassed and helpless, like sheep without a shepherd. 9.37 Then he said to his disciples, "The harvest is plentiful, but the laborers are few; 9.38 pray therefore the Lord of the harvest to send out laborers into his harvest."

[While Matthew left the earlier Sermon on the Mount Speech pretty much alone, he or someone does mix in his other material here. I have separated it out.]

> 10.5. Do not go among the Gentiles or enter any town of the Samaritans. 6. Go rather to the lost sheep of Israel.
> 10.9. Do not take along any gold or silver or copper in your belts; 10. take no bag for the journey, or extra tunic, or sandals or a staff; for the worker is worth his keep. 11. Whatever town or village you enter, search for some worthy person there and stay at his house until you leave. 12. As you enter the home, give it your greeting. 13. If the home is deserving, let your peace rest on it; if it is not, let your peace return to you. 14. If anyone will not welcome you or listen to your words, shake the dust off your feet when you leave that home or town. 15. I tell you the truth; it will be more bearable for Sodom and Gomorrah on the day of judgment than for that town. 16. I am sending you out like sheep among wolves. Therefore be as shrewd as snakes and as innocent as doves. 17. Be on your guard against men; they will hand you over to the local councils and flog you in their synagogues. 18. On my account you will be brought before governors and kings as witnesses to them and to the Gentiles. 19. But when they arrest you, do not worry about what to say or how to say it. At that time you will be given what to say, 20. for it will not be you speaking,

THE EVOLUTION OF CHRISTS AND CHRISTIANIES

but the Spirit of your Father speaking through you. 21. Brother will betray brother to death, and a father his child; children will rebel against their parents and have them put to death. 22. All men will hate you because of me, but he who stands firm to the end will be saved. 23. When you are persecuted in one place, flee to another. I tell you the truth, you will not finish going through the cities of Israel before the Son of Man comes. 24. A student is not above his teacher, nor a servant above his master. 25. It is enough for the student to be like his teacher, and the servant like his master

11.7. What did you go out into the desert to see? A reed swayed by the wind? 8. If not, what did you go out to see? A man dressed in fine clothes? No, those who wear fine clothes are in kings' palaces. 9. Then what did you go out to see? A prophet? Yes!

11.12. From the days of Moses until now the kingdom of heaven has suffered violence, and men of violence take it by force. 13. For all the prophets and the law prophesied until now; 14. and if you are willing to accept it, I am Eli'jah who is to come. 15. He who has ears to hear, let him hear.

11.16. To what can I compare this generation? They are like children sitting in the market-places and calling out to others: 17. 'We played the flute for you, and you did not dance; we sang a dirge, and you did not mourn.'

11.21. Woe to you, Korazin! Woe to you, Bethsaida! If the miracles that were performed in you had been performed in Tyre and Sidon, they would have repented long ago in sackcloth and ashes. 22. But I tell you, it will be more bearable for Tyre and Sidon on the day of judgment than for you. 23. And you, Capernaum, will you be lifted up to the skies? No, you will go down to the depths. If the miracles that were performed in you had been performed in Sodom, it would have remained to this day. 24. But I tell you that it will be more bearable for Sodom on the day of judgment than for you. 25. I praise you, Father, Lord of heaven and earth, because you have hidden these things from the wise and learned, and revealed them to little children. 26. Yes, Father, for this was your good pleasure. 27. All things have been committed to me by my Father. No-one knows the Son except the Father, and no-one knows the Father except the Son and those to whom the Son chooses to reveal him. 28. Come to me, all you who are weary and burdened, and I will give you rest. 29. Take my yoke upon you and learn from me, for I am gentle and humble in heart, and you will find rest for your souls. 30. For my yoke is easy and my burden is light.

12.1. His disciples were hungry and began to pick some ears of corn and eat them. 2. When the Pharisees saw this, they said to him, Look! Your disciples are doing what is unlawful on the Sabbath. Haven't you read what David did when he and his companions were hungry? 4. He entered the house of God, and he and his companions ate the consecrated bread—which was not lawful for them to do, but only for the priests. 5 Or haven't you read in the Law that on the Sabbath the priests in the temple desecrate the day and yet are innocent? 6 I tell you that one greater than the temple is here. 7. If you had known what these words mean, 'I desire mercy, not sacrifice,' you would not have condemned the innocent. 8. For the Son of Man is Lord of the Sabbath.

12.34. You brood of vipers, how can you who are evil say anything good? For out of the overflow of the heart the mouth speaks. 35. The good man brings good things out of the good stored up in him, and the evil man brings evil things out of the evil stored up in him. 36. But I tell you that men will have to give account on the day of judgment for every careless word they have spoken. 37. For by your words you will be acquitted, and by your words you will be condemned

12.38. Then some of the Pharisees and teachers of the law said to him, Teacher, we want to see a miraculous sign from you. 39. He answered, A wicked and adulterous generation asks for a miraculous sign! But none will be given it except the sign of the prophet Jonah. 40. For as Jonah was three days and three nights in the belly of a huge fish, so the Son of Man will be three days and three nights in the heart of the earth. 41. The men of Nineveh will stand up at the judgment with this generation and condemn it; for they repented at the preaching of Jonah, and now one greater than Jonah is here. 42. The Queen of the South will rise at the judgment with this generation and condemn it; for she came from the ends of the earth to listen to Solomon's wisdom, and now one greater than Solomon is here. 43. When an evil spirit comes out of a man, it goes through arid places seeking rest and does not find it. 44. Then it says, 'I will return to the house I left.' When it arrives, it finds the house unoccupied, swept clean and put in order. 45. Then it goes and takes with it seven other spirits more wicked than itself, and they go in and live there. And the final condition of that man is worse than the first. That is how it will be with this wicked generation.

13.2 Such large crowds gathered round him that he got into a boat and sat in it, while all the people stood on the shore. 3. And he told them many things in parables[459], saying: "A sower went out to sow. 4. And as he sowed, some seeds fell along the path, and the birds came and devoured them. 5. Other seeds fell on rocky ground, where they had not much soil, and immediately they sprang up, since they had no depth of soil, 6. but when the sun rose they were scorched; and since they had no root they withered away. 7. Other seeds fell upon thorns, and the thorns grew up and choked them. 8. Other seeds fell on good soil and brought forth grain, some a hundredfold, some sixty, some thirty. 9. He who has ears, let him hear." 10. Then the disciples came and said to him, "Why do you speak to them in parables?" 11. And he answered them, "To you it has been given to know the secrets of the kingdom of heaven, but to them it has not been given. 12. For to him who has will more be given, and he will have abundance; but from him who has not, even what he has will be taken away. 13. This is why I speak to them in parables, because seeing they do not see, and hearing they do not hear, nor do they understand. 14. With them indeed is fulfilled the prophecy of Isaiah which says: 'You shall indeed hear but never understand, and you shall indeed see but never perceive. 15. For this people's heart has grown dull, and their ears are heavy of hearing, and their eyes they have closed, lest they should perceive with their eyes, and hear with their ears, and understand with their heart, and turn for me to heal them[460].' 16. But blessed are your eyes, for they see, and your ears, for they hear. 17. Truly, I say to you, many prophets and righteous men longed to see what you see, and did not see it, and to hear what you hear, and did not hear it. 18. "Hear then the parable of the sower. 19. When any one hears the word of the kingdom and does not understand it, the evil one comes and snatches away what is sown in his heart; this is what was sown along the path. 20. As for what was sown on rocky ground, this is he who hears the word and immediately receives it with joy; 21. Yet he has no root in himself, but endures for a while, and when tribulation or persecution arises on account of the word, immediately he falls away. 22. As for what was sown among thorns, this is he who hears the word, but the cares of the world and the delight in riches choke the word, and it proves unfruitful. 23. As for what was sown on good soil, this is he who hears the word and understands it; he indeed bears fruit, and yields, in one case a hundredfold, in another sixty, and in another thirty." 24. Another parable he put before them, saying, "The kingdom of heaven may be compared to a man who sowed good seed in his field; 25. But while men were sleeping, his enemy came and sowed weeds among the wheat, and went away. 26. So when the plants came up and bore grain, then the weeds appeared also. 27. And the servants of the householder came and said to him, 'Sir, did you not sow good seed in your field? How then has it weeds?' 28. He said to them, 'An enemy has done this.' The servants said to him, 'Then do you want us to go and gather them?' 29. But he said, 'No; lest in gathering the weeds you root up the wheat along with them. 30. Let both grow together until the harvest; and at harvest time I will tell the reapers, Gather the weeds first and bind them in bundles to be burned, but gather the wheat into my barn.'" 31. Another parable he put before them, saying, "The kingdom of heaven is like a grain of mustard seed which a man took and sowed in his field; 32. it is the smallest of all seeds, but when it has grown it is the greatest of shrubs and becomes a tree, so that the birds of the air come and make nests in its branches." 33. He told them another parable. "The kingdom of heaven is like leaven which a woman took and hid in three measures of flour, till it was all leavened." 44. The kingdom of heaven is like treasure hidden in a field, which a man found and covered up; then in his joy he goes and sells all that he has and buys that field. 45. "Again, the kingdom of heaven is like a merchant in search of fine pearls, 46.who, on finding one pearl of great value, went and sold all that he had and bought it. 47. "The kingdom of heaven is like a net which was thrown into the sea and gathered fish of every kind 48.when it was full, men drew it ashore and sat down and sorted the good into vessels but threw away the bad. 49. So it will be at the close of the age. The angels will come out and separate the evil from the righteous, 50. and throw them into the furnace of fire; there men will weep and gnash their teeth. 51. "Have you understood all this?" They said to him, "Yes." 52. And he said to them, "Therefore every scribe who has been trained for the kingdom of heaven is like a householder who brings out of his treasure what is new and what is old."

THE EVOLUTION OF CHRISTS AND CHRISTIANIES

14.1. At that time Herod the tetrarch heard about the fame of Jesus [John]; 14.2. and he said to his servants, "This is John the Baptist [Eli'jah], he has been raised from the dead; that is why these powers are at work in him."

15.2. Then some Pharisees and teachers of the law came... from Jerusalem and asked, Why do your disciples break the tradition of the elders? They don't wash their hands before they eat! 3. ... Jesus [John] replied, And why do you break the command of God for the sake of your tradition? 4. For God said, 'Honour your father and mother' and 'Anyone who curses his father or mother must be put to death.' 5. But you say that if a man says to his father or mother, 'Whatever help you might otherwise have received from me is a gift devoted to God,' 6. he is not to 'honour his father' with it. Thus you nullify the word of God for the sake of your tradition. 7. You hypocrites! Isaiah was right when he prophesied about you: 8. 'These people honour me with their lips, but their hearts are far from me. 9. They worship me in vain; their teachings are but rules taught by men. 10. And he called the people to him and said to them, "Hear and understand: 11. not what goes into the mouth defiles a man, but what comes out of the mouth, this defiles a man." 12. Then the disciples came to him and asked, Do you know that the Pharisees were offended when they heard this? 13. He replied, Every plant that my heavenly Father has not planted will be pulled up by the roots. 14. Leave them; they are blind guides. If a blind man leads a blind man, both will fall into a pit.

18.2. He called a little child and had him stand among them. 3. And he said: I tell you the truth, unless you change and become like little children, you will never enter the kingdom of heaven. 4. Therefore, whoever humbles himself like this child is the greatest in the kingdom of heaven. 5. And whoever welcomes a little child like this in my name welcomes me. 6. But if anyone causes one of these little ones who believe in me to sin, it would be better for him to have a large millstone hung around his neck and to be drowned in the depths of the sea. 7. Woe to the world because of the things that cause people to sin! Such things must come, but woe to the man through whom they come! 8. If your hand or your foot causes you to sin, cut it off and throw it away. It is better for you to enter life maimed or crippled than to have two hands or two feet and be thrown into eternal fire. 9. And if your eye causes you to sin, gouge it out and throw it away. It is better for you to enter life with one eye than to have two eyes and be thrown into the fire of hell. 10-11. See that you do not look down on one of these little ones. For I tell you that their angels in heaven always see the face of my Father in heaven. 12. What do you think? If a man owns a hundred sheep, and one of them wanders away, will he not leave the ninety-nine on the hills and go to look for the one that wandered off? 13. And if he finds it, I tell you the truth, he is happier about that one sheep than about the ninety-nine that did not wander off. 14. In the same way your Father in heaven is not willing that any of these little ones should be lost. 15. If your brother sins against you, go and show him his fault, just between the two of you. If he listens to you, you have won your brother over. 16. But if he will not listen, take one or two others along, so that 'every matter may be established by the testimony of two or three witnesses.' 17. If he refuses to listen to them, tell it to the church; and if he refuses to listen even to the church, treat him as you would a pagan or a tax collector. 18. I tell you the truth, whatever you bind on earth will be bound in heaven, and whatever you loose on earth will be loosed in heaven. 19. Again, I tell you that if two of you on earth agree about anything you ask for, it will be done for you by my Father in heaven. 20. For where two or three come together in my name, there am I with them. 21. Then Peter came up and said to him, "Lord, how often shall my brother sin against me, and I forgive him? As many as seven times? 22. Jesus [John] said to him, "I do not say to you seven times, but seventy times seven. 23. Therefore, the kingdom of heaven is like a king who wanted to settle accounts with his servants. 24. As he began the settlement, a man who owed him ten thousand talents was brought to him. 25. Since he was not able to pay, the master ordered that he and his wife and his children and all that he had be sold to repay the debt. 26. The servant fell on his knees before him. 'Be patient with me,' he begged, 'and I will pay back everything.' 27. The servant's master took pity on him, cancelled the debt and let him go. 28. But when that servant went out, he found one of his fellow—servants who owed him a hundred denarii. He grabbed him and began to choke him. 'Pay back what you owe me!' he demanded. 29. His fellow—servant fell to his knees and begged him, 'Be patient with me, and I will pay you back.' 30. But he refused. Instead, he went off and had the man thrown into prison until he could pay the debt. 31. When the other servants saw what had happened, they were greatly distressed and went and told their master everything that had happened. 32. Then the master called the servant in. 'You wicked servant,' he said, 'I cancelled all that debt of yours because you begged me to. 33. Shouldn't you have had mercy on your fellow—servant just as I had on you?' 34. In anger his master turned him over to the jailers to be tortured, until he should pay back all he owed. 35. This is how my heavenly Father will treat each of you unless you forgive your brother from your heart.

21.23 while he was teaching, the chief priests and the elders of the people came to him. By what authority are you doing these things? they asked. And who gave you this authority?

21.28. What do you think? There was a man who had two sons. He went to the first and said, 'Son, go and work today in the vineyard.' 29. 'I will not,' he answered, but later he changed his mind and went. 30. Then the father went to the other son and said the same thing. He answered, 'I will, sir,' but he did not go. 31 Which of the two did what his father wanted? The first, they answered. 33. "Hear another parable. There was a householder who planted a vineyard, and set a hedge around it, and dug a wine press in it, and built a tower, and let it out to tenants, and went into another country. 34. When the season of fruit drew near, he sent his servants to the tenants, to get his fruit; 35. and the tenants took his servants and beat one, killed another, and stoned another. 36. Again he sent other servants, more than the first; and they did the same to them. 37. Afterward he sent his son to them, saying, 'They will respect my son.' 38. But when the tenants saw the son, they said to themselves, 'This is the heir; come, let us kill him and have his inheritance.' 39. And they took him and cast him out of the vineyard, and killed him. 40. When therefore the owner of the vineyard comes, what will he do to those tenants?" 41. They said to him, "He will put those wretches to a miserable death, and let out the vineyard to other tenants who will give him the fruits in their seasons." 42. Jesus [John] said to them, "Have you never read in the scriptures: 'The very stone which the builders rejected has become the head of the corner; this was the Lord's doing, and it is marvelous in our eyes'? 43. Therefore I tell you, the kingdom of God will be taken away from you and given to a nation producing the fruits of it." 44. And whosoever shall fall on this stone shall be broken: but on whomsoever it shall fall, it will grind him to powder. 45. When the chief priests and the Pharisees heard his parables, they perceived that he was speaking about them. 46. But when they tried to arrest him, they feared the multitudes, because they held him to be a prophet.

22.2 The kingdom of heaven is like a king who prepared a wedding banquet for his son. 3. He sent his servants to those who had been invited to the banquet to tell them to come, but they refused to come. 4. Then he sent some more servants and said, 'Tell those who have been invited that I have prepared my dinner: My oxen and fattened cattle have been slaughtered, and everything is ready. Come to the wedding banquet.' 5. But they paid no attention and went off—one to his field, another to his business. 6. The rest seized his servants, ill-treated them and killed them. 7. The king was enraged. He sent his army and destroyed those murderers and burned their city. 8. Then he said to his servants, 'The wedding banquet is ready, but those I invited did not deserve to come. 9. Go to the street corners and invite to the banquet anyone you find.' 10. So the servants went out into the streets and gathered all the people they could find, both good and bad, and the wedding hall was filled with guests. 11. But when the king came in to see the guests, he noticed a man there who was not wearing wedding clothes. 12. 'Friend,' he asked, 'how did you get in here without wedding clothes?' The man was speechless. 13. Then the king told the attendants, 'Tie him hand and foot, and throw him outside, into the darkness, where there will be weeping and gnashing of teeth.' 14. For many are invited, but few are chosen. 15. Then the Pharisees went out and laid plans to trap him in his words. 16. They sent their disciples to him along with the Herodians. Teacher, they said, we know you are a man of integrity and that you teach the way of God in accordance with the truth. You aren't swayed by men, because you pay no attention to who they are. Tell us then, what is your opinion? Is it right to pay taxes to Caesar or not? 18 ... said, You hypocrites, why are you trying to trap me? 19. Show me the coin used for paying the tax. They brought him a denarius, 20. and he asked them, Whose portrait is this? And whose inscription?

21. Caesar's, they replied. Then he said to them, Give to Caesar what is Caesar's, and to God what is God's. 22. When they heard this, they were amazed. So they left him and went away. 23. That same day the Sadducees, who say there is no resurrection, came to him with a question. 24. Teacher, they said, Moses told us that if a man dies without having children, his brother must marry

the widow and have children for him. 25. Now there were seven brothers among us. The first one married and died, and since he had no children, he left his wife to his brother. 26. The same thing happened to the second and third brother, right on down to the seventh. 27. Finally, the woman died. 28. Now then, at the resurrection, whose wife will she be of the seven, since all of them were married to her? 29. [John] replied, "You are in error because you do not know the Scriptures or the power of God. 30. At the resurrection people will neither marry nor be given in marriage; they will be like the angels in heaven. 31. But about the resurrection of the dead—have you not read what God said to you, 32. 'I am the God of Abraham, the God of Isaac, and the God of Jacob'?" 33. And when the crowd heard it, they were astonished at his teaching. He is not the God of the dead but of the living. 34. But when the Pharisees heard that he had silenced the Sad'ducees, they came together. 35. And one of them, a lawyer, asked him a question, to test him. 36. "Teacher, which is the great commandment in the law?" 37. And he said to him, "You shall love the Lord your God with all your heart, and with all your soul, and with all your mind. 38. This is the great and first commandment. 39. And a second is like it, You shall love your neighbor as yourself.

40. On these two commandments depend all the law and the prophets." 41. Now while the Pharisees were gathered together, Jesus [John] asked them a question, 42. saying, "What do you think of the Christ? Whose son is he?" They said to him, "The son of David."

43. He said to them, "How is it then that David, inspired by the Spirit, calls him Lord, saying, 44. 'The Lord said to my Lord, Sit at my right hand, till I put thy enemies under thy feet'? 45. If David thus calls him Lord, how is he his son?"

46. And no one was able to answer him a word, nor from that day did any one dare to ask him any more questions.

23.1. Jesus [John] said to the crowds and to his disciples: 2 The teachers of the law and the Pharisees sit in Moses' seat. 3. So you must obey them and do everything they tell you. But do not do what they do, for they do not practise what they preach. 4. They tie up heavy loads and put them on men's shoulders, but they themselves are not willing to lift a finger to move them. 5. Everything they do is done for men to see: They make their phylacteries wide and the tassels on their garments long; 6. they love the place of honour at banquets and the most important seats in the synagogues; 7. they love to be greeted in the marketplaces and to have men call them 'Rabbi'. 8. But you are not to be called 'Rabbi', for you have only one Master and you are all brothers. 9. And do not call anyone on earth 'father', for you have one Father, and he is in heaven. 10. Nor are you to be called 'teacher', for you have one Teacher, the Christ. 11. The greatest among you will be your servant. 12. For whoever exalts himself will be humbled, and whoever humbles himself will be exalted. 13. Woe to you, teachers of the law and Pharisees, you hypocrites! You shut the kingdom of heaven in men's faces. You yourselves do not enter, nor will you let those enter who are trying to. 15. Woe to you, teachers of the law and Pharisees, you hypocrites! You travel over land and sea to win a single convert, and when he becomes one, you make him twice as much a son of hell as you are. 16 Woe to you, blind guides! You say, 'If anyone swears by the temple, it means nothing; but if anyone swears by the gold of the temple, he is bound by his oath.' 17. You blind fools! Which is greater: the gold, or the temple that makes the gold sacred? 18. You also say, 'If anyone swears by the altar, it means nothing; but if anyone swears by the gift on it, he is bound by his oath.' 19. You blind men! Which is greater: the gift, or the altar that makes the gift sacred? 20. Therefore, he who swears by the altar swears by it and by everything on it. 21. And he who swears by the temple swears by it and by the one who dwells in it. 22. And he who swears by heaven swears by God's throne and by the one who sits on it. 23. Woe to you, teachers of the law and Pharisees, you hypocrites! You give a tenth of your spices—mint, dill and cummin. But you have neglected the more important matters of the law—justice, mercy and faithfulness. You should have practiced the later, without neglecting the former. 24. You blind guides! You strain out a gnat but swallow a camel. 25. Woe to you, teachers of the law and Pharisees, you hypocrites! You clean the outside of the cup and dish, but inside they are full of greed and self-indulgence. 26. Blind Pharisee! First clean the inside of the cup and dish, and then the outside also will be clean. 27. Woe to you, teachers of the law and Pharisees, you hypocrites! You are like whitewashed tombs, which looks beautiful on the outside but on the inside are full of dead men's bones and everything unclean. 28. In the same way, on the outside you appear to people as righteous but on the inside you are full of hypocrisy and wickedness. 29. Woe to you, teachers of the law and Pharisees, you hypocrites! You build tombs for the prophets and decorate the graves of the righteous. 30. And you say, 'If we had lived in the days of our forefathers, we would not have taken part with them in shedding the blood of the prophets.' 31. So you testify against yourselves that you are the descendants of those who murdered the prophets. 32. Fill up, then, the measure of the sin of your forefathers! 33. You snakes! You brood of vipers! How will you escape being condemned to hell? 34. Therefore I am sending you prophets and wise men and teachers. Some of them you will kill and crucify; others you will flog in your synagogues and pursue from town to town. 35. And so upon you will come all the righteous blood that has been shed on earth, from the blood of righteous Abel to the blood of Zechariah son of Berakiah, whom you murdered between the temple and the altar. 36. I tell you the truth, all this will come upon this generation. 37. O Jerusalem, Jerusalem, you who kill the prophets and stone those sent to you, how often I have longed to gather your children together, as a hen gathers her chicks under her wings, but you were not willing. 38. Look, your house is left to you desolate. 39. For I tell you, you will not see me again until you say, 'Blessed is he who comes in the name of the Lord.'

Conclusions and New Beginnings: Drawing John the Baptist and Jesus Christ from Eleazar and Joshua, Coloring from the Book of Malachi

> Suppose the figure of the pre-Easter Jesus is to be found under the alias of John the Baptist. When we impose this outlandish paradigm onto the gospels, we get some interesting results. A number of things make new sense[461].
>
> Robert M. Price

Robert M. Price has perceptively noted the similarities between Jesus and John the Baptist and has pointed out that a large section of people really believed that Jesus was John resurrected. He suggests that a split occurred within the John the Baptist movement between those who believed John had been resurrected as a Christ and those who simply held John as a prophet without resurrection. This comes very close to our position. We believe that a split came within the John movement between those who regarded John as a prophet and those who regarded him as the Christ. Only when the fictional character of Mary's play about Christ was incorporated into John the

Baptist Material did the idea that Jesus was John reincarnated pop up. Within the John movement, the question was first "Was he just a prophet or Elijah reincarnated?"

Price brilliantly and insightfully suggests that John the Baptist was an historical figure, while Jesus Christ is just a legend about him. In the sense that we have historical evidence from Josephus that a follower of Moses led a Samaritan revolt and was captured and executed by Pilate, and we may deduce that his name was John, John did exist. This is technically correct. However, I think the literary character John the Baptist is also made of the same literary stuff as Jesus Christ. He is made up of bits and pieces out of the Book of the Prophet Malachi (which means, I believe, "My Messenger"). Here are the relevant passages recycled to bring John the Baptist and his resurrected alter ego Jesus to literary life.

> Another thing you do: You flood the LORD's altar with tears. You weep and wail because he no longer pays attention to your offerings or accepts them with pleasure from your hands. You ask, Why? It is because the LORD is acting as the witness between you and the wife of your youth, because you have broken faith with her, though she is your partner, the wife of your marriage covenant. Has not the LORD made them one? In flesh and spirit they are his. And why one? Because he was seeking godly offspring. So guard yourself in your spirit, and do not break faith with the wife of your youth. I hate divorce, says the LORD God of Israel . . . [462]

John the Baptist's as well as Jesus' well known opposition to divorce comes from these lines.

> See, I will send my messenger, who will prepare the way before me. Then suddenly the Lord you are seeking will come to his temple; the messenger of the covenant, whom you desire, will come, says the LORD Almighty. But who can endure the day of his coming? Who can stand when he appears? For he will be like a refiner's fire or a launderer's soap. He will sit as a refiner and purifier of silver; he will purify the Levites and refine them like gold and silver[463].

John the Baptist as the preparer of the way of the Lord, as well as Jesus' dividing the chaff from the wheat proverbs come from these lines.

> Surely the day is coming; it will burn like a furnace. All the arrogant and every evildoer will be stubble, and that day that is coming will set them on fire, says the LORD Almighty. Not a root or a branch will be left to them. But for you who revere my name, the sun of righteousness will rise with healing in its wings. And you will go out and leap like

> calves released from the stall. Then you will trample down the wicked; they will be ashes under the soles of your feet on the day when I do these things, says the LORD Almighty. Remember the law of my servant Moses, the decrees and laws I gave him at Horeb for all Israel. See, I will send you the prophet Elijah before that great and dreadful day of the LORD comes. He will turn the hearts of the fathers to their children, and the hearts of the children to their fathers; or else I will come and strike the land with a curse.

Here we get the idea of the kingdom of God being at hand and John the Baptist as Elijah *redividus*. We also get the idea of Jesus coming to set fire and turning children and fathers against each other, as a curse from God.

Likely Zechariah is John's father because the Book of Zechariah comes just before the Book of Malachi and the two books seem related as father to son. The mother Elizabeth comes from Exodus—Aaron married Elisheba, daughter of Amminadab and sister of Nahshon, and she bore him Nadab and Abihu, Eleazar and Ithamar[464].

It is her role as mother of Eleazar that Elizabeth lands the role of the mother of John. Eleazar became the first High Priest of the Hebrews after Aaron. Most importantly, he blessed and worked with Joshua the Anointed One (Jesus Christ in Greek).

> So the LORD said to Moses, "Take Joshua son of Nun, a man in whom is the spirit, and lay your hand on him. Have him stand before Eleazar the priest and the entire assembly and commission him in their presence. Give him some of your authority so the whole Israelite community will obey him[465].

So the choice of Elizabeth as the name of John's mother comes from Elisheba the mother of Eleazar who gave his authority to Joshua the Christ, who won great military victories for the Hebrews, while the name of the father comes from the (prophetic) father of Malachi who predicted the coming of the day of the Lord. Thus John the Baptist comes from a marriage of the Torah and the Prophets. It is a marriage made not on Earth or Heaven, but in the scriptoriums of the Scribes.

While it is likely the events in the life of the historical figure of John, the Nazarene inspired the material about him, much of that material was derived from the scriptures and lives of the people who wrote about him.

Gravestone. Magician Christ Raises Lazarus with a Wand

Gravestone of Datus, 3rd century. The image eloquently shows the desire for a return to life.

Chapter 8

The Birth of John/Jesus

We have so far ignored the birth material at the beginning of the gospels of Luke and Matthew. While added late to the canonical gospels, they represent a very early layer of material.

But first, let us examine more closely the relationship of John the Baptist and Jesus Christ. One quickly notices certain odd chronological parallels. The Angel Gabriel told Jesus' father that he is going to have a holy son[466] a few months after he told John the Baptist's father that he is going to have a holy son[467]. Jesus is born a few months after John the Baptist is born[468]. Jesus receives the word of God a few months after John the Baptist[469] receives the word of God. Jesus begins to preach the Kingdom of God is near a few months after John the Baptist[470] begins to preach. Jesus starts baptizing people a few months after John the Baptist[471] starts baptizing people. Andrew (and perhaps Peter) becomes a disciple of Jesus a few months after becoming a disciple of Jesus[472]. Jesus dies by order of a high Roman official a few months after John the Baptist dies by order of a high Roman official. Events in Jesus' life duplicate John's life like an echo.

Theologically, both during the time the gospels were produced and today, this echoing is taken as proof that John the Baptist was the forerunner of Jesus. If we do not take this as history, we may see these coincidences rather as the development of literary narratives designed to show John the Baptist as the forerunner of Jesus. More importantly, they indicate that just as the gospel writers had no speeches for Jesus and had to borrow speeches from John the Baptist, the gospel writers had no details of the life of Jesus and had to borrow them from a narrative of the life of John the Baptist. In this literary sense, John the Baptist really was the forerunner of Jesus the Christ.

The birth narrative is borrowed and revised from John material, the baptism narrative is borrowed and revised, the transfiguration on the Mountain material is

411

borrowed and revised, and possibly even some of the trial material is borrowed and revised. On the other hand, the magician and miracle material seems to come from an entirely independent tradition.

But the term "borrowing" is misused here. Under modern copyright laws, it would be considered "stealing." Yet neither of these concepts really apply. Borrowing implies something owned by another will be returned. The Jesus worshippers who used the John the Baptist materials did not intend to return it. Copyright laws did not exist before the 18th Century. Using or rewriting material from others was fine from a legal standpoint. There was no commandment "Thou shall not copy other people's material."

However, copying well known material and putting your name on it was considered forgery and would get you a bad reputation. What was not considered forgery but a positive and creative act was taking material from different sources and compiling it, reusing it in new ways so that new connections could be seen. If one had material from source "A" and material from source "B," one could make a thesis explaining material "A" and "B" and add material "C" to prove it. Someone else could then take material "A," "B,"and "C" and write a different thesis explaining it and add "D" material to it. If the material from "A," "B," and "C" was well known, one could just give the thesis, add "D" to prove it and allow the reader to refer back to "A," "B," and "C". The "D" additions did not have to be exactly the same form as the "A," "B," or "C" material. Minor additions to the prior material "A," "B," or "C" was also quite acceptable. In fact, this was not just acceptable but considered scholarly *Midrash*.

This process of new thesis and additional material to prove it can be seen in the development of the gospels (birth announcements) of Jesus and John. The original model material for these gospels we find in the Hebrew Scriptures in Genesis 16.7-12, 17.15-21, and 18.10-15:

> The angel of the LORD found Hagar near a spring in the desert; it was the spring that is beside the road to Shur. And he said, "Hagar, servant of Sarai, where have you come from, and where are you going?" "I'm running away from my mistress," Sarai, she answered. Then the angel of the LORD told her, "Go back to your mistress and submit to her." The angel added, "I will so increase your descendants that they will be too numerous to count." The angel of the LORD also said to her, "You are now with child and you will have a son. You shall name him Ishmael, for the LORD has heard of your misery. He will be a wild donkey of a man; his hand will be against everyone and everyone's hand against him, and he will live in hostility towards all his brothers."
>
> God also said to Abraham, "As for Sarai your wife, you are no longer to call her Sarai; her name will be Sarah. I will bless her and will surely give you a son by her. I will bless her so that she will be the mother of nations; kings of peoples will come from her." Abraham fell facedown;

he laughed and said to himself, "Will a son be born to a man a hundred years old? Will Sarah bear a child at the age of ninety?" And Abraham said to God, "If only Ishmael might live under your blessing!" Then God said, "Yes, but your wife Sarah will bear you a son, and you will call him Isaac. I will establish my covenant with him as an everlasting covenant for his descendants after him. [20] And as for Ishmael, I have heard you: I will surely bless him; I will make him fruitful and will greatly increase his numbers. He will be the father of twelve rulers, and I will make him into a great nation. But my covenant I will establish with Isaac, whom Sarah will bear to you by this time next year."

Then the LORD said, "I will surely return to you about this time next year, and Sarah your wife will have a son." Now Sarah was listening at the entrance to the tent, which was behind him. Abraham and Sarah were already old and well advanced in years, and Sarah was past the age of childbearing. So Sarah laughed to herself as she thought, "After I am worn out and my master is old, will I now have this pleasure?" Then the LORD said to Abraham, "Why did Sarah laugh and say, 'Will I really have a child, now that I am old?' Is anything too hard for the LORD? I will return to you at the appointed time next year and Sarah will have a son." Sarah was afraid, so she lied and said, "I did not laugh." But he said, "Yes, you did laugh."

This material, with a few other motifs, are mixed together to get the birth announcement of John the Baptist early in Luke at 1.05-20:

In the days of Herod, king of Judea, there was a priest named Zechari'ah, of the division of Abi'jah; and he had a wife of the daughters of Aaron, and her name was Elizabeth. And they were both righteous before God, walking in all the commandments and ordinances of the Lord blameless. But they had no child, because Elizabeth was barren, and both were advanced in years. Now while he was serving as priest before God when his division was on duty, according to the custom of the priesthood, it fell to him by lot to enter the temple of the Lord and burn incense. And the whole multitude of the people were praying outside at the hour of incense. And there appeared to him an angel of the Lord standing on the right side of the altar of incense. And Zechari'ah was troubled when he saw him, and fear fell upon him. But the angel said to him, "Do not be afraid, Zechari'ah, for your prayer is heard, and your wife Elizabeth will bear you a son, and you shall call his name John. And you will have joy and gladness, and many will rejoice at his birth; for he will be great before the Lord, and he shall drink no wine nor strong drink, and he will be filled with the Holy Spirit, even from his mother's womb. And he will turn many of the sons of Israel to the Lord their God, and he will go before him in the spirit and power of Eli'jah, to turn the hearts of the fathers to the children, and the disobedient to the wisdom of the just, to make ready for the Lord a people prepared." And Zechari'ah said to the angel, "How shall I know this? For I am an old man, and my wife is advanced in years." And the angel answered him, "I am Gabriel, who stand in the presence of God; and I was sent to speak to you, and to bring you this good news. And behold, you will be silent and unable to speak until the day that these things come to pass, because you did not believe my words, which will be fulfilled in their time."

Like Abraham, Zechariah is elderly and does not believe a son is possible. It is quite fantastic that a devout Jew, already knowing the story of Abraham, would have such an attitude upon a visitation from an angel, and coincidentally virtually repeat the skeptical words of Abraham. It is evident that the editor of Luke was using material from John the Baptist followers already in existence. He kept the story of John's birth pretty well intact, simply interspersing the new material about the birth of Jesus between large sections, just as the editor of Matthew had done with the speech of John the Baptist. In fact since the *modus operandi* is so similar between this beginning material and the rest of Matthew, I would suggest it is possible that the beginning birth material now in Luke was originally attached to the Gospel of Matthew. The John the Baptist birth material continues at Luke 1.57:

57. Now the time came for Elizabeth to be delivered, and she gave birth to a son.
58. And her neighbors and kinsfolk heard that the Lord had shown great mercy to her, and they rejoiced with her. 59. And on the eighth day they came to circumcise the child; and they would have named him Zechari'ah after his father, 60. but his mother said, "Not so; he shall be called John." 61. And they said to her, "None of your kindred is called by this name." 62. And they made signs to his father, inquiring what he would have him called. 63. And he asked for a writing tablet, and wrote, "His name is John." And they all marveled. 64:And immediately his mouth was opened and his tongue loosed, and he spoke, blessing God. 65. And fear came on all their neighbors. And all these things were talked about through all the hill country of Judea; 66. and all who heard them laid them up in their hearts, saying, "What then will this child be?" For the hand of the Lord was with him. 67. And his father Zechari'ah was filled with the Holy Spirit, and prophesied, saying, 68. "Blessed be

THE EVOLUTION OF CHRISTS AND CHRISTIANIES

the Lord God of Israel, for he has visited and redeemed his people, 69. and has raised up a horn of salvation for us in the house of his servant David, 70. as he spoke by the mouth of his holy prophets from of old, 71. that we should be saved from our enemies, and from the hand of all who hate us; 72. to perform the mercy promised to our fathers, and to remember his holy covenant, 73. the oath which he swore to our father Abraham, 74. to grant us that we, being delivered from the hand of our enemies, might serve him without fear, 75. in holiness and righteousness before him all the days of our life. 76. And you, child, will be called the prophet of the Most High; for you will go before the Lord to prepare his ways, 77. to give knowledge of salvation to his people in the forgiveness of their sins, 78. through the tender mercy of our God, when the day shall dawn upon us from on high 79. to give light to those who sit in darkness and in the shadow of death, to guide our feet into the way of peace." 80. And the child grew and became strong in spirit, and he was in the wilderness till the day of his manifestation to Israel.

These two paragraphs about John the Baptist probably formed the prologue to the "Teachings of John the Baptist, which begins (Matthew 3.1) "In those days came John the Baptist, preaching in the wilderness of Judea." The Jesus birth material is created to give a new explanation of the idea that "the prophet of Most High . . . will go before the lord to prepare his ways." The writer has closely modeled his material on the prior material (Luke 1:24-54).

24. After these days his wife Elizabeth conceived, and for five months she hid herself, saying, 25."Thus the Lord has done to me in the days when he looked on me, to take away my reproach among men." 26. In the sixth month the angel Gabriel was sent from God to a city of Galilee named Nazareth, 27. to a virgin betrothed to a man whose name was Joseph, of the house of David; and the virgin's name was Mary. 28. And he came to her and said, "Hail, O favored one, the Lord is with you!" 29. But she was greatly troubled at the saying, and considered in her mind what sort of greeting this might be.
30. And the angel said to her, "Do not be afraid, Mary, for you have found favor with God. 31. And behold, you will conceive in your womb and bear a son, and you shall call his name Jesus. 32. He will be great, and will be called the Son of the Most High; and the Lord God will give to him the throne of his father David, 33. and he will reign over the house of Jacob for ever; and of his kingdom there will be no end." 34. And Mary said to the angel, "How shall this be,

since I have no husband?" 35. And the angel said to her, "The Holy Spirit will come upon you, and the power of the Most High will overshadow you; therefore the child to be born will be called holy, the Son of God. 36. And behold, your kinswoman Elizabeth in her old age has also conceived a son; and this is the sixth month with her who was called barren. 37. For with God nothing will be impossible."

38. And Mary said, "Behold, I am the handmaid of the Lord; let it be to me according to your word." And the angel departed from her. 39. In those days Mary arose and went with haste into the hill country, to a city of Judah, 40. and she entered the house of Zechari'ah and greeted Elizabeth. 41. And when Elizabeth heard the greeting of Mary, the babe leaped in her womb; and Elizabeth was filled with the Holy Spirit

42. and she exclaimed with a loud cry, "Blessed are you among women, and blessed is the fruit of your womb! 43. And why is this granted me, that the mother of my Lord should come to me? 44. For behold, when the voice of your greeting came to my ears, the babe in my womb leaped for joy. 45. And blessed is she who believed that there would be a fulfilment of what was spoken to her from the Lord." 46. And Mary said, "My soul magnifies the Lord, 47. and my spirit rejoices in God my Savior, 48. for he has regarded the low estate of his handmaiden. For behold, henceforth all generations will call me blessed; 49. for he who is mighty has done great things for me, and holy is his name.

50. And his mercy is on those who fear him from generation to generation. 51. He has shown strength with his arm, he has scattered the proud in the imagination of their hearts,

52. he has put down the mighty from their thrones, and exalted those of low degree; 53. he has filled the hungry with good things, and the rich he has sent empty away. 54. He has helped his servant Israel, in remembrance of his mercy, 55. as he spoke to our fathers, to Abraham and to his posterity for ever." 56. And Mary remained with her about three months, and returned to her home.

Elizabeth is old like Sarah; Mary is young like Hagar, the young fertile handmaid of Abraham. She even calls herself the "Handmaid of the Lord" to further associate herself with Hagar who obeyed the angel and gave birth to Ismael. Again playing upon the well known Genesis stories, the angel announces that John will be the prophet of the Most High, while Jesus will be the Son of the Most High, very like Ismael will be honored as the founder of great nations and Isaac will be the legitimate son and founder/father of Israel. Note the reversal in the positions, while Elizabeth plays the role of Sarah and Mary replaces Hagar, the children are reversed, John plays Ismael to Jesus' Isaac.

This contradiction in roles is an indication that the editor has played around with the story. Logically if Elizabeth is Sarah, she should be giving birth to Jesus/Isaac and Mary as Hagar should give birth to the illegitimate son John/Ismael.

Three indications help us to understand how the original has been changed. First the vagueness of the term *kinswoman*. There is a relationship between Mary and Elizabeth, but that relationship is obscured rather than brought out by the term. If Elizabeth is a cousin, we have to account for the great age differences. Elizabeth is described as too old to give birth putting her in her late 40's, while Mary is probably age 12, the age that virgin Jewish girls were engaged but not yet married. For a young girl to travel by herself from Galilee to "the hill country of Judea" or anywhere for that matter to visit a pregnant cousin or aunt is quite daring, even shocking. We should also note that Jesus and John the Baptist seem quite unaware that they are related or their mothers are related in the rest of the Gospels. Even more problematical is Elizabeth's greeting "And why is this granted me, that the mother of my Lord should come to me?" There is nothing to indicate that Elizabeth should know that Jesus will be her Lord. The reference only makes sense if the woman she is talking to is the mother of Zechariah. Thirdly, Mary's Magnificat speech is quite misplaced as she is an unmarried, alone and pregnant. She possibly faces death for her transgression of Jewish marital laws. God has not done anything good for her. Some ancient manuscripts have Elizabeth delivering this speech, which is much more appropriate for a woman in her situation[473]. In fact the speech comes originally from a barren women. It is from Hannah, the barren wife of Elkanah in 1 Samuel I[474].

> **And Hannah prayed, and said, My heart rejoiceth in the LORD, mine horn is exalted in the LORD: my mouth is enlarged over mine enemies; because I rejoice in thy salvation. There is none holy as the LORD: for there is none beside thee: neither is there any rock like our God. Talk no more so exceeding proudly; let not arrogancy come out of your mouth: for the LORD is a God of knowledge, and by him actions are weighed. The bows of the mighty men are broken, and they that stumbled are girded with strength. They that were full have hired out themselves for bread; and they that were hungry ceased: so that the barren hath born seven; and she that hath many children is waxed feeble. The LORD killeth, and maketh alive: he bringeth down to the grave, and bringeth up. The LORD maketh poor, and maketh rich: he bringeth low, and lifteth up. He raiseth up the poor out of the dust, and lifteth up the beggar from the dunghill, to set them among princes, and to make them inherit the throne of glory: for the pillars of the earth are the LORD's,**

and he hath set the world upon them. He will keep the feet of his saints, and the wicked shall be silent in darkness; for by strength shall no man prevail. The adversaries of the LORD shall be broken to pieces; out of heaven shall he thunder upon them: the LORD shall judge the ends of the earth; and he shall give strength unto his king, and exalt the horn of his anointed. And Elkanah went to Ramah to his house. And the child did minister unto the LORD before Eli the priest.

All these problems disappear when we assign the visitation of the angel to Elizabeth and recognize the visitor as Elizabeth's mother-in-law, Mary. The statement "the mother of my lord" can only refer to the mother of Zachariah. Therefore, I suggest that it may refer to the mother of Zachariah—Mary. The earlier passage may have read something like this:

Reconstruction of Birth Narrative

After these days his wife Elizabeth conceived, and for five months she hid herself, saying, "Thus the Lord has done to me in the days when he looked on me, to take away my reproach among men." In the sixth month the angel Gabriel was sent And he came to her and said, "Hail, O favored one, the Lord is with you!" But she was greatly troubled at the saying, and considered in her mind what sort of greeting this might be. And the angel said to her, "Do not be afraid, Elizabeth, for you have found favor with God. And behold, you will conceive in your womb and bear a son, and you shall call his name John. He will be great, and will be called the Prophet of the Most High; and the Lord God will give to him the throne of his father David, and he will reign over the house of Jacob for ever, and of his kingdom there will be no end." And Elizabeth said to the angel, "How shall this be, since I am barren. And the angel said to her, "The Holy Spirit will come upon you, and the power of the Most High will overshadow you; therefore the child to be born will be called holy, the Son of God. And behold, your mother-in-law, Mary, in her old age has also conceived a son; and this is the sixth month with her who was called barren. For with God nothing will be impossible." And Elizabeth said, "Behold, I am the handmaid of the Lord; let it be to me according to your word." And the angel departed from her. In those days Mary arose and went with haste into the hill country, to a city of Judah, and she entered the house of Zechari'ah and greeted Elizabeth. And when Elizabeth heard the greeting of Mary, the babe leaped in her womb; and Elizabeth was filled with the Holy Spirit and she exclaimed with a loud cry, "Blessed are you among women, and blessed is the fruit of your womb! And why is this granted me, that the mother of my Lord should come to me? For behold, when the voice of your greeting came to my ears, the babe in my womb leaped for joy. [Mary said] And blessed is she who believed that there would be a fulfilment of what was spoken to her from the Lord." And Elizabeth said, "My soul magnifies the Lord, and my spirit rejoices in God my Savior, for he has regarded the low estate of his handmaiden. For behold, henceforth all generations will call me blessed; for he who is mighty has done great things for me, and holy is his name. And his mercy is on those who fear him from generation to generation. He has shown strength with his arm, he has scattered the proud in the imagination of their hearts, he has put down the mighty from their thrones, and exalted those of low degree; he has filled the hungry with good things, and the rich he has sent empty away. He has helped his servant Israel, in remembrance of his mercy, as he spoke to our fathers, to Abraham and to his posterity for ever." And Mary remained with her about three months, and returned to her home.

We now have Mary as the Sarah figure, giving birth in her old age to Isaac, while Elizabeth is the Hagar figure, giving birth to his wildman brother Ismael. This leaves us with a couple of problems. First, Zachariah has previously said that Elizabeth was barren and both were advanced in age, earlier in the narrative. Second, Mariam (Mary) was the sister of Moses and Aaron, and therefore not the Mother-in-Law of Elizabeth, but the sister-in-law.

The first problem gets resolved by supposing that in the original story, Elizabeth was both barren and old and no Mary existed. It was the next stage of the text that had Elizabeth as barren and Mary as old." The text of the Koran (19:7-8) asserts that Zachariah was advanced in old age, but says nothing about Elizabeth being old.

O Zakariya! surely We give you good news of a boy whose name shall be Yahya: We have not made before anyone his equal.

He said: O my Lord! when shall I have a son, and my wife is barren, and I myself have reached indeed the extreme degree of old age?

While not necessarily more accurate than Biblical texts, it would seem that the Koran had no reason to change this bit of information, that instead of both Zachariah and Elizabeth being old, only Zechariah is old. The Koran text reflects this second stage.

The fact that Mariam was the sister-in-law of Elizabeth and the young virgin sister that saved Moses from the Pharoah by placing him on the river presented a real problem for the text. The solution came with the reading of the famous passage Isaiah 7.14: "Therefore the Lord himself will give a sign: The virgin will be with child and will give birth to a son."

The appropriate changes were made and the rest is history. Well, actually not history, but literature that evolves and resembles history, and can influence history.

Fresco. Actor-Magician Christ Raises Lazarus with a Glove.

Catacomb of St. Priscilla, Rome, Italy, 3rd century. Unlike other Christ-Lazarus scenes, Christ has his back turned to Lazarus. He is facing the viewer. This is how the scene would be staged for an audience at a play.

Chapter 9

John the Disciple of the Lord, Papias and Eusebius

A good hypothesis helps us to understand its immediate phenomena, but more importantly other phenomena which are inexplicable without it. The hypothesis that the name of the original leader of the disciples was John helps us to unravel other puzzles in this way. In fact it helps us even to understand and explain the methodology of Eusebius.

In the third book of his history, Eusebius tells us that a man named Papias wrote a book called "Expositions of Oracles of the Lord[475]." The book apparently was quite influential as Papias claimed to be an actual hearer of someone named John, the Disciple of the Lord. Papias tells us that someone named Mark was a follower and interpreter of Peter and that someone named Matthew wrote a work on "Oracles of the Lord" in Hebrew[476]. There is no reason to connect either of these works with the gospels by Mark or Matthew. It is much more likely that people reading Papias mistakingly attributed the gospels to Mark and Matthew based on Papias saying they had written early Christian material.

Using Papias, Eusebius (*H.E.*, book 5) tries to convince us of the existence of a Presbyter John, whom he declares a distinctly different personage from the Apostle John. He does this, most likely to explain certain heretical ideas in the writings of the early Christian Papias. Eusebius writes as follows about him.

> 1   There are extant five books of Papias, which bear the title Expositions of Oracles of the Lord. Irenaeus makes mention of these as the only works written by him, in the following words: These things are attested by Papias, an ancient man who was a

> hearer of John and a companion of Polycarp, in his fourth book. For five books have been written by him." These are the words of Irenaeus.
>
> 2 But Papias himself in the preface to his discourses by no means declares that he was himself a hearer and eye-witness of the holy apostles, but he shows by the words which he uses that he received the doctrines of the faith from those who were their friends.
>
> 3 He says: "But I shall not hesitate also to put down for you along with my interpretations whatsoever things I have at any time learned carefully from the elders and carefully remembered, guaranteeing their truth. For I did not, like the multitude, take pleasure in those that speak much, but in those that teach the truth; not in those that relate strange commandments, but in those that deliver the commandments given by the Lord to faith, and springing from the truth itself.
>
> 4 If, then, any one came, who had been a follower of the elders, I questioned him in regard to the words of the elders,-what Andrew or what Peter said, or what was said by Philip, or by Thomas, or by James, or by John, or by Matthew, or by any other of the disciples of the Lord, and what things Aristion and the presbyter John, the disciples of the Lord, say. For I did not think that what was to be gotten from the books would profit me as much as what came from the living and abiding voice."
>
> 5 It is worth while observing here that the name John is twice enumerated by him. The first one he mentions in connection with Peter and James and Matthew and the rest of the apostles, clearly meaning the evangelist; but the other John he mentions after an interval, and places him among others outside of the number of the apostles, putting Aristion before him, and he distinctly calls him a presbyter[477].

Eusebius's proof of the existence of the Presbyter John amounts to one line where Papias uses the expression "Presbyter John" and then strangely lists him as one of the disciples of the Lord together with the apostles, including another John.

Eusebius's case is extremely weakened by the fact that the writer of *Against Heresies*, taken by him, to be Irenaeus, Bishop of Lyon, circa 200, does not know of this Presbyter John, but appears to be familiar with Papias. The writer of *Heresies* uses the expression "John, the disciple of the Lord," some fourteen times. (*Heresies* 1:8.5, 2:2.5, 2:22.5, 2:23.3, 3.1.1., 3.3.4, 3.11.1, 3:16.5, 3:22.2, 4.20.11, 4:30.4, 5:18.2, 5:33.3). There is absolutely no indication that he is referring to anybody but the Apostle John. From this fact alone, we may be suspicious that the term "Presbyter John" is an invention of Eusebius.

Eusebius confuses the Apostle John and the Presbyter John in a story[478] he takes from the ending of Clement of Alexandria's "Can the Rich Man be Saved." We may suspect that some such story was in Papias and Eusebius changed and interpolated it into the *Rich Man* text.

The stilted language of Papias also indicates this. Let us examine Papias' text more closely.

> "But I shall not hesitate also to put down for you along with my interpretations whatsoever things I have at any time learned carefully from the elders and carefully remembered, guaranteeing their truth. For I did not, like the multitude, take pleasure in those that speak much, but in those that teach the truth; not in those that relate strange commandments, but in those that deliver the commandments given by the Lord to faith, and springing from the truth itself.
>
> 4 If, then, any one came, who had been a follower of the elders, I questioned him in regard to the words of the elders,-what Andrew or what Peter said, or what was said by Philip, or by Thomas, or by James, or by John, or by Matthew, or by any other of the disciples of the Lord, and what things Aristion and the presbyter John, the disciples of the Lord, say. For I did not think that what was to be gotten from the books would profit me as much as what came from the living and abiding voice.

Papias seems to say that he is getting his information first from elders and second from any one who came who had been "a follower of the elders." He does not tell us who these elders are. However the phrase "words of the elders" seems to be put in apposition to "what Andrew or what Peter said, or what was said by Philip, or by Thomas, or by James, or by John, or by Matthew, or by any other of the disciples of the Lord, and what things Aristion and the Presbyter John the disciples of the Lord say." In other words, when he heard the "words of the elders" he heard what "the apostles say." He does not identify who the elders are, so we may take it that he is using the term as identical with Apostles. Papias is just using the term "the elders" as another name for the disciples of the lord.

Papias' list of apostles has to be suspect. He names seven and then says "any other of the disciples of the Lord." He would have been specific and named all twelve or he should have named a few major ones and for space/time sake just said "any other of the disciples of the Lord." Since John is repeated twice without sufficient separation between John the disciple of the Lord and Presbyter John the disciple of the lord, we may take it that John was not on the list of specific names at this point and neither was Matthew.

Papias also needlessly repeats the term disciples of the Lord twice. Logically, he should have included Aristion and the Presbyter John in the list of disciples of the lord starting with Andrew.

The term "Aristion" has no other reference in history. We may assume it comes from the word, "Aristos," meaning "the best." Based on this we may reconstruct the original text this way:

> If, then, any one came, who had been a follower of the elders, I questioned him in regard to the words of the elders,-what Andrew or what Peter said, or what was said by Philip, or by Thomas, or by James, what things the best and John, the disciple of the Lord, say. For I did not think that what was to be gotten from the books would profit me as much as what came from the living and abiding voice.

What is clear is that the term John is being separated from "the best," which refers to the other disciples. If this reconstruction is correct, we may take it that Papias was referring to John, the disciple of the Lord and his apostles, Andrew, Peter, Philip, Thomas, and James. We may take it that Papias claimed to have been an ear witness to John, the Nazarene and his five apostles.

We can see the evolution of ideas out of this text. Irenaeus cannot understand that Papias is referring to the apostles when he is referring to "the elders." He therefore takes it that Papias was referring to Elders who saw the apostles. He writes:

> all the elders testify; those who were conversant in Asia with John, the disciple of the Lord, [affirming] that John conveyed to them that information. And he remained among them up to the times of Trajan. Some of them, moreover, saw not only John, but the other apostles also, and heard the very same account from them[479].

He mixes up John the disciple of the Lord for the John in the story in the Gospel of John, "Afterwards, John, the disciple of the Lord, who also had leaned upon His breast, did himself publish a Gospel."

Eusebius repeats this mistake.

> as the elders who saw John, the disciple of the Lord, related that they had heard from him how the Lord used to teach in regard to these times, and say: The days will come, in which vines shall grow, each having ten thousand branches, and in each branch ten thousand twigs, and in each true294 twig ten thousand shoots, and in each one of the shoots ten thousand dusters, and on every one of the clusters ten thousand grapes, and every grape when pressed will give five and twenty metretes of wine. And when any one of the saints shall lay hold of a cluster,295 another shall cry out, "I am

a better cluster, take me; bless the Lord through me." In like manner [the Lord declared] that a grain of wheat would produce ten thousand ears, and that every ear should have ten thousand grains, and every grain would yield ten pounds (quinque bilibres) of clear, pure, fine flour; and that all other fruit-bearing trees, 296 and seeds and grass, would produce in similar proportions (secundum congruentiam iis consequentem); and that all animals feeding [only] on the productions of the earth, should [in those days] become peaceful and harmonious among each other, and be in perfect subjection to man.

4. And these things are bone witness to in writing by Papias, the hearer of John, and a companion of Polycarp, in his fourth book; for there were five books compiled (suntetagme/na) by him[480].

Eusebius then adds his own mistake by making "John the disciple of the Lord" into the "Presbyter John, the disciple of the Lord." In fairness to Eusebius, it is possible the original text read John the Baptist, the disciple of the Lord. Eusebius, perhaps took it for a scribal error as he did the word "Aristion" and rewrote in a way to make sense to himself.

We cannot be sure about the author Papias' claim that he heard John and the other disciples of the Lord. It is most likely a rhetorical claim by the book's author in order to increase the value of the testimony within the work. However we can be sure that an early group referred to John as "the Disciple of the Lord" and believed that he had five followers Andrew, Peter, Philip, Thomas and James. Since there is no reference to Jesus here, we may assume that John was a disciple of the Jewish Lord—the creator God. This is extremely important. It tells us that Papias is writing before the Christian-Jewish Split in the Jewish community.

Irenaeus tells us that the heretical Valentinians also referred to John as the Disciple of the Lord:

> "Further, they teach that John, the disciple of the Lord, indicated the first Ogdoad, expressing themselves in these words: John, the disciple of the Lord, wishing to set forth the origin of all things, so as to explain how the Father produced the whole, lays down a certain principle,- that, namely, which was first-begotten by God, which Being he has termed both the only-begotten Son and God, in whom the Father, after a seminal manner, brought forth all things[481]."

From this we gather that John, the Nazarene, was known by the name "John, the Disciple of the Lord" before he became the Christ and probably before he became known as John, the Baptist.

While Eusebius distorts Papias, we also have to thank him for preserving some of Papias as it gives us a window into the early world of John. It is apparent that this window was too clear for the leaders of Rome and the Roman Catholic Church of the fourth century. His works disappeared. As Eusebius indicates that he himself understands the importance of them, we should conclude that their destruction was deliberate.

Papias and John the Disciple of the Lord

What evidence is there that Papias provides us an early window on John the Nazarene? The answer is that the things he writes matches what Josephus tells us about John, the Nazarene. Josephus tells us that the man who led the Samaritan revolt on Mount Gerizim was "one who thought lying a thing of little consequence, and who contrived every thing so that the multitude might be pleased[482]." In our reconstruction of the original *Testimonium* of Josephus, we proposed that Josephus originally said this about John:

> "And when Pilate at the suggestion of the principal men amongst us, had arrested him, those that loved him at the first did not forsake him for he appeared to them to be a prophet and foretold ten thousand wonderful things."

Papias tells us precisely what some of those ten thousand wonderful things were. We learn this from both Eusebius and Irenaeus. Eusebius writes:

> The same writer gives also other accounts which he says came to him through unwritten tradition, certain strange parables and teachings of the Saviour, and some other more mythical things.
> To these belong his statement that there will be a period of some thousand years after the resurrection of the dead, and that the kingdom of Christ will be set up in material form on this very earth. I suppose he got these ideas through a misunderstanding of the apostolic accounts, not perceiving that the things said by them were spoken mystically in figures[483].

Irenaeus gives us more information on this [Note that the term "Lord" should be read as referring to the Jewish Creator God and not Jesus Christ]:

> as the elders who saw John, the disciple of the Lord, related that they had heard from him how the Lord used to teach in regard to these times, and say: The days will come, in which vines shall grow, each having ten

thousand branches, and in each branch ten thousand twigs, and in each true twig ten thousand shoots, and in each one of the shoots ten thousand clusters, and on every one of the clusters ten thousand grapes, and every grape when pressed will give five and twenty metretes of wine. And when any one of the saints shall lay hold of a cluster, another shall cry out, "I am a better cluster, take me; bless the Lord through me." In like manner [the Lord declared] that a grain of wheat would produce ten thousand ears, and that every ear should have ten thousand grains, and every grain would yield ten pounds (*quinque bilibres*) of clear, pure, fine flour; and that all other fruit-bearing trees, and seeds and grass, would produce in similar proportions (*secundum congruentiam iis consequentem*); and that all animals feeding [only] on the productions of the earth, should [in those days] become peaceful and harmonious among each other, and be in perfect subjection to man.

John is making rather exaggerated promises about how great the harvests are going to be when the Kingdom of the Lord comes. One imagines him as a politician-prophet trying to get himself elected king. Note that Papias has John/Jesus explaining statements from Hebrew scriptures especially ones using animal allegories.

At other points in his text, Irenaeus gives us more clues to the teachings of John:

4. And these things are bone witness to in writing by Papias, the hearer of John, and a companion of Polycarp, in his fourth book; for there were five books compiled (suntetagme/na) by him. And he says in addition, "Now these things are credible to believers." And he says that, "when the traitor Judas did not give credit to them, and put the question, 'How then can things about to bring forth so abundantly be wrought by the Lord?' 'the Lord declared, 'They who shall come to these [times] shall see.'" When prophesying of these times, therefore, Esaias says: "The wolf also shall feed with the lamb, and the leopard shall take his rest with the kid; the calf also, and the bull, and the lion shall eat together; and a little boy shall lead them. The ox and the bear shall feed together, and their young ones shall agree together; and the lion shall eat straw as well as the ox. And the infant boy shall thrust his hand into the asp's den, into the nest also of the adder's brood; and they shall do no harm, nor have power to hurt anything in my holy mountain." And again he says, in recapitulation, "Wolves and lambs shall then browse together, and the lion shall eat straw like the ox, and the serpent earth as if it were bread; and they shall neither hurt nor annoy anything in my holy mountain, saith the Lord[484]."

Eusebius tries to deny what Irenaeus is relating from Papias. He writes, "not perceiving that the things said by them were spoken mystically in figures." While Eusebius denies Papias' interpretation, he does not deny what was said. In fact, there seems to be no reason to believe that John did not say these things. It seems to correspond very well with Josephus's description of him.

Irenaeus gives us this further insight into John's political plans and ambitions:

> To the same purpose did the Lord also declare, "Heaven and earth shall pass away." When these things, therefore, pass away above the earth, John, the Lord's disciple, says that the new Jerusalem above shall [then] descend, as a bride adorned for her husband; and that this is the tabernacle of God, in which God will dwell with men. Of this Jerusalem the former one is an image-that Jerusalem of the former earth in which the righteous are disciplined beforehand for incorruption and prepared for salvation. And of this tabernacle Moses received the pattern in the mount; and nothing is capable of being allegorized, but all things are steadfast, and true, land substantial, having been made by God for righteous men's enjoyment[485]. And as the presbyters say, Then those who are deemed worthy of an abode in heaven shall go there, others shall enjoy the delights of paradise, and others shall possess the splendour of the city; for everywhere the Saviour shall be seen according as they who see Him shall be worthy.
>
> [They say, moreover], that there is this distinction between the habitation of those who produce an hundred-fold, and that of those who produce sixty-fold, and that of those who produce thirty-fold: for the first will be taken up into the heavens, the second will dwell in paradise, the last will inhabit the city; and that was on this account the Lord declared, "In My Father's house are many mansions." For all things belong to God, who supplies all with a suitable dwelling-place; even as His Word says, that a share is allotted to all by the Father, according as each person is or shall be worthy. And this is the couch on which the guests shall recline, having been invited to the wedding. The presbyters, the disciples of the apostles, affirm that this is the gradation and arrangement of those who are saved, and that they advance through steps of this nature; also that they ascend through the Spirit to the Son, and through the Son to the Father, and that in due time the Son will yield up His work to the Father, even as it is said by the apostle, "For He must reign till He hath put all enemies under His feet. The last enemy that shall be destroyed is death." For in the times of the kingdom, the righteous man who is upon the earth shall then forget to die. "But when He saith, All things shall be subdued unto Him, it is manifest that He is excepted who did put all things under

THE EVOLUTION OF CHRISTS AND CHRISTIANIES

Him. And when all things shall be subdued unto Him, then shall the Son also Himself be subject unto Him who put all things under Him, that God may be all in all."

John, therefore, did distinctly foresee the first "resurrection of the just," and the inheritance in the kingdom of the earth; and what the prophets have prophesied concerning it harmonize [with his vision][486].

Note importantly that Irenaeus uses this discourse apparently from Papias to demonstrate that "John . . . did distinctly foresee the first "resurrection of the just." We must assume that in the second century there was a debate about whether John had foreseen the resurrection. We will suggest why this question may have been debated in the next section. For now, we'll note that this discourse and the one above matches closely with the discourse in the *Book of Revelations*:

Then I saw a new heaven and a new earth; for the first heaven and the first earth had passed away, and the sea was no more.

And I saw the holy city, new Jerusalem, coming down out of heaven from God, prepared as a bride adorned for her husband; and I heard a loud voice from the throne saying, "Behold, the dwelling of God is with men. He will dwell with them, and they shall be his people, and God himself will be with them; he will wipe away every tear from their eyes, and death shall be no more, neither shall there be mourning nor crying nor pain any more, for the former things have passed away."

And he who sat upon the throne said, "Behold, I make all things new." Also he said, "Write this, for these words are trustworthy and true."

And he said to me, "It is done! I am the Alpha and the Omega, the beginning and the end. To the thirsty I will give from the fountain of the water of life without payment.

He who conquers shall have this heritage, and I will be his God and he shall be my son.

But as for the cowardly, the faithless, the polluted, as for murderers, fornicators, sorcerers, idolaters, and all liars, their lot shall be in the lake that burns with fire and sulphur, which is the second death[487]."

Both Papias and *Revelations* tell us that John preached a New Jerusalem coming down from heaven to Earth. Was this the position of John or the followers of John? The writer of the *Revelations* explicitly identifies himself as John, (22.8) "I, John, am he who heard and saw these things." We cannot take this at face value. It is most probably a follower of John writing in his name years later. The important thing here is that the author does not have to tell us very much about John. His audience already knows him as a prophet, so there is no need to give more information since the character is presented as a prophet. The author does give us the important information that he is writing from exile on the island of Patmos. We know from Josephus that John was exiled to Macherus. Was the castle at Marcherus turned into the Island at Patmos as the place of exile for John? I believe we can equate Patmos and Macherus. Josephus describes Macherus as a fantastic place:

> ... Lucilius Bassus ... resolved to make war upon Macherus; for it was highly necessary that this citadel should be demolished, lest it might be a means of drawing away many into a rebellion, by reason of its strength; for the nature of the place was very capable of affording the surest hopes of safety to those that possessed it, as well as delay and fear to those that should attack it; for what was walled in was itself a very rocky hill, elevated to a very great height; which circumstance alone made it very hard to he subdued. It was also so contrived by nature, that it could not be easily ascended; for it is, as it were, ditched about with such valleys on all sides, and to such a depth, that the eye cannot reach their bottoms, and such as are not easily to be passed over, and even such as it is impossible to fill up with earth. For that valley which cuts it on the west extends to threescore furlongs, and did not end till it came to the lake Asphaltitis; on the same side it was also that Macherus had the tallest top of its hill elevated above the rest. But then for the valleys that lay on the north and south sides, although they be not so large as that already described, yet it is in like manner an impracticable thing to think of getting over them; and for the valley that lies on the east side, its depth is found to be no less than a hundred cubits. It extends as far as a mountain that lies over against Macherus, with which it is bounded.
>
> Now when Alexander [Janneus], the king of the Jews, observed the nature of this place, he was the first who built a citadel here, which afterwards was demolished by Gabinius, when he made war against Aristobulus. But when Herod came to be king, he thought the place to be worthy of the utmost regard, and of being built upon in the firmest manner, and this especially because it lay so near to Arabia; for it is seated in a convenient place on that account, and hath a prospect toward that country; he therefore surrounded a large space of ground with walls and towers, and built a city there, out of which city there was a way that led up to the very citadel itself on the top of the mountain; nay, more than this, he built a wall round that top of the hill, and erected towers at the corners, of a hundred and sixty cubits high; in the middle of which place he built a palace, after a magnificent manner,

wherein were large and beautiful edifices. He also made a great many reservoirs for the reception of water, that there might be plenty of it ready for all uses, and those in the properest places that were afforded him there. Thus did he, as it were, contend with the nature of the place, that he might exceed its natural strength and security (which yet itself rendered it hard to be taken) by those fortifications which were made by the hands of men[488].

In short, it is the perfect place to exile a popular holy man to. It is a place of great beauty and hardly a prison, yet it would be difficult for him to escape. If Herod had decided to release John instead of killing him, John could not claim ill treatment. It is also the perfect place for that holy man to have heavenly visions. Josephus also tells us these most interesting facts about Macherus:

But still in that valley which encompasses the city on the north side there is a certain place called Baaras, which produces a root of the same name with itself its color is like to that of flame, and towards the evenings it sends out a certain ray like lightning. It is not easily taken by such as would do it, but recedes from their hands, nor will yield itself to be taken quietly, until either the urine of a woman, or her menstrual blood, be poured upon it; nay, even then it is certain death to those that touch it, unless any one take and hang the root itself down from his hand, and so carry it away. It may also be taken another way, without danger, which is this: they dig a trench quite round about it, till the hidden part of the root be very small, they then tie a dog to it, and when the dog tries hard to follow him that tied him, this root is easily plucked up, but the dog dies immediately, as if it were instead of the man that would take the plant away; nor after this need any one be afraid of taking it into their hands. Yet, after all this pains in getting, it is only valuable on account of one virtue it hath, that if it be only brought to sick persons, it quickly drives away those called demons, which are no other than the spirits of the wicked, that enter into men that are alive and kill them, unless they can obtain some help against them. Here are also fountains of hot water, that flow out of this place, which have a very different taste one from the other; for some of them are bitter, and others of them are plainly sweet. Here are also many eruptions of cold waters, and this not only in the places that lie lower, and have their fountains near one another, but, what is still more wonderful, here is to be seen a certain cave hard by, whose cavity is not deep, but it is covered over by a rock that is prominent; above this rock there stand up two [hills or] breasts, as it were, but a little distant one from another, the one of which sends

> out a fountain that is very cold, and the other sends out one that is very hot; which waters, when they are mingled together, compose a most pleasant bath; they are medicinal indeed for other maladies, but especially good for strengthening the nerves. This place has in it also mines of sulfur and alum[489].
>
> As for the mystery of the seven stars which you saw in my right hand, and the seven golden lampstands, the seven stars are the angels of the seven churches and the seven lampstands are the seven churches[490].

Josephus tells us in *Antiquities* that John was exiled to Macherus[491]. We may presume that people associated the popular prophet John with Macherus, a place with a root called Baaras which "brought to sick persons, it quickly drives away those called demons." Could the association of John/Jesus with curing demons have actually come from John/Jesus' association with Macherus, and Macherus' association with the Baaras root that cures illness by driving out demons? I would suggest that it is a real possibility.

We should also note that the writer of Mark has John imprisoned apparently for a while, (Mark 6.17-19), "Herod had sent and seized John, and bound him in prison . . . for Herod feared John, knowing that he was a righteous and holy man, and kept him safe." The statement that he "kept him safe," agrees quite well with what Josephus tells us about Herod's treatment of John.

Deconstructing *Revelation* or Revealing the Revealing

The *Book of Revelations* provides a great deal of evidence for our major hypothesis that a man named John was the basis for the Jesus Christ myth.

The work appears to be written by two quite different writers interesting in making different points. The earlier writer has written mainly chapters 4 through 22. In it he describes a trip to a heavenly place where he is told the future. The second writer has rewritten mainly chapters one, two and three. This section is a partisan Christian attack against other Christians disguised as a letter to seven churches. Perhaps the easiest way to see the difference between the two writers is to look at their interpretation of the phrases "seven spirits of God" and "seven stars."

> 1:13-16. on turning I saw seven golden lampstands, and in the midst of the lampstands One like a son of man . . . in his right hand he held seven stars.
>
> 1:20. As for the mystery of the seven stars which you saw in my right hand, and the seven golden lampstands, the seven stars are the angels of the seven churches and the seven lampstands are the seven churches.

THE EVOLUTION OF CHRISTS AND CHRISTIANIES

One would expect that the writer would have waited till the end to reveal the meaning of the symbols. The second writer is anxious to give us his meaning.

The term "angels of the seven churches" is never used again in the work. We do however hear of "seven angels who stand before God," "seven angels who had the seven trumpets," "seven angels with the seven plagues," and seven angels with seven golden bowls full of the wrath of God"

- 8:2 Then I saw the seven angels who stand before God, and seven trumpets were given to them.
- 8:6. Now the seven angels who had the seven trumpets made ready to blow them.
- 15:1 Then I saw another portent in heaven, great and wonderful, seven angels with seven plagues
- 15:6 and out of the temple came the seven angels with the seven plagues, robed in pure bright linen, and their breasts girded with golden girdles
- 15:7 And one of the four living creatures gave the seven angels seven golden bowls full of the wrath of God who lives for ever and ever
- 16:1 Then I heard a loud voice from the temple telling the seven angels, "Go and pour out on the earth the seven bowls of the wrath of God."

It is hard to tell if the author means one group of seven angels, who "stand before God, are given "trumpets," and carry "plagues," and carry "bowls of wrath," or there are three different groups of angels. But it is hard to see that the same writer would attribute seven angels to the son of man and call them the angels of the seven churches and have John write letters to them. For the first writer, angels directly carry out the will of the Jewish creator God in bringing an apocalypse. For the second writer, the angels are a codename for the heads of the seven churches. The second writer has Jesus promising them life and power and threatening them with death if they disobey. Essentially, the angels are not ethereal beings for the second writer, but rebellious satraps of the king's territories.

It is easy to see that the second writer/rewriter conceives of angels as men and not celestial instruments of the will of God by how he promises and threatens these men (Revelations 3.1-6):

> And to the angel of the church in Sardis write:'The words of him who has the seven spirits of God and the seven stars. "'I know your works; you have the name of being alive, and you are dead.
>
> Awake, and strengthen what remains and is on the point of death, for I have not found your works perfect in the sight of my God.

> Remember then what you received and heard; keep that, and repent. If you will not awake, I will come like a thief, and you will not know at what hour I will come upon you.
>
> Yet you have still a few names in Sardis, people who have not soiled their garments; and they shall walk with me in white, for they are worthy.
>
> He who conquers shall be clad thus in white garments, and I will not blot his name out of the book of life; I will confess his name before my Father and before his angels.
>
> He who has an ear, let him hear what the Spirit says to the churches.'

Notice that the son of man offers the threat/promise of coming in person to deal with the situation. It is obvious that these angels are not in heaven with the churches on earth. We find the same threats/promises in Paul's letters to the churches (1Corinthians, 1.4 and 2 Corinthians 13:1-3

> 19. But I will come to you soon, if the Lord wills, and I will find out not the talk of these arrogant people but their power.
> 20. For the kingdom of God does not consist in talk but in power.
> 21. What do you wish? Shall I come to you with a rod, or with love in a spirit of gentleness?
>
> 1. This is the third time I am coming to you. Any charge must be sustained by the evidence of two or three witnesses.
> 2. I warned those who sinned before and all the others, and I warn them now while absent, as I did when present on my second visit, that if I come again I will not spare them—

One could argue that the same writer is just using the term angel in two different senses, the Creator God's celestial agents and Jesus' human agents on Earth. But the writer links the churches' angels and churches themselves to heavenly stars and lamps (20), "As for the mystery of the seven stars which you saw in my right hand, and the seven golden lampstands, the seven stars are the angels of the seven churches and the seven lampstands are the seven churches." This linkage mitigates against this interpretation. The original writer certainly had these passage in mind from the *Book of Enoch* (7 and 21):

> And beyond that abyss I saw a place which had no firmament of the heaven above, and no firmly founded earth beneath it: there was no water upon it, and no 13 birds, but it was a waste and horrible place. I saw there seven stars like great burning mountains, and to me, when I

inquired regarding them, The angel said: 'This place is the end of heaven and earth: this has become a prison for the stars and the host of heaven. And the stars which roll over the fire are they which have transgressed the commandment of the Lord in the beginning of their rising, because they did not come forth at their appointed times. And He was wroth with them, and bound them till the time when their guilt should be consummated (even) for ten thousand years.'

"And I saw there something horrible: I saw neither a heaven above nor a firmly founded earth, but a place chaotic and horrible. And there I saw seven stars of the heaven bound together in it, like great mountains and burning with fire. Then I said: 'For what sin are they bound, and on what account have they been cast in hither?' Then said Uriel, one of the holy angels, who was with me, and was chief over them, and said: 'Enoch, why dost thou ask, and why art thou eager for the truth? These are of the number of the stars of heaven, which have transgressed the commandment of the Lord, and are bound here till ten thousand years, the time entailed by their sins, are consummated.'

It makes sense to anyone who has read the *Enoch* that the son of man would be holding the seven rebellious stars in his hand. Here is a passage about the son of man in *Enoch*:

And there I saw One who had a head of days,
And His head was white like wool,
And with Him was another being whose countenance had the appearance of a man,
And his face was full of graciousness, like one of the holy angels.
And I asked the angel who went with me and showed me all the hidden things, concerning that 3 Son of Man, who he was, and whence he was, (and) why he went with the Head of Days? And he answered and said unto me:
This is the son of Man who hath righteousness,
With whom dwelleth righteousness,
And who revealeth all the treasures of that which is hidden,
Because the Lord of Spirits hath chosen him,
And whose lot hath the pre-eminence before the Lord of Spirits in uprightness for ever.

It is clear that the original writer of *Revelation* is playing off the symbols and imagery in *Enoch*. Apparently the second writer did not understand this, otherwise he would not have turned the symbol of the seven stars, (seven angels that rebelled against God) into the symbol of Jesus Christ's seven churches on Earth.

Additionally, we should note that John is apparently in the Temple at Jerusalem when he has his vision. We can base this on the line, (1:13-16) "on turning I saw seven golden lampstands, and in the midst of the lampstands . . ." Josephus tells us that seven golden lamps were among the spoils the Romans took from the Jerusalem Temple after the war.

> On the top of every one of these pageants was placed the commander of the city that was taken, and the manner wherein he was taken. Moreover, there followed those pageants a great number of ships; and for the other spoils, they were carried in great plenty. But for those that were taken in the temple of Jerusalem, they made the greatest figure of them all; that is, the golden table, of the weight of many talents; the candlestick also, that was made of gold, though its construction were now changed from that which we made use of; for its middle shaft was fixed upon a basis, and the small branches were produced out of it to a great length, having the likeness of a trident in their position, and had every one a socket made of brass for a lamp at the tops of them. These lamps were in number seven, and represented the dignity of the number seven among the Jews; and the last of all the spoils, was carried the Law of the Jews[492].

This knowledge by the first writer of the seven golden lampstands may suggest that he was a priest at the Jerusalem Temple during the war. However, we cannot be sure that it was not common knowledge during the period that the Temple contained these golden lampstands.

It seems pretty clear that while the second author wants to critique heretical Christian Churches in Asia, the intent of the first author is to explain, update and revise some unfulfilled historical predictions in the book of *Daniel* by using symbolism and ideas from the *Enoch*. *Daniel* (c.164 B.C.E.) predicted that after the overthrow of the Greek King Antiochus IV, the Last Judgment would come. The historian Robin Lane Fox describes this important prediction:

> The author gave a fine impression of the terrors of a vision and the effects of fasting for too long: perhaps his own experiences were behind the ones which he ascribed to Daniel. Certainly, they impinged on the final chapters (10-12). From another mighty angel, Daniel here learns a very specific sweep of history which had already occurred since the death of Alexander the Great. Hindsight improved its apparent foresight, but the author then risked some future details. King Antiochus would

THE EVOLUTION OF CHRISTS AND CHRISTIANIES

be rebuffed by Rome (this had already happened in Egypt): he would return however, to conquer Egypt and would then turn east and north on diverting news. Finally, he would encamp in Syria where Michael, Israel's angel, would defeat him spectacularly. A time of awful trouble would follow, 'such as never was'; then, many of those who had died would awake. The unrighteous would be shamed for ever, bu the righteous would shine like the stars in eternal life. There would be no mistaking the two groups: sinners and eternal glow-worms, their names were already written in a heavenly book.

The author put a time limit to this extremely turbulent future from the ending of the Temple cult to the Last Judgment there would be 1,290 days (in a postscript, a later author extended the number to 1,335). They ran, therefore, from December 167 to spring 163: the author, presumably, was writing in early 164 (perhaps when the first prophecy of 'three times and a half' was looking too optimistic). Undeterred, he foresaw mayhem with Michael, victory, appalling suffering and then the rewards for those in the virtuous columns of God's heavenly book[493].

Under normal circumstances, the fact that the angel Michael did not come and defeat Antiochus in 163 would not matter much. However, in a time of war, when people were asked to risk their lives for God with the promise of a second life for those who died valiantly, it might certainly present an embarrassing failure of prediction and would need to be explained. Like *Daniel*, the date of *Revelations* can be pinpointed almost to the month.

First we should note that one verse (2.13) states that the Church at Pergamum, "did not deny my faith even in the days of Antipas. Antipas died circa 39 C.E. The writer indicates the days of Antipas are in the past, so that is our *terminus a quo*. There is no reference to the destruction of Jerusalem or the burning of the Temple, which one would expect if written post 70 C.E. So between 39 and 70 seems our first time window.

There are more clues that helps us to zero in further on the date. It comes from symbolical references to Rome that the text itself helps us to discipher. The Roman Empire is a beast with ten horns and seven heads and the city of Rome is a woman sitting on "Seven Mountains" (the seven hills of Rome) in Revelations (17:9-10.):

The writer appears to be predicting the Roman-Jewish War that started in 66 C.E. Such a prediction would be pretty chancy if made before the war actually broke out. While there was tremendous tension over taxes between Judea and Rome, Judea did not have any kind of fighting force to launch a war before this time. A prediction of a full scale war would probably have seemed far fetched, if not ridiculous much before the actual beginning of the war. This allows us to put the composition after 66. Since he apparently thinks the Jews will win the war, we have to place the composition before the year 70 when the Jewish defeat became obvious.

The reference to "five kings fallen" is another clue. If we assume the writer is aware of Roman history, and take this literally, we may assume he is referring to the seven emperors of Rome: Augustus, Tiberius, Caligula, Claudius, Nero, Galba and Otho. The author knows that Galba, the sixth emperor of Rome ruled "only a little while." Galba ruled from June 8th 68 to January 15, 69, or just over about five months. The seventh emperor Otho ruled from January 15, 69 to April 14, 69, less than four months. If the writer was writing after the time of Otho, we may assume he would have mentioned that both the sixth and seventh emperors had short reigns. On the basis of this we may suppose that this work was composed during the reign of the seventh emperor, Otho, between January 15 and April 14 of 69.

We also have this important clue about the beast (Rome) exercising authority for forty-two months:

> This calls for a mind with wisdom: the seven heads are seven mountains on which the woman is seated; they are also seven kings, five of whom have fallen, one is, the other has not yet come, and when he comes he must remain only a little while. As for the beast that was and is not, it is an eighth but it belongs to the seven, and it goes to perdition. And the ten horns that you saw are ten kings who have not yet received royal power, but they are to receive authority as kings for one hour, together with the beast. These are of one mind and give over their power and authority to the beast; they will make war on the Lamb, and the Lamb will conquer them, for he is Lord of lords and King of kings, and those with him are called and chosen and faithful."
>
> Men worshiped the dragon, for he had given his authority to the beast, and they worshiped the beast, saying, "Who is like the beast, and who can fight against it?" And the beast was given a mouth uttering haughty and blasphemous words, and it was allowed to exercise authority for forty-two months;

Nero gave Vespasian command in February of 67. If the author is writing around February of 69, then perhaps he is predicting that Vespasian will stick around for another eighteen months, that is another year and a half for a total of three and a half years. It is possible that the author is applying the words of Daniel (27) to Vespasian, "for half of the week he shall cause sacrifice and offering to cease; and upon the wing of abominations shall come one who makes desolate, until the decreed end is poured out on the desolator." The author is taking the term "half of the week," to mean three and a half years. We must admire the ingenuity of the author who seems to be applying the unfulfilled prediction of the apocalypse to his time in the same way that the Maccabean composers did in 165 B.C.E.

The writer is making a fake prediction about the war, since the war has already started. It is not a prediction at all, but his predictions that Judea will win the war and there will be an apocalypse in a short time are real predictions.

Now, the fact that the war is presented as a prediction of a future event means that the audience must know the alleged narrator John lived in the past. Like Daniel he is getting his future report in a dream from Heaven. We may assume that John was a famous figure in the past so that the audience would believe that the last two predictions (the destruction of Rome and the apocalyptic arrival of the heavenly city of Jerusalem) were foreseen by him and would come true, just as his prediction of the war had done.

Now the only John who can fit the role is the prophet John whom Josephus tells us was beheaded at Macherus circa 36-37. There are no references to any crucifixion in *Revelations*, but there is this reference to beheadings, "Also I saw the souls of those who had been beheaded for their testimony to Jesus and for the word of God, and who had not worshiped the beast or its image and had not received its mark on their foreheads or their hands."

Why and Where Patmos?

This hypothesis that the John intended as the author in Revelations is the character we've been referring to as John the Nazarene fits all the evidence exceedingly well, except for one thing. We are not told that John was exiled to the castle at Macherus. We are told that he was on the island of Patmos. While it is not expressly stated he was exiled to Patmos, this seems to be the implication of the text: (1.8):

> I John, who also am your brother, and companion in tribulation, and in the kingdom and patience of Jesus Christ, was in the isle that is called Patmos, for the word of God, and for the testimony of Jesus Christ.

What could the statement that John was in or on the island of Patmos have meant to the readers of this text. What connotations would it arouse in the minds of the readers? The writer says nothing more about Patmos so we must assume it was known by the readers. If it was not known we would expect John to at least mention its location.

The island of Patmos is known to have been mentioned by three ancient text, Thucydides (*History*, 3:33), Strabo (*Geography*, 10.5), and Pliny (*Natural History*, 4.23).

Only these three ancient writers mention Patmos and each mentions them only once. While it is possible that all three references are later Christian changes, in the case of Thucydides it is obvious. Here is his reference:

> ... As Ionia was unfortified, great fears were felt that the Peloponnesians coasting along shore, even if they did not intend to stay, might make descents in passing and plunder the towns; and now the Paralian and

439

> Salaminian, having seen him at Clarus, themselves brought intelligence of the fact. Paches accordingly gave hot chase, and continued the pursuit as far as the Isle of Patmos, and then finding that Alcidas had got on too far to be overtaken, came back again. Meanwhile he thought it fortunate that, as he had not fallen in with them out at sea, he had not overtaken them anywhere where they would have been forced to encamp, and so give him the trouble of blockading them.
>
> On his return along shore he touched, among other places, at Notium, the port of Colophon,

Ships generally traveled in sight of land and the phrase "on his return along shore" seems to indicate that this was the situation here. The first island off the Ionian coast that Paches would have come to in his chase of Alcidas is Samos. Since Paches knew he could not blockade them once they reached an island, one would expect them to turn back as soon as Peloponnesians reached the first island of Samos. Thucydides mentions Samos three times in book one and forty times in his final book. There is no other mention of Patmos.

It seems quite likely that the mention of Patmos here is simply a Christian scribal error. The readers of Thucydides would have immediately known where Samos was. It is extremely doubtful they would have attached any meaning to the statement that Paches "continued the pursuit as far as the Isle of Patmos. This leaves only two actual references to Patmos in antiquity.

Here is Strabo's testimony:

> [12] And there is Amorgos, one of the Sporades, the home of Simonides the iambic poet; and also Lebinthos, and Leros:
>
> *And so says Phocylides:'the Lerians are bad, not one, but every one, all except Procles; and Procles is a Lerian.'*
>
> For the natives of the island were reproached with being unprincipled.
>
> [13] Nearby are both Patmos and the Corassiae; these are situated to the west of Icaria, and Icaria to the west of Samos. Now Icaria is deserted, though it has pastures, which are used by the Samians. But although it is such an isle as it is, still it is famous, and after it is named the sea that lies in front of it, in which are itself and Samos and Cos and the islands just mentioned—the Corassiae and Patmos and Leros. Famous, also, is the mountain in it, Cerceteus, more famous than the Ampelus, which is situated above the city of Samians.

Strabo makes the definite statement that Patmos is west of Icaria (which is to the west of Samos.) The current location of the island of Patmos is southeast of Icaria. It is hard to understand how Strabo could be correct about the location of Icaria being west of Samos, but wrong about the direction of Patmos from Icaria.

The last reference by Pliny is the most interesting:

> After we pass these, no regular order can be well observed; the rest must therefore be mentioned indiscriminately. There is the island of Scyro, and that of Ios, eighteen miles distant from Naxos, and deserving of all veneration for the tomb there of Homer; it is twenty-five miles in length, and was formerly known by the name of Phœnice; also Odia, Oletandros, and Gyara, with a city of the same name, the island being twelve miles in circumference, and distant from Andros sixty-two. At a distance of eighty miles from Gyara is Syrnos, then Cynæthus, Telos, noted for its unguents, and by Callimachus called Agathussa, Donusa, Patmos, thirty miles in circumference, the Corassiæ, Le—binthus, Leros, Cinara ; Sicinus, formerly called Œnoe ; Hieracia, also called Onus; Casos, likewise called Astrabe; Cimolus, or Echinussa; and Melos, with a city of that name, which island Aristides calls Memblis, Aristotle Zephyria, Callimachus Mimallis, Heraclides Siphis and Acytos. This last is the most circular in form of all these islands. After this comes Machia, then Hypere, formerly Patage, or, as others have it, Platage, but now called Amorgos, Polyægos, Phyle, and Thera, known as Calliste when it first sprang from the waves.

Pliny says he can observe no special order and it seems he is naming them in no special arrangement. This makes it impossible to locate where he thought Patmos lay. However he does say that the circumference of Patmos was only 30 miles. This would be Roman miles which are about half our modern mile, so Patmos has a circumference of 15 miles for Pliny. The current island called Patmos has a circumference of about 45 miles. We may also note that Pliny says nothing about it, neither that it has a city, nor what god/goddess it is associated with in mythology.

Given its indefinite location and tiny size, it is hard to see what the readers of *Revelation* would have made of it. The original intended audience, living in Judea during the war would certainly have not known anything about it. On the other hand the second author intended the work for an audience in the Ephesian area. They may have heard of it or had some unknown association with it.

We can suggest that the original writer wrote, "I, John, am an exile in the castle at Macherus." a later writer changed it to the island of Patmos. It is also possible that a prior editor had written "island of Samos," not Patmos. Samos is a much larger island just North of Patmos. Unlike Patmos, Samos was well known by every literate person in the Greece and Rome. It has an important and long history: Zeus's wife Hera,

Pythagoras, Aristarchus, Epicurus, Herodotos and Aesop are all associated with the island. Herodotus was exiled to the island circa 465 B.C.E. The Athenian Democrats in exile on Samos launched a successful revolution in 400 B.C.E. A man writing from exile in Samos would be a man worth listening to. Samos is directly opposite Ephesus, which, based on its central location of the letters of Paul was an early postwar center of Christianity. We therefore may suggest that Macherus was changed to Samos and Samos was changed to Patmos.

Unlike the obscure Patmos, all people in Judea in 69 would have known the famous castle of Macherus. Also note that Josephus tells us, "This place has in it also mines of sulfur and alum." Marius Victorinus of Pettau, circa 355, writes that John was "condemned to the labour of the mines by Caesar Domitian[494]"

Now, it is hard to know where Victorinus got this information from, but he was apparently a leading scholar of his day and so we should take it with some seriousness. Now, Patmos almost certainly did not have mines. If John was sent to a place with mines, again, it is likely to have been Macherus. Yet, Victorinus tells us this only in passing as part of a Commentary on the text of *Revelation*.

Victorinus' Commentary and John the First Born of the Dead

Victorinus' *Commentary* is a fascinating document because it makes clear the evolution of *Revelation*. If one takes out all of his commentary and just leaves in the lines that he quotes, we get a version of *Revelation* that is simpler, more direct, more Jewish, and clearer.

The opening chapters may be reconstructed this way:

Reconstruction of the Opening of Revelation

> The Revelation of Jesus Christ, which God gave to Him, and showed unto His servants things which must shortly come to pass, and signified it. Blessed are they who read and hear the words of this prophecy, and keep the things which are written.
>
> Grace unto you, and peace, from Him which is, and which was, and which is to come.
>
> And from Jesus Christ, who is the faithful witness, the first-begotten of the dead.
>
> And He made us a kingdom and priests unto God and His Father. Behold, He shall come with clouds, and every eye shall see Him.
>
> And I turned, and saw seven golden candlesticks; and in the midst of the seven golden candlesticks one like unto the Son of man.
>
> As it were the Son of man walking in the midst of the golden candlesticks.
>
> Clothed with a garment down to the ankles.

And He was girt about the paps with a golden girdle. And His head and His hairs were white as it were white wool, and as it were snow.
His eyes were as a flame of fire.
And in His face was brightness as the sun.
His feet were like unto yellow brass, as if burned in a furnace.
And out of His mouth was issuing a sharp two-edged sword.
And His voice as it were the voice of many waters.
And He had in His right hand seven stars.

Compare this with the opening from the *New Testament* version. I have placed the additions that the second writer of *Revelation* probably made in Italics.

1. **The revelation of Jesus Christ, which God gave him to show to his servants what must soon take place;** *and he made it known by sending his angel to his servant John,*
2. *who bore witness to the word of God and to the testimony of Jesus Christ, even to all that he saw.*
3. **Blessed is he who reads aloud the words of the prophecy, and blessed are those who hear, and who keep what is written therein; for the time is near.**
4. *John to the seven churches that are in Asia:* **Grace to you and peace from him who is and who was and who is to come,** *and from the seven spirits who are before his throne,*
5. **and from Jesus Christ the faithful witness, the first-born of the dead,** *and the ruler of kings on earth. To him who loves us and has freed us from our sins by his blood*
6. **and made us a kingdom, priests to his God and Father,** *to him be glory and dominion for ever and ever. Amen.*
7. **Behold, he is coming with the clouds, and every eye will see him, every one who pierced him; and all tribes of the earth will wail on account of him. Even so. Amen.**
8. *"I am the Alpha and the Omega," says the Lord God, who is and who was and who is to come, the Almighty.*
9. *I John, your brother, who share with you in Jesus the tribulation and the kingdom and the patient endurance, was on the island called Patmos on account of the word of God and the testimony of Jesus.*
10. *I was in the Spirit on the Lord's day, and I heard behind me a loud voice like a trumpet*
11. *saying, "Write what you see in a book and send it to the seven churches, to Ephesus and to Smyrna and to Per'gamum and to Thyati'ra and to Sardis and to Philadelphia and to La-odice'a."*

12 Then I turned to see the voice that was speaking to me, and on turning I saw seven golden lampstands,
13 and in the midst of the lampstands one like a son of man, clothed with a long robe and with a golden girdle round his breast;
14 his head and his hair were white as white wool, white as snow; his eyes were like a flame of fire,
15 his feet were like burnished bronze, refined as in a furnace, and his voice was like the sound of many waters;
16 in his right hand he held seven stars, from his mouth issued a sharp two-edged sword, and his face was like the sun shining in full strength.

The first text says nothing about John receiving the revelation. Yet one can see that the Christology is much lower. Jesus is simply the faithful witness and first born of the dead. He is not "the ruler of kings on Earth." He has not "freed us from our sins by his blood." One can hardly imagine followers of Jesus taking out these lines about Jesus Christ, so they could only have been added in later. Thus, it is clear that the New Testament *Revelations* comes after Victorinus' *Revelations*. There is coherence to the added material. We may take this as a separate early letter that was reworked and placed into the separate document Victorinus read and called *Revelations*.

Why mix the two documents together? Why mix a letter by John with a revelation by Jesus the Christ? Why would followers of Jesus change a revelation made to Jesus Christ by God and directly transmitted to his servants into one transmitted through John?

We can clear up the mystery by supposing that Victorinus did have the earlier text, and that text was a revelation from John, the prophet and Christ. So the earlier text read:

Second Reconstruction of the Beginning of *Revelation*

The Revelation of John, the Christ, which God gave to Him, and showed unto His servants things which must shortly come to pass, and signified it. Blessed are they who read and hear the words of this prophecy, and keep the things which are written.

Grace unto you, and peace, from Him which is, and which was, and which is to come.

And from John, the Christ, who is the faithful witness, the first-begotten of the dead.

And He made us a kingdom and priests unto God and His Father.

Behold, He shall come with clouds, and every eye shall see Him.

The first change in the second generation of the text would have been to simply change John to Jesus. This explains Jesus Christ (John the Christ) being called "the faithful witness." We have to assume that at this point in time members of the John cult believed that John had been reborn in heaven and that he would be the one to fulfill Messianic prophesy and would "come with clouds, and every eye shall see him."

Under this reconstruction, the phrase "He made us a kingdom and priests unto God and His Father" make much more sense. John had preached the coming kingdom of God. His cult grew into a large enough group that they considered themselves a separate kingdom and gave John credit for making that kingdom. Note that the text reads "priests unto God and His Father," not "His Father God." In this text, the terms "God" and "his father" appear as two separate terms denoting two separate beings. John's father was the High Priest Zachariah. We may assume that John's followers felt that they were following his father Zachariah as well. Who was Zachariah?

We may go back to the *Clementine Recognitions* for an answer. That work tells us this:

> For when the rising of Christ was at hand for the abolition of sacrifices, and for the bestowal of the grace of baptism, the enemy, understanding from the predictions that the time was at hand, wrought various schisms among the people, that, if haply it might be possible to abolish the former sin, the latter fault might be incorrigible. The first schism, therefore, was that of those who were called Sadducees, which took their rise almost in the time of John. These. as more righteous than others, began to separate themselves from the assembly of the people, and to deny the resurrection of the dead, and to assert that by an argument of infidelity, saying that it was unworthy that God should be worshipped, as it were, under the promise of a reward. The first author of this opinion was Dositheus; the second was Simon. Another schism is that of the Samaritans; for they deny the resurrection of the dead, and assert that God is not to be worshipped in Jerusalem, but on Mount Gerrizim. They indeed rightly, from the predictions of Moses, expect the one true Prophet; but by the wickedness of Dositheus they were hindered from believing that Jesus is He whom they were expecting. The scribes also, and Pharisees, are led away into another schism; but these, being baptized by John, and holding the word of truth received from the tradition of Moses as the key of the kingdom of heaven, have hid it from the hearing of the people. Yea, some even of the disciples of John, who seemed to be great ones, have separated themselves from the people, and proclaimed their own master as the Christ. But all these schisms have been prepared, that by means of them the faith of Christ and baptism might be hindered[495]."

The Sadducees are started almost in the time of John. This suggests that it was started a few years before John. The Sadducees deny the resurrection of the dead. The Samaritans agree but also believe in the coming of the Christ and the true worship of

God at Mount Gerizim and not in the Jerusalem temple. We can now go back to what Josephus tells us about Jewish sects:

> Yet was there one Judas, a Gaulonite, of a city whose name was Gamala, who, taking with him Sadduc, a Pharisee, became zealous to draw them to a revolt, who both said that this taxation was no better than an introduction to slavery, and exhorted the nation to assert their liberty...
>
> ... Such were the consequences of this, that the customs of our fathers were altered, and such a change was made, as added a mighty weight toward bringing all to destruction, which these men occasioned by their thus conspiring together; for Judas and Sadduc, who excited a fourth philosophic sect among us, and had a great many followers therein, filled our civil government with tumults at present, and laid the foundations of our future miseries, by this system of philosophy, which we were before unacquainted withal, concerning which I will discourse a little, and this the rather because the infection which spread thence among the younger sort, who were zealous for it, brought the public to destruction...
>
> ... the doctrine of the Sadducees is this: That souls die with the bodies; nor do they regard the observation of any thing besides what the law enjoins them; for they think it an instance of virtue to dispute with those teachers of philosophy whom they frequent: but this doctrine is received but by a few, yet by those still of the greatest dignity. But they are able to do almost nothing of themselves; for when they become magistrates, as they are unwillingly and by force sometimes obliged to be, they addict themselves to the notions of the Pharisees, because the multitude would not otherwise bear them.

Since Judas came from Gamala and Josephus just says he took Sadduc with him, we may assume that Sadduc too came from the city of Gamala. Gamala is in Galilee. The association of Galilee with John/Jesus the Christ probably stems from this fact.

However, the most important point is that Sadduc and his followers, the Sadducees, did not believe in the resurrection of the dead. Apparently, not believing in the resurrection of the dead was an heretical opinion ("they began to separate themselves from the assembly of the people") to the majority of Jews.

The Hebrew term *Saddiq* means righteous. The Sadducees existed historically in the second century B.C.E., but we may assume that Sadduc was a new leader or title given to the new leader, and that he revived the movement.

Now we can understand the statement in *Revelations* that Jesus/John was "the first born of the dead." Such a statement would only be made by a group that did not believe in the general resurrection of the dead. We may assume that John and his first followers were followers of Sadduc of Gamala and did not believe in the resurrection of the dead. The later followers of John, those who proclaimed him the Christ must have felt that he was the first of the dead to be resurrected. Knowing that he had preached that there was no resurrection of the dead, it was the greatest honor they could bestow on him to make him the first of the dead to be reborn.

It is the greatest of ironies that the man John whose life and preachings resulted in the founding of Christianity did not believe in the resurrection of the dead.

What Really Happened to John and How He Became John the Christ

We may take it that Sadduc and John were extremely close in their ideological outlook. We may speculate that Sadduc is the historical model for John's fictional father Zechariah. Thus the idea that John was a son of Sadduc was taken literally in the material that found its way into the beginning of the *Gospel of Luke* (1:5-6).

> In the days of Herod, king of Judea, there was a priest named Zechariah, of the division of Abijah; and he had a wife of the daughters of Aaron, and her name was Elizabeth. And they were both righteous before God, walking in all the commandments and ordinances of the Lord blameless.

Note that Zechariah was of the "division of Abijah" As with many terms in the Bible, this has multiple references and possible meanings. The most obvious is found in *2 Chronicles* (29-30):

1. Hezekiah began to reign when he was twenty-five years old, and he reigned twenty-nine years in Jerusalem. His mother's name was Abijah the daughter of Zechari'ah.
1. And he did what was right in the eyes of the Lord, according to all that David his father had done.

The writer is associating the father of John with a righteous king—Hezekiah and he is associating him with David. Also, through the reference to the daughter of the high Priest Aaron, the writer is associating Zechariah with Moses. While associating Zechariah and his son John with the righteous king Hezekiah, students of the Hebrew Scriptures would also have associated them with King Abijah. Abijah was the son of a king of Judah called Rehoboam (2Chronicles 18-20), who fought a victorious war against the King of Israel called Jeroboam (2Chronicles 13):

3: Abijah went out to battle having an army of valiant men of war, four hundred thousand picked men; and Jerobo'am drew up his line of

> battle against him with eight hundred thousand picked mighty warriors. 4: Then Abijah stood up on Mount Zemaraim which is in the hill country of Ephraim, and said, "Hear me, O Jeroboam and all Israel! 5: Ought you not to know that the LORD God of Israel gave the kingship over Israel for ever to David and his sons by a covenant of salt? Yet Jeroboam the son of Nebat, a servant of Solomon the son of David, rose up and rebelled against his lord;

The text tells us that Mount Zemaraim is in the hill country of Ephraim. It is the place where Abijah, a descendent of David, declared war against a usurper of the kingship of Israel named Jeroboam. Now compare this to Josephus's description of what the man we have identified as John, the Nazarene did.

> 1. But the nation of the Samaritans did not escape without tumults. The man who excited them to it was one who thought lying a thing of little consequence, and who contrived every thing so that the multitude might be pleased; so he bid them to get together upon Mount Gerizzim, which is by them looked upon as the most holy of all mountains, and assured them, that when they were come thither, he would show them those sacred vessels which were laid under that place, because Moses put them there. So they came thither armed, and thought the discourse of the man probable; and as they abode at a certain village, which was called Tirathaba, they got the rest together to them, and desired to go up the mountain in a great multitude together; but Pilate prevented their going up, by seizing upon file roads with a great band of horsemen and foot-men, who fell upon those that were gotten together in the village; and when it came to an action, some of them they slew, and others of them they put to flight, and took a great many alive, the principal of which, and also the most potent of those that fled away, Pilate ordered to be slain[496].

Mount Gerizzim or Gerizim is in the hill country of Ephraim. We may take it as the later name of Mount Zemaraim, the place where Abijah declared war against the usurper king Jeroboam. It is hard to determine if John simply led people to the mountain to show them sacred vessels or if he was going there to declare war against Herod Agrippa. Probably Agrippa thought that John was going to copy Abijah and declare war on the mountain. He asked Pilate to intervene. Apparently, the situation was serious enough that Pilate ordered some of the men he captured to be slain.

However, it is quite important to note that John himself was not one of the men Pilate ordered killed. John was sent to the castle at Macherus. It is possible that "the most potent of those that fled away" may be a reference to a man named Jesus and that Pilate ordered him executed. This would account for the fleeing, escape and coming to Jerusalem-in-secret motifs that we find in Mark. Our supposition here depends on how much truth Mary put into her passion play. If we had that play instead of just radically changed material from John and Mark based on it, we could judge more definitely if Mary based her material on the death of a follower of John named Jesus or on John himself (the son of a high priest—Caiphas/Jesus represents Zechariah/John). If there was an actual man named Jesus, his arrest, trial and execution would have taken place over a period of several days or months. In writing the play, Mary took Aristotle's advice for writing tragedy and placed all the events in a single day (Aristotle, *Poetics* 5), "for Tragedy endeavors, as far as possible, to confine itself to a single revolution of the sun, or but slightly to exceed this limit,"

In any case, we can suppose that most of the people were intensely interested in the fate of John, as both our biblical and historical sources (Josephus and *Clementine Recognitions*) indicate he had a large following. We may take as true the reports that Antipas respected and feared John. If this was the case then the people were expecting the return of John at any moment. They were disappointed. John did not return from Macherus.

Was he beheaded? It is probable. Josephus tells us he was, but all the story material tells us that Antipas was reluctant to do it, blaming the death on his wife and daughter, and some rather unclear and obtuse violation of some Jewish incest law. We may take this as an attempt to cover up the political reasons for John's death (leading a revolution) with personal reasons (marrying a dead brother's wife) which seem to have been required by Jewish law rather than prohibited[497].

In all three of the synoptic gospels, we have interesting passages about Herod that take place after John's death. He is Luke (9:6-9):

> And they departed and went through the villages, preaching the gospel and healing everywhere. Now Herod the tetrarch heard of all that was done, and he was perplexed, because it was said by some that John had been raised from the dead, by some that Eli'jah had appeared, and by others that one of the old prophets had risen. Herod said, "John I beheaded; but who is this about whom I hear such things?"

Compare this with Matthew (14:1-2):

> At that time Herod the tetrarch heard about the fame of Jesus; and he said to his servants, "This is John the Baptist, he has been raised from the dead; that is why these powers are at work in him."

And Mark (6:14-16)

> King Herod heard of it; for Jesus' name had become known. Some said, "John the baptizer has been raised from the dead; that is why these

> powers are at work in him." But others said, "It is Eli'jah." And others said, "It is a prophet, like one of the prophets of old." 16: But when Herod heard of it he said, "John, whom I beheaded, has been raised."

Mark and Matthew link the statements about John to Herod hearing about Jesus. However Luke says Herod heard about the activities of disciples and became perplexed. We may take it that Luke is reporting more accurately. Otherwise, why would he change a specific reference to Jesus to a reference to his followers? Since our previous analysis of Matthew revealed that it was John who sent his followers out to do miracles, we may take it that in the earlier text it reported that Herod heard about the followers of John and "he was perplexed, because it was said by some that John had been raised from the dead, by some that Elijah had appeared, and by others that one of the old prophets had risen."

We may take it that this was a debate carried on within the John community after his death. Once we understand that this community was a Sadducee Community that did not believe that the dead lived again, this debate makes sense. The first position is that John had been raised from the dead. As noted, *The Book of Revelation* refers to him as the first born of the dead. This went against the notion of the community that the dead were not raised. It exalted John, but at the same time it can be seen as a capitulation to the wider Judean community that believed the dead were raised. This is the "yes he really died but God raised him position." The second position is that he had appeared as Elijah. Elijah did not die but was carried up to heaven (2 Kings 11). This is preshadowed in the scene which we reconstructed in which John went to the mountain with two of his disciples:

> And after six days Jesus took with him Peter and James and John, and led them up a high mountain apart by themselves; and he was transfigured before them, and his garments became glistening, intensely white, as no fuller on earth could bleach them. And there appeared to them Eli'jah with Moses; and they were talking to Jesus. And Peter said to Jesus, "Master, it is well that we are here; let us make three booths, one for you and one for Moses and one for Eli'jah."

Noting that Josephus tells us that John led the Samaritans to Mount Gerizim to look for vessels of Moses, we may take it that in the original version of the tale, John led his two disciples Peter and James to the mountain where he was transformed into Elijah and spoke with Moses. In the original text, Peter's request to build three booths was probably rejected as only two booths were needed since John and Elijah was the same.

This second position may be called the "No, John did not die, but rose to heaven like/as Elijah" position. The third position on the issue of what happened to John is the "One of the Old Prophets has risen" position. This agrees with the second position that John did not die and was raised to heaven, but it argues that he was not specifically

Elijah. Actually, chronologically the third position probably proceded the second, so we get this order:

1. John, a prophet, died but was the first person raised to heaven.
2. John, a prophet, did not die, but like Elijah he was taken to heaven
3. John, a prophet, did not die, but he was really Elijah and he was taken to heaven

Besides figuring out what happened to John, the Sadducees had another problem. They believed in the prophesies that God would send a messiah to save the Jews. However, since they did not believe in resurrection, it could not be any Jew from the past. The messianic prophesy in Daniel (7:14) identified the messiah as a son of man, which is another way of saying "a man".

> I kept looking in the night visions,
> And behold, with the clouds of heaven
> One like a Son of Man was coming,
> And he came up to the Ancient of Days
> And was presented before Him. And to Him was given dominion,
> Glory and a kingdom,

So a man was coming to save the Jews (not an angel). But he was coming from heaven, not the earth. If, like the Sadducean Samaritans, you do not believe that any of the dead are resurrected, this presents a serious difficulty. Who is this man coming from Heaven and how did he get to heaven? This is not a problem for the Pharisees who believed like the Greeks in an after life and judgment. The first solution that the Sadducean followers of John came up with was that John was the one and only exception to the rule. Greater than all human beings before him, he was the first born of the dead. He will be the man coming from heaven. However, it was, perhaps, a little depressing to think that God did not save/preserve this man who was so good and let him die. If God lets even the best die, what chance do us sinners have that God will preserve us in battle. So the second solution was to agree that John would return as the Messiah (the man from heaven), but to deny his death at all. The rule of no resurrection of the dead could be kept if God preserved John and took him directly to heaven before death. The precedent had been set by God taking up Elijah directly to heaven.

This is fine but things are getting complicated and problematical here. For the followers of John, it must have seemed that the Essenes were right after all and there would be two advents of the Messiah, one coming in peace and the other in war. The Community Rule document (1QS) found among the Dead Sea Scrolls reads "[they] shall be ruled by the primitive precepts in which the men of the Community were first instructed until there shall come the Prophet and the Messiahs of Aaron and Israel"

It is at this point that the John community produces the story of the holy birth of John through the miraculous pregnancy of Elizabeth. John had a miraculous birth and was the Messiah of Aaron this time around. He did not die but was raised to heaven to await further instructions. Next time he will come again from heaven.

This seems to explain things nicely. However, now you have two men in heaven who can be the coming Messiah, Elijah and John. Which one would God choose? An alternative explanation was produced which resolves this problem. While being baptized, God sent the spirit of Elijah in the form of a dove into John. This way John who was taken up to heaven was actually Elijah. The two were one. Elijah's first Aaronic turn as Messiah was as the lowly John. The next advent straight from heaven would be as the Davidic Messiah.

While John was first born holy through Elizabeth and than in a competing mythology made holy through the dove/spirit of Elijah; the exact reverse appears to be the case with the Jesus Messiah story. First the story of the dove/spirit from heaven was transformed to make Jesus into the Messiah and later the second story of John's miraculous birth from Elizabeth was transformed into a story including the miraculous birth from Mary.

We see how the imprisonment of the historical John at Macherus led to anxiety among his followers. We see how the hopes for the return of the living John were dashed with the news of his death. This led to the hope of his return from the dead. As this conflicted with the Saducean ideology of no return from the dead, his followers spread the story that he had been taken alive up to heaven like Elijah. This led to a story of John's miraculous birth. To resolve the conflict between the old Jews who believed that Elijah would come as the Messiah and the John community who believed that John would come, John was turned into Elijah through the magical dove from heaven trick.

The Historical John and the Mythology of John

The mythology that was created after John has to be vigorously separated from the historical life of John. We know that John was a Sadducee who did not believe in the resurrection of the dead. He believed, not that people would go to the kingdom of heaven when they died, but that God would bring the kingdom of heaven to Earth while they were still alive. God would then increase food production thousands of times and abolish death.

It is highly probable that he was the son of a priest. Our reconstruction of Mary's play (messiah as high priest's son) as well as the gospel of Luke points to this. We know that he was a devoted follower of Moses and he was arrested for leading a mass of people in a political demonstration at Mount Gerizim in Samaria. We know that he was sent to prison around 35-36 C.E. Josephus, as well as the gospels point to this. He was probably beheaded by Herod Antipas although we cannot be certain of this. Although

THE EVOLUTION OF CHRISTS AND CHRISTIANIES

all our sources agree on this, there are no good descriptions of any execution. It is possible that he died of natural causes, or he quietly went to live elsewhere under a different identity. It may have been the enemies of Antipas who made this proposition into a fact of history.

Is there anything else we can say about the historical John? One important fact that I think we can be reasonably certain about is his nationality. I think we can say that he was a Samaritan. There are some strong clues pointing in this direction. First, it is unlikely that the Samaritans would have followed a non-Samaritan leader in a revolt. They seemed to be quite suspicious and independent of their Galilean and Judean neighbors. Another clue is the statement by Josephus (*Antiquities*, 18.4.1) that "the nation of the Samaritans did not escape without tumults." This line only makes sense if the reader should expect that the Samaritans should without tumults. The only way the reader should expect that the Samaritans should escape without tumults is if Josephus had described John as a Samaritan previously before going on to describe his evil deeds to other people. Other indications of the Samaritan nationality of John is his friendly seductive encounter with the Samaritan woman near Mount Gerizim (*John*, 4), the line in John (8:48) "The Jews answered him, "Are we not right in saying that you are a Samaritan and have a demon?", Luke's (6:30-36) Good Samaritan story, and the grateful Samaritan Story (Luke 17:11-19). Matthew's attack on Samaritans, 'These twelve Jesus sent out, charging them, "Go nowhere among the Gentiles, and enter no town of the Samaritans,"' may also be taken as a strong indication that John was a Samaritan, for if John was a Samaritan, the Jesus cult would not have made much headway in Samaria.

Basically, at this point, we can say this much about Jesus Christ. The material in the gospels come primarily out of two groups, a large John Community and a small Mary community. The John community followed a popular Samaritan Sadducean leader named John. He did not believe in the resurrection of the dead, but he appears to have prepared the Samaritans for an armed uprising to bring God's kingdom of heaven to earth.

A play by Mary seems to have been the core text of the gospel. Canonical gospel writers seem to have heavily edited it and added text about John by simply changing the name John to Jesus in most cases. Once we separate out the approximately 85% of the text that comes from John sources, it is difficult to know what to make of the 15% coming from the Mary source. Unfortunately, the Mary source text seems to have been reworked so much that it is difficult to know how much historical information was in it. As she seems to have studied Aristotle, it is probable that she was more interested in dramatic storytelling than in presenting historical facts.

Sculpture. Christ Raises Lazarus, Mary Anoints His Foot.

Sarcophagus in Lateran Museum, Rome, circa 340. Beardless Jesus with short curly hair uses a curved wand to raise Lazarus. A diminutive Mary pours ointment on his foot.

Chapter 10

Paul through a Mirror Darkly

Earlier I noted that it was a mistake to try to understand Paul's letters as a starting point for Christianity. In fact, it is only after we understand the origin of the gospels and the Book of Revelation that we can understand where Paul's letters come in. Some letters may have been composed before much of the gospel material but they too have been well scrubbed.

The Seven Inauthentic Authentic Letters of Paul

The writer of the letter 1 Corinthians makes a direct attack on those in the Church of Corinth who propose, like the Sadducees, that there is no resurrection of the dead: Here is the relevant text from chapter 16.

12. Now if Christ is preached as raised from the dead, how can some of you say that there is no resurrection of the dead?
13. But if there is no resurrection of the dead, then Christ has not been raised;
14. if Christ has not been raised, then our preaching is in vain and your faith is in vain.
15. We are even found to be misrepresenting God, because we testified of God that he raised Christ, whom he did not raise if it is true that the dead are not raised.
16. For if the dead are not raised, then Christ has not been raised.
17. If Christ has not been raised, your faith is futile and you are still in your sins.
18. Then those also who have fallen asleep in Christ have perished.

19. If for this life only we have hoped in Christ, we are of all men most to be pitied.
20. But in fact Christ has been raised from the dead, the first fruits of those who have fallen asleep.
21. For as by a man came death, by a man has come also the resurrection of the dead.
22. For as in Adam all die, so also in Christ shall all be made alive.
23. But each in his own order: Christ the first fruits, then at his coming those who belong to Christ.
24. Then comes the end, when he delivers the kingdom to God the Father after destroying every rule and every authority and power.
25. For he must reign until he has put all his enemies under his feet.
26. The last enemy to be destroyed is death.
27. "For God has put all things in subjection under his feet." But when it says, "All things are put in subjection under him," it is plain that he is excepted who put all things under him.
28. When all things are subjected to him, then the Son himself will also be subjected to him who put all things under him, that God may be everything to every one.
29. Otherwise, what do people mean by being baptized on behalf of the dead? If the dead are not raised at all, why are people baptized on their behalf?
30. Why am I in peril every hour?
31. I protest, brethren, by my pride in you which I have in Christ Jesus our Lord, I die every day!
32. What do I gain if, humanly speaking, I fought with beasts at Ephesus? If the dead are not raised, "Let us eat and drink, for tomorrow we die."
33. Do not be deceived: "Bad company ruins good morals."
34. Come to your right mind, and sin no more. For some have no knowledge of God. I say this to your shame.
35. But some one will ask, "How are the dead raised? With what kind of body do they come?"
36. You foolish man! What you sow does not come to life unless it dies.
37. And what you sow is not the body which is to be, but a bare kernel, perhaps of wheat or of some other grain.
38. But God gives it a body as he has chosen, and to each kind of seed its own body.
39. For not all flesh is alike, but there is one kind for men, another for animals, another for birds, and another for fish.

40. There are celestial bodies and there are terrestrial bodies; but the glory of the celestial is one, and the glory of the terrestrial is another.
41. There is one glory of the sun, and another glory of the moon, and another glory of the stars; for star differs from star in glory.
42. So is it with the resurrection of the dead. What is sown is perishable, what is raised is imperishable.
43. It is sown in dishonor, it is raised in glory. It is sown in weakness, it is raised in power.
44. It is sown a physical body, it is raised a spiritual body. If there is a physical body, there is also a spiritual body.
45. Thus it is written, "The first man Adam became a living being"; the last Adam became a life-giving spirit.
46. But it is not the spiritual which is first but the physical, and then the spiritual.
47. The first man was from the earth, a man of dust; the second man is from heaven.
48. As was the man of dust, so are those who are of the dust; and as is the man of heaven, so are those who are of heaven.
49. Just as we have borne the image of the man of dust, we shall also bear the image of the man of heaven.
50. I tell you this, brethren: flesh and blood cannot inherit the kingdom of God, nor does the perishable inherit the imperishable.
51. Lo! I tell you a mystery. We shall not all sleep, but we shall all be changed,
52. in a moment, in the twinkling of an eye, at the last trumpet. For the trumpet will sound, and the dead will be raised imperishable, and we shall be changed.
53. For this perishable nature must put on the imperishable, and this mortal nature must put on immortality.
54. When the perishable puts on the imperishable, and the mortal puts on immortality, then shall come to pass the saying that is written: "Death is swallowed up in victory."
55. "O death, where is thy victory? O death, where is thy sting?"
56. The sting of death is sin, and the power of sin is the law.
57. But thanks be to God, who gives us the victory through our Lord Jesus Christ.
58. Therefore, my beloved brethren, be steadfast, immovable, always abounding in the work of the Lord, knowing that in the Lord your labor is not in vain.

We may take it that the Corinth Church still believed in the Samaritan/Sadducee principles of no resurrection of the dead. Paul insists that there will be a resurrection.

Notice that the writer is hitting themes we find are prevalent in *Revelations*: Christ is "the first fruits" Compare this with *Revelations*, 1.5, "the first born of the dead," *Revelation*, 14.4, "one hundred and forty-four thousand . . . have been redeemed from mankind as first fruits for God and the Lamb." Paul knows that the resurrection will happen after the "last trumpet will sound." Compare this (*Revelation*, 8:2): "Then I saw the seven angels who stand before God, and seven trumpets were given to them.," and *Revelation*, 10.7, "but that in the days of the trumpet call to be sounded by the seventh angel, the mystery of God, as he announced to his servants the prophets, should be fulfilled." and Paul say, "Lo I tell you a mystery." Compare this (*Revelation* 1:20): "As for the mystery of the Seven Stars," and (*Revelation*, 17:7) "I will tell you the mystery of the woman, and of the beast with seven heads and ten horns that carries her."

The writer is also denying the doctrines of the original writer of *Revelations*. He says that flesh and blood cannot inherit the kingdom of God, while Revelations postulates precisely this, that flesh and blood humans will inherit the kingdom of God with a New Jerusalem (the kingdom of God) coming down to Earth. We may take it that *Revelation*, written circa 69 C.E. is already a well known and important document for Paul and the group of people that he is writing to.

Now this contradiction of basic Christian doctrine must have caused quite a deep split in the Corinthian community. The writer tells us about divisions in the community in the first chapter (1:11-16):

> For it has been reported to me by Chloe's people that there is quarreling among you, my brethren. What I mean is that each one of you says, "I belong to Paul," or "I belong to Apollos," or "I belong to Cephas," or "I belong to Christ." Is Christ divided? Was Paul crucified for you? Or were you baptized in the name of Paul? I am thankful that I baptized none of you except Crispus and Gaius; lest any one should say that you were baptized in my name. (I did baptize also the household of Stephanas. Beyond that, I do not know whether I baptized any one else.)

The writer tries to overcome these contradictions by saying that it doesn't matter who did the actual baptism, but only that everyone belongs to Christ (1 Corinthians 3):

> 21. So let no one boast of men. For all things are yours,
> 22. whether Paul or Apollos or Cephas or the world or life or death or the present or the future, all are yours;
> 23. and you are Christ's; and Christ is God's.

Apparently, Paul has been accused of baptizing people in his name. Paul admits to only three baptisms.

> 1.13. Is Christ divided? Was Paul crucified for you? Or were you baptized in the name of Paul?
> 14. I am thankful that I baptized none of you except Crispus and Gaius;
> 15. lest any one should say that you were baptized in my name.
> 16. (I did baptize also the household of Stephanas. Beyond that, I do not know whether I baptized any one else.)

The claim of limited baptisms appears to *Acts* (18:8), "Crispus, the ruler of the synagogue, believed in the Lord, together with all his household; and many of the Corinthians hearing Paul believed and were baptized." He has also forgotten to mention the people at Ephesus who were baptized after listening to him (19:1-5).

Paul, perhaps, has also forgotten Lydia of Thyatira and her family in Philippi, as recorded in *Acts* (16:12-15):

> and from there to Philip'pi, which is the leading city of the district of Macedo'nia, and a Roman colony. We remained in this city some days; and on the sabbath day we went outside the gate to the riverside, where we supposed there was a place of prayer; and we sat down and spoke to the women who had come together. One who heard us was a woman named Lydia, from the city of Thyatira, a seller of purple goods, who was a worshiper of God. The Lord opened her heart to give heed to what was said by Paul. And when she was baptized, with her household, she besought us, saying, "If you have judged me to be faithful to the Lord, come to my house and stay." And she prevailed upon us.

Regardless of whom and how many people Paul baptized, it is apparent that the Apollos members of the Church are planning to, or have already filed some kind of law suit against the writer. Although this is not stated explicitly, one certainly gets the idea that he is the target by the vehement opposition of the writer.

> 4.3. But with me it is a very small thing that I should be judged by you or by any human court. I do not even judge myself.
> 4. I am not aware of anything against myself, but I am not thereby acquitted. It is the Lord who judges me.

The writer may not be aware or may be pretending not to be aware of the details of the case ("I am not aware of anything against myself"). He pleads with the Apollos members of the Corinth Church to drop the suit against him.

> 6.3 Do you not know that we are to judge angels? How much more, matters pertaining to this life!
> 4: If then you have such cases, why do you lay them before those who are least esteemed by the church?
> 5: I say this to your shame. Can it be that there is no man among you wise enough to decide between members of the brotherhood,
> 6: but brother goes to law against brother, and that before unbelievers? To have lawsuits at all with one another is defeat for you. Why not rather suffer wrong? Why not rather be defrauded?

Paul in defending himself is trying all kinds of tactics. He tries especially to evoke pity by pointing out how well they are doing in comparison to himself:

> 8. Already you are filled! Already you have become rich! Without us you have become kings! And would that you did reign, so that we might share the rule with you!
> 9. For I think that God has exhibited us apostles as last of all, like men sentenced to death; because we have become a spectacle to the world, to angels and to men.
> 10. We are fools for Christ's sake, but you are wise in Christ. We are weak, but you are strong. You are held in honor, but we in disrepute.
> 11. To the present hour we hunger and thirst, we are ill-clad and buffeted and homeless,
> 12. and we labor, working with our own hands. When reviled, we bless; when persecuted, we endure;
> 13. when slandered, we try to conciliate; we have become, and are now, as the refuse of the world, the offscouring of all things.

Paul is clearly an outsider to the members of the church. He argues that as an outsider he should not be judged. He says (5.13), "God judges those outside. Drive out the wicked person from among you." Instead of facing the charges that have been laid against him, Paul tries to shift the problem to a man who is "living with his father's wife." (5.1). He calls for him to be "delivered to Satan for the destruction of the flesh" (5.5).

It is doubtful if this strategy of evasion actually worked. The church apparently had written him a letter with a series of specific question aimed at trapping him. If he contradicted what he had told members in the letter, they would have witnesses against him. If he repeated what he had said to members privately, he would convict himself. Paul has to be very careful about his reply. The order of the topics is an important clue to what the members of the Corinthian (or some other) church were charging him with.

The first question had to do with marriage and sexual relations (chapter 7).

> Now concerning the matters about which you wrote. It is well for a man not to touch a woman. But because of the temptation to immorality, each man should have his own wife and each woman her own husband. The husband should give to his wife her conjugal rights, and likewise the wife to her husband. For the wife does not rule over her own body, but the husband does; likewise the husband does not rule over his own body, but the wife does. Do not refuse one another except perhaps by agreement for a season, that you may devote yourselves to prayer; but then come together again, lest Satan tempt you through lack of self-control. I say this by way of concession, not of command. I wish that all were as I myself am. But each has his own special gift from God, one of one kind and one of another. To the unmarried and the widows I say that it is well for them to remain single as I do. But if they cannot exercise self-control, they should marry. For it is better to marry than to be aflame with passion. To the married I give charge, not I but the Lord, that the wife should not separate from her husband. (but if she does, let her remain single or else be reconciled to her husband)—and that the husband should not divorce his wife.

Paul is against marriage. He is certainly not against sex. In fact he denounces sexless marriages, "do not refuse one another except for a season." His position regarding sex appears to be the normal Greek position of this time as moderation and self-control as Plato and Aristotle both taught it. One should engage in sex moderately, neither too much nor too little. It is best not to marry. If one cannot control one's self and must have a lot of sex, then it is best to marry to get the sex drive under control. When you marry, your spouse has some control over how much sex you have. She or he determines how often and with whom. Jewish men could easily separate from their wives by accusing them of adultery. This would eliminate the moderation effect of marriage on sex. Therefore Paul calls for this loophole to be closed.

In reading this text, to understand Paul's position, we should take the early story of Thecla and Paul quite seriously. In that story Paul seduces the fiancé of Thamyris, an important person in the town of Iconium. While the details of the story, such as Thecla's heroic antics fighting lions and supernatural martyrdom are certainly additions, the original tale of Paul seducing her may have become a known and scandalous fact. Being too well known to be denied, it became a wonderful fable about Thecla's devotion and heroism. Ordinarily one would expect the story to end with Thecla, after showing her saintliness, to end up marrying Paul. We should expect that Paul's anti-marriage position was well known and therefore the story could not end on that happy note.

In any case, the next question the church asked Paul to clarify was his position on circumcision. He downplays its importance, saying (7.19), "For neither circumcision counts for anything nor uncircumcision, but keeping the commandments of God." We must assume, since he mentions nothing about his own circumcision that the letter writer is neither Jewish nor circumcised. We may take it that the Church in Corinth still had a rule that members were to be circumcised.

The next question he answers has to do with eating food prepared for idols. Again, Paul downplays the importance of the question (8.8), "Food will not commend us to God. We are no worse off if we do not eat, and no better off if we do." We may take it that he was charged with eating food prepared for idols. Paul basically admits the charge, but he promises to correct his ways if it bothers the church (8.16), "Therefore, if food is a cause of my brother's falling, I will never eat meat, lest I cause my brother to fall."

The charges of sexual impropriety, non-circumcision and eating idol meat are just leading up to perhaps the most serious charge against Paul—thievery. Apparently Paul has been charged with scamming money from the church. Paul becomes indignant over this, claiming that he has every right to make money off of his teachings (9.7).

> Am I not free? Am I not an apostle? Have I not seen Jesus our Lord? Are not you my workmanship in the Lord? If to others I am not an apostle, at least I am to you; For you are the seal of my apostleship in the Lord. This is my defense to those who would examine me. Do we not have the right to our food and drink? Do we not have the right to be accompanied by a wife, as the other apostles and the brothers of the Lord and Cephas? Or is it only Barnabas and I who have no right to refrain from working for a living? Who serves as a soldier at his own expense? Who plants a vineyard without eating any of its fruit? Who tends a flock without getting some of the milk?

It is interesting that Paul calls the church the "seal of my apostleship in the Lord." It indicates that he has not been recognized or given a seal of approval by any other group.

It is at this point in the text that the writer apparently admits he was not Jewish (9.20-21):

> To the Jews I became as a Jew, in order to win Jews; to those under the law I became as one under the law—though not being myself under the law—that I might win those under the law.
>
> To those outside the law I became as one outside the law—not being without law toward God but under the law of Christ—that I might win those outside the law.

THE EVOLUTION OF CHRISTS AND CHRISTIANIES

There is some subtlety here that appears a bit confusing. Paul is not saying he scammed both Jews and non-Jays. He is saying he scammed three groups: 1) Jews, 2) those under the law, and 3) those not under the law. If Paul was a Jew one could understand him saying that he scammed the last two groups, but the fact that he scammed the first into believing he was Jewish indicates clearly he was not a Jew.

One might ask about the statement in Romans (11.1) "I ask, then, has God rejected his people? By no means! I myself am an Israelite, a descendant of Abraham, a member of the tribe of Benjamin." We should not take this for a fact, but rather as an example of his scamming the Jews by pretending to be Jewish.

Starting with chapter 11, there is a long discussion primarily centered on the difference between speaking in tongues and prophecy. The term speaking in tongues refers to speaking Hebrew or some other ancient language which God would be expected to communicate in. Paul is trying to explain how he can be a prophet, or be filled with the holy spirit, and not know Hebrew. The reference to Jews demanding signs (1:22) probably refers to this that the Jews are skeptical of Paul because of his lack of knowledge of Hebrew.

We may suppose that there was a woman prophet speaking in Hebrew in this church. Her knowledge was an embarrassment to Paul and therefore Paul gives the order (14.34), "women should keep silent in the churches. For they are not permitted to speak, but should be subordinate."

Finally, in chapter 16, we have an appeal for a contribution for "the Saints."

1. Now concerning the contribution for the saints: as I directed the churches of Galatia, so you also are to do.
2. On the first day of every week, each of you is to put something aside and store it up, as he may prosper, so that contributions need not be made when I come.
3. And when I arrive, I will send those whom you accredit by letter to carry your gift to Jerusalem.
4. If it seems advisable that I should go also, they will accompany me.

It is evident that Paul knows the Corinthians do not trust him. Therefore the Corinthians will accredit people with a letter and Paul will accompany them if they permit it. It is strange that Paul is asking the Corinthians to spend money raised for the Saints on traveling expenses. Would it not be better for Paul to save that money by taking it himself?

The letter at this point contains a clue that it is being written after the destruction of the Jerusalem temple.

5. I will visit you after passing through Macedo'nia, for I intend to pass through Macedo'nia,

> 6. and perhaps I will stay with you or even spend the winter, so that you may speed me on my journey, wherever I go.
> 7. For I do not want to see you now just in passing; I hope to spend some time with you, if the Lord permits.
> 8. But I will stay in Ephesus until Pentecost,
> 9. for a wide door for effective work has opened to me, and there are many adversaries.

If the temple existed, one would expect that the Jews of Corinth would want to make the trip to Jerusalem to sacrifice for Passover. It was the one time of year when Jews from all over traveled to Jerusalem to sacrifice in the temple. Paul intends to stay the winter so he is evidently writing before the winter. In fact, he is writing before Pentecost, which indicates he is writing in Spring. Paul mentions nothing about the important Passover Holiday. Now, do the members of Paul's church, which he calls the Church of God, the church of the Saints make sacrifices in the Jewish Temple? Written before the war this should be a major issue, virtually impossible to ignore in a letter dealing specifically with Jewish versus Christian customs. If this letter was written after the war when the temple no longer existed for sacrifice, the whole question would be mute, so the silence would be explained.

Likewise, the verses in the third chapter (16 and 17), "Do you not know that you are God's temple and that God's Spirit dwells in you? If any one destroys God's temple, God will destroy him. For God's temple is holy, and that temple you are," is another big clue that this text is post temple destruction, i.e. post 70. So it is not only the author's knowledge of Revelations written circa 69 C.E. that dates these letters, but also the references to the Jerusalem temple or lack thereof.

The epistle 2 Corinthians is another letter by the same author written about a year later with Paul now in Macedonia on his way to Corinth. Paul still hasn't come to Corinth, but he has sent Titus who apparently has calmed down the Corinthians' hostility towards Paul so they are no longer suing or threatening to sue him in law courts, but they are willing to accept another visit. Apparently, it is on the condition that he does not ask for money for himself, which Paul tells us is his normal mode of operating.

> 11.8. I robbed other churches by accepting support from them in order to serve you.
> 9. And when I was with you and was in want, I did not burden any one, for my needs were supplied by the brethren who came from Macedo'nia. So I refrained and will refrain from burdening you in any way.

But even though Paul did not engage in his usual custom of having the church he visited support him and his entourage, they still apparently thought he was scamming He further writes in 2 Corinthians (2:12-21):

15. I will most gladly spend and be spent for your souls. If I love you the more, am I to be loved the less?
16: *But granting that I myself did not burden you, I was crafty, you say, and got the better of you by guile.*
17. Did I take advantage of you through any of those whom I sent to you?
18. I urged Titus to go, and sent the brother with him. Did Titus take advantage of you? Did we not act in the same spirit? Did we not take the same steps?
19: Have you been thinking all along that we have been defending ourselves before you? It is in the sight of God that we have been speaking in Christ, and all for your upbuilding, beloved.
20. For I fear that perhaps I may come and find you not what I wish, and that you may find me not what you wish; that perhaps there may *be quarreling, jealousy, anger, selfishness, slander, gossip, conceit, and disorder.*
21. I fear that when I come again my God may humble me before you, and I may have to mourn over many of *those who sinned before and have not repented of the impurity, immorality, and licentiousness which they have practiced.*

We may surmise that the Corinthians, after Paul's second visit thought that he was "crafty" and somehow tricked them. We may also surmise that his second visit led to "quarreling, jealousy, anger, selfishness, slander, gossip, conceit and disorder." Paul's response apparently was to charge those who were upset with "impurity, immorality, and licentiousness."

How Many Trips to Corinth Did Paul Make?

In 1 Corinthians, Paul has already visited Corinth once and now plans to make another visit in the coming year (16.5) "I will visit you after passing through Macedonia, for I intend to pass through Macedonia."

According to 2 Corinthians, Paul planned on going to Corinth first and then to Macedonia, then back to Macedonia for a total of three visits (16-18).

> I wanted to visit you on my way to Macedonia, and to come back to you from Macedonia and have you send me on my way to Judea. Was I vacillating when I wanted to do this? Do I make my plans like a worldly man, ready to say Yes and No at once? As surely as God is faithful, our word to you has not been Yes and No.

Paul is apologizing profusely for not following through on his plan to visit Corinth before visiting Macedonia. This is a bit strange because we do not have any evidence in 1 Corinthians that he promised this. In fact, in 1 Corinthians, he distinctly says (16.5), "I will visit you after passing through Macedo'nia, for I intend to pass through Macedo'nia,"

Apparently, Paul has not made his promised second trip to Corinth, so this only makes sense if he is writing from Macedonia. This is confirmed when he brags in the letter about collecting money from the Macedonians (9:1-5):

> Now it is superfluous for me to write to you about the offering for the saints, for I know your readiness, of which I boast about you to the people of Macedonia, saying that Achaia has been ready since last year; and your zeal has stirred up most of them. But I am sending the brethren so that our boasting about you may not prove vain in this case, so that you may be ready, as I said you would be; lest if some Macedonians come with me and find that you are not ready, we be humiliated—to say nothing of you—for being so confident. So I thought it necessary to urge the brethren to go on to you before me, and arrange in advance for this gift you have promised, so that it may be ready not as an exaction but as a willing gift.

Now there is no problem in the number of visits until we come to chapter 13 in 2 Corinthians. At the beginning of this chapter Paul says:

> "This is the third time I am coming to you. Any charge must be sustained by the evidence of two or three witnesses. I warned those who sinned before and all the others, and I warn them now while absent, as I did when present on my second visit, that if I come again I will not spare them"

Our first thought is that we have simply made a mistake in assuming that Paul had only visited Corinth once before. He had visited twice and we only assumed he had visited it once. There is nothing in 1 Corinthians or 2 Corinthians up to this point to indicate the number of visits. Still, it is strange that we could get the impression so easily that Paul seems only to be speaking of one visit throughout 1 Corinthians when he had visited twice.

We are assured in the Epistle to the Romans that Paul was successful in his third trip to Corinth (Romans, 15:25-26):

> At present, however, I am going to Jerusalem with aid for the saints. For Macedonia and Achaia have been pleased to make some contribution for the poor among the saints at Jerusalem;

Paul may have had a falling out with the Corinthians of Achaia after his second visit, but they came through on his third visit and sent him on his way Jerusalem. All's well that ends well.

Paul is so pleased by the results of his trip to Corinth that he is already planning another trip. This time he is planning on going all the way to Spain. He tells us this in Romans (15:19-26):

> by the power of signs and wonders, by the power of the Holy Spirit, so that from Jerusalem and as far round as Illyricum I have fully preached the gospel of Christ, thus making it my ambition to preach the gospel, not where Christ has already been named, lest I build on another man's foundation, but as it is written, "They shall see who have never been told of him, and they shall understand who have never heard of him." This is the reason why I have so often been hindered from coming to you. But now, since I no longer have any room for work in these regions, and since I have longed for many years to come to you, I hope to see you in passing as I go to Spain, and to be sped on my journey there by you, once I have enjoyed your company for a little. At present, however, I am going to Jerusalem with aid for the saints. For Macedo'nia and Acha'ia have been pleased to make some contribution for the poor among the saints at Jerusalem;

It appears quite amazing that just a few years after the Christ's death, Paul has to go all the way to Spain to find territory where the Christ has not been named. Since he was the appointed apostle to the Gentiles and apparently nobody else had the franchise, it appears even more amazing.

Now, we have three things that are disturbing: 1) Paul's does not mention his two visits to Corinth and 2) Paul has already run out of territory to preach the Gospel, after hitting only two or three (if one includes Philippia) cities in Greece, and 3) Paul claims to have told the Corinthians that he would visit them before the Macedonians, but his first letter to the Corinthians states exactly the opposite that he will visit them afterwards.

Our solution to all three problems comes from the line in Romans (15.25-26):

> "I hope to see you in passing as I go to Spain and to be sped on my journey there by you, once I have enjoyed your company for a little. At present, however, I am going to Jerusalem with aid for the saints. For Macedonia and Achaia have been pleased to make some contribution for the poor among the saints at Jerusalem

We have a missing promise made by Paul to visit Corinth before visiting Macedonia. What if this text was originally the missing promise. In others words, an editor has simply substituted Spain for Macedonia. The second part of the text would not have read "Macedonia" and "Achaia," but must have read Thessaloniki and Philippea, the two cities in Macedonia that Paul visited before his visit to Corinth. Here is the way I propose the original text read:

> "I hope to see you in passing as I go to Macedonia and to be sped on my journey there by you, once I have enjoyed your company for a little. At present, however, I am going to Jerusalem with aid for the saints. For Thessaloniki and Phillipea have been pleased to make some contribution for the poor among the saints at Jerusalem

This now solves all three of our problems. Paul does not mention his two previous visits to Corinth in 1 Corinthians because there was only one. Paul has run out of room to preach the Gospel in Macedonia. It is only in the far reaches of Achaia (Corinth) that people have not yet heard the name of the Christ. Paul did promise the Corinthians he would visit them before visiting Macedonia, so he did have something to apologize for when he said that he would not visit them.

We may go further and say that the document we call Romans was actually Paul's first letter to the Corinthians before it was re-addressed to the Romans. The document we call 1 Corinthians is actually the second letter and the document called 2 Corinthians was actually the third letter.

To prove that this is the case, we may look at another line from Romans (16:1):

> I commend to you our sister Phoebe, a deaconess of the church at Cenchreae, : that you may receive her in the Lord as befits the saints, and help her in whatever she may require from you, for she has been a helper of many and of myself as well.

Cenchreae is the port city near Corinth. It makes no sense for Paul to be commending her to the Church at Rome. It makes perfect sense for Paul to be commending her to the Church at Corinth.

This helps us to understand also the provenance of the earlier writer. He obviously wants to say that Thessaloniki and/or Philippea was first in receiving Paul before the Corinthians. Further he wants to say that the Corinthians rejected Paul. We must assume that the Church at Corinth had published some kind of letter by Paul saying that he intended to visit them.

This letter goes through the hands of an editor from Thessaloniki. He says that Paul will first be delivering contributions from Thessaloniki and Philippea to Rome before going to Corinth.

THE EVOLUTION OF CHRISTS AND CHRISTIANIES

The beginning of the first epistle to the Thessalonians confirms this:

> Paul, Silva'nus, and Timothy, To the church of the Thessalo'nians in God the Father and the Lord Jesus Christ: Grace to you and peace. We give thanks to God always for you all, constantly mentioning you in our prayers, remembering before our God and Father your work of faith and labor of love and steadfastness of hope in our Lord Jesus Christ. For we know, brethren beloved by God, that he has chosen you; for our gospel came to you not only in word, but also in power and in the Holy Spirit and with full conviction. You know what kind of men we proved to be among you for your sake. And you became imitators of us and of the Lord, for you received the word in much affliction, with joy inspired by the Holy Spirit; so that you became an example to all the believers in Macedo'nia and in Acha'ia. For not only has the word of the Lord sounded forth from you in Macedo'nia and Acha'ia, but your faith in God has gone forth everywhere, so that we need not say anything.

The Church of Thessalonica is an example for all Macedonia and Achaia. This sentiment gets repeated in the second epistle:

> Paul, Silva'nus, and Timothy, To the church of the Thessalo'nians in God our Father and the Lord Jesus Christ:
> Grace to you and peace from God the Father and the Lord Jesus Christ.
> We are bound to give thanks to God always for you, brethren, as is fitting, because your faith is growing abundantly, and the love of every one of you for one another is increasing.
> Therefore we ourselves boast of you in the churches of God for your steadfastness and faith in all your persecutions and in the afflictions which you are enduring.

Again we find extreme praise from Paul to the Church at Thessaloniki. The other Church in Macedonia near Thessaloniki, the Church of the Philippians, appears also to be wildly praised (1.3-7):

> I thank my God in all my remembrance of you, always in every prayer of mine for you all making my prayer with joy, thankful for your partnership in the gospel from the first day until now.
> And I am sure that he who began a good work in you will bring it to completion at the day of Jesus Christ.

> It is right for me to feel thus about you all, because I hold you in my heart, for you are all partakers with me of grace, both in my imprisonment and in the defense and confirmation of the gospel.

In fact the letter contains a put-down of the Church at Thessaloniki (3.15-18):

> And you Philippians yourselves know that in the beginning of the gospel, when I left Macedonia, no church entered into partnership with me in giving and receiving except you only; for even in Thessalonica you sent me help once and again.
> Not that I seek the gift; but I seek the fruit which increases to your credit.
> I have received full payment, and more; I am filled, having received from Epaphrodi'tus the gifts you sent, a fragrant offering, a sacrifice acceptable and pleasing to God.

The phrase "in the beginning of the gospel" is the key to understanding things here. Apparently the gospel begins with Paul leaving Macedonia after visiting Thessaloniki. This occurs only in one place at the end of Romans. Here is the passage that apparently came at the beginning of Paul's Gospel (Romans, 25-33):

> At present, however, I am going to Jerusalem with aid for the saints. For Macedonia and Achaia have been pleased to make some contribution for the poor among the saints at Jerusalem; they were pleased to do it, and indeed they are in debt to them, for if the Gentiles have come to share in their spiritual blessings, they ought also to be of service to them in material blessings.
> When therefore I have completed this, and have delivered to them what has been raised, I shall go on by way of you to Spain; and I know that when I come to you I shall come in the fulness of the blessing of Christ.
> I appeal to you, brethren, by our Lord Jesus Christ and by the love of the Spirit, to strive together with me in your prayers to God on my behalf, that I may be delivered from the unbelievers in Judea, and that my service for Jerusalem may be acceptable to the saints, so that by God's will I may come to you with joy and be refreshed in your company.
> The God of peace be with you all. Amen.

As noted before, Romans was originally written to the Corinthians, with the terms "Macedonia" and "Achaia" actually being Thessaloniki and Philippia. We may assume that the same person who made changes to *Romans* also made changes to the *Epistle to*

THE EVOLUTION OF CHRISTS AND CHRISTIANIES

the Philippians. We base this on the fact that as presented in Philippians, the description of Paul's relationship with the Philippians ("the only church to enter into partnership with me") not only contradicts the information in both Thessalonikian Epistles, but they also contradict what happens to Paul in Acts.

Here is the description of Paul's first trip to Greece. Notice that the reception in Philippia is less than cordial:

> And he came also to Derbe and to Lystra. A disciple was there, named Timothy, the son of a Jewish woman who was a believer; but his father was a Greek. He was well spoken of by the brethren at Lystra and Iconium. Paul wanted Timothy to accompany him; and he took him and circumcised him because of the Jews that were in those places, for they all knew that his father was a Greek. As they went on their way through the cities, they delivered to them for observance the decisions which had been reached by the apostles and elders who were at Jerusalem. So the churches were strengthened in the faith, and they increased in numbers daily. And they went through the region of Phrygia and Galatia, having been forbidden by the Holy Spirit to speak the word in Asia. And when they had come opposite Mysia, they attempted to go into Bithynia, but the Spirit of Jesus did not allow them; so, passing by Mysia, they went down to Troas.
>
> And a vision appeared to Paul in the night: a man of Macedonia was standing beseeching him and saying, "Come over to Macedonia and help us." And when he had seen the vision, immediately we sought to go on into Macedonia, concluding that God had called us to preach the gospel to them. Setting sail therefore from Troas, we made a direct voyage to Samothrace, and the following day to Neapolis, and from there to Philippi, which is the leading city of the district of Macedonia, and a Roman colony. We remained in this city some days; and on the sabbath day we went outside the gate to the riverside, where we supposed there was a place of prayer; and we sat down and spoke to the women who had come together. One who heard us was a woman named Lydia, from the city of Thyatira, a seller of purple goods, who was a worshiper of God. The Lord opened her heart to give heed to what was said by Paul. And when she was baptized, with her household, she besought us, saying, "If you have judged me to be faithful to the Lord, come to my house and stay." And she prevailed upon us. As we were going to the place of prayer, we were met by a slave girl who had a spirit of divination and brought her owners much gain by soothsaying. She followed Paul and us, crying, "These men are servants of the Most High God, who proclaim to you the way of salvation." And this she did for many days.

> But Paul was annoyed, and turned and said to the spirit, "I charge you in the name of Jesus Christ to come out of her." And it came out that very hour.
>
> But when her owners saw that their hope of gain was gone, they seized Paul and Silas and dragged them into the market place before the rulers; and when they had brought them to the magistrates they said, "These men are Jews and they are disturbing our city. They advocate customs which it is not lawful for us Romans to accept or practice." The crowd joined in attacking them; and the magistrates tore the garments off them and gave orders to beat them with rods. And when they had inflicted many blows upon them, they threw them into prison, charging the jailer to keep them safely. Having received this charge, he put them into the inner prison and fastened their feet in the stocks. But about midnight Paul and Silas were praying and singing hymns to God, and the prisoners were listening to them, and suddenly there was a great earthquake, so that the foundations of the prison were shaken; and immediately all the doors were opened and every one's fetters were unfastened. When the jailer woke and saw that the prison doors were open, he drew his sword and was about to kill himself, supposing that the prisoners had escaped. But Paul cried with a loud voice, "Do not harm yourself, for we are all here." And he called for lights and rushed in, and trembling with fear he fell down before Paul and Silas, and brought them out and said, "Men, what must I do to be saved?" And they said, "Believe in the Lord Jesus, and you will be saved, you and your household." And they spoke the word of the Lord to him and to all that were in his house. And he took them the same hour of the night, and washed their wounds, and he was baptized at once, with all his family. Then he brought them up into his house, and set food before them; and he rejoiced with all his household that he had believed in God. But when it was day, the magistrates sent the police, saying, "Let those men go." And the jailer reported the words to Paul, saying, "The magistrates have sent to let you go; now therefore come out and go in peace." But Paul said to them, "They have beaten us publicly, uncondemned, men who are Roman citizens, and have thrown us into prison; and do they now cast us out secretly? No! let them come themselves and take us out."

First, we should note that we are dealing with events that sound like events in the canonical gospels: visions, exorcisms, baptisms, imprisonments, and earthquakes. Paul is certainly leading an exciting life.

Secondly note the switch to the first person "we" in this text. While many explanations may be given for this, I would suggest that the simplest one is editor's fatigue. The editor was changing this Gospel from a first person narrative to a third person narrative and simply skipped a few lines.

The author of 1 Thessalonians knows about this bad treatment at Philippi and also uses the "we" style (2.1-2):

> For you yourselves know, brethren, that our visit to you was not in vain; but though we had already suffered and been shamefully treated at Philippi, as you know, we had courage in our God to declare to you the gospel of God in the face of great opposition.

Paul makes his trip to Macedonia with Silvanus (shortened to Silas in *Acts*) and Timothy. We must assume that the "we" would include an "I," either Silvanus or Timothy. As it describes the forced circumcision of Timothy rather casually, we may assume that the letters were purportedly coming from Silvanus. We may assume that both the/an editor of *Acts* and the editor of at least six of Paul's letters, Romans, 1 and 2 Corinthians, 1 and 2 Thessaloneans, and Philippeans, (who was probably a Church official from Thessaloniki) both used this earlier text. This text appears to have been a gospel in the form of letters. It starts with Paul returning from Macedonia to Jerusalem. Apparently it describes in a series of letters how Paul came to make a successful, but wild and dangerous trip to Greece starting from his home in Cilicia.

This "Gospel of Silvanus" in the form of letters seems to know almost nothing of the canonical gospels. It does incorporate an ideology taken directly from *the Book of Revelation*. We may take it as being written roughly 100 C.E. and the Thessalonian letters of Paul developing between this time and around 150.

Since the letter in its current form is contradicting *Acts* and passages in it from the *Gospel of Silvanus*, we may propose that the following passage has been tampered with by a later editor.

> 15: And you Philippians yourselves know that in the beginning of the gospel, when I left Macedo'nia, no church entered into partnership with me in giving and receiving except you only;
> 16: for even in Thessalonica you sent me help once and again.
> 17: Not that I seek the gift; but I seek the fruit which increases to your credit.

It makes no sense for Paul to be talking about "when I left Macedonia" and talking about a trip to Thessalonica in the next sentence. Thessalonica is right next to Philippia. Sending help once and again would be no big deal. We may reconstruct the original passage this way:

> 15: And you Thessalonians yourselves know that in the beginning of the gospel, when I left Macedo'nia, no church entered into partnership with me in giving and receiving except you only;
> 16: for even in Corinth you sent me help once and again.
> 17: Not that I seek the gift; but I seek the fruit which increases to your credit.

The passage now makes sense. He is putting the good treatment of the Thessalonians even when he "left Macedonia" in opposition to the bad treatment of the Corinthians who treated him badly even when he stayed there. We know that Paul complains in 2 Corinthians that the Corinthians did not support him (11.9):

> And when I was with you and was in want, I did not burden any one, for my needs were supplied by the brethren who came from Macedonia. So I refrained and will refrain from burdening you in any way.

We have seen that the epistle to the Romans was originally the first letter to the Corinthians. It appears now that the epistle to the Philippians, was a third letter to the Thessalonians. We thus have three letters to the Corinthians and three letters to the Thessalonians. What about the letter to the Galatians?

We may take the beginning of the letter and its description of Paul's trip to Jerusalem to be designed to establish Paul's relationship with the Jerusalem movement. This section bares no relationship to the rest of the letter and appears to be added in later. The real letter begins at chapter three:

> O foolish Galatians! Who has bewitched you, before whose eyes Jesus Christ was publicly portrayed as crucified? Let me ask you only this: Did you receive the Spirit by works of the law, or by hearing with faith? Are you so foolish? Having begun with the Spirit, are you now ending with the flesh? Did you experience so many things in vain?—if it really is in vain. Does he who supplies the Spirit to you and works miracles among you do so by works of the law, or by hearing with faith?

The man who supplies miracles "by works of the law" could very well be Apollos, the same man we heard about in Corinth. Beside 1 Corinthians, Acts talks about him (18:24-28, 19:1-5):

> While Apollos was at Corinth, Paul passed through the upper country and came to Ephesus. There he found some disciples. And he said to them, "Did you receive the Holy Spirit when you believed?" And they said, "No, we have never even heard that there is a Holy Spirit." And he

said, "Into what then were you baptized?" They said, "Into John's baptism." And Paul said, "John baptized with the baptism of repentance, telling the people to believe in the one who was to come after him, that is, Jesus." On hearing this, they were baptized in the name of the Lord Jesus. While Apollos was at Corinth, Paul passed through the upper country and came to Ephesus. There he found some disciples.

Apollos, the Jewish follower and preacher of John the Baptist baptized into the spirit of repentance. He did not preach about the Holy Spirit. We may take it that in this text, which we have called the "Gospel of Sylvanus," the Holy Spirit is the dividing line between Jews and Christians. Perhaps we may more accurately term the two groups Jewish Christians and Holy Spirit Christians.

In any case, *Galatians* contains these important lines (18:4):

12: Brethren, I beseech you, become as I am, for I also have become as you are. You did me no wrong;

13: you know it was because of a bodily ailment that I preached the gospel to you at first;

14: and though my condition was a trial to you, you did not scorn or despise me, but received me as an angel of God, as Christ Jesus.

15: What has become of the satisfaction you felt? For I bear you witness that, if possible, you would have plucked out your eyes and given them to me.

16: Have I then become your enemy by telling you the truth?

17: They make much of you, but for no good purpose; they want to shut you out, that you may make much of them.

18: For a good purpose it is always good to be made much of, and not only when I am present with you.

Although the epistle is addressed to the Churches of Galatia, this appears to be a description of a visit to a single Church/city.

It is hard to know exactly what condition Paul is talking about when he says "my condition was a trial to you." The phrase, "if possible, you would have plucked out your eyes and given them to me" suggests that it was blindness. Paul says in 1 Corinthians (2.3),"And I was with you in weakness and in much fear and trembling . . ." We may suggest that both letters are talking about one and the same visit, the first visit to Corinth. We may suggest that our later editor has taken the second letter to Corinth from the Thessalonean Pauline author and revised it to read as if it was to the churches in Galatia. He has changed "Oh, foolish Corinthians" to "Oh, foolish Galatians." The similarity in the criticisms of the church in 1 Corinthians and Galatian suggests this.

Thus, it appears that the Thessalonian author wrote seven letters, four to the Church at Corinth and three to the church at Thessalonica. A later editor changed one of the Thessalonican letters to Philippia, and changed the first two Corinthian letters to Roman and Galatians.

Proof from Acts that Apollos was First to Preach the Gospel to the Gentiles

The writer of the seven epistles from Thessalonika is anxious to discredit Apollos as the first teacher of the Corinthians. If the Corinthians are holding to the teachings of Apollos and he is their first teacher, the founding father of their church, you can hardly blame them for continuing in his ways. However, if it can be proved that Paul was the real original teacher, then the Corinthians are traitors to their true heritage. Portraying the Corinthians as traitors to their heritage seems to be the approach that the Thessalonian writer has decided to take. It is likely that he is giving tit for tat and answering a charge made against himself by the Corinthians.

Can we be sure that this is the real status quo in Corinth at the time of the letters? Is this a real historical situation? I think we can be reasonably sure based on information given in *Acts*.

The editor of *Acts* wants to also tell us that Paul was first in Corinth. However it creates a fabulous contradiction in telling the tale. The text inadvertently praises Apollos for converting the Corinthians away from the Gospel of Paul and back to the Gospel of John. To figure out how this came about, we may examine the relevant text at the point where Apollos enters the picture. Acts (18) tells us that Paul traveled with Priscilla and Aquilla from Corinth to Ephesus.

> 18. After this Paul stayed many days longer, and then took leave of the brethren and sailed for Syria, and with him Priscilla and Aq'uila. At Cen'chre-ae he cut his hair, for he had a vow.
> 19. And they came to Ephesus, and he left them there; but he himself went into the synagogue and argued with the Jews

After this the writer relates how Priscilla and Aquila met Apollos.

> 24. Now a Jew named Apol'los, a native of Alexandria, came to Ephesus. He was an eloquent man, well versed in the scriptures.
> 25. He had been instructed in the way of the Lord; and being fervent in spirit, he spoke and taught accurately the things concerning Jesus, though he knew only the baptism of John.
> 26. He began to speak boldly in the synagogue; but when Priscilla and Aq'uila heard him, they took him and expounded to him the way of God more accurately.

27. And when he wished to cross to Acha'ia, the brethren encouraged him, and wrote to the disciples to receive him . . . .

After this, Apollos, apparently armed with the gospel of Priscilla and Aquila which they got from Paul, heads for Corinth. Since Paul has just preached in Corinth allegedly we expect that he should get a warm welcome. The text supports this idea.

27 . . . . When he arrived, he greatly helped those who through grace had believed,
28. for he powerfully confuted the Jews in public, showing by the scriptures that the Christ was Jesus.

The lucky Corinthians are now getting to hear Paul's gospel a second time. This time they are getting it from Apollos who heard it from Priscilla and Aquila, who heard it from Paul. One should suspect that the Corinthians should be correcting him if he makes any mistakes as they received it before he did. But wait, something has gone terribly wrong (*Acts*, 19):

1. While Apol'los was at Corinth, Paul passed through the upper country and came to Ephesus. There he found some disciples.
2. And he said to them, "Did you receive the Holy Spirit when you believed?" And they said, "No, we have never even heard that there is a Holy Spirit."
3. And he said, "Into what then were you baptized?" They said, "Into John's baptism."
4. And Paul said, "John baptized with the baptism of repentance, telling the people to believe in the one who was to come after him, that is, Jesus."
5. On hearing this, they were baptized in the name of the Lord Jesus.
6. And when Paul had laid his hands upon them, the Holy Spirit came on them; and they spoke with tongues and prophesied.
7. There were about twelve of them in all.

Apollos heard the good news from Priscilla and Aquila. They wrote to the Corinthians about him. They apparently received him well. The text next tells us "When he arrived, he greatly helped those who through grace had believed." How can this be? It turns out he was preaching John's gospel of Baptism, i.e., the wrong gospel. If the Corinthians had Paul set them on the right track and then Apollos set them on the wrong track, why does the text say that "he greatly helped those who through grace had believed."

Perhaps, we are reading the chronology wrong. Perhaps he went to Corinth before Paul and met Priscila and Aquila afterwards. But no, the text very clearly says (19:1) "While

Apol'los was at Corinth, Paul passed through the upper country and came to Ephesus." Paul stays at Ephesus apparently the next two years (19:9). After two years, Paul takes a trip to Macedonia, but never makes it to Corinth. Instead he returns to Jerusalem.

There is simply no resolving this contradiction. If Paul taught first in Corinth, how can the Johanine teachings of Apollos have been a positive thing for the Corinthians. Also how could he be preaching to the Corinthians John's baptism after Priscilla and Aquila had set him straight? Perhaps he did not accept Priscilla and Aquila's Pauline Gospel and lied to them about it to get them to write positive letters to the Corinthians to make his trip possible. On this assumption it becomes even more incomprehensible for the text to be praising him.

The text has an equally insoluble problem at in the lines that follow:

8. And he entered the synagogue and for three months spoke boldly, arguing and pleading about the kingdom of God;
9. but when some were stubborn and disbelieved, speaking evil of the Way before the congregation, he withdrew from them, taking the disciples with him, and argued daily in the hall of Tyran'nus.
10. This continued for two years, so that all the residents of Asia heard the word of the Lord, both Jews and Greeks.

The Hall of Tyrannus can only be referring to the Hall of Oedipus Tyrannus, Corinth's most famous king. Paul is at Ephesus. How can he be at Ephesus and in Corinth at the same time?

This problem and the problem of the text praising Apollos for teaching a regressive gospel are solved if we assume the scenic cut back from Apollos in Corinth to Paul in Ephesus is an interpolation. By simply changing Paul to Apollos we can understand the original text.

These problems disappear if we assume that Apollos alone was the first to bring John the Baptist's Gospel to Corinth and the editor of Acts is just rewriting an accurate historical text about Apollos to give the credit to Paul. Reconstructing the original we get this text which not only eliminates the problems mentioned but explains how the text knows Gallio was the Proconsul in Corinth: Only a couple of lines (18:1 and 19:26) have to be rearranged for better sense. Here is the reconstructed text:

Reconstruction of Acts 19

Now a Jew named Apol'los, a native of Alexandria, came to Ephesus.
He was an eloquent man, well versed in the scriptures.

He had been instructed in the way of the Lord; and being fervent in spirit, he spoke and taught accurately the things concerning Jesus, though he knew only the baptism of John.

And when he wished to cross to Acha'ia, the brethren encouraged him, and wrote to the disciples to receive him.

{19:1} After this he left Ephesus and crossed to Corinth

When he arrived, he greatly helped those who through grace had believed, for he powerfully confuted the Jews in public, showing by the scriptures that the Christ was John....

...And he found a Jew named Aq'uila, a native of Pontus, lately come from Italy with his wife Priscilla, because Claudius had commanded all the Jews to leave Rome. And he went to see them; and because he was of the same trade he stayed with them, and they worked, for by trade they were tentmakers.

{18.26} He began to speak boldly in the synagogue; but when Priscilla and Aq'uila heard him, they took him and expounded to him the way of God more accurately.

And he argued in the synagogue every sabbath, and persuaded Jews and Greeks.

When Silas and Timothy arrived from Macedo'nia, Apollos was occupied with preaching, testifying to the Jews that the Christ was John.

And when they opposed and reviled him, he shook out his garments and said to them, "Your blood be upon your heads! I am innocent. From now on I will go to the Gentiles."

And he left there and went to the house of a man named Titius

Justus, a worshiper of God; his house was next door to the synagogue.

Crispus, the ruler of the synagogue, believed in the Lord, together with all his household; and many of the Corinthians hearing Apollos believed and were baptized.

And the Lord said to Apollos one night in a vision, "Do not be afraid, but speak and do not be silent;

10: for I am with you, and no man shall attack you to harm you; for I have many people in this city."

And he stayed a year and six months, teaching the word of God among them.

But when Gallio was proconsul of Acha'ia, the Jews made a united attack upon Apollos and brought him before the tribunal, saying, "This man is persuading men to worship God contrary to the law."

But when Apollos was about to open his mouth, Gallio said to the Jews, "If it were a matter of wrongdoing or vicious crime, I should have reason to bear with you, O Jews; but since it is a matter of questions about words and names and your own law, see to it yourselves; I refuse to be a judge of these things."

And he drove them from the tribunal.

And they all seized Sos'thenes, the ruler of the synagogue, and beat him in front of the tribunal. But Gallio paid no attention to this.

After this Apollos stayed many days longer, and then took leave of the brethren and sailed for Syria, and with him Priscilla and Aq'uila...

...And they came to Ephesus, and he left them there; but he himself went into the synagogue and argued with the Jews.

When they asked him to stay for a longer period, he declined; but on taking leave of them he said, "I will return to you if God wills," and he set sail from Ephesus.

When he had landed at Caesare'a, he went up and greeted the church, and then went down to Antioch.

After spending some time there he departed and went from place to place through the region of Galatia and Phryg'ia strengthening all the disciples.

We can now see what happened. The editor of *Acts* took an old historical text that referred to Apollos and made it refer to Paul.

We have left out one small section at the beginning of chapter 19 that seems to have been more extensively played with.

1. While Apol'los was at Corinth, he passed through the upper city and came to Cenchreae. {18.18} At Cenchreae he cut his hair, for he had a vow.
   There he found some disciples.
2. And he said to them, "Did you receive the Holy Spirit when you believed?" And they said, "No, we have never even heard that there is a Holy Spirit."
3. And he said, "Into what then were you baptized?" They said, "Into John's baptism."

4. And Apollos said, "John baptized with the baptism of repentance, telling the people to believe in the one who was to come after him, that is, Jesus."
5. On hearing this, they were baptized in the name of the Lord Jesus.
6. And when Apollos had laid his hands upon them, the Holy Spirit came on them; and they spoke with tongues and prophesied.
7. There were about twelve of them in all.

At first I considered Apollos baptizing in the name of the Lord Jesus was an interpolation. It is certainly surprising that the name would be used so early. The baptisms seem to be taking place around 50 or 51 C.E. when Gallio was proconsul. Shouldn't Apollos be baptizing in the name of John?

My thinking is that John was considered the Christ or anointed one (meaning king) shortly after 39 C.E. when the Romans appointed Herod Grippa king. John's followers would have balked at this and declared him king/Christ. Mary has the witty scene of Mary Magdalene anointing Jesus in her play, and Peter/Judas criticizing her for wasting money.

The key thing to notice is that Jesus is not referred to as Christ here, simply Lord. Jesus. He is the Lord of the Angels who is still to come. It is improbable that John knew the name Jesus as the Lord of the Angels. The concept is not strongly associated with John. Most likely he just believed God would send or raise some messiah/savior. By 69 C.E., in the Book of Revelations, it is clear that the head angel has been given the name of Jesus. It is not improbable that sometime between the death of John circa 36 and 50, the followers of John determined that Jesus (Joshua) was the name of the head of the angels in heaven. This was easily derived from figuring that God had sent a man Jesus (Joshua Nun) to save Israel before in the time of Moses, so God would again send someone named Jesus. Since John had been raised to heaven and sat at the right hand of God, it was probable that the great Joshua had also been raised to heaven and made chief of the angels. If Joshua/Jesus was lord of the angels in the kingdom of God and John had said that the kingdom of God would be brought to Earth, it was obvious that Joshua/Jesus would come and rule the Kingdom of God on Earth. Therefore baptizing in the name of the lord Jesus would simply be baptizing in the name of the present king/lord of heaven and the future king/lord of Earth. We may take the concept of the Lord Jesus as developing in the 40's among the followers of John the Nazarene/Baptist.

Note also that we have Apollos making a vow and cutting his hair, i.e., becoming a Nazarene at Cenchrae. He also baptizes twelve disciples. Note too that we have the concept of the proconsul Gallio not judging the dispute between the Alexandrian Jew Apollos and the other Jews. Both of these elements make it into the New Testament tales with the idea that Jesus had twelve disciples and that Pilate refused to judge the case between the Jews and Jesus.

We may take it as a probable historical fact that Apollo, in the year 51 when Gallio was proconsul of Corinth, baptized men in the name of Lord Jesus as far away as Corinth. We may also take it as highly probable that they were expecting an important angel named Jesus, the lord of heaven to come.

The narrative text regarding Apollos sounds like a history written by an historian. I may conjecture that it is from a work called *A Chronicle of the Kings of the Jews in the form of a genealogy*, by Justus of Tiberias. Photius, in the ninth century described him this way:

> He came from Tiberias in Galilee, from which he took his name. He begins his history with Moses and carries it down to the death of the seventh Agrippa of the family of Herod and the last of the Kings of the Jews. His kingdom, which was bestowed upon him by Claudius, was extended by Nero, and still more by Vespasian. He died in the third year of Trajan, when the history ends. Justus' style is very concise and he omits a great deal that is of utmost importance. Suffering from the common fault of the Jews, to which race he belonged, he does not even mention the coming of Christ, the events of his life, or the miracles performed by Him. His father was a Jew named Pistus; Justus himself, according to Josephus, was one of the most abandoned of men, a slave to vice and greed. He was a political opponent of Josephus, against whom he is said to have concocted several plots; but Josephus, although on several occasions he had his enemy in his power, only chastised him with words and let him go free. It is said that the history which he wrote is in great part fictitious, especially where he describes the Judaeo-Roman war and the capture of Jerusalem[498].

Photius could not understand how a Jewish historian could not mention the coming of Christ. He ascribes this omission to a Jewish conspiracy. However, Justus could not have left out a description of the movement that Josephus blames for the war. This is simply another piece of evidence that no-one had ever heard of Jesus of Nazareth before the War. Josephus, in his autobiography, himself gives us a great deal of important information about Justus of Tiberias:

- (*The Life of Flavius Josephus*, 9) **But as for Justus, the son of Pistus, who was the head of the third faction, although he pretended to be doubtful about going to war, yet was he really desirous of innovation, as supposing that he should gain power to himself by the change of affairs.**
- (17) **But when John was come to the city of Tiberias, he persuaded the men to revolt from their fidelity to me, and**

THE EVOLUTION OF CHRISTS AND CHRISTIANIES

to adhere to him; and many of them gladly received that invitation of his, as ever fond of innovations, and by nature disposed to changes, and delighting in seditions; but they were chiefly Justus and his father Pistus, that were earnest for their revolt from me, and their adherence to John. But I came upon them, and prevented them; for a messenger had come to me from Silas, whom I had made governor of Tiberias, as I have said already, and had told me of the inclinations of the people of Tiberias, and advised me to make haste thither; for that, if I made any delay, the city would come under another's jurisdiction.

- (35) Now the men of Tiberias, after I was gone to Taricheae, perceived what stratagem I had used against them, and they admired how I had put an end to their foolish sedition, without shedding of blood. But now, when I had sent for some of those multitudes of the people of Tiberias out of prison, among whom were Justus and his father Pistus, I made them to sup with me; and during our supper time I said to them, that I knew the power of the Romans was superior to all others, but did not say so [publicly] because of the robbers. So I advised them to do as I did, and to wait for a proper opportunity, and not to be uneasy at my being their commander; for that they could not expect to have another who would use the like moderation that I had done. I also put Justus in mind how the Galileans had cut off his brother's hands before ever I came to Jerusalem, upon an accusation laid against him, as if he had been a rogue, and had forged some letters; as also how the people of Gamala, in a sedition they raised against the Babylonians, after the departure of Philip, slew Chares, who was a kinsman of Philip, and withal how they had wisely punished Jesus, his brother Justuses sister's husband [with death]. When I had said this to them during supper time, I in the morning ordered Justus, and all the rest that were in prison, to be loosed out of it, and sent away.

- (65) And now I am come to this part of my narration, I have a mind to say a few things to Justus, who hath himself written a history concerning these affairs, as also to others who profess to write history, but have little regard to truth, and are not afraid, either out of ill-will or good-will to some persons, to relate falsehoods. These men do like those who compose forged deeds and conveyances; and because they are not brought to the like punishment with them, they have no regard to truth. When, therefore, Justus undertook to write about these facts, and about the Jewish war, that he might appear to have been an industrious man, he falsified in what he related about me, and could not speak truth even about his own country; whence it is that, being belied by him, I am under a necessity to make my defense; and so I shall say what I have concealed till now. And let no one wonder that I have not told the world these things a great while ago. For although it be necessary for an historian to write the truth, yet is such a one not bound severely to animadvert on the wickedness of certain men; not out of any favor to them, but out of an author's own moderation. How then comes it to pass, O Justus! thou most sagacious of writers, (that I may address myself to him as if he were here present,) for so thou boastest of thyself, that I and the Galileans have been the authors of that sedition which thy country engaged in, both against the Romans and against the king [Agrippa, junior] For before ever I was appointed governor of Galilee by the community of Jerusalem, both thou and all the people of Tiberias had not only taken up arms, but had made war with Decapolis of Syria...

- (65) But if thou art so hardy as to affirm, that thou hast written that history better than all the rest, why didst thou not publish thy history while the emperors Vespasian and Titus, the generals in that war, as well as king Agrippa and his family, who were men very well skilled in the learning of the Greeks, were all alive? for thou hast had it written these twenty years, and then mightest thou have had the testimony of thy accuracy. But now when these men are no longer with us, and thou thinkest thou canst not be contradicted, thou venturest to publish it.

It is obvious that Josephus despises Justus. He denounces his history as false, at least in the things relating to the Roman war. However, we should not lose sight of the fact that they were comrades in their youth, fighting together on the same side against the Romans. Josephus tells us that Justus wrote his history while Vespasian was still alive. Vespasian died in 79. This means that Justus wrote his history in the 70's. We may suppose that Josephus wrote his *Antiquities* in response to the publication of Justus's work. If we take this to be 93-95 C.E., then deducting the twenty years between writing and publication, we get a date of 73-75 C.E. for Justus writing his work. Photius tells us that the work goes up to the third year of Trajan when the History ends. We may suppose that Justus added later to his original work.

Josephus tells us that Justus became a follower of John of Gischala and supported those in favor of "innovation" (Josephus's code word for Christians). Thus Justus is a follower of the Jewish Christian movement. He writes his history probably in the early to mid 70's and hides it for twenty years because he is afraid that it will offend the Roman emperors. This is an indication that he was trying to be truthful rather than appeasing to the Romans. It may have been because of its truthfulness that it mysteriously disappeared after Photius read it in the ninth century. If we are correct in our assumption that the editor of *Acts* is re-editing and rewriting Justus' work, we may take *Acts* as quite accurate historically, at least as far as it has preserved information from Justus intact. We have to remember that Acts, if it is getting its information primarily from Justus has been heavily edited.

Note also that Josephus says that he made Silvas governor of Tiberias (17). This Silvas may very well be the author of the work I called "The Gospel of Silvanus" which described his travels with Paul and Timothy, only now we may take it that Silvas traveled with Apollos. Justus of Tiberius probably got his information about Apollos directly from Silvas (Silvanus) of Tiberius.

The Seven Inauthentic Inauthentic Epistles of Paul

Ephesians and *Colossians* are dull letters. Unlike the seven letters from Thessalonian author, there does not appear to be specific reason for Paul to write these letters as he has not visited either place. Curiously, the epistle to the Ephesians is not addressed to the Ephesians. We must assume there was originally an address and someone has erased it. Why?

In *Colossians*, we have several references to Laodicea, but no reference to Ephesus.

- (2.1) For I want you to know how greatly I strive for you, and for those at La-odice'a, and for all who have not seen my face.
- (4.12) Ep'aphras, who is one of yourselves, a servant of Christ Jesus, greets you, always remembering you earnestly in his prayers, that you may stand mature and fully assured in all the will of God.
- (4.13) For I bear him witness that he has worked hard for you and for those in La-odice'a and in Hi-erap'olis.

Tertullian refers to Laodicea in his work *Against Marcion*, "We have it on the true tradition of the Church, that this epistle was sent to the Ephesians, not to the Laodiceans. Marcion, however, was very desirous of giving it the new title."

It appears to be much more likely that Laodicea was in the beginning of the epistle and that Tertullian erased it.

Tertullian also tells us that in the case of Philemon, "To this epistle alone did its brevity avail to protect it against the falsifying hands of Marcion" It is possible that Marcion himself wrote the letters to the Laodiceans (Ephesians), Colossians and Philemon to bring the seven previous epistles he published from the Thessalonian writer up to ten. However, it is also possible that he got the three letters from an earlier source.

Tertullian tells us further, "he rejected the two epistles to Timothy and the one to Titus, which all treat of ecclesiastical discipline. His aim, was, I suppose, to carry out his interpolating process even to the number of (St. Paul's) epistles."

The evidence is a little long to go into at the moment, but we may take it that Tertullian likewise wanted to surpass his arch-enemy Marcion in the number of authentic Pauline letters he could point to, so he himself wrote the two letters to Timothy, and the letter to Titus.

The most interesting part that gives us a clue to the author's identity is this passage from 1 Timothy (2.8-15):

> I desire then that in every place the men should pray, lifting holy hands without anger or quarreling; also that women should adorn themselves modestly and sensibly in seemly apparel, not with braided hair or gold or pearls or costly attire but by good deeds, as befits women who profess religion. Let a woman learn in silence with all submissiveness. I permit no woman to teach or to have authority over men; she is to keep silent. For Adam was formed first, then Eve; and Adam was not deceived, but the woman was deceived and became a transgressor. Yet woman will be saved through bearing children, if she continues in faith and love and holiness, with modesty.

The misogynistic attitude is clear, "Let a woman learn in silence with submissiveness." This ideology closes matches the misogynist ideology expressed by Tertullian in his writings in *de cultu feminarum*:

> But Christians always, and now more than ever, pass their times not in gold but in iron: the stoles of martyrdom are (now) preparing: the angels who are to carry us are (now) being awaited! Do you go forth (to meet them) already arrayed in the cosmetics and ornaments of prophets and apostles; drawing your whiteness from simplicity, your ruddy hue from modesty; painting your eyes with bashfulness, and your mouth with silence; implanting in your ears the words of God; fitting on your necks the yoke of Christ. Submit your head to your husbands, and you will be

> enough adorned. Busy your hands with spinning; keep your feet at home; and you will "please" better than (by arraying yourselves) in gold. Clothe yourselves with the silk of uprightness, the fine linen of holiness, the purple of modesty. Thus painted, you will have God as your Lover!

Tertullian is writing this circa 207. We may take it that Marcion included 10 letters in his New Testament. We may assume that the Church of Thessaloniki had 7 letters of Paul. At some point in the third century after this, the Church at Rome added the Pauline *Epistle to the Hebrews* to bring its total of Pauline letters to 14, double what the Greeks possessed. Tertullian thought that *Hebrews* was written by Barnabus (De Pudicitia, 20). I will discuss this important epistle later.

Tertullian is the most likely suspect in changing the first two Corinthian letters by the Thessalonikian writer into Romans and Galatians, and changing the third Thessalonikian letter into Philippians, as well as changing Marcion's *Laodiceans* into *Ephesians*.

Incidentally we may take it that he also wrote 1 Peter. The misogynist ideology at the beginning of chapter three fits him like a glove. Compare this with the misogynist ideology of *de cultu feminarum* above:

> Likewise you wives, be submissive to your husbands, so that some, though they do not obey the word, may be won without a word by the behavior of their wives, when they see your reverent and chaste behavior. Let not yours be the outward adorning with braiding of hair, decoration of gold, and wearing of fine clothing, but let it be the hidden person of the heart with the imperishable jewel of a gentle and quiet spirit, which in God's sight is very precious. So once the holy women who hoped in God used to adorn themselves and were submissive to their husbands,

In fact all the many calls for women's submission in Paul's epistles may be attributed directly to Tertullian. Apparently, although he loved his wife dearly, and she was a Christian, she was not as obedient to him or as modest as he wished. Therefore he had to place reminders inside of letters allegedly by apostles to remind her. It is probable that she could not herself read, otherwise she would have detected the forgery herself.

Summary:

- A writer from Thessaloniki, circa 100-150, writes seven letters, three to Thessaloniki and four to Corinth in the name of Paul.
- Marcion, circa 160, adds Colossians, Laodiceans (Ephesians) and Philemon, which come from earlier source material.

- Tertullian, circa 207, revises and edits the letters and adds the Pasturals (1 and 2 *Timothy* and *Titus*. He also takes perhaps an old treatise regarding High Priests, and by adding four lines at the end changes it into the fourteenth epistle, *To the Hebrews*.

How the Seven Epistles of Ignatius Evolved from Seven Asia Minor Epistles of Paul

After deriving our understanding about the letters of Paul, we find something curious. Only two letters are to churches in Asia Minor, Colossians and its sister letter Laodiceans. As apostle to the gentiles, one would expect that Paul would have first written letters to the churches in Asia Minor that would have spread out from Judea and Syria and started long before the churches on the mainland in Greece. Recall that the revised *Book of Revelation*, circa 100, knew of seven churches in seven cities in this area: Ephesus, Smyrna, Per'gamum, Thyati'ra, Sardis, Philadelphia and Laodicea." In *Revelations*, we find seven short letters written by John to these Churches.

I think it is significant that Tertullian apparently has changed a letter addressed to the seventh church at Laodicea into the first church at Ephesus. One has to wonder, "Where are the other letters by Paul to Churches in Asia Minor?" If the Thessalonikian writer had Paul write seven letters to Churches in Greece, we may suspect that he was copying seven previous letters written by Paul to churches in Asia Minor. Yet we do not have these letters, instead we have seven letters by another Christian named Ignatius.

There are many coincidences between Paul and Ignatius besides their writing letters to Christian churches. Like Paul, Ignatius goes to Rome under arrest for his faith in Christ and writes letters while under arrest. Like Paul he fights with beasts (1 Corinthians 15:32, "I have fought with beasts at Ephesus," *Ignatius To the Romans*, Chapter 5, "From Syria even unto Rome I fight with beasts")

Looking at the Ignatius's *Letter to the Ephesians*, we find this passage:

> If Jesus Christ shall graciously permit me through your prayers, and if it be His will, I shall, in a second little work which I will write to you, make further manifest to you [the nature of] the dispensation of which I have begun [to treat], with respect to the new man, Jesus Christ, in His faith and in His love, in His suffering and in His resurrection.

Ignatius tells us he is going to write another work. Where is this second little work which manifests further the "dispensation" of the "new man, Jesus Christ?" We do not find the term used again in any of the Ignatian corpus. However we find the term three times in the Pauline corpus, once in Colossians, and twice in Ephesians (Laodiceans):

- (Ephesians, 2.15) Having abolished in his flesh the enmity, even the law of commandments contained in ordinances; for to make in himself of twain one **new man**, so making peace.
- (Colossians, 3.10) And put on the **new man**, which is renewed in knowledge after the image of him that created him:
- Ephesians, 4.24) And that ye put on the **new man**, which after God is created in righteousness and true holiness.

Note how similar the last two (Col. 3:10 and Ephesians 4:24) are to each other. The term in Ephesians (2:15) is being used slightly differently. These three sentences come from paragraphs which indicate the same relationship. Here they are in the same order (Eph. 2, Col 3, Eph 4):

11   Wherefore remember, that ye being in time past Gentiles in the flesh, who are called Uncircumcision by that which is called the Circumcision in the flesh made by hands; 12 That at that time ye were without Christ, being aliens from the commonwealth of Israel, and strangers from the covenants of promise, having no hope, and without God in the world: 13 But now in Christ Jesus ye who sometimes were far off are made nigh by the blood of Christ. 14 For he is our peace, who hath made both one, and hath broken down the middle wall of partition between us; 15 Having abolished in his flesh the enmity, even the law of commandments contained in ordinances; for to make in himself of twain one new man, so making peace; 16 And that he might reconcile both unto God in one body by the cross, having slain the enmity thereby: 17 And came and preached peace to you which were afar off, and to them that were nigh. 18 For through him we both have access by one Spirit unto the Father.

5   Mortify therefore your members which are upon the earth; fornication, uncleanness, inordinate affection, evil concupiscence, and covetousness, which is idolatry: 6 For which things' sake the wrath of God cometh on the children of disobedience: 7 In the which ye also walked some time, when ye lived in them. 8 But now ye also put off all these; anger, wrath, malice, blasphemy, filthy communication out of your mouth. 9 Lie not one to another, seeing that ye have put off the old man with his deeds; 10 And have put on the new man, which is renewed in knowledge after the image of him that created him: 11 Where there is neither Greek nor Jew, circumcision nor uncircumcision, Barbarian, Scythian, bond nor free: but Christ is all, and in all.

> 17 This I say therefore, and testify in the Lord, that ye henceforth walk not as other Gentiles walk, in the vanity of their mind, 18 Having the understanding darkened, being alienated from the life of God through the ignorance that is in them, because of the blindness of their heart: 19 Who being past feeling have given themselves over unto lasciviousness, to work all uncleanness with greediness. 20 But ye have not so learned Christ; 21 If so be that ye have heard him, and have been taught by him, as the truth is in Jesus: 22 That ye put off concerning the former conversation the old man, which is corrupt according to the deceitful lusts; 23 And be renewed in the spirit of your mind; 24 And that ye put on the new man, which after God is created in righteousness and true holiness.

Notice that the last one is a commandment. In *Ephesians*, chapter four, the writer says "henceforth walk not as other Gentiles walk . . . put on the new man" In Colossians, chapter three, we also have a commandment to "lie not to one another, seeing that ye have put off the old man with his deeds and have put on the new man." Note the movement from future tense to past tense. The Ephesians addressed by the first author have not yet put on the *new man*. The Colossians addressed by the second writer have already put on the *new man*. In Ephesians, chapter two, the author has the Ephesians remember a time in the past when they were Gentiles. It is God who has made himself into a new man.

We can see the development of the writing. First comes chapter four in *Ephesians* Where the audience is told to become new men, then chapter three in Colossians where the audience is told not to lie because they have become new men. Finally we have chapter two in *Ephesians* where the audience has to remember back to when God made himself into a new man.

Our conclusion is that chapter two is an interpolation written a long time after chapter four. Chapter Four of *Ephesians* (Laodiceans) was written first with *Colossians* chapter three being a later clone.

As importantly, in *Colossians*, we have this line (2:1), "For I want you to know how greatly I strive for you, and for those at Laodicea, and for all who have not seen my face. The "you" refers to the leaders of the church he is addressing, while "Laodicea" tells us the church he is addressing. The phrase "all who have not seen my face" would indicate that he has never been to Laodicea. We may take it that *Colossians* was originally addressed to the church at Laodicea.

We have the evidence repeated later (4:12-13):

> Epaphras, who is one of yourselves, a servant of Christ Jesus, greets you, always remembering you earnestly in his prayers, that you may stand

mature and fully assured in all the will of God. For I bear him witness that he has worked hard for you and for those in Laodicea and in Hierapolis.

In both these cases, we should have the author associating Colossus with Laodicea, if he meant both Colossus and Laodicea. As it stands, it is apparent that the original author only meant to say Laodicea. There is a third instance that proves Laodicea is the intended address of the letter at Colossians 4:15, "Give my greetings to the brethren at Laodicea, and to Nympha and the church in her house." Asking someone in Colossus to give greetings to someone in Laodicea is a little like asking someone in New York to give greetings to someone in Boston. The line only makes sense if Nympha has her Church in the same city where the letter is being sent, Laodicea.

We do find a slight problem with this reading (15-17).

> Give my greetings to the brethren at Laodicea, and to Nympha and the church in her house. And when this letter has been read among you, have it read also in the church of the Laodiceans; and see that you read also the letter from Laodicea. And say to Archippus, "See that you fulfil the ministry which you have received in the Lord."

Apparently, the Colossians should read this letter in the Church at Laodicea as well as the Church at Colossus. But note that the letter does not say to read it in the church at Colossus first and then Laodicea. Since the writer has just mentioned the church of Nympha, we may suppose that he meant that after the addressees have read it, they should share it with Nympha and the Church at her house. We may reconstruct the passage this way:

> Give my greetings to the brethren at Laodicea, and to Nympha and the church in her house. And when this letter has been read among you, have it read also in her church and see that you read also the letter from her. And say to Archippus, "See that you fulfil the ministry which you have received in the Lord."

It appears from this reconstruction that Paul has received a letter from Nympha who has a house church in Laodicea and that she has given a ministry to Archippus. The writer adds his authority to the ministry Nympha has given to Archippus by telling him to fulfill his ministry. We may take it that Nympha was the first leader (Bishop, so to speak) of the Church at Laodicea.

In the fragmentary *Acts of Paul*, a woman named Nympha lives in Smyrna and is the wife of a man named Hermocrates. Paul cures Hermes of dropsy, but his sons Hermocrates and Dion are angered instead of happy. They attack Paul. Pual kills one

491

and blinds the other. Nympha pleads with Paul to help her sons Paul raises Dion from the dead and restores Hermippus' sight. Based on this text, we may suggest that Nympha was a powerful and rich woman known in Smyrna as well as in Laodicea.

In any case, it appears that we start out with a letter or series of letters addressed to the church at Laodicea. This/these get changed into the Epistles to the Ephesians and the Colossians.

If the letter of the *Colossians* is a later clone using parts of *Ephesians* (Laodoceans), the third letter added by Marcion to the Pauline corpus, Philemon, copies, but condenses the closing greeting part of *Colossians*. Here is *Colossians* (10-14):

> *Aristarchus* my fellow prisoner greets you, and *Mark* the cousin of Barnabas (concerning whom you have received instructions—if he comes to you, receive him), and Jesus who is called Justus. These are the only men of the circumcision among my fellow workers for the kingdom of God, and they have been a comfort to me. *Epaphras*, who is one of yourselves, a servant of Christ Jesus, greets you, always remembering you earnestly in his prayers, that you may stand mature and fully assured in all the will of God. For I bear him witness that he has worked hard for you and for those in Laodicea and in Hierapolis. *Luke* the beloved physician and *Demas* greet you.

Compare with Philemon (23-24):

> **Epaphras, my fellow prisoner in Christ Jesus, sends greetings to you, and so do Mark, Aristarchus, Demas, and Luke, my fellow workers.**

Note that the writer assumes the reader of Philemon has already read *Colossians*, so there is no longer any need to inform the reader who these people are. Conversely, it may be that Colossians is expanding the name list from Philemon. *Colossians* is addressed to "the saints and faithful brethren in Christ at Colossus," (2). However it instructs the addressee, "And say to Archippus, 'See that you fulfil the ministry which you have received in the Lord,'" (4:17). Here the addressees in Colossus are being asked to speak with Archippus who has a ministry apparently at Colossus. In *Philemon*, we have this address:

> **Paul, a prisoner of Christ Jesus, and Timothy our brother, to Philemon our beloved and fellow worker, and Apphia our sister and Archippus our fellow soldier, and the church in your house:**

Since the saints and brethren at Colossus are instructed to speak to Archippus in *Colossians*, we may assume he lives in Colossus. Since the author is writing to Archippus in *Philemon*, we may assume that this letter is also being sent to Colossus/Laodicea and Philemon, Apphia (our sister) and Archippus are the leaders of the house church at Colossus/Laodicea. Based on our knowledge that the epistle was originally written to the Church at Laodicea, We may assume that Archippus, Philemon and Apphia had a house church at Laodicea.

Timothy, the Useful Real Son of Paul

Most theologians say that the Letter to Philemon is about Paul pleading with someone named Philemon not to be harsh with a runaway slave. This allegedly shows how kindhearted Paul was towards slaves. It is an absurd interpretation which involves substituting a metaphorical interpretation for obvious and literal ones.

There is no evidence in the letter that Onesimus is a runaway slave. He is simply referred to as Paul's son. He has been born after Paul became a Christian. There is a joke about Onesimus refreshing the bowels of Saints. The bowels is both where the human body excretes waste products, but also where children come from. It does not make any sense for Paul to be talking about "refreshing the bowels of the Saints" with Philemon unless Onesimus is his actual son from his own bowels.

It is apparent that Philemon is a Christian teacher. Paul sent his son Onesimus to him. Philemon sent him back calling him "useless." Paul is trying to get Philemon to take him back as a student. Paul is making some kind of joke by calling him "Onesimus" which means "useful" or "profitable"

Now, the only other person who Paul refers to as his son is Timothy (*1 Corinthians*, 2.22, *Philippians*, 1:4, *1 Timothy*, 1:18 and *2 Timothy* 2:1). We may take it that Timothy is "Onesimus" (the useful one).

We may recall at this point what *Acts* first tells us about Timothy (16:1-3):

> And he came also to Derbe and to Lystra. A disciple was there, named Timothy, the son of a Jewish woman who was a believer; but his father was a Greek. He was well spoken of by the brethren at Lystra and Iconium. Paul wanted Timothy to accompany him; and he took him and circumcised him because of the Jews that were in those places, for they all knew that his father was a Greek.

Notice that upon the first introduction of Timothy, we are given important information about his mother and father, but oddly, no names. Also notice that the explanation for the circumcision makes no sense. How did the people outside of Lystra know that Timothy had a Greek father? We may take it that the people, in the places where Paul traveled knew that Paul/Apollos was Greek. Introducing Timothy as his son, they would immediately know that he too was Greek. Who was the Jewish woman who gave birth to Timothy?

The *Acts of Paul and Thecla* start in Iconium, a small town on the road between Antioch and Lystra. Titus gives a man who has never met Paul a description of him. The man takes Paul to his house where Thecla overhears him talking and gets swept away by his eloquence. We may suggest that in the original story Thecla of Iconium fell in love with Paul and the result was the child Titus, and that is why Titus knows what Paul looks like. The coincidences of Thecla and Titus/Timothy being from the same town, and a story of Thecla falling in love with Paul in that town, is quite suggestive.

In the epistle *Titus*, the author writes, "Titus, my true child in a common faith." Richard Fellows has well argued that Timothy is also actually Titus[499]. He writes, "It is possible that 'Titus' was just a nickname, but it is perhaps more likely that it was a genuine Latin praenomen[500]."

We may take it that the four letters, *1 Timothy*, *2 Timothy*, *Titus* and *Philemon* were originally a series of three or four letters about Paul/Apollos and his relationship to his son Timothy/Titus. Further evidence of this comes from the Catholic Encyclopedia which tells us, "Some of the Greek MSS. end the First Epistle to Timothy with these words: "Written at Laodicea, metropolis of Phrygia Pacatiana"[501]. While the pastoral letters, as I proposed were rewritten by Tertullian (and I based this on their Tertullianic misogynist ideology), it appears he was working from pre-existing material.

Going back to *Philemon*, we may understand its purpose better now that we understand what it is really about. Let us assume that Nympha's church at Laodicea was well-known and popular. A rival church in the same city run by the Master Philemon, Minister Achippus and his wife/Prophetess Apphia might have trouble attracting the faithful. If Apollos or Paul and his son Timothy were well known, it would be quite useful to show them as clients of Philemon. The letter may be seen as an advertisement for Philemon. It tells us that not only did Philemon have the son of Paul/Apollos as his student, but that Nympha has personally endorsed Achippus' ministry.

We may therefore propose that Philemon himself was the originator of the Philemon letter and that much of the material in the pastorals also comes from him. If Philemon writes the letter as an advertisement for his school, we may also take it that he wrote the three letters addressed to Paul's son Timothy/Titus.

Actually when we take out the material that was added by Tertullian and reflects themes that are prevalent in his work (e.g., subordinate position of women, martyrdom as a crown of glory won by an athlete), we get an incredibly coherent and smooth rhethoric performance delivered in a single letter. Tertullian has cut the first part of the letter to create Titus and the middle to create 1 Timothy and the end to make 2 Timothy.

Tertullian changed the address of Titus to Crete, reflecting material in *Acts*, (27.12), "And because the harbor was not suitable to winter in, the majority advised to put to sea from there, on the chance that somehow they could reach Phoenix, a harbor of

THE EVOLUTION OF CHRISTS AND CHRISTIANIES

Crete, looking northeast and southeast, and winter there." He is trying to have us believe that Paul wrote to his son from Crete while on his way to Rome as a prisoner. His son rushed to him in Crete, but he had been moved to Rome, from where he writes another letter.

In fact, once we remove the Tertullian material, it appears that Paul is writing to Titus in Laodicea, apparently still under the tutelage of Philemon. Figuring out where the letter is supposed to be coming from is a little difficult. The story of Paul and Thecla takes place in Iconium. Now, in *Acts* (14.21-23), we find:

> **When they had preached the gospel to that city and had made many disciples, they returned to Lystra and to Ico'nium and to Antioch, strengthening the souls of the disciples, exhorting them to continue in the faith, and saying that through many tribulations we must enter the kingdom of God. And when they had appointed elders for them in every church, with prayer and fasting they committed them to the Lord in whom they believed.**

The construction Lystra and Iconium and to Antioch is quite awkward. The idea that they appointed elders in every church is the same idea that Tertullian has placed in *Titus*. I take it that Tertullian edited both works at the same time. He is mixing together stories and emphasizing Antioch at the expense of Iconium (where the story about Paul in *Paul and Thecla* takes place. We may reconstruct the original passage this way:

> When they had preached to that city and had made many disciples, they returned to Lystra and to Ico'nium, strengthening the souls of the disciples, exhorting them to continue in the faith, and saying that through many tribulations we must enter the kingdom of God. With prayer and fasting they committed them to the Lord in whom they believed.

This is exactly what we would expect from followers of John the Baptist. The awkward grammatical construction is eliminated with the elimination of Antioch in the sentence and we now have a text that matches the main location of the tale of Paul and Thecla—Iconium. We may take it that Paul is writing to Titus from Iconium. The letter probably is supposed to take place before the events in the beginning of *Paul and Thecla*, where Paul returns to Iconium and meets his son Titus.

However, Iconium as the letter's place of origin has gone through a couple of changes. The text we now have has Paul telling Titus to meet him in Nicopolis (*Titus* 3:12)> He is writing to Titus who is in Crete (1.5). In *2 Timonthy*, (4.13), the writer asks, "When you come, bring the cloak that I left with Carpus at Tro'as, also the books, and above all the parchments." Now assuming this is all one letter, Titus would have to travel about 400 miles in a Northeastern direction from Crete to retrieve Paul's cloak and bring it to him in Nicopolis which is Northwest from Crete. Likewise, if Titus is in Laodicea and going to Nicopolis, he is still making a 200 mile detour. On the other hand, if the town is Neopolis instead of Nicopolis and Titus is in Laodicea, then Troas is directly on the route that Titus would take to reach him there. The idea of Neopolis in Macedonia, not Nicopolis in Achaia being the meeting place for Paul and Titus matches well with the beginning of Timothy, which has "As I urged you when I was going to Macedonia, remain at Ephesus." Someone writing from Thessalonica and going to winter at Neopolis would be moving in the direction of either Ephesus or Laodicea. So it would make sense as a rendevous place. We may take it that the letter is coming from Thessalonica. We may take it as well the Thessalonian writer of the seven authentic letters of Paul also edited this one (Titus/1and 2 Timothy), making the point of origin for the letter Thessalonica.

We may take it that the original letter writer was Philemon and Iconium was the original rendevous point between Titus and Paul/Apollos. It was changed by the Thessalonian writer to Neopolis and changed by Tertullian to Nicopolis.

Reconstruction of Epistle of Paul to Titus, by Philemon of Laodicea:

Here is a reconstruction of the original letter written by Philemon that I believe Tertullian changed into the three Pauline letters: *Titus*, and *1 and 2 Timothy*. Brackets indicate where I believe Tertullian has interpolated material. Words that I think Tertullian changed are in brackets too. Lines that Tertullian rearranged out of order in his three epistles are noted in parentheses:

> (Titus 1). Paul, a servant of God { }, to further the faith of God's elect and their knowledge of the truth which accords with godliness, { }
> 3. and at the proper time manifested in his word through the preaching with which I have been entrusted by command of God our Savior;
> 4. To Titus, my true child in a common faith: Grace and peace from God {} and Christ Jesus our Savior.
> 5. This is why I left you in {Crete} Laodicea, that {you} Philemon might amend what was defective, { }
> 6. if any man is blameless, { } and not open to the charge of being profligate or insubordinate. { }
> 8. but hospitable, a lover of goodness, master of himself, upright, holy, and self-controlled;
> 9. he must hold firm to the sure word as taught, so that he may be able to give instruction in sound doctrine and also to confute those who contradict it.

10. { } especially the circumcision party;
13. { } Therefore rebuke them sharply, that they may be sound in the faith,
14. instead of giving heed to Jewish myths or to commands of men who reject the truth.
15. To the pure all things are pure, but to the corrupt and unbelieving nothing is pure; their very minds and consciences are corrupted.
16. They profess to know God, but they deny him by their deeds; they are detestable, disobedient, unfit for any good deed.
1. But as for you, teach what befits sound doctrine.
2. Bid the older men be temperate, serious, sensible, sound in faith, in love, and in steadfastness.

(1 Tim 51). Do not rebuke an older man but exhort him as you would a father; treat younger men like brothers,
6. { } Likewise urge the younger men to control themselves.
7. Show yourself in all respects a model of good deeds, and in your teaching show integrity, gravity,
8. and sound speech that cannot be censured, so that an opponent may be put to shame, having nothing evil to say of us.

{ } (1 Tim 6.1). Let all who are under the yoke of slavery regard their masters as worthy of all honor, so that the name of God and the teaching may not be defamed.
2: Those who have believing masters must not be disrespectful on the ground that they are brethren; rather they must serve all the better since those who benefit by their service are believers and beloved. Teach and urge these duties.
9. Bid slaves to be submissive to their masters and to give satisfaction in every respect; they are not to be refractory,
10. nor to pilfer, but to show entire and true fidelity, so that in everything they may adorn the doctrine of God our Savior.
3.1. Remind them to be submissive to rulers and authorities, to be obedient, to be ready for any honest work,
2. to speak evil of no one, to avoid quarreling, to be gentle, and to show perfect courtesy toward all men.
3. For we ourselves were once foolish, disobedient, led astray, slaves to various passions and pleasures, passing our days in malice and envy, hated by men and hating one another;
4. but when the goodness and loving kindness of God our Savior appeared,
5. he saved us, not because of deeds done by us in righteousness, but in virtue of his own mercy, by the washing of regeneration { }

8. { } I desire you to insist on these things, so that those who have believed in God may be careful to apply themselves to good deeds; these are excellent and profitable to men. { }
14. And let our people learn to apply themselves to good deeds, so as to help cases of urgent need, and not to be unfruitful. { }

(1 Timothy 4.7.) Have nothing to do with godless and silly myths. Train yourself in godliness;
8. for while bodily training is of some value, godliness is of value in every way, as it holds promise for the present life and also for the life to come. { }

(1 Tim 5.6.) There is great gain in godliness with contentment;
7. for we brought nothing into the world, and we cannot take anything out of the world;
8. but if we have food and clothing, with these we shall be content.
9. But those who desire to be rich fall into temptation, into a snare, into many senseless and hurtful desires that plunge men into ruin and destruction.
10. For the love of money is the root of all evils; it is through this craving that some have wandered away from the faith and pierced their hearts with many pangs. { }

(1 Tim 6.17). As for the rich in this world, charge them not to be haughty, nor to set their hopes on uncertain riches but on God who richly furnishes us with everything to enjoy.
18. They are to do good, to be rich in good deeds, liberal and generous,
19. thus laying up for themselves a good foundation for the future, so that they may take hold of the life which is life indeed.

(1 Tim 6.11). But as for you, man of God, shun all this; aim at righteousness, godliness, faith, love, steadfastness, gentleness. { }
14. I charge you to keep the commandment unstained and free from reproach until the appearing of our Lord Jesus Christ;
15. and this will be made manifest at the proper time by the blessed and only Sovereign, the King of kings and Lord of lords,
16. who alone has immortality and dwells in unapproachable light, whom no man has ever seen or can see. To him be honor and eternal dominion. Amen.

(1 Tim 4.9). The saying is sure and worthy of full acceptance.
10. For to this end we toil and strive, because we have our hope set on the living God, who is the Savior of all men, especially of those who believe.
11. Command and teach these things.

12. Let no one despise your youth, but set the believers an example in speech and conduct, in love, in faith, in purity.
13. Till I come, attend to the public reading of scripture, to preaching, to teaching.
14. Do not neglect the gift you have, which was given you by prophetic utterance when the council of elders laid their hands upon you.
15. Practice these duties, devote yourself to them, so that all may see your progress.
16. Take heed to yourself and to your teaching; hold to that, for by so doing you will save both yourself and your hearers. { }

(2 Timothy 1.6). Hence I remind you to rekindle the gift of God that is within you through the laying on of my hands; { }
7. for God did not give us a spirit of timidity but a spirit of power and love and self-control. { }

(1 Timothy 5.22). Do not be hasty in the laying on of hands, nor participate in another man's sins; keep yourself pure.
23. No longer drink only water, but use a little wine for the sake of your stomach and your frequent ailments.
24. The sins of some men are conspicuous, pointing to judgment, but the sins of others appear later.
25. So also good deeds are conspicuous; and even when they are not, they cannot remain hidden.

(2 Timothy 1.15). You are aware that all who are in Asia turned away from me, and among them Phy'gelus and Hermog'enes.
16. May the Lord grant mercy to the household of Onesiph'orus, for he often refreshed me; he was not ashamed of my chains, { }
18. may the Lord grant him to find mercy from the Lord on that Day—and you well know all the service he rendered at Ephesus. { }

(2 Timothy 2.1). You then, my son, be strong in the grace that is in Christ Jesus, { }
15. Do your best to present yourself to God as one approved, a workman who has no need to be ashamed, rightly handling the word of truth.
16. Avoid such godless chatter, for it will lead people into more and more ungodliness,
17. and their talk will eat its way like gangrene. Among them are Hymenaeus and Philetus,
18. who have swerved from the truth by holding that the resurrection is past already. They are upsetting the faith of some.

19. But God's firm foundation stands, bearing this seal: "The Lord knows those who are his," and, "Let every one who names the name of the Lord depart from iniquity."
20. In a great house there are not only vessels of gold and silver but also of wood and earthenware, and some for noble use, some for ignoble.
21. If any one purifies himself from what is ignoble, then he will be a vessel for noble use, consecrated and useful to the master of the house, ready for any good work.
22. So shun youthful passions and aim at righteousness, faith, love, and peace, along with those who call upon the Lord from a pure heart.
23. Have nothing to do with stupid, senseless controversies; you know that they breed quarrels.
24. And the Lord's servant must not be quarrelsome but kindly to every one, an apt teacher, forbearing,
25. correcting his opponents with gentleness. God may perhaps grant that they will repent and come to know the truth,
26. and they may escape from the snare of the devil, after being captured by him to do his will.

(2 timothy 1.3). I thank God whom I serve with a clear conscience, as did my fathers, when I remember you constantly in my prayers.
4. As I remember your tears, I long night and day to see you, that I may be filled with joy.
5. I am reminded of your sincere faith, a faith that dwelt first in your grandmother Lois and your mother Eunice and now, I am sure, dwells in you. { }

(2 Tim 4.9). Do your best to come to me soon.
12. Tychicus I have sent to Ephesus.

Titus 3.12. When I send Artemas or Tychicus to you, do your best to come to me at _____, for I have decided to spend the winter there.
14. Alexander the coppersmith did me great harm; the Lord will requite him for his deeds.
15. Beware of him yourself, for he strongly opposed our message.
16. At my first defense no one took my part; all deserted me. May it not be charged against them!
17. But the Lord stood by me and gave me strength to proclaim the message fully, that all the Gentiles might hear it. So I was rescued from the lion's mouth.
18. The Lord will rescue me from every evil and save me for his heavenly kingdom. To him be the glory for ever and ever. Amen.

19. Greet Prisca and Aq'uila, and the household of Onesiphorus.
20. Erastus remained at Corinth; Trophimus I left ill at Miletus.
21. Do your best to come before winter. Eubulus sends greetings to you, as do Pudens and Linus and Claudia and all the brethren.
22. The Lord be with your spirit. Grace be with you.

Now, we should immediately note that there is nothing about Jesus Christ being the son in this reconstruction. Jesus is simply the lord of the angels who God will send to save the Jews. There is nothing beyond the ideology of John except for the fact that Jesus is the name of the coming savior. The line at *2 Tim* 4.9 for example "The Lord will rescue me from every evil and save me for his heavenly kingdom," is exactly what a devout Jew would write.

Notice this line (*Tim* 2.24): "And the Lord's servant must not be quarrelsome but kindly to every one, an apt teacher, forbearing," It is interesting that being the lord's servant is associated with both being kindly to every one and being a forbearing teacher. On the assumption that the letter to Philemon was really about asking forbearance of a teacher who had a wayward student, this idea fits in quite well. Also note we find the same sentiment expressed in *Hebrews* (12.14), "Strive for peace with all men."

Hebrews also ties into the idea of a forbearing teacher. We read (5.12), "For though by this time you ought to be teachers, you need some one to teach you again the first principles of God's word. You need milk, not solid food." We may take it that the writer of Hebrews, the original Titus and Philemon thought of himself as a servant of God and a teacher.

Who Was Untimely Born?

We need to go back to *1 Corinthians* to solve a mystery we found in the *Gospel of Mark*. In deconstructing that gospel we found two groups at odds with each over the sayings of Jesus, each producing one saying of a couplet. We were afterwards able to see that one of the groups believed in the resurrection of the dead and the other did not. From 1 Corinthians we may find the leaders of these two groups.

We focus in on the late chapter 15 which seeks to remind us of Paul's fundamental principles, something one should have expected much earlier in the letter.

1. Now I would remind you, brethren, in what terms I preached to you the gospel, which you received, in which you stand,
2. by which you are saved, if you hold it fast—unless you believed in vain.
3. For I delivered to you as of first importance what I also received, that Christ died for our sins in accordance with the scriptures,
4. that he was buried, that he was raised on the third day in accordance with the scriptures,

5. and that he appeared to Cephas, then to the twelve.
6. Then he appeared to more than five hundred brethren at one time, most of whom are still alive, though some have fallen asleep.
7. Then he appeared to James, then to all the apostles.
8. Last of all, as to one untimely born, he appeared also to me.

This list quite contradicts the gospels and even *Acts* regarding the resurrection appearances of Jesus. We may take the list to be derived from a different source. How was it derived? Traditionally, people suggests that the odd form of this statement proves that it comes from oral history and reflects some kind of truth or that it reflects the fact that the author made it up. In fact, it neither comes from oral history nor is it made up by the author. Its bizarre nature helps us to solve the riddle.

First, we should note that we have two lists.

List One:
1. Cephas
2. The twelve
3. Five hundred

List Two:
1. James
2. All the Apostles
3. Me, one untimely born

List one is complete with Jesus' appearance to five hundred people. It shows that Jesus appeared to a great number of people after his death. The second list does not add anything to this fact. Actually, the second list confuses everything. Was James included in the twelve? Seemingly, then we are talking about a second round of visits. Logically, the author should say, "then he was seen again by James and all the Apostles." Apparently, the author was untimely born because he was not one of the five hundred who saw him the first time, and not one of the apostles who saw him twice. Since Cephas and James are themselves Apostles, we may take it that they saw him three times. On the other hand, the one untimely born got a private personal visit, so he has to be classed with James and Cephas as specially chosen. Therefore, apparently, he was not so untimely born.

Note the lists are quite balanced with Cephas balancing James and the Twelve balancing the Apostles. It is only when we get to the third names on the list that we get a wild imbalance with the author seemingly comparing himself to five hundred people. This makes us suspicious that the third element of list one has been tampered with. In fact, the use of the term the Twelve and the Five Hundred are suspicious. If the first list was intended as a numbers list, where the numbers visited after death was of significance, we should have the author saying that Christ first appeared to one man, then twelve, then five hundred. The list is not written this way. We may take it that the first list was not a numbers list. It originally read Cephas, the Apostles and someone else (as the third element of the second list is singular, we may take it that the third element of the first list was originally singular also).

THE EVOLUTION OF CHRISTS AND CHRISTIANIES

We now have this.

List One:	List Two:
1. Cephas	1. James
2. All the Apostles	2. All the Apostles
3. ?	3. Me, one untimely born

The text continues:

9. For I am the least of the apostles, unfit to be called an apostle, because I persecuted the church of God.
10. But by the grace of God I am what I am, and his grace toward me was not in vain. On the contrary, I worked harder than any of them, though it was not I, but the grace of God which is with me.
11. Whether then it was I or they, so we preach and so you believed.

It is interesting that the writer does not mention his name at this point. It is really a perfect opportunity to say "I, Paulus Antonius Julianus, was the last to see the Christ and the least of the Apostles" or whoever he is. Instead he puts himself in opposition to the Apostles to indicate that the speaker is supposed to be the well known opponent of the Church of God—Saul/Paul. In any case, this does not tell us who was originally on the second list. It appears that just as the author has changed the third name on the first list, he has changed the third name on the second list. This leaves us with

List One:	List Two:
1. Cephas	1. James
2. All the Apostles	2. All the Apostles
3. ?	3. ?

Now the two lists clearly show Cephas being put into opposition with James. The writer of the Pauline epistles clearly knows about the opposition between the two and exploits them. We may assume the opposition was real. If the split in the Jerusalem group was between Cephas/Simon and James, we should expect that each would attempt to prove that he was the first to see the Christ and the other was the last. We may fill in the third names on the lists to reflect this.

List One:	List Two:
1. Cephas	1. James
2. All the Apostles	2. All the Apostles
3. James	3. Cephas

The second list is just a mirror of the first one. The next passage in the text confirms that the original list came from followers of Cephas (Simon AKA Peter).

> 11: Whether then it was I or they, so we preach and so you believed.
> 12: Now if Christ is preached as raised from the dead, how can some of you say that there is no resurrection of the dead?
> 13: But if there is no resurrection of the dead, then Christ has not been raised;
> 14: if Christ has not been raised, then our preaching is in vain and your faith is in vain.
> 15: We are even found to be misrepresenting God, because we testified of God that he raised Christ, whom he did not raise if it is true that the dead are not raised.

The issue that the text is again debating is the old one of raising the dead that Josephus tells us divided the Pharisees from the Sadducees. The rival lists show intense rivalry between the two groups. We may suppose that this issue of the resurrection of the dead divided them bitterly. It is a good bet that the couplets we found in the *Gospel of Mark* that formed the basic sayings of Jesus came from these rival factions. From this we may suppose that Cephas or Simon Peter believed the dead rose, while James did not. However, this may be a later revision. What is safer to say is that one of them probably supported the idea of resurrection from the dead while the other opposed it.

The replacement of Cephas-Simon-Peter in this list by Paul reminds us of the substitution of Paul for Peter as the lead character in Chapter 12 of *Acts*. Paul replaces Peter after Herod Agrippa executes James and imprisons Peter. In the text, an angel helps Peter escape from prison on the eve of his execution. We may take it that the escape from prison is a pious fantasy. Peter appears again briefly in chapter 15, but that scene is out of order. It should take place at the beginning of Paul's career when he would first become interested in the Jerusalem Christ cult. We have to explain the disappearance of Peter from the text after Herod puts him in prison circa 43 or 44 C.E. The obvious answer is that Peter was not rescued by an angel. Herod executed him.

Another clue that Peter died at this time lies in the way the text tells us of his arrest:

> 1: About that time Herod the king laid violent hands upon some who belonged to the church.
> 2: He killed James the brother of John with the sword;
> 3: and when he saw that it pleased the Jews, he proceeded to arrest Peter also. This was during the days of Unleavened Bread.

4: And when he had seized him, he put him in prison, and delivered him to four squads of soldiers to guard him, intending after the Passover to bring him out to the people.

There is a noticeable lack of parallelism here. He kills James, but only arrests Peter. Amazingly, the death of James is only mentioned in passing. Apparently Herod's popular killing of James means he can hand over Peter to the Jews who will put him to death on the day after Passover. There seems to be some confusion around Antipas and Herod the tetrarch here. The coincidence of John the Baptist having his head cut off with a sword and his brother James dying by the sword is too great for the author not to take note of it. We may take it that the original read "John" and not "James the brother of John." This story is about Peter/Simon's escape from Herod the Tetrarch. Reconstructed we get:

1: About that time Herod the Tetrarch laid violent hands upon some who belonged to the church.
2: He killed John the brother of James with the sword;
3: and when he saw that it pleased the Jews, he proceeded to kill Peter also.

This means that Peter died around the same time that John was killed. This is quite astonishing. Is there any other evidence that this is true? There is definite evidence that the text is lying to us at this point. We have another contemporary source that tells us that James was not killed by Herod the king. The source is Hegesippus.

The Secret Identity of the Crucified Man

Eusebius quotes this quite extensive passage from Hegesippus regarding the death of James (*History*, II.23)

3   The manner of James' death has been already indicated by the above-quoted words of Clement, who records that he was thrown from the pinnacle of the temple, and was beaten to death with a club. But Hegesippus, who lived immediately after the apostles, gives the most accurate account in the fifth book of his Memoirs. He writes as follows:

4   "James, the brother of the Lord, succeeded to the government of the Church in conjunction with the apostles. He has been called the Just by all from the time of our Saviour to the present day; for there were many that bore the name of James.

5   He was holy from his mother's womb; and he drank no wine nor strong drink, nor did he eat flesh. No razor came upon his head; he did not anoint himself with oil, and he did not use the bath.

6   He alone was permitted to enter into the holy place; for he wore not woolen but linen garments. And he was in the habit of entering alone into the temple, and was frequently found upon his knees begging forgiveness for the people, so that his knees became hard like those of a camel, in consequence of his constantly bending them in his worship of God, and asking forgiveness for the people.

7   Because of his exceeding great justice he was called the Just, and Oblias, which signifies in Greek, 'Bulwark of the people' and 'Justice,' in accordance with what the prophets declare concerning him.

8   Now some of the seven sects, which existed among the people and which have been mentioned by me in the Memoirs, asked him, 'What is the gate of Jesus?' and he replied that he was the Saviour.

9   On account of these words some believed that Jesus is the Christ. But the sects mentioned above did not believe either in a resurrection or in one's coming to give to every man according to his works. But as many as believed did so on account of James.

10 Therefore when many even of the rulers believed, there was a commotion among the Jews and Scribes and Pharisees, who said that there was danger that the whole people would be looking for Jesus as the Christ. Coming therefore in a body to James they said, 'We entreat thee, restrain the people; for they are gone astray in regard to Jesus, as if he were the Christ. We entreat thee to persuade all that have come to the feast of the Passover concerning Jesus; for we all have confidence in thee. For we bear thee witness, as do all the people, that thou art just, and dost not respect persons.

11 Do thou therefore persuade the multitude not to be led astray concerning Jesus. For the whole people, and all of us also, have confidence in thee. Stand therefore upon the pinnacle of the temple, that from that high position thou mayest be clearly seen, and that thy words may be readily heard by all the people. For all the tribes, with the Gentiles also, are come together on account of the Passover.'

12 The aforesaid Scribes and Pharisees therefore placed James upon the pinnacle of the temple, and cried out to him and said: 'Thou just one, in whom we ought all to have: confidence, forasmuch as the people are led, astray after Jesus, the crucified one, declare to us, what is the gate of Jesus.

13 And he answered with a loud voice, 'Why do ye ask me concerning Jesus, the Son of Man? He himself sitteth in heaven

at the right hand of the great Power, and is about to come upon the clouds of heaven.'

14 And when many were fully convinced and gloried in the testimony of James, and said, 'Hosanna to the Son of David,' these same Scribes and Pharisees said again to one another, 'We have done badly in supplying such testimony to Jesus. But let us go up and throw him down, in order that they may be afraid to believe him.'

15 And they cried out, saying, 'Oh! oh! the just man is also in error.' And they fulfilled the Scripture written in Isaiah, 'Let us take away the just man, because he is troublesome to us: therefore they shall eat the fruit of their doings.'

16 So they went up and threw down the just man, and said to each other, 'Let us stone James the Just.' And they began to stone him, for he was not killed by the fall; but he turned and knelt down and said, 'I entreat thee, Lord God our Father, forgive them, for they know not what they do.'

17 And while they were thus stoning him one of the priests of the sons of Rechab, the son of the Rechabites, who are mentioned by Jeremiah the prophet, cried out, saying, 'Cease, what do ye? The just one prayeth for you.'

18 And one of them, who was a fuller, took the club with which he beat out clothes and struck the just man on the head. And thus he suffered martyrdom. And they buried him on the spot, by the temple, and his monument still remains by the temple.

Note the important end statement that his monument still remains by the temple. This means that the temple was still standing when Hegesippus wrote, so we may take this as a pre-70 CE account. Later in his *History*, Eusebius will impeach the credibility of Hegesippus by having him testify to second century events. We may ignore that and recognize that at this stage, Eusebius has more or less faithfully recorded this text, although he evidently did not understand its content.

At first glance it appears simply that James is killed for testifying to Jesus. However, a closer reading indicates that he was killed for what he said and did not say about Jesus. The Pharisees and Scribes, who we know do believe in the resurrection of the dead are asking James about "Jesus, the crucified" James answers about "Jesus, the Son of Man." James simply repeats what all Jews know about Jesus from the book of Enoch, that he is in heaven and will come upon the clouds. The Pharisees and Scribes want him to say that the crucified man was Jesus. It is because James denies the resurrection of Jesus or that he was a man on Earth that he is put to death by the Christian Pharisees and Scribes. This also explains why the Jews would build a monument to him on the spot of his death. We may take it that James was a Sadducee who did not believe in the resurrection of the dead.

In Josephus (*Antiquities*, 20.9.1), we are told that a Sadducee named Ananus killed James.

> And now Caesar, upon hearing the death of Festus, sent Albinus into Judea, as procurator. But the king deprived Joseph of the high priesthood, and bestowed the succession to that dignity on the son of Ananus, who was also himself called Ananus[502]. Now the report goes that this eldest Ananus proved a most fortunate man; for he had five sons who had all performed the office of a high priest to God, and who had himself enjoyed that dignity a long time formerly, which had never happened to any other of our high priests. But this younger Ananus, who, as we have told you already, took the high priesthood, was a bold man in his temper, and very insolent; he was also of the sect of the Sadducees. who are very rigid in judging offenders, above all the rest of the Jews, as we have already observed; when, therefore, Ananus was of this disposition, he thought he had now a proper opportunity [to exercise his authority]. Festus was now dead, and Albinus was but upon the road; so he assembled the sanhedrim of judges, and brought before them the brother of Jesus, who was called Christ, whose name was James, and some others, [or, some of his companions]; and when he had formed an accusation against them as breakers of the law, he delivered them to be stoned: but as for those who seemed the most equitable of the citizens, and such as were the most uneasy at the breach of the laws, they disliked what was done; they also sent to the king [Agrippa], desiring him to send to Ananus that he should act so no more, for that what he had already done was not to be justified; nay, some of them went also to meet Albinus, as he was upon his journey from Alexandria, and informed him that it was not lawful for Ananus to assemble a sanhedrim without his consent. Whereupon Albinus complied with what they said, and wrote in anger to Ananus, and threatened that he would bring him to punishment for what he had done; on which king Agrippa took the high priesthood from him, when he had ruled but three months, and made Jesus, the son of Damneus, high priest.

This occurs in 52 CE. We may take it for the moment that James was John (the Baptist's) brother and ruled the followers of John from 37 to 52 CE. The contradiction between the report in Josephus that Sadducees killed James by stoning and the report in Hegesippus that Scribes and Pharisees killed James by stoning can easily be reconciled if we assume the lines about being one of the sect of Sadducees applied to James not Ananus. Thus, reconstructed we get this:

THE EVOLUTION OF CHRISTS AND CHRISTIANIES

> And now Caesar, upon hearing the death of Festus, sent Albinus into Judea, as procurator. But the king deprived Joseph of the high priesthood, and bestowed the succession to that dignity on the son of Ananus, who was also himself called Ananus [Ananias][503]. Now the report goes that this eldest Ananus proved a most fortunate man; for he had five sons who had all performed the office of a high priest to God, and who had himself enjoyed that dignity a long time formerly, which had never happened to any other of our high priests., But Ananus was a bold man in his temper, and very insolent; this younger Ananus [Ananias], who, as we have told you already, took the high priesthood, was of this disposition, so when therefore he thought he had now a proper opportunity to exercise his authority, Festus was now dead, and Albinus was but upon the road; he assembled the sanhedrim of judges, and brought before them the brother of John, who was called Christ, whose name was James, he was also of the sect of the Sadducees. who are very rigid in judging offenders, above all the rest of the Jews, as we have already observed; and some others, and when he had formed an accusation against them as breakers of the law, he delivered them to be stoned: but as for those who seemed the most equitable of the citizens, and such as were the most uneasy at the breach of the laws, they disliked what was done;

The reference "also" in the phrase "also of the sect of Sadducees" would refer to John being a Sadducee and James also being one. This would confirm what we have deduced previously from the phrase about Jesus being the "first born of the dead." It is now evident that the Pharisees and Scribes are divided from the Sadducees over the issue of resurrection of the dead and the nature of the Christ. The Pharisees and Scribes support the idea that Jesus had come down to Earth and risen. It is the denial of this by the Sadducee James that leads to his death at the hands of the Pharisee High Priest Ananus and his followers.

Now, the Pharisees are upset with the brother of John for not saying that the Christ was crucified. It seems a little harsh that they would kill John for not declaring his brother John the Christ. Obviously James knew him best and knew quite well he was not a god. Whom did this group of Pharisees believe had been the incarnation of the lord Jesus? If *Acts* is telling us the truth that Herod killed Peter shortly after killing John, this means that Peter must be the historical model for Jesus, crucified man. We may deconstruct the sections of *Acts* dealing with Peter to see if this is correct.

Fresco. Christ as Good Shepherd.

Catacomb of St. Priscilla, early 3rd century. Birds, trees and animals are typical of afterlife paradise settings. Probably, people were expecting and hoping to see this gentle image of Christ after they died. Probably this idea predates the idea of Christ as afterworld judge.

Chapter 11

Peter was Simon, But who Was Simon?

We have only scratched the surface in discussing the problems with *Acts'* chapter 12 as it stands. As we noted there is the fact that Peter's career shuts off abruptly after he supposedly escapes from prison. There is the coincidence of James and John the Baptist being executed by the sword by Herod and no remark on the part of the author to this effect. There is the misuse of Herod's name instead for Antipas. There is the contradiction between this text and texts of Hegesippus and Josephus that claim James was stoned and not killed by Herod. There is the fact that Peter asks people to tell James about his escape after James is dead (12.17). In chapter 15 James suddenly becomes alive again and makes a speech.

To solve some of these problems an apostle named James the lesser or James son of Alphaeus has been invented. This apostle plays no part in any story and has just been made up for the specific purpose of explaining away some of the contradictions in the text. This creates a new problem of imagining that the author of Acts would be so thoughtless as to mention the death of one of two James and not tell which one it was. The invention of the second James, called "James, Son of Alphaeus" in the disciple list in the first chapter of *Acts* creates a contradiction with Mark (2.14) where we are told of the disciple "Levi, the son of Alphaeus."

All of these problems disappear when we suppose that the original text spoke of the imprisonment and death of Peter happening immediately after Herod killed John (not his brother James) with the sword. We propose changing Acts 12.2 to read "He killed John the brother of James with the sword." from "He killed James the brother of John with the sword." This makes it match perfectly with the information in Mark (6.16) "But when Herod heard of it he said, "John, whom I beheaded, has been raised."

As further proof that *Acts* referred originally to the death of John not James, we may note that the text mentions no action of James in the eleven chapters leading up to this point. He is only mentioned once on an apostle list which could easily have been added to the text at any point over the next two centuries. On the other hand, the text shows Peter and John together often and indicates that they are both the leaders of the church. In chapters one and two, only Peter speaks for the apostles. At the beginning of chapter three, Peter and John go together to the temple to pray. Both are asked for alms by a crippled man. It is Peter who heals him. The fact that he's the spokesperson and miracle worker indicates that this is being written by followers of Peter, but that they acknowledge John as the co-leader of the Church. We really must assume that when the text says that Herod attacked the church in chapter twelve, it originally said that he attacked the leaders of the church Peter and John, and not some unknown apostle (unknown even to any of the gospel authors) named James.

By tracing the career of Peter in *Acts* up to the point where he gets arrested by Herod in 36/37 CE, shortly after the death of John, we can understand who he was and how he became what he became.

As mentioned Peter is presented as the real leader of the group. He delivers four speeches of approximately 55 lines, orders an election to be held to replace Judas and performs a miracle of healing a cripple, before another apostle even speaks. When another apostle does speak for the first time in chapter four, it is actually John and Peter speaking together only one line (4.19-20). In chapter five, Peter and the Apostles speak three lines. The Apostles, presumably including Peter, speak one line in chapter six. Essentially, in the first six chapters of *Acts* Peter speaks every apostolic statement, about 60 lines. In the narrative, he is the main speaker for the church and the main leader of the church.

Chapter six changes focus. It concerns eight other apostles (6.5), "they chose Stephen, a man full of faith and of the Holy Spirit, and Philip, and Prochorus, and Nicanor, and Timon, and Parmenas, and Nicolaus, a proselyte of Antioch." We may take it that these are disciples from a secondary sect. The text is trying to merge the two stories of these eight disciples and the other twelve. We may provisionally suggest that these disciples belong with Peter. Just as Peter has been associated with the twelve disciples and given a dominant role, these followers of Peter have been associated with the twelve disciples. One gets this from the way this pro-Peter text refers to them. For example, it says (6.8), "And Stephen, full of grace and power, did great wonders and signs among the people. None of the canonical gospel writers have such nice things to say about the twelve apostles.

In chapters six and seven Stephen delivers a long speech seemingly against some specific Jewish groups (6.9), "some of those who belonged to the synagogue of the Freedmen (as it was called), and of the Cyre'nians, and of the Alexandrians, and of those from Cili'cia and Asia," Notice that the people against Stephen are ex-slaves and foreigners.

THE EVOLUTION OF CHRISTS AND CHRISTIANIES

The ending of the speech, as it stands is confusing with two contradictory ideas put forward against the ex-slaves and foreigners 1) (52)they murdered "the righteous one" and 2) (53) they did not obey the law. The point of the long speech that Stephen gives is that (7.53) "you who received the law as delivered by angels and did not keep it." It appears that someone has added some text before this point. The text as it now stands reads:

> 51: "You stiff-necked people, uncircumcised in heart and ears, you always resist the Holy Spirit. As your fathers did, so do you.
> 52: Which of the prophets did not your fathers persecute? And they killed those who announced beforehand the coming of the Righteous One, whom you have now betrayed and murdered,
> 53: you who received the law as delivered by angels and did not keep it."

The uncircumcised in hearts and ears is a Pauline motif and the Holy Spirit is a Montanist/Tertullianic theme. In almost fifty lines of text before this, Stephan has not said one word about Jews persecuting prophets. On the other hand he has talked about Jews in the desert not obeying the laws of Moses. We may speculate that the original read this way:

> 51: "You stiff-necked people, As your fathers did, so do you.
> 53: you who received the law as delivered by angels and did not keep it."

Stephan is defending the law of Moses against the ex-slaves and foreigners who he and presumably Peter believe are attacking it.

The description of the attack matches fairly closely to the attack against James as described by Hegesippus. James speech apparently ends with James saying, "'Why do ye ask me concerning Jesus, the Son of Man? He himself sitteth in heaven at the right hand of the great Power, and is about to come upon the clouds of heaven.'" Stephen's speech ends with him saying (56), "Behold, I see the heavens opened, and the Son of man standing at the right hand of God." The crowd throws James off of the temple and then stone him, while the crowd (7.56) casts Stephen out of the city and then stones him. Even this may not be considered a different description, as the temple may have risen above the city gates and throwing someone off the temple would land them outside the city.

Hegesippus tells us that James was killed by a fuller's club. A fuller was a lowly position involving cleaning clothes. We may take it as a likely job for an ex-slave, a member of the "synagogue of freedmen." We may take the death of Simon to be a Petrine retelling of the death of James.

513

In chapter eight, Philip, the second of the eight apostles, goes into Samaria. He does a multitude of miracles.

> 5: Philip went down to a city of Sama'ria, and proclaimed to them the Christ.
> 6: And the multitudes with one accord gave heed to what was said by Philip, when they heard him and saw the signs which he did.
> 7: For unclean spirits came out of many who were possessed, crying with a loud voice; and many who were paralyzed or lame were healed.
> 8: So there was much joy in that city.

He baptizes a man called Simon the magician. Simon has also impressed the Samaritans.

> 9: But there was a man named Simon who had previously practiced magic in the city and amazed the nation of Samaria, saying that he himself was somebody great.
> 10: They all gave heed to him, from the least to the greatest, saying, "This man is that power of God which is called Great."
> 11: And they gave heed to him, because for a long time he had amazed them with his magic.
> 12: But when they believed Philip as he preached good news about the kingdom of God and the name of Jesus Christ, they were baptized, both men and women.
> 13: Even Simon himself believed, and after being baptized he continued with Philip. And seeing signs and great miracles performed, he was amazed.

The problem is we have two miracle workers. But why should Simon be amazed? After all, everybody was saying "from the least to the greatest" that Simon was "the power of God which is called Great." It makes much more sense to see Philip as being impressed with Simon the Magician. We may conjecture that the original read this way.

> 5: Philip went down to a city of Samaria,
> 9: But there was a man named Simon who had previously practiced magic in the city and amazed the nation of Samaria, saying that he himself was somebody great.
> 10: They all gave heed to him, from the least to the greatest, saying, "This man is that power of God which is called Great."

THE EVOLUTION OF CHRISTS AND CHRISTIANIES

11: And they gave heed to him, because for a long time he had amazed them with his magic.

7: For unclean spirits came out of many who were possessed, crying with a loud voice; and many who were paralyzed or lame were healed.
And seeing signs and great miracles performed, he [Philip] was amazed.

12: But when they believed Philip as he preached good news about the kingdom of God and the name of Jesus Christ, they were baptized, both men and women.

13: Even Simon himself believed, and after being baptized he continued with Philip.

6: And the multitudes with one accord gave heed to what was said by Philip, and [he] proclaimed him [Simon] the Christ, when they heard him and saw the signs which he [Simon] did.

8: So there was much joy in that city.

Just as the Stephen stoning story was a version of the James stoning story, the baptism of Philip-Simon story appears to be a version of the John-Jesus baptism story. It is evident that the character of John has been changed to Philip as he does nothing but baptize and forgive sins. Why has John been changed to Philip? Apparently an/the early editor realized that the baptism of Simon Magus by John would be recognized as the baptism of Jesus of Nazareth by John. To disguise it, he changed the name of John to Philip.

Did followers of Simon change the story of the baptism from Jesus of Nazareth to Simon or did followers of Jesus change the story from Simon to Jesus? The fact that the text tells us that Simon openly proclaimed himself to be the Christ and that he was enormously popular with all layers of the people and the Petrine rewriter has not bothered to disguise nor dispute these facts tends to indicate that indeed Simon was a well known Christ figure before his alleged encounter with John. Obviously John did not baptize both someone named Jesus and someone named Simon and proclaim both of them the Christ. We may take it as most probable that the story of John's baptism of Simon Magus preceded the story of and was the basis for John's baptism of Jesus of Nazareth.

The next lines in *Acts* talk about the persecution of Simon by John and Peter.

14: Now when the apostles at Jerusalem heard that Samaria had received the word of God, they sent to them Peter and John,

15: who came down and prayed for them that they might receive the Holy Spirit;

16: for it had not yet fallen on any of them, but they had only been baptized in the name of the Lord Jesus.

> 17: Then they laid their hands on them and they received the Holy Spirit.
> 18: Now when Simon saw that the Spirit was given through the laying on of the apostles' hands, he offered them money,
> 19: saying, "Give me also this power, that any one on whom I lay my hands may receive the Holy Spirit."
> 20: But Peter said to him, "Your silver perish with you, because you thought you could obtain the gift of God with money!
> 21: You have neither part nor lot in this matter, for your heart is not right before God.
> 22: Repent therefore of this wickedness of yours, and pray to the Lord that, if possible, the intent of your heart may be forgiven you.
> 23: For I see that you are in the gall of bitterness and in the bond of iniquity."
> 24: And Simon answered, "Pray for me to the Lord, that nothing of what you have said may come upon me."

The contradiction here is obvious. Peter and John are spreading the faith by laying on of hands. Philip has already baptized Simon. Now Peter and John are refusing to lay hands on Simon although he has even offered them money. One should expect that they would be overjoyed to have to have such an important person as a convert. Since everybody in Samaria already worships Simon as the Christ, it would certainly be the best way for Peter and John to spread the holy spirit.

The laying on of hands and the talk of the Holy Spirit again at this point is a Montanist editorial, probably put in by Tertullian. The text has introduced Saul as a persecutor at the beginning of this chapter. It is most probable that the original text involved Saul going to Samaria. We may reconstruct at least a portion of the text this way:

Reconstructing Saul's Trip

> 14: Now when the officials at Jerusalem heard that Samaria had received the word of God, they sent to them Saul,
> 18: Now when Saul saw that the Spirit was given through baptism, he offered them money,
> 19: saying, "Give me also this power, that any one whom I baptize may receive the Holy Spirit."
> 20: But John said to him, "Your silver perish with you, because you thought you could obtain the gift of God with money!
> 21: You have neither part nor lot in this matter, for your heart is not right before God.

22: Repent therefore of this wickedness of yours, and pray to the Lord that, if possible, the intent of your heart may be forgiven you.
23: For I see that you are in the gall of bitterness and in the bond of iniquity."
24: And Saul answered, "Pray for me to the Lord, that nothing of what you have said may come upon me."

This reconstruction or at least something compatible gets confirmed when the narrative continues in the next line:

25. Now when they had testified and spoken the word of the Lord, they returned to Jerusalem, preaching the gospel to many villages of the Samaritans.
26: But an angel of the Lord said to Philip, "Rise and go toward the south to the road that goes down from Jerusalem to Gaza." This is a desert road.

We have been told that Simon traveled with Philip (8.13). The narrative continues with Philip and Simon returning to Jerusalem, not Peter and John. If we lay out the characters in the scenes, starting from chapter 8, this becomes clear.

8.1-4. Saul in Jerusalem
8.5-13 Philip goes to Samaria and meets Simon in Samaria
8.14-24. Peter and John go to Samaria and meet Philip and Simon in Samaria
8.25. Philip and ? go to Jerusalem
8.26-40. Philip and Eunuch going towards Joppa in Samaria
9.1-9. Saul on the road to Damascus

It is ridiculous that Philip would return from Samaria to Jerusalem only to be told by an angel to head back to Samaria. If we put the scene of Philip meeting the Eunuch at the beginning of this chapter and assume Saul, not Peter and John went to Samaria, everything makes sense.

8.1-4. Saul in Jerusalem
8.26-40. Philip (John) and Eunuch going towards Joppa in Samaria
8.5-13. Philip (John) meets Simon in Samaria
8.14-24. Saul goes to confront Philip and Simon in Samaria
8.25. Philip and Simon go to Jerusalem.

In reconstructing the ninth and tenth chapters, we find that again the order of events make no sense. Saul goes to Damascus to hunt or arrest someone. Then Peter gets called to Damascus to baptize the gentiles. The narrative makes sense if Peter goes to Damascus first and then Saul follows him there to arrest him.

Before reconstructing the scenes in this order, we should carefully examine our already reconstructed scene between Paul and John and Simon.

> 20: But John said to him, "Your silver perish with you, because you thought you could obtain the gift of God with money!
> 21: You have neither part nor lot in this matter, for your heart is not right before God.
> 22: Repent therefore of this wickedness of yours, and pray to the Lord that, if possible, the intent of your heart may be forgiven you.
> 23: For I see that you are in the gall of bitterness and in the bond of iniquity."
> 24: And Saul answered, "Pray for me to the Lord, that nothing of what you have said may come upon me."

It is clear from Saul's response, "Pray for me to the Lord, that nothing of what you have said may come upon me," that John has said something terrible was going to happen to him. John is a prophet and is just doing what prophets do by predicting the future. What John said is missing at this point in the text. We know that Saul will go blind shortly in the next scene on his way to Damascus. We may assume that John predicted that Saul would go blind at this point in the text.

There are actually two blinding scenes

> 1. **Now in the church at Antioch there were prophets and teachers, Barnabas, Simeon who was called Niger, Lucius of Cyrene, Manaen a member of the court of Herod the tetrarch, and Saul.**
> 2: **While they were worshiping the Lord and fasting, the Holy Spirit said, "Set apart for me Barnabas and Saul for the work to which I have called them."**
> 3: **Then after fasting and praying they laid their hands on them and sent them off.**
> 4: **So, being sent out by the Holy Spirit, they went down to Seleucia; and from there they sailed to Cyprus.**
> 5: **When they arrived at Salamis, they proclaimed the word of God in the synagogues of the Jews. And they had John to assist them.**
> 6: **When they had gone through the whole island as far as Paphos, they came upon a certain magician, a Jewish false prophet, named Bar-Jesus.**
> 7: **He was with the proconsul, Sergius Paulus, a man of intelligence, who summoned Barnabas and Saul and sought to hear the word of God.**

THE EVOLUTION OF CHRISTS AND CHRISTIANIES

8: But Elymas the magician (for that is the meaning of his name) withstood them, seeking to turn away the proconsul from the faith.
9: But Saul, who is also called Paul, filled with the Holy Spirit, looked intently at him
10: and said, "You son of the devil, you enemy of all righteousness, full of all deceit and villainy, will you not stop making crooked the straight paths of the Lord?
11: And now, behold, the hand of the Lord is upon you, and you shall be blind and unable to see the sun for a time." Immediately mist and darkness fell upon him and he went about seeking people to lead him by the hand.
12: Then the proconsul believed, when he saw what had occurred, for he was astonished at the teaching of the Lord.
13: Now Paul and his company set sail from Paphos, and came to Perga in Pamphyl'ia. And John left them and returned to Jerusalem;

The line "will you not stop making crooked the straight paths of the Lord?" is a line that should be associated with John as John is known for making straight the path for the Lord. Note the opening of the Gospel of Mark.

1: The beginning of the gospel of Jesus Christ, the Son of God.
2: As it is written in Isaiah the prophet, "Behold, I send my messenger before thy face, who shall prepare thy way;
3: the voice of one crying in the wilderness: Prepare the way of the Lord, make his paths straight—"

The line about "stop making crooked the straight paths of the Lord" works much better if directed at someone persecuting John. If John is making the Lord's paths straight, then anybody attacking John is "making crooked the straight paths of the Lord." We may take it that the lines are aimed at Saul and were originally not part of the scene in Pampylia, but part of the blinding of Saul scene on the way to Damascus. The term "Elymas Magus" was probably originally "Elias Magus," referring to the Old Testament miracle worker Elias.

3: Now as he journeyed he approached Damascus, and suddenly a light from heaven flashed about him.
4: And he fell to the ground and heard a voice saying to him, "Saul, Saul, why do you persecute me?"
5: And he said, "Who are you, Lord?" And he said, "I am Elias the Magician, whom you are persecuting; You son of the devil, you enemy of all righteousness, full of all deceit and

519

> villainy, will you not stop making crooked the straight paths of the Lord? And now, behold, the hand of the Lord is upon you, and you shall be blind and unable to see the sun for a time."
>
> 6: but rise and enter the city, and you will be told what you are to do." Immediately mist and darkness fell upon him and he went about seeking people to lead him by the hand.
>
> 7: The men who were traveling with him stood speechless, hearing the voice but seeing no one.
>
> 8: Saul arose from the ground; and when his eyes were opened, he could see nothing; so they led him by the hand and brought him into Damascus.

The reference to Elias the magician at this point, which we assume was changed by the editors to Elymas the magician when the text was made part of the Pampylia scene, is important. It indicates a connection between Simon Magus and the Old Testament prophet Elias. This helps to explain several references to Elias (also known as Elijah) in the text of Mark:

> 6.14: King Herod heard of it; for Jesus' name had become known. Some said, "John the baptizer has been raised from the dead; that is why these powers are at work in him."
> 15: But others said, "It is Elijah."
>
> 8.27: And Jesus went on with his disciples, to the villages of Caesarea Philippi; and on the way he asked his disciples, "Who do men say that I am?"
> 28: And they told him, "John the Baptist; and others say, Elijah;
>
> 9.2: And after six days Jesus took with him Peter and James and John, and led them up a high mountain apart by themselves; and he was transfigured before them,
> 3: and his garments became glistening, intensely white, as no fuller on earth could bleach them.
> 4: And there appeared to them Elijah with Moses
>
> 9.11: And they asked him, "Why do the scribes say that first Elijah must come?"
> 12: And he said to them, "Elijah does come first to restore all things; and how is it written of the Son of man, that he should suffer many things and be treated with contempt?

13: But I tell you that Elijah has come, and they did to him whatever they pleased, as it is written of him."

15.34: And at the ninth hour Jesus cried with a loud voice, "Eloi, Eloi, lama sabachthani?" which means, "My God, my God, why hast thou forsaken me?"
35: And some of the bystanders hearing it said, "Behold, he is calling Elijah."
36: And one ran and, filling a sponge full of vinegar, put it on a reed and gave it to him to drink, saying, "Wait, let us see whether Elijah will come to take him down."

We may take it as probable that Simon the Samaritan magician identified himself as Elias or claimed to have the same powers as Elias.

As mentioned, the movement of Saul to Damascus makes far more sense coming after the movement of Simon/Peter to Damascus in chapter nine of *Acts*. Since the movement of Philip/John towards Samaria at the end of chapter 8 comes earlier in the text and the movement of Saul to Damascus at the beginning of chapter 9, comes later, the text from 8.25 should run right into 9.31.

8.25: Now when they had testified and spoken the word of the Lord, they returned to Jerusalem, preaching the gospel to many villages `of the Samaritans.
9.32: Now as Peter went here and there among them all, he came down also to the saints that lived at Lydda.
33: There he found a man named Aeneas, who had been bedridden for eight years and was paralyzed.
34: And Peter said to him, "Aeneas, Jesus Christ heals you; rise and make your bed." And immediately he rose.
35: And all the residents of Lydda and Sharon saw him, and they turned to the Lord.
36: Now there was at Joppa a disciple named Tabitha, which means Dorcas. She was full of good works and acts of charity.
37: In those days she fell sick and died; and when they had washed her, they laid her in an upper room.
38: Since Lydda was near Joppa, the disciples, hearing that Peter was there, sent two men to him entreating him, "Please come to us without delay."
39: So Peter rose and went with them. And when he had come, they took him to the upper room. All the widows stood beside him weeping, and showing tunics and other garments which Dorcas made while she was with them.

40: But Peter put them all outside and knelt down and prayed; then turning to the body he said, "Tabitha, rise." And she opened her eyes, and when she saw Peter she sat up.
41: And he gave her his hand and lifted her up. Then calling the saints and widows he presented her alive.
42: And it became known throughout all Joppa, and many believed in the Lord.
43: And he stayed in Joppa for many days with one Simon, a tanner.

The similarities of these healings to those of Jesus in *Mark* is quite obvious:

22: Then came one of the rulers of the synagogue, Jairus by name; and seeing him, he fell at his feet,
23: and besought him, saying, "My little daughter is at the point of death. Come and lay your hands on her, so that she may be made well, and live."
24: And he went with him. And a great crowd followed him and thronged about him . . .
35: While he was still speaking, there came from the ruler's house some who said, "Your daughter is dead. Why trouble the Teacher any further?"
36: But ignoring what they said, Jesus said to the ruler of the synagogue, "Do not fear, only believe."
37: And he allowed no one to follow him except Peter and James and John the brother of James.
38: When they came to the house of the ruler of the synagogue, he saw a tumult, and people weeping and wailing loudly.
39: And when he had entered, he said to them, "Why do you make a tumult and weep? The child is not dead but sleeping."
40: And they laughed at him. But he put them all outside, and took the child's father and mother and those who were with him, and went in where the child was.
41: Taking her by the hand he said to her, "Talitha cumi"; which means, "Little girl, I say to you, arise."
42: And immediately the girl got up and walked (she was twelve years of age), and they were immediately overcome with amazement.
43: And he strictly charged them that no one should know this, and told them to give her something to eat.

Just as the later editors needed to change John to Philip to disguise Simon's baptism, they needed to change Simon to Peter to disguise his miracles. The last line about Simon staying in Joppa with a Tanner named Simon makes no sense. We may conjecture the following ending was much more likely.

> 40: But Simon put them all outside and knelt down and prayed; then turning to the body he said, "Tabitha, rise." And she opened her eyes, and when she saw Simon she sat up.
> 41: And he gave her his hand and lifted her up. Then calling the saints and widows he presented her alive.
> 42: And it became known throughout all Joppa, and many believed in the Lord.
> 43: And she stayed in Joppa for many days with Simon who was a tanner.

The question of whether Simon was a tanner is an important one. In the received text, Peter stays at the house of Simon the Tanner. Since Peter is Simon, there is no reason to believe that the house of Simon the Tanner is not the house of Simon the Magician. A tanner was a lowly position. It is possible that the enemies of Simon gave him this description. It is likely that the position of tanner was so low that when the story of Simon's doing miracles was switched to Jesus the job description of tanner was switched to carpenter.

In any case, we may note that the text we are following has Simon baptized by John and then doing miracles. Later, Herod puts him to death shortly after killing John. It appears that *Acts* is revising an early version of the canonical gospel story with Simon as the Christ character. We hypothesized earlier that Mark's gospel combines two descriptions of the death of Jesus. While we found one written by Mary, we did not find the other one. We may take it that this other text involving Simon contained the second description of the Jesus/Simon arrest.

In chapters nine and ten of *Acts*, we have two men sent on parallel missions.

> 9.10: Now there was a disciple at Damascus named Ananias. The Lord said to him in a vision, "Ananias." And he said, "Here I am, Lord."
> 11: And the Lord said to him, "Rise and go to the street called Straight, and inquire in the house of Judas for a man of Tarsus named Saul;
>
> 10.1: At Caesare'a there was a man named Cornelius, a centurion of what was known as the Italian Cohort,
> 2: a devout man who feared God with all his household, gave alms liberally to the people, and prayed constantly to God.
> 3: About the ninth hour of the day he saw clearly in a vision an angel of God coming in and saying to him, "Cornelius."

4: And he stared at him in terror, and said, "What is it, Lord?" And he said to him, "Your prayers and your alms have ascended as a memorial before God.
5: And now send men to Joppa, and bring one Simon who is called Peter;
6: he is lodging with Simon, a tanner, whose house is by the seaside."

Notice first that whereas Saul is identified as a man from Tarsus, Peter is not identified with any other city but Joppa. We may take it that Simon/Peter was identified with the Samarian city of Joppa. As noted we may conjecture that Peter does not live with Simon the tanner, but that he is in fact Simon the tanner.

Second, note that Saul stays at the house of Judas. We are not told what the relationship of Saul is to this house. We may take it that this is a relative's house. Being a relative from the house of Judas, we can assume his name to be Saul Judas. The House of Judas is being set up as the opposition to Jesus with both Judas and Saul coming from there.

A great deal of chapter ten is taken up by the baptism of the centurian Cornelius. The description of him is quite interesting, "a devout man who feared God with all his household, gave alms liberally to the people, and prayed constantly to God." The text is anxious to explain to us that the baptism of Cornelius came at God's instigation. Not only does an angel visit Cornelius, but an angel visits Simon/Peter as well to make sure that he carries out the baptism. Not only are we told twice that the baptism was a response to a demand by God, but when Simon reaches Cornelius, Simon again repeats the tale for a third time. When put on trial by his Jewish brethren, Simon repeats that he baptized Cornelius in response to holy orders for a fourth time.

We may suppose that this apologetic defense by Simon comes from a real historical incident. Apparently people believed that the Centaurian Cornelius had bribed Simon to give him the secret of the holy spirit and/or baptize him. This would have been a great crime and betrayal of the Johanine society. The defenders of Simon must have been very sensitive to this accusation. They pronounce that Simon was obeying an order by God four times. They also show that Saul tried to bribe him to get the secret of baptism and the holy spirit and that he absolutely refused. We may assume that Simon was accused of selling out the brotherhood and this *Gospel of Simon* made a robust defense against that accusation.

We can glimpse the main conflict in the earlier text between Simon the Samaritan and Saul Judas (the Jew). Saul kills James/Stephen (6.8-8.1). John baptizes Simon the Samaritan (8.5-13). Simon refuses to baptize Saul despite an offer of a bribe (8.19-24). Instead Simon blinds Saul (9.1-9, 13.7-12). God orders Ananias to restore the sight to Saul (9.10-13) and baptize him. Saul disappears from the narrative in chapter 13, but we may assume that Saul Judas is the Judas that betrays Jesus in the later Gospels. It

THE EVOLUTION OF CHRISTS AND CHRISTIANIES

turns out that Simon was right about Saul and he was only interested in obtaining the secret of baptism to make money.

We may take this as a layer of text deriving from a pro-Simon source responding to attacks against Simon. What were these attacks? Apparently Simon has been charged with selling the magical powers that go along with baptism to Saul. Saul then became one of the Twelve and used them to betray, persecute and defeat John and/or Simon.

A small piece of the Clementine Recognitions helps us to see the opposition between Simon and Saul (1.70):

> "And when matters were at that point that they should come and be baptized, some one of our enemies, entering the temple with a few men, began to cry out, and to say, 'What mean ye, O men of Israel? Why are you so easily hurried on? Why are ye led headlong by most miserable men, who are deceived by Simon, a magician?'
>
> "While he was thus speaking, and adding more to the same effect, and while James the bishop was refuting him, he began to excite the people and to raise a tumult, so that the people might not be able to hear what was said.
>
> "Therefore he began to drive all into confusion with shouting, and to undo what had been arranged with much labour, and at the same time to reproach the priests, and to enrage them with revilings and abuse, and, like a madman, to excite every one to murder, saying, 'What do ye? Why do ye hesitate? Oh sluggish and inert, why do we not lay hands upon them, and pull all these fellows to pieces?'
>
> "When he had said this, he first, seizing a strong brand from the altar, set the example of smiting. Then others also, seeing him, were carried away with like readiness. Then ensued a tumult on either side, of the beating and the beaten. Much blood is shed; there is a confused flight, in the midst of which that enemy attacked James, and threw him headlong from the top of the steps; and supposing him to be dead, he cared not to inflict further violence upon him."

What is interesting is the statement that the apostles are "most miserable men, who are deceived by Simon, a magician?" one would expect the text to say Jesus, a magician.

A disciple named Aquila gives us this biographical information about Simon (2.7).

> "This Simon's father was Antonius, and his mother Rachel. By nation he is a Samaritan, from a village of the Gettones; by profession a magician yet exceedingly well trained in the Greek literature; desirous of glory, and boasting above all the human race, so that he wishes himself to be

believed to be an exalted power, which is above God the Creator, and to be thought to be the Christ, and to be called the *Standing One*.

Later, Simon himself contradicts this and adds important information:

'Do not think that I am a man of your race. I am neither magician, nor lover of Luna, nor son of Antonius. For before my mother Rachel and he came together, she, still a virgin, conceived me, while it was in my power to be either small or great, and to appear as a man among men.

One has to ask why the Christian writer of this text would be setting up Simon as a demi-God in this way. There is no reference to Jesus being born a virgin and no hint of irony in the pronouncement by Simon. We may take it that the writer did not know that Jesus had been born of a virgin. The story of Jesus' virgin birth probably migrated from tales of Simon the Magician to Jesus.

We have so far based our identification of Jesus with Simon the Samaritan on material from *Acts* and the *Clementine Recognitions*. There are strong hints in the canonical gospels themselves to back up this hypothesis.

Hints of Jesus' Simon Identity in the Canonical Gospels

As we all know Jesus is from Nazareth in Galilee. However, we may suppose that this identity was invented rather late. There are clues in these later canonical gospel texts that suggest earlier texts pointed way from Jesus and towards Simon and clues that point away from Nazareth and towards Samaria.

The first hint from the canonical gospels of Jesus' Simon of Samaria identity is the large number of characters named Simon. There are far more characters with the name Simon than any other name. One can almost see this as a subconscious process: having replaced Simon with the name Jesus, the name reappears constantly around the outer edges of the story.

There are eight characters with the name Simon:

1. Simon Peter (*John*, 1, 6, 13, 18, 21, Mark 1, 14, Matthew, 14, 10, 16, 17, Luke, 4, 5, 6, 7, 22, 24),
2. Simon Iscariot (John, 13),
3. Simon the Cananaean (Mark, 3, Matthew, 10),
4. Simon who was called the Zealot (Luke, 6),
5. Simon, Jesus' brother (Mark, 6, Matthew, 13),
6. Simon the leper (Mark, 14, Matthew, 26),
7. Simon of Cyrene (Mark, 15, Matthew 27, Luke, 23).

THE EVOLUTION OF CHRISTS AND CHRISTIANIES

8. Simeon. We may also include Simeon, the devout man who blesses the baby Jesus in Luke (2) as Simeon is apparently just a variant spelling of Simon. We have evidence of this from the epistle *2 Peter*, where the author refers to himself as Simeon Peter.

When we analyze the function of each of these Simons in the story, we see the importance of the name to the general story. Simon the Cananaean and Simon the Zealot are the same character. Luke has just renamed him Zealot after Mark and Matthew call him the Cananaean. Both are the last identified apostle in their apostle lists. The only purpose that Simon the Cananaean or Simon the Cannaanite serves is to explain the fact that Simon Peter has two names while all the other apostles have only one. By having a second apostle named Simon, the text implies that the reason for calling Simon, Simon—Peter was to avoid confusion between the two apostles named Simon. The *Gospel of Mark* (3:16) and *Luke* (6:14) give this fact and then give the apostle list with Simon Peter at the beginning and the second Simon at the end. We can conclude from this that the texts want us to believe that Simon got the name Peter to distinguish him from Simon the Cananaean. *Matthew* (4:10) just tells us that Simon "is called Peter," but doesn't bother to tell us that Jesus named him that. *John* is the only gospel to actually show the renaming (1:42), "He brought him to Jesus. Jesus looked at him, and said, 'So you are Simon the son of John? You shall be called Cephas' (which means Peter)."

Besides the implied explanation of distinguishing Simon Peter from Simon the Cananaean/Zealot, we are given no explanation for the renaming. This is strange as renaming is an excellent opportunity to associate the character with some dramatic event or trait. Simon is the only case of renaming in the canonical gosepls. We may suppose that the renaming did not grow out of organic elements of the narrative, but rather out of a need to combine the characters Simon and Peter from two different stories into one. Simon may have been an apostle associated with John ("Simon, the son of John"), while Peter may have been an apostle associated with Simon the Magician. If we assume only one Simon to begin with, then Simon the Cananaean would have been the name of the original Apostle. He has been demoted from number one apostle/son of John in the earlier tales to the number twelve apostle in the canonicals. The name Simon the Cananaean itself may be taken as a disguise for Simon the Samaritan. While I could find no evidence of it being used as an epithet for Samaritans, given the Samaritan's preference for ancient worshipping, and dislike for the more modern Jews of Judea, one can easy see the term Cananaean as being a derogatory epithet for Samaritan.

Simon Iscariot, mentioned only in John (13) as the father of Judas Iscariot, may be taken also as the same character as Simon the Cananaean/Zealot. The text suggests that the son of this Simon was the betrayer of Jesus. We may take it that in an earlier text, Simon the Samaritan was betrayed by his own son Judas. We may see this as a

527

Samaritan allegory of how the Jews, the sons of the Samaritans ended up betraying them. It is a possibility that this early theme of son betraying the father gets reversed into the theme of a father sacrificing his son in the later gospels.

Mark (14) and *Matthew* (16) both mention the house of Simon the leper in Bethany. Jesus gets anointed by a woman in the house. The writer of John is kind enough to tell us that Mary was the woman (11:2). He also tells us that Mary lived in the village of Bethany (11:1). Luke changes the story significantly:

> 36: One of the Pharisees asked him to eat with him, and he went into the Pharisee's house, and took his place at table.
> 37: And behold, a woman of the city, who was a sinner, when she learned that he was at table in the Pharisee's house, brought an alabaster flask of ointment,
> 38: and standing behind him at his feet, weeping, she began to wet his feet with her tears, and wiped them with the hair of her head, and kissed his feet, and anointed them with the ointment.
> 39: Now when the Pharisee who had invited him saw it, he said to himself, "If this man were a prophet, he would have known who and what sort of woman this is who is touching him, for she is a sinner."
> 40: And Jesus answering said to him, "Simon, I have something to say to you." And he answered, "What is it, Teacher?"

Note that the owner of the house questions Jesus' actions. But Jesus addresses his answer to Simon. There is no pretence of Peter being Simon here. The coincidence of Simon the leper owning the house and Jesus addressing the owner of the house as Simon his apostle indicates that Simon the leper is just a cover for Simon Peter. Apparently, the writers of *Mark* and *Matthew* wanted to hide the fact that Simon had a house in Bethany. How could Simon a poor Galilean fisherman afford a house in Bethany, a suburb of Jerusalem? For the sake of narrative continuity, they changed Simon Peter into Simon the Leper. It should be noted that in this early version of the story Simon is a Pharisee and Mary acts the role of a prostitute. The ending of the scene gives us another clue to the original story:

> 44: Then turning toward the woman he said to Simon, "Do you see this woman? I entered your house, you gave me no water for my feet, but she has wet my feet with her tears and wiped them with her hair.
> 45: You gave me no kiss, but from the time I came in she has not ceased to kiss my feet.
> 46: You did not anoint my head with oil, but she has anointed my feet with ointment.

47: Therefore I tell you, her sins, which are many, are forgiven, for she loved much; but he who is forgiven little, loves little."
48: And he said to her, "Your sins are forgiven."
49: Then those who were at table with him began to say among themselves, "Who is this, who even forgives sins?"
50: And he said to the woman, "Your faith has saved you; go in peace."

Forgiving of sins is the speciality of John the Baptist. The washing of the feet, an aquatic motif would also be appropriate for him. We may take it that this story derives from a tale originally about him.

The next Simon character we encounter is the brother of Jesus named Simon. He only exists as the name for a brother. It is just a reference in Mark and Matthew to indicate that that the people of Jesus' hometown are familiar with the names of Jesus' brothers. It is significant that of all the names they could have chosen, they picked Simon. We may suppose some people were under the impression that Jesus and Simon the Magician were one person. The writer, by naming Jesus' brother Simon, would suggest to these people that they have mistaken two brothers for one person. Thus, it may be a means of distinguishing Jesus the Christ from Simon the Christ.

Simon the Cyrene carries Jesus' cross for him according to the synoptic gospels. Almost a combination of the words Christ and Nazarene, the odd fact of a complete stranger carrying the cross of Jesus may be a reference to an earlier tale of Simon the Samaritan carrying his cross on the way to crucifixion.

The Simeon character we find mentioned in the second chapter in Luke seems to be extracted from Anna the prophetess. The editor of Luke did not like the idea of a woman prophesizing the future greatness of Jesus, so he invented Simeon and gave him her lines and actions.

All these transformations of Simon shows not only the fluidity of the text on the level of each incident, but also suggests someone named Simon was an essential part of the earlier narratives.

The text of John (1.40-42) gives us an even stronger clue:

40. One of the two who heard John *speak* and followed Him, was Andrew, Simon Peter's brother. 41. He found first his own brother Simon and said to him, "We have found the Messiah" (which translated means Christ). 42. He brought him to Jesus. Jesus looked at him and said, "You are Simon the son of John; you shall be called Cephas" (which is translated Peter).

The "him" in this statement is ambiguous. It seems to be referring to Simon, but it could be referring to the other of the "two who heard John speak." Since the text mentions Philip in the next line (43) without explaining who he is, we may assume that Philip is the second of the "two who heard John speak." If this is the case, Andrew finds the Christ when he finds his brother Simon, and explains it to Philip. It makes sense that he would take him to John and John would bless him by changing his name. We may reconstruct the original text this way.

> One of the two who heard John speak and followed him was Andrew, Simon Peter's brother. He found his own brother Simon and said to Philip, "We have found the Messiah (which translated means Christ). He brought him to John. John looked at him and said, "You are Simon, the Son of John, you shall be called Cephas (which is translated Peter).

This narrative now makes sense. Andrew gets excited from hearing John speak about the Christ. He declares his own brother Simon to be the Christ and brings him to John. John adopts Simon as his son and renames him Peter. In this way, stories about Peter, the disciple of John, can now be told about Simon and stories about Simon can now be told about Peter with the explanation that they are really one and the same character under two different names.

The clues pointing away from Nazareth as the hometown of the Savior in early gospel stories are also strong.

It is well known that no text before the canonical gospels refer to any town named Nazareth. The attempts by some to paint it as a small obscure village contradict *Matthew* (2:23) and *Luke* (1:26) who declares it a city, and somewhat controverts John (1.41) who has a disciple named Nathanael from Cana Galilee state, "Can anything good come out of Nazareth?" which implies that it is well known as a place where bad things come from.

John never mentions Jesus being in Nazareth. Nor does Mark. Matthew has only this brief reference.

> 11: Then the devil left him, and behold, angels came and ministered to him.
> 12: Now when he heard that John had been arrested, he withdrew into Galilee;
> 13: and leaving Nazareth he went and dwelt in Capernaum by the sea, in the territory of Zebulun and Naphtali,

Jesus is in the desert for 40 days after being baptized by John. Mark has Jesus going directly to the area around Capernaum:

> 14: Now after John was arrested, Jesus came into Galilee, preaching the gospel of God,

15: and saying, "The time is fulfilled, and the kingdom of God is at hand; repent, and believe in the gospel."
16: And passing along by the Sea of Galilee, he saw Simon and Andrew the brother of Simon casting a net in the sea; for they were fishermen.

The author of *Matthew* or an editor has interpolated *Nazareth* into Jesus' trip from the Wilderness to Capernaum. Whoever put it in does not bother to invent a story or even a reason for Jesus going to Nazareth. It is evident that the interpolator expects the reader to know that Nazareth is Jesus' hometown. The purpose of the interpolation seems to be simply to associate Jesus with Nazareth.

It is in the beginning of the *Gospel of Luke* that we find several scenes set in Nazareth and learn that Mary and Joseph come from there. We may suppose that the writers of the gospels of John, Mark, and Matthew never heard of Nazareth. If this were the case, we need to explain about five references in each of them to Jesus of Nazareth.

In *Acts* (2:22), we read "'Men of Israel, hear these words: Jesus of Nazareth, a man attested to you by God with mighty works and wonders and signs which God did through him in your midst, as you yourselves know."

We are fortunate in that the church father Tertullian quotes for us the same line in his *On Modesty*, "Men of Israel, let what I say sink into your ears, Jesus the Nazarene, a man destined by God for you . . ."

We see that the line Tertullian around 205 C.E. included the phrase: "Jesus the Nazarene," instead of the phrase "Jesus of Nazareth." Based on this interpolation we may suggest that in the fifteen or so cases where Jesus of Nazareth appears in the gospels of John, Mark, and Matthew, the original phrase was Jesus the Nazarene.

We can also understand how the change came about through the writings of Tertullian. Tertullian, writing some 800 pages about Jesus and Christianity only mentions the term Nazareth once. He does this in the context of talking about Marcion's Gospel in *Against Marcion* (4:7):

[1] The Christ of the Creator had to be called a *Nazarene* according to prophecy; whence the Jews also designate us, on that very account, *Nazerenes* after Him. For we are they of whom it is written, "Her Nazarites were whiter than snow; "even they who were once defiled with the stains of sin, and darkened with the clouds of ignorance. But to Christ the title Nazarene was destined to become a suitable one, from the hiding-place of His infancy, for which He went down and dwelt at Nazareth, to escape from Archelaus the son of Herod. This fact I have not refrained from mentioning on this account, because it behoved Marcion's Christ to have forborne all connection whatever with the *domestic* localities of the Creator's Christ, when he had so many towns in Judaea which had not been by the prophets

> thus assigned to the Creator's Christ. But Christ will be (the Christ) of the prophets, wheresoever He is found in accordance with the prophets. And yet even at Nazareth He is not remarked as having preached anything new, whilst in another *verse* He is said to have been rejected by reason of a simple proverb.

This passage refers to this statement in Matthew:

> 22: But when he heard that Archelaus reigned over Judea in place of his father Herod, he was afraid to go there, and being warned in a dream he withdrew to the district of Galilee.
> 23: And he went and dwelt in a city called Nazareth, that what was spoken by the prophets might be fulfilled, "He shall be called a Nazarene."

What is truly astonishing is that Tertullian is telling us that this passage which is currently in our gospel of Matthew was originally in Marcion's Gospel. Further, he is giving Marcion credit for inventing the passage. Tertullian, writing here around 207 C.E., criticizes Marcion for connecting Jesus with Old Testament prophecy in this way. Since Marcion did not believe that Jesus came in fulfillment of Old Testament prophecy, he should not have had him living in Nazareth and fulfilling the Old Testament prophecy.

We may take it that Tertullian did not know anything about Jesus' parents being from Nazareth and that the early sections of Luke containing this idea were added to the gospel of Luke sometime after 207 C.E. Secondly we may take it that the beginning of Matthew came from Marcion's Gospel and that he invented the idea of Jesus coming from Nazareth.

Why did Marcion do this? It is not hard to figure out the answer. Jesus was known as *Jesus the Nazarene*. A Nazarene was a devout Jew, someone who had made a vow to God to accomplish something. Marcion wanted to disassociate Jesus from Judaism. He therefore invented the city of Nazareth and claimed that Jesus had lived there as a young child and that is how he acquired the name Jesus the Nazarene. The passage about Jesus going to Nazareth has been lifted from Marcion's gospel and put in Matthew's. We may conjecture that it was Tertullian himself who changed the text from Marcion's Gospel to Matthew's gospel and added the line "that what was spoken by the prophets might be fulfilled, "He shall be called a Nazarene." We deduce this from the fact that Tertullian wants to emphasize that Jesus came in fulfillment of the prophesies of the Hebrew Scriptures in opposition to Marcion. Moving the line about Jesus being from Nazareth to the gospel of Matthew and adding the line about it being in fulfillment of Hebrew Scripture completely trumps Marcion. The followers of Marcion cannot argue that Marcion had secret information about where Jesus lived and why he was called the Nazarene, as Tertullian now has a text that is older, Matthew's

Gospel, that knows that he was from Nazareth and that declares this in fulfillment of the Hebrew Scriptures[504].

If Jesus did not come from Nazareth and it was a late third century addition to the canonical gospels based on Marcion's gospel, where did Jesus originally come from? The answer appears to be Capernaum. That is apparently what Mark wishes us to believe. He immediately has Jesus going to Capernaum after returning from the desert. He preaches in the synagogue in Capernaum. *Matthew* and *Luke* changes this synagogue scene to Nazareth, but we may take it that Mark is giving us the earlier version of the story (Mark 1):

> 21: They went into Capernaum; and immediately on the Sabbath He entered the synagogue and *began* to teach. 22: They were amazed at His teaching; for He was teaching them as *one* having authority, and not as the scribes. 23: Just then there was a man in their synagogue with an unclean spirit; and he cried out, 24: saying, "What business do we have with each other, Jesus of Nazareth? Have You come to destroy us? I know who You are—the Holy One of God!" 25: And Jesus rebuked him, saying, "Be quiet, and come out of him!" 26: Throwing him into convulsions, the unclean spirit cried out with a loud voice and came out of him. 27: They were all amazed, so that they debated among themselves, saying, "What is this? A new teaching with authority! He commands even the unclean spirits, and they obey Him." 28: Immediately the news about Him spread everywhere into all the surrounding district of Galilee. 29: And immediately after they came out of the synagogue, they came into the house of Simon and Andrew, with James and John. 30: Now Simon's mother-in-law was lying sick with a fever; and immediately they *spoke to Jesus about her. 31: And He came to her and raised her up, taking her by the hand, and the fever left her, and she waited on them. 32: When evening came, after the sun had set, they *began* bringing to Him all who were ill and those who were demon-possessed. 33: And the whole city had gathered at the door.

We may put this information together with Mark 2.1:

> 1. When He had come back to Capernaum several days afterward, it was heard that He was at home.

Here, *Mark* directly refers to Capernaum as Jesus' home. Since Jesus comes from the desert directly to Capernaum, we may take it that the writer of Mark wanted to give us the idea that Jesus was from Capernaum. This explains why the editor of *Matthew*

(Tertullian most probably) immediately has Jesus in Nazareth after his encounter with the devil in the wilderness. He had to counter the idea found in both *Mark* and *Matthew* that Jesus' hometown was Capernaum.

Besides going directly from the desert to Capernaum, we have other clues. Jesus teaches in the synagogue of Capernaum. It is hard to imagine that strangers coming from the desert would be allowed to preach in a strange synagogue. It makes sense to assume that it was his hometown synagogue. Mark also tells us that Jesus first becomes famous in Capernaum, another indication that it is his hometown. The cursing of Capernaum in Matthew (11:23, repeated in Luke 10:15) "And you, Capernaum, will not be exalted to heaven, will you? You will descend to Hades; for if the miracles had occurred in Sodom which occurred in you, it would have remained to this day," only makes sense if we assume that for the first writer of *Matthew* Capernaum was Jesus' hometown.

But we should note that the first miracle that Mark records about Jesus is his curing Simon's mother-in-law who lived in Capernaum (1.30). As we have suggested, the stories of Simon the Christ predated the gospels and so the fact that his mother-in-law lived in Capernaum could be evidence that he came from Capernaum or that he was visiting her there. The first miracle in the gospel of John takes place at the wedding in Cana. This might suggest Cana as the hometown of Jesus for John. This supposition gets support from John's statement, "This beginning of *His* signs Jesus did in Cana of Galilee, and manifested His glory, and His disciples believed in Him," (2.11). The next passage in John tells us, "After this He went down to Capernaum, He and His mother and *His* brothers and His disciples; and they stayed there a few days," (John 2:12). This would seem to indicate that Cana was only a short distance from Capernaum. On the supposition that Simon was Jesus, it is possible that Simon/Jesus was going to his mother-in-law's house in Capernaum for a few days after the wedding at Cana and then returning to Cana. John also has Jesus returning from Jerusalem to Cana (4:46), another indication that Cana is Jesus' hometown, or at least it is what the author of *John* wants us to believe.

We have this migration of the home/birthplace of Jesus from Cana to Capernaum to Nazareth in the canonical gospels, but did Jesus have perhaps another hometown before any of these? As we have seen by the way *John* combined the characters and sources of Simon and Peter, even the earliest writer of *John* had source texts which he changed to suit his own purposes. The key is perhaps in the reconstruction of the original scene about the Samaritan Woman. Here is the scene as it has come down to us in its Kin James version:

> 1. Therefore when the Lord knew that the Pharisees had heard that Jesus was making and baptizing more disciples than John 2. (although Jesus Himself was not baptizing, but His disciples were), 3. He left Judea and went away again into Galilee. 4. And He had to pass through

Samaria. 5. So He *came to a city of Samaria called Sychar, near the parcel of ground that Jacob gave to his son Joseph; 6. and Jacob's well was there. So Jesus, being wearied from His journey, was sitting thus by the well. It was about the sixth hour. 7. There *came a woman of Samaria to draw water. Jesus *said to her, "Give Me a drink." 8. For His disciples had gone away into the city to buy food. 9. Therefore the Samaritan woman *said to Him, "How is it that You, being a Jew, ask me for a drink since I am a Samaritan woman?" (For Jews have no dealings with Samaritans.) 10. Jesus answered and said to her, "If you knew the gift of God, and who it is who says to you, `Give Me a drink,' you would have asked Him, and He would have given you living water." 11. She *said to Him, "Sir, You have nothing to draw with and the well is deep; where then do You get that living water? 12. "You are not greater than our father Jacob, are You, who gave us the well, and drank of it himself and his sons and his cattle?" 13. Jesus answered and said to her, "Everyone who drinks of this water will thirst again; 14. but whoever drinks of the water that I will give him shall never thirst; but the water that I will give him will become in him a well of water springing up to eternal life." 15. The woman *said to Him, "Sir, give me this water, so I will not be thirsty nor come all the way here to draw." 16. He *said to her, "Go, call your husband and come here." 17. The woman answered and said, "I have no husband." Jesus *said to her, "You have correctly said, `I have no husband'; 18. for you have had five husbands, and the one whom you now have is not your husband; this you have said truly." 19. The woman *said to Him, "Sir, I perceive that You are a prophet. 20. "Our fathers worshiped in this mountain, and you *people* say that in Jerusalem is the place where men ought to worship." 21. Jesus *said to her, "Woman, believe Me, an hour is coming when neither in this mountain nor in Jerusalem will you worship the Father. 22. "You worship what you do not know; we worship what we know, for salvation is from the Jews. 23. "But an hour is coming, and now is, when the true worshipers will worship the Father in spirit and truth; for such people the Father seeks to be His worshipers. 24. "God is spirit, and those who worship Him must worship in spirit and truth." 25. The woman *said to Him, "I know that Messiah is coming (He who is called Christ); when that One comes, He will declare all things to us." 26. Jesus *said to her, "I who speak to you am *He*." 27. At this point His disciples came, and they were amazed that He had been speaking with a woman, yet no one said, "What do You seek?" or, "Why do You speak with her?" 28. So the woman left her waterpot, and went into the city and *said to the men, 29. "Come, see a man who told me all the things that I *have* done; this is not the Christ, is it?" 30. They went out of the city, and were coming to Him. 31. Meanwhile the disciples were urging Him, saying, "Rabbi, eat." 32. But He said to them, "I have food to eat that you do not know about." 33. So the disciples were saying to one another, "No one brought Him *anything* to eat, did he?" 34. Jesus *said to them, "My food is to do the will of Him who sent Me and to accomplish His work. 35. "Do you not say, 'There are yet four months, and *then* comes the harvest'? Behold, I say to you, lift up your eyes and look on the fields, that they are white for harvest. 36. "Already he who reaps is receiving wages and is gathering fruit for life eternal; so that he who sows and he who reaps may rejoice together. 37. "For in this *case* the saying is true, 'One sows and another reaps.' 38. "I sent you to reap that for which you have not labored; others have labored and you have entered into their labor." 39. From that city many of the Samaritans believed in Him because of the word of the woman who testified, "He told me all the things that I *have* done." 40. So when the Samaritans came to Jesus, they were asking Him to stay with them; and He stayed there two days. 41. Many more believed because of His word; 42. and they were saying to the woman, "It is no longer because of what you said that we believe, for we have heard for ourselves and know that this One is indeed the Savior of the world." 43. After the two days He went forth from there into Galilee. 44. For Jesus Himself testified that a prophet has no honor in his own country. 45. So when He came to Galilee . . .

The first quirk to notice in the text is in the final lines, "After two days, he went forth from there into Galilee, for Jesus himself testified that a prophet has no honor in his own country." Why would he go into Galilee if a prophet has no honor in his own country, if Galilee was his own country? The lines only make sense if Samaria was his own country and Galilee was a foreign country. He goes to Galilee to achieve the honor he could not get in his own country.

Secondly, we should note the phrase (John 4:43) "After two days, he went from there into Galilee." We find this chronologically related to another, earlier sentence in John (2.1), "On the third day there was a wedding in Cana of Galilee, and the mother of Jesus was there." We may suggest that the author of *John* has rewritten the order of these two events. Jesus spent two days with the woman at the well at Sychar in Samaria and on the third day he married her at Cana in Galilee. The currently identified site of Cana is almost 45 miles from Sychar. This would make it too far for a wedding party to travel in one day, but the tradition for this location of Cana dates back only to the eight century[505]. If it was a real city, we would have to place it closer to Sychar in order for the wedding party to reach it on the third day. Japha (modern day Joffa) is a city about 37 miles northwest of Sychar. We know that it existed in this time period because Josephus tells us it was "the largest village of all Galilee, and encompassed with very strong walls, and had a great number of inhabitants in it."[506] In coming from Jerusalem, one would almost certainly pass through Sychar to reach Japha. *Acts* (9:36-40) tells us that Peter brought Tabitha back from the dead there. The name sounds very much like Joppa (modern day Yafa) in Samaria where an angel sought out Peter (Simon as we reconstructed it) in the house of Simon the tanner to preach the gospel to non-Jews. We may take it that this is not a coincidence. We can suppose that later story tellers found Japha and Joppa too close, (it could lead people to associate Peter with Simon the Samaritan) so Japha became Cana in the canonical gospel texts.

Besides this clue of the Samaritan identity of Simon Peter/Jesus, we find this interesting convoluted statement in the Samaritan at the well scene:

10. **Jesus answered and said to her, "If you knew the gift of God, and who it is who says to you, 'Give Me a drink,' you would have asked Him, and He would have given you living water."**

The sentence seems to forget that it is Jesus asking the woman for a drink and not the woman asking Jesus. How could the sentence get so tangled. The sentence only makes sense if the woman had asked Jesus for a drink previously and Jesus replied, "If you knew the gift of God and who it is who you are speaking to, you would have asked God to give you a drink and he would have given you living water."

We also have a problem with the food that the disciples bring back and Jesus does not eat. The scene does not make sense as presented. The disciples go off to the city to get food for Jesus, so it is obvious that he was hungry and too weak to go with them. They return and are amazed that he is longer hungry. The text seems to be telling us that Jesus did not need to eat food, but why did the disciples believe him to be hungry and go off to get him food if this is the case? Why didn't he just tell them that he does not need food and save them the trip. It is apparent that Jesus received food between the time that the disciples left and the time that the disciples returned. One has to conclude that the woman he met gave him food and the disciples were mystified by the fact that it seemed that he did not need food.

Based on this we may assume that it is the woman who asks Jesus for a drink and that she gave him food.

Finally we have to explain why Jesus' disciples were amazed that Jesus was talking to a woman and why Jesus offers the parable he does to explain his actions. It is hard to believe that the simple act of talking to a woman could amaze the disciples. One can imagine men living in a monastery having no verbal contact with women, with for anyone who traveled around, it is hard to believe that a man would not be coming constantly into contact with women and needing to verbally communicate with them, if only to ask for directions or a price of an item. Jesus was an adult male and there is no suggestion that he did not engage in the ordinary activities of men of that period which would include talking to women. Simply talking with a woman could not have amazed the disciples. Likewise one has to ask why Jesus explains his actions by giving the parable he does about sewing and reaping. It is plainly a hedonist parable saying that the time has come for people to reap the harvest, although others may have sewn it. Basically it is saying take what you want now. Such a parable would be out of place if Jesus had merely talked with the woman. We may propose that both these problems are solved if the disciples came back and found Jesus kissing the woman. It would explain why they were amazed and it would explain why Jesus felt the need to tell his hedonist parable suggesting the time had come to take what want. The Gospel of Philip tells us that Jesus "used to kiss her often on her . . . [507]"

Taking into account all these factors; who asked for the water, how Jesus got food, and what amazed the disciples, we may reconstruct the scene this way:

> Therefore when the Lord knew that the Pharisees had heard that Jesus was making and baptizing more disciples than John (although Jesus Himself was not baptizing, but His disciples were), He left Judea and went away again into Samaria. So He *came to a city of Samaria called Sychar, near the parcel of ground that Jacob gave to his son Joseph; and Jacob's well was there. So Jesus, being wearied from His journey, was sitting thus by the well. For His disciples had gone away into the city to buy food. It was about the sixth hour. There *came Mary to draw water.
>
> He said to her, "Give me food."
>
> She said to him, "Give Me a drink."
>
> Therefore the Samaritan said to her, "How is it that You, being a Jew, ask me for a drink since I am a Samaritan man[508]? Our fathers worshiped in this mountain, and you people say that in Jerusalem is the place where men ought to worship. You worship what you do not know; we worship what we know, for salvation is from the Samaritans[509].
>
> The woman said, "Sir, believe Me, an hour is coming when neither in this mountain nor in Jerusalem will you worship the Father. But an hour is coming, and now is, when the true worshipers will worship the Father in spirit and truth; for such people the Father seeks to be His worshipers. "God is spirit, and those who worship Him must worship in spirit and truth." "I know that Messiah is coming (He who is called Christ); when that One comes, He will declare all things to us."
>
> Jesus *said to her, "I who speak to you am He."
>
> She said to him, "You are not greater than our father Jacob, are You, who gave us the well, and drank of it himself and his sons and his cattle?"

Jesus answered and said to her, "If you knew the gift of God, and who it is who says to you, 'Give Me food,' you would have asked Him, and He would have given you living water."

She *said to Him, "Sir, You have nothing to draw with and the well is deep; where then do You get that living water?

Jesus answered and said to her, "Everyone who drinks of this water will thirst again; but whoever drinks of the water that I will give him shall never thirst; but the water that I will give him will become in him a well of water springing up to eternal life."

The woman *said to Him, "Sir, give me this water, so I will not be thirsty nor come all the way here to draw."

He *said to her, "Go, call your husband and come here."

The woman answered and said, "I have no husband."

Jesus *said to her, "You have correctly said, 'I have no husband' for you have had five husbands, and the one whom you now have is not your husband; this you have said truly."

The woman *said to Him, "Sir, I perceive that You are a prophet.

[She gave him food and he kissed her[510].] At this point His disciples came, and they were amazed that He had been kissing a woman, yet no one said, "What do You seek?" or, "Why do You speak with her?"

So the woman left her waterpot, and went into the city and *said to the men, "Come, see a man who told me all the things that I have done; this is not the Christ, is it?" They went out of the city, and were coming to Him.

Meanwhile the disciples were urging Him, saying, "Rabbi, eat."

But He said to them, "I have food to eat that you do not know about."

So the disciples were saying to one another, "No one brought Him anything to eat, did he?"

Jesus *said to them, "My food is to do the will of Him who sent Me and to accomplish His work. Do you not say, 'There are yet four months, and then comes the harvest'? Behold, I say to you, lift up your eyes and look on the fields, that they are white for harvest. "Already he who reaps is receiving wages and is gathering fruit for life eternal; so that he who sows and he who reaps may rejoice together. [511].]

From that city many of the Samaritans believed in Him because of the word of the woman who testified, "He told me all the things that I have done."

> So when the Samaritans came to Jesus, they were asking Him to stay with them; and He stayed there two days.
>
> Many more believed because of His word; and they were saying to the woman, "It is no longer because of what you said that we believe, for we have heard for ourselves and know that this One is indeed the Savior of the world."
>
> After the two days He went forth from there into Joppa. On the third day a wedding took place in Joppa"[12].

It is not hard seeing this reconstruction as being part of the Passover Gospel play that Mary wrote. Taking this as the first scene between Jesus and Mary, we may understand why Mary plays such a big role at the end of the gospels.

The scene refers directly to Jesus or Simon being a Samaritan, which was unacceptable to the writer of John. His ingenious solution was to turn Mary into the Samaritan and Jesus into the Jew. The later gospel writers, probably uncomfortable with Jesus being so clearly identified with being a Jew, just cut the important scene altogether. But without this scene one can hardly understand the ending of any of the gospels.

The scene, in its present form presents enough clues that we may reconstruct it to show a Samaritan Jesus preceded the Galilean Jesus in the earliest gospel texts.

Christ as Young Good Shepherd and Lamb of God

Catacomb of St. Sebastian, Rome, Italy, circa 3rd century. This Christ has lamb's hair, which probably is a reference to his being the *Lamb of God*. This graphic reference is not found in other Good Shepherd images.

Chapter 12

The Shepherd and the Church of God Before Jesus

We have already seen how two groups, the followers of Simon and the followers of John, helped to create the Christ mythology and the idea of a human Christ on Earth. They were not, however, the only Christian groups around in the first century. Examining the related concepts within *The Book of Revelation, The Epistles of Paul, The Epistle of Barnabus,* and most importantly *The Shepherd* of *Hermas* allows us to say that the largest early Christian group of the first half of the first century did not believe in an Earthly Christ let alone a Jesus of Nazareth. This Judaic-Christian group called itself the Church of God. It considered itself Jewish and had members in cities throughout the Roman Empire, even in Rome. While *Barnabus* and the *Shepherd* were later dropped from the canon of the Roman Catholic Church, the *Epistles of Paul* and *Revelation* remained. Yet all of these book are productions of the Church of God.

Barnabus is relatively short and therefore not of great significance. By itself, it is dismissible as an aberration. The writer of the Pauline epistles associate Paul directly with the Church of God[513]. However, as I have already noted about the Pauline epistles, they were written and edited by five hands over a period of nearly a century and a half, from the late first to the early third century, They do not give us a clear picture of the first century Church of God. It is to the text of *the Shepherd* we must go if we want a clear picture of the Church of God around the middle of the first century.

In support of the idea of the importance of this text, we may note that the earliest images we have of Christ are as a magician with a wand and as a good shepherd carrying a lamb on his back. The magician image we can trace back to the miracles in the gospels, but the shepherd image is a little peculiar as there are no scenes in the gospels where Jesus dresses or acts like a shepherd. There are numerous metaphorical

542

passages comparing Jesus to a shepherd, but why should those metaphorical expressions represent Christ rather than actual events from the gospels. It seems more reasonable to assume that these early images are not based on metaphorical expressions in any gospels, but from a text which actually does portray the Christ as a shepherd: *The Shepherd* by Hermas.

Quite significantly, this book was included as the final book in perhaps the earliest copy of the Bible that we possess, the *Codex Sinaiticus*, which is generally dated to the fourth century. One may conclude from this that even in the fourth century the text was still widely considered canonic, that is, of equal authority as the gospels. This is a great mystery if we try to understand it within the framework of Eusebean History. Not only does this text never mention Jesus or any of the Apostles, but it purports to show the dreams of a slave that offer a route to salvation that in no way involves Jesus. How does it come to be included in what is one of the earliest manuscripts of the New Testament? Did Eusebius' ever-vigilant church guardians of the holy message have a temporary lapse in judgment?

It is true that *Shepherd* was not universally recognized as canonic. Tertullian in the early third century denounced it as a forgery and either started or participated in a campaign to have it removed from the canon of the Church at Rome. We shall examine why in a moment. More evidence of the anti-*Shepherd* campaign comes from a fragment of a book leaf commonly called the *Muratorian Canon*, discovered by Ludovico Antonio Muratori in the eighteenth century. This text calls it a forgery and dates *Shepherd* to the mid-second century. However, this text, by an unknown author, seems designed to promote certain texts as canonical and to reject others. Even when we do not consider the real possibility that it is itself an ancient or modern forgery, its factual representations can hardly be considered significant evidence regarding the origins of *the Shepherd*. No other ancient author speaks of *the Shepherd* as being the work of the brother of the tenth pope, Pope Pius. The existence of such a Pope itself may be doubted as nothing about him was known in antiquity. We would suspect that Tertullian who attacked *the Shepard* should have heard and communicated the information that Pius' brother had concocted it, but he never mentions this. Knowing that there was a campaign against *the Shepherd* as early as the beginning of the third century, we must take this document as merely being more evidence for such an ongoing campaign.

Tertullian himself gives striking evidence of the importance of *the Shepherd* for the Roman Church while discussing the subject of praying. He writes[514]:

> Again, for the custom which some have of sitting when prayer is ended, I perceive no reason, except that which children give. For what if that Hermas, whose writing is generally inscribed with the title *The Shepherd*, had, after finishing his prayer, not sat down on his bed, but done some other thing: should we maintain that also as a matter for observance? Of course not. Why, even as it is the sentence, "When I had prayed, and

> had sat down on my bed," is simply put with a view to the order of the narration, not as a model of discipline. Else we shall have to pray nowhere except where there is a bed!

Tertullian here suggests that if you ask a Christian child why he prays, he will say because Hermas did it in *the Shepherd*. Tertullian takes this proposition as self-evident and traditional. This indicates that for a long time the Church was using *Shepherd* to teach children and holding up Hermas as a role model for its youngest members.

The Shepherd was very clearly a part of the orthodox Canon of the Church of Rome long after the first years of the third century when Tertullian raised objections to it. As mentioned before, *The Epistle of Barnabus* is another document that like *Shepherd* appears to have been part of the canon at the Church of Rome at this time. It also can be found in the *Codex Sinaiticus* and like *Shepherd*, it has an unknown Christ as its central figure. Looking at the *Epistles of Paul, Barnabus* and *Shepherd*, it seems we have a significant group of texts held to be canonical till the fourth century by the Church of Rome and showing virtually no knowledge of or interest in an earthly Jesus of Nazareth. We must believe either the Church fell away from a human Jesus ideology and adopted an unknown Christ as the object of its worship, or that the Church adopted a human Christ after beginning with a non-human Christ/Jesus ideology. The later appears to be the case if *the Shepherd* predates the canonical gospels.

As we will show in a moment, *the Shepherd* appears to be the source text for many of the ideas about Jesus in the canonical gospels. This makes it almost certain as well as logical that the Church of God (Paul's Church) first worshipped a nonhuman non-Jesus of Nazareth, an unknown Christ as its central figure of worship. There was apparently a large international Christian Church movement before the leadership or most members of that Church had ever read or heard about Jesus of Nazareth.

Tertullian Attacks *the Shepherd*

Rev. F. Crombie, the 19th century translator of the Shepherd for the Ante-Nicene Fathers book series, notes the importance of *the Shepherd* and that Tertullian is alone in his fervent opposition to the text:

> In ancient times two opinions prevailed in regard to the authorship. The most widely spread was, that the Pastor of Hermas was the production of the Hermas mentioned in the Epistle to the Romans. Origen states this opinion distinctly, and it is repeated by Eusebius and Jerome.
>
> Those who believed the apostolic Hermas to be the author, necessarily esteemed the book very highly; and there was much discussion as to whether it was inspired or not. The early writers are of

opinion that it was really inspired. Irenaeus quotes it as Scripture; Clemens Alexandrinus speaks of it as making its statements "divinely;" and Origen, though a few of his expressions are regarded by some as implying doubt, unquestionably gives it as his opinion that it is "divinely inspired." Eusebius mentions that difference of opinion prevailed in his day as to the inspiration of the book, some opposing its claims, and others maintaining its divine origin, especially because it formed an admirable introduction to the Christian faith. For this latter reason it was read publicly, he tells us, in the churches.

The only voice of antiquity decidedly opposed to the claim is that of Tertullian. He designates it apocryphal, and rejects it with scorn, as favouring anti-Montanistic opinions. Even *his* words, however, show that it was regarded in many churches as Scripture.

It is a tribute to the power of Tertullian's rhetoric and influence in the Church of Rome that he apparently succeeded in getting the Shepherd renounced as holy scripture and eliminated from the canon. Tertullian's most vigorous argument against the text appears in his work *On Modesty*[515]:

[9] Come, you rope-walker upon modesty, and chastity, and every kind of sexual sanctity, who, by the instrumentality of a discipline of this nature remote from the path of truth, mount with uncertain footstep upon a most slender thread, balancing flesh with spirit, moderating your animal principle by faith, tempering your eye by fear; [10] why are you thus wholly engaged in a single step? Go on, if you succeed in finding power and will, while you are so secure, and as it were upon solid ground. For if any wavering of the flesh, any distraction of the mind, any wandering of the eye, shall chance to shake you down from your equipoise, "God is good." [11] To His own (children), not to heathens, He opens His bosom: a second repentance will await you; you will again, from being an adulterer, be a Christian! These (pleas) you (will urge) to me, most benignant interpreter of God. [12] But I would yield my ground to you, if the scripture of "the Shepherd," which is the only one which favours adulterers, had deserved to find a place in the Divine canon; if it had not been habitually judged by every council of Churches (even of your own) among apocryphal and false (writings); itself adulterous, and hence a patroness of its comrades; from which in other respects, too, you derive initiation; to which, perchance, that" Shepherd," will play the patron whom you depict upon your (sacramental) chalice, (depict, I say, as) himself withal a prostitutor of the Christian sacrament, (and hence) worthily both the idol of drunkenness, and the

prize of adultery by which the chalice will quickly be followed, (a chalice) from which you sip nothing more readily than (the flavour of) the "ewe" of (your) second repentance! [13] I, however, imbibe the Scriptures of that Shepherd who cannot be broken. Him John forthwith offers me, together with the layer and duty of repentance; (and offers Him as) saying, "Bear worthy fruits of repentance:and say not, We have Abraham (as our) father"—for fear, to wit, lest they should again take flattering unctions for delinquency from the grace shown to the fathers— "for God is able from these stones to raise sons to Abraham." [14] Thus it follows that we too (must judge) such as "sin no more" (as) "bearing worthy fruits of repentance." For what more ripens as the fruit of repentance than the achievement of emendation? But even if *pardon* is rather the" fruit of repentance," even pardon cannot co-exist without the cessation from sin.

Tertullian's rhetorical wordplay here is spectacular. He tells us that because *the Shepherd* favors forgiveness of sins, it encourages them. Thus, because it favors adultery it is an "adulterous" book. The followers of *the Shepherd* apparently drink wine from a chalice and this leads to getting drunk and adultery, and thus it contributes to prostitution (both physical and the spiritual prostitution of the Christian sacrament), and thus the book itself is a prostitute ("patroness").

On the other hand, going beyond the wordplay, we find that Tertullian is giving us important information about the status of the book. By claiming it does not belong in the divine canon ("If *the Shepherd* . . . had deserved to find a place in the divine canon"), Tertullian acknowledges that at the time of writing (circa 215), the book is part of the divine canon at Rome (which the *Codex Sinaiticus* confirms). His argument that all Church councils including the ones at Rome have found the book "apocryphal and false," should be taken as part of his rhetoric. Most likely the question discussed at these councils (whenever or whatever they were) was simply authorship and if the narrator Hermas was the actual author of the text. Apparently those who included it in the canon felt that it was still "divine" even if Hermas was not the real author. Since Hermas describes himself as a slave, one can imagine that the freemen of the church councils would have a problem with giving a slave credit for writing a holy work and might want to assign it to an unknown author. This anti-slave attitude did not stop them from recognizing its spirituality and usefulness to the Church.

It appears that authorship is not a question prompting Tertullian's opposition, rather it is the text's doctrine that he objects to. The text, according to him takes the position that Christians should be forgiven multiple times for their sins. Tertullian takes the position that Christians should be forgiven only once and if the same sin gets repeated the sinner should be banned from the Church and salvation.

We may gather from what Tertullian tells us that *the Shepherd* is not only a part of the canon, but that it is being appealed to as holy writ on the important question of church membership. What he does not say about the text is also important. He does not say that only some churches recognize the text as holy and he does not say that the document was recently imported into the canon. Both of these arguments would have been important to discredit the document and its doctrines. Tertullian makes neither of them. This suggests that the use of the text was widespread and that its use did not begin at a definite fixed point in the second half of the second century, but must have begun earlier. How early?

The Recycled Proposition Principle

Let us say we have two texts containing the same or similar propositions. Let us call the proposition D. In one text the proposition is presented as part of an orderly and close chain of propositions in an argument: A, B, C, D, E, F, F, H. In another text, the proposition is presented in an argument filled with propositions presented in a rhetorical manner without an orderly or close chain of propositions: H, D, X, Y. I say that the text where the proposition is presented in an orderly fashion is the original text. The text where the proposition gets presented in a disorderly fashion is the later proposition, referencing the original proposition. We may call this *the Recycled Proposition Principle*.

Based on this, we can say that many propositions in the gospels are recycled from arguments in the Shepherd.

The Smoking Gun Parable

There are dozens of lines, concepts and sayings in Shepherd that are similar to lines, concepts and sayings in the *Gospels* and *Paul's epistles*. In no case does the Shepherd give any credit to any of these sources. It is difficult to imagine why a church which already had the *Gospels* or *Paul's epistles* would adapt text that had drastically changed some of the most important sayings by Jesus and gave no credit to him for anything. It is easy to see the development going the other way. With a later Church adopting later text that attributed to Jesus many concepts and sayings in *Shepherd*. In one case, involving an important parable, it is particularly clear that the *Shepherd* text is the source and the gospels the borrower and editor. This is the parable of the Absent Vineyard Owner. We actually have five versions, from all three synoptic gospels, *Thomas* and *Shepherd*. Mark declares it to be Jesus' first parable. Here is the parable in each text in the order of its development from *Shepherd*, *Thomas* (65), *Mark* (12.1-9), *Matthew* (21.33-46) and *Luke* (20.9-16):

Shepherd:

"Hear the similitude which I am about to narrate to you relative to fasting. A certain man had a field and many slaves, and he planted a certain part of the field with a vineyard, and selecting a faithful and beloved and much valued slave, he called him to him, and said, 'Take this vineyard which I have planted, and stake it until I come, and do nothing else to the vineyard; and attend to this order of mine, and you shall receive your freedom from me.' And the master of the slave departed to a foreign country. And when he was gone, the slave took and staked the vineyard; and when he had finished the staking of the vines, he saw that the vineyard was full of weeds. He then reflected, saying, 'I have kept this order of my master: I will dig up the rest of this vineyard, and it will be more beautiful when dug up; and being free of weeds, it will yield more fruit, not being choked by them.' He took, therefore, and dug up the vineyard, and rooted out all the weeds that were in it. And that vineyard became very beautiful and fruitful, Having no weeds to choke it. And after a certain time the master of the slave and of the field returned, and entered into the vineyard. And seeing that the vines were suitably supported on stakes, and the ground, moreover, dug up, and all the weeds rooted out, and the vines fruitful, he was greatly pleased with the work of his slave. And calling his beloved son who was his heir, and his friends who were his councillors, he told them what orders he had given his slave, and what he had found performed. And they rejoiced along with the slave at the testimony which his master bore to him. And he said to them, 'I promised this slave freedom if he obeyed the command which I gave him; and he has kept my command, and done besides a good work to the vineyard, and has pleased me exceedingly. In return, therefore, for the work which he has done, I wish to make him co-heir with my son, because, having good thoughts, he did not neglect them, but carried them out.' With this resolution of the master his son and friends were well pleased, viz., that the slave should be co-heir with the son. After a few days the master made a feast, and sent to his slave many dishes from his table. And the slave receiving the dishes that were sent him from his master, took of them what was sufficient for himself, and distributed the rest among his fellow-slaves. And his fellow-slaves rejoiced to receive the dishes, and began to pray for him, that he might find still greater favour with his master for having so treated them. His master heard all these things that were done, and was again greatly pleased with his conduct. And the master again calling; together his friends and his son, reported to them the slave's proceeding with regard to the dishes which he had sent him. And they were still more satisfied that the slave should become co-heir with his son."

Thomas:

He said, A [. . .] person owned a vineyard and rented it to some farmers, so they could work it and he could collect its crop from them. He sent his slave so the farmers would give him the vineyard's crop. They grabbed him, beat him, and almost killed him, and the slave returned and told his master. His master said, "Perhaps he didn't know them." He sent another slave, and the farmers beat that one as well. Then the master sent his son and said, "Perhaps they'll show my son some respect." Because the farmers knew that he was the heir to the vineyard, they grabbed him and killed him. Anyone here with two ears had better listen!

Mark:

1: And he began to speak to them in parables. "A man planted a vineyard, and set a hedge around it, and dug a pit for the wine press, and built a tower, and let it out to tenants, and went into another country.
2: When the time came, he sent a servant to the tenants, to get from them some of the fruit of the vineyard.
3: And they took him and beat him, and sent him away empty-handed.
4: Again he sent to them another servant, and they wounded him in the head, and treated him shamefully.
5: And he sent another, and him they killed; and so with many others, some they beat and some they killed.
6: He had still one other, a beloved son; finally he sent him to them, saying, 'They will respect my son.'
7: But those tenants said to one another, 'This is the heir; come, let us kill him, and the inheritance will be ours.'
8: And they took him and killed him, and cast him out of the vineyard.
9: What will the owner of the vineyard do? He will come and destroy the tenants, and give the vineyard to others.

Matthew:

33: "Hear another parable. There was a householder who planted a vineyard, and set a hedge around it, and dug a wine press in it, and built a tower, and let it out to tenants, and went into another country.

34: When the season of fruit drew near, he sent his servants to the tenants, to get his fruit;

35: and the tenants took his servants and beat one, killed another, and stoned another.

36: Again he sent other servants, more than the first; and they did the same to them.

37: Afterward he sent his son to them, saying, 'They will respect my son.'

38: But when the tenants saw the son, they said to themselves, 'This is the heir; come, let us kill him and have his inheritance.'

39: And they took him and cast him out of the vineyard, and killed him.

40: When therefore the owner of the vineyard comes, what will he do to those tenants?"

41: They said to him, "He will put those wretches to a miserable death, and let out the vineyard to other tenants who will give him the fruits in their seasons."

42: Jesus said to them, "Have you never read in the scriptures: 'The very stone which the builders rejected has become the head of the corner; this was the Lord's doing, and it is marvelous in our eyes'?

43: Therefore I tell you, the kingdom of God will be taken away from you and given to a nation producing the fruits of it."

45: When the chief priests and the Pharisees heard his parables, they perceived that he was speaking about them.

46: But when they tried to arrest him, they feared the multitudes, because they held him to be a prophet.

Luke:

9: And he began to tell the people this parable: "A man planted a vineyard, and let it out to tenants, and went into another country for a long while.

10: When the time came, he sent a servant to the tenants, that they should give him some of the fruit of the vineyard; but the tenants beat him, and sent him away empty-handed.

11: And he sent another servant; him also they beat and treated shamefully, and sent him away empty-handed.

12: And he sent yet a third; this one they wounded and cast out.

13: Then the owner of the vineyard said, 'What shall I do? I will send my beloved son; it may be they will respect him.'

THE EVOLUTION OF CHRISTS AND CHRISTIANIES

14: But when the tenants saw him, they said to themselves, 'This is the heir; let us kill him, that the inheritance may be ours.'

15: And they cast him out of the vineyard and killed him. What then will the owner of the vineyard do to them?

16: He will come and destroy those tenants, and give the vineyard to others." When they heard this, they said, "God forbid!"

The parable in *the Shepherd* is extremely upbeat. The slave goes beyond his master's expectations for the fields and he's rewarded beyond his expectations. The slave shares his good fortune with his fellow slaves and the master increases the reward. The owner here represents God and the slaves, all obedient slaves.

In *Thomas*, instead of a tale of a slave giving extra, we have a tale of a master trying to get something for nothing. He wants to get the produce of the field simply because he owns it. He is so greedy that he does not recognize the anger of the tenant farmers. In his blindness and greed, he ends up sacrificing his son. The owner here represents Rome and the tenants represent the Jews. We may take it that this is written before, but near the start of the Judeo-Roman War.

In *Mark*, the farmer himself does the labor to make the field productive. This is an important change that he has made from *Thomas*. Now he has a right to "some of the fruit" and the tenants act wickedly by beating and killing his servants, but the owner does not see the evilness of the tenants. The servants kill the owner's beloved son. Mark proposes that the patience of the good father has run out. He will come and destroy them. The owner again represents God and the tenants represent the Jews killing God's prophets.

Matthew simply makes explicit what is implicit in Mark's parable. The Jews will lose their kingdom, "Therefore I tell you, the kingdom of God will be taken away from you and given to a nation producing the fruits of it."

Luke has the Jews recognize their crime by saying "God forbid."

It is hard to imagine the changes of the text in any other order. The joy of the Hermas parable almost has to be mediated by the Thomas parable to reach the bitterness of the last three parables. This, plus the fact that the Shepherd never refers directly to anything in gospels, makes it a certainty for me that it predates the gospels. As Thomas seems to be pre-war before 66 C.E., we should probably give a date of around 50-55 C.E. for *the Shepherd*.

The Shepherd as a Source for the Gospel Writers

It is certainly worth going through the entire text of *the Shepherd* to demonstrate that it predates much of the gospel and Pauline text, and that it is the source for many important concepts in the gospels and epistles.

551

The prologue to the work has the author, Hermas explains that he is a slave owned by someone named Rhoda in Rome. He apparently still sees the mistress who raised him and one he helps her out of the Tiber River where we may assume she was bathing nude. He thinks only that it would be nice to be married to someone as beautiful as her. Apparently, he thinks she may have gotten the impression he wanted to sleep with her, as that night he dreams that he goes to heaven and she accuses him of wanting her. Now we should keep in mind that she is a freewoman and he is merely a slave, so his desiring her would be considered quite inappropriate and he could be severely punished if she did tell on him. We should also keep in mind that he says that she "raised him," which indicates that she may have played the roll of a mother towards him. So this would make any desire he showed for her even worse. He would be breaking both strict class rules and oedipal family taboos by desiring her.

When she accuses him in his dream, the woman says:

> "The desire of wickedness arose within your heart. Is it not your opinion that a righteous man commits sin when an evil desire arises in his heart? There is sin in such a case, and the sin is great," said she; "for the thoughts of a righteous man should be righteous. For by thinking righteously his character is established in the heavens, and he has the Lord merciful to him in every business. But those who entertain wicked thoughts in their minds are bringing upon themselves death and captivity; and especially is this the case with those who set their affections on this world, and glory in their riches, and look not forward to the blessings of the life to come. For many will their regrets be; for they have no hope, but have despaired of themselves and their life. But do thou pray to God, and He will heal thy sins, and the sins of thy whole house, and of all the saints."

One immediately thinks of the Sermon of the Mount saying by Jesus (*Matt.* 5: 27-28): "You have heard that it was said, `You shall not commit adultery.' But I say to you that every one who looks at a woman lustfully has already committed adultery with her in his heart." Now we should note that the woman does not quote or refer to Jesus at all. In fact the woman attributes the belief to Hermas—"your opinion."

The idea presented here that Hermas has committed *thought adultery* fits in exactly with the situation and reflects the situation. On the other hand when the gospel of Matthew uses the concept, it is simply a saying designed to illustrate the heightened morality of Christians. None of the other gospels contain it. Why doesn't Jesus explain the concept? The equivalence of thought and action is not clear in any sense. Perhaps Matthew does not have to explain it because the concept would be quite familiar to anybody who has already read *the Shepherd*.

THE EVOLUTION OF CHRISTS AND CHRISTIANIES

If there were other attributions of concepts or lines to Jesus' within the text, we might say that the lack of attribution of this saying to Jesus was simply an oversight. As there is no attribution at all of any concept or saying to Jesus, we have to say that the concept is independent of the gospels. Note also that the woman takes it as the norm for people to believe this, at least the norm for people of Hermas' persuasion, presumably Jewish/Christian. This suggests that Jesus was not the originator of the concept of "thought adultery," but that it was a common concept among Jewish/Christians when the Jesus character mentioned it.

Herma continues his dream recitation by telling of an old woman he meets. When he tells her about the accusation against him, she tells him:

> Far be such a deed from a servant of God. But perhaps a desire after her has arisen within your heart. Such a wish, in the case of the servants of God, produces sin. For it is a wicked and horrible wish in an all-chaste and already well-tried spirit to desire an evil deed; and especially for Hermas so to do, who keeps himself from all wicked desire, and is full of all simplicity, and of great guilelessness. But God is not angry with you on account of this, but that you may convert your house, which have committed iniquity against the Lord, and against you, their parents. And although you love your sons, yet did you not warn your house, but permitted them to be terribly corrupted.

The old woman quickly agrees that it is a sin for someone as good as Hermas to have such thoughts, but she quickly dismisses the charge as something not serious. The real problem for God is not any accidental lust in the heart, but the way he has raised his two sons. She tells Hermas to give daily advice to her sons and, "Cease not therefore to admonish your sons; for I know that, if they will repent with all their heart, they will be enrolled in the Books of Life with the saints." The sons can still be saved.

She adds that God:

> has surrounded His creation with beauty, and by His strong word has fixed the heavens and laid the foundations of the earth upon the waters, and by His own wisdom and providence has created His holy Church, which He has blessed, lo! He removes the heavens and the mountains, the hills and the seas, and all things become plain to His elect, that He may bestow on them the blessing which He has promised them, with much glory and joy, if only they shall keep the commandments of God which they have received in great faith."

Now, we should note that she is not talking about Jesus at all here. She is talking about the creator God. It is by keeping the commandments of the creator God that

Hermas and his sons will be put in the Books of Life. She can only mean at this point that Hermas and his two sons must obey Mosaic Law to be saved.

A year later, Hermas again encounters the same old woman in a dream. The woman asks him to copy and deliver a letter for the "Elect of God," apparently the leaders of this Jewish Church. After fifteen days of prayer and fasting Hermas remembers the contents of the letter. The gentiles have till the last day to repent, but the Jews have a time limit. If they do repent they will get all the good things he promised, "Stand steadfast, therefore, ye who work righteousness, and doubt not, that your passage may be with the holy angels." We should note that there is nothing about eternal life here, but only that the passage from life to death will be made easier for the righteous.

This full passage is quite extraordinary:

> Stand steadfast, therefore, ye who work righteousness, and doubt not, that your passage may be with the holy angels. Happy ye who endure the great tribulation that is coming on, and happy they who shall not deny their own life. For the Lord hath sworn by His Son, that those who denied their Lord have abandoned their life in despair, for even now these are to deny Him in the days that are coming. To those who denied in earlier times, God became gracious, on account of His exceeding tender mercy.

We can immediately point to a similar text in Mark (8:34-38, also Matt: 16:24-27 Luke 9:23-26 and John):

> 34: And he called to him the multitude with his disciples, and said to them, "If any man would come after me, let him deny himself and take up his cross and follow me.
> 35: For whoever would save his life will lose it; and whoever loses his life for my sake and the gospel's will save it.
> 36: For what does it profit a man, to gain the whole world and forfeit his life?
> 37: For what can a man give in return for his life?
> 38: For whoever is ashamed of me and of my words in this adulterous and sinful generation, of him will the Son of man also be ashamed, when he comes in the glory of his Father with the holy angels."

First, notice the reversal in meaning of denial. In the first text the ones who "shall not deny their own life" will be happy. The second text commands, "let him deny himself." In the second text, the author is tripping over himself, unsure of his meaning, he contradicts the command to sacrifice his life, saying "what does it profit a man, to gain the whole world and forfeit his life." The second author is trying to expand on the concept of the first by quoting from the Hebrew Scriptures, but the lines are out of place.

The expression "For the Lord has sworn by his son" seems to be referring to Jesus, but if you examine the next sentences it is clear that it cannot be a reference to Jesus.

> "But as for you, Hermas, remember not the wrongs done to you by your children, nor neglect your sister, that they may be cleansed from their former sins. For they will be instructed with righteous instruction, if you remember not the wrongs they have done you. For the remembrance of wrongs worketh death. And you, Hermas, have endured great personal tribulations on account of the transgressions of your house, because you did not attend to them, but were careless and engaged in your wicked transactions. But you are saved, because you did not depart from the living God, and on account of your simplicity and great self-control.

Hermas will be saved because of his "simplicity and great self-control." He will be saved because he will "remember not the wrongs done" to him by his children and sister. There is absolutely nothing about being saved as a result of God sacrificing his son. It is forgiveness of other people's wrongs that leads to salvation. This makes sense when we read the prior expression "God has sworn by his son" as simply a metaphor. It means that the situation is such that if God had a son, he would swear to sacrifice his life if he does not keep his promise. In order words, it means simply that God is absolutely serious about forgiving people.

Finally, the old woman has this message for Maximus who is apparently Hermas' wicked son, "Blessed are all they who practice righteousness, for they shall never be destroyed. Now you will tell Maximus: Lo! Tribulation cometh on. If it seemeth good to thee, deny again." So Hermas should give his sons one last chance.

Chapter four moves in a new direction:

> Now a revelation was given to me, my brethren, while I slept, by a young man of comely appearance, who said to me, "Who do you think that old woman is from whom you received the book?" And I said, "The Sibyl." "You are in a mistake," says he; "it is not the Sibyl." "Who is it then?" say I. And he said, "It is the Church." And I said to him, "Why then is she an old woman?" Because," said he, "she was created first of all.

It is amusing that Hermas has confused the Church with the Sibyl. It is a reminder that prophetic entities were grouped together in people's minds: "On this account is she old. And for her sake was the world made." It is fascinating that this document gives the place of first creation to the Church. This line gets echoed in the *Gospel of*

Thomas (14), "The disciples said to Jesus, "We know that You will depart from us. Who is to be our leader?" Jesus said to them, "Wherever you are, you are to go to James the Righteous, for whose sake heaven and earth came into being." We cannot make the connection directly from this, but the commonality of the forms suggest that the Church we are talking about is the Church of James the Righteous.

The old woman returns in another dream and they arrange a meeting to take place in the country outside the city. This time the woman advises Hermas, "cease praying continually for your sins; pray for righteousness, that you may."

She bids him to sit down on her left. She says, "Are you vexed, Hermas? The place to the right is for others who have already pleased God, and have suffered for His name's sake; and you have yet much to accomplish before you can sit with them." This idea is echoed in *Mark* (14:62): And Jesus said, "I am; and you will see the Son of man seated at the right hand of Power, and coming with the clouds of heaven." Again, Hermas' text explains what the sitting at the right hand means. We may presume *Mark* knows his readers are familiar with the concept from reading *the Shepherd* and he does not have to explain it again.

The old woman elaborates on what one has to go through in order to sit at the right hand of God:

> "What have they borne?" said I. "Listen," said she: "scourges, prisons, great tribulations, crosses, wild beasts, for God's name's sake. On this account is assigned to them the division of sanctification on the right hand, and to every one who shall suffer for God's name: to the rest is assigned the division on the left. But both for those who sit on the right, and those who sit on the left, there are the same gifts and promises; only those sit on the right, and have some glory. You then are eager to sit on the right with them, but your shortcomings are many. But you will be cleansed from your shortcomings; and all who are not given to doubts shall be cleansed from all their iniquities up till this day."

Again, we should note that there is no mention of Jesus suffering and going to sit at the right hand of God. Apparently anybody who suffers for the God's name makes it to the right hand of God.

Next the old woman shows Hermas a tower being constructed:

> And in this way the building of the tower looked as if it were made out of one stone. Those stones, however, which were taken from the earth suffered a different fate; for the young men rejected some of them, some they fitted into the building, and some they cut down, and cast far away from the tower. Many other stones, however, lay around the tower, and the young men did not use them in building; for some of them were

rough, others had cracks in them, others had been made too short, and others were white and round, but did not fit into the building of the tower. Moreover, I saw other stones thrown far away from the tower, and falling into the public road; yet they did not remain on the road, but were rolled into a pathless place. And I saw others falling into the fire and burning, others falling close to the water, and yet not capable of being rolled into the water, though they wished to be rolled down, and to enter the water.

The woman goes on to explain that the tower is the Church. She explains her parable about the stones. The story seems to be the basis for two gospel parables. The Gospel of Thomas has taken from this story the line, "Jesus said, 'Show me the stone which the builders have rejected. That one is the cornerstone.'" *Matthew* (21:42) has changed this to "The very stone which the builders rejected has become the head of the corner; this was the Lord's doing, and it is marvelous in our eyes." We may suggest that *Thomas* also derived the scattering of seeds parable from this (*Thomas*: 9) from where *Mark* picked it up (4:4-9).

In general, the point of the parable is that God will use some stones/people to build his church and he will smash other stones that are disobedient. The old woman continues the vision by introducing seven women around the tower: Faith, Self-restraint, Simplicity, Guilelessness, Chastity, Intelligence and Love. She notes, "The deeds, then, of these are pure, and chaste, and divine. Whoever devotes himself to these, and is able to hold fast by their works, shall have his dwelling in the tower with the saints of God." Again, it is important to note that the text says nothing about following Jesus. One gets to heaven by following seven Goddesses.

In this scene, Hermas asks about the end of this age, and he tells us "She cried out with a loud voice, 'Foolish man! Do you not see the tower yet building? When the tower is finished and built, then comes the end" This concept of God fulfilling a task before the endtime gets repeated and changed in Mark (13:10) "And the gospel must first be preached to all nations."

The old woman sends Hermas off commanding him to preach to the Saints of the Church. In the following chapter (9), we find him addressing both his sons and Church authorities. He argues for charity, and against overeating and for an end to dissension.

Hermas wants to find out why the woman kept getting younger each of the three times she appeared to him. He fasts and prays again and in his next dream. This time he sees a young man who tells him that the woman reflected his own spirit in each appearance. Apparently when he heard that there was an inheritance for him in heaven, his spirit grew younger and when he heard the good news that he would be forgiven, his spirit grew younger still: "For, just as when some good news comes suddenly to one who is sad, immediately he forgets his former sorrows, and looks for nothing else than the good news which he has heard, and for the future is made strong for good, and his spirit is renewed on account of the joy which he has received; so ye also have received the renewal of your spirits by seeing these good things."

In other words, Hermas had received the good news (gospel) that he was forgiven. Again note that there is absolutely no Jesus involved in this gospel.

Hermas says that twenty days later he was praying for more revelations while walking on a deserted area of the Campanion road in the country. He sees a hundred foot beast like a whale. He goes past the beast and encounters a virgin dressed in white as if coming from the bridal chamber. He recognizes her as the Church in an even more youthful form. She tells him that because of his faith, God sent an angel named Segri to close the mouth of the beast. He asks about the four colors of the beast black, red, gold and white. She tells him that black is this world, red is for the blood and fire that will destroy it, gold is for those who will survive, and white is the world to come.

After four visions of the church as a woman, Hermas has a completely different fifth vision back at his home, "a man of glorious aspect, dressed like a shepherd, with a white goat's skin, a wallet on his shoulders, and a rod in his hand . . ." Hermas identifies the man as "The Angel of Repentence". The man orders him to write down some "commandments and similitudes."

The Twelve Commandments of the Angel of Repentence

The first commandment is to believe in one creator God. Surprisingly, after comes "Be simple and guileless, and you will be as the children who know not the wickedness that ruins the life of men." We find a similar child reference in *Matthew* (18:3) "Truly I say to you unless you turn and be like children, you will never enter the kingdom of heaven." It is also found in *Thomas* (22) and *Luke* (18:17). The third commandment is not to speak slander. The fourth is to practice goodness, by giving to the needy in simplicity. The fifth is to speak truth and do not lie. The sixth is to "guard your chastity, and let no thought enter your heart of another man's wife, or of fornication, or of similar iniquities; for by doing this you commit a great sin. But if you always remember your own wife, you will never sin."

If the wife continues to commit adultery, the Shepherd advices:

> "The husband should put her away, and remain by himself. But if he put his wife away and marry another, he also commits adultery. And I said to him, "What if the woman put away should repent, and wish to return to her husband: shall she not be taken back by her husband?" And he said to me, "Assuredly. If the husband do not take her back, he sins, and brings a great sin upon himself; for he ought to take back the sinner who has repented. But not frequently. For there is but one repentance to the servants of God. In case, therefore, that the divorced wife may repent, the husband ought not to marry another, when his wife

has been put away. In this matter man and woman are to be treated exactly in the same way."

We may compare this to what Jesus says in Matthew (19.8-9), ""For your hardness of heart Moses allowed you to divorce your wives, but from the beginning it was not so. And I say to you: whoever divorces his wife, except for unchastity, and marries another, commits adultery." Again we find that the saying makes perfect sense in *the Shepherd*, but makes no sense in the gospels. It is as if someone had half remembered the pronouncement of *the Shepherd* and gave it as a nonsensical paraphrase to Jesus without bothering to copy the explanation.

The text next takes a neutral position on the question of remarriage:

> And again I asked him, saying, "Sir, since you have been so patient in listening to me, will you show me this also?" "Speak," said he. And I said, "If a wife or husband die, and the widower or widow marry, does he or she commit sin?" "There is no sin in marrying again," said he; "but if they remain unmarried, they gain greater honour and glory with the Lord; but if they marry, they do not sin. Guard, therefore, your chastity and purity, and you will live to God.

Paul echoes this position in *1 Corinthians* (7:8-9), "To the unmarried and the widows I say that it is well for them to remain single as I do. But if they cannot exercise self-control, they should marry. For it is better to marry than to be aflame with passion."

The Shepherd next tells Hermas to be patient and avoid anger. After this he talks about "two angels that reside in man one of righteousness, and the other of iniquity." He tells Hermas how to recognize the second:

> When anger comes upon you, or harshness, know that he is in you; and you will know this to be the case also, when you are attacked by a longing after many transactions, and the richest delicacies, and drunken revels, and divers luxuries, and things improper, and by a hankering after women, and by overreaching, and pride, and blustering, and by whatever is like to these. When these ascend into your heart, know that the angel of iniquity is in you.

Not surprisingly, the Shepherd urges Hermas to follow the angel of righteousness. He also urges him to fear "the lord and keep his commandments." He then gives us a laundry list of things to stay away from, "adultery and fornication, from unlawful reveling, from wicked luxury, from indulgence in many kinds of food and the extravagance of riches, and from boastfulness, and haughtiness, and insolence, and lies, and backbiting, and hypocrisy, from the remembrance of wrong, and from all slander." Soon he add to the list, "theft, lying, robbery, false witness, overreaching, wicked lust, deceit, vainglory, boastfulness, and all other vices like to these." He follows this with a positive to do list including, "faith, then fear of the Lord, love, concord, words of righteousness, truth, patience." He sums up the two angel problem, "'You see, then,' says he, 'that, faith is from above—from the Lord—and has great power; but doubt is an earthly spirit, coming from the devil, and has no power.'"

Surprisingly, the angel next tells Hermas that grief "crushes out the Holy Spirit." He describes how a man doubts, fails and becomes angry. This causes grief to the Holy Spirit. The angel advices Hermas to cleanse himself from this grief, and "put on all cheerfulness."

The angel then warns of "false prophets." He provides a method for spotting the false prophets:

> the man who seems to have the Spirit exalts himself, and wishes to have the first seat, and is bold, and impudent, and talkative, and lives in the midst of many luxuries and many other delusions, and takes rewards for his prophecy; and if he does not receive rewards, he does not prophesy.

He suggests that the false prophets are powerless because they come from the earth and the powers of the sky are greater than the Earth.

> Take a stone, and throw it to the sky, and see if you can touch it. Or again, take a squirt of water and squirt into the sky, and see if you can penetrate the sky." "How, sir," say I, "can these things take place? for both of them are impossible." "As these things," says he, "are impossible, so also are the earthly spirits powerless and pithless. But look, on the other hand, at the power which comes from above. Hail is of the size of a very small grain, yet when it falls on a man's head how much annoyance it gives him!

The angel tells Hermas to walk in the twelve commandments he has given him, and warns him "If you do not keep them, but neglect them, you will not be saved, nor your children, nor your house . . ." Note once again that salvation does not in any way depend upon Jesus, but only on following the twelve commandments of the angel of repentance:

> The angel warns again to watch out for the devil. When a man has filled very suitable jars with good wine, and a few among those jars are left empty, then he comes to the jars, and does not look at the full jars, for he knows that they are full; but he looks at the empty, being afraid lest they have become sour. For empty jars quickly become sour, and the goodness

THE EVOLUTION OF CHRISTS AND CHRISTIANIES

> of the wine is gone. So also the devil goes to all the servants of God to try them. As many, then, as are full in the faith, resist him strongly, and he withdraws from them, having no way by which he might enter them. He goes, then, to the empty, and finding a way of entrance, into them, he produces in them whatever he wishes, and they become his servants.

It is hard to know if this has any relationship to Jesus' first miracle in John regarding filling wine jars. If it does, it suggests that the character of Jesus may have evolved from a devilish character. The original story may have something about the devil filling wine jars with water and making people believe it was wine.

The shepherd next tells Hermas that he is like a foreigner in his earthly city:

> you know your city in which you are to dwell, why do ye here provide lands, and make expensive preparations, and accumulate dwellings and useless buildings? He who makes such preparations for this city cannot return again to his own. Oh foolish, and unstable, and miserable man! Dost thou not understand that all these things belong to another, and are under the power of another?

This concept gets repeated in Mark (10:21) when Jesus advices a young follower, "sell what you have, and give to the poor, and you will have treasure in heaven . . ." Jesus's advice also reflects the relationship between the rich and poor that the angel soon tells Hermas about:

> "The rich man has much wealth, but is poor in matters relating to the Lord, because he is distracted about his riches; and he offers very few confessions and intercessions to the Lord, and those which he does offer are small and weak, and have no power above. But when the rich man refreshes the poor, and assists him in his necessities, believing that what he does to the poor man will be able to find its reward with God—because the poor man is rich in intercession and confession, and his intercession has great power with God—then the rich man helps the poor in all things without hesitation; and the poor man, being helped by the rich, intercedes for him, giving thanks to God for him who bestows gifts upon him.

The Shepherd next denounces fasting:

> Listen," he continued: "God does not desire such an empty fasting? For fasting to God in this way you will do nothing for a righteous life; but offer to God a fasting of the following kind: Do no evil in your life, and

serve the Lord with a pure heart: keep His commandments, walking in His precepts, and let no evil desire arise in your heart; and believe in God. If you do these things, and fear Him, and abstain from every evil thing, you will live unto God; and if you do these things, you will keep a great fast, and one acceptable before God.

We can relate this to Mark (31: 33) who simply changes the anti-fasting message to an anti-sacrifice message, "and to love him with all the heart, and with all the understanding, and with all the strength, and to love one's neighbor as oneself, is much more than all whole burnt offerings and sacrifices."

The Reward of the Flesh: the Founding Myth of All Christianities

At this point the author gives us the parable of the absentee landlord (see section Smoking Gun Parable above). The angel relates it to fasting. Fasting is an extra sacrifice. It is acceptable if you eat nothing but bread and water on a fast day and give the money you save to the poor. Under persistent questioning by Hermas, the angel reveals more precisely the meaning of the parable:

> the Lord of the field is He who created, and perfected, and strengthened all things; [and the son is the Holy Spirit;] and the slave is the Son of God; and the vines are this people, whom He Himself planted; and the stakes are the holy angels of the Lord, who keep His people together; and the weeds that were plucked out of the vineyard are the iniquities of God's servants; and the dishes which He sent Him from His able are the commandments which He gave His people through His Son; and the friends and fellow-councilors are the holy angels who were first created; and the Master's absence from home is the time that remains until His appearing."

The surprising thing here is that the slave turns out to be the son of god. Hermas questions how the Son of God can take the form of a slave. The explanation that the angel gives is quite amazing:

> "God planted the vineyard, that is to say, He created the people, and gave them to His Son; and the Son appointed His angels over them to keep them; and He Himself purged away their sins, having suffered many trials and undergone many labours, for no one is able to dig without labour and toil. He Himself, then, having purged away the sins of the people, showed them the paths of life by giving them the law

which He received from His Father. [You see," he said, "that He is the Lord of the people, having received all authority from His Father.] And why the Lord took His Son as councilor, and the glorious angels, regarding the heirship of the slave, listen. The holy, pre-existent Spirit, that created every creature, God made to dwell in flesh, which He chose. This flesh, accordingly, in which the Holy Spirit dwelt, was nobly subject to that Spirit, walking religiously and chastely, in no respect defiling the Spirit; and accordingly, after living excellently and purely, and after labouring and co-operating with the Spirit, and having in everything acted vigorously and courageously along with the Holy Spirit, He assumed it as a partner with it. For this conduct of the flesh pleased Him, because it was not defiled on the earth while having the Holy Spirit. He took, therefore, as fellow-councilors His Son and the glorious angels, in order that this flesh, which had been subject to the body without a fault, might have some place of tabernacle, and that it might not appear that the reward [of its servitude had been lost], for the flesh that has been found without spot or defilement, in which the Holy Spirit dwelt, [will receive a reward].

What we have here is the metaphysics and birth of the Son of God, but without the story of Mary and Jesus. Keeping in mind the parable of the absentee landlord, we can follow the steps of what occurs.

1. There is a Holy Spirit. It is pre-existent (existing before the creation of the heavens and the earth)
2. This Holy Spirit creates every creature
3. God chose flesh for the Holy Spirit to dwell in. Apparently flesh here means a substance like water or air or earth.
4. Flesh is subject to the Holy Spirit. The Holy Spirit controls the flesh.
5. Flesh performs nobly, "In no sense defiling the spirit, behaving religiously and chastely."
6. God is pleased with Flesh and rewards it by making it a partner with the Holy Spirit. He does this because Flesh "was not defiled on the earth while having the Holy Spirit."
7. God takes Flesh combined with Holy Spirit as his councilor. This flesh joins the Holy Spirit (which is the Son of God) and the glorious angel and becomes a co-councilor of God. He does this because Flesh "has been found without spot or defilement."

Perhaps the most important phrase here is "For this conduct of the flesh pleased Him, because it was not defiled on the Earth while having the Holy Spirit." Later this line will be applied to Jesus Christ's time on Earth. However in the context of this paragraph it clearly means that the flesh was not on the Earth. Apparently, this combining of Flesh and Holy Spirit took place before the creation of the Earth. Flesh was obedient to the Holy Spirit and thus got the position of co-son of God along with Holy Spirit. We may surmise that it was only when it was put on Earth that flesh became corrupted.

One can easily see how this myth of flesh and spirit becomes the basis for both Gnostic Christianity and Roman Catholic Christianity. The Gnostics emphasize the split between God and Holy Spirit. The Holy Spirit does become corrupted by flesh and thus becomes a lesser God when it creates the Earth. The Roman Catholics emphasize the way God puts flesh on spirit. They mix in the story of Jesus the Christ with it by having the Holy Spirit enter Mary to become flesh.

One could point out that the thinkers who creates the ideology of the Roman Catholic Church in opposition to the Gnostic Marcionites has gotten the story wrong and that flesh was rewarded with the title son of God before the creation of the Earth. But the simple answer to that would be that God might have redeemed flesh generally before the creation of the earth, but specifically it needed redemption again after its pollution with the earth. So we find this denounciation of flesh in Paul's Roman Epistle (8.2-14):

> For the law of the Spirit of life in Christ Jesus has set me free from the law of sin and death. For God has done what the law, weakened by the flesh, could not do: sending his own Son in the likeness of sinful flesh and for sin, he condemned sin in the flesh, in order that the just requirement of the law might be fulfilled in us, who walk not according to the flesh but according to the Spirit. For those who live according to the flesh set their minds on the things of the flesh, but those who live according to the Spirit set their minds on the things of the Spirit. To set the mind on the flesh is death, but to set the mind on the Spirit is life and peace. For the mind that is set on the flesh is hostile to God; it does not submit to God's law, indeed it cannot; and those who are in the flesh cannot please God. But you are not in the flesh, you are in the Spirit, if in fact the Spirit of God dwells in you. Any one who does not have the Spirit of Christ does not belong to him. But if Christ is in you, although your bodies are dead because of sin, your spirits are alive because of righteousness. If the Spirit of him who raised Jesus from the dead dwells in you, he who raised Christ Jesus from the dead will give life to your mortal bodies also through his Spirit which dwells in you. So then, brethren, we are debtors, not to the flesh, to live according to the flesh—for if you live according to the flesh you will die, but if by the Spirit you put to death the deeds of the body you will live. For all who are led by the Spirit of God are sons of God.

THE EVOLUTION OF CHRISTS AND CHRISTIANIES

The irony here is that Hermas imagines a glorious mixing of spirit with flesh, due to its ability to bring pleasure exceeding expectations, raised to the same level as spirit, while this epistle proclaims a radical Platonic separation between the two only bridgeable by following the spirit of Jesus. While the Catholic Church rejected Marcion's separation between Good God and evil creator spirit, they adopted his separation between flesh and spirit. Tertullian probably sensed the contradiction between Marcion and Hermas and unconsciously, following his nemesis Marcion, started the process of eliminating the early Hermasian ideals of universal forgiveness and equality of flesh and spirit, and substituting the ideal of good emperor God/spirit in total control of a slave mass of evil flesh.

Still the stoic ideal of maximum obedience to superior authority is found in its purest form in *the Shepherd* itself. Here, not Jesus, but only God can unite the two. After being informed of the meaning of the absentee landlord, the angel of repentance proclaims:

> "Keep this flesh pure and stainless, that the Spirit which inhabits it may bear witness to it, and your flesh may be justified. See that the thought never arise in your mind that this flesh of yours is corruptible, and you misuse it by any act of defilement. If you defile your flesh, you will also defile the Holy Spirit; and if you defile your flesh [and spirit], you will not live."

Note that the individual here is portrayed as a mixture. There's you (soul), flesh and holy spirit. By the time of DesCartes the Holy Spirit has flown off to God, replaced by the more inclusive concept of "thought." DesCartes merges soul into thought to create "mind" and flesh becomes "body," thus coming up with the mind/body duality.

Hermas Meets the Shepherd

Up to this point Hermas has met an old woman who grew progressively younger on each meeting and the angel of repentance who gave him twelve commandments and two parables (the stones for the Church and the absentee landlord). He now sees a joyous Shepherd, "clothed in a suit of garments of a yellow colour," feeding many happy sheep. The angel of repentance warns him that "this is angel of luxury and deceit" His sheep have turned from away from God and enjoy material luxury. He then sees a second shepherd, "a tall shepherd, somewhat savage in his appearance, clothed in a white goatskin, and having a wallet on his shoulders, and a very hard staff with branches, and a large whip." This second shepherd is punishing his sheep.

Hermas starts talking with a shepherd. It is not clear if the angel of repentance has turned into a shepherd or if this is the shepherd of luxury and deceit. In any case the angel tells him that for every hour the sheep of the first shepherd receive pleasure, they receive a month of pain from the second shepherd, or for every day of pleasure, they receive a year of torment. When Hermas asks what kinds of things the sheep are punished for, the Shepherd tells him:

> "Every act of a man which he performs with pleasure," he replied, "is an act of luxury; for the sharp-tempered man, when gratifying his tendency, indulges in luxury; and the adulterer, and the drunkard, and the back-biter, and the liar, and the covetous man, and the thief, and he who does things like these, gratifies his peculiar propensity, and in so doing indulges in luxury. All these acts of luxury are hurtful to the servants of God. On account of these deceits, therefore, do they suffer, who are punished and tortured.

It is hard to imagine the kind of mind that believes it is part of God's plan or the natural order that a day's worth of pleasure leads to a year's worth of pain. It seems probable that the writer is in fact a slave who does find his days of pleasure comparatively few in comparison with his days of pain. If Hermas was a slave and this document is the most important document in the founding of Christianity, then we can say that Friedrich Nietzsche got things upside. He said "it was the Jews who started the slave revolt in morals[516]." He should have said, "it was a slave who started the revolt in Jewish morals."

A few days later, he sees someone, the Angel of Repentance again, although, exactly whom he sees is a bit fuzzy. It may be the Sheperd of Punishment. In any case, Hermas asks someone to take the Angel/Shepherd of Punishment from his house. The angel says he has been delivered to the Angel of Punishment because of his children, but he will intervene and lighten Hermas' coming punishment

The angel then tells another parable. This one is about people who are given branches from a tree. Different people return the branches in different conditions and receive reward and punishment based on it. The angel explains the symbolism in the parable:

> "This great tree that casts its shadow over plains, and mountains, and all the earth, is the law of God that was given to the whole world; and this law is the Son of God, proclaimed to the ends of the earth; and the people who are under its shadow are they who have heard the proclamation, and have believed upon Him. And the great and glorious angel Michael is he who has authority over this people, and governs them; for this is he who gave them the law into the hearts of believers: he accordingly superintends them to whom he gave it, to see if they have kept the same. And you see the branches of each one, for the branches are the law.

THE EVOLUTION OF CHRISTS AND CHRISTIANIES

Note that it is the law that is the son of God, not Jesus, and the angel Michael has delivered the law to the people, again not Jesus. This is just more evidence that we are dealing with a pre-Jesus document.

The Angel of Repentence tells how the good people who returned their branches green get to go into the tower/church. It is at this point, in the narrative, that the Angel of Repentance gets replaced by the Shepherd of Punishment as Hermas' teacher. The Shepherd suggests that they plant the branches of those who did not make it into the tower and to see if they will still grow. He compares the tree to a Willow because of its tenacious ability to grow in poor circumstances. He calls on Hermas to summon the men who brought back the branches and line them up in rows according to the condition of the branches. The Shepherd tells where each row/type of people will go in relationship to the tower (Church). Here are the ten types of people according to the condition of the branches they returned.

Branches	People Types
1. Green with fruit	Those who have suffered on account of the law. Winners of Crown from the angel.
2. Green, and with offshoots, but without fruit	Afflicted on account of the law, but who have not suffered nor denied their law. Venerable and just.
3. Green, as they had received them from the angel	Majority. [unstated, but apparently these are the ordinary good members of the church.]
4. Green, but having the tips withered and cracked	Always good, and faithful, and distinguished before God; but they sinned a very little through indulging small desires
5. Two-thirds green and one-third withered	Faithful who acquired wealth and went over to the heathen, some repenting and some not.
6. Two-thirds withered and one-third green	Faithful, who denied, repented, hesitated and doubted.
7. Green and cracked	Faithful and good, yet envious of each other about their place in the church fame.
8. Half-withered and cracked	Waverers and slanderers
9. Withered and undecayed	Hypocrites, and introducers of strange doctrines, and subverters of the servants Of God
10. Withered and Moth eaten	Apostates and traitors of the Church

It is the last seven who the Shepherd of Punishment tests by planting their branches to see if they will grow. They all apparently have a chance, although the chance of the branch growing and the people getting admitted to the tower diminishes as we go down the list, with the tenth and last having the least chance of redemption. Besides the church, the tower also appears to symbolize life.

A few days later, the Angel of Repentence comes back once again. He tells Hermas:

> I wish to explain to you what the Holy Spirit that spake with you in the form of the Church showed you, for that Spirit is the Son of God. For, as you were somewhat weak in the flesh, it was not explained to you by the angel. When, however, you were strengthened by the Spirit, and your strength was increased, so that you were able to see the angel also, then accordingly was the building of the tower shown you by the Church. In a noble and solemn manner did you see everything as if shown you by a virgin; but now you see [them] through the same Spirit as if shown by an angel.

Note that there is no trinity of Gods here. The Holy Spirit is the Son of God. It spoke to Hermas in the form of a virgin. The Virgin (apparently meant to mean a young girl without understanding) shows Hermas the form of the tower, but it is the Angel who gives him understanding of it. This introduction of the concept of a Virgin is very important. The concept of a revelation of the true form of the church through a virgin will come to be associated with Jesus' mother later. It appears that the creators of the Jesus story were not taking their inspiration from Hebrew Scriptures, but were using the Hebrew Scriptures to match the Jesus story to the dreams of Hermas.

The Shepherd takes Hermas to a high hill in Arcadia and shows him twelve mountains. He also shows him a rectangular white rock capable of holding the whole world. The rock has a gate with twelve linen-clad virgins in front. Six "tall and distinguished men" "summon a multitude" of man to build a tower. The six men summon ten stones from a pit that the virgins carry. The virgins go through the gate and give the stones to the men to build the foundation for the tower. The process gets repeated with twenty-five, thirty-five stones, and forty stones. The stones are of different color but they all change to white when handled by the virgins. Other stones are not handled by the virgins and do not change their color so they are eliminated from the tower. Building on the tower ceases, as everybody waits for the Lord to come to give his approval.

A "Glorious Man," the lord of the tower, who is taller than the tower comes and rejects some of the stones. Hermas asks the Shepherd, ", "Can these stones return to the building of the tower, after being rejected?" The Shepherd assures Hermas that he can make them acceptable. In light of this tale, we can suggest a relationship with the saying in Thomas (66) "Show me the stones which the builder has rejected, that one has become the cornerstone." And Mark (12.10), "Have you not read the scripture the very stone which the builders rejected has become the cornerstone?"

The Shepherd says he will fix the rejected stones:

> Let us go, and after two days let us come and clean these stones, and cast them into the building; for all things around the tower must be cleaned, lest the Master come suddenly? and find the places about the tower dirty, and be displeased, and these stones be not returned for the building of the tower, and I also shall seem to be neglectful towards the Master."

I think the fact that the Shepherd of Punishment speaks like a slave here is important. If only one character in the text, Hermas, spoke like a slave, we would have to consider that the writer was not a slave but just producing the stylistic thought patterns of a slave to give an accurate and natural portrayal of the character. When more than one character speaks in the same style, it suggests that the writer himself is just following his natural thought patterns. This is evidence that Hermas is not a fictional character, but the actual author of the text.

The Shepherd gives a detailed description of how he will fix the rejected stones and finish the tower. He orders Hermas, "Go and bring unslacked lime and fine-baked clay, that I may fill up the forms of the stones that were taken and thrown into the building; for everything about the tower must be smooth." The Shepherd fixes the stones and replaces them in the tower with the help of the Virgins and some "fierce women" with "hair disheveled," dressed in black. The detailed nature of the description suggests that the author himself was involved in the building trade.

The Shepherd leaves Hermas alone with the Virgins and there is some interesting interaction:

> "You will sleep with us," they replied, "as a brother, and not as a husband: for you are our brother, and for the time to come we intend to abide with you, for we love you exceedingly!" But I was ashamed to remain with them. And she who seemed to be the first among them began to kiss me. [And the others seeing her kissing me, began also to kiss me], and to lead me round the tower, and to play with me. And I, too, became like a young man, and began to play with them: for some of them formed a chorus, and others danced, and others sang; and I, keeping silence, walked with them around the tower, and was merry with them. And when it grew late I wished to go into the house; and they would not let me, but detained me. So I remained with them during the night, and slept beside the tower. Now the virgins spread their linen tunics on the ground, and made me lie down in the midst of them; and they did nothing at all but pray; and I without ceasing prayed with them, and not less than they. And the virgins rejoiced because I thus prayed

Since their linen tunics were laid on the ground, I suppose we are to imagine that the virgins were naked as Hermas prayed with them.

When he comes back the next day, the Shepherd talks more about the Son of Christ in terminology that will later be applied to Jesus:

> This rock," he answered, "and this gate are the Son of God." "How, sir?" I said; "the rock is old, and the gate is new." "Listen," he said, "and understand, O ignorant man. The Son of God is older than all His creatures, so that He was a fellow-councilor with the Father in His work of creation: for this reason is He old." "And why is the gate new, sir?" I said. "Because," he answered, "He became manifest in the last days of the dispensation: for this reason the gate was made new, that they who are to be saved by it might enter into the kingdom of God

The rock (*Petros*) symbolizes the Holy Spirit that was God's councilor in creating the world. The gate symbolizes the Holy Spirit's latest appearance to Hermas as the old/de-aging woman to tell him that these are the last days that God will grant forgiveness before the deadline. After telling Hermas that both the gate and rock are symbolic of the Son of God, he adds yet another symbol for the Son of God:

> "If, then, you cannot enter into the city except through its gate, so, in like manner, a man cannot otherwise enter into the kingdom of God than by the name of His beloved Son. You saw," he added, "the multitude who were building the tower?" "I saw them, sir," I said. "Those," he said, "are all glorious angels, and by them accordingly is the Lord surrounded. And the gate is the Son of God. This is the one entrance to the Lord. In no other way, then, shall any one enter in to Him except through His Son. You saw," he continued, "the six men, and the tail and glorious man in the midst of them, who walked round the tower, and rejected the stones from the building?" I saw him, sir," I answered. "The glorious man," he said, "is the Son of God,

The term "name of his beloved son" does not indicate that the Holy Spirit has a name, let alone the name "Jesus." The term seems to merely indicate that you have to be familiar enough with the Holy Spirit to know his name to enter the kingdom of God. In other words the name of the Son of God is a magical password. The fact that the "Son of God" can also be immediately described as a magical gate that leads to God again indicates that we are dealing with a pre-Jesus Christ and pre-Jesus of Nazareth concept.

"Beloved Son" would be the equivalent of the first son in a society where primogeniture dominates. The first son would often be given the same name as the father. Pronouncing God's name may have been a sin, but pronouncing the name of his first-born son may have been an acceptable alternative, as it would be the functional equivalent of the name of God.

The Shepherd next informs Hermas that the virgins he saw were also "holy spirits." He adds that the rejected stones "bore his name" but the rejected stones did not put on the clothing of the virgins. He explains that the clothing of the virgins are their names, and "Every one who bears the name of the Son of God, ought to bear the names also of these; for the Son Himself bears the names of these Virgins." Some of the rejected stones/people went with the fierce women in black with disheveled hair and left the Virgins. Because these people were persuaded by the fierce women, the building of the tower came to a halt. They may come back in the house if they go back to the Virgins.

Under further questioning, the Shepherd reveals the names of the Virgins and the Women in Black.

> **The first is Faith, the second Continence, the third Power, the fourth Patience. And the others standing in the midst of these have the following names: Simplicity, Innocence, Purity, Cheerfulness, Truth, Understanding, Harmony, Love. He who bears these names and that of the Son of God will be able to enter into the kingdom of God. Hear, also," he continued, "the names of the women who had the black garments; and of these four are stronger than the rest. The first is Unbelief, the second: Incontinence, the third Disobedience, the fourth Deceit. And their followers are called Sorrow, Wickedness, Wantonness, Anger, Falsehood, Folly, Backbiting, Hatred.**

Hermas then asks about the number of stones that formed the foundation of the Church/Tower. The Shepherd answers that the first ten, "are the first generation, and the twenty-five the second generation, of righteous men; and the thirty-five are the prophets of God and His ministers; and the forty are the apostles and teachers of the preaching of the Son of God." Again, we should note that this matches nothing in any of the gospels.

'The Shepherd explains how the dead rise by ascending through water:

> "before a man bears the name of the Son of God s he is dead; but when he receives the seal he lays aside his deadness, and obtains life. The seal, then, is the water: they descend into the water dead, and they arise alive. And to them, accordingly, was this seal preached, and they made use of it that they might enter into the kingdom of God."

In light of later ideology, we may see this as a reference to the practice of baptism. In fact, it appears to predate baptism in the group and baptism may have been adopted based on this line. Note that a man has to die before he gets the name of "the son of God."

The Shepherd then discusses the twelve mountains and the people/stones that come from them. This is quite similar to the description of the ten returned branches and the personalities of the people who returned them. For example, he calls the people from the first mountain that was black, "apostates and blasphemers against the Lord, and betrayers of the servants of God." The people from the mountains get better as the color of the mountain lightens until we get to the twelfth mountain which is white:

> they are as infant children, in whose hearts no evil originates; nor did they know what wickedness is, but always remained as children. Such accordingly, without doubt, dwell in the kingdom of God, because they defiled in nothing the commandments of God; but they remained like children all the days of their life in the same mind. All of you, then, who shall remain stedfast, and be as children, without doing evil, will be more honored than all who have been previously mentioned; for all infants are honorable before God, and are the first persons with Him. Blessed, then, are ye who put away wickedness from yourselves, and put on innocence. As the first of all will you live unto God."

Out of this came the saying in the Gospel of Matthew (18.3-4) "Truly, I say to you, unless you turn and become like children, you will never enter the kingdom of heaven. Whoever humbles himself like this child, he is the greatest in the kingdom of heaven."

After urging people to behave like children, the Angel of Repentence shows up suddenly. This short section appears to be a later interpolation, calling for peace among the Church leadership. He asks the church leaders to lay aside their bitterness and be of one spirit. They will be judged and cannot blame their "flock" for their problems. He says that he himself is a shepherd who is responsible for rendering an account.

He finishes with one last parable and similitude of a fuller (cleaner) who tears a garment while cleaning it. This naturally ruins it. In the same way God will punish you if you do not give him back a "sound spirit."

The Angel of Repentence leaves the house of Hermas, but he promises that the Shepherd (of Punishment) and the Virgins will return.

Summary of What We Learn from this Founding Document

There is not the slightest indication that the author of *the Shepherd* is familiar with any story involving Jesus of Nazareth or a Christ on Earth. The document shows no knowledge of the crucifixion, the Eucharist or Baptism. The document shows no animosity towards Romans as *Revelation* (circa 69 C.E.) does and no animosity towards Jews as virtually all late first and second century Christian documents do. The lack of any anti-Jewish ideology would suggest it was written before the Judeo-Roman War (66-73 C.E.) The lack of animosity towards Rome would suggest a time a date before 62 (C.E.). The persistant use of metaphorical language can be compared to the mid-first century writer Philo. We may suggest a rough date of around 50 C.E. If it was much later, we would expect to see evidence of some knowledge of the Judeo-Roman conflicts or at least some knowledge of other first century prophets and their ideology.

The contents suggest that there was an international Jewish Church called the Church of God operating at this time. The Church had a strong emphasis on a program involving redemption and salvation in the afterlife. It preached reaching the Kingdom of God in Heaven and some form of afterlife by following twelve commandments. These include, believing in one God, opposing adultery and being cheerful (or at least not angry). The Church may have referred to its members as Sons of God and thought of the Holy Spirit as the original Son of God and co-creator of the Earth.

Many of the parables and theological ideas (i.e., children entering the kingdom of heaven) told by the lead character, the Angel of Repentance end up being transferred to the mouth of Jesus in the synoptic gospels and Thomas. The use of some of the Hebrew Scripture in the New Testament seems to be to connect the Jesus stories with the ideas in the visions of Hermas.

The fact that the Church of Rome still recognized this document in the third century as Holy Scripture on a par with the canonical gospels suggest that it was a primary document of the Church of Rome and that the Church of Rome grew out of the Jewish Church of God. It appears that the Jesus gospels and Apostle Epistles were added over a long period of time to the Shepherd Document to form the canon.

Once the gospels and letters were part of the Canon, there appears to have been an ultimately successful attempt to remove the earlier Shepherd Document from the canon starting with Tertullian and continuing to the time of the Muratorian Canon.

There is nothing to suggest that we should not take the authorship at face value and believe that a slave named Hermas wrote the document. His description of tower building suggests someone who has participated in building projects. His dominant ideology that pleasure gets punished by much longer lasting pain in this life reflects a kind of primitive stoicism that would be appropriate for a slave.

Psychoanalyzing Hermas

Hermas' writing are quite extraordinary. However we should not treat him as a philosopher brilliantly manipulating abstract concepts, or a mystic giving us new religious insight. Instead, I suggest, we treat him as a slave truthfully relating his dreams. When we take this approach, we find that by psychoanalyzing his dreams, we can discover a great deal about the *modus operandi* of the early Church of God, probably around 50 C.E.

Hermas dreams about four woman, each woman getting progressively younger who visit him. These women later reveal themselves as The Church of God. He also dreams of repeated visits from the Angel of Repentance, and his two agents, the Shepherd of Pain and the Shepherd of Pleasure.

Let us assume that these dream visions represent real experiences in the life of Hermas. Instead of each figure being the Church of God, the dream figures in Hermas' dream represent real living representatives from the Church of God to Hermas' household.

It is important that the first visit was from an elderly woman. We may take it from his description that Hermas was owned by a wealthy widow. It is logical that the Church would first send an elderly woman to a wealthy woman's household. The church could not send a man to a woman's house as that would be a severe breach of social etiquette. Sending a younger woman on a first introductory visit would not be productive. An elderly woman widow might feel superior to a younger woman and reject any advice she had to offer. Thus an approach by a peer, an elderly woman, would be the socially accepted protocol. The elderly woman would discuss basic ideas about the religion, but mainly act as a spy, gathering information about the household. Most likely she would show some interest in the slaves and ask about any trouble that the woman might be having with them. Talk would quickly turn to the sexuality of the slave and how the matriarch kept it under control. Such talk would play into the matriach's fears and desires. In *Shepherd*, Hermas tells how he was accused of sexual impropriety for simply helping his nude mistress out of a bath.

After the initial visit by an elderly widow to introduce the woman to the Church of God, the Church would send progressively younger women back on visits, probably ending with a visit by a virgin orphan girl, (possibly as young as eleven or twelve years old). This would have a very positive effect on the matriarch as she would feel a sense of growing security, power and trust as the visitors became younger. Also, it would make her remember her own younger days and probably make her feel more desirable. This would play into the important theme of sexual danger from her own slaves. At this point, it is likely that she would allow her slaves to undergo some form of religious training by the Church of God, even if she herself did not wish to participate.

Hermas next tells us about the "angel" and his two "shepherds," new and different representatives of the Church of God. Apparently, the "Angel of Repentence" would instruct the slave in obedience to the doctrines of the religion, while the two shepherds played what we nowadays call a "good cop-bad cop" role. One of the shepherds, the "Shepherd of Pleasure," would be friendly and helpful to the slave, while the other shepherd, the "Shepherd of Pain," would beat and torture the slave when he disobeyed his "Angel of Repentance." Apparently these visits went on for quite some time, possibly a year or more. The slave was told that after death, God would judge him and would again send shepherds of pleasure or pain to him.

We may take it that this marketing strategy was quite effective in both bringing large numbers of obedient slaves into the religion and raising money for the group from wealthy matriarchs.

Relationship of Paul to Hermas

Was Paul a Slave?

Hermas identifies himself as a slave in *Shepherd*. We should not be surprised that a slave could be so well educated as to write an influential religious treatise. We may consider the models of Terence the comic play-write and Epictetus the stoic philosopher to guide us. Being slaves did not stop them from creating great literature. Also as evidence that slaves could rise to positions of influence and respect, we may point to this testimony by Pliny the Younger, in a letter he writes to his colleague Valerius Paulinus about his freedman Zosimus,

> As I know how mildly you treat your own servants I the more frankly confess to you the indulgence I shew to mine. I have ever in my mind that line of Homer's," Like to a father's was his gentle sway," and that expression in our own language, "father of a household." But were I naturally of a rough and hardened temper, the ill state of health of my freedman Zosimus (who has the stronger claim to humane treatment, as he now stands the more in need of it) would suffice to soften me. He is honest and well-educated; but his profession, his certified accomplishments, one might say, is that of comedian, wherein he highly excels. He speaks with great emphasis, judgement, propriety, and some gracefulness; and also plays the lyre more skilfully than a comedian need do. To this I must add, he reads history, oratory, and poetry, as well as if he had singly applied himself to that art.
>
> I am particular in enumerating these qualifications to let you see how many and agreeable services I receive from this one man's hand[517].

Like Hermas, Paul and other apostles also identify themselves as slaves, although not precisely in the same way. We may look at the opening of some canonical epistles:

1. Romans: Paul, a **servant** of Jesus Christ, called to be an apostle, set apart for the gospel of God.
   παυλος **δουλος** ιησου χριστου κλητος αποστολος αφωρισμενος εις ευαγγελιον θεου

2. Titus: Paul, a **servant** of God and an apostle of Jesus Christ, to further the faith of God's elect and their knowledge of the truth which accords with godliness.
παυλος **δουλος** θεου αποστολος δε ιησου χριστου κατα πιστιν εκλεκτων θεου και επιγνωσιν αληθειας της κατ ευσεβειαν
3. Philippians: Paul and Timothy, **servants** of Christ Jesus.
παυλος και τιμοθεος **δουλοι** χριστου ιησου
4. James: James, a **servant** of God and of the Lord Jesus Christ.
ιακωβος θεου και κυριου ιησου χριστου **δουλος**
5. Jude: Judas, a **servant** of Jesus Christ, and brother of James.
ιουδας ιησου χριστου **δουλος** αδελφος δε ιακωβου
6. 2 Peter: Simeon Peter, a **servant** and apostle of Jesus Christ.
σιμων πετρος **δουλος** και αποστολος ιησου χριστου

Also Note:

7. 1 Corinthians 3.5: What then is Apollos? What is Paul? **Servants** through whom you believed.
τι ουν εστιν απολλως τι δε εστιν παυλος **διακονοι** δι ων επιστευσατε
8. 1 Corinthians 4.1: This is how one should regard us, as **servants** of Christ and stewards of the mysteries of God.
ουτως ημας λογιζεσθω ανθρωπος ως **υπηρετας** χριστου

Notice that the word translated as servant in most English bible translations is δουλος. The word means "Born Bondsman or slave" according to LSJ[518]. In relevant works like Euripides *Bacchae* (1026) and Epictetus ("*Peri eleutherias*," *Works* 4.1.7) the word gets translated as *slave*. The terms in 1 Corinthians, διακονοι, (servant, official or attendant) υπηρετας, (rower, underling, servant, attendant) show that the writers could easily have chosen other words if they meant servant instead of slave. We may suggest that in all these passages, *slave* should be substituted for *servant*.

What is interesting is how the terms *slave, apostle, God* and *Jesus Christ* change positions. It is hard to see why an apostle would degrade himself by calling himself a slave. It is however easy to see how a slave would gladly exchange the lowly title of *slave* for the higher one of *Apostle*. In fact we see in later works that the writer(s) of the canonical epistles drop the slave description and adopt the Apostle title:

1 Corinthians: Paul, called by the will of God to be an **apostle** of Christ Jesus
Colossians: Paul, an **apostle** of Christ Jesus by the will of God
Galatians: Paul an **apostle**—not from men nor through man, but through Jesus Christ and God the Father

THE EVOLUTION OF CHRISTS AND CHRISTIANIES

1 Timothy: Paul, an **apostle** of Christ Jesus by command of God our Savior and of Christ Jesus our hope
1 Peter: Peter, an **apostle** of Jesus Christ

We may suppose that there was an evolution in self perception within the Church of God. The first members called themselves slaves of God. Only later they added the ideas of Jesus Christ and apostleship. They forgot their slave origins and ended up calling themselves apostles of Jesus Christ. Here are the meanings in Henry George Liddell and Robert Scott, *A Greek-English Lexicon*:

Apostole: *sending off or away, dispatching, sending forth on their journey, shooting, discharge, discharge from service, payment of tribute, expedition.*
Apostollo: *to send off or away from*
Apostoleus: *one who dispatches*
Apostolos: *messenger, ambassador, envoy, commander of a naval force, messenger from God,*

The term *apostle* is not used in the *Gospel of John*. It is used only once in the *Gospel of Mark* (6.30), "The apostles returned to Jesus, and told him all that they had done and taught." Jesus has sent out his twelve disciples on a mission to various earlier in the chapter. It appears that the author is not using the term "apostles" in any technical sense, but simply describing people sent out on a mission. Similarly, we find the term only once in the *Gospel of Matthew* (10.2) to describe the same mission. He uses the opportunity to give a list of names of the twelve disciples. This usage seems to be a transition point between Mark's non-technical usage and Luke's use of the term as a title for the twelve disciples (6.13), "And when it was day, he called his disciples, and chose from them twelve, whom he named apostles." In the book *Acts of the Apostles*, the dead Jesus sends the disciples out on a seemingly open-ended mission, and it is in light of this that the disciples get the title apostles.

We may summarize our findings by saying that the disciples are not called apostles in the earliest canonical gospel of *John*, while in *Mark* the term *apostle* refers descriptively to a single simple mission that Jesus has his twelve disciples perform. Matthew and Luke associate the term more closely with the disciples. In *Acts of the Apostles*, instead of a living Jesus sending some of his disciples out one time to do some exorcisms (healings for money?), we have a dead Jesus sending his disciples on an endless mission to spread the gospel, thus giving them the permanent title of apostle.

We find the term *apostle* over forty times in the various letters of Paul. There does not appear to be any reference to either the specific apostolic mission of the living Jesus found in the gospels or the after-death apostolic mission of *Acts*. In fact, the term seems to be used to describe any person on an authorized mission. For example, in *Hebrews*, we find the term used only once (3.1) and applied to Jesus Christ, "Therefore, holy brethren, who share in a heavenly call, consider Jesus, the apostle and high priest of our confession. He was faithful to him who appointed him, just as Moses also was faithful in God's house."

Likewise, the four uses in *Romans* show no precise connection to the twelve disciples.

1. 1.1 Paul, a servant of Jesus Christ, called to be an **apostle**, set apart for the gospel of God.
2. 1.4-5 Jesus Christ our Lord, through whom we have received grace and **apostle**ship to bring about the obedience of faith for the sake of his name among all the nations ...
3. 11.13 Now I am speaking to you Gentiles. Inasmuch then as I am an **apostle** to the Gentiles, I magnify my ministry
4. 16.7 Greet Andronicus and Junias, my kinsmen and my fellow prisoners; they are men of note among the **apostles**, and they were in Christ before me.

The "setting apart" in the first reference seems to refer to the idea of being an apostle (i.e. sent on a mission). Apparently the mission was to preach the gospel of God. There is nothing about Jesus Christ sending him on his mission. The second reference, tells us that his mission is to bring obedience of faith among all the nations. In the third reference he simply confirms that it is a mission from Jews to non-Jews. Note that he calls himself just "an apostle to the Gentiles," not "the apostle," so we may take it that his mission is not unique. In the fourth reference, we have him naming Andronicus and Junias as other apostles. Obviously Andronicus and Junias were not among the twelve original disciples of Jesus. From this we conclude that Paul is using the term apostle in its general meaning of anybody sent on a mission and specifically referring to people sent on missions by his particular Church of God.

There does appear to be some question as to the legitimacy of Paul's mission. He does not really give us much in the way of specifics about who sent him and what he is to accomplish. He acknowledges a problem in 1 Corinthians (9.2), "If to others I am not an **apostle**, at least I am to you; for you are the seal of my **apostle**ship in the Lord." This is a rather odd argument that somehow the fact that he has accomplished something with the Corinthians proves that he has been sent on a mission. It certainly does not give us much confidence that he has been sent on a mission.

But if Paul's mission was real or imagined by himself, we still need to know what he did before he was sent on his missions (i.e. became an apostle). *Acts* (18) tells us that he was a tentmaker:

> 2: And he found a Jew named Aquila, a native of Pontus, lately come from Italy with his wife Priscilla, because Claudius had commanded all the Jews to leave Rome. And he went to see them;

3: and because he was of the same trade he stayed with them, and they worked, for by trade they were tentmakers.

This, however, tells us nothing about Paul. We have no reason to trust this statement. First, because we do not know where the author is getting his/her information and if it is reliable, second, because in our earlier reconstruction it appeared that it was Apollos who was the tentmaker who associated with Aquila and Priscilla, and third, because it does not explain Paul's silence about his own occupation in his many works which often touch on his own life.

There are a number of clues in the epistles that point strongly to what appears to be Paul's real situation. We can begin with this statement in Hebrews (3.1-6)

> Therefore, holy brethren, who share in a heavenly call, consider Jesus, the apostle and high priest of our confession. He was faithful to him who appointed him, just as Moses also was faithful in God's house. Yet Jesus has been counted worthy of as much more glory than Moses as the builder of a house has more honor than the house. (For every house is built by some one, but the builder of all things is God.) Now Moses was faithful in all God's house as a servant, to testify to the things that were to be spoken later, but Christ was faithful over God's house as a son. And we are his house if we hold fast our confidence and pride in our hope.

Notice the dichotomy between Moses called "the servant" and Christ called "the son." Significantly the same dichotomy appears in Hermas' parable in *The Shepherd* of the vacationing landlord and the faithful servant who eventually becomes a son. In the parable, remember that even the legitimate son agrees that the good servant/slave should be adopted and made co-heir.

2[55]:7 And he saith to them; "I promised this servant his freedom, if he should keep the commandment which I commanded him; but he kept my commandment and did a good work besides to my vineyard, and pleased me greatly. For this work therefore which he has done, I desire to make him joint-heir with my son, because, when the good thought struck him, he did not neglect it, but fulfilled it."

2[55]:8 In this purpose the son of the master agreed with him, that the servant should be made joint-heir with the son.

Hermas' optimistic vision is that he will do such good work as a slave that he will become a son in God' household and be accepted by the current son. Paul, working in a later Church of God, has lost that hope. Now it is a question of who is the real son of

God's household. Obviously Jews, who called themselves sons of God, would not think of Moses as a mere obedient servant. Why is Paul accusing the Jews of being mere servants of God, while his followers of Jesus are the real sons of God?

This approach makes sense if Paul and the Church of God are servants of God and separate from the Jews who consider themselves sons of God. Paul is reversing this perception. It is not the Jews who are the sons of God, but the followers of Jesus Christ. It is not the followers of Jesus Christ who are the servants of God, but they are the actual sons of God. How and why did the Jews believe that the followers of Jesus Christ were servants of God and not sons of God. The most logical answer is because they were servants/slaves of God. We may propose that the Church or Assembly of God started off as a special organization of slaves/servants.

In Aristophanes' play *Ecclesiazusa*, we have an assembly of woman. It is an absurdist notion for the people of Athens in the early fourth century B.C. However, an assembly of slaves in first century C.E. would be an extremely useful organization. Its open purpose could not have been to help slaves become free, but rather to make slaves more obedient to their masters. This is exactly what we find in the writings of Paul. As the Catholic Encyclopedia notes:

> St. Paul recommends slaves to seek in all things to please their masters, not to contradict them, to do them no wrong, to honour them, to be loyal to them, so as to make the teaching of God Our Saviour shine forth before the eyes of all, and to prevent that name and teaching from being blasphemed (cf. I Tim, vi, 1; Tit., ii, 9, 10)[519]

The same article also notes this:

> The apostolic writings show how large a place slaves occupied in the Church. Nearly all the names of the Christians whom St. Paul salutes in his Epistles to the Romans are servile *cognomina*: the two groups whom he calls "those of the household of Aristobulus and "those of the household of Narcissus" indicate Christian servitors of those two contemporaries of Nero. His Epistle, written from Rome to the Philippians (iv, 22) bears them greeting from the saints of Caesar's household, i.e. converted slaves of the imperial palace.

Once we assume that Paul was himself a slave working within an organization primarily for slaves (Church of God), the history of early Christianity becomes clear. Based on the ideology displayed in *Shepherd* and Paul's writings, we can suggest that the organization was probably set up by Jews in order to bring wayward Jewish slaves back into the Jewish religious social order. It used both Platonic and Jewish moral and educational principles. After a period of time, it became a society open to all slaves (not just the Jewish ones). As slaves themselves often acquired their freedom through purchase or their masters' wills, the society soon would include slaves and free people.

Since Moses was well known as a leader of a Hebrew slave revolt, he could not be the principal model. Apparently, his protégé, the Anointed Joshua (Latinized, it became Jesus Christ) was the primary model[520]. This worked well as he was not only a model of obedience, but also a model of self-sacrifice and military leadership, all things that the Jews would be looking for in their slaves to combat Roman domination.

Under this scenario, we can make sense out of much of the ideology and events in the Pauline epistles. For example, we read in King James 2 Corinthians (11.23-27):

> Are they ministers of Christ? (I speak as a fool) I am more; in labours more abundant, in stripes above measure, in prisons more frequent, in deaths oft. Of the Jews five times received I forty stripes save one. Thrice was I beaten with rods, once was I stoned, thrice I suffered shipwreck, a night and a day I have been in the deep; In journeyings often, in perils of waters, in perils of robbers, in perils by mine own countrymen, in perils by the heathen, in perils in the city, in perils in the wilderness, in perils in the sea, in perils among false brethren; In weariness and painfulness, in watchings often, in hunger and thirst, in fastings often, in cold and nakedness.

Labors, stripes, prison and death; this is not a description of the life of a tentmaker or a Jew from an upperclass family. It does describe the life of a slave and perhaps a runaway slave.

We find this connection with slavery implicit in the ideology throughout the epistles. Examine these famous lines of Romans (6.16-23):

> Do you not know that if you yield yourselves to any one as obedient slaves, you are slaves of the one whom you obey, either of sin, which leads to death, or of obedience, which leads to righteousness? But thanks be to God, that you who were once slaves of sin have become obedient from the heart to the standard of teaching to which you were committed, and, having been set free from sin, have become slaves of righteousness. I am speaking in human terms, because of your natural limitations. For just as you once yielded your members to impurity and to greater iniquity, so now yield your members to righteousness for sanctification. When you were slaves of sin, you were free in regard to righteousness. But then what return did you get from the things of which you are now ashamed? The end of those things is death. But now that you have been set free from sin and have become slaves of God, the return you get is sanctification and its end, eternal life. For the wages of sin is death, but the free gift of God is eternal life in Christ Jesus our Lord.

Paul is not speaking metaphorically when he talks about people being slaves but literally. They cared about their bodies and that was why they were enslaved. Now that they care about righteousness, they are slaves to the lord. They have exchanged the slavery of man for the slavery of God. In so doing they have found freedom. We can find this same idea of a slave's freedom in God applied to Paul himself in Galatians (2.1-7):

> Then after fourteen years I went up again to Jerusalem with Barnabas, taking Titus along with me. I went up by revelation; and I laid before them (but privately before those who were of repute) the gospel which I preach among the Gentiles, lest somehow I should be running or had run in vain. But even Titus, who was with me, was not compelled to be circumcised, though he was a Greek. But because of false brethren secretly brought in, who slipped in to spy out our freedom which we have in Christ Jesus, that they might bring us into bondage—to them we did not yield submission even for a moment, that the truth of the gospel might be preserved for you. And from those who were reputed to be something (what they were makes no difference to me; God shows no partiality)—those, I say, who were of repute added nothing to me;

Notice that Paul does not appeal to his own reputation against those leaders of the Church from Jerusalem. Paul attacks the idea of reputation itself ("God shows no partiality"). He also perhaps implies that the Jerusalem's leaders might also be slaves ("what they were makes no difference to me").

He notes that people spied on him to bring him into bondage. But how could Paul have been brought into bondage unless he was a slave in the first place? One may argue that he is speaking here of Judaism as bondage, but that idea does not preclude the idea that he is also speaking of literal bondage. Examine these lines from *Hebrews* (13.4-7):

> In your struggle against sin you have not yet resisted to the point of shedding your blood. And have you forgotten the exhortation which addresses you as sons?—"My son, do not regard lightly the discipline of the Lord, nor lose courage when you are punished by him. For the Lord disciplines him whom he loves, and chastises every son whom he receives." It is for discipline that you have to endure. God is treating you as sons; for what son is there whom his father does not discipline?

This matches the ideology of *the Shepherd* exactly. Slaves undergo earthly discipline so that they may become sons of God in the afterlife in heaven. Paul also plays around with this motiff of slavery being a form of sonship in Galatians 4.1-9):

THE EVOLUTION OF CHRISTS AND CHRISTIANIES

> I mean that the heir, as long as he is a child, is no better than a slave, though he is the owner of all the estate; but he is under guardians and trustees until the date set by the father. So with us; when we were children, we were slaves to the elemental spirits of the universe. But when the time had fully come, God sent forth his Son, born of woman, born under the law, to redeem those who were under the law, so that we might receive adoption as sons. And because you are sons, God has sent the Spirit of his Son into our hearts, crying, "Abba! Father!" So through God you are no longer a slave but a son, and if a son then an heir. Formerly, when you did not know God, you were in bondage to beings that by nature are no gods; but now that you have come to know God, or rather to be known by God, how can you turn back again to the weak and beggarly elemental spirits, whose slaves you want to be once more?

This makes perfect sense if we assume that Paul was a slave, at least as a child, who is addressing slaves. Paul cannot blame God for his slavery, so he assumes that slavery is a form of disciple instituted by God the father on his sons.

In *1 Corinthians* (7.20-24), we have another important reference to slavery:

> Every one should remain in the state in which he was called. Were you a slave when called? Never mind. But if you can gain your freedom, avail yourself of the opportunity. For he who was called in the Lord as a slave is a freedman of the Lord. Likewise he who was free when called is a slave of Christ. You were bought with a price; do not become slaves of men. So, brethren, in whatever state each was called, there let him remain with God.

There is a clear contradiction here. Paul first says that one should remain as called and then says that slaves should take the opportunity to get free. This seems to indicate that the writer does not take his own rhetoric very seriously. On a rhetorical level, human slavery does not make a difference, but Paul is sympathetic enough to the plight of slaves that he knows that freedom is better.

Paul and the Obedience School for Slaves

Paul tells us that he was Jewish and he persecuted the Church of God (Galatians 1), but nothing about his profession either before or after conversion. Why does he not tell us his profession? If he was from a wealthy noble family, so as not to need to work, that would have been an important and positive fact. Why not state such a thing openly. Instead of telling us that he is from a good family and independently wealthy, he appears to tell us that he obtained needed money from his preaching. He tells us this explicitly in *2 Corinthians* (11.7-9):

> Did I commit a sin in abasing myself so that you might be exalted, because I preached God's gospel without cost to you? I robbed other churches by accepting support from them in order to serve you. And when I was with you and was in want, I did not burden any one, for my needs were supplied by the brethren who came from Macedonia. So I refrained and will refrain from burdening you in any way.

The author tells us that he had to accept support (money) from other churches in order to preach in Corinth. The term *robbed* is quite strong. If it was his ordinary habit of taking money from churches then to say he robbed them by taking money from them would be absurd. He was not apparently in the habit of taking money from Churches. On the other hand, if he had a source of income from his profession, why did he need to take money from the churches? We may assume he took money from the churches in exchange for his preaching. By not preaching to the churches that paid him, but by preaching to a church that did not pay him, he was not giving the churches that paid him their money's worth. Thus he was robbing them.

In *1 Corinthians* (9.18-19), Paul seems to directly contradict this idea that he took money from churches:

> What then is my reward? Just this: that in my preaching I may make the gospel free of charge, not making full use of my right in the gospel. For though I am free from all men, I have made myself a slave to all, that I might win the more.

Paul appears to be lying to the Corinthians when he claims here that he does not to take money for his preaching of the gospel. It seems that he is being more honest in 2 Corinthians where he claims that it is only his acceptance of money from other churches that allows him to preach to the stingy Corinthians.

When he says that he is free from all men and has made himself a slave to all, he may again be deceiving the Corinthians. This claim of being free from all men sounds very much like Paul's claim in Galatians (1.11-12), "the gospel which was preached by me is not man's gospel for I did not receive it from man, nor was I taught it, but it came through a revelation of Jesus Christ."

We may assume in both cases that Paul is exaggerating his independence. Instead, we may take it that Paul was a Jewish slave and that men did teach him the gospel of salvation through belief in Jesus Christ (the Anointed Joshua of Nun who descended to hell and rose to heaven after his death). Paul's innovation seems to have been to modify this gospel to make it acceptable to Greek slaves as well as Jewish ones.

At this point we may ask the question if slaves could have afforded to finance trips like Paul's. He apparently had a perpetual entourage, Timothy and Barnabus, among others. (His Angels of Pleasure and Pain, perhaps?) Slaves were generally quite poor and when they did get money they would save it and use it to finance their freedom. One can imagine slaves being able to host guests with a place to sleep and food, but could they really finance expensive voyages for preachers who showed up at their door and stayed a few months. The answer is most probably not. Then, we have to ask where Paul did get his money?

While the concept of equalitarian churches with everybody contributing a few pennies to the common good is a nice ideal, in the real world, it rarely happens. Usually churches are substained by a small group of wealthy donors who actually contribute the great majority of funds. These wealthy donors get power, influence, control and name recognition in exchange. We may take it that the Church of God also had its wealthy donors. But why would wealthy people contribute to an organization of slaves? The answer is in the character and charter of that organization. The organization's purpose was to make slaves more religious, i.e. more obedient. Wealthy people, especially slave owners, would see this as a positive achievement worth paying for.

Slaves-owners, especially Jewish ones, would naturally have trouble with their slaves, who were most likely believers in mystery gods and members of mystery cults. The slaves would have seen their Jewish masters as believers in outdated superstitions, old fools not up to date with the latest religious fashions. They would hardly be inclined to obey masters that they considered fools. Wealthy widowed women slave-owners would be even more vulnerable. The solution was to reform the slaves through the Church of God.

This may help to explain how the Church of God was able grow and finance itself. It was the slave masters themselves who paid for the religious education of their slaves. The famous house churches of early Christianities were nothing more than houses where the slave-owners paid to have their slaves trained for obedience. Based on an examination of its early ideology, we can suggest that the Church of God was essentially an obedience training school for slaves. This would explain why the primary ideology of the Church was obedience to masters in this life for great rewards in the afterlife.

This also explains why the Anointed Joshua of Nun (Jesus Christ) was the primary hero (model and God) for the Church as opposed to Moses. Moses led a slave rebellion. He would never work as a figure preaching obedience. The good servant, Joshua, who carried out all orders without question would be the preferable model. Likewise, the commandments and laws of Moses could not be a part of the teaching. There was too much debate in the Jewish community about their precise application in day to day life. This was replaced in early Christianity by a supererogatory Platonic/Stoic dedication to duty. Christianity in the form created by the Church of God was not the slave's religion, but the religion of slavemasters created for slaves.

The question is can we determine who started this church of slaves and why? I think we can.

Fresco. Christ as Lanky Good Shepherd Carrying a Pot.

Catacomb of Saint Callistus, Rome, 286.

CHAPTER 13

JAMES AND THE CHURCH OF GOD

Eusebius tells us there were fifteen bishops in the Church of Jerusalem. The first two he names are James and Symeon[521]. He says that Symeon, was "a cousin" of the lord[522], from Joseph's (Jesus' father) brother Clopas. Symeon is simply an errant spelling of Simon and Simon is the original or real name of Peter. The close association of James and Peter in the gospel texts and *Acts* allows us to assume that Eusebius, although he cites no source, is being accurate. James and Simon (Peter) are the founders of the Jerusalem Church (assembly) of God. We may assume that John, the other great disciple of Jesus in the tales, was the brother of James and also the cousin of Peter. As we noted previously John got sent off to the mountain retreat/fortress Macherus where God only knows what happened to him. Eusebius, citing Hegesippus, has Simon Peter living to the ripe old age of one hundred and twenty before the Emperor Trajan crucifies him. What became of Simon, the apparent founder and first Bishop of the Church?

Eusebius tells us that he was stoned after declaring for Jesus to a crowd of Jews[523]. It is a dramatic retelling and difficult to know how true the details of the story are, but essentially we have a story of the leaders and priests of the Jews killing the founder of the Church of God.

In *Acts* we have a similar story but it is assigned to somebody named Stephen. Yet, while allowing Stephen to give a long speech, reciting the history of Judaism which ends with him being stoned, the text strangely tells us nothing about why he was singled out of such treatment. It is also surprising that his death would cause a scattering of the other disciples. Also interesting is that the Disciple John disappears from the story after the death of Stephen. Ultimately, rather than believing two people were stoned by Jews after witnessing for Jesus, it is simpler to believe that the editor of *Acts* has changed the name of James to Stephen. In fact, the disappearance of John from the story after the death of Stephen indicates that John himself was a substitute for James. Apparently the editor of *Acts* was trying to cover up James' role in the founding of the Church of God.

Acts tells this about the situation[524]:

> *1:* Now in these days when the disciples were increasing in number, the Hellenists murmured against the Hebrews because their widows were neglected in the daily distribution.
>
> *2:* And the twelve summoned the body of the disciples and said, "It is not right that we should give up preaching the word of God to serve tables.
>
> *3:* Therefore, brethren, pick out from among you seven men of good repute, full of the Spirit and of wisdom, whom we may appoint to this duty.
>
> *4:* But we will devote ourselves to prayer and to the ministry of the word."
>
> *5:* And what they said pleased the whole multitude, and they chose Stephen, a man full of faith and of the Holy Spirit, and Philip, and Prochorus, and Nicanor, and Timon, and Parmenas, and Nicolaus, a proselyte of Antioch.
>
> *8:* And Stephen, full of grace and power, did great wonders and signs among the people.
>
> *9:* Then some of those who belonged to the Synagogue of the Freedmen (as it was called), and of the Cyrenians, and of the Alexandrians, and of those from Cilicia and Asia, arose and disputed with Stephen.
>
> *10:* But they could not withstand the wisdom and the Spirit with which he spoke.
>
> *11:* Then they secretly instigated men, who said, "We have heard him speak blasphemous words against Moses and God."
>
> *12:* And they stirred up the people and the elders and the scribes, and they came upon him and seized him and brought him before the council,
>
> *13:* and set up false witnesses who said, "This man never ceases to speak words against this holy place and the law;
>
> *14:* for we have heard him say that this Jesus of Nazareth will destroy this place, and will change the customs which Moses delivered to us."
>
> *15:* And gazing at him, all who sat in the council saw that his face was like the face of an angel.

Note the use of the terms Hellenic (ελληνιστων) and Hebrew (εβραιους). Both are terms referring to ancient peoples. This probably indicates that we are dealing with two types of Jews rather than Jews and gentile Greeks. The exact meaning of the terms "daily distributions" and "serve tables" is hard to figure out. It has something to do with taking care of the everyday needs of the widows. Serving tables was a job for slaves. The twelve did not want to be slaves, but wanted to be free to pray and preach the word of God. The twelve appoint a task force of seven people to take care of the problem. They leave it apparently to the body of disciples to choose/select or elect the seven.

If this was simply a matter of uneven food distribution, the solution to increase food for the Hellenics would have been simple. However, this was a serious problem which apparently prevented the twelve from being free to work normally. Since Cyenians, Alexandrians, Cilicians, and Asians are involved, it is possible that we are talking about an international problem rather than a simple problem in Jerusalem. If so, it would involve mass transportation of a great amount of food to a great many ports and cities. Perhaps the Synagogue of the Freedmen were involved in this massive charity project run by the seven.

Note the title of the accusers, "Synagogue of the Freedmen." Was this an organization of ex-slaves or was it an organization of slaves who were free because they believed again in the Jewish God? Were the Cyrenians, Alexandrians, Cilicians and Asians part of the Synagogue of Freedmen, or are they separate accusers? It seems probable they are part of it, as it seems probable that the Synagogue of Freedmen is somehow involved in the problem of taking care of the widows. Slaves or ex-slaves would want to gain a good reputation by participating in such a charity project, whether on an international or local scale.

Now one has to ask why the accusers in the Synagogue of the Freedmen did not come to the twelve disciples to accuse Stephan. Since the twelve appointed him, logically they were responsible for any of his offensive actions. We are told that the accusers put him on trial before "the council." Who is this council? Logically, it should be the twelve who sent him. If not them, then why do none of the twelve appear at the trial to defend him? Again, it does not make sense. Stephan can just say that he is following the orders and teaching what the twelve disciples of Jesus taught him. In which case, it is the twelve who should be put on trial. If Stephan is breaking out on his own and preaching in opposition to the twelve than why do not any of the twelve appear to denounce him.

The situation makes more sense if the twelve who appointed Stephan was a council of Jewish High Priests and they themselves are the ones who are judging him. Thus there are no twelve disciples to appeal to or to support him or denounce him.

In any case notice that the charges against him are that "Jesus of Nazareth will destroy this place and will change the customs which Moses delivered to us"

These are basically the same charges that the same false witnesses make against Jesus in the gospels.

> Now the chief priests and the whole council sought testimony against Jesus to put him to death; but they found none. For many bore false witness against him, and their witness did not agree. And some stood up and bore false witness against him, saying, "We heard him say, 'I will destroy this temple that is made with hands, and in three days I will build another, not made with hands[525].'

The gospel of John declares "For the law was given through Moses; grace and truth came through Jesus Christ[526]." Compare this with line 8 "And Stephen, full of grace and power, did great wonders and signs among the people." The description of Stephen could easily fit Jesus. Stephan is accused of opposition to Moses just as Jesus was.

At the end of the trials we also have similar visions by Stephan and Jesus.

- Mark (14:61-65) But he was silent and made no answer. Again the high priest asked him, "Are you the Christ, the Son of the Blessed?" And Jesus said, "I am; and you will see the Son of man seated at the right hand of Power, and coming with the clouds of heaven." And the high priest tore his garments, and said, "Why do we still need witnesses? You have heard his blasphemy. What is your decision?" And they all condemned him as deserving death. And some began to spit on him, and to cover his face, and to strike him
- Acts (7:54-58): Now when they heard these things they were enraged, and they ground their teeth against him. But he, full of the Holy Spirit, gazed into heaven and saw the glory of God, and Jesus standing at the right hand of God; and he said, "Behold, I see the heavens opened, and the Son of man standing at the right hand of God." But they cried out with a loud voice and stopped their ears and rushed together upon him. Then they cast him out of the city and stoned him;

We may also note the dying words of Jesus and Stephan:

Note Jesus' last words in the Gospel of Luke after crucifixion compared with the last words of Stephan after stoning.

- Luke (23:34) And Jesus said, "Father, forgive them; for they know not what they do."
- Acts (7:60) And he knelt down and cried with a loud voice, "Lord, do not hold this sin against them."

THE EVOLUTION OF CHRISTS AND CHRISTIANIES

So we have similar descriptions of the accused, similar accusations, similar paid witnesses before a similar unnamed Jewish council, similar visions of Jesus in heaven next to God at the end of the trial and similar last words after execution.

Who is copying whom? If the writers of Acts were copying the gospels, there would have been some indication that these things happened to Jesus, earlier. We may take it as most probable that the charges against Jesus were actually the charges against Stephen/James. It is most probable that the gospel writers have gotten their material from the history of Stephan, which was originally the history of James, the Just. This explains the necessity for the name change from the famous James the Just to the unknown Stephan.

Look again at the accusation, "We have heard him speak blasphemous words against Moses and God." One would expect that Stephan/James would speak in defense of this charge and assert that he would never spoke anything against Moses. But he makes no apology. Instead he accuses the Jews of continual disobedience to their God from the beginning. He delivers a fantastic revisionist interpretation of Jewish history.

He says that God gave Abraham no inheritance in the land of Israel, "not even a foot's length[527]," God only forced his progeny to be circumcised and promised to enslave them and ill-treat them for four hundred years[528]." The Jews ended up as slaves in Egypt. God sent Moses to free them, but they rejected him, saying, 'Who made you a ruler and a judge over us?' God appointed the rejected Moses to lead the Jews out of Egypt. Moses "performed wonders and signs in Egypt and at the Red Sea, and in the wilderness for forty years[529]," and predicted the coming of another prophet after him[530]. The Jews "refused to obey him, but thrust him aside, and in their hearts they turned to Egypt[531]." David did find favor with God, but Solomon had the audacity to build him a temple. God, the most high, who created everything, has no need for temples[532]. Then we get this:

> **Ye stiffnecked and uncircumcised in heart and ears, ye do always resist the Holy Ghost: as your fathers [did], so [do] ye. Which of the prophets have not your fathers persecuted? and they have slain them which shewed before of the coming of the Just One; of whom ye have been now the betrayers and murderers: Who have received the law by the disposition of angels, and have not kept [it]. When they heard these things, they were cut to the heart, and they gnashed on him with [their] teeth. But he, being full of the Holy Ghost, looked up steadfastly into heaven, and saw the glory of God, and Jesus standing on the right hand of God[533],**

The reference to "the Just One" may be taken as a self reference. The speaker is James the Just. He is saying that all the prophets predicted his coming and that the

Jews have betrayed and murdered all the prophets. The term "gnashed on him with their teeth" apparently means that they denounced him. His response is to look up steadfastly into heaven. This is another way of saying that he did not answer them. He was silent. Compare with *Mark* (14:61-62):

> But he held his peace, and answered nothing. Again the high priest asked him, and said unto him, Art thou the Christ, the Son of the Blessed? And Jesus said, I am: and ye shall see the Son of man sitting on the right hand of power, and coming in the clouds of heaven.

Again, it is quite clear that the canonical gospel's description of the trial of Jesus is coming out of the trial of James the Just. It is the Christ Joshua of Nun that James sees when he looks up to heaven. The original split between Christianity and Judaism is the split between Jewish followers of the action and faith orientated resurrected Joshua of Nun and the Jewish followers of Moses and his legalisms. The Jews killed James after he declared them enemies of God and declared himself the prophet from God that Moses and the prophets had said God would send.

But again we have to be careful with equating the text with an accurate history. This text is being written after the Temple's destruction. Thus it is Post 70 CE. James' death seems to have taken place around 52 CE. The text is trying to establish that James predicted the destruction of the temple. This would have made him a legitimate prophet. This is most likely false. What does seem likely to be true about the story is that James was a popular Jewish leader in charge of an important food distribution project involving widows. There was a famine around 42-44 CE, so this is likely the time of the project. Paul's Galatians' epistle has Paul claiming that he reached the doctrine of Jesus the resurrected three years before he met James and that he met James again after 14 more years. We may assume that the writer of the epistle is trying to one-up James. Still, this suggests that the writer of the epistle thought James was at his post for at least the ten year period from 42-52.

It seems that before blaming the Jewish leadership of killing their God/Man founder Jesus Christ, an earlier group of Christians, just after the Roman War blamed the leadership of the Jews for killing their founder James the Just. Have we hit the bedrock of History? Did this really happen? Or was this too only a fantasy created to explain the defeat of the Christians in the War?

Apparently the death of James was portrayed as a *casus belli* for the Roman War. At least it was in Josephus' works in the third century in the time of Origin. He writes this:

> And James is he whom Paul says in the Epistle to the Galatians that he saw, "But other of the Apostles saw I none, save James the Lord's brother." And to so great a reputation among the people for righteousness did this James rise, that Flavius Josephus, who wrote the "Antiquities of the

Jews" in twenty books, when wishing to exhibit the cause why the people suffered so great misfortunes that even the temple was razed to the ground, said, that these things happened to them in accordance with the wrath of God in consequence of the things which they had dared to do against James the brother of Jesus who is called Christ. And the wonderful thing is, that, though he did not accept Jesus as Christ, he yet gave testimony that the righteousness of James was so great; and he says that the people thought that they had suffered these things because of James[534].

Now this writer, although not believing in Jesus as the Christ, in seeking after the cause of the fall of Jerusalem and the destruction of the temple, whereas he ought to have said that the conspiracy against Jesus was the cause of these calamities befalling the people, since they put to death Christ, who was a prophet, says nevertheless-being, although against his will, not far from the truth—that these disasters happened to the Jews as a punishment for the death of James the Just, who was a brother of Jesus (called Christ)—the Jews having put him to death, although he was a man most distinguished for his justice[535].

Here we stop. We have found another important stream of early Christianity. This one flows from the first Christian Martyr James the Just and the Church of God (perhaps growing out of the Synagogue of the Freedmen), most likely starting in the 40's.

Gravestone. Christ as Husky Good Shepherd Carrying a Pot.

Gravestone of Mouses and his wife. Rome, 3rd Century. The hand to the ear would probably indicate that the Good Shepherd has heard the prayers of the woman.

CHAPTER 14

STILL JESUS AFTER ALL THESE YEARS

Historical and potentially historical evidence from the late first and second centuries speaks of Christianity as a recent, temporary and local phenomenon, basically the struggling remnants of the school of a beloved, but unlucky teacher.

Our historical sources for Christianity outside the canonical gospels are Post-Christian. They announce or predict the possible death of Christianity. In a sense they are "Baspels" (bad spells—bad news). If the Gospels announce the birth of the King/Kingdom of God, all our potential historical sources give brief announcements of the death of the King/Kingdom of God.

> It was then that he learned the wondrous lore of the Christians, by associating with their priests and scribes in Palestine. And—how else could it be?—in a trice he made them all look like children, for he was prophet, cult-leader, head of the synagogue, and everything, all by himself. He interpreted and explained some of their books and even composed many, and they revered him as a god, made use of him as a lawgiver, and set him down as a protector, next after that other, to be sure, whom[11] they still worship, the man who was crucified in Palestine because he introduced this new cult into the world.
>
> Lucian
> *Passing of Peregrinus*
> (circa 180 C.E.)

"Now there was about this time Jesus, a wise man, if it be lawful to call him a man, for he was a doer of wonderful works, a teacher of such men as receive the truth with pleasure. He drew over to him both many of the Jews, and many of the Gentiles. He was the Christ; and when Pilate, at the suggestion of the principal men amongst us, had condemned him to the cross, those that loved him at the first did not forsake him, for he appeared to them alive again the third day, as the divine prophets had foretold these and ten thousand other wonderful things concerning him; and the tribe of Christians, so named from him, are not extinct to this day."

Eusebius,
"Testamonium Flavianum"
Evangelical Demonstration 3.5
Ecclesiastical History 1.11,
(circa 320 C.E.)
Josephus?
Wars (93 C.E.)

... Others named by the informer declared that they were Christians, but then denied it, asserting that they had been but had ceased to be, some three years before, others many years, some as much as twenty-five years. They all worshipped your image and the statues of the gods, and cursed Christ.

They asserted, however, that the sum and substance of their fault or error had been that they were accustomed to meet on a fixed day before dawn and sing responsively a hymn to Christ as to a god, and to bind themselves by oath, not to some crime, but not to commit fraud, theft, or adultery, not falsify their trust, nor to refuse to return a trust when called upon to do so. When this was over, it was their custom to depart and to assemble again to partake of food—but ordinary and innocent food. Even this, they affirmed, they had ceased to do after my edict by which, in accordance with your instructions, I had forbidden political associations. Accordingly, I judged it all the more necessary to find out what the truth was by torturing two female slaves who were called deaconesses. But I discovered nothing else but depraved, excessive superstition.

Pliny
Letter to Trajan
(circa 112 C.E.)

THE EVOLUTION OF CHRISTS AND CHRISTIANIES

Consequently, to get rid of the report, Nero fastened the guilt and inflicted the most exquisite tortures on a class hated for their abominations, called Christians by the populace. Christus, from whom the name had its origin, suffered the extreme penalty during the reign of Tiberius at the hands of one of our procurators, Pontius Pilatus, and a most mischievous superstition, thus checked for the moment, again broke out not only in Judaea.

Tacitus
Annals 15.44
(circa 115 C.E.)

But there stood up one in the council, a Pharisee, named Gamaliel, a doctor of the law, had in honor of all the people, and commanded to put the men forth a little while. And he said unto them, Ye men of Israel, take heed to yourselves as touching these men, what ye are about to do. For before these days rose up Theudas, giving himself out to be somebody; to whom a number of men, about four hundred, joined themselves: who was slain; and all, as many as obeyed him, were dispersed, and came to nought. After this man rose up Judas of Galilee in the days of the enrolment, and drew away *some of the* people after him: he also perished; and all, as many as obeyed him, were scattered abroad. And now I say unto you, Refrain from these men, and let them alone: for if this counsel or this work be of men, it will be overthrown: but if it is of God, ye will not be able to overthrow them; lest haply ye be found even to be fighting against God. And to him they agreed: and when they had called the apostles unto them, they beat them and charged them not to speak in the name of Jesus, and let them go.

Luke?
Acts of the Apostles 5:34-40.
(circa 50-200 C.E.?)

Lucian has the Christians worshipping Peregrinus on a par with Christ. They "still worship" the lawgiver, Christ, but Lucian implies it is just a matter of time before the next charlatan comes along and the Christians convert to a new hero. "The Flavorium Testamonium" seems surprised that the Christians are not extinct yet, a position possibly partly reflecting the thought of Eusebius who believed it was a miracle the Christians survived all the persecutions. Pliny is also astonished that the Christian outbreak that he's investigating has lasted for some 25 years (87-112 C.E?). He announces that the age of Christianity is over and the worship of the ancient Gods has been restored:

> **For the contagion of this superstition has spread not only to the cities but also to the villages and farms. But it seems possible to check and cure it. It is certainly quite clear that the temples, which had been almost deserted, have begun to be frequented, that the established religious rites, long neglected, are being resumed, and that from everywhere sacrificial animals are coming, for which until now very few purchasers could be found. Hence it is easy to imagine what a multitude of people can be reformed if an opportunity for repentance is afforded.**

Tacitus (or Eusebius's interpolation) treats Christianity as a disease that broke out in Judea due to the ineptitude of Tiberius Caesar's agent Pilate and spread to Rome due to the degeneracy of Nero, although I have suggested that he's talking about Judaism. The legendary Pharisee Gamaliel represents the Jewish position that Jews need do nothing about Christianity as it will fade away like the rebellions of Theudas and Judas. The author of *Acts* is being perhaps ironical knowing that Christianity did not pass away immediately, but it is quite probable that many Jews of the first and second century held this position that Christianity was a passing phenomenon of the moment.

It is difficult to get much knowledge of Christianity from these and similarly scattered sources outside the gospels, at least much knowledge beyond the fact that Christianity was considered to be a transitory phenomenon. The Christians thought the apocalypse would come any day and put an end to Christianity, while everyone else just thought it was a really bizarre cult. All the ancients, apparently even the Christians, if Eusebius is any clue, were surprised that it did not pass away.

One need not attribute this longevity to intrinsic supernatural characteristics. Rather one should consider the ability of the ideology to adopt to a variety of situations. This ability to adopt can be traced to its fortunate birth as the product of diverse cultures. Greek drama, Roman triumphalism and Jewish mysticism all meet in the gospels.

One might compare this to the James Bond movie phenomenon. Dozens of feature length spy, detective and secret agent movies were made in the decades of the 30's, 40's and 50's, but none were remotely as successful as James Bond who was a combination of many of these earlier characters[536]. His success led to the creation of hundreds of spy movies in the 1960's and early 1970's. All of these characters had a short life span of one or a few movies over a few years, but James Bond movies continued to be produced steadily for over 40 years. Future historians circa 4,000 CE might believe that the success of James Bond had something to do with a real James Bond who was the model for the movies. They might carefully sift through the movies to get clues to a real historical James Bond. One can imagine a liberal Bondian historian of the future saying, "Nobody believes the real James Bond smashed all the evil conspiratorial organizations that the movies portray, but there must have been a real James Bond who smashed at least one evil conspiratorial organization at some point in the late twentieth century." They might point to the fall of the Soviet Union as an act brought about by James Bond.

One can also imagine this not happening. There is no desire to historicize James Bond. It is hard to see a power base developing within a community that requires belief in an historical James Bond to continue to exist and expand. This was precisely the situation in the Christian communities: the belief in an historical Jesus was a necessary condition for the continuation of Christianity. That belief had to be generated by faith (command) for the evidence certainly did not exist.

The letter by Simon Peter gets to the heart of the situation and paradoxically the lack of any evidence for the human existence of Jesus Christ.

> **We did not follow cleverly invented stories when we told you about the power and coming of our Lord Jesus Christ, but we were eyewitnesses of his majesty.** [17]**For he received honor and glory from God the Father when the voice came to him from the Majestic Glory, saying, "This is my Son, whom I love; with him I am well pleased. "We ourselves heard this voice that came from heaven when we were with him on the sacred mountain**[537].

Looking at it critically, one can easily see the incredibility of Simon Peter's testimony. Indeed, the character is telling the truth when he says he has not followed cleverly invented stories. The use of the same adoption formula in a totally different setting, in the Baptism of Jesus stories in the gospels, shows the story to be a cliché. This is not a cleverly invented story, but a well known, old fashioned traditional story—man hears God speaking on mountaintop. Because it is so well known, not even the most minimal details are given. Who are the "we" who were with you? What were you doing on the sacred mountain? Which sacred mountain? This is not eyewitness testimony, but simply a reference to Hebrew Scriptures and prophetic tradition and a pronouncement of such testimony as being eyewitness. As an eyewitness testimony of a dream it is fine, but as eyewitness testimony of a history it is fantastic.

Also note, technically, this is not eyewitness testimony, but earwitness testimony. All that the speaker is saying is that God spoke to him like the prophets of old and that is how he knows that it is true. But almost immediately the speaker realizes that others who contradict him make the same claim of God-given knowledge.

> But there were also false prophets among the people, just as there will be false teachers among you. They will secretly introduce destructive heresies, even denying the sovereign Lord who bought them—bringing swift destruction on themselves. Many will follow their shameful ways and will bring the way of truth into disrepute[538].

Instead of explaining how his information is more trustworthy, he launches into an angry tirade denouncing other prophets. Basically he is just saying, believe me because I am a true prophet hearing the voice of God, while they are false prophets. It is not a rational argument, but a rhetorical performance. Celsus, a Roman Epircurean writing around 180 C.E., describes it well, "Christians weave together erroneous opinions drawn from ancient sources, and trumpet them aloud, and sound them before men, as the priests of Cybele clash their cymbals in the ears of those who are being initiated in their mysteries[539].

Such pre-gospel arguments as those found in the epistles of Paul and the other apostles were essentially demagogic and would hardly have been successful in the long run. Rather, the nurturing attitudes of a host of early women Christian leaders probably helped the Mystery Cults of Jesus Christ to be born, stay alive and grow in the early years. Celsus mentions five women as leaders of Jesus Christ Mystery Cults, Helene, Marcellina, Salome, Mariamme, and Martha:

> Certain Simonians exist who worship Helene, or Helenus, as their teacher, and are called Helenians, certain Marcellians, so called from Marcellina, and Harpocratians from Salome, and others who derive their name from Mariamme, and others again from Martha and Marcionites, whose leader was Marcion.

Men did take control of the Jesus Mystery Cults movement. Rewriting earlier material, they created the canonical gospels. The inclusion of numerous stories of Jesus' encounters with women probably reflects the earlier matriarchal period.

Possibly more than any other factor, around this time, 90-170 CE, the creation of biographies of the Man/God Jesus Christ in the gospels contributed to the popularity and longevity of the cult. Once the gospels were in place, an intellectual class (Tatian, Justin Martyr, Tertullian, Origen, Eusebius to name a few members of this class) rushed to the aid of the beleaguered Christians, developing increasingly sophisticated arguments, proving the historicity of the gospels, Jesus and other associated phenomena

In some sense the search for the historical Jesus movements in the 19th, 20th and now 21st centuries are the continuation of debates started around the gospels in the mid 2nd century. The crumbling and destabilization of the Roman Empire in the third century and, ironically, the seizure of power by Christians in the early fourth century suppressed the dialectical process that might have led to a better understanding of the Christian phenomenon.

Among other things, this work has analyzed just a small amount of material and concluded that a rather creative woman was responsible for the general form of the original story of the Word of God becoming Flesh. It also found that most of the words of Jesus, traditionally considered authentic and coming from an historical Jesus tradition, actually come from treatises originally written with John the Nazarene/Baptist as the speaker. It appears that disaffected elements from the John the Nazarene/Baptist community are responsible for much of the unique form and plot of the canonical gospels as we now have them. Finally, the Church of God possibly founded by James the Just, also played a significant role in creating the uniquely slave orientated ideology of Christianity. This is, at least to me, a unique and singularly important discovery.

Movies, Mickey Mouse and Jesus Christ: The Confusion of the *Sitz-Im-Leben* and the *Mise-en-Scene*

In his recent work, *The Christian Myth: Origins, Logic, and Legacy*, Burton L. Mack suggests radical reforms for not only the way we discuss early Christian history, but religion in general, and even socio-political relations today. It is a sweeping programatic vision of change that matches the divine madness of the early Christians he discusses.

Mack wrote in an earlier book called *Who Wrote the New Testament*[540] about the discovery that the earliest layer of the *Q* document surprisingly and strikingly revealed the influence of a cynic philosophy at the base of the Canonical Gospels. He finds that many historical Jesus researchers have been unable to account for this finding or "give a convincing account based on the narrative logic of the gospels[541]:

> "This must mean that the textual data for reconstructing the historical Jesus are inadequate or have been wrongly construed, or that the texts available for a reconstruction of the historical crucifixion are inadequate or wrongly construed. What if both sets of data are inadequte and incompatable because they are the products of early Christian mythmaking?

Mack believes many biblical scholars are dedicated to supporting the images of Jesus from the gospels. He derisively calls them "the Guild." Mack's findings of cynic philosophy at the base of the Canonical Gospels did not fit their gospel inspired notions of Jesus and therefore they ignored or rejected it. He notes:

> The catch-22 is that, for Christian mentality, the New Testament is taken as proof for the conventional picture of Christian origins, and the conventional picture is taken as proof for the way in which the New Testament came to be written[542].

In this case the scholars seem to be acting like Jesus when he says in John (18:18), "I bear witness to myself, and the Father who sent me bears witness to me." The gospels prove the historical Jesus and the historical Jesus accounts for there being gospels. As Mack writes in opposition to this circular methodology, "the critical scholar tries to account for the gospel story itself as one among many different myths of origin that emerged in the movements that claimed Jesus as their founder."

If I may generalize, the main problem is a fundamental misunderstanding of the social imaginary production process. It is a confusion of the Sitz-Im-Leben (the real life conditions of a work's production) with the Mise-En-Scene (the time-place setting within a work of art)

If I go to a movie such as Martin Scorsese's *Last Temptation of Christ*, or Mel Gibson's *Passion of Christ*, I know that I cannot use the images in it as evidence for the historical activities of Jesus Christ. Yet scholars find no problem using the images in the books of the *New Testament* as evidence for an historical Jesus Christ. They naively accept the mise-en-scene of these gospels and epistles as the setting and conditions for their production. It is quite like the thousands of people who confused Orson Wells' 1939 broadcast of H.G. Wells' "War of the Worlds" with a real Martian invasion. Unfortunately we are not born with a special sense that tells us what is human produced illusion and what is non-human nature produced reality, and the creases between them are sometimes quite difficult to discern. Nevertheless, we should recognize the books of the Bible as complex productions created for the entertainment and improvement by the social imagination and the protection/defense/desire of specific groups.

Chop up every frame of Scorsese or Gibson's movie and rearrange them anyway you like, you cannot provide any evidence from it for an historical Jesus Christ. Likewise chop up every word from the gospels (any version you wish) and rearrange them anyway you like and you cannot come up with any evidence for an historical Jesus Christ. This is because the gospels do not claim to be and are not historical records. This is not to say that such a technique is not helpful if used

THE EVOLUTION OF CHRISTS AND CHRISTIANIES

to understand the production of the work. For example, knowing that the writer of the *Gospel of Mark* relied on a text originally written for John the Baptist certainly helps us in reconstructing the production process. It is as if we had read a first draft of a script for the movie *Pirates of the Carribean*, and found that instead of both leading heroic characters of Jack Sparrow and Will Turner, there was only Will Turner. We learn about the development of the movie from this, but we learn nothing about the history of pirates from this. We learn about the development of the gospels by seeing developments within them, We do not learn about the lives of the people involved in the real early Christian movements.

It is when we imagine without any evidence that the lead gospel character Jesus Christ was really a cynic philosopher and that the writers of the gospels somehow got these cynical sayings from him that we cross the line from research to fantasy. It is like imagining that Moses told Cecil B DeMille how to stage the Red Sea Parting in *The Ten Commandments* or Luke Skywalker gave George Lucas his light saber to use in *Star Wars*.

A fine scholar, Gerd Lüdemann has produced a far more comprehensive work than this one, going over every line in the canonical Gospels, the *Gospel of Thomas*, and other apocryphal material and sifting out a number of sayings and actions of Jesus which he believes to be authentic. He has followed a very good and clear methodology. He lists the following six "Criteria of authenticity."

> *First*, many sayings and actions of jesus may be demonstrated to be authentic on the basis of the criterion of offensiveness . . .
>
> *Secondly*, the criterion of difference is a plausible way of discovering authentic Jesus material. Its use relates to the question of whether sayings and actions of Jesus can be derived from the post-Easter communities. If the answer to this is negative, when there is a difference between the communities and Jesus, the later may be taken to have spoken the words or performed the action in question. One example is Jesus' rejection of fasting, which differs from the community's later practice of fasting (cf. Mark 2.18-22).
>
> *Thirdly*, the criterion of growth offers a good opportunity to identify authentic Jesus material. The final form of a text can be compared with an onion from which one layer after another can be peeled. The older a unit of text is, the more densely it is covered with later tradition. There are examples of this in the ethical radicalisms of the Sermon on the Mount. Thus Jesus' absolute prohibition of swearing oaths (Matt. 5.34a) is supplemented with several instructions by 'Jesus' (Matt. 5.34b-37) which in fact result in the abolition of this prohibition.

> *Fourthly*, mention should be made of the criterion of rarity, which relates to those actions and sayings of Jesus that have few parallels in the Jewish sphere. Jesus' absolute prohibition against judging (Matt. 7.1) is a candidate for this.
>
> *Fifthly*, the criterion of wide attestation offers some assurance that sayings and actions of Jesus which are attested by sources independently of one another may be authentic.
>
> *Sixthly*, the criterion of coherence can be used to bring out authentic sayings of Jesus:in each instance this asks whether there is a seamless link between a particular statement or action and assured Jesus material.

Now all of these criteria are really quite reasonable. Put together, they do form a powerful tool of getting at a series of actions and sayings that seem to represent a different and earlier tradition about Jesus than the ones commonly represented in the gospel material.

The problem is that Lüdemann never asks the question if this is sufficient to reach an historical Jesus. Might not these criteria only give us an earlier characterization of a literary character? Lüdemann has accepted on faith, without examining the presupposition, that the earlier Jesus picture found would be the picture of a real character and not just another fictional construct representing a community.

This error is quite categorical. Using his criteria we may discover the historical Mickey Mouse. The original Mickey Mouse cartoon character of 1928 was rude. He played roughly and even sadistically with other cartoon characters. In the second Mickey Mouse cartoon, "Plane Crazy," he demands a kiss from Minnie Mouse, endangers her life to scare her when he does not get it, and finally just grabs her and kisses her. This is something the gentle and mild mannered "good host" Mickey Mouse of the 1940's and 1950's would never do. This fits the criteria of "offensiveness." This character is drawn differently, without shoes or gloves, and cannot be derived from the later Mickey Mouse cartoons or the community he inhabits. Thus, the second criterion of "difference" fits this early Mickey Mouse. Mickey certainly exhibits the third criteria of "growth" in the later cartoons, turning away from the nasty behavior that marks the earlier ones. The early Mickey also fits the "rarity" category, being one of the first talking animated cartoons and among the first to use camera movements. Fifthly, there is wide attestation that these are authentic Mickey Mouse cartoons by many independent sources. Sixthly, we certainly have seamlessness between the Mickey Mice portrayed in all these early cartoons. Under the six "Criteria of Authenticity," we have found the authentic Mickey Mouse. The problem is that Mickey Mouse is not an historical human being. It is a fictional character. As we saw, the popular comic/movie character Batman also evolved from the Bat of writer Mary Roberts Rinehart to the Bat-man of the comic book artist Bob Kane. The Bat is still not an historical person.

While the criteria used by Lüdemann and many other historical Jesus researchers is quite good for determining earlier from later material, it cannot distinguish between real and fictional characters. What we can get from this criteria are facts such as the fact that the Jesus character spoke through the voice of John the Baptist, just as the early Mickey Mouse cartoon character spoke with the voice of Walt Disney. The difference is we have historical evidence that Walt Disney existed, while we cannot tell if the earlier John the Baptist character existed.

Christ with Wand Performing Miracles.

Child-size sarcophagus from the Catacombs of Saint Callixtus, Rome, mid-4th century.

On the top level, two men are led to the heavenly throne of God which is surrounded by angels. One man carries a petition and the other carries an offering, perhaps a child in a cradle symbolizing the dead child. In the lower register, in the middle, a man prays. He is probably the father of the dead child. Two men, perhaps representatives of the Church instruct him. On the left and right we see what he is praying for. On the left, we have the miracle of Daniel and the Lion. God protected the naked Daniel from the lions. Probably this represents protection from the wild forces of nature. On the right, we see a Christ changing water to wine, possibly representing wealth. On the extreme right we have Christ raising Lazarus from the dead. It seems that the man in the middle is praying for protection, abundance and for his child to be brought back to life. At the extreme right a tiny figure, probably meant to represent both Mary and the man's wife is on her knees at the feet of the savior showing her devotion, and perhaps adding to the prayers of the man.

One can see the bargain that the man is making with God. He is giving the soul of the child in exchange for protection, wealth and a return to life after death. This was the deal that Christian Churches of the fourth century offered people. Many people thought it a good deal and bought it.

Chapter 15

Bringing It All Back Home

> Jesus taken serious by the many
> Jesus taken joyous by a few
>
> Leonard Cohen
> "Jazz Police"
> *I'm Your Man*, Sony CD (1988)

Good News: Jesus did not Die in the Original Story. Bad News: He Died in Real Life.

In chapter 3, we reconstructed the original ending of what we believe was the earliest gospel, a comedic play by a woman. We did not know then that the Jesus character was the son of Caiaphas. It is evident that the two women who prepared the body for burial were Simon's mother, Mary Caiaphas and his lover, Mary Magadalene. We can now fill in what we left blank and reconstruct the original ending.

Second Reconstruction of the UrTomb Scene

John 19.38. Later, Mary Caiaphas asked Pilate for the body of Jesus. With Pilate's permission, she came and took the body away.

39. She was accompanied by Mary, who earlier had visited Jesus at night[543]. Mary brought a mixture of myrrh and aloes, about seventy-five pounds.

40. Taking Jesus' body, the two of them wrapped it, with the spices, in strips of linen. This was in accordance with Jewish burial customs.

41. At the place where Jesus was crucified, there was a garden, and in the garden a new tomb, in which no-one had ever been laid.
42. Because it was the Jewish Passover and since the tomb was near by, they laid Jesus there. Then the Gardner rolled a stone against the entrance of the tomb.
Mark 15.47. Mary Magdalene and Mary Caiaphas saw where he was laid.
16.1. Mary Magdalene and Mary Caiaphas bought spices so that they might go to anoint Jesus' body
2. just after sunrise, they were on their way to the tomb and they asked each other, Who will roll the stone away from the entrance of the tomb?
John 20.1. Mary Magadalene went to the tomb and saw that the stone had been removed from the entrance.
2. So Mary, the one whom Jesus loved, came running to the other Mary, and said, "They have taken my Lord away, and I don't know where they have put him."
3. So Mary and Jesus' mother started for the tomb.
4. Both were running, but the mother outran Mary Magdalene and reached the tomb first.
5. She bent over and looked in at the strips of linen lying there but did not go in.
6. Then Mary, who was behind her, arrived and went into the tomb,. She saw the strips of linen lying there,
7. as well as the burial cloth that had been around Jesus' head. The cloth was folded up by itself, separate from the linen.
8. Finally, the mother who had reached the tomb first, also went inside. She saw and believed.
10. Then the mother went back to her home,
11. But Mary stood outside the tomb crying. As she wept, she bent over to look into the tomb
12. and saw two men in white, seated where Jesus' body had been, one at the head and the other at the foot.
13. They asked her, "Woman, why are you crying?"
"They have taken my Lord away," she said, and "I don't know where they have put him."
14. At this, she turned round and saw Jesus standing there, but she did not realise that it was Jesus.
15. Woman, he said, why are you crying? Who is it you are looking for? Thinking he was the gardener, she said, "Sir,

16. Jesus said to her, Mary. She turned towards him and cried out in Aramaic, "Rabboni! "(which means "Teacher"). She ran to him and kissed him, clasped his feet and worshipped him.

17. Jesus said, "Do not hold on to me, for I have not yet returned to the Father. Go instead to my brothers and tell them, 'I am returning to my Father and your Father, to my God and your God.'"

18. Mary Magdalene went to the disciples with the news: I have seen the Lord! And she told them that he had said these things to her. Mark 16.11. When they heard that Jesus was alive and that she had seen him, they did not believe it.

Note the words, "my father and your father" would refer to the living fathers of Jesus and Mary, the Jewish Chief Priests Caiaphas and Annas. By returning to them, Jesus, is returning to the fold and the God of the Samaritans and Jews, or as he puts it, "My God and your God." There is nothing supernatural going on here. The crucifixion was stopped before Jesus/Simon died. The two men at the tomb were not angels but priests sent by Caiaphas to revive his son.

Throughout this book, we have been getting two competing dates for the death of the messiah character. One is 36/37 and the other is 45. The earliest gospel texts seems to be giving us the date of around 36/37 for the crucifixion, and the historical texts, like *Josephus*, *Acts* and others seem to be giving us the date of 45. The best solution for the moment is that the actual Christ character, Simon bar Caiaphas, was executed in 45. On the other hand the play written by Mary (probably shortly thereafter) was set about a decade earlier in 36/37.

We may suggest that the play shyly left open the possibility that Simon although crucified might still be alive. This would certainly ease the pain of his distraught followers. The play also points to Mary as the legitimate heir and leader of whatever movement Simon led.

Evolution of the True Gospel

Examining the evolution of the early references for the term "gospel" may help us to see the evolution of Christianity itself. Here is a list showing the changing of the meanings of the term in the order and times that I believe they occurred:

o 20's: The term "gospel," (*evangel*, in Greek) if used in Judea at all in this period, probably refers to the announcement that the son of God and savior of the world, Augustus Caesar, has been born. The Priene inscription from 9 BCE reads:

> The providence which has ordered the whole of our life, showing concern and zeal, has ordained the most perfect consummation for human life by giving to it Augustus, by filling him with virtue for doing the work of a benefactor among men, and by sending in him, as it were, a saviour for us and those who come after us, to make war to cease, to create order everywhere . . . ; the birthday of the god [Augustus] was the beginning for the world of the glad tidings that have come to men through him.

- 30's: The *gospel* is the pronouncement by the prophet/priest John that God is coming to take over Judea and give birth to the Kingdom of God. This reflects a conservative priestly Jewish moment in opposition to Roman rule.
- 40's: The *gospel* is the news that the Kingdom of God is within all of us. It involves simplicity and getting back to nature and acting naturally. This reflects a liberal Hellenic-based movement, probably involving the followers of Simon Magus, including Mary and Thomas.
- Late 40's early 50's: The *gospel* means the idea that slaves can become sons of God and inherit the Kingdom of God in heaven after they die. This salvation involves strict obedience to authority and acceptance of punishment and suffering in this life. This reflects the Church of God or the Synagogue of Freedmen and its leader James the Just.
- Late 50's: The *gospel* is the birth announcement that an angel of the lord gives to John's mother Elizabeth that a prophet named John will be born. This will be changed a century and a half later into the birth announcement for Jesus Christ delivered to Mary.
- Circa 69: The *gospel* is the news that God is sending his chief angel Jesus to destroy the Romans and put an end to the current order of this world. It is the time of the Apocalypse. This reflects the desperate dreams of the Jewish-Christian rebels fighting a losing war against the much larger, better trained and more powerful Roman army.
- 70's: The *gospel* is the news that God himself punished the Jews for their disobedience by destroying the Jerusalem temple and selecting Vespasian to be Emperor of. (This is the gospel of Josephus).
- 80's: The *gospel* is the news that God crucified his chief angel Jesus while he was on Earth so that he may go down to hades and release the soles of the dead to live with him in Heaven. Jesus will return and judge the living and the dead in the final Apocalypse. This is the gospel of Paul and the international Church of God.
- 90's: The *gospel* is that the Jews and not God crucified Jesus on Earth and for this reason, he destroyed Jerusalem and its temple.

- Late 90's: The *gospel* is the record of Jesus the Christ on Earth from the time he entered the body of a follower of John the Baptist to the time he was crucified. This is the *gospel* of the writer of the *Gospel of Mark*.
- Early 100's The *gospel* is any story of the Christ on Earth
- Early 200's: The *gospel* is each of the four "gospels" of the followers of Jesus: John, Mark, Matthew, and Luke.
- Late 200's and early 300's: The *gospel* is the text of the New Testament, including the four canonical *gospels*, *Acts of the Apostles*, *Book of Revelation*, *Epistles of Paul, James, John, Jude, Peter* and *Barnabus*, and *the Shepherd of Hermas*.
- Mid 300's: The *gospel* is the text of the New Testament minus the *Epistle of Barnabus* and *the Shepherd of Hermas*.

Basis for a New Interpretation of Early Christian Development

I originally divided this text into five main sections corresponding to five main hypotheses. Thus we have the *Eusebis Master Forger* hypothesis, *Mary Author of Passion Comedy* hypothesis, the *Jesus Words in Matthew Came from John the Nazarene* hypothesis, the *Simon Magus Jesus Model* hypothesis and *James, the Just's Church of God Slave Indoctrination School* hypothesis. We met a number of other important hypotheses along the way.

Here is a time table of the main events developed out of these hypotheses:

- **Circa 35 C.E.** From Josephus, we get the story that a follower of Moses, and possibly a high priest was thrown out of Judea for breaking Jewish laws. He went to Rome and flimflammed the wife of a leading Roman Citizen into supplying him with clothes and possibly money to produce a scam in Jerusalem. Although the man's name has been erased from this text, we may conclude from a reconstruction and other evidence that the man's name was very possibly John.
- **Circa 37.** Josephus tells us that this man lead Samaritans on Mount Gezzerim in an armed uprising of some sort. It was attacked and put down by Pontius Pilate. Herod the Tetrarch had the man executed at Macherus fearing his growing popularity.
- **Circa 45/46.** According to Josephus, two leading Jews, James and Simon are executed. I suggest that these were sons of the high priest Joseph Caiaphas. Our reconstruction of the gospel texts indicates that a woman (possibly named Mary, and possibly the daughter of a Jewish high priest) apparently wrote an allegorical comic play in which she describes the word of God coming to Earth and possessing the real son of the Jewish High Priest Caiaphas, Simon bar Caiaphas. In the play, Mary Magdalene is the wife of Caiaphas and stepmother of this Jewish Savior. She carries on a secret love affair with him. When the

Savior becomes popular, Caiaphas tricks Pilate into crucifying his son in order to unite the people of Judea against the Romans. While undergoing arrest and crucifixion, the Savior accidentally goes through a ceremony that makes him King of the Jews. Apparently, the crucifixion was not supposed to be a real sacrifice, but a subterfuge, a clever plan by Caiaphas to get rid of Pontius Pilate. Mary sees him alive again at the tomb. The disciples do not believe her when she tells them this. The audience for the play, having seen Jesus and Mary together at the tomb, knows she is telling the truth. If the authoress did have a real life model in mind for the main character, it was most probably Simon bar Caiaphas who probably should also be associated with Simon Magus, the Samaritan magician.

- **Circa 46-2005.** Multiple Gnostic-Mystery cults grow from the material in Mary's play, including orthodox Christianity.
- **Circa 40-52 C.E.** The Church of God, possibly formed out of the Synagogue of the Freedmen becomes active throughout the Roman World. James the Just seems to have been associated with this group. They seem to have started out as a Jewish task force designed to aid widows. They seem to have adopted Joshua Nun (Jesus Christ) as their primary hero, asserting that he had been raised to heaven after his death and would return. At some point after the Roman War, they claimed that the destruction of the temple was due to the Jews killing the prophet James the Just.
- **Circa 37-65.** The executed John the Nazarene develops a cult following who practice daily bathing rituals and soon call him John the Baptist. He is considered a great prophet. They create or perhaps record his sayings and ideas. A faction of the group develops the idea that he was the Jewish prophet Elijah reincarnated. Soon, another section of the group proclaims him the Christ (Messiah).
- **Circa 62-66.** Mary's scandalous play gets rewritten as a straight narrative by a follower of John the Nazarene. Mary's role gets minimized. This is the basis for the *Gospel of John*. It probably contained more material that the writer of the *Gospel of Mark* has hijacked, either using it in his own work or destroying it.
- **Circa 90-100.** A scribe from Capernaum secretly writes a revised Gospel by expanding a small number of sayings and counter-sayings probably from the two John the Baptist factions and cutting it into a reduced version of the *Gospel of John*. He makes the Jesus character into a Galilean from the town of Capernaum. He adds in material from the later parts of Mary's play, again using the *Gospel of John* as his guide.
- **Circa 95-150.** The author of the *Gospel of Matthew* adds a long speech (called perhaps *The Sayings of John the Nazarene,*" and some other material to the gospel of Mark and comes up with a more popular gospel. He changes the expression

Jesus the Nazarene to *Jesus from Nazareth*. Most of the sayings of Jesus in this gospel come from sayings originally written for John the Nazarene.
- **Circa 140-175**. The writer of Luke writes a gospel appealing to a more cosmopolitan, international and Roman audience. It is very possible that Marcion wrote the original using the previous three gospels of John, Mark, Matthew and his own material.
- **Circa 210**. The birth of Jesus tale gets added at the beginning of Luke and Matthew, probably introduced by the North African writer Tertullian. Also added is the first draft of *Acts of the Apostles*, probably a drastic revision of the history of Justus of Tiberius. The names of many characters are changed to try and get the material to match the gospel stories and epistles of Paul.
- **Circa 300-335**. Eusebius creates a *History* based on forged documents, interpolations, and misguided interpretations. We may assume he creates it specifically for the Emperor Constantine. His purpose is to show that the Roman Catholic Church is the only true church directly transmitting the words and spirit of Jesus the Christ. Also at this time, Eusebius probably edits other historical works by different authors, including Josephus' works, to give a new Christian interpretation to events.

This hopefully provides a solid working alternative to the widely accepted, but fantastic Eusebean version of early Christian history. Admittedly, this version depends heavily on deconstructing much early material, but we should keep in mind that the well-documented destruction, both purposeful and accidental, of much material from this period. This makes such a deconstructive process, followed by a reconstructive process absolutely necessary for a real understanding of the period. Without doing this hard work, we cannot hope to get a reasonable understanding of the complex evolution of the Christs and Christianities from this time period. I hope others will build on this foundation as I have built on the foundation of others.

We are acting naively if we look to the *New Testament* to provide us with evidence for the existence of a single church or a biography of its founder. Like, Eusebius, we must ignore or misunderstand a great deal of it to use it in this fashion. Instead, we may open our eyes and see that it provides excellent evidence for the evolution of abstract theoretical concepts like *Christ, Jesus, messiah, son of God* and *God*, and their use among people living at those times and places. It also provides evidence of the diverse groups that used these terms to gain social power. Taken together with the mass of non-Biblical evidence, we can determine the different attitudes, social conditions and perhaps, finally, the precise interactions of these groups. When we have done this, we will able to provide a much truer and more accurate history of this period.

At the end of the day, we have found three interesting groups. The first were followers of the Samaritan Simon Magus, including an important woman writer probably named Mary, who probably did not believe in any future Kingdom of God or Christ, but believed that Simon was the word of God incarnate and that the Kingdom of God was within us. In her comic play, Simon, the son of the Jewish High Priest Caiaphas claimed to be the Christ. He had an affair with Mary, the daughter of Annas, who was the second wife of Caiaphas. Caiaphas found out and turned him over to the Romans for crucifixion. He underwent a mock coronation and crucifixion, whereby he ended up becoming king of the Jews. At the same time, we found baptizing followers of a high priest named John who believed that Elijah would be the future returning Christ, although some of his followers came to believe that John himself had been the Christ and would return. Lastly, we found the followers of the Church of God and James the Just who believed that Joshua of Nun would be the coming Christ. It is out of the struggles and interactions of these three major groups that the the complex character of Jesus the Christ/Jesus of Nazareth developed.

We end with a straight answer to the question "Was Jesus of Nazareth a myth or an historical figure?" The answer is that Simon bar Caiaphas seems to be the name of the real historical character that the earliest layer of the gospel text refers to. However, when we talk about all the layers of the gospels, we have to say that Jesus was a fictional character in a series of first and/or early-to-mid second century literary works. The final character was constructed as a blend of at least four prior literary characters: Joshua of Nun, Simon Magus, John the Baptist, and James the Just. It is difficult to determine if any or all of these four Christ characters were based on living people or were simply literary characters. Based on our reconstructions, it seems most probable that they were literary characters, but meant to be references to actual, well-known living people. The names, words, deeds, actions and events associated with these people were drastically and repeatedly changed for dramatic and theological purposes.

ENDNOTES

1. Santayana, George, *The Philosophy of Santayana*, "Reason in Religion," edited with an introductory essay by Irwin Edman, Modern Library, 1936, pg. 167.
2. Myers, Ernest, *The Extant Odes of Pindar Translated Into English*, 1904, retrieved August 26, 2004 on The Project Gutenberg EBook of *The Extant Odes of Pindar, by Pindar*. Release Date: January 14, 2004 [EBook #10717], http://www.gutenberg.net/dirs/1/0/7/1/10717/10717-8.txt
3. Tertullian, De praescriptione haereticorum, 18. (Holmes' translation)
4. *Catholic Encyclopedia*, "Eusebius," Retrieved September 20, 2004, http://www.newadvent.org/cathen/05617b.htm.
5. It is quite coincidental that in each case these women are named Mary or have names derived from Mary. I chose them based on their work and the importance of their contributions, not their names. My explanation for this phenomenon is that the name "Mary" was closely associated with the Virgin Mary and the concepts of virtue and honor at the time of their childhoods, and thus they were more likely to choose the path of authorship, which was also associated with virtue and honor.
6. Kaufmann, Walter, *Tragedy and* Philosophy, Princeton University Press, New Jersey, 1979.
7. Eisenman, Robert, James the Brother of Jesus, Penguin Books, New York, 1997, pp. 140, 141-145, et al.
8. Since Tertullian does not seem to know about this scene when he explains the calling of Jesus' family to him, we may suspect that Tertullian himself, sometime after writing *De Carne Christi* in the early third century rewrote this scene in the *Gospel of Luke* to rehabilitate Mary. He apparently created and/or developed the notion that Mary was the new Eve. Therefore he would have a motive for wanting to rehabilitate her.
9. H.E., 1:4.
10. *Theophania* 5:48-49.
11. The rumor that Eusebius was a slave of Pamphilius should perhaps be taken seriously. His rise from slave to head of a prominent Christian church would explain his sympathy for rags to riches stories that he finds in the Gospels and repeats in his *History*.

[12] H.E., 1:1-3.
[13] Chadwick, Henry, *the Church in Ancient Society*, Oxford University Press, 2002, p. 186.
[14] Barnes, Timothy, *Eusebius and Constantine*, Cambridge, Harvard University Press, 1981, pp. 277,278.
[15] H.E., 1:5.
[16] Ibid. 2:3.1-2.
[17] Barnes, Constantine and Eusebius, pg. 142.
[18] H.E., 1:13.5.
[19] Bauer, Walter, *Orthodoxy and Heresy In Earliest Christianity, Translated and supplemented under the direction of Robert A. Kraft and Gerhard Kroedel (Philadelphia: Fortress 1971)from the 2nd German edition edited and supplemented by Georg Strecker(Tübingen: J.C.B.Mohr 1964 [original ed 1934]); electronic edition periodically updated by Robert A. Kraft (since 1993).* Viewed January 02, 2005, http://ccat.sas.upenn.edu/rs/rak/publics/new/BAUER01.htm
[20] Sidney Griffith of the Catholic University of America gives a similar assessment that this work is based on Eusebius and not a Eusebean source in a recent detailed examination of this text. Griffith, Sidney H., "The *Doctrina Addai* as a Paradigm of Christian Thought in Edessa in the Fifth Century," from Hugoye: Journal of Syriac Studies, Vol. 6, No. 2, July 2003. Viewed January 02, 2005, http://syrcom.cua.edu/Hugoye/Vol6No2/HV6N2Griffith.html
[21] This also explains similar changes we find in Eusebius to works like Josephus' *Antiquities* and Tertullian's *Apology*. The alternative explanation that we find in each case that Eusebius was the dupe of earlier unknown Christian forgers and the works underwent further changes at the hands of unknown later Christian forgers I consider an ad hoc apologetic defense of Eusebius. Bauer ends up blaming Eusebius' contemporary, Bishop Kûnê of Edessa, for the forgery. This would be credible if so much other material in Eusebius did not present similar problems.
[22] *H.E.*, 1:13.5.
[23] I believe Eusebius added the phrase "so-called brother of the lord" to the James text in Josephus (*Antiquities* 20:9.1). Logically reconstructing the passage, the James mentioned originally by Josephus apparently was the brother of Jesus Damneus. Eusebius uses the phrase "James, the so-called brother of the lord" in H.E. 4:5.5 Like the Testimonium Flavorium, Eusebius is the first in history to mention this passage (H.E. 2:23.3 and 2:23.21) He also talks about the "so-called epistle of James (H.E. 3:25.3)."
[24] Ibid. 2:1.4.
[25] Ibid.1:12.1-3.
[26] Ibid. 9:2.3.
[27] *Stromata* 1.1.
[28] Ibid. 6.8.
[29] Acts 6:2.
[30] Ibid. 6:8.

31 "If therefore any one should, after all this, impugn the truth and dare disingenuously to affirm, that the Christ of God was not (such) as we believe He was, but was a magician, seducer, and impostor; we would present to him, as an infant in mind, those things which we also formerly investigated..." *Theophania*, 5.1.
32 Josephus, *Wars*, 4:5.2.
33 Ibid. 4:5.4.
34 H.E., 2:22.16-20.
35 Ibid. 2:23.1.
36 It is hard to know if Eusebius has wholly made up the text of Hegessipus or has drastically changed the text of a real historian to reflect his point of view. Since nobody else mentions Hegesippus before Eusebius and it is difficult to say if anybody ever read him after Eusebius, the more sober judgment for the moment is that he never existed. Eusebius is just taking text from other sources to create him.
37 One may counter that the text of Origin also contains references to this James death responsibility passage in Josephus. We may suggest that placing these passages in Origin was a simple and necessary task, in case copies of *Wars* were discovered showing Ananus rather than James in the honored position.
38 H.E., 3:11.1-2.
39 Ibid. 3:22.
40 Ibid. 1:2.
41 Ibid. 4:22.2.
42 Ibid. 3:20.1-8.
43 Ibid. 3:32.3.
44 Ibid. 3:32.6.
45 Ibid. 3:11.2-12.
46 Ibid. 3:17.
47 One may suppose that Domitian was made heavy in Eusebius' novel because Tertullian describes him as persecuting Christians. However, as we shall see later, there is good evidence that Eusebius inserted that passage into Tertullian's *Apology*.
48 Ibid. 3:35.
49 Ibid. 5:-4.
50 Ibid. 5:22.
51 Ibid. 5:23.2.
52 Ibid. 6:19.17.
53 Ibid. 6:27.1.
54 Ibid. 6:46.3.
55 Ibid. 7:32.21.
56 Ibid. 8:3.1.
57 Ibid. 4:30.1
58 Ibid. 4:31.2-3
59 Ibid. 3:31.5.

[60] Ibid. 2:25.6.
[61] Acts 6.5.
[62] Ibid. 21:7-12.
[63] Ibid. 8:3-6.
[64] H.E., 4:31.2-3
[65] Acts 13.5-12.
[66] Ibid. 10.
[67] Acts, 8:5.
[68] Ibid. 11:19-20.
[69] Ibid. 23:25-33.
[70] Romans 15:19
[71] Barnes, *Constantine and Eusebius*, pg. 141.
[72] *H.E.*, 6:14.10.
[73] *Praeparatio*, 7.22.
[74] *H.E.*, 5:27.
[75] Origen, *The Philocalia of Origen: A Compilation of Selected Passages From Origen's Works Made by St. Gregory of Nazianzus and St. Basil of Caesarea*, Translated into English by Rev. George Lewis, Printed by Morrison and Gibb Limited for T. & T. Clark, Edinburgh, London: Simpkin, Marshall, Hamilton, Kent, and Co. Limited, New York: Charles Scribner's Sons, 1911. Viewed January 10, 2005, http://www.tertullian.org/fathers/origen_philocalia_01_intro.htm.
[76] *H.E.*, 6:23.4.
[77] Ibid. 6:32.3.
[78] *Praeparatio*, 6:10.
[79] The same passages on matter are found in a work attributed to Methodius., a bishop contemporary with Eusebius. It is difficult to say how this came about. Was someone trying to discredit Methodius, a known enemy of Origen by suggesting that he plagiarized his work? In any case, it suggests how one piece of writing can be assigned to three different people, thus tripling the number of Christian writers on a subject, and making the early Church seem more literate than it was.
[80] Post-Nicene Fathers, Series II, Volume III, *Translation of Pamphilus' Defence of Origen, Rufinus's Epilogue to Pamphilus the Martyr's Apology for Origen, Rufinus's Apology in Defense of Himself, The Apology of Rufinus, Jerome's Apology for Himself Against the Books of Rufinus*, and *Jerome Letter LXXXIV*.
[81] *H.E.*, 6:33.4.
[82] Jerome, Letter LXXXIV.
[83] Jerome, *Jerome's Apology for Himself Against the Books of Rufinus*, 8.
[84] Ibid. 9
[85] Jerome, Illustrious Men, LXXV.
[86] Blavatsky, Helena Petrovna, *Apollonius Tyaneus and Simon Magus, Theosophist*, June 1881, retrieved June 12, 2005 from http://theosophy.org/tlodocs/hpb/ApolloniusTyaneusAndSimonMagus.htm.

87 For example, here is Walter Bauer's defense. "Although we cannot be absolutely sure from his statement that he himself had translated the material from the Syriac, we can be certain that the material was given to him with the express assurance that it came from the public records of Edessa. It is well to note that it is not Jerome or some other questionable person that is speaking here, but a man whose devotion to truth and whose honesty are above suspicion. Thus for me, what he describes to be the state of affairs is reliable." Bauer, Walter, *Orthodoxy and Heresy in Earliest Chritianity*, Fortress Press, Philadelphia, 1971, pg. 15.

88 Eusebius, *Ecclesiastical History*, 2:2.6.

89 Barnes, Constantine and Eusebius, Harvard University Press, 1981, pp. 40-141.

90 H.E,.2:7.

91 K. A. Olson, "Eusebius and the *Testimonium Flavianum*," *Catholic Biblical Quarterly*, 61 (1999): 305-322. Also online, Olson, Ken, *Eusebian Fabrication of the Testimonium*, 2001, retrieved November 10, 2004, at. http://f4.grp.yahoofs.com/v1/IHsDQyIFp-ce0I3z4_DLlyL664tb1OCO6sEJ9pPPmF4oKFPYXeO00waWQ4_XtAhsfJydcy4RFVHFld21YYMO/%22Eusebian%20Fabrication%20of%20the%20Testimonium%22

92 Ferguson, Everett, *Christian History*, "The Problem of Eusebius," Nov, 2001, Vol. 20 Issue 4, p8, 4p, 6c

93 Holmes, David, *Stylometry: Its Origins, Development and Aspirations*, viewed November 10, 2004 on http://www.cs.queensu.ca/achallc97/papers/s004.html

94 Eusebius, *Theophania*, Book 4.1.

95 Ibid. 5:45.

96 The little detail of an orthodox Christian Church functioning in Jerusalem for some 100 years after the death of Christ is one that Josephus and every other writer before Eusebius failed to notice. There is no evidence that such a church existed beyond the word of Eusebius. He repeats this in *H.E.* (4::5.1), listing the names without giving any source.

97 Note the popularity of Apollonius. Apparently, it was so great that Eusebius felt compelled to write a treatise specifically against him. Robin Lane Fox points to an Oracle at Oenoanda, where a man asks Apollo if he could come near to the Gods through self examination and gets the reply that this privilege belongs only to "Egyptian Hermes, "Moses of the Hebrews" and "the wise man of the Mazacenes." The last epithet is a reference to Apollonius. Thus we find that at least one priest thought Apollonius to be the equivalent of Moses and Hermes Trismegistus. Fox, Robin Lane, *Pagans and Christians*, Alfred Knopf, New York, 1986, pg. 191.

98 Eusebius, *The Treatise of Eusebius, the Son of Pamphilus, Against the Life of Apollonius of Tyana Written by Philostratus, Occasioned by the Parallel Drawn By Hierocles Between Him and Christ*, VII.

99 Ibid. 3:31.

100 Ibid. 4:16.

101 Ibid. 5:52.

102 Eusebius, *Demonstratio Evangelica*, 1.1.

[103] H.E., 1:1.5.
[104] Ibid. 1:3.19.
[105] Ibid. 2:1.7.
[106] Ibid. 2:25.5.
[107] Ibid. 3:39.6.
[108] Ibid. 4.23.9.
[109] Ibid. 4:3.1.
[110] Ibid. 4:3.3.
[111] Ibid. 4:24.3. Tertullian writes a five-book work against Marcion in 207 C.E. If Theophilus whom Eusebius says was a Bishop of Antioch in 169 C.E. wrote a book against Marcion, it is surprising that Tertullian does not mention him. In fact, nobody quotes anything from this book against Marcion.
[112] Ibid. 5:23.1.
[113] Ibid. 7:18.2.
[114] Ibid. 7:19.1.
[115] Ibid. 7:32.29.
[116] Ibid. 1:11.7-8.
[117] Ibid. 4:8.3.
[118] Ibid. 4:8.2.
[119] Ibid. 2:23.4.
[120] Eusebius will forget he has told us this and assign his historian Hegesippus to the late second century later in his History. As nobody ever read and quoted this first Christian Historian before Eusebius, and it seems probable that nobody read him afterwards, we must assign Hegesippus to the category of fictional characters.
[121] Ibid. 4:3.1.
[122] Ibid. 4:11.9.
[123] Ibid. 5:8.6.
[124] Perhaps the Emperor Severus.
[125] Ibid. 5:28.8.
[126] Ibid. 5:5.1.
[127] Ibid. 5:5.5-6.
[128] Tertullian, *Apology*, Chapter 5.
[129] Ibid. 6:42.3.
[130] Ibid. 7:11.25.
[131] Ibid. 10:5.23.
[132] Ibid. 1:9.2-3. One may suspect that Eusebius has forged this information too into Josephus.
[133] Ibid. 9:5.
[134] Ibid. 9:7.1.
[135] After refuting a long list of attacks against Jesus and the Apostles, in Theophania (1-43), Eusebius quotes Josephus's *Testimonium*. Since he refutes the *Acts of Pilate and Jesus* text by quoting the same passage from Josephus, one may suppose it likely that the attacks

136. *Theophania*, 5:8.
137. Ibid. 5:33.
138. *Ad Martyres, Ad Nationes, Ad Scapulam, Ad Uxorem, Adversus Hermogenem, Adversus Iudaeos, Adversus Marcionem, Adversus Praxean, Adversus Valentinianos, Apologeticum, De anima, De Baptismo, De Carne Christi, De Corona Militis, De Cultu Feminarum, De Exhortatione Castitatis, De Fuga in Persecutione, De Idololatria, De Ieiunio Adversus Psychicos, De Monogamia, De Oratione, De Paenitentia, De Pallio, De Patientia, De Praescriptione Haereticorum, De Pudicitia, De Resurrectione Carnis, De Spectaculis, De Testimonio Animae, De Virginibus Velandis, Scorpiace,* found at *http://www.tertullian.org/*
139. *Address to Martyrs*, VI.
140. *Adversus Judaeos*, 13.
141. *De spectaculis*, VI.
142. *De virginibus velandis*, III.1.
143. *Apologeticum*, V.
144. If Justin Martyr had written any *Apology*, one would expect Tertullian to mention it or quote from it in his Apology. He does not. Could an educated Christian writing an apology to an emperor be unaware that another Christian had written an apology to the emperor fifty years before?
145. Tacitus, *Annals*, 15.44.
146. Suetonius, *Lives*, Nero, 16.
147. Suetonius does say "As the Jews were making constant disturbances at the instigation of Chrestus, he expelled them from Rome," *The Life of Claudius*, 25.4. This may be a changed or inserted reference to Christ and may mean Christians. It think this is highly probable, but let us for the moment treat it as just a reference to Jews.
148. Severus, Sculpitius, *Sacred History*, Book 2, chap. 29.
149. Doughty, Darrell, *Tacitus' Account of Nero's Persecution of Christians*, retrieved January 14, 2005, http://www.courses.drew.edu/sp2000/BIBST189.001/Tacitus.html
150. A Christian would be unlikely to use the term extreme penalty in reference to the execution of Jesus, so we may suppose the interpolator found it there.
151. Josephus, *Ant.*, 20:8.5. *Yet did Felix catch and put to death many of those impostors every day, together with the robbers.* Unlike the Prefect Pontius Pilate, Porcius Festus was a "procurator." We may note also that Tacitus was writing "Annals" accounts of events year by year. He would have been likely to have included a reference to Pilate in an earlier book. One would have expected Tacitus to refer back to this earlier mention. He does not.
152. A Chirstian would have referred to Bethlehem or Nazareth as the source of Christianity. We may suppose that the term Judea was in the original.
153. Tacitus, *Annals*, 15:43.
154. H.E., 2:25.2.
155. Ibid. 10:9.5-9.

[156] See Clement of Alexandria's Stromata, Book III, for a description of the Carpocratean free sex ideology.
[157] Fox, Robin Lane, *Pagans and Christians*, Alfred A. Knopf, Inc. New York, 1989, pg. 309.
[158] Ibid. pg. 310.
[159] This is the original Nicene Creed as presented by Eusebius of Caesarea, a man who was extremely influential in creating the official history of Christianity. Note that it contains no mention of Mary, and the only suggestion of an historical Jesus is the phrase "lived and suffered amongst men" which can just as well refer to a God. (from *Nicene and Post Nicene Fathers, Series II, Vol XIV*, retrieved August 31, 2004, http://www.ccel.org/fathers2/NPNF2-14/Npnf2-14-10.htm#P522_112870:

> We believe in one only God, Father Almighty, Creator of things visible and invisible; and in the Lord Jesus Christ, for he is the Word of God, God of God, Light of Light, life of life, his only Son, the first-born of all creatures, begotten of the Father before all time, by whom also everything was created, who became flesh for our redemption, who lived and suffered amongst men, rose again the third day, returned to the Father, and will come again one day in his glory to judge the quick and the dead. We believe also in the Holy Ghost We believe that each of these three is and subsists; the Father truly as Father, the Son truly as Son, the Holy Ghost truly as Holy Ghost; as our Lord also said, when he sent his disciples to preach: Go and teach all nations, and baptize them in the name of the Father, and of the Son, and of the Holy Ghost.

[160] The discussion of the text, "The Apocalypse of John" by Dionysius in Eusebius's *History* (7.25) reveals that the New Testament Canon had not been adopted before 250 C.E. Around this time, Dionysius writes, "But I could not venture to reject the book, as many brethren hold it in high esteem." It is apparent that Bishops in each city in the third century chose their own texts and there was no question of a fixed canon. The Muratorian Canon fragment which placed the canon in the second century for most scholars in the twentieth century has now been traced to the fourth century. See Hahneman, Geoffrey Mark, *The Muratorian Fragment and the Development of the Canon* (Clarendon Press, Oxford, 1992), Numerous websites still use it to prove an early canon and a Big Bang type development of Christianity.
[161] If this alternative history had a creed, it would be, "I believe Jesus Christ was written about by a woman, possibly named Mary, shortly after the time of Pontius Pilate. Her texts were crucified (edited, to be less dramatic) as part of the complex development of the Christian Religion and the Jesus Mythology . . . " Through deconstruction, figuring out how the Gospel texts were constructed, we can recognize her work again, and perhaps write a truer history of the development of early Christianity.
[162] Tertullian, *De praescriptione haereticorum*, 30

163. Ibid. 37
164. Tertullian, *Adversus Marcionem*, 5.1.
165. Ibid. 5.4.
166. Ibid.
167. Ibid. 5.14.
168. Ibid. 5.17.
169. Ibid. 5.18.
170. Ibid. 5.31.
171. Ibid. 5.13.
172. H.E., 4.20.
173. *Adversus Marcionem*, 4.5. Ernest Evans translation, Oxford University Press, 1972.
174. Possibly inserted by Tertullian himself.
175. Again, these three lists are possibly inserted by Tertullian himself.
176. Ibid. 4.4.
177. *Adversus Praxean*, 1.
178. *De ieiunio adversus psychicos*, 10.
179. *De carne Christi*, 20, 22.
180. Doherty, Earl, *The Jesus Puzzle: Did Christianity Begin with a Mythical Christ?*, Canadian Humanist Publications, 1999.
181. Origen, *Commentary on John*, Book I 7.
182. He also takes great pains to suppress an earlier narrative that he is using and revising. This earlier gospel seems to have been written by a woman and has a woman named Mary as the true lover and disciple of the Word of God in human form. We will demonstrate this later.
183. For example, the beginnings of the Gospels may be said to be John-the-Baptist-centered
184. Wikipedia, the free encyclopedia, viewed Decemeber 16, 2004, http://en.wikipedia.org/wiki/Damnatio_memoriae
185. Wikipedia,, Retrieved Decemeber 16, 2004, http://en.wikipedia.org/wiki/Hatshepsut
186. While it does not explicitly say that Peter was afraid in this scene, the fact that he called down curses upon himself and swore that he did not know Jesus would tend to indicate that he was afraid. Admittedly, one may read the scene as him being cool and clever.
187. Jesus tells the man just to tell his family what God has done for him. Instead, he spreads the word about Jesus throughout the whole region of Decapolis.
188. Here Jesus lies to the crowd that the child is asleep. He does not even trust all his disciples with the secret of his resurrection power, only taking Peter, James and John with him.
189. Pilate probably represents a typical Roman, who, having heard that the Jews awaited a Messiah, would be quite surprised to hear the secret that he was already dead.
190. Jesus dies in secret, his death only witnessed by a single Christian Centurion and some of his women followers from a distance.
191. The burial place is also a secret, known only by a Christian named Joseph and the women followers of Jesus.

[192] Justin Martyr, *Dialogue with Trypho*, 108.

[193] It appears that Celsus, writing sometime between 150-180 was aware of the Gospel of Matthew and Gospel of John endings, "there came an angel to the tomb of this said being—according to some, indeed, one, but according to others, two—who answered the women that he had arisen. For the Son of God could not himself, as it seems, open the tomb, but needed the help of another to roll away the stone." From Origen, *Against Celsus*, 1.52. Mark has one man at the tomb, Matthew has one angel, Luke has two men and John has two angels.

[194] Theissen, Gerd, *The Gospels in context*, T. & T. Clark Publishers, 1999, pp 167-168.

[195] Hale, Sarah Josepha, *The Juvenile Miscellany*, September/October, 1830, retrived May 23, 2005 from *Recess* on the internet at http://www.recess.ufl.edu/transcripts/2003/1029.shtml

[196] Deut 21:23.

[197] Richard Carrier in *Jewish Law, the Burial of Jesus, and the Third Day* suggests this is exactly what must have happened. Retrieved July 7, 2004, http://www.secweb.org/asset.asp?AssetID=125#3. It is a far more plausible interpretation in light of the Jewish legal requirement which he notes that executed criminals be buried in a special graveyard.

[198] Matthew 28.9.

[199] Mark also inserts an odd scene in which Jesus arrives at the temple too late to do anything. This seems to have more to do with Mark often being personally late or perhaps fearing he is too late in writing this text to do much good. In any case, lateness, like fear of God and silence is an odd motif that we have to associate with Mark's personality rather than any objective narrative needs.

[200] Act 1, Scene 5.

[201] In Mark's revision of the story, this line makes no sense. Why did the women go to the tomb if they knew there was a stone in front of the tomb that they could not move? In fact, the stone would have been relatively small to cover a small entrance. Here the question means which of the women are going to move the stone. Mary volunteers. This shows Mary as a take charge kid of person. It is meant to show Mary as the leader of the group.

[202] The original in John has Mary say, "They have taken the Lord out of the tomb, and we don't know where they have put him!" Since Mary has not been in the tomb to see the Lord has been taken out this cannot be the original line. The line that Mary says to the angels later on, "They have taken my Lord away, and I don't know where they have put him," seems to fit perfectly. John has changed the "I" to "we" just as he has pluralized the number of Marys in the scene. When we reconstruct the line this way, we see that it is actually quite affecting that Mary repeats the same line twice, first to her two companions and then to the two angels. It indicates that she is in shock and just repeats the same sad lines over and over.

[203] John 12.3.

[204] There is nothing to suggest that this visit did not take place the previous night. This suggests that a scene took place after the arrest of Jesus where Mary went to visit him.

THE EVOLUTION OF CHRISTS AND CHRISTIANIES

205 Tertullian, *de spectaculis*, 30. One should note Tertullian's list carefully. They show that many Jewish objections were incorporated into later additions of the Gospels and answered.

206 James, M.R. (Trans), *The Apocryphal New Testament*, Oxford: Clarendon Press, 1924, *The Book of the Resurrection of Christ by Bartholomew the Apostle.*

207 Mark 14:58.

208 The author of *Refutation of All Heresies* (in Book 5:1) tells us about an early Christian group the Nassenes who had a saying also relating a son in a half relationship to a father, "And concerning this (nature) they hand down an explicit passage, occurring in the Gospel inscribed according to Thomas, expressing themselves thus: "He who seeks me, will find, me in children from seven years old; for there concealed, I shall in the fourteenth age be made manifest." This, however, is not (the teaching) of Christ, but of Hippocrates, who uses these words: "A child of seven years is half of a father." And so it is that these (heretics), placing the originative nature of the universe in causative seed, (and) having ascertained the (aphorism) of Hippocrates, that a child of seven years old is half of a father, say that in fourteen years, according to Thomas, he is manifested."

209 Matthew does his best to Judaize the line by trying to make it refer to Jonah 1:17 and being in the belly of the whale for three days and three nights, but Jonah was never really dead, so this just adds to the confusion.

210 Mark 14:1-2.

211 Ibid.14:48-49.

212 Camus, Albert, The Myth of Sisyphus and Other Essays, Vintage Books, (translated by Justin O'Brien, New York, 1955, *The Minotaur*, Pg. 132. Note that Camus does not realize that the disciples did not fall asleep on the Mount of Olives but in the Garden of Gesemene. Note also that John places the scene of Jesus' pronouncement at the Last Supper (John 13.36) and immediately says, "Let not your hearts be troubled."

213 If Gethsemane was supposed to be a place on the Mount of Olives, as some suppose, Mark would likely have told us. As he did not, we may suppose it to be an entirely different place coming from a different narrative.

214 We must note also that the cock crowing here in John is out of place. As mentioned, in John's Gospel, the phrase "cock crow" just means "sunrise" It is not a literal cock crow. In Mark, it makes sense. Peter starts to weep, so the cock crow brings about a realization on Peter's part that he has betrayed Jesus. Here there is no reaction by Peter to the cock crow. The cock crow here serves no narrative function. The listener already understands that it is night and Peter has betrayed Jesus. The cock crowing is superfluous and adds nothing to our understanding. Whoever added it was just trying to harmonize the two gospels.

215 Later in the scene, Mary says, "They have taken my Lord away, she said, and I don't know where they have put him." It is unbelievable that she would use "we" for no reason in the first sentence, and "I" in the identical second sentence. Logically, she must have used "I" in both cases. The "I" has been changed to "we" for purposes of harmonization between gospels.

216 The reference to remaining alive as opposed to "remaining" seems to be a change for theological purposes. It is designed to bolster the idea that Jesus could grant eternal life. It suggests perhaps that Mary lived to a ripe old age and seemed immortal. Hopefully, she lived with good health into her seventies or eighties and rumors spread that the Savior had given her the gift of eternal life.

217 I will fill me this blank later.

218 It makes no sense for the beloved disciple to lean against Jesus' breast at this point in the narrative. Peter's gesture to the beloved disciple to ask him who the betrayer was could not have gone unnoticed by Jesus if she was lying on his breast. Only if Jesus was lying on Mary's breast could Peter gesture without Jesus seeing. The eroticism of Jesus leaning against Mary's breast has been subverted by reversing the situation and having the beloved disciple lean against Jesus' male breast. This may be another reason for the switch. As usual, in cases of editors changing text, the editor has made a "double switch," not only changing the sex of the beloved disciple, but also who leaned against whose breast.

219 If Jesus is rebuking Peter, it is doubtful he would end by saying "Follow me." John has completely gotten things upside down by having Mary (the other disciple following). Once we put the scene into its correct position in the narrative before going to Annas' house, and once we see that Jesus and Mary enter the courtyard together, and Peter, coming afterwards, remains outside, it appears obvious that Peter must have been the one following. The changing of the man into the woman and the woman into the man in this scene, matches the way John changes a woman into a man at the tomb, leaning against Jesus' breast at the last supper, the washing of the disciples' feet scene and even in the raising of Lazarus (which was originally, I believe, the raising of Mary from the dead).

220 I will fill me this blank later.

221 Jesus saying that he does not want to be crucified is a theological problem for the editor(s). They change Jesus' prediction of his own crucifixion into a prediction of Peter's crucifixion. By changing the text into a prediction of Peter's death, the editor(s) solved their theological problem, but garbled the sense of the text. The following line, "Jesus said this to indicate the kind of death by which he would glorify God," only makes sense if the previous line referred to Jesus's death and not Peter's.

222 The writer gives the name of the servant to show he has concrete exact knowledge of the event. If s/he did or just wants people to believe s/he did is difficult to judge.

223 The writer gives the name of the servant to show he has concrete knowledge of the event. If s/he did or just wants people to believe s/he did is difficult to judge.

224 This line interrupts the narrative flow. The command to release Peter is simply an heroic gesture, not a fulfillment of prophesy.

225 Actually, John has him say, "I am not" in response to the question "You are one of his disciples, are you not?" Mark does not give Peter's response, but just says, "He denied it." If Peter's disavowal and Jesus' avowal are in the same scene it is most probable that they were mirror images of one another with just the word not put in.

226 Mark 18.12.

227 Josephus, *Antiquities*. 18:2.2, "Tiberius Nero...He was now the third emperor; and he sent Valerius Gratus to be procurator of Judea, and to succeed Annius Rufus. This man deprived Ananus of the high priesthood, and appointed Ismael, the son of Phabi, to be high priest. He also deprived him in a little time, and ordained Eleazar, the son of Ananus, who had been high priest before, to be high priest; which office, when he had held for a year, Gratus deprived him of it, and gave the high priesthood to Simon, the son of Camithus; and when he had possessed that dignity no longer than a year, Joseph Caiaphas was made his successor. When Gratus had done those things, he went back to Rome, after he had tarried in Judea eleven years, when Pontius Pilate came as his successor."

228 Josephus tells us that Annas was the only person to have five sons as High Priests. "Now the report goes that this eldest Ananus proved a most fortunate man; for he had five sons who had all performed the office of a high priest to God, and who had himself enjoyed that dignity a long time formerly, which had never happened to any other of our high priests." (Ant. 20:9.1)

229 from http://articles.jerusalemperspective.com/articles/DisplayArticle.aspx?ArticleID=1632, viewed July 24, 2004. Riech, Ronnie, *Jerusalem Prospective Online*, "Ossuary Inscriptions from the Caiaphas Tomb"

230 Younan, Paul David, *Use of Orbg in Classical and Contemporary Aramaic Thought*, viewed April 21, 2005 at http://www.peshitta.org/bethgazza/Gabra.htm.

231 Josephus, *Ant*, 19.343-350.

232 The name Cantheras may be the source for the legend that Jesus was fathered by a Roman soldier named Pantera or Pandira.

233 Ibid. 19:8.1.

234 Josephus, *Ant*, 19.9.1.

235 Ibid. 20.1.3.

236 It seems that Menachem, the brother of Simon was welcomed into Jerusalem as a Messiah some 20 years later in 66 C.E. See Josephus, Wars, 2.17.8.

237 Mark 14:42.

238 Jospehus, *Wars*, 13:4-5.

239 Josephus, *Ant*, 10:8.6.

240 Tacitas, *Annals*, 12:54.

241 Josephus, *War*, 2:13.2.

242 Josephus, *Ant*, 20:7.5.

243 Ibid. 20:9.1.

244 War, 3:3.9.

245 Josephus, Life, 12 *et al*.

246 These cults may have later combined and become known as the Simon Magus cult.

247 Eisenman, Above, pg. 475.

248 Eusebius, H.E., 5:22.4.

[249] Ibid 3:23.1.
[250] Ant. 20:5.2.
[251] My speculation would be that in the original tale Jairus was a widower and Jairus's daughter had her first menstrual.flow. Jairus, in his ignorance of women, thought that she was dying. In other words, Jairus and his bumpkin fiends took her menstrual flow as a deadly disease. The original authoress of the tale thought it was comical that people would believe that a touch of Jesus' gown had cured her. She was making fun of both Jewish ignorance of women and ignorance of magic. The author of Mark was probably upset by the reference to the phony miracle, so he broke the story up into two real miracles, a real stopping of a serious menstrual flow and a real raising from the dead of the daughter. He tried to keep some humor in the story by saying that the woman had been bleeding for twelve years, simply a reverse of the idea that the girl had not bled for twelve years.
[252] Orczy, Emmuska, *the Scarlet Pimpernel*, Ch. 12.
[253] John 11:56-57.
[254] Orczy, *Pimpernel*, Ch. 1.
[255] To create her hero, Baroness Orczy took elements from Sherlock Holmes, the legends of Robin Hood and the novels of Alexandre Dumas, but then added a final ingredient of her own: the secret identity. The notion of unlikely heroes finding hidden reserves of courage is as old as *The Frog Prince, Beauty and the Beast*, or *David and Goliath*. But Orczy introduced a new idea into the collective consciousness: a heroic figure who creates a lounging, foppish alter ego to hide his (or her) true, heroic nature. It was as if Orczy saw that the Age of Heroism was over, and that the 20th century would be controlled by bureaucrats and small men. For the hero to survive, he would have to hide behind a mild-mannered mask. From Royston, Peter, *The Hidden Hero: Baroness Orczy and the Myth of the Secret Identity*, reprinted in Center Stage Magazine, Winter 2000, viewed Dec. 05, 2004, http://www.moveweb.com/Guidewrite/hiddenhero.html
[256] Springer, Nancy, *Scarlet Pimpernel*, Foreword, "A Biography of Baroness Orczy," 1988,
[257] From Blakeney manor at http://www.blakeneymanor.com/accuracy.html, viewed November 05, 2004.
[258] The bourgeois writer, Ian Fleming, did a similar thing in the 50's and 60's with his James Bond books portraying communists as evil villains and terrorists, and secret government spies as sexy supermen heroes. Unlike Orczy, he never used real names for his major characters.
[259] Oliver, Myrna, LA Times, November 5, 1998, *Bob Kane creator/artist*, obituary, retrieved June 30, 2005 from http://www.teako170.com/kane.html.
[260] Macleod, Charlotte, *Had She But Known*, The Mysterious Press, New York, 1994, pg. 153
[261] From Geometry.net online store. Retrieved July 1, 2005 from http://www.988.com/authors/rinehart_mary_roberts_page_no_4.php
[262] "The Batman," *People Weekly Magazine*, July 31, 1989.
[263] Rinehart, Mary Roberts, The Circular Staircase, Bobbs-Merrill, 1908, Indianapolis, chapter 23,

[264] Grost, Michael E., *Gender Intergration and the Mystery*, Retrieved July 1, 2005 from http://members.aol.com/MG4273/bigthree.htm.
[265] Rinehart, Mary Roberts, and Hopwood, Avery, The Bat, Samuel French, New York, no date, page 9.
[266] Grost, Michael E., *The Rogue School*, above.
[267] Rinehart, Mary Roberts, *The Bat*, Kensington, 1998, pp.10-11.
[268] Frye, Northrop, The Great Code: The Bible and Literature, HBJ, 1983, pg. 90.
[269] Ibid. pg. 91.
[270] The spearing of Jesus' side (19:34-37) is a later addition to the text. It is designed to show that Jesus was a God with a mixture of blood and water in his veins. It also tries to establish that the teller of the tale is a Roman soldier. This idea of a roman narrator apparently went nowhere. But a study of soldier narrations might help us pinpoint a date for this addition.
[271] Kaufmann, Walter, *Tragedy and Philosophy*, Princeton, New Jersey, 1968, pg. 85.
[272] I consider it slightly possible that these letters were invented shortly after Mary's death and written in her name and then changed. However the style is so feminine and close to parts of the Gospel of John, the Gospel of Mary, which I believe Mary wrote that it must have been written by someone who knew her very well. Notice that the editors have changed the name of the writer to "The Elder." To change it to "John" would have been to directly lie, while this change may be considered only a partial deception as those who know that the Elder is Mary would not be deceived.
[273] Mark 8:27-29.
[274] Numerous editions of text found in the Dead Sea Scrolls seem to contradict this statement, but we should consider that many of the editions were written much earlier than the first century.
[275] Richard Gere in the movie musical, *Chicago* (2002).
[276] Wikipedia, http://www.fact-index.com/b/be/beulah_annan.html, viewed August 22, 2004.
[277] Watkins, Maureen, *Chicago*, Edited and with an Introduction by Pauly, Thomas H., Southern Illinois University Press, 1997, pg. 122, Woman plays Jazz Air as Victim Dies," Chicago Tribune, April 4, 1924, pg. 1.
[278] Ibid. She was drunk at the time and may have perceived her lover as her husband, or she may have considered killing her husband too.
[279] Rodgers, Ginger, *Ginger, My Story*, Harper Collins, 1991, pg. 240.
[280] Bob Fosse was a great fan of Fred Astaire and Ginger Rodgers. It was perhaps Ginger Rodgers' connection with the movie *Roxie Hart* and the dance numbers that she added that drew him to the material.
[281] Reinking was the real life girl friend of Bob Fosse. She also played his girlfriend in Fosse's semi-biographical film, *All That Jazz* (Fosse, 1979).
[282] One may conjecture that the competitive relationship was actually between Gwen Verdon and Chita Rivera, the two stars of the original 1975 musical play. Gwen Verdon had become popular in 1955 starring in the Broadway musical *Damn Yankees*, Chita Rivera

starred in 1957 in the Broadway musical West Side Story. In 1966, Gwen Verdon starred in the title role of Sweet Charity on Broadway, in 1967, Chita Rivera starred in the title role of the national touring company of the same play. Bob Fosse used neither of them, but Shirley Maclaine in the 1969 movie version.

[283] Ebb, Fred, and Fosse, bob, Chicago: A Musical Vaudeville, Samuel French, Inc. New York, 1976, Act 1, Scene 1, pp.12-13.

[284] We can find another strange name coincidence here. Paul gets mistakened for the God Hermes in Acts 14:11-13. "When the crowd saw what Paul had done, they shouted in the Lycaonian language, "The gods have come down to us in human form!" Barnabas they called Zeus, and Paul they called Hermes because he was the chief speaker. The priest of Zeus, whose temple was just outside the city, brought bulls and wreaths to the city gates because he and the crowd wanted to offer sacrifices to them."

[285] In another bit of irony, apparently Maurine Watkins became religious and "left her fortune of over $2,000,000 to found chairs at university for Biblical studies." [from an article in wikipedia—http://www.fact-index.com/m/ma/maurine_dallas_watkins.html, viewed Oct. 20, 2004.] On the other hand, we also have this: Watkins' life-long interests in classical studies and creative writing set the stage for her philanthropic interests. To this day, students of Latin and Greek in 130 colleges and universities across the continent compete for Maurine Dallas Watkins Prizes, administered by the collegiate honorary society Eta Sigma Phi. Competitive scholarships also are available for students attending the American School of Classical Studies at Athens and the American Academy in Rome, partially due to her benevolence. Watkins established Ernest Woodruff Delcamp Essay Awards, to honor the college's late Department of English chairman. And classical studies programs at both Harvard and the University of Iowa benefited greatly from her largess. [from http://people.hsc.edu/organizations/etasigmaphi/03spring/nuntius2.html]

[286] There are a few seconds in Rob Marshall's 2002 movie version where we do feel some fear for/with Roxie. It is when she spends her first night in prison. The heavy echoing sounds of the Cook County jail briefly cuts against the light tone of much of the rest of the movie.

[287] And also striking, it was two women, I believe, Maurine Watkins, and Mary, who were responsible for the spread and popularity of the material. In each case the women portraying themselves as characters in the narrative.

[288] Ebb, *Chicago: A Musical Vaudeville*, Act II, Scene 8.

[289] Some parallels are a bit spooky, almost mystical, Beulah's husband Annan was the first to hear her case. In the Gospel of John, the Jewish High Priest who is the first to hear Jesus' case is named Ananus. The Jesus Christ story became a big broadway musical, *Jesus Christ, Superstar*, in the 1970's, as did the Beulah Annan story.

[290] Rowling, J.K., *Biography*, J.K. Rowling Official Site. Retrieved on June 15, 2005 from http://www.jkrowling.com/textonly/biography.cfm.

[291] Hadaway, Diane, *Biography: J. K. Rowling, Author of Harry Potter Books From Single Mom Writer to Global Phenomenon*, retrieved on June 15, 2005, from http://singleparents.about.com/cs/booksandmovies/l/aajkrowlingbio1.htm

292 Nietzsche, Friedrich, *The AntiChrist*, Alfred Knopf, New York, 1920, chapter 44.
293 Gospel of Thomas 3.
294 Mark 1.13-14.
295 Origen, *Contra Celsus*, Book II.LIX.
296 Matthew 28.8-10.
297 Origen, *Contra Celsus*, Book II.LX.
298 H.E., 3:26.11, *Ep. ad Smyr.* Ch. 3. Origen. *de prin.* praef. 8 Jerome, *de vir. ill.* 16,
299 We know this from the Gospel of Mary.
300 Dixon, Suzanne, *Reading Roman Women:Sources, Genres and Real Life*, Duckworth, 2002, pg. xi.
301 Ibid. pg. X.
302 Evans, Craig, "Mark's Incipit And The Priene Calendar Inscription From Jewish Gospel To Greco-Roman Gospel," JGRChJ 1 (2000) 67-81, pg. 70.
303 P.Oxy. 1021, translated by Hanson, K.C., http://www.kchanson.com/ANCDOCS/greek/nero.html, viewed August 10, 2004.
304 Note that the Gospel of John never uses the word "Gospel." to refer to itself or anything else.
305 Mk, 1:14, 15.
306 A good example of this is the movie *Speed* (1994, Jan De Bont) in which much of the movie takes place on a runaway bus and then switches near the end to a subway train.
307 *New Oxford Annotated Bible with the Apocrypha: New Revised Standard Version*. Ed. Michael D. Coogan. 3rd ed. New York: Oxford University Press, 2001.
308 Xenophon, Memorabilia, 1.1.
309 Ibid., 4.8.
310 John 1.1.
311 Ibid. 21.20-25.
312 Scott, Jean, *The Dr. Gene Scott Bible Collection*, from http://www.drgenescott.com/stn33.htm, viewed on August 10, 2004.
313 There's no logical connection.
314 Recall that Aristotle's *Poetics* placed drama squarely in the category of poetry. It is only the naturalistic prose style of play writing of the last two centuries that has removed drama from the category of poetry.
315 Jones, Michel Ridgway, "Natural" Women: The Mima and the Construction of Gender," http://duke.usask.ca/~porterj/abstracts/jones.html, viewed on September 13, 2004.
316 Terence, *The Complete Comedies of Terence: Modern Verse Translations by Palmer Bovie, Constance Carrier, and Douglass Parker*, Rutgers University Press, 1974, ending from *The Self Tormentor*.
317 Ibid. ending from *The Girl From Andros*.
318 From http://www.ancientroute.com/cities/caesarea.htm:

> **In the very south of the city Herod had a theater built, one of the earliest theaters in the Near East. It faces the sea, with it's thousands of seats**

rising on vaulting, a Roman invention. The stage floor, at first just covered with plaster, was eventually overlain with marble. An inscription stone has been found indicating Pontius Pilate helped in the financing, or at least was given a dedication mention. According the Josephus, Herod Agrippa, the grandson of Herod the Great, died by choking at this theater.

[319] Josephus, *Life*, 1:3.

[320] Cornelia Gracchus, (circa 190-100 B.C.E.), daughter of Scipio Africanus Major, hero of Carthaginian War, mother of Tiberius and Gaius Gracchus, popular tribunes of plebian rights. Agrippina, (15-59 C.E.), related to three emperors, wife of Claudius, sister of Caligula, mother of Nero,

[321] Cross, Suzanne, *Imperial Women Of Ancient Rome*, from http://dominae.fws1.com/imperial_women/Index.html, viewed August 11, 2004.

[322] Fraschetti, Augusto, *Roman Women*, University of Chicago Press, 2002, "Lycoris the Mime," by Traina, Giusto, pg. 86.

[323] Ibid. pg. 83.

[324] Jones, Michael, "Natural" Women: The Mima and the Construction of Gender," abstract, *http://duke.usask.ca/~porterj/abstracts/jones.html*, viewed September 15, 2004.

[325] James M. Robinson, ed., *The Nag Hammadi Library*, "The Thunder, Perfect Mind," translated by MacRae, George W,.revised edition. HarperCollins, San Francisco, 1990.

[326] Dixon, Above, pg. 16.

[327] Lucian, The Works of Lucian of Samosata: Vol. 2, "On Pantomime," translated by Fowler, Oxford University Press, 1905, pg. 240.

[328] Suetonius, *Life of Augustus*, 94.

[329] From http://didaskalia.open.ac.uk/issues/vol1no2/wslater.html, viewed Setemeber 14, 2004, "Pantomimes," Slater, William.

[330] Frost, Frank, Transactions and Procedings of the American Philological Assoication, 38: 49-56.

[331] Ibid.

[332] 2 Pet. 1:16, We did not follow cleverly invented stories when we told you about the power and coming of our Lord Jesus Christ, but we were eye-witnesses of his majesty.

[333] Imagine Achilles never meeting Hector, Aeneas never meeting Turnus, Orestes and Electra never meeting Clytemnestra, Captain Ahab never meeting Moby Dick, Batman never confronting the Joker, or Luke Skywalker never meeting Darth Vader. In the present *Gospel of John* we have Jesus never meeting the mastermind of his death Caiaphas. We just these insipid interpolations that he was taken to Caiaphas and he left the next morning from Caiaphas' house.

[334] See below the interpretation of that scene.

[335] *Encyclopedia Britannica*.

[336] Josephus, *Ant*, 18:5.3., 18:6.7, *War*, 2:9.5

337. *Ant*, 18:6.10.
338. Jefferys, William H., AST 309—Time Easter, Rosh Hashanah and Passover, viewed on July 27, 2004 at http://quasar.as.utexas.edu/BillInfo/ReligiousCalendars.html
339. Pliny. *Natural History*, XIX, 1.
340. Philo in "Embassy to Gaius" (36) has Agrippa point out, that the news of Gaius' emperorship reached Jerusalem first, before other Asia cities: "It was at Jerusalem, O emperor! that your most desirable succession to the empire was first announced; and the news of your advancement spread from the holy city all over the continent on each side, and was received with great gladness." This may be hyperbole.
341. Blatt, Heather, "Some Notes on the Historical and Physical Context of Letters," viewed July 27, 2004, http://www.people.cornell.edu/pages/heb4/letters.html
342. Tacitus, *Annals*, 11.8.
343. Josephus, *Wars*, 9:4.2
344. Ibid. 9:4.3.
345. Josephus, *Ant*, 18:5.3.
346. Ibid. 18:3.5.
347. There are a number of Gospel scenes with just four men: Jesus, Peter, James and John.
348. Ibid., *Ant*, 18:4.1.
349. Ibid., 18:4.2.
350. One may easily imagine that he was welcomed with flowers as the savior of the Jews from Pilate.
351. Josephus, *Ant*. 18:4.3.
352. Ibid. 18:4.4.5.
353. Ibid. 18:5.1.
354. Ibid. 18:5.3.
355. Tacitus, Annals, 6:31.
356. Ibid. 6:38.
357. Tacitus gives a slightly different version from Josephus, but for us the dating is important not precisely what happened.
358. Josephus, *Ant*, 15:11.4.
359. Ibid. 18:5.1.
360. Tacitus, *Annals*, bk. 6.
361. Jospehus, *Wars*, 2:9.4-5.
362. *Wars*, 2:9.1, *Antiquities*, 18:3.1.
363. Philo, *Embassy to Gaius*, 38.
364. Ibid.
365. Josephus, *Wars*, 2:9.1-2.
366. Ibid. 2:9.4.
367. Josephus, *Ant*, 18:3.1-2.
368. Cassius Dio, *Roman History*, Book 57
369. *Ant* 18:3.5-4.1.

[370] Ibid. 18:4.2.
[371] Kurt Aland and Barbara Aland, *The Text of the New Testament*, pp. 275-276, retrieved July 6, 2004 on http://www.earlham.edu/~seidti/iam/text_crit.html.
[372] Mark 9:12.
[373] Ibid. 9:4.
[374] One should consider seriously that this work strongly influenced the presentation of the Jesus character, the way Charlie Chaplin influenced comedians in the early silent films or the James Bonds movies of the 1960's became a paradigm for spy movies in the following decades.
[375] Cassius Dio, *Roman* history, 69.12.1-14.3
[376] Jerome, *Commentary on the Bible*, Matthew 24:15, "the statue of the mounted Hadrian, which stands to this very day on the site of the Holy of Holies." Jerome implies that the Jews of his time took this statue to be the *Abomination of Desolation* and still performed ceremonies related to it. A traveler called Bordeaux Pilgrim also left from his visit to Jerusalem in 333 testifying to Hadrian's statue.
[377] Collins, Adela Yarbro, *Biblical Research*, Vol. 41, 1996, *The Apocalyptic Rhetoric of Mark 13 in Historical Context*, pg. 22.
[378] Ibid. Pg. 36.
[379] Botha, Pieter, J.J., *Journal for the Study of the New Testament*, No. 51, 1993, *The Historical Setting of Mark's Gospel: Problems and Possibilities*, Pg. 38.
[380] The "distress" that Jesus refers to here is at 9.12, the suffering and rejection of the Son of Man. Remember, this dialogue is originally a continuation of the post transfiguration-coming down from the mountain scene.
[381] *Clementine Recognitions*, Book 1.14.
[382] Probably, "If the Lord will not shorten those days" reflects the original intent. Mark seems to have started to change the sentence to the past tense, but became distracted.
[383] Josephus, Wars, 4:3.7.
[384] Ibid. 4:3.10.
[385] Ibid. 6:9.1.
[386] Ibid. 7:1.1.
[387] Mark 14.58.
[388] Ibid. 15:29-30.
[389] Matthew 26:60-61.
[390] Ibid. 27:39-40.
[391] Ibid. 14:55-61.
[392] John 18:22.
[393] Camus, Albert, *The Myth of Sisyphus and Other Essays*, Vintage Books, New York, 1955, pg. 72, "Absurd Creation: Philosophy and Fiction"
[394] Mark 10:45.
[395] Ibid. 8:31.
[396] Ibid.14:58.
[397] Shakespeare, William, Romeo *and Juliet*, Act II, Scene II.

[398] 1 Kings 17.1.
[399] John 4:7, 2:1-11, 6:1-14.
[400] 1 Kings 17:8-15.
[401] Ibid. 17-24.
[402] John 4:46-54.
[403] Matthew 8:6-13.
[404] Matthew 25:57.
[405] 1 Kgs 19:19.
[406] II Kgs. 3:11.
[407] Dart, John, *Decoding Mark*, Trinity Press International, A Continuum Imprint, 2003, pg. 28-30.
[408] II Kgs. 9.14-34.
[409] Ibid. 10:17.
[410] Ibid. 10:18.
[411] Ibid. 13:20-21.
[412] Retreaved July 5, http://www.hope.edu/academic/religion/bandstra/RTOT/CH17/CH17_2A.HTM, 2004.
[413] One should take this "Son" statement to be reference to the Son of Man, the angel of God, as opposed to the Son of God.
[414] Boorstin, Daniel J., *The Creators*, Vintage Books, New York, 1992, pg. 111.
[415] Zimet, David, "Jewish Magic in the Roman Bathhouse," retrieved June 12, 2005, from http://www.winds.org/~frost/words/writings/magic.html.
[416] Mark 2:10,28; 8:31,38; 9:9,12,31; 10:33,45; 13:26; 14:21,41,62.
[417] Ibid. 3:11, 5:7, 15:39. The last is very possibly an interpolation. The Roman plays no other part in the story and we are not even given his name.
[418] Ibid.14:60-62
[419] Smith, Morton, *Jesus The Magician*, Harper & Row, New York, 1978, pg. 85.
[420] Wink, Walter, *The Human Being: Jesus and the Enigma of the Son of Man*, Minneapolis: Fortress, 2002, XI.
[421] "Testament of Solomon," Translation by F. C. Conybeare, *Jewish Quarterly Review*, October, 1898, pg. 20.
[422] Mark 12.35.
[423] Segal, Alan F, "Review and Appreciation: Walter Wink's The Human Being," *Cross Currents*, Summer 2003, Vol. 53, No 2.
[424] Burkett, Delbert, *The Son of Man Debate: A History and Evaluation*, Cambridge University Press, 1999, pg. 96.
[425] Ibid. pg. 119.
[426] Ibid. pg. 120.
[427] Fletcher-Louis, H.T. Crispin, First Oxford Lecture On The Development Of Christology, on website http://www.st-andrews.ac.uk/~www_sd/med_oxford1.html, Web Page on Divine Mediator Figures in the Biblical World by Davila, James R.

[428] Boyarin, Daniel, "The Gospel of the Memra: Jewish Binitarianism and the Prologue to John," **HTR**, July, 2001.
[429] Philo, Somn. 2.242-45.
[430] From http://www.jewishencyclopedia.com/index.Sp, Jewish Encyclopedia originally published 1901-1906.
[431] Not to mention that they do not use the name Jesus of Nazareth at all. For good, albeit polemical, arguments that Paul and the other early Christian writers worshipped a God named Jesus Christ and did not know Jesus of Nazareth, read Earl Doherty's *The Jesus Puzzle*. Above.
[432] Col. 1:18.
[433] *Proverbs* 8:22-30.
[434] Holding, James Patrick, "Jesus: God's Wisdom," from http://www.tektonics.org/JPH_AOA.html
[435] Goodspeed, Edgar J., *The Apocrypha*, Vintage Books, 1959, "The Wisdom of Sirach," 2:1-2:6, pg. 227
[436] Price, Robert M., *Deconstructing Jesus*, Prometheus Books, Amherst, New York, 2000, pg. 161.
[437] Mack, Burton, *Who Wrote the New Testament*, Harper San Francisco, 1995, pg. 153.
[438] Luigi Casioli has noted that the Christ was originally called "John the Nazarene." He writes, "The name John, replaced with the generic names of Christ (Kristos meaning Anointed) and Lord, was finally changed to Jesus in about the year 180 as shown in a book written by Celsus against the Christians which said: "The one you gave the name Jesus to was really just the head of a band of bandits." *John the Nazarene*, retrieved February 28, 2005, at http://www.anti-religions.org/eng/prove2.php. He associates the name John the Nazarene with John, the son of Judas the Gaulonite. I think it is highly probable, but the issue lies beyond the scope of this book.
[439] Price, Robert M., The Incredible Shrinking Son of Man, Prometheus Books, Amherst, New York, 2003, pg. 132.
[440] Probably the writer of this epistle means a metaphorical crucifixion.
[441] Mark 8:11-13.
[442] Ur was the original city of Abraham. It usually means earliest, and thus the word 'Ur' for the title UrMark Gospel. "Q" comes from the latin word "Quelle" meaning source. Since the 19th century it has been applied to a sayings gospel perhaps used by Matthew and Luke.
[443] *Gospel of Thomas*, 22.
[444] Mack, above, pg. 59-60.
[445] *Clementine Recognitions*, Book 1.14. Compare this with Josephus's *Antiquities* 18:3.5-6. Compare the phrase "word of truth received from the tradition of Moses as the key of the Kingdom of heaven," in *Clementine* with "professed to instruct men in the wisdom of the laws of Moses," in *Antiquities*.
[446] Schweitzer, Albert, *the Quest of the historical Jesus*, Fortress Press, Minneapolis, 2001, pg. 434.

THE EVOLUTION OF CHRISTS AND CHRISTIANIES

447   The orginal would have been, "Was baptism from heaven or earth?

448   2.21-47, 3.34-99, 4.3-9, 4.9-33, 4.26-21, 6.4-31, 7.14-14, 8.11-50, 9.35-46, 9.43-22, 9.49-10, 10.14-46, 10.14-46, 11.22-106, 12.1-65, 12.17-100, 12.34-82.

449   The response seems to mean, "My baptism was from God, not men."

450   "Perhaps the most remarkable picture of a baptism is in the ceiling of the Baptistry of the Orthodox at Ravenna. In this case the picture of John baptizing Jesus in the dome of the baptistry had by this time become a convention. By A.D. 450, when this mosaic was put into place, the philosophy of the icon was developing rapidly. Everything in the baptistry was built as the setting for the baptismal mysteries of the Christian Passover. Clearly the baptisms performed in this baptistry were immersions. In the center of the room was a large pool obviously built for immersions. How is it, then, that the picture of the baptism of Christ in the ceiling, put there to be seen by those being baptized as they were laid into the water, is a baptism not by immersion but by pouring? The answer is very simple. The traditional picture of baptism had evolved at a time when pouring was the normal way to baptize. The traditional icon must have evolved in the second century; by the third century we find traces of it all over the Empire. Here we have clear evidence that in the second century baptism was most often performed by pouring."

Hughes Oliphant Old, *The Shaping of the Reformed Baptismal Rite in the Sixteenth Century* (Grand Rapids: William B. Eerdmans Publishing Company, 1992), pages 1-3. Quoted in The Mode of Baptism, by Grover Gunn, August 23, 2005 <http://www.capo.org/cpc/mode.htm>.

451   Neusner, Jacob, *Rabbinic Literature & the New Testament*, Trinity Press International, 1994, pg. 67.

452   Several of the cut points I am unsure about. I might have made mistakes and the reader should take the opportunity to correct them. However, the general structure I have found of a single speech and a terrific one at that, makes it certain, at least to my mind, that an UrMatthew document has been found.

453   The use of King James here is arbitrary. The translations of these passage are pretty much the same in most Bibles and do not seriously affect the points I am making.

454   This will be revealed in the reconstructed text of UrMatthew. It is a great irony that the first editor of Matthew seems to have spent only a few hours pasting the large pieces of texts together, while many people have devoted thousands of hours to puzzling over each line of the text.

455   Matthew 9:1-5.

456   Mark 4:7-13.

457   John refers most likely to the Son of Man angel at this point, not anybody named Jesus.

458   Luke 11:1-4 also tells us that these lines are from John the Baptist:

> One day Jesus was praying in a certain place. When he finished, one of his disciples said to him, "Lord, teach us to pray, just as John taught his disciples." He said to them, "When you pray, say:" 'Father, hallowed

be your name, your kingdom come. Give us each day our daily bread. Forgive us our sins, for we also forgive everyone who sins against us. And lead us not into temptation.'"

[459] These Parables form a separate text, but I assume they were already included in the "Teachings of John the Nazarene" by the time the editor of Matthew used them.

[460] Mark 4.12 has "lest they should turn again and be forgiven." instead of "turn for me to heal them." Possibly Mark has the earlier ending.

[461] Price, Robert M., "Was Jesus John the Baptist Raised from the Dead?" http://www.courses.drew.edu/sp2000/BIBST189.001/pricejj.html, retrieved December 12, 2003. Prices' insightful essay overlaps some of the material in this section and actually offers similar conclusions.

[462] Malachi 1:13-16.

[463] Ibid. 3:1-3.

[464] Exodus 6:23.

[465] Numbers 18:27-29

[466] Matthew 1:20-23.

[467] Luke 1:12-15.

[468] Ibid.1:36.

[469] They are born months apart and both die violently at the same age months apart. Their tombstones would read the same.

[470] Luke 3:1-2: In the fifteenth year of the reign of Tiberius Caesar—when Pontius Pilate was governor of Judea, Herod tetrarch of Galilee, his brother Philip tetrarch of Iturea and Traconitis, and Lysanias tetrarch of Abilene&—during the high priesthood of Annas and Caiaphas, the word of God came to John son of Zechariah in the desert.

[471] John 3:22. After this Jesus and his disciples went into the land of Judea; there he remained with them and 23. John also was baptizing at Ae'non near Salim, because there was much water there; and people came and were baptized 24. For John had not yet been put in prison. 25. Now a discussion arose between John's disciples and a Jew over purifying 26. And they came to John, and said to him, "Rabbi, he who was with you beyond the Jordan, to whom you bore witness, here he is, baptizing, and all are going to him." There is a ridiculous interpolation put in at John 4.2 "although Jesus himself did not baptize, but only his disciples," which clearly contradicts the previous embarrassing assertion that Jesus baptized.

[472] John 1:35. The next day again John was standing with two of his disciples; 140 One of the two who heard John speak, and followed him, was Andrew, Simon Peter's brother. 141 He first found his brother Simon, and said to him, "We have found the Messiah" (which means Christ).

[473] Price, Above.

[474] 1Samuel 2.1.

[475] *H.E.*, 3:39.1

[476] Ibid. 3:39.15-16.
[477] Ibid. 3:39.3-4.
[478] Ibid. 3:23.7-19. Eusebius calls the same character Apostle (23.5) and Presbyter (23.8).
[479] Irenaeus, Against Heresies, 2:22.5.
[480] Ibid. 5:33.3.
[481] *Heresies*, 1:8.5.
[482] *Ant.*, 18:4.1.
[483] H.E., 3:39.11-12.
[484] Against Heresies, 5:33.3.
[485] Ibid., 5:35.2.
[486] Ibid., 5:36.1-3.
[487] Revelation 21.1-8.
[488] Josephus, *Wars*, 7:6.1-2.
[489] Ibid., 7:6.3.
[490] Ibid. 7:6.4.
[491] Josephus, *Ant*, 18:5.2.
[492] Josephus, *Wars*, 7.5.5.
[493] Fox, Robin Lane, *The Unauthroized Version*, Knopf, 1992, pp. 335. 11. Above, *Wars*, 7:6.2
[494] Victorinus, *Commentary on the Apocalypse of the Blessed John*, 10.11.
[495] *Clementine Recognitions*, 1.54.
[496] Josephus, *Ant*, 18:4.1.
[497] One could argue that the problem was that Antipas had married Herodias prior to her husband Philip's death. If John was arguing this, it was an extremely trivial point and like hundreds of other questions about the observance of Jewish laws, teachers could be found who could argue all sides of the issue. It is hardly a reason that Herod could or would have used to imprison John. This argument is simply meant to obscure the political nature of John's arrest.
[498] Photius, *Justus of Tiberius*, Reviewed April 15, 2005 at http://www.tertullian.org/rpearse/justus.htm.
[499] Fellows, Richard, *Was Titus Timothy?*, JSNT 81 (2001) p33-58.
[500] Ibid. pp 33.
[501] Catholic Encyclopedia, *Laodicea*, Reviewed April 16, 2005, http://www.newadvent.org/cathen/08794a.htm
[502] As the following passage talks about the high priest Ananias, it is likely that Ananias and not Ananus should be the reading in this passage The next passages go on to tell how robbers called Sicarri kidnapped Ananias's son and servants and held them for ransom. We may take it that these were the Christian followers of James getting revenge for what Ananias had done to James.
[503] As the following passage talks about the high priest Ananias, it is likely that Ananias and not Ananus should be the reading in this passage The next passages go on to tell how

robbers called Sicarri kidnapped Ananias's son and servants and held them for ransom. In *Acts*

[504] We may take it that Tertullian also added the first two chapters in Luke to create our present Luke out of Marcion's gospel. He did this also to discredit Marcion. He created these chapters out of a birth narrative about John the Baptist. He probably did this many years after changing the gospel of Matthew to support earlier minor changes he made in that text. Proving this will require a different book which I hope to write in the future.

[505] *The Catholic Encyclopedia*, Volume III, Copyright © 1908 by Robert Appleton Company, Reviewed on June 4, 2005 at http://www.saint-mike.org/Library/Papal_Library/Definitions/Cana.html

[506] Josephus, *Life of Josephus*, 45

[507] My best guess would be "breast" for the lacuna. The scene where Jesus lay on Mary's breast (as we have reconstructed it) would point in this direction.

[508] There is no need to explain that Jews have no dealings with Samaritans as a later interpolation does. When reconstructed in this way the antagonism between the Samaritans and Jews is obvious. Only after the later editor mixes up the lines between Mary and Jesus (to avoid giving the impression that Jesus is Samaritan) do we need an explanation of this antagonism.

[509] Note the chiastic construction of this speech when reproduced in this form. It is a signature mark of Mary's writing.

[510] It is possible that more material regarding kissing and eating and living water were here in the earlier material.

[511] I have left out, "For in this case the saying is true, `One sows and another reaps.' "I sent you to reap that for which you have not labored; others have labored and you have entered into their labor" This section of the parable makes little sense, except as a pointless put-down of the disciples. It was probably added later to the earlier section of the parable, which is an apology for Jesus' hedonism.

[512] Whether the wedding took place in Joppa, Samaria or Japha, Galilee, both 37 miles from Sychar or Cana 45 miles from Sychar, we still have a problem with the distance traveled in one day. The earlier text probably suggested that the wedding took place on the third day after the two days spent in Sychar.

[513] 1 Corinthians, 1:10, 11:15, 2 Corinthians 1, Galatians 1, Acts, 20.

[514] Tertullian, *De Oration*, 16.

[515] Tertullian, *De pudicitia*, 10.

[516] Nietzsche, Friedrich, *The Genealogy of Morals*, Doubleday Anchor, N.Y., 1974, p. 168.

[517] Pliny, *Letters of Pliny the Younger*, Loeb, 1915, Book 5, letter 19, to Valerius Paulinus, Retrieved August 4, 2005 from http://www.vroma.org/~hwalker/Pliny/Pliny05-19-E.html

[518] Henry George Liddell, Robert Scott, *A Greek-English Lexicon*, retrieved August 4, 2005 at http://www.perseus.tufts.

[519] *Slavery and Christianity*, Catholic Encyclopedia, retrieved August 8, 2005 from http://www.newadvent.org/cathen/14036a.htm.

[520] For evidence of the Joshua Christology, see Kraft, Robert A, *Was There a "Messiah-Joshua" Tradition at the Turn of the Era, Ioudaios*, June, 1992, retrieved August 9, 2005, from http://listserv.lehigh.edu/lists/ioudaios-l/Articles.html. Also see Magee, M.D. *The Pre-Christian Joshua Cult*, retrieved August 9, 2005 from http://www.askwhy.co.uk/christianity/0190JoshuaCult.html#The%20Pre-Christian%20Joshua%20Cult

[521] Eusebius, *H.E.*, 4.5.

[522] Ibid., 3.21.4.

[523] Ibid. 2.23.

[524] Acts 6.

[525] Mark 14:56-58.

[526] John 1:17.

[527] Acts, 7:5.

[528] Ibid. 7:6.

[529] Ibid. 7:36

[530] Ibid. 7:37

[531] Ibid. 7:39.

[532] Ibid. 7:49-50.

[533] Ibid. 7:51-55

[534] Origen, *Matthew* 10:17

[535] Origen, *Against Celsus* 1.47.

[536] Turning Freudian for a moment, I would speculate that a masculine (or closet homosexual) sexuality that holds sex with women in low regard contributed to the popularity of James Bond movies. Likewise, I would speculate that a masculine (or closet homosexual) sexuality that holds sex with women in low regard contributed to the popularity of Christianity.

[537] 2 Peter 1:16-18.

[538] Ibid. 2:1-2.

[539] Origen, *Against Celsus*, 3:16.

[540] Mack, Burton L, *Who Wrote the New Testament*, Harper Collins, NY 1995.

[541] Mack, Burton L., *The Christian Myth: Origins, Logic, and Legacy*, Continuum, NY, 2001, pp. 137.

[542] Ibid. pg. 64.

[543] There is nothing to suggest that this visit did not take place the previous night. This suggests that a scene took place after the arrest of Jesus where Mary went to visit him.

[544] There is nothing to suggest that this visit did not take place the previous night. This suggests that a scene took place after the arrest of Jesus where Mary went to visit him.

Bibliography

Barnes, Timothy. *Eusebius and Constantine*. Cambridge: Harvard University Press, 1981.

Bartholomew. "The Book of the Resurrection of Christ by Bartholomew the Apostle." Trans: James, M.R. *The Apocryphal New Testament*. Oxford: Clarendon Press, 1924,

Bauer, Walter. Orthodoxy and Heresy In Earliest Christianity. Translated and supplemented under the direction of Kraft, Robert A., and Gerhard Kroedel. Philadelphia: Fortress, 1971 from the 2nd German edition edited and supplemented by Strecker Georg, (Tübingen: J.C.B.Mohr, 1964 [original ed 1934]), electronic edition, January 02, 2005, <http://ccat.sas.upenn.edu/rs/rak/publics/new/BAUER01.htm>

Blatt, Heather. "Some Notes on the Historical and Physical Context of Letters," July 27, 2004 <http://www.people.cornell.edu/pages/heb4/letters.html>.

Blavatsky, Helena Petrovna. "Appolonius Tyraneus and Simon Magus." *Theosophist*. June 1881. June 12, 2005 <http://theosophy.org/tlodocs/hpb/ApolloniusTyaneusAndSimonMagus.htm.>.

Boorstin, Daniel J. *The Creators*, New York: Vintage Books, 1992.

Botha, Pieter, J.J. "The Historical Setting of Mark's Gospel: Problems and Possibilities."*Journal for the Study of the New Testament*. No. 51, 1993.

Boyarin, Daniel. "The Gospel of the Memra: Jewish Binitarianism and the Prologue to John." *HTR*, July, 2001.

Burkett, Delbert. *The Son of Man Debate: A History and Evaluation*, Cambridge, England: Cambridge University Press, 1999.

Camus, Albert. "The Minotaur." "Absurd Creation: Philosophy and Fiction." Trans. O'brien, Justin. *The Myth of Sisyphus and Other Essays*. New York: Vintage Books, 1955.

Casioli, Luigi. "John the Nazarene." *The Lawsuit*. February 28, 2005 <http://www.anti-religions.org/eng/prove2.php>.

Cassius Dio, *Roman History*. August 18, 2005 <http://penelope.uchicago.edu/Thayer/E/Roman/Texts/Cassius_Dio/home.html>.

Catholic Encyclopedia, "Eusebius." September 20, 2004, <http://www.newadvent.org/cathen/05617b.htm>.

Catholic Encyclopedia. "Slavery and Christianity." August 8, 2005 <http://www.newadvent.org/cathen/14036a.htm.>.

Catholic Encyclopedia. "Laodicea." April 16, 2005, <http://www.newadvent.org/cathen/08794a.htm>.

Catholic Encyclopediea. "Cana." Volume III, Robert Appleton Company, 1908. June 4, 2005 <http://www.saint-mike.org/Library/Papal_Library/Definitions/Cana.html>.

Chadwick, Henry. *the Church in Ancient Society*, New York: Oxford University Press, 2002.

Clement of Alexandria. "Stromata." *Anti-Nicene Fathers: Vol. II*. August 17, 2005 <http://www.ccel.org/fathers2/>.

Clement. "*Clementine Recognitions.*" *Anti-Nicene Fathers*. August 18, 2005 <http://www.ccel.org/fathers2/ANF-08/anf08-31.htm#TopOfPage>.

Cohen, Leonard, "Jazz Police." *I'm Your Man*, Sony Catalog: #44191, 1988

Collins, Adela Yarbro. "The Apocalyptic Rhetoric of Mark 13 in Historical Context." *Biblical Research*, Vol. 41, 1996.

Cross, Suzanne. "Imperial Women Of Ancient Rome." August 11, 2004 <http://dominae.fws1.com/imperial_women/Index.html>.

Dart, John. *Decoding Mark*. Harrisburg, PA: Trinity Press International, A Continuum Imprint, 2003.

Dixon, Suzanne, *Reading Roman Women:Sources, Genres and Real Life*. Duckworth, 2002.

Doherty, Earl, *The Jesus Puzzle: Did Christianity Begin with a Mythical Christ?*. Ottawa, Ontario, Canada: Canadian Humanist Publications, 1999.

Doughty, Darrell J. "Tacitus' Account of Nero's Persecution of Christians. *Annals* 15.44.2-8." January 14, 2005 <http://www.courses.drew.edu/sp2000/BIBST189.001/Tacitus.html>

Ebb, Fred and Bob Fosse. *Chicago: A Musical Vaudeville*. New York: Samuel French, Inc., 1976.

Eisenman, Robert. *James the Brother of Jesus*. New York, NY: Penguin Books, 1997.

Eusebius," The Treatise of Eusebius, the Son of Pamphilus, Against the Life of Apollonius of Tyana Written by Philostratus, Occasioned by the Parallel Drawn By Hierocles Between Him and Christ," Philostratus, *Life of Apollonius of Tyana*, pp. 404-605. London: Loeb Classical Library, 1912, August 17, 2005 <http://www.tertullian.org/fathers/>.

Eusebius. "Demonstratio Evangelica." *The Proof of the Gospel; Two Volumes in One*. Ed. Ferrar, W.J. Wipf and Stock., 2001. August 17, 2005 <http://www.tertullian.org/fathers/eusebius_de_00_epreface.htm>.

Eusebius. "The Church History." *Nicene and Post-Nicene Fathers, Series II, Vol 1*. <http://www.ccel.org/fathers2/NPNF2-01/TOC.htm>.

Eusebius. "Theophania." Trans. Lee, Samuel. Cambridge: Cambridge University Press. August 17, 2005 <http://www.tertullian.org/fathers/>.

Evans, Craig. "Mark's Incipit And The Priene Calendar Inscription From Jewish Gospel To Greco-Roman Gospel." *JGRChJ*. 1 (2000) pp 67-81.

Fellows, Richard. "Was Titus Timothy?" *JSNT* 81 (2001) p33-58.

Ferguson, Everett. "The Problem of Eusebius," *Christian History*. Vol. 20 Issue 4, Nov, 2001,

Fletcher-Louis, H.T. Crispin. "First Oxford Lecture On The Development Of Christology." August 18, 2005 <http://www.st-andrews.ac.uk/~www_sd/med_oxford1.html>.

Fox, Robin Lane. *Pagans and Christians*. New York, N.Y.: Alfred Knopf, 1986.

Fox, Robin Lane. *The Unauthorized Version*. New York, N.Y.: Alfred A. Knopf Incorporated, 1992.

Frye, Northrop. *The Great Code: The Bible and Literature*. New York: Harcourt Brace Jovanovich HBJ, 1983.

Geo.metry the Online Learning Center. "Rinehart Mary Roberts." July 1, 2005, <http://www.988.com/authors/rinehart_mary_roberts_page_no_4.php>.

Goodspeed, Edgar J. "The Wisdom of Sirach." *The Apocrypha*, New York: Vintage Books, 1959.

Griffith, Sidney H. "The Doctrina Addai as a Paradigm of Christian Thought in Edessa in the Fifth Century," *Hugoye: Journal of Syriac Studies*. Vol. 6, No. 2, July 2003. January 02, 2005 <http://syrcom.cua.edu/Hugoye/Vol6No2/HV6N2Griffith.html>.

Grost, Michael E. "Gender Intergration and the Mystery." July 1, 2005 <http://members.aol.com/MG4273/bigthree.htm.>

Hadaway, Diane. "Biography: J. K. Rowling, Author of Harry Potter Books, From Single Mom Writer to Global Phenomenon." June 15, 2005 <http://singleparents.about.com/cs/booksandmovies/l/aajkrowlingbio1.htm>.

Hahneman, Geoffrey Mark. *The Muratorian Fragment and the Development of the Canon*. Oxford: Clarendon Press, 1992.

Hale, Sarah Josepha. "The Juvenile Miscellany." September/October, 1830. May 23, 2005 <http://www.recess.ufl.edu/transcripts/2003/1029.shtml>.

Hanson, K.C, "P.Oxy. 1021," August 10, 2004 <http://www.kchanson.com/ANCDOCS/greek/nero.html>.

Holding, James Patrick. "Jesus: God's Wisdom." August 18, 2005 <http://www.tektonics.org/JPH_AOA.html>.

Holmes, David. "Stylometry: Its Origins, Development and Aspirations." November 10, 2004 <http://www.cs.queensu.ca/achallc97/papers/s004.html>

Jefferys, William H. "Time Easter, Rosh Hashanah and Passover." July 27, 2004 <http://quasar.as.utexas.edu/BillInfo/ReligiousCalendars.html>.

Jerome. "Jerome's Apology for Himself Against the Books of Rufinus," "Jerome Letter LXXXIV." "Illustrious Men" *Post-Nicene Fathers, Series II, Volume III*.

Theodoret, Jerome and Gennadius, Rufinus and Jerome, August 17, 2005 <http://www.ccel.org/fathers2/>

Jones, Michael. "Natural" Women: The Mima and the Construction of Gender." September 15, 2004 <http://duke.usask.ca/~porterj/abstracts/jones.html>.

Jones, Michel Ridgway. "Natural" Women: The Mima and the Construction of Gender." September 13, 2004 <http://duke.usask.ca/~porterj/abstracts/jones.html>.

Josephus. *War of the Jews. Antiquities. Life.* Trs. William Whiston. August 17, 2005, <http://www.ccel.org/j/josephus/JOSEPHUS.HTM>.

Kaufmann, Walter. *Tragedy and Philosophy*, Princeton, New Jersey: Princeton.University Press, 1979

Kaufmann, Walter. *Tragedy and Philosophy*. Princeton, New Jersey: Princeton University Press, 1968.

Kraft, Robert A. "Was There a "Messiah-Joshua" Tradition at the Turn of the Era." *Ioudaios*, June, 1992, August 9, 2005 <http://listserv.lehigh.edu/lists/ioudaios-l/Articles.html>.

Liddle, Henry George and Robert Scott. "δουλος"*?A Greek-English Lexicon*. August 4, 2005 <http://www.perseus.tufts>.

Lucian, "On Pantomime." *The Works of Lucian of Samosata: Vol. 2*, trans. Fowler, H.W. and F.G. Fowler. Oxford: At the Clarendon Press, 1905.

Mack, Burton L. *The Christian Myth: Origins, Logic, and Legacy*. New York, NY, U.S.A: Continuum, 2001.

Mack, Burton. *Who Wrote the New Testament*. San Francisco: Harper, 1995.

Macleod, Charlotte. *Had She But Known*. New York: The Mysterious Press, 1994

Magee, M.D. "The Pre-Christian Joshua Cult." August 9, 2005 <http://www.askwhy.co.uk/christianity/0190JoshuaCult.html#The%20Pre-Christian%20Joshua%20Cult>.

Martyr, Justin. "Dialogue with Trypho."*Ante-Nicene Fathers. Vol. 1*. August 19, 2005 <http://www.ccel.org/fathers2/ANF-01/anf01-48.htm#P4043_787325>.

Myers, Ernest. *The Extant Odes of Pindar Translated Into English*. 1904. *The Project Gutenberg EBook of The Extant Odes of Pindar, by Pindar*. August 26. 2004, <http://www.gutenberg.net/dirs/1/0/7/1/10717/10717-8>txt>.

Neusner, Jacob. *Rabbinic Literature & the New Testament*. Valley Forge, PA: Trinity Press International, 1994.

New Oxford Annotated Bible with the Apocrypha: New Revised Standard Version. Ed. Michael D. Coogan. 3rd ed. New York: Oxford University Press, 2001.

Nietzsche, Friedrich. *The AntiChrist*. New York: Alfred Knopf, 1920.

Nietzsche, Friedrich. *The Genealogy of Morals*. New York, N.Y.:Doubleday Anchor, 1974.

Oliver, Myrna, "Bob Kane creator/artist, obituary." *LA Times*, November 5, 1998, June 30, 2005 <http://www.teako170.com/kane.html>.

Olson, K.A., "Eusebius and the *Testimonium Flavianum*." *Catholic Biblical Quarterly*, 61 (1999): 305-322. November 10, 2004 <http://f4.grp.yahoofs.com/v1/IHsDQyIFp-ce0l3z4_DLlyL664tb1OOO6sEJ9pPPmF4oKFPYXeO00waWQ4_XtAhsfJydcy4RFVHFld21YY MO/%22Eusebian%20Fabrication%20of%20the%20Testimonium%22>.

Orczy, Baroness Emmuska. *The Scarlet Pimpernel*. August 18, 2005, <http://www.classicreader.com/booktoc.php/sid.1/bookid.421/>.

Origen, *The Philocalia of Origen: A Compilation of Selected Passages From Origen's Works Made by St. Gregory of Nazianzus and St. Basil of Caesarea*. Trs. Lewis, George, Edinburgh: T. & T. Clark, London: Simpkin, Marshall, Hamilton, Kent, and Co. Limited, New York: Charles Scribner's Sons, 1911. January 10, 2005 <http://www.tertullian.org/fathers/origen_philocalia_01intro.htm>.

Origen. "Origen Against Celsus." Ante-Nicene Fathers. Vol. 4. Book 1 Volume 54. August 17, 2005 <http://www.ccel.org/fathers2/ANF-04/anf04-55.htm#TopOfPage>.

Origen. "*Origen's Commentary on the Gospel of John*." *Ante-Nicene Fathers, Vol. X*. August 17, 2005 <http://www.ccel.org/fathers2/ANF-10/anf10-37.htm#P6092_924944>.

People Weekly Magazine. Vol 32. #5. July 31, 1989. "The Batman." August 18, 2005 <http://www.geocities.com/Athens/8580/bobkane.html>.

Philo, "Embassy to Gaius." August 18, 2005 <http://www.earlychristianwritings.com/yonge/book40.html>

Photius. "Justus of Tiberius." April 15, 2005 <http://www.tertullian.org/rpearse/justus.htm>.

Pliny, "Letter 19, to Valerius Paulinus." *Letters of Pliny the Younger*, Loeb, Book 5, 1915. August 4, 2005 <http://www.vroma.org/~hwalker/Pliny/Pliny05-19-E.html>.

Price, Robert M. "Was Jesus John the Baptist Raised from the Dead?" December 12, 2003 <http://www.courses.drew.edu/sp2000/BIBST189.001/pricejj.html>.

Price, Robert M. *Deconstructing Jesus*. Amherst, New York: Prometheus Books, 2000.

Price, Robert M. *The Incredible Shrinking Son of Man*. Amherst, New York: Prometheus Books, 2003.

Richard Carrier, Richard. "Jewish Law, the Burial of Jesus, and the Third Day." July 7, 2004 <http://www.secweb.org/asset.asp?AssetID=125#3>.

Riech, Ronnie. "Ossuary Inscriptions from the Caiaphas Tomb." *Jerusalem Prospective Online*. July 24, 2004, <http://articles.jerusalemperspective.com/articles/DisplayArticle.aspx?ArticleID=1632>

Rinehart, Mary Roberts and Avery Hopwood. *The Bat*. New York: Samuel French, nd.

Rinehart, Mary Roberts. *The Bat*. E Rutherford, New Jersey: Kensington Publishing Corporation, 1998.

Rinehart, Mary Roberts. *The Circular Staircase*. Indianapolis: Bobbs-Merrill, 1908.

Rodgers, Ginger. *Ginger, My Story*. New York: Harper Collins, 1991.

Rowling, J.K. "Biography." *J.K. Rowling Official Site*. June 15, 2005, *<http://www.jkrowling.com/textonly/biography.cfm>*.

Royston, Peter. "The Hidden Hero: Baroness Orczy and the Myth of the Secret Identity." Center Stage Magazine, Winter 2000. Dec. 05, 2004 <http://www.moveweb.com/Guidewrite/hiddenhero.html>.

Rufinus. "Translation of Pamphilus' Defence of Origen," "Rufinus's Epilogue to Pamphilus the Martyr's Apology for Origen," "Rufinus's Apology in Defense of Himself," "The Apology of Ruinus." *Post-Nicene Fathers, Series II, Volume III. Theodoret, Jerome and Gennadius, Rufinus and Jerome,* August 17, 2005, <http://www.ccel.org/fathers2/>.

Santayana, George. "Reason in Religion." Edman, Irwin, ed. *The Philosophy of Santayana.* Modern Library, 1936.

Schweitzer, Albert. *the Quest of the historical Jesus,* Minneapolis: Fortress Press, 2001.

Scott, Jean. "The Dr. Gene Scott Bible Collection." August 10, 2004 <http://www.drgenescott.com/stn33.htm>.

Segal, Alan F. "Review and Appreciation: Walter Wink's *The Human Being.*" *Cross Currents.* Summer 2003, Vol. 53, No 2.

Severus, Sculpitius, "Sacred History," Book 2, *Nicene and Post-Nicene Fathers, Series II, Vol. XI.* August 17, 2005 <http://www.ccel.org/fathers2/NPNF2-11/Npnf2-11-24.htm#P1272_561883>.

Shadows and Fog. Dir. Woody Allen. Orion Pictures Corporation, 1992.

Shakespeare, William. *Romeo and Juliet,* Act II, Scene II, August 18, 2005 <http://www.online-literature.com/shakespeare/romeo_and_juliet/>.

Smith, Morton. *Jesus The Magician.* New York: Harper & Row, 1978.

Springer, Nancy, "Scarlet Pimpernel, Foreword, A Biography of Baroness Orczy," 1988, <August 18, 2005 <http://www.blakeneymanor.com/orczy2.html>.

Suetonius. "*De Vita Caesarum.*" J. C. Rolfe, ed., *Suetonius,* (London: William Heinemann, and New York: The MacMillan Co., The Loeb Classical Library, 1914), II.87-187.

Tacitus. *Annals.* Trs. Church, Alfred John, and William Jackson Brodribb. London: Macmillan, 1906. August 17, 2005 <http://classics.mit.edu/Tacitus/annals.html>.

Terence, *The Complete Comedies of Terence: Modern Verse Translations by Palmer Bovie, Constance Carrier, and Douglass Parker.* New Brunswick, New Jersey: Rutgers University Press, 1974.

Tertullian. "De praescriptione haereticorum." "Ad martyras." "Adversus Judaeos." De spectaculis." "Apologeticum." "Adversus Marcionem." "De ieiunio adversus psychicos." "Adversus Praxean." "De carne Christi." "De spectaculis." "*De pudicitia.*" "De Oratione." Eds. Roberts, Alexander, and James Donaldson. *Ante-Nicene Fathers Volume IV, Fathers of the Third Century.* September 20, 2004, <http://www.tertullian.org/anf/anf03/anf03-24.htm>.

"Testament of Solomon." Trans. Conybeare, F.C. *Jewish Quarterly Review,* October, 1898. August 18, 2005 <http://www.esotericarchives.com/solomon/testamen.htm>.

"The Thunder, Perfect Mind," Ed. Robinson, James M. James M. Robinson. *The Nag Hammadi Library.* San Francisco: HarperCollins, 1990.

Theissen, Gerd, and Linda M. Maloney. *The Gospels in Context: Social and Political History in the Synoptic Tradition.* T. & T. Clark Publishers, 1999.

Thomas. "Gospel of Thomas." *The Nag Hammadhi Library*, August 18, 2005 <http://www.gnosis.org/naghamm/gosthom.html>.

Traina, Giusto. "Lycoris the Mime." Ed. Fraschetti, Augusto. *Roman Women.* University of Chicago Press, 2002.

Victorinus, *"Commentary on the Apocalypse of the Blessed John."* Anti-Nicene Fathers. Vol. 7. August 18, 2005 <http://www.ccel.org/fathers2/ANF-07/anf07-30.htm#P4546_1741041>.

Watkins, Maureen. *Chicago.* Ed: Pauly, Thomas H. Carbondale, Illinois: Southern Illinois University Press, 1997.

Watkins, Maureen. Woman plays Jazz Air as Victim Dies." *Chicago Tribune.* April 4, 1924. pg.1.

Wikipedia, the free encyclopedia, "*Damnatio memoriae.*" Decemeber 16, 2004, <http://en.wikipedia.org/wiki/Damnatio_memoriae>.

Wikipedia. "Beulah Annan." August 22, 2004 <http://www.fact-index.com/b/be/beulah_annan.html>.

Wikipedia. Maureen Watkins. Oct. 20, 2004 <http://www.fact-index.com/m/ma/maurine_dallas_watkins.html >.

Wink, Walter. *The Human Being: Jesus and the Enigma of the Son of Man.* Minneapolis: Fortress, 2002.

Zimet, David, "Jewish Magic in the Roman Bathhouse." June 12, 2005 < http://www.winds.org/~frost/words/writings/magic.html>.